The Legacy of Muslim Spain

The Legacy of Muslim Spain

VOLUME 2

Salma Khadra Jayyusi

BRILL
LEIDEN • BOSTON • KOLN

This journal is printed on acid-free paper.

Design: TopicA (Antoinette Hanekuyk), Leiden

Library of Congress Cataloging-in-Publication Data

The Library of Congress Cataloging-in-Publication Data
are also available.

ISBN 90 04 11992 2 (volume 1)
ISBN 90 04 11993 0 (volume 2)
ISBN 90 04 11945 0 (set)

PRINTED IN THE NETHERLANDS

MUSIC

MUSIC IN MUSLIM SPAIN

OWEN WRIGHT

Consideration of the nature and history of music in Muslim Spain, and the question of its possible influence on Christian Europe, whether in the domain of instruments, repertoire, structures or concepts, had best begin with a review of sources. What dominates the picture, it should be admitted from the outset, is the stark fact that the music itself can not be disinterred. Central to any study of music in medieval Europe is the extensive corpus of surviving notations, whatever the difficulties of interpretation that surround it; but for Muslim Spain, in contrast, just as for the Middle East, there is no equivalent corpus: the exclusively aural transmission of the repertoire meant that even if techniques of notation were known to theorists, for the practising musician they were superfluous, and consequently no notated record remains. Doubtless certain legitimate inferences can be drawn from the modern successor traditions in the Maghrib, but it would be vain to expect these to contain, as if mounted behind exhibition glass, perfectly preserved specimens of the Andalusī music of five or more centuries before. The material from which any conclusions must be drawn is therefore essentially secondary and falls broadly into three categories: documentary—historical, literary, even legal works in which music or musicians are discussed or incidentally referred to; lexical—the vocabulary of music, including Arabic loan words in European languages; and iconographic—paintings or carvings containing depictions of musical instruments and activities.

Our principal source is, inevitably, the written word, of especial importance being references to music in literary and historical works. For the parallel (but quite separate) history of music in the Middle East such references, valuable as they are, are essentially ancillary: for technical matters it is to the extensive theoretical literature produced by such major figures as al-Kindī (d.*c*. 252/866), al-Fārābī (d.*c*. 339/950), Ibn Sīnā (370/980-428/1037) and Ṣafiyy al-Dīn 'l-Urmawī (d. 693/1294) that we turn in the first instance, while for information on repertoire, transmission, and social context the vast riches of the *Kitāb al-aghānī* by Abū 'l-Faraj al-Iṣbahānī (284/897-356/967) can be ransacked. For Muslim Spain, however, such scattered and incidental materials are virtually all we have. Theoretical works certainly existed—that by Ibn Bājja (d. 533/1139) was said to rival al-Fārābī's monumental *Kitāb al-mūsīqī al-kabīr*—but if we discount two chapters of a 7th/13th century encyclopaedia by al-Tīfāshī, to be considered below, those few that survive are late, brief, and not very informative.[1]

With such exiguous sources it is hardly surprising to find that next to nothing is known of the early history of music in Muslim Spain. There can be no firm answers to a number of key questions concerning its development during the 2nd/8th century, only conjectures. Given the ethnic composition of the first Muslim wave of settlement, it would have been of interest to know, for example, whether Berber styles were influential, or whether the more purely Arab culture symbolised by the importation of various musicians from the Ḥijāz was to dominate from a very early stage. Connected with this would be the question of the alacrity with which the emerging art-music tradition of Medina was adopted, occasioning an at least incipient stylistic cleavage between the pre-existing folk-song traditions and that of the court. There is, further, the more general and perhaps more important question of the extent and rate of cultural exchange between the immigrant communities and the much larger (and also ethnically mixed) indigenous population, whether Christian or convert.

During the first half of the 3rd/9th century the picture becomes, apparently, rather clearer, at least as far as court music is concerned, the period being dominated by the key figure of Abū 'l-Ḥasan ʿAlī b. Nāfiʿ, nicknamed Ziryāb. But despite the various innovations attributed to him and his reputed prominence as a court favourite, his significance is by no means easy to determine. Both Arab and Western scholars have been happy to accept as authoritative the full and detailed account of his career presented by al-Maqqarī (986/1578-1041/1632), whose source is the historian Ibn Ḥayyān (377/987-8-469/1076), quoted, we are to assume, verbatim.[2] But Ibn Ḥayyān is still at a considerable temporal remove from his subject, and it would be prudent to regard his account as in certain respects exemplary rather than factual.

Ziryāb's biography, as related by al-Maqqarī from Ibn Ḥayyān, can be summarised quite briefly. Incurring the jealousy of his eminent teacher Isḥāq al-Mawṣilī (150/767-235/850) as a result of his brilliant debut recital given before Hārūn al-Rashīd (170/786-193/809), he was obliged to leave Baghdad and seek his fortune elsewhere. On his arrival in North Africa he was invited to the Umayyad court at Córdoba, where he swiftly established himself not only as the leading performer and teacher of the day, but also as a general arbiter of taste who was to have an enduring influence in such areas as dress, hair-style and even culinary habits. Successful both materially and artistically, he taught in addition to his own children many competent pupils who survived him to perpetuate and disseminate his distinctive musical style and repertoire.[3]

On the surface there is nothing controversial or incoherent about Ibn Ḥayyān's narrative, and we may add that the historical importance of Ziryāb was still recognised in the 7th/13th century by al-Tīfāshī, according to whom he introduced a style that was to dominate until the 5th/11th century.[4] Nevertheless, on closer scrutiny a number of the statements made about him appear less than convincing. For example, the circumstances of his supposed contretemps with Isḥāq al-Mawṣilī are somewhat curious, to say the least. We are expected to believe that Isḥāq was startled and dismayed by the quality of Ziryāb's performance, but it is difficult to credit either that he could have been so unaware that his pupil possessed gifts outstanding enough to make him a potential rival or, alternatively, that Ziryāb should have wished to conceal his talent (and, presumably, his technological improvements to the lute) and succeeded in doing so for so long, even though he came to Isḥāq having already had lessons with his father, Ibrāhīm al-Mawṣilī. It is the latter explanation that is offered by the text, Hārūn excusing Isḥāq for not having brought Ziryāb to his attention before on the grounds that he accepted that he had kept his abilities secret, but, not surprisingly, no convincing motivation for such strange behaviour is forthcoming. The inherent implausibility of the whole episode is reinforced by the final touch of Isḥāq's appeal, in the course of explaining away Ziryāb's disappearance, to the motif of inspiration through supernatural visitation that had earlier—as al-Maqqarī's text explicitly recognises elsewhere—been associated with his own father.

Suspicion is sharpened by the existence of a parallel anecdote reported about him by Ibn ʿAbd Rabbihī (246/860-328/940), at least a century earlier, therefore, than Ibn Ḥayyān's account.[5] Here we are presented with essentially the same thematic core: a performance provokes anger resulting in the musician being told to flee or face death. For Ibn ʿAbd Rabbihī, however, the person issuing the threat is not Ziryāb's teacher but a patron, the Aghlabid Ziyādat Allāh I (201/817-223/838); and he, together with this whole episode, is conspicuously absent from Ibn Ḥayyān's narrative, which, we may conclude, is most probably an artfully embellished transplant. Support for this interpretation may be drawn, further, from the existence of an intermediate stage in the evolution of the story. This is provided by Ibn al-Qūṭiyya (d. 367/977), whose brief notice on Ziryāb's background retains the motif of princely displeasure but incorporates the crucial transfer of locale to Baghdad.[6] There is, however, no Hārūn al-Rashīd: Ziryāb is said, rather, to have been an intimate of al-Amīn (193/809-198/813) but to have incurred the enmity of his brother al-Maʾmūn (198/813-218/833), so that on the death of al-Amīn he fled to Spain. According to the chronology of this relocated version the Hārūn/Isḥāq plot would have to be a later fabulation and there is, accordingly, no reference to it. Nor is there any mention of either plot in Ibn ʿAbd Rabbihī's original version, where the story is framed by the bald information that Ziryāb had been a slave and pupil of Ibrāhīm al-Mawṣilī and that he subsequently went to the court of ʿAbd al-Raḥmān II (206/822-237/852).[7] In the light of the above it will come as no surprise to find, in the major source for the biography of Isḥāq, the *Kitāb al-aghānī*, that there is no mention of Ziryāb.

To draw attention to such likely transformation and embroidery of earlier narrative in the account reproduced by al-Maqqarī is by no means to show that the crucial importance ascribed to Ziryāb as performer, teacher and setter of cultural standards is without historical foundation. But if we leave the more obviously literary elements aside and turn to technical matters, it is equally the case that not all the particular musical innovations attributed to him are to be given uncritical acceptance. The changes he is said to have introduced to the structure of the lute, for example, involved not merely the use of thinner wood for increased resonance but also rather unusual substitutions in the materials chosen for the plectrum and strings: the previous wooden pick was replaced by an eagle's quill and, alongside the two upper strings of silk (no longer prepared in the traditional way), the lower two were now made of the gut of a lion cub. Wild life may well have been abundant, but even for the connoisseur market one can imagine supplies of commodities such as these being rather hard to come by. Nevertheless, if the details are hardly credible we may still reasonably give assent to the underlying notion of a move towards improvements allowing enhanced sonority, increased durability and, perhaps most important, greater technical finesse.

Ziryāb is further credited with the addition of a fifth string to the lute. But to the immediate question of what the practical function of such an innovation might have been there is no answer. It certainly does not appear that the intention was to extend the range of the instrument, one of the usual reasons for such additions, for the extra string was inserted in the middle and, as no mention is made of any change in accordatura to accommodate this interloper, it is difficult to see how the melodic resources of the instrument might have been enhanced. What is referred to, rather, is the colour (red) of the string and what it represents: the soul. It is a further development of the integration of music into cosmological schemes being elaborated at the same time in the East by al-Kindī, and articulated in terms of the four strings of the lute, with which various standard four-fold sets were associated. The fifth string thus has a purely conceptual, symbolic value, complementing the equally colour-coded representation of the four humours by the other strings.[8]

The importance of Ziryāb himself, it might be argued, is also primarily symbolic. According to this view he embodies the introduction, establishment and diffusion of a certain tradition in a way that confirmed the nascent cultural equality between Córdoba and Baghdad and the increasing self-confidence that went with it—even if still expressed partly in terms of covert comparisons with the East. We may note that he is seen on arrival eclipsing such gifted performers as Qalam, who represented the Eastern tradition in its earlier Umayyad Medinese form;[9] and he further embodies not merely the introduction of the current Baghdad style but also implied parity with the East, or even, in that he is depicted as someone who might have bested the supreme exponent of the early Abbasid school, potential superiority. The innovations he is credited with introducing as an arbiter of taste, whether vestimentary or gastronomic, run parallel to his technical improvements to the lute, reflecting as they do the increasing material prosperity and sophistication of Cordoban life during the reign of ʿAbd al-Raḥmān II. Finally, implicit in his fame as a teacher renowned for developing new methods of voice training is the notion of encouraging access, thereby promoting the diffusion of the tradition beyond the immediate confines of the performer's own family circle.

Whatever their semiological import for cultural self-assertion, a number of the innovations ascribed to Ziryāb thus appear to be either exaggerated or fanciful. But one that has not yet been mentioned points to a genuine historical development (even if, quite likely, of later origin): the emergence of the *nawba*, the suite form still characteristic of the classical traditions of the Maghrib. However, as Ibn Ḥayyān does not use the word in this context it would be more precise to speak in relation to Ziryāb of a proto-*nawba*. This consisted of a conventional sequence marked by a progression from initial slow pieces (*nas̲h̲īd*, which appears in Spanish as *anaxir*, then *basīṭ*) to final fast ones (*muḥarrakāt* followed by *ahzāj*) and, even if now more elaborate, the same basic plan is retained in the modern *nawba*.[10] But whatever the date of the institutionalising of the form, it is clear that the general progression from slow to fast is an ancient feature, and certain specifics may be traced back to early Abbasid practice. Thus the sequence *nas̲h̲īd*, *basīṭ* is already mentioned in connexion with Ziryāb's teacher Isḥāq al-Mawṣilī,[11] although rather than being two separate types of song they appear to be contrasting sections within the same song, and the mention of an internal transition from one to the other by al-Ḥasan b. ʿAlī al-Kātib (late 4th/10th to early 5th/11th century) indicates that such was still the case at the end of the 4th/10th century.[12] In addition to referring to this particular sequence al-Ḥasan also mentions that the beginning should be in slow tempo, with a *nas̲h̲īd* or *istihlāl* (which differs from the *nas̲h̲īd* in being based on even smaller fragments of the text, possibly no more than a single word—thereby, it may be conjectured, providing an opportunity for the singer to demonstrate skill in improvisation). The lighter, quicker rhythms *ramal* and *hazaj*, in contrast, come towards the end of the performance.[13]

Even if we have here no specification of the total sequence, and no mention of the *nawba* as such, the typological resemblance is clear. Nevertheless, unless we are to suppose that the crystallisation of the *nawba* into a suite form consisting of a specific number of movements, each with particular conventional musical (and possibly also textual) characteristics, took place considerably earlier in Spain than elsewhere, it may be concluded that it is unlikely to have reached a stable, well-recognised form before the 5th/11th century. In the earliest surviving description of a contemporary *nawba*, that of Aḥmad b. Yūsuf al-Tīfāshī (580/1184-651/1253), we encounter not the *muḥarrakāt* and *ahzāj* attributed to Ziryāb but *muwashshaḥāt* and *azjāl*, that is, song-types relating to the strophic verse forms which emerged most probably during the 3rd/9th and 4th/10th centuries,[14] and we must suppose either that these newly introduced forms eventually ousted older ones from a pre-existing *nawba* structure or, rather more likely, that it was only after their ready entry into a looser slow to fast sequence of pieces that others were shed, allowing the *nawba* to emerge as a stable entity.

According to al-Tīfāshī, the *nawba* consists of the sequence *nashīd*, *ṣawt*, *muwashshaḥ* and *zajal*, the *nashīd* incorporating an *istihlāl*, the *ṣawt* not.[15] These first two movements evidently incorporate for al-Tīfāshī, who has a keen sense of differing regional styles and an equally clear conception of what is ancient and what modern, the oldest layer of the contemporary music of Muslim Spain, and he is in general keen to stress the conservative core of this tradition, contrasting it with that of the East, which he stigmatises as having become so indebted to Persian modes and styles that its singers are generally incapable of performing the ancient Arab repertoire. Indeed, they are said to be unable to pronounce Arabic properly, and even when they can cope with the text they are unable to sing it in the old style which, it is implied, was more complex.[16] Differences between East and West in the ability to perform ancient songs (or song texts) are matched (and, presumably, reinforced) by differences of melodic habit, in relation to which al-Tīfāshī again stresses the modernity of the modal and compositional procedures (*ṭarāʾiq talḥīn*) in the East. Although, unfortunately, no technical details are given, he makes it clear that in his day East and West had evolved separate modal systems. That of the East provides in its nomenclature clear evidence of the incorporation of Persian elements, and is already organised into the two sets of 12 and 6 modes which will receive their canonical form in the 7th/13th century descriptions of Ṣafiyy al-Dīn,[17] and which are prefigured in the works of earlier Eastern writers.[18]

For the West, however, al-Tīfāshī mentions no more than four modes: *khusrawānī*, *muṭlaq*, *mazmūm* and *mujannab*.[19] Traces of this nomenclature may still be found in later Eastern theoretical treatises, but it is evident that it is there considered both marginal and ancient.[20] Further indications to support al-Tīfāshī's claim that the tradition to which these terms relate is more conservative than the Eastern one may be found in al-Ḥasan's treatise, which cites three of them and implies that two, despite certain innovations affecting their structure, are essentially survivals from the early modal system that received its definitive codification at the hands of Isḥāq al-Mawṣilī.[21] It is also of some interest to note that for al-Ḥasan the beginning pieces of a sequence (i.e. those occupying what for al-Tīfāshī are the *nashīd* and *basīṭ* slots) should be in either *mazmūm* or *muṭlaq*, and if this association between forms and modes were later extended to cover *khusrawānī* and *mujannab* as well it could be that al-Tīfāshī's list is incomplete and that, as comparisons with both earlier and later practice would suggest, there were other modes in existence at the time, for the passage in question is not designed as an exhaustive account of the modal system, but rather as an anthology of song texts specific to the *nashīd* and *basīṭ* forms: there are no examples of *muwashshaḥ* and *zajal* texts and, consequently, no mention of any modes that might have been particularly associated with these forms.[22] But whatever the range of modes employed in Muslim Spain in the 7th/13th century, it is certain that the modern Maghribi system is considerably different. Indeed, of the four mode names mentioned by al-Tīfāshī only two, *mazmūm* and *mujannab*, survive into the modern period.[23] It is true that discontinuity of nomenclature should not necessarily be interpreted as indicating discontinuity of structure or repertoire, but the present set of mode names certainly includes later additions, some of them imports from the East introduced during the period of Turkish ascendency. Of the 25 modes recorded by al-Ḥā'ik, and current therefore in the 12th/18th century, at least six may be adjudged to be of Eastern provenance, and it follows that little or nothing of Andalusī origin is likely to survive in these.

Sketchy as the material may be that relates to form or mode, it is at least greater than that for rhythm. On this topic al-Tīfāshī is unfortunately silent, and the history of the rhythmic cycles employed in the Maghribi tradition, the majority of which are peculiar to it, remains obscure. Integral to the early Abbasid system codified by Isḥāq al-Mawṣilī were the rhythmic cycles described, with varying degrees of precision and complexity, first by al-Kindī and then by al-Fārābī, and it is these that would have been introduced into Muslim Spain by Ziryāb and the other musicians who came from the East.

But how they might have developed there is impossible to say. Even in the East, where several later theorists provide definitions of the rhythmic cycles in use in their day, the historical changes affecting them are by no means easy to determine. The rhythmic cycles described in the 7th/13th century by Ṣafiyy al-Dīn are explicitly stated to be those used by the Arabs, contrasting therefore with others favoured by the Persians,[24] but there is no evidence to suggest that they should also be considered representative of the rhythms of court music in the West, and there is certainly little that could link them to the cycles now found in the Maghrib, most of which are considerably shorter, i.e. have fewer time units per cycle.[25] If we consider *khafīf*, the one instance of the survival of an early cycle name, we find that whereas in Tunisia it now has the form 6/4 ♩ 𝄽 ♪ ♪ ♪ 𝄽,[26] in Turkey it is a cycle of no fewer than 32 time units, and it is of this latter form that the versions provided by earlier theorists are precursors.[27] It is thus by no means unlikely that by the 7th/13th century, if not before, there were differences between West and East in the rhythmic cycles used as well as in the modal system. The emergence of quite distinct repertoires that such separate lines of development would encourage is further reflected in the fact that by the time of al-Tīfāshī the East also differed from the West in the identity of the movements that made up the *nawba*, so that in virtually every aspect of style and structure it provided a contrast with what he sees as the retention of the old style (*al-ṭarīq al-qadīm*) in Muslim Spain, thereby rendering unlikely any continuation of the diffusion eastwards of *muwashshaḥ* and *zajal* songs that had been witnessed in earlier centuries.[28] It may be noted that al-Tīfāshī further distinguishes an intermediate style in Tunisia (Ifrīqiya) which is lighter than the Spanish but melodically more florid (*akthar naghaman*) than the Eastern.

But what is meant by the heavy, complex Spanish style? Evidently, we are not dealing with a generalisation covering all genres. The characterisation almost certainly refers in the first instance to the slower, more solistic *nashīd* and *ṣawt* forms—the only ones for which al-Tīfāshī identifies texts and composers—and it is again primarily to this segment of the repertoire that his remarks about performance features and the training of performers must be deemed to relate. Thus, having listed the first lines of the songs of the ancient (and evidently, for him, prestigious) repertoire, he emphasises that such songs were designed for court performance,[29] and proceeds to mention anecdotes underlining their technical difficulty and potentially enormous duration. In the performance of a single line by one Andalusī singer he claims to have counted no fewer than 74 *hazzāt* ("vibrations", meaning presumably something like a shake), while on another grand occasion at which he was present a singing girl spent no less than two hours on one line. With all due allowance for exaggeration, we have here an indication that in this area at least the expert performer operated towards the improvisation end of the improvisation-composition continuum. For al-Tīfāshī such expertise was concentrated in Seville and, more interestingly (another contrast with the East), was in the hands of elderly female singers who had established a monopoly, transmitting their arts to slave-girls who would then be sold at a price, we are assured, determined solely by their musical accomplishments. Their value (from 1000 Maghribi *dīnār*s upwards) was underwritten by an accompanying catalogue of the repertoire they had mastered, thus demonstrating that skill in improvisation had at least to be matched, if not exceeded, by the ability to memorise a vast number of compositions.

These normally comprised not just the difficult classical songs for competent performers of which the wealthy cultured élites were prepared to pay such high prices, but also whole *nawba*s, sometimes as many as 500, it is claimed, and included therefore the *muwashshaḥ* and *zajal* repertoire also. Now, it is clear that although certain complex forms required the skills of highly trained experts who, in all probability, would only be appreciated by a sophisticated minority, there is no reason to suppose that the *muwashshaḥ* and *zajal* fell into this category, and we are faced therefore with the question of whether there was a significant gulf between court music and folk music and, if so, of the extent to which the *nawba* (and its specialist performers) might bridge it. Certainly there is no particular problem in positing an audience part sophisticated, part popular nor, indeed, in accepting the possibility of what may have been originally a folk-music form, characterised by alternating solo and chorus sections, gradually gaining acceptance at court. We are not, it may be assumed, faced with a contrast as stark as that between highly virtuosic coloratura arias and the simplest of hymn tunes: a more reasonable analogy could perhaps be found in the modern Iraqi *maqām* tradition, where in the typical performance context of a family celebration the expertise of the solo singer would be listened to attentively only by the cognoscenti, while the whole audience would enthusiastically join in the lighter *pasta* which rounds off each group of *maqām*s (*faṣl*).

If we now edge towards the question of how Arab musical styles might have been accepted or indeed adopted by the Christian population, and vice versa, we may note, first, that there is some evidence, in anecdotes of singing slave-girls adorning Christian courts or households,[30] to point to the most sophisticated style of Arab singing finding enthusiastic reception. But such evidence is by no means conclusive: anecdotes of this kind may be preserved because they represented the exception rather than the rule, and where such singers were acquired through conquest they may have resembled mounted trophies, tokens of victory indicating ostentation rather than comprehension. In any case, it may be assumed that the kind of cultural contact that would lead to significant and durable exchange was more likely to have involved popular styles and to have occurred at the popular level.[31] That such contact, and exchange, may have begun at a very early date is suggested by al-Tīfāshī, whose historical perception—even if unbuttressed by source references—is striking in its clear acceptance of the confluence of two cultural streams. For him the old Andalusī song, that is, the music of the first decades of the Muslim conquest, before even Ziryāb's predecessors from the East arrived, was either Christian in style or was the song of Arab camel-drivers, the *ḥudā'*. It is reasonable to suppose that the primary purpose of this reference to the *ḥudā'* was to reflect the quite commonly expressed view that it was the earliest genre of singing known to the Arabs, antedating the emergence of *ghinā'*, the ultimate forebear of court music, and consequently to imply that the only genres the first immigrants brought with them were those of folk song.

The reference to a Christian style is less easy to interpret. But on the assumption that al-Tīfāshī would hardly dwell on indigenous forms that were unknown to the Muslim population we may detect here the first signs of cultural influence, probably in the form of contrafact songs resulting from the adaptation of Arabic words to tunes that originally had Latin or, more likely, proto-Romance texts.[32] Al-Tīfāshī goes on to tell us that the style of

Ziryāb then held sway for some two centuries until, in a crucial new stage of cultural interaction, Ibn Bājja "fused Christian song with Eastern song, thereby creating a style found only in Spain",[33] and further refinements to this base resulted in the final apotheosis of the compositions of Abū 'l-Ḥusayn b. al-Ḥāsib al-Mursī (fl. ca. 600/1200). The reported fact of Ibn Bājja's innovation is of considerable importance, for such integration can only be possible in the context of a degree of similarity between the types of music practised by the two communities rendering them mutually permeable. But concerning the nature of the resulting changes we can, unfortunately, only speculate. Ibn Bājja is noted as a composer of distinction as well as a theorist, and texts for several of his songs are recorded by al-Tīfāshī, who also states that he refined (*tahdhīb*) the *istihlāl* and *ʿamal* (thus demonstrating, incidentally, that the former was now viewed as a fully composed section).[34] Of his individual style, however, nothing is said, so that the nature of the Christian component remains elusive.

But equally elusive, in many respects, is the nature of the Eastern, Muslim component. It is therefore hardly surprising to find, just as with the cognate question of whether Arabic models influenced the development of troubadour poetry with regard to both thematic resources and strophic structures, that attitudes towards the possibility of significant Arab musical influences on medieval Europe have varied between ardent espousal and unyielding rejection. Discussion of the degree to which such contrary conclusions have been shaped by cultural bias had perhaps best proceed within the context of a critique of orientalism, and will not be pursued here; but what is abundantly clear is that differing, indeed diametrically opposed, hypotheses can best flourish where, as has sadly been shown to be the case with regard to music, the ground is uncluttered by significant amounts of evidence.

In certain areas, nevertheless, it is possible to be more specific, and we may consider first the domain of theory. With regard to the core topics of sound, intervals and their various combinations (approached in a way that justified the inclusion of music among the mathematical sciences, the medieval quadrivium), rhythmic analysis, and the classification and discussion of instruments, it appears that the debt of Western Europe to Muslim Spain is negligible. For all the considerable amount of translation from Arabic into Latin that survives in technical fields such as medicine and philosophy, there is no evidence that any of the major musicological treatises of al-Kindī and al-Fārābī were ever translated. Of al-Kindī there is no trace, while virtually all that we have of al-Fārābī is a general classificatory work, the *Iḥṣāʾ al-ʿulūm*, which happens to contain a brief section on music.[35] Borrowings from this appear in the *De Divisione Philosophiae* of Gundisalvi (fl. 1130-50), and also in 13th- and 14th-century musical treatises such as the *De Musica* of Jerome of Moravia and the *Quatuor Principalia Musicae* of Simon Tunstede, but as a contribution to the development of musical thought it does little more than supply (or resuscitate) a conceptual distinction between theory (*musica speculativa*) and practice (*musica activa*).[36] Of the elaborate theories of mode and rhythm nothing was transferred to Western Europe, and it would be reasonable to speculate that the cause, straightforwardly, was not that the existence of such a literature was wholly unknown to the translators but rather that its subject matter did not engage them sufficiently to merit attention, particularly when aspects of the Greek theoretical heritage were already available in the form given them by Boethius.[37] What filters through from al-Fārābī is thus not only minor but incidental, and results from a general intellectual indebtedness rather than a specifically musical one.

Instances of Arabic elements of vocabulary derived from other sources may also be encountered, but again without necessarily indicating a musical influence. A particularly striking case is that of the terms *elmuarifa* and *elmuahym*, of evident Arabic origin even if the etyma are not immediately apparent, which occur in a passage of Anonymous IV dealing with mensural notation. From their presence in this context the conclusion was drawn (with hindsight one can fairly say jumped to) by Farmer that they provided evidence of an Arab influence affecting, if not indeed inspiring, the emergence of the medieval rhythmic modes.[38] Closer inspection reveals, however, that these terms relate not to notational function but to note design, and that they are derived from the Arabic terms for the relevant geometric shapes—*al-munḥarif* ("trapezium") and *al-muʿayyan* ("rhombus"). The influence, therefore, lies in the field of mathematics, and the appearance of these terms in a musical text is fortuitous.[39]

If imported concepts here impinge on a musical text, we may find elsewhere instances of notions relating to music appearing in generally non-musical contexts. The musical influence of Ibn Sīnā, for example (whose large-scale chapter in the *Kitāb al-S̲h̲ifāʾ* was, like the other major theoretical treatises, evidently unknown in the West), is confined to the medical dictum "inter omnia exercitia sanitatis cantare melius est" behind which lurks an interesting and complex set of ideas on musical therapeutics linked to notions of physical and psychic equilibrium and, through them, to cosmological schemata. A further, if rather mysterious, instance of these—reminiscent, conceptually, of the representation of the soul through Ziryāb's fifth string—is the set of *chordae* recorded by Odo of Cluny, among which we find the evidently Arabic-derived *scembs*, *caemar*, and *nar*. While some of the other terms may also reasonably be considered of Arabic origin it must, however, be conceded that no model is known for the set as a whole: its precise origin, and hence the significance of Arab musical cosmology as an influence, is unclear.[40] Such cosmological ideas, it should be stressed, were not just the recondite playthings of specialists, but part of the general intellectual climate within which the performance of music was comprehended. A theory of appropriate times of day for the performance of various modes has still not been entirely lost from the Islamic world today, and one may note that in the Maghrib the modes are known not as *maqāmāt* but as *ṭubūʿ*, a term that implies the notion of affective character and, through that, potentially, the broader concept of ethos and the ramifications of cosmological associations.

The most tangible evidence for Arab influence lies, however, neither in the realm of concepts and attitudes, nor in that of modal and rhythmic structures, but in the wide range of instruments that medieval Europe acquired from Islamic sources. Here lexical and iconographic evidence comes to the fore. The extensive vocabulary of Arabic origin found not only in Iberian languages but also in French and even English is itself a sufficient indication of cultural indebtedness: lute (*ʿūd*), rebec (*rabāb*) and nakers (*naqqāra*) are only the most obvious of a whole series of linguistic borrowings demonstrating that a significant proportion of the medieval European instrumentarium was made up of instruments either directly of Spanish-Arab provenance or sufficiently affected by contact with similar types used in Muslim Spain for the Arabic name to be adopted in place of the indigenous one.

The historical importance of the introduction of the *ʿūd* to Europe is clear: it was to become the major vehicle of domestic music making throughout the Renaissance. But that of the *rabāb* was perhaps even greater, for although the characteristically boat-shaped vertically held form still used in the Maghrib was to survive in Europe only as a folk instrument, the new concept of bowing that it introduced was enthusiastically applied to other types of lute, often now braced against the chest, thus leading to the emergence of the viol family which would later challenge the dominance of the lute. Terms such as *guitarra morisca* show that the *ʿūd* was not the only plucked lute of Arab provenance, while a further type of string instrument that was to prove influential is represented by the *qānūn*, psaltery.

Percussion and wind instruments also figure prominently in the list of borrowings. Among the former we find, in addition to nakers, cymbals (*ṣunūj>sonajas*), frame-drum (*al-duff>adufe*) and drum (*al-ṭabl>atabal*), and among the latter trumpet (*al-nafīr>añafil*) and hornpipe (*al-būq>albogue*). The list could be continued,[41] and the degree of cultural indebtedness it indicates can hardly have been restricted to the mere acquisition of the instrument itself: we are dealing not with exotic objects mysteriously deposited at the end of a trade route but with ones that centuries of close contact had rendered thoroughly familiar, and it is sensible to assume that along with them were adopted for the most part their characteristic sounds and playing techniques. In this connexion we may mention the celebrated 7th/13th-century miniatures of the *Cantigas de Santa Maria* which, in addition to providing invaluable information about the form, dimensions and sometimes even playing technique of various instruments, demonstrate that Christian and Moorish musicians played together at the court of Alfonso el Sabio, king of

León and Castile (1252-1284).[42] There must have been, therefore, either a common repertoire or, failing that, at least sufficient similarity of musical language to ensure mutual appreciation and acceptance, and that being so it is difficult to resist the conclusion that a certain amount of melodic material—if not whole pieces then at least commonly used and idiomatic phrases—must have been taken over with the instruments.

It is here that we reach the most difficult area of the debate on influence. It concerns the core problem of the extent to which the early secular music of Europe may have been indebted to Muslim Spain not only for certain aspects of what might be called its mentality—ideas about the nature, power and associations of music—and, more importantly, for many of the instruments on which it was played, but also for part of its melodic substance. Not surprisingly, given the paucity of evidence to hand, the question has provoked diametrically opposed responses, as witness on the one hand the claims of Ribera that the rhythmic structures of the *Cantigas de Santa Maria* bear unmistakable signs of Arab inspiration,[43] and on the other the denial of any such influence by scholars such as Ursprung.[44] It is, further, in this area that we approach, through the parallelism of musical and poetic forms, the equally contentious and intractable issue of possible literary borrowings. In short, given that we are dealing with poetic genres that were normally sung, if there were literary influences should we expect there to have been musical influences also; or, indeed, could cultural interchange have operated initially at the level of the song, musical material even acting as a conduit for the transfer of literary motifs? Alternatively if, despite the considerable weight of circumstantial evidence, the case for literary influences cannot be established, should we regard it as more likely that any melodic borrowings that took place should have been without textual trammels?

The main genre in relation to which arguments for literary influence have been articulated is the troubadour *canso*. For this a number of melodies have survived, and the evidence they supply is further reinforced by that derivable from the much larger number of songs that have survived for its North French counterpart, the trouvère *chanson*. Further, setting aside in the present context any consideration of the possible origins of the topoi of courtly love to examine only the musical dimension, we may add to the above a further corpus of melodies originating within Spain itself, that of the thematically quite distinct *Cantigas de Santa Maria*, many of which are in *zajal* form, providing therefore further evidence of a strophic song type characteristic of 13th-century Christian culture. But for Muslim Spain there is no equivalent evidence. We may accept that the *muwashshaḥ* and *zajal* were normally sung, and can reasonably presume that the formal structure of the song coincided with that of the verse, the most characteristic feature being the recurrence, at the end of each strophe, of a refrain, while at least partially contrasting material would be used to set the intervening verses of each strophe.[45] But any claim about the melodic nature of the setting can only be based on inference, appeal being made either to the evidence of theoretical and other writings or to that provided by the possible survival of parts of the Andalusī musical repertoire in North Africa.

The former, as we have seen, is of little help. With regard to the latter, we may note first that the tradition itself lays claim to be Andalusī, even making very specific connexions, so that the style of Seville, for example, is said to be perpetuated in Tunis, that of Granada in Fez and Tétouan, and that of Córdoba in Tlemcen. But more important than any such hypothetical twinnings —which are to be treated with the greatest reserve—is the general phenomenon of several centuries of mutual contact reinforced by the frequently itinerant way of life of the professional minstrel and, in particular, by the diffusion of the Spanish court repertoire throughout the urban centres of the Maghrib brought about by the agency of slave girls such as those described by al-Tīfāshī. In the 5th/11th and 6th/12th centuries contact would have been further facilitated by the creation of political union at the hands of the Almoravid and Almohad dynasties and, as the *reconquista* gained momentum during the following centuries, would have been given fresh impetus by the influx of Spanish Muslims caused by emigration and, finally, expulsion. There is more, therefore, to the claim of Andalusī origins than the possibly recent elaboration of a psychology of cultural nostalgia; and insofar as this element is present it would, in any case, have helped to preserve whatever residue of Andalusī material may have survived by reinforcing the prevailing conservative attitudes, noted by 19th- and 20th-century observers, which place considerable emphasis on the faithful reproduction of an inherited corpus to which no fresh additions may be made.[46] In addition to this defensive ideological framework we may note the conservatism of the Maghribi tradition, when compared with its Eastern equivalent, with regard to technical features such as the accordatura of the lute[47] or the retention of a more ancient modal nomenclature.

But potentially far more significant than such essentially circumstantial evidence is the fact that certain texts have remained within the musical repertoire over long periods of time. A 7th/13th century *muwashshaḥ*, for example, is cited by al-Maqqarī as still current in his day, appears again in the 12th/18th-century song text anthology of al-Ḥā'ik, and survives in the present day Moroccan repertoire.[48] This appears to be a powerful indication of continuity within the tradition which, when read against the background of the conservatism previously observed by al-Tīfāshī, suggests that it is not unreasonable to hope that the melodic properties of the setting now current might provide some insight into the practice of earlier centuries. Any such hope must, nevertheless, be entertained with extreme diffidence, for continuity is not to be equated with lack of development and change. The historical evolution of the *nawba*, within which these pieces occur, has already been mentioned: it is today a more complex structure, with a greater number of parts, than its medieval precursor. Performance practice has also changed in certain respects, for even if solo singing still occurs, the dominant alternation is now that between chorus and orchestra, and although *ʿūd* and *rabāb* remain prominent, the great variety of instruments mentioned in medieval literary sources and illustrated in miniature paintings is no longer to be found. The instrumental palette of modern Maghribi art music is relatively narrow, and one of its primary colours, in an interesting reversal of instrumental borrowing, is that of the violin. For al-Tīfās͟hī, in contrast, one of the most popular instruments, held in high esteem and frequently used to accompany dancing and singing, was the *būq*, a form of hornpipe, and that it was also used in court performances is shown by its being depicted in one of the miniatures of the *Cantigas de Santa Maria*. But there is no trace of this instrument in the art-music ensembles of today. Thus certain changes can be documented, however sketchily, and there is every reason to suppose that the repertoire was similarly affected, not merely by loss and substitution, but by developments of a more general order. Indeed, comparison with the traditions of the Islamic Middle East would suggest that stylistic and structural change could on occasion be quite rapid and far-reaching in its effects.

There can thus be no certainty that the settings of ancient texts now current preserve ancient features. However, if such features survive anywhere it is in these songs that they are most likely to be found, and we may note that the current repertoire contains ten pieces that have been identified as settings of classical *muwas͟hs͟haḥāt*.[49] But accepting that they are most unlikely to be essentially unaltered survivals of Andalusī originals, the immediate issue is one of considering whether there are any available criteria that might enable us to evaluate the extent to which they could derive from early pieces or, failing that, at least be paradigmatically representative in that they exhibit certain of the melodic and formal properties of the songs of the medieval period.

In seeking indicators of period more precise than subjective impressions we may turn first to features of modal and rhythmic structure. Thus one of the two *muwas͟hs͟haḥāt* that al-Ḥilw considers to be authentic Andalusī pieces, *man ḥabbak yaṣʿub ʿalayh al-tajāfī*, is, encouragingly, in *al-dīl*, one of the core ancient modes. But at the same time it is in the rhythmic cycle *samāʿī t͟haqīl*, and it is clear from the evidence of Eastern theorists of the 10th/16th and 11th/17th centuries that *samāʿī t͟haqīl* only emerges towards the end of this period. Further, it is equally clear from the examples of notation of ca. 1110/1700 made by Demetrius Cantemir that early pieces in this cycle do not exhibit the melodic patterns—that is, the particular ways in which the melody matches the rhythmic articulation of the cycle—which are now typical of *samāʿī t͟haqīl* pieces and which are exemplified by this *muwas͟h-s͟haḥ*. The contrast is made apparent in fig. 1, which presents the first sect-

(i)

(ii)

(iii)

Figure 1

ions of (i) the *muwashshaḥ*,[50] (ii) an Ottoman *samāʿī thaqīl* piece attributed to an 11th/17th-century composer, and (iii) a *samāʿī thaqīl* piece notated by Cantemir. Now, a number of the instrumental compositions recorded by Cantemir have survived in the repertoire, but very considerably altered: their modern forms are characterised by significant accretions of melodic material, that is, they have a considerably higher number of pitch changes per rhythmic cycle.[51] The difference between (iii) and (i) is analogous, the average figures being 5.4 and 12 respectively, while (ii), with 7.5, shows an intermediate stage of development (note, however, the close resemblance in the melodic-rhythmic profile of cycle 2 between (ii) and (i)). From such general stylistic criteria, therefore, we may determine that *man ḥabbak* must be assigned to the second half of the 12th/18th century at the earliest, and it may be added that the layout of the melody is atypical in that it begins not at the commencement of the cycle but half way through, an innovatory feature suggesting that in its current form it is essentially a 13th/19th century composition: what it most assuredly is not is an ancient piece of Andalusī provenance.

Stylistic evidence of such a conclusive kind is, unfortunately, only rarely forthcoming and with the other pieces we are on less firm ground. Nevertheless, modal identity may be considered a sound initial indicator, especially when we find that the Andalusī *muwashshaḥāt* identified by Stern in late collections are all in modes that predate the Ottoman period.[52] Thus although the possibility of a piece being reassigned in the course of its history to another mode cannot be discounted altogether, we may accept that those in modes known not to be ancient are in principle unlikely to preserve authentic Andalusī material. Of the pieces under consideration, no less than five fall into this category: the four in *ṣīka* and the one in *kurdī*. These are late additions to the Maghribi mode stock, being first mentioned in Eastern sources, *ṣīka* (‹ *segāh*) in a Persian work of c. 700/1300, *kurdī* in theoretical treatises of no earlier than the 9th/15th century, and their arrival in the West was probably posterior to the extinction of the kingdom of Granada (and certainly some centuries later than the period of potential Arab musical influence in Spain).

Setting these five pieces aside as dubious we are left with just four. One of them is first attested in al-Ḥā'ik, and has since undergone considerable textural reformulation, while the others are settings of texts by two poets of the 7th/13th century (al-Shushtarī and Ibn Sahl) and one of the 8th/14th century (Ibn al-Khaṭīb). Consequently, even in the most unlikely eventuality of the present form of these songs preserving, miraculously, the original setting in all essentials, there would still be no guarantee that they were stylistically representative of those earlier centuries during which Arab musical influences might, hypothetically, have affected the early formulation of troubadour and trouvère art-song; and that they do not in fact preserve the original form of the setting is indicated not simply by stylistic analogy with the piece discussed above (it could be contended that there is insufficient uniformity to adduce this as a conclusive argument) but, crucially, by the textual erosion that they exhibit. Of the three or (normally) five strophes of the original only one or at most two survive, and the most convincing explanation for such dramatic truncation is that loss of text occurs as a result of melodic amplification causing a gradual increase in the duration of each strophe. The total length of the song can then only be kept within reasonable bounds by sacrificing one or more strophes.[53] Accordingly, we must consider unrealistic the hope that the current repertoire might provide the key to the specifics of compositional practice in Muslim Spain.

In consequence, influence at the level of melody can be neither demonstrated nor disproved: the evidence is simply insufficient. No doubt the possibility might be entertained the more readily if the melodic character of these Maghribi songs, despite the process of elaboration which, it has been suggested, they have undergone, still evinced similarities (beyond formal properties relatable to common strophic structures) to that of known troubadour, trouvère and *Cantigas* melodies. But that any similarities there may be are inadequate to form the basis of a case can be shown by a brief consideration of two crucial, interrelated aspects, melodic-rhythmic structure and techniques of word-setting. As previously indicated, the history of the rhythmic cycles of the Maghribi tradition cannot be traced with any certainty. The vital point is not, however, that the names of most of the cycles occurring in the pieces in question are not attested in early sources but rather that each piece is throughout in a stable rhythmic cycle, a feature that must also be considered typical of medieval practice in Muslim Spain. Such rhythmic regularity is less easy to detect in the troubadour/trouvère songs, however. Indeed, it has been argued that their melodies are not subject to a particular rhythmic cycle at all, but are essentially isosyllabic, single notes or ligatures being associated with each syllable of the text without being subjected to the straitjacket of a uniform metre.[54] (With regard to the *Cantigas*, Ribera's attempt to discern Arab rhythmic structures has been, rightly, rejected: apart from anything else it relies on unjustifiable interpretations of Arabic sources.)[55]

In word setting we also encounter marked differences. However elaborately melismatic vocal styles might be in other genres, the troubadour melodies rarely exhibit more than two pitch changes to a single syllable, while in the modern *muwashshaḥ* six or seven may be encountered and, furthermore, a significant proportion of the whole may be taken up with internal repetitions and, equally characteristically, strings of nonsense syllables inserted between the various segments of the verse text, features alien to the *canso/chanson* or *cantiga*. It is true that if the argument for melodic accretion through time is accepted such features may well have been equally absent from the medieval *muwashshaḥ*, but all we could then presume is that there were fewer stylistic contrasts, leaving a number of broad (and bland) similarities—a predominant diatonicism, analogous melodic procedures, preference for stepwise melodic movement usually within the range of an octave or less—indicative of nothing more precise than the existence of a common area of musical discourse within which influence (in either direction) might readily be exerted. In any event, even if the negative arguments marshalled above are dismissed as extravagant extrapolations from the flimsiest of evidence, to maintain the case for an Arab musical influence affecting the medieval European strophic song one still has to answer the question of what might have been not only the nature but also the cultural roots of the music to which the *muwashshaḥ* and *zajal* were sung, and, in view of the simple fact that there is no indication of the emergence of strophic songs in the Umayyad and early Abbasid court music to which that of Muslim Spain was heir, we must conclude that, like the verse form, the song form is likely to have been a local innovation. In the absence of specific evidence to the contrary it might well be thought that the fusion of Eastern and Christian elements to which al-Tīfāshī refers in relation to Ibn Bājja could also serve as a reasonable encapsulation of the musical processes giving rise to these forms. Indeed, given that the *muwashshaḥ* and *zajal* replace, in the *nawba* as described by al-Tīfāshī, the earlier *muḥarrakāt* and *ahzāj* associated with Ziryāb and therefore presumably representative of the purely Arab inheritance, it might well be considered that it was here that the Christian contribution would have been felt most strongly. If so, we may assume that it was not only the *rondeau* and *virelai* song forms that were taken over, but also, at least in the early stages, a number of existing tunes, so that the early Arab examples were likely, accordingly, to have been contrafacts.

It must be emphasised, however, that what is being put forward here is no stronger than reasonable conjecture. What musical evidence we have is essentially neutral, and although it certainly does not run counter to the hypothesis that the *zajal* (and through that, subsequently, the *muwashshaḥ*) was calqued on a pre-existing Romance strophic form with refrain, equally it cannot provide strong support. We are dealing, at the end of the day, with nothing more specific than a balance of probabilities. Comparison with the (admittedly much later) complex song forms that are recorded in Eastern anthologies shows that text sections were often repeated in ways that could have been adapted without difficulty to provide a refrain in a strophic structure, and there is no reason to suppose that such a structure could not have evolved in response to the invention of a new verse form, but if it is accepted that the emergence of the song form was not consequent upon that of the verse form it seems more convincing to suppose that it was taken over from some pre-existing model, evolving thereafter as part of what may well have been a common musical heritage.

At a certain point it is obviously proper—but at the same time comfortably (and comfortingly) vague—to speak of a degree of cultural symbiosis involving Muslim, Christian and Jew. But in the realm of music it is difficult, apart from the undeniable evidence for a strong Arab impact on the medieval instrumentarium, to evaluate their respective contributions. Miniature paintings may provide additional visual confirmation of the collaboration and mutual comprehensibility that documentary evidence implies, but for Muslim Spain the music that lies behind picture and page remains as elusive and enigmatic as ever.

[1] An annotated list may be consulted in M. Guettat, *La musique classique du Maghreb*, (La Bibliothèque Arabe), Paris, 1980, pp.181-82. For broader bibliographical coverage see H. G. Farmer, *The Sources of Arabian Music*, Bearsden, 1940, 2nd ed., Leiden, 1965 and A. Shiloah, *The Theory of Music in Arabic Writings (c. 900-1900)* (Répertoire International des Sources Musicales: B X), Munich, 1979; and for a survey of Islamic iconographical materials (including some examples from Spain) see H. G. Farmer, *Islam* (Musikgeschichte in Bildern. Band III: Musik des Mittelalters und der Renaissance, Lieferung 2), Leipzig, 1976.

[2] *Nafḥ al-ṭīb*, ed. I. ʿAbbās, Beirut, 1968, III, 122-33. Ibn Ḥayyān is not mentioned by name, but the whole lengthy passage is introduced by *qāla fī 'l-Muqtabis*.

[3] There is no mention of dates of birth or death. For Farmer ("Ziryāb", *Encyclopaedia of Islam*, first ed., supp.) these are unknown, while Muḥsin Mahdī (*Nafḥ*, III, 122n.), on the authority of *Al-Muqtabis*, states that he died 40 days before ʿAbd al-Raḥmān II (although the year given is not 237 but 238).

[4] M. b. T. al-Ṭanjī, "Al-Ṭarā'iq wa-'l-alḥān al-mūsīqiyya fī Ifrīqiya wa 'l-Andalus", *Al-Abḥāth: Quarterly Journal of the American University of Beirut*, 21/2,3, 4, 1968, pp. 114-15. Al-Tīfāshī calls him *al-imām al-muqaddam*, and states that he *jā'a bi-mā lam taʿhadhu 'l-asmāʿ wa-ttukhidhat ṭarīqatuh maslakan wa-nusiya ghayruhā*. Save to note his origin as a *ghulām* of Isḥāq al-Mawṣilī and his arrival at the court of ʿAbd al-Raḥmān II no biographical information is given. A translation of the text of al-Tīfāshī's two chapters included by al-Ṭanjī may be consulted in B. M. Liu and J. T. Monroe, *Ten Hispano-Arabic Strophic Songs in the Modern Oral Tradition* (Modern Philology, 125), Berkeley-Los Angeles-London, 1989, pp. 36-44.

[5] Ibn ʿAbd Rabbihī, *Al-ʿIqd al-farīd*, ed. A. Amīn *et al.*, Cairo, 1949, VI, 34.

[6] J. M.Nichols, *The* History of the Conquest of al-Andalus *by Ibn al-Qūṭīya the Cordovan: Translation and Study*, Ph.D thesis, University of North Carolina, Chapel Hill, 1975, pp. 148-50. (I am indebted to Mr F. al-Qaisī for drawing my attention to this source.)

[7] Farmer, "Ziryāb", produces a composite narrative deriving from both al-Maqqarī and Ibn ʿAbd Rabbihī. Ibn al-Qūṭiyya is ignored, despite being included in the references.

[8] For further details see Guettat, *op. cit.*, pp. 110-13. He notes that the central fifth string would not extend the range, and suggests that the accordatura was *embrassé*, i.e. of the type (for four strings) *C-A-D-G*. But this is unlikely. If an Eastern accordatura had been introduced (whether or not by Ziryāb is immaterial) it would have been in ascending fourths: *D-G-c-f*, and this is the type noted by al-Tīfāshī in relation to Ibn Bājja (with some variation for the lowest string: al-Ṭanjī, *op. cit.*, p. 115). "Ziryāb's" fifth string is not necessarily purely notional in origin, however. It should be regarded, most probably, as a symbolic reinterpretation of a real fifth string added above the highest pitch string which it would either reinforce (following al-Tīfāshī), being the first step towards introducing the now standard double courses, or exceed by a further fourth in order to facilitate extension of the range to a full two octaves.

[9] Although herself of Spanish (Basque) origin (*Nafḥ*, III, 140), so that she can be seen as a combination of Eastern polish and Western talent.

[10] For details of the main regional variations see Guettat, *op.cit.*, pp. 193-231.

[11] Abū 'l-Faraj al-Iṣbahānī, *Kitāb al-aghānī*, Cairo, 1932, V, 427.

[12] Al-Ḥasan b. Aḥmad b. ʿAlī 'l-Kātib, *Kamāl adab al-ghinā'*, ed. Gh. ʿA. Khashaba and M. A. al-Ḥifnī, Cairo, 1975, p. 28; trans. in A.Shiloah, *La perfection des connaissances musicales*, Paris, 1972, pp. 55-56.

[13] *Ibid.*, pp. 126/176; 82-83/128-29.

[14] For the relationship between music and verse in the *muwashshaḥ* and *zajal* see Liu and Monroe, *op. cit.*, the most up to date survey of the field. It also (pp. 8-9) advances the thesis that

the *muwashshah* was derived from the *zajal*. The argument is pursued in J. T. Monroe, "Which Came First, the *Zajal* or the *Muwaššaḥa*? Some Evidence for the Oral Origins of Hispano-Arabic Strophic Poetry", *Oral Literature*, 4/1-2, 1989, pp. 38-64 which (like the present chapter) tries to build a case from disconnected and unpromising fragments. If its conclusions are accepted, the emergence of the *zajal* must be dated earlier. Less convincing is the suggestion by I. ʿAbbās ("Akhbār al-ghinā' wa 'l-mughannīn fī 'l-Andalus", *Al-Abḥāth: Quarterly Journal of the American University of Beirut*, 1963/1, pp. 10, 13) that the melodic/formal diversity (*al-tanwīʿ fī 'l-alḥān*) within the *nawba* may have been one of the causes of the emergence of the *muwashshaḥ* verse form.

15 This Western *nawba* contrasts with an Eastern one consisting of five movements: *qawl*, *ghazal*, *tarānā* (sic), *zamanāh* (?) and *qawl(-i) dīgar* (al-Ṭanjī, *op. cit.*, p. 97). This will later be reduced to four, the last two being replaced by a movement called *firūdasht*. It may also be noted that the Eastern *nawba*, at least as described by the theorists, does not exhibit a clear slow to fast progression.

16 *Fa-ammā annahum yughannūn fī shay' min al-ashʿār al-ʿaṣriyya al-ʿajamiyya aw al-ʿarabiyya aw al-dūbaytī bi-ghinā' qadīm wa ʿamal kabīr fa-dhālik ayḍan maʿdūm ʿindahum* (al-Ṭanjī, *op. cit.*, p. 97).

17 Ṣafī 'l-Dīn ʿAbd al-Mu'min al-Urmawī 'l-Baghdādī, whose two treatises, the *Kitāb al-adwār* and the *Risāla al-sharafiyya* (both including definitions of these modes), may be consulted in R. D'Erlanger, *La musique arabe*, Paris, 1938, Vol. III. As al-Tīfāshī's mode names differ in certain respects from those of Ṣafī 'l-Dīn we may suspect a degree of local variation within the Eastern tradition at this period.

18 Kay Kā'ūs, *Qābūs-nāma*, ed. R. Levy (E. W. J. Gibb memorial series, new series, 18), London, 1951, pp. 112-13; Niẓāmī (J. C. Bürgel, *The Feather of Simurgh*, New York-London, 1988, p. 97). One or two are already mentioned by Ibn Sīnā.

19 Al-Ṭanjī's text has *mujtathth* but (as pointed out by Liu and Monroe, *op. cit.*, p. 41) this is a misreading. To judge from the number of texts listed, the repertoire for *mujannab* was significantly smaller than that for the other three modes.

20 See O. Wright, *The Modal System of Arab and Persian Music A. D. 1250-1300* (London Oriental series, 28), Oxford, 1978, pp. 249-52. However, they are also cited in a 6th/12th- or 7th/13th-century Geniza fragment, in which there is no suggestion of their being marginal: see H. Avenary, "Paradigms of Arabic Musical Modes in the Geniza Fragment Cambridge, T. S. N. S. 90, 4", *Yuval*, 4, 1982, pp. 11-25.

21 *Mujannab* is essentially not an independent mode but a process affecting already existing modes whereby for the note produced by the first finger fret another, somewhat lower in pitch, is substituted. But *muṭlaq* and *mazmūm* (al-Ḥasan, *op. cit.*, p. 112; Shiloah, *op. cit.*, pp. 159-60) are fully independent modes. Of *khusrawānī* there is no mention.

22 Certainly, the existence of more than four modes may be suspected: Guettat (*op. cit.*, p. 169) cites an 8th/14th-century poem in which 13 are mentioned. It should, however, be noted that although al-Ḥasan may be cited in support of the notion of particular modes being preferred for beginning and ending a song sequence, the contrast of emotional effect involved is not quite the same as al-Tīfāshī's slow/serious followed by fast/gay: the movement is rather from activity (*nashāṭ*) to repose (*rāḥa, sukūn*) (al-Ḥasan, *op. cit.*, pp. 126-27; Shiloah, *op. cit.*, pp. 176-77).

23 The latter only in the combination *mujannab al-dīl* (see the mode lists quoted in Liu and Monroe, *op. cit.*, pp. 25-26).

24 Of which just one is listed. D'Erlanger, *op. cit.*, pp. 173-76.

25 A list of these cycles may be consulted in Guettat, *op. cit.*, pp. 292-95.

26 *Ibid.*

27 The earliest (c. 700/1300) being that of Quṭb al-Dīn Shīrāzī, who defines it as a cycle of 16 time units.

28 Ibn Quzmān, for example, speaks of his *zajal*s being sung in the East (Liu and Monroe, *op. cit.*, p. 2). But in the later Eastern *nawba* there is no *muwashshaḥ* or *zajal*; nor are any included in Eastern song-text collections. On the diffusion of the *muwashshaḥ*, including later literary developments, see in general S. M. Stern, *Hispano-Arabic Strophic Poetry*, ed. L. P. Harvey, Oxford, 1974, pp. 72-80.

29 *Fī majālis al-mulūk wa 'l-ru'asā' ʿalā 'l-sharāb wa-ghayrih* (al-Ṭanjī, *op. cit.*, p. 102).

30 A. Y. Mansoor, *Die arabische Theorie. Studien zur Entwicklungsgeschichte des abendländischen Minnesangs*, Heidelberg, 1966, pp. 162-63.

31 Insight into this area may be gained from the materials relating to performances at festivities and ceremonies assembled in J. Ribera y Tarragó, *La música de las Cantigas*, Madrid, 1922, pp. 75-95.

32 Cf. Liu and Monroe, *op. cit.*, p. 6. For a further, explicit indication of musical borrowings from Christians see I. ʿAbbās, *op. cit.*, p. 18 (citing *Masālik al-abṣār*, I, 385).

33 *Mazaja ghinā' al-naṣārā bi-ghinā' al-Mashriq wa-khtaraʿ ṭarīqa lā tūjad illā bi 'l-Andalus* (al-Ṭanjī, *op. cit.*, p. 115).

34 He is also, incidentally, reported as having added to the *istihlāl* and *ʿamal* of a piece that Ziryāb had sung.

35 See H. G. Farmer, "The Influence of al-Fārābī's 'Ihsa' al-ʿulum'(*De Scientiis*) on the Writers on Music in Western Europe", *JRAS*, 1932, pp. 561-92. A similar but slighter work, the *De Ortu Scientiarum*, has also been attributed to al-Fārābī. On this see H. G. Farmer, "A Further Arabic-Latin Writing on Music", *JRAS*, 1933, pp. 307-22.

36 For further information on the diffusion of this material see E. R. Perkuhn, *Die Theorien zum arabischen Einfluss auf die europäische Musik des Mittelalters* (Beiträge zur Sprach- und Kulturgeschichte des Orients, 26), Walldorf-Hessen, 1976, pp. 38-45. This work provides the most thorough and judicious assessment to date of the evidence for and against Arab influences.

37 See the entry in S. Sadie (ed.), *The New Grove Dictionary of Music and Musicians*, London, 1980.

38 H. G. Farmer, "Clues for the Arabian Influence on European Musical Theory", *JRAS*, 1925/1, pp. 61-80.

39 See Perkuhn, *op. cit.*, pp. 63-66 and C. Burnett, "The Use of Geometric Terms in Medieval Music: Elmuahim and Elmuarifa and the Anonymous IV", *Sudhoffs Archiv*, 70/2, 1986, pp. 198-205. Further areas in which (generally unconvincing) claims have been made are solmisation (Perkuhn, *op. cit.*, pp. 67-72), alphabetical notation (*ibid.*, pp. 46-58) and lute tablature (*ibid.*, pp. 59-61).

40 For a more extensive discussion of this area see Perkuhn, *op. cit.*, pp. 73-82. For the similar situation resulting from the parallel Arab-European contact in Sicily see C. Burnett, "Teoria e pratica musicali arabe in Sicilia e nell'Italia meridionale in età normanna e sveva", *Nuove Effemeridi*, 11, 1990, pp. 79-89.

41 For a fuller catalogue, including cases where Arabic etymologies have been suggested which have failed to find general acceptance, see H. Hickmann, "Die Musik des arabisch-islamischen Bereichs" in *Orientalische Musik* (Handbuch der Orientalistik, Erste Abteilung, Ergänzungsband IV), Leiden-Cologne, 1970, pp. 129-33. See also the discussion and detailed evaluation in Perkuhn, *op. cit.*, pp. 133-213.

42 A point confirmed by the identity of the musicians employed, nine years after his death, at the court of his son, no less than half of them being non-Christian (Sadie, *op. cit.*, art. "cantiga") With regard to the miniatures, it may be observed that although due account must always be taken of both conventions of representation and influences (and that one or two show clear compositional parallels with the Ḥarīrī *maqāmāt* miniatures (Paris MS f. ar. 5847) has been shown by G.Menéndez Pidal ("Los manuscritos de las cantigas", *Boletín de la Real Academia de la Historia*, 150/1, 1962, pp. 25-51)) there is no obvious reason to think that the instruments are depicted in other than a realistic manner.

43 *Op. cit.*, pp. 95-121.

44 O.Ursprung, "Um die Frage nach dem arabischen Einfluss auf die abendländische Musik des Mittelalters", *Zeitschrift für Musikwissenschaft*, 16, 1934, pp. 129-41, 355-57. But what is essentially denied is the existence of evidence.

45 Modern examples are mainly of the *rondeau* type: see J. S. Pacholczyk, "The Relationship between the Nawba of Morocco and the Music of the Troubadours and Trouvères", *The World of Music*, 25/2, 1983, pp. 5-16.

46 See e.g. A.Chottin, *Tableau de la musique marocaine*, Paris, 1939, p. 98.

47 But the present tuning (e.g. *C-A-D-G*) is a Maghribi feature not, as al-Tīfāshī notes, an Andalusī one.

48 The textual sources are given by Stern (*op. cit.*, p. 71), the music by Liu and Monroe (*op. cit.*, p. 95). The former speaks justifiably of continuity, the latter (p. 3), with more enthusiasm than accuracy, of "an unbroken chain of earwitness accounts".

49 Liu and Monroe, *op. cit.*, pp. 83-101.

50 Copied from Liu and Monroe, *op. cit.*

51 See O. Wright, "Aspects of Historical Change in the Turkish Classical Repertoire" in R. Widdess (ed.), *Musica Asiatica*, 5, 1988, pp. 1-108.

52 *Op. cit.*, pp. 70-71.

53 Liu and Monroe, who provide a most valuable review of sources, and are generally sound in their conclusions, are here left with the unreconciled juxtaposition of the embellishment already noted by al-Tīfāshī on the one hand, and on the other what they call "melodic erosion" (*op. cit.*, pp. 32-33). Embellishment may lead, rather, to eventual formal erosion.

54 J. Stevens, *Words and Music in the Middle Ages: Song, Narrative, Dance and Drama, 1050-1350*, Cambridge (England), 1986, pp. 500-04.

55 See the discussion in Perkuhn, *op. cit.*, pp. 116-32. However, the solutions of his chief critic, Anglès, the doyen of Cantigas studies, have not themselves found universal acceptance.

BIBLIOGRAPHY

ʿAbbās, I., "Akhbār al-ghinā' wa-'l-mughannīn fi 'l-Andalus", *Al-Abḥāth: Quarterly Journal of the American University of Beirut*, 1963/1, pp. 3-22.

Anglès, H., *La música de las Cantigas de Santa María del rey Alfonso el Sabio*, Barcelona: Diputación Provincial de Barcelona: Biblioteca Central, 1958.

Avenary, H., "The Hebrew Version of Abu 'l-Ṣalt's Treatise on Music", *Yuval*, 3, 1974, pp. 7-81.

Braune, G., "Musik in Orient und Okzident", *Europa und der Orient 800-1900: eine Ausstellung des 4. Festivals der Weltkulturen Horizonte '89, 28. Mai-27. August, 1989*, Berlin, 1989, pp. 210-30.

Burnett, C., "Teoria e pratica musicali arabe in Sicilia e nell'Italia meridionale in età normanna e sveva", *Nuove Effemeridi*, 11, 1990, pp. 79-89.

——, "The Use of Geometric Terms in Medieval Music: Elmuahim and Elmuarifa and the Anonymous IV", *Sudhoffs Archiv*, 70/2, 1986, pp. 198-205.

Chottin, A., *Tableau de la musique marocaine*, Paris: Geuthner, 1939.

D'Erlanger, R., *La musique arabe*, Paris: Geuthner, 1959, Vol. VI.

Farmer, H. G., "Clues for the Arabian Influence on European Musical Theory", *JRAS*, 1925/1, pp. 61-80.

——, "The Evolution of the Ṭanbūr or Pandore", *Transactions of the Glasgow Universitie Oriental Society*, 5, 1923-1928, pp. 26-28.

——, "A Further Arabic-Latin Writing on Music", *JRAS*, 1933, pp. 307-22.

——, *Historical Facts for the Arabian Musical Influence*, London: Reeves, n.d..

——, *A History of Arabian Music to the XIIIth Century*, London: Luzac, 1929, repr. 1973.

——, "The Influence of al-Fārābī's 'Ihsa' al-'ulum' (*De Scientiis*) on the Writers on Music in Western Europe", *JRAS*, 1932, pp. 561-92.

——, *Islam* (Musikgeschichte in Bildern. Band III: Musik des Mittelalters und der Renaissance, Lieferung 2), Leipzig: VEB Deutscher Verlag für Musik, 1976.

——, "The Music of Islam", in E.Wellesz (ed.),*The New Oxford History of Music*, London: Oxford University Press, 1957, Vol. I.

——, "An Old Moorish Lute Tutor", *JRAS*, 1931, pp. 349-66, 1932, pp. 99-109, 379-89, 897-904.

——, *The Sources of Arabian Music*, Bearsden, 1940, 2nd ed., Leiden, 1965.

——, *Studies on Oriental Musical Instruments*, London, 1931, Glasgow, 1939.

——, "Ziryāb", *Encyclopaedia of Islam*, 1st ed., supp.

Al-Faruqi, L. I., "Muwashshaḥ: a Vocal form in Islamic Culture", *Ethnomusicology*, 19, 1975, pp. 1-29.

Abū Zayd ʿAbd al-Raḥmān b. ʿAlī al-Fāsī, *Al-Jumūʿ fī ʿilm al-mūsīqī wa 'l-ṭubūʿ*, ed. H. G. Farmer in *Collection of Oriental Writers on Music*, Glasgow, 1933, Vol. I.

Le Gentil, P., *Le virelai et le villancico: le problème des origines arabes*, Paris: Les Belles Lettres, 1954.

Guettat, M., *La musique classique du Maghreb* (La Bibliothèque Arabe), Paris: Sindbad, 1980.

ʿAlī al-Ḥajjī, ʿA., *Tārīkh al-mūsīqā 'l-Andalusiyya*, Beirut: Dār al-Inshād, 1969.

Hickmann, H., "Die Musik des arabisch-islamischen Bereichs" in *Orientalische Musik* (Handbuch der Orientalistik, Erste Abteilung, Ergänzungsband IV), Leiden-Cologne: E. J. Brill, 1970, pp. 1-134.

Al-Ḥifnī, M. A., *Ziryāb. Abū 'l-Ḥasan ʿAlī b. Nāfiʿ, mūsīqār al-Andalus* (Aʿlām al-ʿArab 54), Cairo: al-Dār al-Miṣriyya li 'l-Ta'līf wa 'l-Tarjama, n. d.

Al-Ḥilw, S., *Al-Muwashshaḥāt al-Andalusiyya: nash'atuhā wa taṭawwuruhā*, Beirut: Dār Maktabat al-ḤayāT, 1965.

Huseby, G. V., "Musical Analysis and Poetic Structure in the *Cantigas de Santa Maria*", *Florilegium Hispanicum: Medieval and Golden Age Studies Presented to Dorothy Clotelle Clarke*, ed. J. S.Geary *et al.*, Madison: The Hispanic Seminary of Medieval Studies, 1983, pp. 81-101.

Ibn ʿAbd Rabbihī, *Al-ʿIqd al-farīd*, ed. Aḥmad Amīn *et al.*, Cairo: Maṭbaʿat Lajnat al-Ta'līf wa 'l-Tarjama wa 'l-Nashr, 1949, Vol VI.

Ibn al-Qūṭiyya: see J. M. Nichols.

Al-Jarrārī, ʿA., *Athar al-Andalus ʿalā Ūrubbā fī majāl al-nagham wa 'l-īqāʿ*, Rabat: Maktabat al-Maʿārif, 1982.

Katz, I. J., "The Study and Performance of the *Cantigas de Santa Maria*: a Glance at Recent Musicological Literature", *Bulletin of the Cantigueros de Santa Maria*, 1/1, 1987, pp. 51-60.

Lisān al-Dīn b. al-Khaṭīb, *Risāla fī 'l-ṭabā'iʿ wa-'t-ṭubūʿ wa-'l-uṣūl*, ed. H. G. Farmer in *Collection of Oriental Writers on Music*, Glasgow 1933, Vol. I.

Liu, B. M., *The Music of the Muwashshaḥ and Zajal* (forthcoming).

Liu, B. M., and J. T. Monroe, *Ten Hispano-Arabic Strophic Songs in the Modern Oral Tradition* (Modern Philology, 125), Berkeley-Los Angeles-London, University of California Press, 1989.

López-Morillas, C., "Was the *Muwashshaḥ* Really Accompanied by the Organ?", *La Corónica*, 14/1, 1985, pp. 40-54.

Al-Maqqarī, *Nafḥ al-ṭīb*, ed. I. ʿAbbās, Beirut: Dār Ṣādir, 1968, Vol. III.

Monroe, J. T., "Poetic Quotation in the *Muwaššaḥa* and its Implications: Andalusian Strophic Poetry as Song", *La Corónica*, 14/2, 1986, pp. 230-50.

——, "The Tune or the Words? (Singing Hispano-Arabic Strophic Poetry)", *Al-Qanṭara*, 8, 1987, pp. 265-317.

——, "Which Came First, the *Zajal* or the *Muwaššaḥa*? Some Evidence for the Oral Origins of Hispano-Arabic Strophic Poetry", *Oral Tradition*, 4/1-2, 1989, pp. 38-64.

Neubauer, E., "Zur Rolle der Araber in der Musikgeschichte des europäischen Mittelalters", *Islam und Abendland. Geschichte und Gegenwart*, ed. A Mercier, Bern-Frankfurt 1976, pp. 111-29.

Nichols, J. M., *The* History of the Conquest of al-Andalus *by Ibn al-Qūṭīya the Cordovan: translation and study*, Ph.D thesis, University of North Carolina, Chapel Hill, 1975.

Pacholczyk, J. S., "The Relationship between the Nawba of Morocco and the Music of the Troubadours and Trouvères", *The World of Music*, 25/2, 1983, pp. 5-16.

Perkuhn, E. R., *Die Theorien zum arabischen Einfluss auf die europäische Musik des Mittelalters* (Beiträge zur Sprach- und Kulturgeschichte des Orients, 26), Walldorf-Hessen: Verlag für Orientkunde, 1976.

Ribera y Tarragó, J., *Historia de la música árabe medieval y su influencia en la española* (Colección de Manuales Hispania, Vol. 1-serie G), Madrid: Editorial Voluntad, 1927, reprinted New York: AMS Press, 1975.

——, *La música de las Cantigas*, Madrid: Real Academia Española, 1922.

Sadie. S. (ed.), *The New Grove Dictionary of Music and Musicians*, London: Macmillan, 1980. Articles: Arab music; cantiga; chanson; flamenco; Spain; troubadours, trouvères; villancico; virelai.

Sadie, S., (ed.), *The New Grove Dictionary of Musical Instruments*, London: Macmillan, 1984. Articles: adufe; alboka; gaita; hornpipe; lute; nakers; rabāb; rebec.

Schneider, M., "A propósito del influjo árabe: ensayo de etnografía musical de la España medieval", *Anuario Musical*, 1, 1946, pp. 31-141.

Schuyler, P. D., "Moroccan Andalusian music", *The World of Music*, 21/1, 1978, pp. 33-46.

Shiloah, A., *The Theory of Music in Arabic Writings (c. 900-1900)* (Répertoire International des Sources Musicales: B X), Munich: Henle, 1979.

Stern, S. M., "Andalusian *Muwashshaḥs* in the Musical Repertoire of North Africa", *Actas del Primer Congreso de Estudios Arabes e Islámicos, Córdoba, 1962*, ed. F. M. Pareja, Madrid: Maestre, 1964, pp. 319-27.

——, *Hispano-Arabic Strophic Poetry*, ed. L. P.Harvey, Oxford: Clarendon Press, 1974.

Stevens, J., *Words and Music in the Middle Ages: Song, Narrative, Dance and Drama, 1050-1350*, Cambridge: Cambridge University Press, 1986.

Al-Ṭanjī, M. b. T., "Al-Ṭarā'iq wa 'l-alḥān al-mūsīqiyya fī Ifrīqiya wa 'l-Andalus", *Al-Abḥāth: Quarterly Journal of the American University of Beirut*, 21/2, 3, 4, 1968, pp. 93-116.

Al-Tīfāshī, Aḥmad, *Mutʿat al-asmāʿ fī ʿilm al-samāʿ*, ch. 10, 11 in al-Ṭanjī.

Ursprung, O., "Um die Frage nach dem arabischen Einfluss auf die abendländische Musik des Mittelalters", *Zeitschrift für Musikwissenschaft*, 16, 1934, pp. 129-41.

Wulstan, D., "The *Muwaššaḥ* and *Zajal* Revisited", *JAOS*, 102/2, 1982, pp. 247-64.

Yafil, N. A., (ed.), *Majmūʿ al-aghānī wa 'l-alḥān min kalām al-Andalus*. Yafil and Seror, Algiers, 1904.

ART AND ARCHITECTURE

TWO PARADOXES IN THE ISLAMIC ART OF THE SPANISH PENINSULA

OLEG GRABAR

Introduction

Of all the lands of the earth which have preserved masterpieces of Islamic architecture, or from which unique monuments of craftsmanship attributable to Muslim artisans or to Muslim patronage have come, two are no longer ruled by Muslims. They are India, the home of the Taj Mahal and of Fatehpur Sikri, and then there is Spain. Of the numerous sub-cultures which shaped European Christian civilisation in the Middle Ages and in pre-modern times, two were for several centuries in close connection with and at times even subjugated by the world of Islam. One is the Eastern and South-Eastern European world of, for the most part, orthodox Christians and the other is a major portion of the Iberian Peninsula, more specifically that part of the Peninsula which has been called al-Andalus, the southern section of which has become the contemporary province of Andalucía; for, in the Middle Ages, al-Andalus was to Arab Muslim writers every part of the Peninsula under Muslim rule and control.

I shall not, in the context of this essay, pursue the parallels between the intercultural contacts of the Iberian Peninsula and those of other parts of the Eurasian and African worlds, though I shall refer to them toward the end of my observations, as they may well provide a useful interpretative framework within which to see and to explain the art of Muslim Spain. What I shall try to show is that the art of Islamic Spain can be seen in two ways. It can be part of a large body of monuments known as "Islamic", that is to say as made by or for people who professed the Muslim faith; or else it can be seen as Spanish or Hispanic, that is as the creation of a land with traditions which would have been, in part at least, independent of the religious, ethnic or cultural allegiances of rulers of the moment.

Good arguments can be made, and have been made in the past, in favour of either one of these positions or approaches toward the arts of Muslim Spain; for indeed each one of them is justified by some at least of the factual characteristics of the monuments involved, but especially by reference to two diametrically opposed ideological positions. I and others in this volume will deal with the monuments. The ideologies are less easy to define. On the one hand, there lies the achievement of a land remote from the centres of Muslim power and creativity; and that achievement can be interpreted as a demonstration of the divinely inspired power of a Muslim ethos or of the brilliantly superior cultural bind that tied together, through a single faith with many variants, as diverse a crowd as Turkified Iranians from Central Asia and the descendants of Arabicised Berbers and of Hispanic women. But there is an alternative position to what may be called a pan-Islamic ideology explaining culture through the forceful mediation of the faith and of the ethic attached to it. From this other point of view, the qualities of a land's art are explained through the permanent operation of a national spirit, of an indefinable attribute of a land and of its past, through the presence of the "earth" and of the "dead", as theoreticians of nationalism defined the nation in the early years of our century.

The debate between these ideologies is not one in which someone who is neither a Spaniard nor a Muslim should intervene, but it is proper to wonder why it is that apparently incompatible attitudes of interpretation have emerged around the art of Islamic Spain, as they had also grown around its culture and indeed its very existence. I shall explore this question by identifying two apparent paradoxes concerning the art of Islamic Spain and by weaving various thoughts and observations around these paradoxes. The first is the apparently unique character, both typologically and aesthetically, of so many works of Spanish Islamic art. The second one is the unusual fit between forms assumed to be Islamic and patrons of art or settings for art which are not. In conclusion I shall return to some of the broader issues brought up at the beginning.

I. *The monuments of Spain*

The Great Mosque in Córdoba is acknowledged as a major masterpiece of Islamic architecture, and many scholars have used it as a prototypical exemplar of the hypostyle mosque which creates large spaces for the whole community by multiplying a single support, in this instance the column with arches, in a flexible manner adjusted to increases and decreases in the population of believers. And it is true that, at a very simple and elementary level, the mosque of Córdoba is planned and designed according to principles comparable to those which created the mosque of Qayrawān in Tunisia, the Azhar or the mosque of ʿAmr in Cairo, the Mosque of the Prophet in Medina, the Aqṣā mosque in Jerusalem, and, in slightly different ways, the large brick mosques of Samarra in Iraq and of Ibn Ṭūlūn in Cairo. All these are buildings earlier than the Cordoban one or roughly contemporary with its latest phase in the 4th/10th century. After the 4th/10th century thousands of mosques, especially the ones in the Muslim West, would continue this hypostyle tradition.

But to see the mosque of Córdoba as "just" another example of a well-known type is to misunderstand the peculiar qualities of the building. As several present-day architects and architectural critics have pointed out, it combines a number of unusual features: a subtle harmony of proportions between elements like thin columns and horse-shoe arches which are not themselves original; a geometry of the arch which gives it a feeling of repose rather than the strain of being a carrier of thrusts; an equilibrium between single supports and mass ensembles like naves; occasionally the conscious breakdown of nuclear forms like arches into segments which can then be recomposed in alternate ways; and, finally, the stunning *miḥrāb* with the three domes in front of it, an ensemble glittering with rich mosaics for the representation of highly composed vegetal motifs and for the copying of long written messages, and yet mysterious in the deep niche of the *miḥrāb* itself, which is like an empty chamber, or else the gate toward another realm than that of man.

Some of these features, like the mosaic technique or the expensive *miḥrāb* area, can be explained by specific local contingencies, namely the politico-cultural relations with the Byzantine world which explain the mosaics themselves and the existence of more elaborate ceremonies than was usually the case around the daily prayers required of all Muslims. In Córdoba, perhaps in imitation of Christian practices, the muezzins came and prayed in front of the *miḥrāb* before calling for prayer. There was in the mosque a gigantic copy of the Quran which required two men to move it, and in which were included four leaves from a Quran attributed to the caliph U<u>th</u>mān, a hero of Umayyad tradition, who had allegedly been assassinated while reading the Holy Book; drops of blood were in fact found on these pages, which had obviously become symbols for something much greater than pages of text. This Quran was carried around at prayer time preceded by an acolyte with a candle, just as the Gospels are carried in a church.

But, even beyond such specific details, which are original to the mosque of Córdoba but which are typologically not different from objects associated with other mosques, two features differentiate the mosque of Córdoba from nearly all other Muslim congregational buildings. One feature is that so much about it has been recorded and maintained even by historians and geographers who wrote much later, after the city had been taken by Christians. It is as though collective memory, Muslim, and probably also Christian since that particular mosque has been preserved, recognised something unique about the Cordoban monument. The second feature is the consistency of aesthetic purposes in the building, that is to say of creating visual effects which would affect the senses, which would give pleasure to the visitor or to the user. Few other mosques (Ibn Ṭūlūn's in Cairo is a major exception) are designed in such a way that everything in it, even later additions like the Christian chapels and the church, has to be done in the harmonic key of the constructions of the early 3rd/9th century. A concern for sensory effectiveness and for visual beauty is a hallmark of Córdoba's mosque in ways that are more consistent, more fully anchored and more gripping than in most examples of congregational buildings within the medieval Muslim tradition.

An even stranger case is that of the ivory objects of the 4th/10th and early 5th/11th centuries. Some twenty small boxes have remained, which were probably used for the storage of precious items, kerchiefs of different types or unguents. Many of them are dated and localised either in Córdoba or in the royal city of Madīnat al-Zahrā' only a few miles from the urban centre itself. Inscriptions often identify the owners of many of them as members of the ruling family or very high officials of the Umayyad state. In itself there is nothing unusual about expensive objects in a rare material being made for members of ruling classes in the Muslim world. Chronicles and other written sources are full of references to the fancy things and the fancy clothes which surrounded the princes and assorted aristocrats in Baghdad, Nishapur, Cairo, Herat, Rayy or Bukhara. But hardly anything has remained from these treasures, and one way of interpreting the Spanish ivories is to argue that they are an accidentally preserved set of princely artifacts of a type which would have existed elsewhere as well. In all likelihood it was the possibility of reusing these objects for church treasures which saved them from being destroyed, or utilised and handled over the centuries to the point of becoming totally worn.

To a certain extent this is probably the correct conclusion to draw. These ivories are indeed aristocratic household objects illustrating the wealth and the taste of the Umayyad court in al-Andalus. But there are several reasons for wondering whether we are not also dealing with a rather unique group of objects reflecting some uniquely local phenomena. I will mention just two peculiarities of these ivories which cannot be explained, at least within our present scholarly capabilities, in terms of a wider Muslim culture. One is that some among this group of objects—for instance the cylindrical casket of 357-8/968 in the Louvre, the 359-60/969-70 one in the Victoria and Albert Museum, and an undated one in the Museo Nazionale in Florence—are very deeply cut, so that the decoration on them appears in high relief, almost like the sculpture on antique and early Christian sarcophagi. This sculpted effect is, especially in the Louvre object, carried to the point where the personages, animals and plants of the design appear almost like free-standing sculptures in the round fixed on an object. Nothing like this is known in Islamic art elsewhere, nor, for that matter, is it known in early medieval Christian art. It is likely in fact that some antique model influenced the patron or artisans of these objects, but it is difficult to imagine how and why such an impression would have been sought.

The second peculiarity of some of these ivories is even more unsettling. The Louvre and Victoria and Albert examples, as well as several others in the Cathedral Treasury of Pamplona, the one in Burgos, and once again in the Victoria and Albert Museum, are decorated with personages and animals either arranged formally and symmetrically, as they often are on textiles, or else in what are clearly narrative or symbolic scenes: a prince enthroned, wrestling, hunting, plucking eggs from a nest, riding elephants, picking dates, and so on. It is, first of all, remarkable that these scenes using personages in a narrative context occur in Spain nearly a century and a half before they become common in Egypt and the rest of the Islamic world. But even more remarkable is the fact that, while some of the representations would eventually become fairly common in Islamic art, most of them are unique. We are thus faced with the strange paradox of being unable to explain images which are easy to describe.

At this stage we can only speculate about the reasons for these peculiarities of the Spanish Islamic ivories of the Umayyad period. They might have reflected, at the height of Umayyad power and wealth, the unusual cultural and artistic depth of the Umayyad court, in which new motifs are invented to give an old look, classical in mode, to the expensive materials brought from Central Africa. A hundred or more years later, under the rule of a Christian king, quintessentially Muslim motifs would adorn the ceiling of the royal chapel in the Norman palace of Palermo in Sicily. This later example suggests that in the Western Mediterranean a cultural mix was perhaps created different from that of places farther east. A couple of minor points would confirm the sense of a difference in the art of Muslim Spain in its earliest and greatest time. The names of artists and craftsmen for objects and for architectural decoration have been preserved from Spain much earlier and much more frequently than from elsewhere in the Muslim world, as though the status of the artisan was higher there. And then it is interesting to note the visibility of the patronage of objects by women, again a phenomenon which is rare elsewhere at that time. The two earliest dated ivory objects were made for daughters of ʿAbd al-Raḥmān III, and one of the later ones was made for a Princess Ṣubḥ.

My third example is that of the most celebrated monument of Islamic art in Spain, the Alhambra. This is not the place to discuss either its archaeology or its stunning features which attract millions of tourists every year. What is important from the point of view I am developing in this essay is that it too is unique in Islamic architecture—even though everyone, from scholars who have written about it to Hollywood or rich Arab patrons from the Gulf who have copied it or imitated it or parts of it a thousand times, regards the Alhambra as so characteristic of Islamic culture that popular as well as sophisticated imagination has, since the early 19th century, woven its orientalist fantasies around it. Yet it is curious that there is no other building, no other part of a known building, which resembles the Alhambra, some later imitations in Morocco in particular notwithstanding. And it requires a considerable stretch of the imagination to see in the Top Kapi Seray in Istanbul, the palace of the Ottoman sultans or the later Safavid palaces of Isfahan and the Mughal palaces of India, more than occasional similarities with Granada's masterpiece. We are less well informed about earlier and contemporary palaces around the Mediterranean, but what is known for instance about the citadel of Cairo in the heyday of Mamlūk rule bears very little relationship to the Alhambra. It is maybe just possible that a dying Muslim dynasty in al-Andalus did not create a "typical" palace belonging to a set which has disappeared elsewhere, but something adapted to its own specific history and to its own specific needs and expectations.

The mosque of Córdoba, the 4th/10th century Umayyad ivories and the 8th/14th century Alhambra are all unique monuments which fit uneasily within the generic cultural types with which they have usually been associated. And yet all three—as well as several additional ones like a number of silks and bronzes, or the small mosque of Bīb Mardūm in Toledo—illustrate functions and tastes which were indeed part of the traditional and classical ethos of the Islamic world: the large congregational mosque, the princely household object of great value, the luxurious setting for the life of rulers. None of these needs, except to a degree the second one, was significant to the medieval Christian world. Their Spanish expression, however, seems to have obeyed other constraints, other forces than those which obtained elsewhere in the Islamic world. Why?

II. *Islamic forms and non-Islamic patrons*

The second paradox I would like to develop is easier to define than the first, but equally difficult to explain. It has long been noted that the forms of Islamic art lingered on in Spain much longer than in Sicily or in the Balkans or Russia, where they had hardly affected the arts of the local population (except in clothes), even during Muslim domination.

Examples abound. Pedro the Cruel's Alcázar in Seville comprises architectural forms associated normally with Islamic art, and, in the decorative cartouches of plaster which appear everywhere, his name is clearly written out in Arabic letters. For several centuries the churches of Toledo and Saragossa utilised real or blind decorative arcades which come out of the facades and minarets of the earlier Islamic tradition. As profoundly Christian a building as the so-called "tempietto" in the monastery of Guadelupe bears unmistakable and obviously deliberately chosen traces of medieval Islamic themes. In Burgos, one of the main centres of Spanish life to escape Muslim rule, and which became one of the centres of the *reconquista*, the monastery of Las Huelgas, in the early 13th century, was designed in part as a commemorative monument for Alfonso VII, one of the main Crusaders against Muslim power in the South. But not only is its stucco decoration entirely taken from Islamic models, but the textiles which had been kept there, often as shrouds, were for the most part either manufactured by Muslims or imitated Muslim types. Ceramic production remained for centuries under the influence of the high lustre techniques developed in the Muslim world and brought relatively late to Spain. And two remarkable synagogues built in

Toledo under Christian rule—one from the 12th century, known today as the church of Santa María la Blanca, the other dated 1357, and transformed into a church under the name of El Tránsito—were decorated in the purest style of Islamic ornament.

This is all well-known, and for over a century now scholars have identified examples of what has been called Mudejar art, an art of Muslim forms within a non-Muslim context. Even its migration into Mexico and Peru has occasionally been noted. What is more puzzling is that this preservation of allegedly Muslim forms often took place while Islam itself and those who professed it were persecuted, often quite brutally, and eventually physically expelled from the Iberian Peninsula. Gothic art coming from the North appeared at times like an outright intruder within a formal system which would have been the accepted genuine local one; and it is only with the Italianate taste of the Renaissance that Islamic motifs began to fade away, as in the lovely House of Pilate in Seville. But, even then, Charles V built his grandiose palace of Granada next to the Alhambra, dominating it no doubt, as a victorious culture would, but recognising something of its values by preserving it. And earlier Alfonso the Wise was deeply imbued with Muslim values and aware of all that went into the making of a cultivated Muslim Arab.

How can one explain the contrast between policies that were leading to the destruction of Islam's presence in the Peninsula and this fascination with forms issuing from Islamic art, which continued quite consciously for several centuries, and, according to some, has remained in the background ever since? What, especially, is it that made Spain so different from other lands?

As most paradoxes do, mine about Islamic art in Spain end up with questions. Both questions imply that something happened in Spain which is different from what happened elsewhere. There does not seem, *a priori*, to be any reason why the Islamic monuments of Spain should be qualitatively and typologically unique within the huge spectrum of Islamic art, even though their functions were not. And it is strange that a land which had invested so much physical and psychic energy in reclaiming from an allegedly alien power what was presumed to be its own would, for several centuries, maintain and carefully nurture the artistic forms of the enemy.

To be able to reach an answer or answers to these questions, we must be willing to explore two propositions which go against well-established assumptions of the history of art, and perhaps of cultural history in general.

The first of these assumptions is that which involves labelling forms with cultural or national identifications. What seem to us today to be valid or even accurate means for the classification of visual evidence from the past, and for the appreciation of that evidence within our own, present-day minds, may not have been the appropriate criterion at the time when the monuments through which this evidence appears were created. If we consider a motif or a type of design as first of all colourful, geometric or vegetal, rather than

Islamic or Gothic or Byzantine, an appreciation of forms emerges which may well correspond more closely to what actually happened than the national and ethnic constructs we have posited. Alternatively, one can consider a motif as "ours", as belonging to a tradition within a land rather than to a system of belief in that land. Analyses freed of prejudices may indeed begin to argue for a complex growth, in medieval Spain, of a common heritage of forms which was, in part if not as a whole, differentiated by its presence in that particular land rather than by its association with religious or national groups in that land. Within that heritage, some specific feature may be charged with an Islamic, Arab, Christian, Castilian or Catalonese connotation, but such distinctions will only be reached after the realisation that there was a common language for the expression of different thoughts and of different tastes and purposes. Perhaps after all it was other factors than those of cultural identification that predominated in the arts of the Middle Ages in Spain, and even elsewhere.

The second issue to be pursued springs not so much from a possibly wrong-headed assumption as from one's awareness of the position of al-Andalus within the huge body of Islamic culture. It was a frontier area, at the outer edges of the *dār al-Islām*, and like all frontier areas it was endowed with a peculiarly paradoxical ethos in which intense identification of differences between groups and allegiances, at times warped by hate and contempt, coexisted with open-minded cohabitation and creative inventiveness. 13th-century Anatolia, 12th-century Sicily, Central Asia until the 16th century, were all frontier areas between opposing and at times warring factions of many different kinds. They were also areas of intense visual (and perhaps other) creativity, in which the desire to show off one's unique qualities went along with competition with others and understanding of various ways of achieving visual effectiveness. With the advent of the rational doctrines issuing from the Renaissance, such tolerance became more difficult to maintain.

It is obvious that these hypotheses and assumptions need elaboration and reflection before they can be fully accepted as explanations for the Islamic arts of the Spanish Peninsula in the Middle Ages. That they can even be raised is a testimony to the extraordinary quality of the centuries which revolutionised a land and expressed some of the best ambitions of a universal religious and ethical system created far away.

BIBLIOGRAPHY

This essay is based on commonly known volumes of information like Vols. III and IV of *Ars Hispaniae* and the monumental E. Kuhnel, *Islamische Elfenbeinskulpturen*, Berlin, 1971. I have much profited from the following more detailed or more recent studies:

Beckwith, John, *Caskets from Cordova*, London, 1960.
Delgado Valero, Clara, *Toledo islámico*, Toledo, 1987.
Gómez Moreno, Manuel, *El Panteón Real de Las Huelgas de Burgos*, Madrid, 1946.
Instituto de Estudios Turolenses, *II Simposio Internacional de Mudejarismo: Arte*, Teruel, 1982.
Moneo, Rafael, and others, "La Mezquita de Córdoba", *Arquitectura*, 66, 1985.
Pavón Maldonado, B., *El arte hispano-musulmán en su decoración geométrica*, Madrid, 1975.
Sánchez Albornoz, C., *L'Espagne musulmane*, French translation of earlier Spanish version, Paris, 1985.
Stern, Henri, *Les mosaïques de Cordoue*, Berlin, 1976.

THE MUDEJAR TRADITION IN ARCHITECTURE

JERRILYNN DODDS

Al-Andalus suffered profound changes to its political authority long before the fall of Granada. Christian forces had been making major and irreversible incursions into Muslim-ruled lands since the late 6th/12th century, and this produced, in many cities in particular, a divergence between the new Christian rule and an existing Islamic social and cultural structure. This was in particular the case in Toledo, where a long-standing tradition of architectural and artistic production established under Muslim rule was inherited by Christian rulers of the Reconquest.

Christian attitudes towards arts perceived as Islamic were variable with the political and social climate. But scholarship has not always considered this to be the case. For some time it was assumed that Mozarabic art, the art of Christians who lived under Islamic rule, must be the unwitting bearer of Islamic artistic culture to Christian Spain. There was at one time even the tendency to define Mozarabic art by the intensity of Islamic formal impact on its works. It is clear, however, that Christian patrons under the Emirate —when the Christian cultural identity was in most peril—exercised a resistance to forms recognisably Islamic, while later, more secure periods saw Christians appropriating Islamic forms to suit their own artistic aims.[1]

The case of Mudejar art is interesting, for it represents a moment of Christian control: Islamic culture no longer posed a threat to Christian identity and existence. Indeed, the word Mudejar suggests an art of subjected Muslims, though the old-fashioned notion that it was executed by Muslim slaves of Christian masters has no basis in fact. In fact they probably included, in their ranks, Christians and Jews as well, all of whom had worked as craftsmen under Muslim power. Mudejar was, however, a style associated with Islamic patronage. It was only the new position of Christian rulers in the political hierarchy of the 6th/12th and 7th/13th centuries—along with a relaxation of the cultural defensiveness which had characterised the Christian attitude towards Islamic arts in the earlier period—that rendered the new widespread appropriation of Islamic crafts and forms possible, allowing the traditional Islamic crafts of Spain to take on new meanings for its new patrons.

An example can be traced in the small mosque of Bāb al-Mardūm near the city walls of Toledo. Constructed on the ruins of a Visigothic church, and even reusing some of the spolia of that Christian sanctuary, its brick construction tradition exploited the thickness of the brick to create planar reveals and textures that enliven a simple and aniconic exterior to this pavilion-like sanctuary. The stucco domes that copy more monumental forms in the Great Mosque of Córdoba use local materials to evoke a grander monument. But sometime in the 590s/1190s, during the Christianisation of Toledo under Alfonso VIII, a voluminous apse was added to that mosque's nine-bay plan, converting it into an axialised church culminating in an altar.

Though figural paintings had transformed the monument's interior, the entire project was executed by masons working within a continuation of the same tradition as that in which the mosque had been built almost two hundred years before. The entire construction is of brick, punctuated by an occasional saw-tooth course as in the earlier work. Its articulation consists of blind arcades that embrace an occasional window as well, all conceived in a multi-planar style defined by the thickness of the brick itself. There are more lobes to the polylobed, pointed arches of the apse decoration than in the mosque construction, but it reads as a continuation of the similarly conceived decoration of the older mosque flanks.

There are of course practical reasons for such borrowing, not the least of which is the need for an existing work force for the job of reconstructing ruined churches and settings for the newly empowered Christian administrators and churchmen. But there is nevertheless a clear interest in some level of visual continuity on the part of patrons, or at least a curious abstinence on their part from distinguishing their new sacred buildings of Christian reconquest by any change in exterior visual vocabulary. It is the buildings' interiors, their use of narrative imagery and a Christian typology in plan, that declares their new identity, but that is an issue seemingly underplayed in their exterior form.

There is, in monuments like the mosque of Bāb al-Mardūm converted into the church of Cristo de la Luz, a tension between the need to lay claim to and transform a site from mosque to church (as indeed it had originally been transformed from church to mosque), and a desire to appropriate some of the power and validity of the indigenous tradition established during Toledo's Muslim domination. It is the dilemma of a new Christian hegemony which finds itself ruling a population including strong vestiges of an enemy culture which the Christians nevertheless held in some awe. It was an admiration suppressed in the years of Islamic control of the Peninsula, but now it seemed that, in the face of political domination, it was safe to give such cultural indenture free reign.

The early use of the Mudejar style in other parts of the country had similar meanings. In Castile the possession of that style, and its subordination to Christian projects, might have been a coded reference to the progress of the Reconquest. Why else, at the height of the development of the Romanesque style in the Christian north, would the important churches of Sahagún be constructed entirely in an imported, brick-based Mudejar style? Once more the practical considerations were significant. Entire communities of Muslim masons and bricklayers had settled in Castile, some of them brought there by Christian monarchs as part of the resettlement of frontier areas.[2] The work they offered was cheaper than the current Romanesque style in vogue. But a curious fact helps us to see the persistent appeal of the style in which they built as well. At San Tirso de Sahagún, a tri-apsed church was begun in ashlar, presumably as a Romanesque church of the pilgrimage road type, a style formed in France and imported into Spain for use in religious establishments like the parochial church at Frómista. However, after six courses of the apse of San Tirso were constructed (and probably the church itself laid out in plan as well), it was completed in an austere version of the brick style of blind arches and cool reveals we associate with Toledo. Though it is possible this abrupt change responded to practical considerations, the resettlement of masons from Toledo in the north was itself a work of propaganda and appropriation.

But further, it is hard to see such a complete divergence in style and technique without positing that there was an appealing meaning to this exotic new type of technique and ornament; for out of the peninsula in which Muslims and Christians lived in constantly shifting tensions came a consciousness concerning artistic styles as bearers of cultural meaning and identification. It allowed both for the gesture of the adoption of Romanesque as a reference to a wholly Christian northern culture, and for an accrued meaning to cling to Mudejar brickwork, a strange imported style and technique associated with Muslim Toledo.

At San Román in Toledo we find another aspect of Mudejar style: its celebration of a shared, indigenous culture, one which at times obscured the original meanings of borrowed form. The church of San Román was constructed in 618/1221 with the same masonry technique that fashioned the apse of Cristo de la Luz, but this time with rather extraordinary figural paintings in its interior. It must have been part of a frenzy of church building following the reconquest of the city. The paintings are large-scale and maladroit, but they contain some fascinating ironies: they are narrative, representing biblical themes, yet they use inscriptions as borders in a manner more typical of Islamic than of Christian monuments. But more surprisingly, the arches of the church's arcades are painted in alternating red and white voussoirs, and Arabic inscriptions are added to the Latin ones. The large-scale narrative paintings were enough to free the church from any possible association with Muslim worship. The use of Latin inscriptions probably represents the absorption of a habit of thinking involving the use of writing in an architectural setting. The alternating voussoirs and the Arabic inscriptions, however, seem to indicate a deeper connection between the builders and users of the church and their context. For there is the suggestion here of a shared culture: certainly of a shared spoken and written language by means of which the city had been administered for years, and a shared language of forms which saw much that began as identifiably Islamic becoming part of a local visual culture, a decoration that witnessed a history and culture belonging to all Toledans.

This seems in particular to have been the case for Jews, whose synagogues are decorated in a Mudejar style quite close to its Granadan predecessors. The earliest of these, the 6th/12th century synagogue of Santa María la Blanca, has been converted into a church, but vestiges of a dispersed mosque-like plan are still visible, with white octagonal piers crowned by wide stucco capitals covered with pine cones and sensual volutes. There is also a restrained stucco relief that follows the extrados and spandrels of the arches and the upper wall of each gallery. The effect of peering laterally into the hall is very much like that of an Almohad mosque, both in elevation and decoration, though without its original furnishings it is difficult to guess at a complete appearance. But it is clear that whatever similarities we see between synagogue and mosque are due not to a melding of ideologies but to a secularisation of artistic form.

This is more easy to discern in the synagogue built in 762/1360 by Samuel Halevi Abulafia, also known as the Synagogue of El Tránsito in Toledo. A wide, open rectangle with niches to the east to receive Torah scrolls, this synagogue possessed a special passage to its patron's home; for it was not intended for community worship but as a kind of palatine chapel for Abulafia, who was finance minister and adviser to King Pedro the Cruel.

The synagogue of Abulafia is covered with opulent painted stucco relief of the Granadan type, rather than reflecting the more Almohad taste noted at the synagogue of Santa María la Blanca. For though Mudejar represents a dialogue which takes place after the overthrow of an Islamic rule, communications with Islamic arts seem not to have ended. On the contrary, Mudejar was more than Islamic-trained masons looking for work; it was part of a web of cultural interdependencies in lands which had known many different rules, and as such involved an idea about art, one that grew and changed and made renewed reference to the Islamic arts which were at its roots.

The references at the synagogue of Abulafia were very current ones: mural surfaces disembodied by ornament, and upper walls festooned with a line of polylobed arches. The synagogue is also covered with a series of inscriptions in Hebrew and in Arabic. The Arabic inscriptions are innocuous invocations that suggest, once again, a shared language. Indeed, for the Jews of Toledo a strategic power lay in their easy working knowledge of the three languages of the city. But the Hebrew inscriptions are of particular interest because, as rather hubristic poems about the building's patron, they recall the use of ornament and inscription at the Alhambra in Granada, and remind one of the extent to which a court Jew conceived of patronage in the mould, not of his Christian lord, but of a Muslim prince.

But perhaps the situation was more complex still. For Abulafia's lord was Pedro the Cruel, who is also known as a primary builder of the palace of the Alcázar in Seville, as it now appears. There, court after court, room upon room presents a palace indentured to the image of an Islamic palace like the Alhambra as a setting for royalty. A confusing and disorienting plan; screens of luxurious interlace held aloft on slender columns; dados of tile in geometric patterns and large panels of stucco with Arabic inscriptions: all are our witness that there could be no complete image of kingship in Spain without reference to the myth of Islamic kingship forged at the Alhambra in the last years of the Islamic hegemony.

Perceived not as a reference to religious or political identification, but rather as it was meant to be, as a virtuoso wielding of cultural power which created an image of kingship more powerful than a thousand military conquests, the Alhambra's myth was perpetuated. It is this that Pedro the Cruel sought to evoke at Seville, and something of the same—perhaps the image of a setting for exclusive, aristocratic life—that Abulafia sought in Toledo: the power of a setting that alludes constantly to privilege and authority.

These associations lead to Mudejar constructions in a number of royal foundations. It is not a coincidence that the military banner of the Almohads, the so-called Banner of Las Navas de Tolosa, was given to the monastery of Las Huelgas in Burgos. Its stuccos, which find elegant birds embedded in intertwining knots, or its marquetry doors, extensions of the same tradition in which the *minbar* of the Kutubiyya mosque was fashioned, all speak of culture captured like booty when it is marked by the arms of the conquering prince. The monarch Alfonso X would build a cathedral in León that copied Reims Cathedral in France—the site of the coronation of French kings; and yet he also personally oversaw the construction of a number of Mudejar monuments in other parts of Spain. The most important is probably the chapel in the reappropriated Great Mosque of Córdoba—now the Cathedral of St. Mary —where he hoped to be buried. There, a tiny cube within a (at that time) largely untransformed mosque space was covered with Mudejar stucco work, polylobed and lambriken arches and geometric designs on mosaic tile dados. It is a work of Mudejar style by Mudejar artists, and it suggests something about Alfonso's ability to use architectural style to express pertinent political moods: the Gothic Cathedral of León expressed his cosmopolitan, imperial concerns, while his Mudejar constructions grow from his constant attempts to create an image of a monarch at home with, and in control of, the vast ethnic and religious diversity which characterised the rapidly growing Spanish Christian kingdoms.

In Aragon the concentration of Mudejar monuments is great, and the style is there swept up as part of a vibrant local tradition. A series of beautiful towers survives from the 8th/14th century, reminding one in many ways of Almohad minarets: simple and geometric in their form, and with the ubiquitous double arched windows and panels of interlace in low, brick relief. But in the tower of San Salvador the motifs are multiplied to include impertinent zig-zags and rosettes, and the whole is punctuated with polychromed ceramic. The geometry and logic that lay at the heart of such decoration under Islamic rule is lost; instead it has become a vibrant local tradition that saw complex surface ornament as part of an indigenous heritage.

Indeed, on the eve of the Renaissance in Spain, most of the decorative principles which entered the Mudejar vocabulary through Almohad or Naṣrid sources were absorbed into a common language of forms shared by Christian and Muslim alike. In Plateresque art, or the peculiar strain of Renaissance architecture found particularly in Salamanca, classical motifs cover the face of a building, creating a sense of horror vacui reminiscent of Islamic stuccos, but with an entirely new, imported decorative vocabulary. The principle of complex, overall surface ornamentation had become a national one, the terms by which other new architectural styles from the outside were transformed. Today elements of the Mudejar style are recognised as national, but marginal. Appearing in cultural expositions and carnival architecture, they represent something traditional and ancient in Spanish history, but also something which is other than the featureless European face Modern Spain at times strives to assume.

But it is clear that Mudejar architecture bears artistic witness to an intensely creative moment in the formation of Spanish culture; it testifies to the tensions of a shifting political and ethnic identification, through the retention of visual forms which began as Islamic but ended as simply indigenous. In many cases, in fact, its meaning became synonymous with Spanish hegemony; this is why colonial architecture in Central and South America, which came to represent the Spanish Christian presence in those newly discovered lands, is actually often called Mudejar. It embodies—in its use of a skin of complex ornament that becomes abstracted because of the complexity and multiplicity of form—the broad extension over time and space of an artistic tradition which began with the advent of Islamic rule in Spain

Mudejar arts began as arts involving conscious association with Islamic society according to historical moment, patron and audience. Subsequently, the theme of reconquest and political appropriation reflected in them gave way, gradually, to myths and principles dissociated from their original, Islamic context: princely, opulent, mystical, indigenous, they became, finally, simply Spanish.

[1] For a development of this idea and examples, see J. Dodds, *Architecture and Ideology in Early Medieval Spain*, University Park-London, 1990.

[2] L. Torres Balbás offers a number of examples in "Arte Mudéjar", *Ars Hispaniae*, 4, Madrid, 1949, p. 257.

BIBLIOGRAPHY

Aguilar, M., *Málaga mudéjar. Arquitectura religiosa y civil*, Málaga, 1979.
Borrás, G., *Arte mudéjar aragonés*, Aragoza, 1985, 3 vols.
Fraga, M., *Arquitectura mudéjar en la Baja Andalucía*, Santa Cruz de Tenerife, 1977.
Martinez Caviró, B., *Mudéjar toledano; palacios y conventos*, Madrid, 1980.
Mogollón, P., *El mudéjar en Extremadura*, Universidad de Extremadura, 1987.
Pavón, B., *Arte toledano islámico y mudéjar*, Madrid, 1973 (2nd ed. 1988).
——, *Arte mudéjar en Castilla la Vieja y León*, Madrid, 1975.
Valdés, M., *Arquitectura mudéjar en León y Castilla*, León, 1981 (2nd ed. 1984).

THE ARTS OF AL-ANDALUS

JERRILYNN DODDS

Introduction

From the 2nd/8th to the 9th/15th century, the western frontier of Islam was al-Andalus, a rich land poised at the mouth of the Atlantic on a peninsula stretched taut between Europe and North Africa. Far from the centre of Islamic rule, and embedded in a peninsula which would always retain a Christian hegemony as well, the patrons and artists of Spanish Islamic society would rely heavily on art and architecture to create and reassert an Islamic cultural identity. Though the formal structures and conscious meanings behind the many styles emerging in those seven centuries are wildly different, the arts of al-Andalus are strung together by the same underlying tension: the need to create forceful forms both to forge a link with Islamic centres and to defy the presence of an encroaching alien culture and religion.

I. The Emirate, the Caliphate and the *Mulūk al-Ṭawā'if*

I.1 *The Emirate*

All of al-Andalus was a frontier during the early years of Islamic occupation, and we know of little art other than common ceramics before the rule of ʿAbd al-Raḥmān I. But with the arrival of that intrepid young prince, the image of Islamic ruler as patron assured the development of courtly arts. The young Umayyad, who escaped the massacre of most of the rest of the Umayyad family at the hands of their successors to the Caliphate, began a programme of building as soon as his hold on the southern half of the Iberian Peninsula was assured. From the very beginning, these gestures would address the issue of creating for the Muslims of al-Andalus a visual profile that might connect them with the sanctity and privilege of their usurped heritage. We know that ʿAbd al-Raḥmān's first palace was a country villa on the outskirts of Córdoba, named Ruṣāfa after a country palace of his grandfather, the caliph Hishām. The name signals for us a recurrent theme in the patronage of al-Andalus for fully three hundred years: a keen nostalgia for Syria, both as homeland and as the seat of a usurped authority; the centre of a culture and polity which were lost to all, yet keen in the memory of the Umayyad rulers of al-Andalus.

But ʿAbd al-Raḥmān's achievement will always be understood through his foundation of the Great Mosque of Córdoba, a monument whose conceptual and formal potency would make it the focus of the entire Islamic community of al-Andalus, and of its most important patrons, for three centuries.[1]

ʿAbd al-Raḥmān I built a wide hypostyle mosque of eleven aisles which ran perpendicular to the *qibla*, in the manner of several important Umayyad mosques, in particular the al-Aqṣā mosque in Jerusalem. Its plan, whose repetition is broken only by a subtle widening of the central aisle, corresponded to some of the earliest and most conservative mosque plans of Islam, which subsume the entire community of the faithful into one vast hall that is remarkably free of authoritative architectural forms. While the aisles run in the direction of the *qibla* there is little axis to create an authoritative body, and no privileged space within the prayer hall. These are of course principles that mark much early mosque planning—indeed they are tied to most early Muslim communities in answering the need for a place in which communal prayer can occur without hierarchy or priestly intermediary. But they are worth reviewing here as we form an idea of the tensions that penetrated the building of the westernmost mosques of Islam, for their remote location and strange, indigenous surroundings produced an elevation as unique as the mosque's plan is familiar.

The repetitive, almost monotonous plan of the mosque of ʿAbd al-Raḥmān I explodes in elevation into a carnival of colour and form: the aisles are defined by doubled arcades, each supporting two vertical levels of horseshoe arches. The arches in turn are reduced to their own component parts, as the voussoirs that compose them alternate brick and stone, red and white, an effect which succeeds in breaking the whole interior into parts; transforming it into a complex, abstract design. This complex and surprising solution springs, at the most fundamental level, from the need to create a monumental and impressive interior for a new Emirate, one which did not resort to figural decoration for its rhetorical power. But the abstract designs were not without meaning for ʿAbd al-Raḥmān and his followers. Though fashioned of brick and stone, the alternating voussoirs were surely meant to evoke, in available materials, the *opus sectile* decoration of Umayyad buildings of the Fertile Crescent, in particular the Great Mosque of Damascus, and conceivably the Dome of the Rock. Once again, a nostalgia for lost rule and a distant land prevails, but it is encased in a form which might seem quite strange to a native of Damascus.

The horseshoe arch is used consistently here for the first time in an Islamic building: this is the heritage of Spain's pre-existing tradition of churchbuilding, called "Visigothic", and it reminds us of the extent to which indigenous craftsmen and traditions of construction must have affected the first appearance of the mosque. The startling piggy-back arches are also without prototype in Islamic architecture. They allow the wooden roof of the hypostyle hall to reach significantly higher than would otherwise have been possible; a kind of monumentality achieved in a different way in the Great

Mosque of Damascus. The prototype, however, was new, and indigenous: Roman aqueducts such as the surviving fragment at Mérida combine both superposed arches and alternating red and white masonry, suggesting the extent to which the new Spanish Emirate appropriated and reused indigenous forms to achieve its goals for its greatest building.

This tension between Umayyad tradition and the appropriation of indigenous form seems to exert a steady hold over subsequent patrons of the mosque. ʿAbd al-Raḥmān II extended this prayer hall eight bays to the south in 222/836, elongating the plan but respecting the elevation and decoration of his predecessor. His addition was completed by his son, Muḥammad I, who restored the early door of St. Stephen. Again and again, we have a sense of the reverence for the past: architectural style becomes in fact the embodiment of the nostalgia sensed since the time of ʿAbd al-Raḥmān I, and the peculiar disposition of the mosque's elevation is retained carefully by each ruler adding to the mosque, as if his own heritage of authority were encased in that continuity.

I.2 *The Caliphate*

The mosque's first minaret had been constructed by Hishām, but the one which can be viewed today is the work of ʿAbd al-Raḥmān III, who ordered that the original minaret be pulled down. The work of the first Umayyad *amīr* to call himself caliph is aimed at monumentalising the mosque, and yet it retains familiar meanings: his rebuilding of the courtyard in 340/951 gave its pillars and columns an alternation reminiscent of, once again, Damascus—not a surprising gesture on the part of the ruler who re-established his family's link with their ancient Umayyad authority.

It was, however, his son, al-Ḥakam II, who gave the mosque its most authoritative forms: he extended the prayer hall twelve bays to the south, and established an elaborate axis culminating in a domed *maqṣūra* pressed against a *qibla* adorned with three doors that glowed with gold, green and blue mosaics. The organisation of the mosque now seems to form around an exclusive, ceremonial space in keeping with the concerns of a new caliphate. The axial aisle of the *maqṣūra* is announced by a domed bay, supported by an elaborate screen of interlacing and polylobed arches which continue the mosque's tradition of superposed arches and alternating colours, but in a wildly mannered interweaving of architectural form that sets this section of the mosque apart from the rest of the prayer hall. This bay organises the space around the *maqṣūra* into a basilical space like that of the ceremonial rooms of ʿAbd al-Raḥmān III's palace at Madīnat al-Zahrā', but with the added surprise of the three-doored *qibla* and the domed *maqṣūra* before it, all of which recalls the Salo Rico at Madīnat al-Zahrā'. Both monuments seem unconsciously to reflect the rhetorical power of contemporary Christian liturgical spaces, in particular the mosque addition, in which three arched openings, a *miḥrāb* in the shape of a room and a deep-bayed *maqṣūra* are all organised like the eastern part of a Mozarabic church.

This is probably a good point to remember that a growing proportion of Córdoba's population was composed of Muwallads, or converted Christians, and to recall the extent to which all the inhabitants of the city were aware of the rhetorical power of Christian ceremony and the architecture in which it took place. However, in this curious piece of appropriation, it was clearly the power of a culminatory, directional effect, rather than any direct allusion to Christian worship, which was sought.

Once again the tensions between a new Islamic art and a still struggling but live indigenous tradition help to form that which is distinctive and vibrant in a very traditional building, but the lustrous spectacle of the mosaic-covered *qibla* owes its presence to the axis of meaning that constantly renewed formal and ideological connections with Damascus. According to Ibn ʿIdhārī, al-Ḥakam II requested a mosaicist from the Byzantine king "in imitation of that which al-Walīd had done at the time of the construction of Damascus".[2] The decoration resembles Damascus only in technique and colour, however, for in contrast with the representational mosaics of the Umayyad mosque of Damascus, there appears here a juxtaposition of floral and geometric patterns into which inscriptions are inserted, their presence at times obscured by their own abstract texture. These Quranic citations and fragments of the building's own history are, as O. Grabar has demonstrated, one of the earliest attempts to create a written iconography for a mosque.[3]

The mosque's dispersed, hypostyle space was reasserted in the last major addition, that of the pretender al-Manṣūr (377-8/987-8). He added eight aisles, this time to the east, deflecting the longitudinal thrust of al-Ḥakam II's plan, but maintaining every other aspect of ʿAbd al-Raḥmān I's original sanctuary. The specific concerns of the early Caliphate had subsided, but the tenacious continuity of forms created to serve a new Islamic polity in the name of an ancient claim are carefully cherished and preserved. By the time of al-Manṣūr, indigenous forms like the horseshoe arch had become as much a part of an absorbed, Spanish Islamic style for religious building as the echoes of building from Damascus.

The symbolic importance of the Great Mosque of Córdoba as a visual centre for Islamic Spain is borne out by the studies of Ewert concerning the private mosque of Bāb al-Mardūm in Toledo.[4] This tiny nine-bay oratory is typical of neighbourhood or private oratories throughout Islam, but once again it is in elevation and articulation that its more immediate and conscious meaning is revealed. Its four columns support an elaborate series of domes whose ribbed decoration evokes the domes of al-Ḥakam II's *maqṣūra*—indeed, the mosque seems to be a reduction of the *maqṣūra* itself, suggesting a reverence for the Cordoban mosque and its meanings.[5] In this way we see the artistic taste of al-Andalus turning in upon itself; the styles born of tensions between indigenous form and Islamic tradition are now the strange hybrids by which Spanish Muslims define their own visual world. Islamic Spain now looks to its own centres; Bāb al-Mardūm is a reflection of the Spanish need to create a strong set of visual forms that might serve as a beacon for Spanish Muslim culture.

The great palaces of al-Andalus were the focus of considerable funds and patronly energies in the same years that the mosque was actively growing. In particular, ʿAbd al-Raḥmān III's patronage was centred on one of the many palatine cities to skirt the edges of Córdoba; Madīnat al-Zahrā', which today is a vast excavation punctuated by a number of intriguing reconstructed buildings, was begun around 325/936.

Madīnat al-Zahrā' can be seen as a continuation of that tradition that saw Umayyad caliphs build palaces outside town, part of the profile of patronage that saw ʿAbd al-Raḥmān I build al-Ruṣāfa. It was a sprawling city organised on three terraces cut into the side of a hill about five miles to the west of Córdoba. Madīnat al-Zahrā' consisted of palaces, pavilions, courtyards, gardens, mosques and buildings providing the town fabric that supported a refined and regal life: baths, workshops and military barracks.

This was an opulent, controlled city, which it was necessary to negotiate in all of its complexity to reach the Caliph. His throne room was embedded deep in a confusing fabric of palaces and courts, rooms and passages, which forged a sense of the ruler's power and remoteness within a dense and circuitous architectural plan. Only upon reaching the throne room or reception hall itself would an organised, axial space culminate in the person of the Caliph. In this respect, the plan of Madīnat al-Zahrā' resembles that of Abbasid palatine cities like Samarra, which tended, in their maze-like form, to buttress the sanctified image of their rulers. Such concerns are understandable for ʿAbd al-Raḥmān III, who, in elevating himself to the rank of caliph, was setting his claim in opposition to that of the Abbasids. This was a case in which the ancient allusion to Umayyad architectural form would not be potent enough to further a political goal: ʿAbd al-Raḥmān III saw that it was to this more mysterious, ceremonial image of caliph that he had to respond, in order to lend credibility to his caliphal claim. But this extraordinary city reminds us not just of a grasp at political authority, but of the continuing dialogue with the centres of Islam: with political groups concerning which Spanish Muslims felt both opposition and identification.

Though the planning of Madīnat al-Zahrā' shows the impact of the Abbasids, the decoration grows clearly from an indigenous Spanish Islamic tradition. The famous *Salón Rico*, a three-aisled columnar basilical structure with lateral rooms, reflects this. Its vocabulary is an indigenous Mediterranean one: corinthian-based capitals and relief sculpture based on vine-scroll types; but these have been flattened and their parts miniaturised and equalised, so that the designs become a complex, abstract skin that hugs the surface of the object to which it adheres, transforming an architectural morpheme into a delicate, precious object of luxury art. Much of the decoration of the *Salón Rico* thus recalls the *maqṣūra* of al-Ḥakam II in the Great Mosque of Córdoba, and with good reason. As ʿAbd al-Raḥmān III's son, al-Ḥakam was a site supervisor at Madīnat al-Zahrāʾ, and later built his own portions of the royal city. But more importantly, this decorative style that used indigenous forms—horseshoe arches, capitals and columns—and enveloped them in an abstraction of mannered and equalised form, had become emblematic of Umayyad patronage in al-Andalus.

By the time of the Caliphate, then, the artistic tensions had shifted: indigenous Mediterranean and Syrian allusions tended to be absorbed into one Spanish Islamic style, which carried a coded meaning both of Syrian heritage and indigenous tradition, for al-Andalus now had a potent Islamic identity of its own. The third cultural axis was now that of the Abbasid court in Iraq, from which the Umayyads of Spain appropriated a number of cultural ideas in a kind of stimulus diffusion that saw them react to the power and meaning of their rivals' courtly culture. Thus, as early as the rule of ʿAbd al-Raḥmān II, the Iraqi musician Ziryāb was enticed to the Spanish court, bringing with him a taste for music, furnishings, dress and even cooking in the sophisticated styles of the Abbasid court.

An admiration for developments in the Abbasid court can be seen in the Caliphal ceramic tradition of al-Andalus, which forms part of the created visual identity of Spanish Islam. There are imitations of Abbasid lustreware and a fine white glazed ceramic, often painted in green and black, primarily known as Elvira or Madīnat al-Zahrāʾ ware, though its manufacture has been demonstrated throughout al-Andalus in the 4th/10th century. The objects and their subject matter have traditionally been treated as banal and trivial in meaning, but I believe they ought to be considered as laden with implications of wealth and sovereignty. The entire field of a plate or basin might be given over to a single subject, such as a fine harnessed horse with a falcon —wings spread—on its back, a subject which points to the possessions and pastimes of an aristocrat or king; and animals such as hare or deer could conceivably provide links with hunting, with implications of land ownership. In a number of pieces a kufic inscription intones *al-mulk*—"the dominion" or "the kingdom"—yet another reminder of the extent to which the patronage of beautiful objects can be tied to royal privilege.

A large bronze deer from Madīnat al-Zahrāʾ probably served as a fountain head; it still retains in its base the tube by which water was propelled through its body and out of its mouth. Might it be part of one of the fountains of which al-Maqqarī later spoke in his account of the history of Madīnat al-Zahrāʾ? He recounts that

> among the wonders of al-Zahrā' ... were two fountains that constituted the principal ornament of the palace. The larger of the two ... was brought to the Caliph from Constantinople ... as to the small one ... it was brought from Syria ... The Caliph fixed on it twelve figures made of red gold and set with pearls and other precious stones. The figures, which were all made in the workshop of Córdoba, represented various animals: the lion, an antelope, a crocodile, an eagle, a dragon, a pigeon, a falcon, a peacock, a hen, a cock, a kite and a vulture. These were ornamented with jewels and the water poured out from their mouths."[6]

The description and the fountain itself recall the importance of fountains and water in the expression of the palace—not only as a place of pleasure and repose, but as a place where water operating through hydraulic systems was conspicuously present in palace settings as a sign of power.

This elegant, stylised deer, etched with a repetitive rinceau pattern, reminds us as well of the persistent ambiguity of Islamic kingship. Its definition often lies in the symbolic privilege of possessing objects and fashion settings that define kingship in terms of a patronage challenging more conservative Islamic attitudes towards the arts, attitudes more characteristic of Roman and Sassanian rule: the making of figural art, hunting, drinking, and, in this case, the creation of an almost monumental representational sculpture.

But nowhere is the linking of patronage and kingship so strong as in the case of the Caliphal ivories of Córdoba. With the reign of 'Abd al-Raḥmān III came the influx of Sudanese gold, and perhaps ivory as well, for it is in this moment that a series of important ivory boxes is crafted in Córdoba and Madīnat al-Zahrā'. Though there are cases of caskets made for other courtly figures, there seems to have been a particular tradition of giving such gifts within the royal family, to figures closely associated with succession.

Two boxes executed for 'Abd al-Raḥmān III's daughter in 349/960 and 351/962 suggest a discrete and elegant tradition already in full swing. Their work is miniature and jewel-like, with a delicate undercut rinceau and inscription appearing against a shadowed ground. The interplay between the inscription and the vegetal decoration creates a formal ambiguity that in concept reminds us of the way the word becomes both part of a puzzle-like ornament and conveyer of meaning in the *miḥrāb* of the Great Mosque.

The best-known of the boxes date to the reign of al-Ḥakam II, and we see in them a divergent imagery: a pyxis made for Princess Ṣubḥ, the mother of a son of al-Ḥakam II, is covered with a tangle of delicate foliage, carved in a single plane and undercut so that it seems to hover above the body of the vessel. As one looks closer, however, one notes peacocks, game birds and deer sprouting heraldically from the trees and vines like animate leaves, camouflaged by their formal sympathy with the vegetal forms. One senses a visual puzzle here, as with inscriptions; the mark of an art which, even when it employs figural decoration, creates with it an intellectual challenge to match the sensual representation.

One of the finest of the Caliphal ivories is a casket of Prince al-Mughīra, al-Ḥakam II's younger brother, who would later become a pretender to the throne. Here, in a medallion, is an image of courtly life encased in another myth of princely pleasure: royal personages sit on a dais, drinking and enjoying music. It is accompanied by other images of princely pursuit, like falconry, as well as the more allusive scenes of date harvest, animals, hunting and fighting that can be associated with possession of the land and a kind of authority of rule, together with the very act of patronage of costly ivory objects.

A large rectangular casket made for ʿAbd al-Malik, a son of al-Manṣūr, is a last great masterpiece, completed in the last moments of the Caliphate. Carved in slightly lower relief than the earlier examples, its eight intertwined medallions offer similar scenes of princely leisure to the al-Mughīra casket, but these are joined by a frontal, authoritative image of the monarch, a scene of him battling lions like an Assyrian king, and more bellicose images of warriors battling from the backs of camels and elephants. One senses that the profile of an effective prince for al-Andalus had changed significantly since the early Caliphate, and that prowess in battle had replaced much of the more sensual iconography of patronage and leisure—symbolism with roots in Islamic rules in Iraq—that had characterised the earlier period.

Indeed, the great dictator who rose during the minority of Hishām II had become an extraordinary general, and in one spectacular campaign after another kept the growing Christian kingdoms at bay, so nurturing the last moments of the culture of the Umayyad Caliphate in Spain.

I.3 *The* Mulūk al-Ṭawāʾif

The 5th/11th century saw a political restructuring of al-Andalus. After a succession of caliphs could no longer retain any semblance of authority, the Caliphate was dissolved by the Cordoban aristocracy. For the next fifty years al-Andalus was composed of about 23 small states, ruled by what were called petty kings (*mulūk al-ṭawāʾif* or *ṭāʾifa*s), each of whom took the title of *ḥājib* to maintain the fiction that he was reigning as a sort of chief minister for a mythical caliph. There was in this period a constant and confusing shifting of alliances between individual *ṭāʾifa* states and of Christian states with their *ṭāʾifa* neighbours, and none of the *ṭāʾifa* states was able to establish an expanding political authority. Their genius instead lay in their mythification and reinterpretation of Caliphal culture, for just as their kings feigned themselves the protectors of a lost Caliphate, so their courts nourished arts which cultivated and yet transformed the Caliphal model.

At the palace of al-Jaʿfariyya, in Saragossa, al-Muqtadir built a fortified royal palace, surrounded by a rectangular wall, cylindrical towers and a large rectilinear defensive tower. Within, rooms are organised around patios, in a plan which culminates in a small mosque. Many details of the design recall Córdoba: the *miḥrāb* which has swollen into an entire horseshoe-shaped room is a direct copy of the Cordoban example, which was the earliest one to take that form. The entrance arch is fashioned of alternating voussoirs, ornately carved with a delicate bas relief that characterised Cordoban stucco work and ivory carving as well.

But there is, throughout the palace, a segregation and celebration of that which is the least logical and quiescent of the Caliphal designs: the architects of al-Jaʿfariyya deconstructed the interlacing arches of the *maqṣūra* of al-Ḥakam II, so that the arches on either side of the *miḥrāb* opening read like a wild calligraphic profile which dips underneath a string course like a penstroke on a page. There is at every impasse an undermining of what architectonic logic these forms had retained in the Caliphal period; a delight in mannered elaboration. The basket shapes of capitals are elongated, their crowns complicated by interlacing foliage or screens of intertwining, polylobed arches; corbels erupt into organic forms at their very centres.

Nowhere is this tendency more evident than in a stucco relief from the palace preserved in the Museo Arqueológico Nacional in Madrid. The two sides of its arch never meet, but are instead subsumed into a jungle of tiny microcosmic arcades, supported in every direction except that indicated by gravity by tiny columns and capitals, these themselves being consumed by the never-ending pilgrimage of the moulding—now polylobed, now twining into a swirling knot—which represents the course of the mythical arch.

In the face of shifting interdependencies with Christian rules, with neither caliph nor political or military substance to support their claims to continuity, the *ṭāʾifa* rulers of Saragossa cultivated the visual culture of the Cordoban Caliphate: they gave it the sustained gaze of their ardent admiration and indulged a sophisticated taste for its architectonic perversions.

Not all of the architectural vestiges of the *ṭāʾifa* kingdoms are so elaborate or mannered. Of the many fortified sites left by these small and insecure rules is numbered the Alcazaba of Almería, its crenellated defensive walls cutting across the countryside, while the Alcazaba of Málaga, constructed around 432/1040, retains an elegant tri-lobed arcade of three horseshoe arches, with alternating voussoirs carved in bas relief that recall entrances to the pavilion-like rooms of Madīnat al-Zahrāʾ.

There is a lively continuation of stone sculpture in the period of the *ṭāʾifa*s, though usually in less luxurious materials. An exception is a marble font which reproduces the Caliphal theme of lions attacking antelopes, perhaps with rather more energy and density than earlier examples. But the most surprising piece is the Font of Játiva, named for the town where it is now found. It is covered with a frieze of dynamic and inventive figural imagery, and seems to come closer than any Caliphal piece preserved to a kind of narrative. Familiar scenes of courtly leisure and combat of warriors and animals are accompanied by more directional compositions suggesting perhaps a kind of offering (which in Roman art would be associated with ownership of the land), in addition to a curious medallion with a nude woman nursing a child. Like the conceivable classical prototype for this last scene, the meaning of the font seems to suggest abundance as an idea linked to the person of a landowner. The forms used to express such concerns are here new and inventive, but they relate to themes alluded to on Caliphal objects like the casket of al-Mughīra.

Clearly the idea that the patronage and possession of beautiful objects was a sign of sovereignty had survived the dissolution of the Spanish Caliphate, though the numerous and dispersed courts were not always the focus of the craft traditions that served them. The manufacture of ivory boxes shifted from Córdoba to Cuenca, where a workshop served a more diverse group of patrons. A casket carved in the workshop of ʿAbd al-Raḥmān b. Zayyān for a governor named Ḥusām al-Dawla shows a shift in imagery and meaning that marks the change in patronage. The fields of decoration here now correspond to the casket shape; gone are the medallions segregating themes of princely life. Instead the heraldic animals and birds remain, but reduced in size; the same scale now as the trees and palmettes of vegetation, they have receded to form part of its pattern, part of an aniconic maze whose attraction to the viewer is intellectual, not symbolic.

But there are also the vestiges of luxurious court arts that remind us of the luxury and refinement typically associated with the *ṭāʾifa* courts. A silver perfume bottle in Teruel made for the ruler of the *ṭāʾifa* kingdom of Albarracín is one of the finest precious metals from any period of Spanish Islamic art. Engraved and decorated in low repoussé, its detail hugs a sensual, glossy form, broken only by tiny animal figures poised impertinently on its handles. With its fine craft, expensive materials and functional implication of personal adornment and pleasure, it characterises much of the myth of the period of the *ṭāʾifa*s.

II. Almoravid and Almohad Rule and the Naṣrid Dynasty

From the beginning of the 5th/11th century, political and social changes occur in al-Andalus that have a profound effect on the way art serves a court and society. For the first time, implied challenges are made to the artistic privilege of kings, who had seemed to derive a symbol of legitimacy from their licence with luxurious possessions, sensual pursuit and figural art laden with allusion or symbolism. Instead, arts would become precious and treasured crafts which, while worthy of contemplation in their own right, were often disembodied by the abstraction of their ornament; veiled by the impossible multiplication of geometric form and the craft used to create it.

Art in the later rules of Islam became part of the creation of an exquisite setting fashioned by unparalleled craft.

By the last quarter of the 5th/11th century, the Islamic presence on the Iberian Peninsula was threatened by the alarming advances of the Christian monarch Alfonso VI. The *ṭā'ifa* kings of Granada, Seville and Badajoz appealed for help to Almoravid rulers of North Africa. The deliverance ended in invasion, with Almoravid jurists justifying their usurpation on the grounds of immorality and the kings' undermining interdependence with the Christians. For Almoravids were bound by a highly conservative attitude towards Islam, involving a puritanical observance of Quranic law; they eschewed the courtly pleasures that seemed to have become emblematic of princely life for the rulers of the Caliphate and *ṭā'ifa* kingdoms. These potent Berber conservatives saw their Spanish counterparts as effete secular cybarites, while they were viewed by the denizens of al-Andalus as rough cretins. Al-Muʿtamid of Seville is thought to have voiced the feelings of his contemporaries when he declared that he would rather herd camels for Almoravids than keep the pigs of Alfonso VI.

It was a juxtaposition of cultural formation and ideological commitment that would change the course of the arts in al-Andalus.

II.1 *Almoravid art and architecture*

Art historians have long struggled with the juxtaposition of Almoravid puritanism—their outspoken criticism of the luxurious and sensual courts maintained by their predecessors in al-Andalus—and their obvious taste for the architectural achievement of Spanish Islamic craftsmen. There is now a growing contention that a shift of patronage occurred during Almoravid hegemony in Spain. During the reign of the ardent reformer Yūsuf b. Tāshfīn (453/1061-500/1106), authors see a frugality and simplicity to artistic production which is broken by his son, ʿAlī b. Yūsuf. Educated in al-Andalus and Arab speaking, he partook in none of the austere theories of his father, and opened the way for artists and architects from al-Andalus to work in the new North African centres.

These were in fact the great centres of Almoravid art, and it was there that Spanish artists realised their finest works at the end of the 5th/11th and beginning of the 6th/12th centuries, in Tlemcen, Marrakesh and Fez. There we find mosques with hypostyle plans of great simplicity and conservatism: at the Great Mosque of Tlemcen, founded by ʿAlī b. Yūsuf in 531/1136, a pillared hypostyle hall of 13 aisles giving onto a small square court features a slightly accentuated *miḥrāb* aisle punctuated by two domes. Like most North African mosques, it would embrace the notion of the *miḥrāb* as a room, first adopted at Córdoba, perhaps as part of the impact of Christian forms. But here that obscure history is forgotten, and it appears as a form sanctified by its history within the Islamic tradition, and becomes part of a restrained and traditional mosque plan.

On first glance, the decoration of a mosque like that of Tlemcen seems anything but restrained: it possessed a fanciful lantern which hovered over the *miḥrāb* bay like a screen of lace, and its slightly pointed horseshoe arches explode at times into complex polylobed profiles and wave-like undulations. But we can see a choice in forms that suggests a shift in taste from the period of the *ṭā'ifa*s: the most sensual and surprising forms are rationed; there is, in the area around the *miḥrāb,* an elegant complexity and invention—in the use of *muqarnas*, and the adaptation of a window screen effect for the vault itself—but the vast fields of mannered plastic relief characteristic of a work like the al-Jaʿfariyya of Saragossa have not found fertile ground even in the more assimilated period of Almoravid hegemony.

From the Almoravid period on the Iberian Peninsula, only military architecture remains standing, and most of the surviving examples were remade or remodelled by their successors, the Almohads. However an excavation called The Castillejo of Monteagudo, located in the suburbs of Murcia, reveals the residence perhaps of an Almoravid chief like Ibn Saʿd b. Mardanī<u>sh</u>. The residence is situated in a large agricultural domain that included a substantial artificial lake and a series of pleasure gardens with vistas. It possessed a rectangular enclosure with towers that might have served for habitation, all organised around a patio of some interest: it is oblong, with two raised walks that cross in the centre, dividing its field into a four-part garden plan of a type known throughout the Islamic world. At either short end, however, a rectangular unit cuts into the space of the court—some believe these units to be pavilions but there is still considerable debate concerning the original disposition[7]—revealing a planned space that provides possible typological precedent for the Court of the Lions of the Alhambra. This *riyāḍ* might possibly be related to a smaller one found in excavations of the palace of ʿAlī b. Yūsuf in Marrakesh (526-7/1131-2), which in turn might be dependent on a Spanish palace: on a now largely destroyed court in the al-Jaʿfariyya in Saragossa. But the key here is a sharing of forms between North Africa and Spain, and the enduring link between garden and privileged residence. It is yet another piece of Western Islamic formal identity depending on a meaning whose roots lie in Abbasid Iraq.[8]

At the Castillejo of Monteagudo traces of stucco decoration remain, together with complex geometric painting, bearing witness to an interest in geometric planning in decoration as well as architectural form, and heralding a period of complex abstraction in ornament. Though geometric ornamentation clearly existed in the early Islamic rules of al-Andalus, and a healthy amount of ornament of Caliphal inspiration survives to the last moments of Muslim hegemony on the Peninsula, the increased interest and development of geometric decoration in painting, tilework and stucco creates a divergent view of the visual world suitable for an Islamic prince, one which would have distinguished progeny in al-Andalus.

Almoravid North Africa was a consumer, as well, of an extraordinary and lively tradition of wood carving from Córdoba. The *minbar* housed until recently in the Kutubiyya Mosque in Marrakesh is the finest of its type, and a witness to an almost entirely lost tradition of Cordoban luxury crafts in wood and ivory. Like most *minbar*s, its composition is conservative: a monumental stair flanked on either side by a balustrade, leading to a platform with a pulpit, a disposition that links it with the most ancient *minbar*s known in Islam. But in its extraordinary decoration—its marquetry of ivory and precious woods in a complex geometric interlace based on a hexagonal grid—is found the finest and most luxurious work known from the Almoravid and Almohad period in Spain.

A kufic inscription on the higher platform supplies the information that the *minbar* was constructed in Córdoba for the Mosque of Marrakesh. Though the year in the inscription is illegible, chronicles ascribe it to the reign of ʿAbd al-Muʾmin (525/1130-559/1163). This places the *minbar* at a significant moment for the study of Spanish arts of the period of the "African Dynasties". It is to this period of more conservative attitudes towards the religious arts at least that is owed the subtle complexity of the decoration, which engages the intellect, drawing the viewer ever closer to discover the puzzle-like ambiguities of the marquetry.

The *minbar* presents us with an illustration in craft as well as architecture of the way al-Andalus, as an indigenous culture—one which had to alter its artistic traditions to fit an invasive ideology—still exercised considerable cultural influence over its aggressors.

The Almoravids were known in particular for their rich and vivid textiles, which were made in the extraordinary manufacturing capital of Almería (chroniclers marvelled at the quality and quantity of the textiles produced there). This opulent textile production is one of our indications that the Almoravids in al-Andalus soon embraced the richest of the *ṭāʾifa* arts, and fragments like the "Lion Strangler" textile conserved in the tomb of San Berenardo Calvo in Vich reveal the power and vitality of their figural designs. That these textiles were considered—both as signs of exaggerated luxury and as carriers of figural design—to be a challenge to the most rigorous religious values becomes clear when the next fundamentalist sect overtakes al-Andalus; the first Almohad rulers would close down the textile factories of the Almoravids and demand that the contents of their warehouses be sold off. The Almoravids had in fact become patrons in the Andalusī tradition —a deviation from religious conservatism the Almohads did not intend to make themselves.

II.2 *Almohad art and architecture*

In the year 540/1145, the victorious Almohad Mahdī ʿAbd al-Muʾmin led troops into the Almoravid mosque of Fez. There they proceeded to whitewash the ornament, leaving the once ornate mosque bathed in an austere, white light. Such were the concerns of the second, even more serious band of reformers to conquer Spain: the rigorous monotheists called Almohads. They crossed to Spain soon after securing the rule of Almoravid lands in North Africa, taking advantage there of a disintegration in Almoravid rule in al-Andalus, which had been weakened by Christian military incursions, and, also, by the disillusion of those who accused the Almoravids of legalistic Mālikism, and (as in the case of the 7th/13th century historian al-Marrākus͟hī) of apathy, obsession with their own comfort and an unrestrained pursuit of women.

It is not a surprise, then, that the most famous textile produced in this moment is the so-called Banner of Las Navas de Tolosa, which is most probably, however, the Almohad military banner captured in the campaigns of Fernando III. It is a bold, completely aniconic design composed of inscriptions, geometric interlace and abstractions. Composed of silks and gold thread, it announces an Islamic presence unsullied by interdependency with Christians: a victory banner for an uncompromised Muslim hegemony.

Once again, military building takes an important position, both because the Almohads were conceived militarily and because of constant tensions with Christians along shifting frontiers. They are characterised by advances conceivably derived from Fāṭimid sources, and refined and perfected in the intense military atmosphere of al-Andalus in the 6th/12th century: second rings of fortification called *barbacanas*, and new types of strategic towers, are but two examples.

That civil and military architects also worked on religious and palatial commissions is clear from the career of one of the few architects known by name from the period of Islamic hegemony on the Iberian Peninsula. Aḥmad b. Bāṣo was a Sevillian who designed a variety of works for his Almohad patrons: lost military and civil constructions in Gibraltar and Córdoba, and an Almohad palace. But we know his work through the vestiges of the Great Mosque of Seville, the only Almohad mosque in Spain of which significant sections survive in elevation.

Built by the Almohad caliph Abū Yaʿqūb Yūsuf (559/1163-580/1184), the Great Mosque of Seville was constructed in the new Almohad capital by Ibn Bāṣo, who is in fact the only architect whose name and history can be connected with a standing Islamic building on the Iberian Peninsula. Begun in 568/1172 when Abū Yaʿqūb Yūsuf summoned Ibn Bāṣo together with a number of master masons from North Africa and other parts of al-Andalus, it was completed some ten years later. Today, only the famous minaret, La Giralda, and sections of the *ṣaḥn* survive; the former was altered in its upper portions during the Renaissance, and the latter encased in the cloister of Seville's cathedral. Originally the mosque extended to seventeen aisles perpendicular to the *qibla*, with a slightly wider aisle aligned with the *miḥrāb*, and a single broad aisle hugging the *qibla*. This T-type hypostyle plan, as it is called, had become common in Almohad mosque construction since the mosque of Tinmal was constructed in 548/1153. It provides a structure for the deep, wide plan, an axis which normally becomes the focal point for decoration. From what can be seen at Tinmal or the second Kutubiyya Mosque in Marrakesh, the subtle planes established by the mosque's brick construction would have been entirely whitewashed, while arches of the axial aisle might have taken a polylobed form, or hidden an occasional carved stucco shell or geometric form in the intrados of its springer. The eastern door into the *ṣaḥn* preserves a *muqarnas* vault. *Muqarnas* is a three-dimensional decorative system composed of sections of cones which combine to form a three-dimensional, suspended surface; a complex, plastic geometric grid usually covering the surface of a vault or arch. Its exploitation in the Almoravid and Almohad periods in Spain is fascinating, for it reveals a desire to make the morphemes of the building itself—the intrinsic geometry of its own parts—the basis of its decorative system. This is at once a traditional attitude towards architectural form—the alternating voussoirs of the Great Mosque of Córdoba function formally in the same way—and a new concern. For in creating a mosque style that relied on pristine, whitewashed surfaces, the building's ornamental interest now depended on planar variations and juxtapositions between flat, mural effects and highly complex three-dimensional surfaces like those created by *muqarnas* to create interest. Indeed, the *muqarnas* vaults, like the bits of hidden stucco carving at Tinmal, are rationed, and placed strategically in Almohad mosques to create a decorative hierarchy that reasserted the T-type plan, culminating in the *qibla*.

In the decoration of Ibn Bāṣo's famous minaret we can see how this more austere attitude toward form transformed an earlier one. The minaret shows great attention to the simplicity and refinement of solid, geometric form. Panels of interlace decoration hug the volume of that form, never breaking its surface or interrupting its flow. Each section possesses an arcade above which is a cool, repetitive pattern of interwoven forms, derived ultimately from the famous mannerist arches of the al-Jaʿfariyya in Saragossa. Their pattern, however, is so regular, that they have lost all architectonic irony; indeed, all connection with the diminutive arcades that support them.

Architectural decoration now conforms to the restrained vocabulary of austere patrons. As in the earliest moments of the Muslim hegemony in Spain, there are tensions between indigenous form and the architectural vocabulary of a foreign home; but now the indigenous architecture is an Islamic one as well, and the arts have become coded—not only with political meaning, but in terms of a structure that uses art and architecture as one of the means by which religious ideology is expressed.

Judging by the Patio del Yeso of the Alcázar of Seville, which was an Almohad achievement, the architectural restraint implied by such an ideology was not applied with the same vigour to palace architecture. A rectangular court bordered on one side by seven arches, the patio uses a Caliphal vocabulary of columns and capitals absent in mosque design, and employs reused Caliphal capitals.

The lambriken arcades of the Patio del Yeso do not support walls, but elaborate screens of open stucco work. Here the design is the same as the panels in the minaret of The Great Mosque, but it is, in contrast, subjected to none of the controls that restrained freedom and sensuality in its forms: here it is neither restricted to cool rectangles on a larger mass nor placed at a distance. Instead it is an opulent and fanciful screen that can be permeated and transformed by light and air.

The arts that have dominated these discussions up to now are those of courts and great rulers; such has been the fate of the arts and civilisation of al-Andalus that these are the objects and monuments that survive to this day. However, recent scholarship, much of it based on archaeological research, has also revealed something of the arts and architecture of less empowered groups—showing, for instance, the highly varied nature of domestic housing types in al-Andalus. It is in these homes that we ought perhaps to picture the rich variety of ceramic forms used in more current daily life, from Málaga to Valencia.

One of the architectural forms known to both prince and common man was the bath; it is in fact to the Islamic presence in Spain that the construction and use of civic baths is due. The bath was initially built to provide for the religious requirement of washing before prayer, but eventually became an important social institution, one used by Christians and Jews as well. The basic plan type, which can be seen in Granada's surviving bath of the 5th/11th century, was not adapted directly from Spanish Roman prototypes but brought from other parts of the Muslim world. It includes a frigidarium (cold water room), a tepidarium (warm area) and a caldarium (hot water room), each function in a single room, as in the palace baths of Umayyad Syria.

What is extraordinary, however, is the way the institution of the bath is appropriated by Christians after their conquest of Islamic lands, though documents do suggest some official disapproval. Post-conquest baths like the Christian one in Gerona are a reminder of the extent to which the fabric of Spanish Christian social life was transformed by the presence of Islam.

II.3 *Naṣrid art and architecture*

The last Islamic kingdom in Spain grew from the detritus of a failed Almohad hegemony. From the 7th/13th century to its fall in 897/1492, its rulers lived by the politics of tribute and alliances, including a persistent relationship with the Christian kingdom of Castile—a reflection of their powerless position.

And yet the Naṣrids created some of the most adroit, opulent works of art to emerge from al-Andalus, works that seem to issue from an artistic tradition of extraordinary confidence and resource. This art develops clearly from the Almohad tradition, in its preference for aniconic form and an ornament which creates an abstract field for contemplation by the intellect, but it seems to have been free of many of the restraints concerning luxury and formal sensuality that characterised the Almohad achievement. The famous Alhambra vases, such as those now in Granada and Palermo, bring the ceramic technique of lustreware to a new level of sophistication and monumentality. The vases do belong to a functional type, but, at 1m20 to 1m70, they were surely meant as ornament, to work with low furniture pieces in an architectural setting. Painted either in metallic lustre or cobalt blue, they are covered with delicate designs based on calligraphy, and primarily vegetal interlace, with occasional heraldic animals obscured within the jungle of foliage, as in the example now in Granada. They are coded in their size, their lack of utilitarian purpose and in their lustrous glow with allusions to wealth; indeed, they seem to follow, in their almost rhetorical opulence, a theme that pervades much of the Naṣrid artistic product.

An enamelled sword and sheath in the Museo del Ejército in Madrid, taken less than a decade before the fall of Granada, is in fact the most spectacular we know: of gilded silver, it is covered with filigree, enamel and ivory inlay. Extraordinary silks of enormous cost, such as the curtain from the Alhambra now in the Cleveland museum, or the countless rich fabrics that now line the interior of reliquaries in the Christian north, attest to a production of fine and costly luxury arts in full swing until the last moment of Islamic hegemony in Spain.

The vases, silks and more practical arts—like a beautiful desk of complex inlay and marquetry in the Museo Arqueológico Nacional in Madrid—all contribute to an elaboration of daily palace life: they are less objects that might have constituted a focus or end in themselves than a working of art into the finest detail of everyday life. Perhaps as part of the attitudes formed under the Almoravid and Almohad rules, they all become part of a highly refined context; and the wider and far more opulent setting of that context is Naṣrid palace architecture.

That context is supplied, of course, by the Royal Palaces of the Alhambra. Built on the site of the "red fortress", a citadel of long standing, it is believed that the Alhambra was preceded by a 5th/11th century residence of Yehoseph b. Nagh̲rīlla, the Jewish vizier to a Berber *ṭā'ifa* king. Its aspect was clearly totally transformed, however, with the Naṣrid construction of the 8th/14th century, when it became a royal city, containing a gardened villa (The "Generalife"), palaces, mosques, schools and various practical functions to support the lofty royal centre.

There is controversy concerning the functions of the various parts of the Alhambra—there are actually as many as seven palaces—with some seeing both a private and a public palace within the same central nucleus of courts and halls of the old royal palace. Two palaces form the nucleus of the old royal palace as it is visited today, and though their construction spans at least two reigns, their planning retains a persistent theme of purposeful ambiguity. As with Madīnat al-Zahrā', the approaches to the innermost rooms of the palace are serpentine and oblique. Courts and rooms are set at odd angles to one another, and access is obtained, often, through inconspicuous doors or dark passages. Here as well the ruler's inaccessibility conduces to his power, and it creates a sense of vulnerability in the viewer. That same equivocal attitude, set at undermining the viewer's control of his or her surroundings, is also evident in elevation.

The main precinct as it stands today includes two palaces: the Comares Palace and the Palace of the Lions, and the facade of the Comares Palace was a gateway to the palace itself. There is, further, some indication that the king might have dispensed judgements there, a tradition that extends at least to Abbasid tradition at Samarra. But the setting is disorienting, and does not offer the standard axial forms one might expect in a palace facade or audience hall. The court is flanked by a corridor-like space with windows giving onto the town. This in turn is pierced by arcades that lead to the roofless court itself, contributing to a constant fluctuation of interior and exterior experience, and a subtle sensation of disorientation stemming from the undermining of the viewer's logical expectations.

That this sense of ambiguity is a part of the formal system of the palace as a whole is suggested in a more literal manner in the facade of the court: the one which would have served as a backdrop to the monarch himself. The wall is bilaterally symmetrical, possessing two large doors, with two double lancet windows above and a smaller, single-arched window between them. Every inch of the wall is covered with decoration: tilework dados and doorframes that use colour to create dozens of geometric figures within one repetitive field; stucco carving in extremely low relief that seems to embrace every non-figural motif—vegetal and geometric—from the history of Islamic Spain in one gaudy skin; inscriptions and a band of *muqarnas* at the top.

The effect is an ostentatious one to be sure, but it all aims at enframing the two gaping and identical doors. Do they both lead into the palace? If they are both identical, how can any one lead to the king, whose entrance must be the greatest? The composition of the facade offers no clue; only the query of a choice, unaided by hierarchy, axis or decoration. The first facade of the Alhambra offers the viewer an architectural version of the sort of geometric puzzle often posed by its abstract systems of ornamentation, which present a design in which the primary forms change before one's eyes because of shifts in a figure-ground relationship, or the interdependency of two divergent geometric constructs on a series of intertwined morphemes. The irony of the choice is accentuated when we discover that one door leads back to the palatial anteroom, and another into the private courts and apartments of the Naṣrid king. The doors have a clear hierarchy in function, but not in form or decoration, so only those who have been initiated can know their secrets. The notion that the Alhambra's form creates a class of privileged and non-privileged viewers is accentuated when we discover that the superior windows in the Cuarto Dorado gave secluded visual access to the proceedings there to members of the Harem. Indeed, there are many interior passages in the royal palace, and much shifting of levels, as if the notion of the palace as a place of intrigue was actively courted.

The plan, elevation and decoration of the Alhambra combine to create the image of a palace full of complexity and mystery. It is more than the continuation of a spirit that extends to the earliest palaces of the Middle East: it is a conscious evocation of such palaces as places of myth.[9] Indeed it was a myth of potency and opulence that was needed to sustain the cultural activity of this last Islamic rule on the Iberian Peninsula, for political realities saw them ever-threatened, and dependent by treaty and tribute on the very infidels who had once been ruled by Muslims in Spain.

The Patio de los Arrayanes, or Court of the Myrtles, provided gracious living quarters for the Sultan and four wives, and the Hall of the Ambassadors is a throne room in which the cupola becomes, with the help of poetic and Quranic inscriptions, the dome of heaven in the long tradition of palaces extending back to Roman and Near Eastern prototypes. This theme is extended in the small rooms arranged around the Court of the Lions. In the Hall of the Two Sisters, a court-like space with a fountain stream flowing to its centre is instead covered with a deep and intricate *muqarnas* cupola set over an octagon. This room was probably a private reception hall, and it contains, in its own decoration, a poem by Ibn Zamrak in which the dome explains itself:

> In here is a cupola which by its height becomes lost from sight; beauty in it appears both concealed and visible ...
> The bright stars would like to establish themselves firmly in it, rather than continue wandering about in the vault of the sky ...
> For it is before your dwelling that it has arisen to perform its service, since he who serves the highest acquired merits thereby.

The notion of a hall in which a monarch sits as in a Dome of Heaven appears here again, but in the more complex, dynamic formal language of the *muqarnas* dome; reminding us of the ways in which architecture can create a persuasive setting that mines both history and myth. The art of that myth has to do with encasing the monarch in a web of caesaropapistic imagery that long antedates Islam, but which might have entered its courtly vocabulary during the Abbasid Caliphate in Baghdad. It is important to remember that

Baghdad was a city of legend: the setting for tales of courtly intrigue and the centre of the memory of an invincible Islamic hegemony. It existed as an allusion, as part of the subconscious meaning of the Alhambra, which is itself a monument seeking to perpetuate the myth in the face of a rapidly eroding power.

We find here, however, not only the notion of the *muqarnas* dome as the Dome of Heaven which gathers around the person of the Sultan, but also a conscious acknowledgement of the effect of the complexity of the *muqarnas* vault for its audience. The principles of architecture and decoration which privileged notions of ambiguity were part of the search for a beauty "both concealed and visible", revealed in their full power only after considerable meditation, and even then not understandable in their full complexity. They were part of a cosmic view which sought solace in belief in a higher order; one perhaps that would somehow avert or explain the imminent collapse of a seven-hundred-year Muslim hegemony in Spain.

The Naṣrids created a palace of mythic style and opulence in defiance of their precarious political power. Almost apotropaic in its ubiquitous catalogue of decorative forms, its litany of poetry and quotations, and its vast inhaling of centuries of Islamic palatial planning and decoration, the royal palace of the Alhambra seems to attempt to defy the precarious plight of Muslims in Spain with a building: with the power of a culture which is old and potent even when the military and political force behind it is weakened.The unseen partner in this exchange is a rapidly encroaching Christian rule.

Grabar in particular has shown one of the themes of the palace inscriptions to be a celebration of the Naṣrid monarchs' military prowess in battle against Christian forces at Algeciras. It makes of that small border skirmish a great victory for an Islamic rule which is rarely able to afford the luxury of making of the Infidel a political other: "and how many infidel lands did you reach in the morning, only to become arbiter of their lives in the evening!"[10] It is, perhaps, a constantly present, always threatening Christian political and cultural hegemony which is denied in the Alhambra, as if that denial might in some way keep Christian Spain from enveloping the last Muslim kingdom on the Iberian peninsula.[11]

The Royal Palace of the Alhambra and the Great Mosque of Córdoba frame any account of the arts of Medieval Spain: the latter representing the establishment of a place of worship that aided the formation of a Spanish Muslim identity in a remote Western land; and the former an extravagant vision of one of the last Islamic palaces built to serve al-Andalus, one that attempts to retain that same Spanish Muslim identity, and its history, in the face of the fall of Islamic Spain. The two monuments certainly represent divergent historical moments, but they also remind us of what is constant in the arts and architecture of al-Andalus: a need to create and retain a cultural identity; a consciousness of the presence and force of the other, of a constant shifting of Islamic and Christian positions which never let any one of the Muslim Spanish rules rest in assured control of its cultural hegemony on the Peninsula. The Caliphal and *ṭā'ifa* rules used indigenous forms as a means of creating an identity in a far-off land. Almoravid and Almohad rules can be seen as intent on purifying an Islamic tradition considered too interdependent with Christian political life and its Mediterranean cultural traditions—a stated stance that would not have been necessary in a land firmly in the control of Muslim forces. Their attitudes also had the effect of clarifying, and making conscious, attitudes towards artistic production as they related to Islamic cultural identity. This politicising of artistic style and content must surely have had an effect on the Naṣrid arts and their meaning; for the Naṣrids, the most threatened and impotent of the rules discussed here, would mine history and myth to take a final stand against a Christian obliteration of Islamic Spain. They offer, in defence, an amalgamation of the cultural identity of al-Andalus in the opulent, complex identity of a Spanish Islamic artistic tradition.

[1] There is a question as to whether the nostalgia for the Umayyad Caliphate in Syria so characteristic of the rule of 'Abd al-Raḥmān I might have coloured the chronicles that tell us of the foundation of the Great Mosque of Córdoba. It is not clear, for instance, if the church of St. Vincent was originally shared by the Muslims and Christians of Córdoba, or if this is a textual tradition created to align with the experience of the first Muslims of Damascus. But certainly the Muslims of Córdoba prayed in a pre-existing structure in 169/785, when it was agreed that the *amīr* 'Abd al-Raḥmān I would purchase its site from the Christians and build a new mosque for Córdoba's Muslim population.

[2] Ibn 'Idhārī, *Al-Bayān al-mughrib fī akhbār al-Andalus wa 'l-Maghrib* (trans. Fagnan), II, 392.

[3] Oleg Grabar, "Notes sur le mihrab de la Grande Mosquée de Cordoue", in *Le Mihrab dans l'architecture et la religion musulmane*, ed. A. Papadopoulo, Leiden, 1988, pp. 115-22.

[4] C. Ewert, "Die Moschee von Bab al-Mardum in Toledo-ein 'Kopie' der Moschee von Cordoba", *Madrider Mitteilungen*, 18, 1977, pp. 287-354.

[5] T. Allen, *Five Essays on Islamic Art*, Sebastopol, 1988, pp. 79-83. See also Ewert, *op. cit.*

[6] Taken from the translation by P. de Gayangos ("The History of the Mohammedan Dynasties in Spain"), London, 1840-43, Vol. 1.

[7] The excavations presently being conducted under the direction of Julio Navarro Palazón promise to resolve a number of problems concerning the Castillejo and its surroundings.

[8] These associations are traced by Hoag, *Islamic Architecture*, New York, 1977, pp. 104-05.

[9] The analysis which follows depends on a number of distinguished scholars of the Alhambra, in particular Oleg Grabar, *The Alhambra*, Cambridge, 1978. See also: J. Bermudez López, *La Alhambra y el Generalife*, Madrid, 1987; and Fernández Puertas, *La fachada del palacio de Comares*, Granada, 1980.

[10] Grabar, *The Alhambra*, pp. 140-41.

[11] For an analysis of the one work of art that clearly shows the impact of Christian culture, in terms of this same set of meanings, see J. Dodds, "Paintings from the Sala de Justicia de la Alhambra: Iconography and Iconology", *The Art Bulletin*, 16/2, 1979, pp. 186-98.

BIBLIOGRAPHY

Basset, H., and H. Terrasse, *Santuaires et forteresses almohades*, Paris, 1932.
Beckwith, J., *Caskets from Cordoba*, London, 1960.
Borrás, G., *El Islam: de Córdoba al Mudéjar*, Madrid, 1990.
Creswell, K. A. C., *Early Muslim Architecture*, II, Oxford, 1932-40 (2nd ed., 1969).

Ewert, C., *Spanisch-islamische Systeme sich kreuzender Bogen*, I, Berlin, 1968.
——, *Forschungen zur almohadischen Moschee. 1. Vorstufen. 2. Die Moschee von Tinmal (Marokko)*, Madrid, 1981, 1984.
Expósito, M., J. Pano and M. Sepúlveda, *La Aljafería de Zaragoza*, Saragossa, 1986 (2nd ed., 1988).
Fernández Puertas, A., *La fachada del palacio de Comares*, Granada, 1980.
Ferrandis, J., *Marfiles árabes de occidente*, Madrid, 1935, 1940, 2 vols.
Golvin, L., *Essai sur l'architecture religieuse musulmane*, Vol. 4: *L'art hispano-musulman*, Paris, 1979.
Gómez-Moreno, M., *Arte árabe español hasta los almohades. Arte mozárabe*, Vol. III of *Ars Hispaniae*, Madrid, 1951.
Grabar, Oleg., *The Formation of Islamic Art*, New Haven, 1973.
——, *The Alhambra*, Cambridge, 1978.
Hernández, F., *Madinat al-Zahra, arquitectura y decoración*, Granada, 1985.
Instituto Velazquez (Madrid), *La casa hispano-musulmana. Aportaciones de la arqueología*, Granada, 1990.
Jiménez Martin, A., and A. Almagro Grobea, *La Giralda*, Madrid, Banco Arabe Español, 1985.
Marçais, G., *L'architecture musulmane d'Occident*, Paris, 1954.
Pavón, B., *El arte hispanomusulmán en su decoración geométrica*, Madrid, 1975.
——, *Estudios sobre la Alhambra*, Granada, 1975, 1977, 2 vols.
Terrasse, H., *L'art hispano-mauresque des origines au XIIIe siècle*, Paris, 1932.
Torres Balbás, L., *Arte almohade. Arte nazarí. Arte mudéjar*, Vol. IV of *Ars Hispaniae*, Madrid, 1949.
——, *Artes almorávide y almohade*, Madrid, 1955.

SPACE AND VOLUME IN NAṢRID ARCHITECTURE

JAMES DICKIE (YAQUB ZAKI)

In the architecture of the Naṣrids volume is expressed by the cubiform organisation of space. Not even the most casual visitor to the Alhambra can fail to remark the intrusive character of the hemicyclical bastions introduced by the Christians after the conquest, like El Cubo, or the structures replacing the Alcazaba Baja, all of which proclaim their alien origins in their sphericity. Naṣrid (but not Zīrid) military architecture used only square defensive towers. Internally the tower defines a cubiform space, frequently part of a palace. This shared cubiformity means that military and domestic architecture overlap. Apart from towers forming part of a palace (Torre de Comares, Torre de Machuca, Torre de las Damas), others comprised complete palaces in themselves (Torre de Homenaje, Torre de la Cautiva, Torre de las Infantas). The Alhambra which, seen from without, appears a jumble of cubiform substructures and pyramidal or prismatic superstructures proves, on closer inspection, to be a sequence of autonomous units individually aligned on axes that relate the architecture to the landscape, blending the natural and the artificial.

The cube or its two-dimensional expression, the square, underlies the basic planning concept of the Alhambra. The Torres de Comares, the rectangular court that precedes it, the façade of the Comares Palace (the south side of the Patio del Cuarto Dorado), the rotated square of the Sala de los Abencerrajes, or the square with chamfered corners opposite, the Sala de las dos Hermanas, all quantify space in a cubic manner.

The nucleus is invariably the courtyard, rectilinear like the pool which sometimes occupies its centre, with, ranged around it, living units axially disposed. The cube as hall or *mirador* (belvedere) terminates a sequence and forms a climax where drama is provided by successive disclosure. Screens, porous to a greater or lesser degree, interrupt the axial progression with a series of receding planes. Arches compose a diaphanous, or transparent, screen, walls an opaque screen. The transparent screen precedes the opaque one, the opacity of which is never total, as it is pierced with an archway, or more than one, as in the triple-arched openings in the Generalife and the ex-Convento de San Francisco. Thus planes before and behind produce an effect comparable to the multiplied perspectives in Regency or Federal interiors, where mirrors are so placed as to reflect each other as well as all the objects in between. This is probably clearer in mosque architecture than in domestic, particularly when the arcades are parallel to the *qibla* wall. A mosque is not monoaxial like a church but spreads the way a forest spreads, and the articulation of space by means of columns means that the perspective will alter with the spectator's position, producing intersecting vistas that open and close as one moves. In the Alhambra the screens define two different kinds of space: longitudinal and transversal, contrastedly shaped zones being part of the drama. Transversal rooms like the (vanished) Sala de las Aleyas and the Sala de la Barca were terminal living quarters situated at opposite ends of a long courtyard, the Patio de los Arrayanes; spatially, however, the Sala de la Barca had the more important role to play in an unfolding sequence leading up to the disclosure of the throne. The Sala de la Barca interposes between the sultan and the spectator, interrupting the route without disrupting the progression, and so prepares him for the emotional climax of the Salón de Embajadores. This differentiation of space by means of screens which interrupt and punctuate the direction not only breaks up the space into apprehensible units but heightens the sense of awe as one approaches the Presence.

Periodic interruption of the axis by transversal walls means that the archways linking up the different spaces form a perspective made up of receding planes: three as a rule, but sometimes four. The Comares tower has a double wall, so two arches are preceded by a third, the entrance into the Sala de la Barca, and even a fourth one (the central arch of the portico) framing the vista. A similar arrangement occurs in the Patio de los Leones, where a transversal passageway replaces the Sala de la Barca, and recurs in the Partal, in addition to the Generalife. In the Generalife the central span of the portico frames a three-arch composition, the central portion of which focuses the window of the *mirador* closing the vista, so that the planes not only recede, they also contract. The Partal lacks a sleeping chamber behind the portico, but the central arch frames a *mirador* punctured with three windows. In each case there is recession of planes in depth, with the dramatic impact magnified in the Sala de los Abencerrajes and the Sala de las Dos Hermanas by the archways being elevated on steps.

A triple recession is standard in Naṣrid architecture. In the baths, as one looks across the Sala de las Camas to the recessed couch, screened by two arches, it is obvious that the architecture is arranged so as to recede on planes; likewise in the Patio de los Leones, as one looks out on to the patio from the Sala de los Reyes, again a triple recession becomes apparent, in which planes are defined by the amount of light falling on any one plane. The number three seems to be significant; apart from its role as a modular ratio for towers and *miradors*, it occurs in porticoes, which can have three, five or even seven arches, although three is the norm. In a *mirador* or hall like the Embajadores, triple embrasures entail a sevenfold division of the wall, a division found also in the Sala de los Reyes, by far the most complex interior in the whole Alhambra and the one offering the deepest and most varied perspectives.

Even in an arcaded courtyard like the Lions, where the modular system takes in all four sides, axial composition remains dominant. On the main axis pavilions replace the central arch, but on the transversal axis the greater height and width of such arches emphasises the axiality and focuses the perspective. The arcades form a porous screen, filtering the light the same way *qamariyyāt* do for a room interior, and at the same time binding and unifying the disparate elements of a highly complex composition. The roofs of the pavilions pick up and prolong on a different axis the three pyramidal roofs of the Sala de los Reyes. The pavilions shorten the visible length of the main axis in the courtyard in relation to the transversal one, whilst their bulk helps equilibrate a composition that would otherwise be thrown off balance by the bulk of the two principal apartments, the Sala de las Dos Hermanas and the Sala de los Abencerrajes.

In the Patio de Comares the Sala de la Barca preceded the main chamber, but in the Sala de las Dos Hermanas the equivalent room, the Sala de los Ajimeces, follows it; however, the principle remains the same: the interruption of the route by the introduction of transversal elements, the route in this case being that leading to the Mirador de Lindaraja, the sultan's favourite retreat. Though in the Comares palace the Sala de la Barca is a sleeping chamber, in the Lions complex the Sala de los Ajimeces has no such function; the single royal bedchamber of the Comares complex has bifurcated to form two lateral chambers, with one bed apiece, opening off the Sala de las Dos Hermanas to right and left.

The ruler's seat is unvaryingly axial: in the Patio del Cuarto Dorado, where a temporary throne occupied a position between the two doors, in the Salón de Embajadores, where a permanent one filled the central embrasure on the north side, and in the Mirador de Lindaraja, where the sultan relaxed. Though the throne is axial, access to the courtyard is always on an angle. Petitioners or litigants wishing to approach the Presence would use the door in the north-west corner of the Patio del Cuarto Dorado, and this door bears the same relation to the Cuarto Dorado courtyard as the Comares entrance does to the Patio de los Arrayanes. The sequence of courtyards in the Generalife, arranged on different axes producing an L-shaped figure, is precisely that of the Comares palace in the Alhambra: initial courtyards set at right angles to the axis of the main courtyard generate a tension resolved in the principal vista. This explains why one enters the Patio de los Arrayanes not, as one might expect, from the south-west but from the north-west. Thus the visitor's first view is the sultan's habitual one, for the south side of the courtyard is even prettier than the north.

Interrupted or discontinuous space is the clue to the planimetry of the Alhambra. Naṣrid architecture is based on the notion of divided and subdivided (as in the Sala de los Reyes) space, In the process of compartmentalising space the square follows the rectangle, which itself follows another rectangle but on a different axis. The cubiform Salón de Embajadores follows after the E-W rectangle of the Sala de la Barca, which follows after the N-S rectangle of the Patio de los Arrayanes. The Generalife has the same arrangement, with a *mirador* replacing the Salón de Embajadores (in reality merely an inflated *mirador*). A variant occurs in the Patio de los Leones, where, though rectangle (the Sala de los Ajimeces) precedes square (the Mirador de Lindaraja), it is itself preceded by another and larger square (the Sala de las Dos Hermanas). Screen succeeds screen until you reach the final screen (the wall of the *mirador*), so that the architecture reaches a climax in the landscape: tension followed by release. The *mirador* is never other than axial; at the same time as it terminates one vista, which is artificial, it opens up another, which is natural. In fact,` it closes a single vista in order to open up three, for the *mirador*, which is a protuberance, is porous on three of its sides. And because it protrudes either into a garden or into a landscape, this means that a compenetration is effected between the architecture and its natural setting. The compenetration is even more complete when the garden contains a pool reflecting the *mirador* on its surface.

In Islamic architecture decoration is always subordinated to form; if form can be said to follow function, in Islamic architecture decoration follows form. In Naṣrid art a wall is merely a stucco tapestry; the purpose of decoration is strictly to enhance the form. Inside the structure, the assorted cubic, pyramidal and prismatic shapes break down into the planes from which they were built up in the first place: cube reverts to square and rectangle; pyramid and prism revert to triangle. Triangles, rectangles and squares divide and subdivide the wall surface into areas designed for contrasting treatments. The cubicity imposes an interior made up of planes in regular arrangement. The surfaces are articulated by vertical or horizontal divisions forming bands or panels, with the squinches forming a sequence of triangles at a higher level. The architecture is crystalline, with polyhedrons like the Abencerrajes and Dos Hermanas exteriors breaking down internally into repetition of their basic structures, like the rotated square, covering the walls in petrified geometry. Abstract form logically translates into abstract decoration.

The function of pattern, whether tilework, stuccowork or honeycombing, is to trap and enmesh the eye. By trapping and enmeshing the eye the decoration engages the spectator, so he becomes absorbed in tracing a pattern or deciphering a description. As such he becomes a participant in the architecture. A defined set of relationships obtains both between the exterior and the interior and between the interior and the observer. This could explain why the aesthetic emotion the Alhambra generates in the beholder differs from that produced by any other building, in the western world at least; and that, even though the onlooker's response is enfeebled by the disappearance of the colour. This basic component of the ensemble is missing everywhere but on the dado. One can only surmise, therefore, what effect light must have had on the chromatic balance intended by the Naṣrid artisans, but it must have been considerable.

Certainly, the architecture would change and become less stable under the impact of light. The prismatic medium of the *muqarnaṣ* fractures the light and entraps it. In Naṣrid architecture the angle of light is always oblique, highlighting patterns or parts of a pattern on the opposite wall in succession as the sun moves round the sky; detail would be alternately vibrant and dormant, whenever a cloud obscured the sun. What all this means is that the architecture was never for a moment static, but constantly unstable. The function of light, especially of filtered light, was to energise an otherwise static mass, as water did in gardens.

A metamorphic architecture changes under the impact of light. The honeycombed vaulting is composed of polyhedrons exactly like a real honeycomb. Honeycombing stands at the opposite remove from the wall surfaces because it is plastically metamorphic. A weightless geometry, energised by light, hangs suspended over a cubiform space. The prismatic medium of the *muqarnas* fractures the light, just as, earlier, the *qamariyyāt* had filtered it on entering. Highlighted surfaces and shadowed concavities break up the space so that volume disintegrates and volumetric analysis becomes an impossibility. It disintegrates then reintegrates as spirit becomes matter and matter assumes form in its descent into phenomenality. Integration takes place as each successive order of stalactites eases the transition from the dome to the plane surfaces of the walls. Matter is no longer perceived as solid or static but as fluid and kinetic. The ceiling of the Sala de las Dos Hermanas is an architectural "black hole" which threatens to draw the spectator up into a vacuum; it is a visual metaphor for the world as seen from the standpoint of Ash'arī metaphysics. Indeed, the Alhambra in its brittle beauty epitomises an attitude explicable only in terms of Islamic philosophy; a work of such fragile elegance could not have been produced by any other civilisation.

BIBLIOGRAPHY

It is not practicable, given the specialised nature of this article, to provide an extensive bibliography. The reader is, however, specifically referred to:

Chueca Goitia, Fernando, *Invariantes castizos de la arquitectura española*, Madrid, 1971.

More generally applicable references may be found in my forthcoming work, *The Alhambra. A Functional Analysis* (in preparation).

ECSTASY AND CONTROL IN ANDALUSĪ ART: STEPS TOWARDS A NEW APPROACH

J. C. BÜRGEL

I

Ecstasy and control are two key elements in Islamic art, and are linked to the two dimensions or poles of the Islamic religion: to the *sharīʿa* or legal system on the one hand and to Sufism or Islamic mysticism on the other—although, as we shall presently see, these two aspects are actually far more intertwined than strictly divided.[1] The dominant role played by geometrical patterns, and by form in general, in the Islamic arts may be seen as a visual counterpart of the rigidity of Islamic law, these abstract forms reflecting the Islamic order *niẓām* which rules in the universe and should prevail on earth, giving structure not only to religious actions, but to arts, sciences, habit and custom, to the public life of the Islamic community and to the daily life of every Muslim.

However, this predominance of abstract forms in the ornamentation of visual objects connected with architecture or handicraft also of course stems from the prohibition of the image, even though this prohibition is actually based on *ḥadīth* rather than on any specific Quranic decree.[2] Why did this prohibition become so strict in Islam? It should be remembered, first of all, that the restrictive attitude of *sharīʿa* was not limited simply to the production of images; with a few exceptions, the three fine arts, poetry, music and painting, were also regarded with suspicion, or even rejected, by the representatives of Islamic law and order. Much speculation has surrounded the reasons for this attitude, and, among other things, various theories of influence have been advanced.[3] The present writer is persuaded that the intrinsic and all-embracing reason lies in the nature of arts as psychic powers or energies, there being, according to Islamic belief, no other might and no other power than by, with or through God.[4] The awareness of the power or, as I call it, the "mightiness" of the arts in traditional Islamic society is reflected in the many testimonies to the power of poetry, music and images to be found in medieval sources.[5]

Before Islam entered the scene, these powers were, in Arabia at least, pagan, with a very frequent magical component. They were—or appeared to be—more or less profane in the cultures conquered by Islam. It is understandable, therefore, that the arts, with their uncontrollable "mightiness", should have provoked suspicion on the part of the new régime which sought to impose its religious rule and sacred control upon everything. At first this concern manifested itself in *ḥadīth*s about painting and poetry, but the visible consequences were soon to follow.[6]

The sober, sometimes even sombre nature of early Islamic architecture is a reflection of this attitude. However, Islam contained, from the very beginning, another, though less palpable dimension in its Holy Scripture and the early collections of *ḥadīth*s: the dimension of ecstasy. If we are seeking areas of ecstatic experience in Islam (before the rise of mysticism), we may discover them in certain rites: in the utter strictness of fasting, in prayer within a large community, in the pilgrimage and in the Holy War.

Some of these rites display a repetitive structure which provides links both with control and with ecstasy. We may think, for example, of certain repeated actions during the pilgrimage, such as the sevenfold circumambulation of the Kaʿba, the throwing of three times seven pebbles at various places in Mina, etc. The Quranic text, too, contains remarkable repetitive structures, notably in Sura 55, and so do certain famous accounts concerning the Prophet, such as the *ḥadīth al-shafāʿa*, or *ḥadīth* of Intercession, and the *ḥadīth al-miʿrāj*, or *ḥadīth* of the Ascension, which in turn reflect repetitive structures existing in time and space according to the Islamic world view: sacred history with its recurrence of prophets and the Quranic universe with its seven spheres, later modified by the more scholarly Ptolemaic concept.[7]

Those concerning themselves with Islamic art are bound, sooner or later, to be struck by the enormous importance of repetitive structures in almost all its manifestations, whether in architecture, ornament, calligraphy, carpets or elsewhere. Far from producing monotony, as a Westerner might expect, repetition is a source of growing delight, culminating, perhaps, in ecstasy. This will, not, of course, apply to any repetition whatever. In art the item repeated must be beautiful, in religion it must be sacred; and in religious art it must be both sacred and beautiful. This applies both to sacred texts —according to Muslim belief, the Quranic text represents an inimitable miracle in itself—and to mystical music or ornaments used in sacred architecture. The impact of repetition is often enhanced by additional stratagems, such as an acceleration of rhythm or a gradual shortening of the elements repeated, a type of structure, which, incidentally, underlies the arrangement of the suras in the Quran, and for which I have proposed the term "conical". Furthermore, the combination of repetition and rhythmic intensification, so typical of Islamic musical performances, represents one of the many examples of the superimposing of two systems—which may be seen as a symbol of mystical or physical union, and thus has, again, much to do with ecstasy.

It is thanks to the efforts of mysticism, with its interiorised stance, that the arts, including, probably, miniature painting, but in particular literature and poetry, became capable of, and acceptable as, the expression of religious feelings in Islam. Mystics began to lay stress on God's being not only a God of majesty (*jalāl*), but also of beauty (*jamāl*);[8] "God is beautiful and loves beauty" is a *ḥadīth* attributed to the Prophet, and it belongs to the favourite set of *ḥadīth*s quoted in mystical circles and writings.[9] God reveals Himself in His creation by dint of his divine emanation (*fayḍ*), a neo-Platonic idea that became central in the context of mystical feeling and aesthetics;[10] for now the artist could indulge in beauty without the fear of creating something provocative, confident of partaking in God's act of revealing divine beauty on earth.

Along with divine beauty, the mystics cultivated sacred ecstasy (*wajd*). Dance and music, once profane and the source of outbursts of uncontrolled ecstasy (*ṭarab*) regarded as satanic, were reintroduced precisely as a means of attaining such ecstasy, now regarded as permissible since it served to foster union with the Beloved, i.e. God. The legalists were, indeed, to look upon these "innovations" with a due degree of suspicion.[11] Yet the mystics were certain that their ecstasy was not only permissible, but divine, although they would warn against any illicit use of the power implicit in it.[12]

How do these general principles apply to Andalusī art? The present approach is so novel that several years of concentrated study would be needed to give a comprehensive answer to this question; only a few glimpses can be offered here.

II

Mysticism existed in al-Andalus as elsewhere in the Islamic world, culminating in the fascinating and enigmatic personality of Ibn ʿArabī, in whose nature control and ecstasy manifested themselves as in any mystic, although his artistic expression—that is, his poetry—does not usually reveal the typical structures of mystical ecstasy such as we find, for instance, in Jalāluddīn Rūmī's ecstatic hymns in praise of his mystical friend Shamsuddīn of Tabriz.[13] However, Ibn ʿArabī matches Rūmī in his claims to "mightiness", which in fact verges on self-deification, and repetitive structures do occur in his prose writings, for example in his *Treatise on the Lights of the Secrets Granted to One Who Undertakes Retreat*, which describes the "Journey to the Lord of Power"; that is, the soul's ascension, structured in accordance with the famous lines of Rūmī:

> I died as mineral and became a plant,
> I died as plant and rose to animal etc.[14]

Every new stage is introduced by Ibn ʿArabī with almost the same formulaic phrase:

> First you will discover the secrets of the mineral world. You will become acquainted with the secret of every stone and its particular harmful and beneficial qualities ... then He will free you from that mode and unveil the vegetal world.

> And if you do not stop, He will reveal the animal world to you.
> Then after this, He reveals to you the infusion of the world of life-force into lives.
> And if you do not stop with this, He reveals to you the "surface signs".
> If you do not stop with this, He reveals to you the light of the ascendant stars.
> And if you do not stop with this, He reveals to you the degrees of speculative sciences.
> And if you do not stop with this, He reveals to you the world of formation and adornment and beauty.
> And if you do not stop with this, He reveals to you the degrees of the *quṭb*.
> And if you do not stop with this, He reveals to you the world of fever and rage and zeal for truth and falsehood.
> And if you do not stop with this, He reveals to you the world of dignity and serenity and firmness.
> And if you do not stop with this, He reveals to you the Gardens.
> And if you do not stop with this, He reveals one of the sanctuaries where spirits are absorbed in the divine Vision. In it they are drunken and bewildered. The power of ecstasy has conquered them, and their state beckons you.
> And if you do not stop with this beckoning ...

There follow several further revelations introduced with the same formula, namely the sons of Adam, the Throne of Mercy, the Pen, identified with the First Intellect, and finally the Mover of the Pen, i.e. God himself. Then the work continues:

> And if you do not stop with this, you are eradicated, then withdrawn, then effaced, then crushed, then obliterated. When the effects of eradication and what follows are terminated, you are affirmed, then made present, then made to remain, then gathered together, then assigned. And the robes of honor which [your degree] requires are conferred upon you, and they are many.[15]

The close link between ecstasy and repetitive structure is obvious in this text, but so is the importance of control, which is never abandoned; and at the end of his spiritual *miʿrāj* the mystic is obliged to realise that he is still in his body, on earth, and must return to his everyday activities.

Repetition is also connected with mirror effects,[16] this link being notably present in the marvellous passage in Ibn Ṭufayl's *Ḥayy ibn Yaqẓān* where the descent of the divine light, proceeding from God and traversing the seven spheres until it reaches the earth, is described as being reflected, at every sphere, as if in a mirror.[17]

III

Let us now, however, turn our attention to some poetical texts in which either ecstasy or control, or the two together, play an important part. The reader should be reminded, first of all, that the dominant form of pre-modern Arabic poetry, and of Islamic poetry generally—a form common to the *qaṣīda* (long poem), the *qiṭʿa* (short poem) and the *ghazal* (short love poem)—was characterised by monorhyme and strict prosody, which obliged the poet to make use of a single meter throughout a poem, and by the absence of stanzas or strophic segments. The formal structure had thus to be chosen in the first line of any poem, and then continued until the last; this naturally entailing (from the historical beginnings of this poetry) a highly repetitive structure, with every line mirroring the preceding and following ones. The monorhyme causes every line to end on the same sound, rather as rays, proceeding from various points, move toward one centre in a fan-like formation; and again, the effect of this acoustic structure is far removed from monotony. The degree of expectation created by the limited number of possibilities in the rhyme activates the hearer, and, if the poem answers favourably to this expectation, the joy to the auditory sense mounts moment by moment, until ecstasy is reached. In other words, a rigid technical control does not exclude ecstasy, but may rather contribute to unleashing it.

This being the case, it would seem reasonable to interpret the formal revolution in Arabic poetry that took place in al-Andalus, with its development of a highly sophisticated strophic form, within this frame of reference.The *muwashshaḥa* may in fact be understood as a hypertrophic *qaṣīda* or *ghazal*. What has been said above also applies to this form, except that the basic structure is repeated not in each line but only in each stanza. The lines of the stanza may vary in length and have different rhymes, yet whatever rhyme pattern and rhythm appears in the first strophe is repeated in the following ones; in other words, the *qaṣīda* line has, so to speak, been stretched into a whole strophe. The process rather resembles a widespread practice in Persian and Turkish literature, where the *ghazal* poets would often divide each line into four segments of equal length, placing interior rhymes at the end of the first three segments, so that the resulting form always displays the pattern (a,b, etc.=interior rhymes, changing from line to line and strophe to strophe ; capitals=monorhyme, followed throughout the poem) aR aR, bbbR, cccR—although this did not in fact need to be strictly followed throughout the poem.

In the *muwashshaḥa*, we find the most variegated strophic structures, e.g.

I. abcd	II. efgh	III. ijkl etc.
abcd	efgh	ijkl
abcd	efgh	ijkl
QRS	QRS	QRS
QRS	QRS	QRS[18]

Those *muwashshaḥāt* which end in the *kharja*, a popular Romance verse or strophe, reveal how this revolutionary pattern actually stems from indigenous Romance poetry, although the *kharja* lends its form only to the second part of the strophe, the so-called *qufl* ("lock") or *simṭ* ("girdle"), and the first part, called a *ghuṣn* ("branch"), is an independent invention (still, its strophic structure resembles that of the *kharja* and, as such, it is evidently inspired by it). The *qufl* takes the place, as it were, of the rhyme, and therefore all *qufl* (or *kharja*) rhymes appear in all strophes, whereas the *ghuṣn* rhymes change from strophe to strophe and take the place of the part preceding the rhyme in traditional verse. Sometimes the *kharja* part precedes the whole poem, as an introduction called a *maṭlaʿ*.

It was thus the *kharja* that broke through the ancient pattern of the *qaṣīda*, enriching it with a variety of meters and rhymes not previously conceivable. In other words, the *muwashshaḥa* comes about through the combination of two systems, the indigenous strophic form being superimposed upon the *ghazal* form, or, rather, merged with it and absorbed by it. As such, it is a fine example of the fusion of two cultures that took place in al-Andalus, and symbolises the Islamic principle of incorporating foreign influences by assimilating them to its own rules; in other words, of offering participation through submission.[19]

At the same time, however, this superimposing of various structural systems is one of the main principles underlying Islamic ornament and Islamic art in general.[20] By superimposing the indigenous strophic form on the *ghazal* pattern, the repetitive elements in the *muwashshaḥa* have become tighter, feverish as it were, with the formal effort or degree of control more pronounced than in the traditional *ghazal*. Again, however, the effect is by no means necessarily insipid, the exercise of technical skill without spirit, but can rather be one of ecstasy. The *muwashshaḥa* thus also symbolises the very Islamic phenomenon of attaining ecstasy through a particularly strong submission to self-imposed rules, or, to put it in religious terms, supererogatory efforts. Without having witnessed any performance, we may yet surmise that the amount of ecstasy unleashed in a listener by a *muwashshaḥa* strongly depended on its musical execution; for, as Monroe and others have pointed out, "musical influences probably lie behind the origin of the new form".[21]

IV

Other aspects of "ecstasy and control" in Andalusī poetry concern its cosmic dimensions and religious overtones; and these we can perceive directly in the texts.

A fine example of the ecstatic cosmic-ranging fantasies created by Andalusī poets (following in the footsteps of earlier Eastern writers) is a short poem by Ibn Khafāja (450/1058-533/1139), known as *al-jannān* ("the Gardener") and esteemed as one of the best composers of nature lyrics in al-Andalus:

> That [young man] "Flame" played with that [maiden] "Wind", till their play turned to earnest.
> He passed the night in the abode of passion, ardent for her and restless.
> I shared his sleeplessness, judging him drunk, while ecstasy [*ṭarab*] trembled in his shoulders.
> Even a mint inspector, now appearing, could not tell if this were burning flame or gold.

The [maiden] "Wind" kisses his bashful cheek, while sparks are watchful eyes
There, at a fire-place, where morning poured [as into wine] its water, bubbles above it [formed] by stars,
Partly [appear] blue cinders, partly the embers below them,
As if the night sky knelt there above them, with meteors sparkling upon it.[22]

As is usually the case with this poet, the writing is rather difficult and defies a convincing translation. Its meaning, however, is not obscure. The poet, although he appears only once for a short moment (in the first half of the third line), not only shares the sleeplessness of the flame, but evidently also its ecstasy, its love, its brightness, and, finally, its dying away; in other words, he projects some of his own emotional experience into the night scene. The "control" pole is provided not by *sharīʿa* elements, to which there is no express reference in this poem, but by a certain sense of melancholy, which is typical not only of this poet but of other Andalusī poets too—and which finally, with its implications of submission to fate and to the cosmic order, has very clear Muslim implications. The gradual extinction of the fire may be understood as a symbol not only of life's transitoriness, but of the impending end of Andalusī glory.

In terms of structure, the poem is a fine example of the superimposing of various systems or levels, in this case the realms of real fire and metaphorical wine, upon which, as a third layer, the love scene is imposed; and finally, again by a daring interlacing of metaphor and reality, earth and cosmos are intertwined, the real sky with its stars providing the water (dew) and the bubbles (stars) for the wine (fire) in the imaginary night-embracing wine glass, while the cinders with the embers beneath them glimmering through the cracks seem to the poet like a tiny night sky flashing with stars or comets or meteors. Microcosm and macrocosm are thus skilfully interwoven. The poet magnifies terrestrial phenomena into celestial ones and vice versa, revealing himself, or rather his fantasy, to be endowed with the cosmic power of a perfect man. But if "the Gardener" views a reflection of his own emotion in the ecstasy of the flame, he also unmasks it as a passing illusion, part of the self-consuming process of life within the flickering spectacle of the universe.[23] All this is a perfect and very tight artistic expression of medieval Islamic ontology, an existence between ecstasy and control, with control meaning submission either to religious laws, or to cosmological forces, or, very often, to both at the same time.

V

The topic of love, only vaguely present in the preceding poem, is of course much more prominent in many other poems, and it is tempting to look at them with our polarity in mind. A few preliminary reflections, however, are advisable to ensure a proper understanding of the subject in its particular Andalusī context.

Love between the sexes is not a major subject in the Quran, but nor is it entirely absent. Yūsuf and Zulaikha figure in the twelfth Sura, and the Prophet himself appears as lover, expressly or by implication, in various revelations.[24] Love and sexual relations had to be sacred, submitted, like everything else in Islam, to the laws of revelation, and this did not in every respect provide a convenient framework for writers of love-lyrics. On the one hand, the *sharīʿa* allowed intercourse with slave-girls—"what your right hand owns" (4, 3); but on the other hand, Islamic matrimonial law is anything but emotional, and, with its leaning towards polygamy, it is in direct conflict with the essential basis of true love, which is a dual and not a one-to-many relation. Whereas Muḥammad Abū Ḥāmid al-Ghazālī (d. 505/1111) in his "Revival of the Sciences of [the Islamic] Religion" cites the Prophet as saying (pointing to his grandson Ḥasan b. ʿAlī with his total of 200 wives): "The best man of my community is he with the greatest number of wives."[25] , Arab poets had to decide whether to continue in pre-Islamic hedonism or cultivate—in their verses, at least—a relationship of authentic monogamous love. Many of them chose the latter, even trying to sacralise their love, or divinise the beloved, or draw parallels between true love and monotheism. The school best known for this attitude was that of the so-called ʿUdhrī poets, who, however, went to the extreme, remaining faithful to the unattainable adored one until death and often even dying from love.[26] In their poems the ecstasy of love is controlled by its sanctity; the submission is not to law, but to love, which takes the place of religion.

Fine examples of this are to be found in the poetry of the great Andalusī poet, philosopher, jurist and theologian Ibn Ḥazm (384/994-456/1064) Consider, for instance, the following lines:

> I love you with a love that knows no waning, whereas some of men's loves are midday mirages.
> I bear for you a pure, sincere love, and in [my] heart there is a clear picture and an inscription declaring my love for you.
> Moreover, if my soul were filled by anything but you, I would pluck it out.[27]

> Are you from the world of the angels, or are you a mortal? Explain this to me, for inability to reach the truth has made a mockery of my understanding.
> I see a human shape, yet if I use my mind, then the body is in reality a celestial one.[28]

> He who claims to love two lyingly commits perjury, just as Mani[29] is belied by his principles.
> In the heart there is no room for two beloveds, nor is the most recent of things always the second.[30]
> Just as reason is one, not recognising any creator other than the One, the Clement,
> Likewise the heart is one and loves only one, though he (she) should put you off or draw you to him.[31]

VI

The *muwashshaha* structure, however, offered a further means of counterbalancing ecstasy: the *kharja* with its popular, sometimes even crude, burlesque or obscene note.

The two elements of divinisation and a stylistic anticlimax provided by the *kharja* appear often, for example in a *muwashshaha* by the "Blind Poet of Toledo", al-Aʿmā al-Tuṭīlī (d. 519-20/1126). The poem is full of ecstatic declarations of love. In the second stanza, the beloved—in all likelihood a girl, even though introduced with the male gender—is compared to the Kaʿba, and the poet declares his intention of making the pilgrimage to him (her) and of being himself the victim for the ceremonial sacrifice. There are several further declarations of devotion and willingness to suffer, and the high style is preserved throughout the rest of the poem, until the *kharja* closes the song in popular Romance style:

> Meu l-habib enfermo de meu amar
> Que no ha d'estar
> Non ves a mibe que s'ha de no llegar?
>
> ("My beloved is sick for love of me. How can he not be so? Do you not see that he is not allowed near me?")[32]

The gushing verses, which display a note of masochism in their talk of unconditional submission to the ruthless lord who is the beloved, thus come to an end very abruptly, and the extravagant feelings are belittled or even belied by the playful turn of the *kharja*—by words, that is, put into the mouth of one of those among the conquered, who were, however, to emerge as victors after long centuries of subjugation. Thus, in this poem, the ecstasy of love is once more hampered by circumstances—or, from an Islamic point of view, due to the poet's submission not to the Lord of the universe, but to a Spanish courtesan. This appears to have more to do with Islamic sexual morals, and with the position of woman in Islam, than with our particular topic. Yet the question remains: what ultimately is the meaning of this strange contrast affecting so many *muwashshaḥāt* and resulting from the superimposing of two cultural traditions? Was the poet merely playing a game, or was he attempting to set out a symbolic truth, or is the truth a mixture of the two?

VII

The superimposing of two systems within Andalusī society, so successful in many respects—engendering as it did social, cultural, and artistic fusions and the delightful offspring of these—ended in ultimate failure for Arabic Spain. Yet it bequeathed many graceful remains, including Andalusī architecture and other works of art. It is, unfortunately, beyond the present writer's competence to deal with this topic within the short space of time available for this volume. It does seem to me, however, that repetition and the superimposing of systems, which are both of all-pervading importance in Islamic ornament and calligraphy, also played a decisive part in the development of Andalusī architecture and other visual arts. Let us recall just a few very famous and conspicuous examples, considering first the Great Mosque of Córdoba, then certain places in Granada. Repetition is marvellously represented by the forest of columns in the prayer-hall of the Great Mosque of Córdoba (though this is, it is true, a common feature of many mosques, from the earliest days of Islam), and the superimposition of systems is likewise among the striking features of this building, manifesting itself in various ways. According to one specialist, "the method of construction with double superimposed arches, which gives the Córdoba mosque an original beauty and a unique character in medieval architecture, is not found in any other mosques".[33] Such superimposed columns are, it is true, to be found in the Hagia Sophia and in the Umayyad Mosque of Damascus, and Titus Burckhardt thinks those in Córdoba may have been inspired by the latter.[34] Nevertheless, these arches are certainly unique in their grace and weightlessness, and the impression may well be described as one of ecstasy built in stone—an impression further enhanced by the particular forms of the Moresque arch, the horseshoe arch, and, even more typical and important in our context, the broken arch, one, that is, into which a number of small arches have been carved; this representing an almost exact counterpart to the *muwashshaḥa* in terms of structure.

Other fine examples are to be seen in Granada, such as the double row of fountains in the Generalife Garden (a wonderful repetitive structure) or the *muqarnas* or stalactite domes in various halls of the Alhambra (a highly sophisticated superimposed structure)—"these small stalactites," one scholar notes, "are created with great variety, and provide a play of line and shadow both rigorous and hallucinating."[35] Here also is found the combination of vegetal motifs with complex geometrical outlines and inscriptions in Kufic and cursive.[36]

Yet, as is often the case with the *muwashshaḥāt*, some of these architectural devices, arches and moulded plasterwork do not convey an impression of lightness and grace, but rather one of mannerism and stiffness.[37] Here and there, what was intended to testify to ecstasy (*wajd*) has become pose, a cramp of ecstasy (*tawajjud*).

Thus the poet king Yūsuf III (810/1408-820/1417), one of the last Arabic poets of Granada, starts and ends one of his *muwashshaḥāt* with the following lines:

O you who have aimed	At my heart with the dart	Of a piercing glance:
Meet one who's dying	One whose eye is shedding	Fast-flowing tears!

In between he praises the infinite beauty of his beloved and recollects the fulfilment granted him by the latter in former days:

He's gained all beauty! Who can vie with him?
He is sweet and licit Would he not make pretexts.
Full of perfection— Praised be his creator! ...

How many a night Did he keep faith with me
While by our union He lodged me in Eden!
He cured the disease Of my languishing heart,

With the deep red lips Whose white snow doth taste sweet Pleasantly cool.
Oft did he heal With a peaceful embrace My broken heart...

Yet the cyclic structure of the poem—and of life as viewed by the poet?—forces him to return to the first lines. So the poem continues:

He lovingly gazed Like a fawn without peer
And yet he had trespassed Killing me by intent.
Then he turned off While I exclaimed in ecstasy (*wajd*):
O you who have aimed etc.[38]

The ecstasy of this love seems doomed by its own laws, and perhaps this was true also of Andalusī culture in general. But what culture is not doomed to perish sooner or later? And why should it not perish after experiencing such ecstasies, ecstasies that reverberate still in its rhymes, and in its vaults, arches, gardens and water-works?[39]

[1] Cf. J. C. Bürgel, "Ecstasy and Control: Two Dominant Elements in Islamic art", in *The Iconography of Islamic art: A Symposium presented by the National Museums of Scotland and the University of Edinburgh*, ed. R. Hillenbrand, forthcoming.

[2] Cf. J. C. Bürgel, *The Feather of Simurgh. The "Licit Magic" of the Arts in Medieval Islam,* New York, 1988, p. 8 *et seq*. and p. 12 *et seq*.

[3] *Ibid*., p. 13 *et seq*.

[4] This is best expressed in the ubiquitous statement *lā ḥawla wa-lā quwwata illā billāh*.

[5] Cf. the source material in Bürgel, *The Feather of Simurgh.*

[6] Examples are Muḥammad's calling poetry "the Quran of Satan", or cursing the makers of pictures along with women who tattoo themselves, those who live from usury and sorcerers; for further material and references, see *The Feather of Simurgh*, p. 11 *et seq.*

[7] See J. C. Bürgel, "Repetitive Structures in Early Arabic Prose", in *Critical Pilgrimages: Studies in the Arabic Literary Tradition*, ed. F. Malti-Douglas, Austin, 1989, pp. 49-64.

[8] Cf. A. Schimmel, *Mystical Dimensions of Islam*, Chapel Hill, 1975, p. 44.

[9] *Ibid*., p. 471.

[10] Cf. T. de Boer, "Fayḍ", in *Shorter Encyclopaedia of Islam.*

[11] Cf. Bürgel, *The Feather of Simurgh*, p. 112 *et seq*.; *idem*, *Allmacht und Mächtigkeit: Religion und Welt im Islam,* Munich, 1991 (forthcoming) (chapter entitled "Einige Fetwas gegen Musik").

[12] See, for example, the chapter on *samāʿ* in G͟hazālī's *Revival of the Sciences of Religion* (*Iḥyāʾ ʿulūm al-dīn*, Cairo, 1387/1967, II, 346-89).

[13] Cf. J. C. Bürgel, "Speech is a Ship and Meaning the Sea: Some Formal Aspects of the *Ghazal* poetry of Rūmī", in *The Heritage of Rūmī, 11th Giorgio Levi Della Vida Biennial Conference*, ed. Amin Banani and George Sabbagh, forthcoming.

14 Schimmel, *op. cit.*, p. 321.

15 Ibn ʿArabī, *Journey to the Lord of Power: A Sufi Manual on Retreat by Muhyiddin Ibn ʿArabī with Notes from a Commentary by ʿAbdul-Karīm Jīli and an Introduction by Sheikh Muzaffer Ozak al-Jerrahi, Translated by Rabia Terri Harris*, London-The Hague, 1981, p. 36 *et seq.*

16 Cf. the chapter "The Magic Mirror: On Some Structural Affinities in Islamic Miniature, Calligraphy, and Literature", in Bürgel, *The Feather of Simurgh*, p. 138 *et seq.*

17 See my "Ibn Ṭufayl and his *Ḥayy ibn Yaqẓān*", in this volume.

18 Monroe, No. 18. Very often, the *ghuṣn* has the structure ababab; cf. the examples in E. García Gómez, *Las jarchas romanes de la serie árabe en su marco*, 2nd ed., Barcelona, 1965.

19 *Teilhabe durch Unterwerfung*, one of the basic assumptions underlying my book *Allmacht und Mächtigkeit.*

20 This is shown in Bürgel, "Ecstasy and Control".

21 Monroe, *op. cit.*, p. 31.

22 Ibn Khafāja, *Dīwān*, ed. S. M. Ghāzī, Alexandria, 1960, No. 29, p.75.

23 Cf. J. C. Bürgel, "Man, Nature and Cosmos as Intertwining Elements in the Poetry of Ibn Khafāja", *Journal of Arabic Literature*, 14, 1983, pp. 31-45.

24 Cf. Quran 24,4; 33,4; 37-40; 66,1-5; 33, 52.

25 *Iḥyāʾ ʿulūm al-Dīn*, II, 38.

26 On *ʿUdhrī* love cf. L. A. Giffen, *Theory of Profane Love Among the Arabs: The Development of the Genre*, New York-London, 1971.

27 Monroe, *op. cit.*, p. 171, No. 8A.

28 *Ibid.*, No. 8C.

29 Mani: the founder of Manichaeism, a religion based on the duality of two opposed forces, and severely persecuted as heresy in Islam.

30 The second half of this line is not clear to me. Possibly *wa-la aḥdathu 'l-umūri bi thāni* should be emended to *wa-la aḥdathi 'l-umūri li-thāni* ("[nor is there room] for that which, more than anything else, leads to splitting [literally: 'produces a second one']", i.e., inconstant love or concupiscence).

31 Monroe, *op. cit.*, No. 8E.

32 *Ibid.*, p. 249, No. 23.

33 Cf. L. Torres Balbás, "Andalusian Art", in *Encyclopaedia of Islam*, new ed., Leiden, 1960–, I, 498a.

34 T. Burckhardt, *L'art de l'Islam: Langage et signification*, Paris, p. 196.

35 H. Terrasse, "Gharnāṭa", in *Encyclopaedia of Islam*, new ed., Leiden, 1960–, II, 1019a.

36 Torres Balbás, *op. cit.*, 500a/b.

37 Terrasse states, with regard to the Alhambra, that "at the end of the 8th/14th century a certain stiffness appears in the moulding and even in the forms". (*op. cit.*, 1018b).

38 Monroe, *op. cit.*, No. 42.

39 On Andalusī garden architecture cf. J. Brookes, *Gardens of Paradise: The History and the Design of the Great Islamic Gardens*, London, 1987, pp. 37-69.

BIBLIOGRAPHY

Boer, T. de, "Fayḍ", in *Shorter Encyclopaedia of Islam.*

Brookes, J., *Gardens of Paradise: The History and the Design of the Great Islamic Gardens*, London: Weidenfeld and Nicolson, 1987.

Burckhardt, T., *L'art de l'Islam: Langage et signification*, Paris: Sindbad.

Bürgel, J. C., *The Feather of Simurgh. The "Licit Magic" of the Arts in Medieval Islam*, New York, 1988.

——, *Allmacht und Mächtigkeit: Religion und Welt im Islam*, Munich, 1991 (forthcoming).

——, "Man, Nature and Cosmos as Intertwining Elements in the Poetry of Ibn Khafāja", *Journal of Arabic Literature*, 14, 1983, pp. 31-45.

——, "Speech is a Ship and Meaning the Sea. Some Formal Aspects of the *Ghazal* Poetry of Rūmī", in *The Heritage of Rūmī, 11th Giorgio Levi Della Vida Biennial Conference*, ed. Amin Banani and George Sabagh, forthcoming.

——, "Ecstasy and Control: Two Dominant Elements in Islamic art", *The Iconography of Islamic Art. A Symposium presented by The National Museums of Scotland and The University of Edinburgh*, ed. R Hillenbrand, forthcoming.
——, "Repetitive Structures in Early Arabic Prose", in *Critical Pilgrimages: Studies in the Arabic Literary Tradition* (Literature East th West), ed. F. Malti-Douglas, Austin, 1989, pp. 49-64.
García Gómez, E., *Las jarchas romanes de la serie árabe en su marco*, 2nd ed., Barcelona, 1965.
Al-Ghazālī, M., *Iḥyāʾ ʿulūm al-Dīn*, Cairo, 1387/1967, 5 vols.
Giffen, L. A., *Theory of Profane Love Among the Arabs: The Development of the Genre*, New York-London, 1971.
Ibn ʿArabī, *Journey to the Lord of Power. A Sufi Manual on Retreat by Muhyiddin Ibn ʿArabī, with Notes from a Commentary by ʿAbdul-Karīm Jīli and an Introduction by Sheikh Muzaffer Ozak al-Jerrahi, Translated by Rabia Terri Harris*, London-The Hague: East West Publications, 1981.
Ibn Khafāja, *Dīwān*, ed. S. M. Ghāzī, Alexandria, 1960.
Monroe, J. T., *Hispano-Arabic Poetry—A Student Anthology*, Berkeley, Los Angeles-London: University of California Press, 1974.
Schimmel, *A., Mystical Dimensions of Islam*, Chapel Hill, 1975.
Terrasse, H., "Gharnāṭa", in *Encyclopaedia of Islam*, new ed., Leiden: E. J. Brill, 1960-, II, 1012a-1020a.
Torres Balbás, L., "Andalusian Art", in *Encyclopaedia of Islam*, new ed., Leiden: E. J. Brill, 1960-, I, 497a-501b.

CALLIGRAPHY IN AL-ANDALUS

ANTONIO FERNÁNDEZ-PUERTAS

INTRODUCTION

Arabic is written and read from right to left, for which reason the pages of their books are read in the opposite direction from a western book, beginning at the back and ending at the front. Even the way of handling an Arabic book is different, as the book is held in the left hand, and on completing the reading of two pages, the leaf is turned over by the honourable "right hand". This is decisive at the moment of creation and of subsequent aesthetic "reading", since a Muslim unconsciously sees, or "reads", a monument correctly. When a westerner approaches Islamic art he instinctively "reads" it the opposite way and misses the original intention.

The new Islamic religion was born in a Semitic surrounding containing different dialects. In the time of the first three of the four *rāshidūn* or caliph companions and followers of the Prophet,[1] a written compilation of the Quran was begun under the first and second caliphs, Abū Bakr and ʿUmar, and it was the third caliph ʿUthmān who probably provided a unified written version. From the early days of the Umayyads, archaic Arabic writing began to separate the angular form of script, known as kufic, from the more flexible free-hand form known as *naskhī*. Kufic prevailed in official writing and Qurans, free of diacriticals or vowels ("scripta defectiva"), reduced to 17 letters out of the 28 sounds pronounced in speech. Confusion and divergent readings entailed the addition of diacritical points round about the middle of the 2nd/8th century, and a system of distinguishing vowels and doubling consonants to fix the meaning of the sacred text in copies of the Quran in Abbasid times (4th/10th century). The form of kufic lettering, free of diacriticals, was the style adopted in artistic Islamic decoration.[2]

Artistic Arabic calligraphy first made its appearance in the Dome of the Rock in Jerusalem, dated 72/691, in the reign of ʿAbd al-Malik.[3] The letters are stiff and primitive but clear because prepared in advance before being executed in mosaic. Far more calligraphic, with better-drawn kufic letters, is the historic inscription on a stone lintel at Qaṣr al-Ḥayr al-Gharbī[4], dated 109/727, which refers to Hishām, Commander of the Faithful, a son of the above ʿAbd al-Malik. Nonetheless, alongside this calligraphy that was first drawn and then executed, there is another type of free-hand calligraphy in inscriptions on Umayyad palaces, bearing the direct impress of the artist's hand, cursive and irregular.[5] This kind of manual writing is to be found in ink on marble, as in Qaṣr al-Ḥayr al-Gharbī,[6] in Khirbat al-Mafjar, or in Mshaṭṭa, dating from the time of al-Walīd II b. Yazīd.[7]

The Iberian Peninsula passed under the dominion of the Umayyads in 92/711, and the dynasty survived there after the conquest of the area in 138/756 by the Umayyad prince ʿAbd al-Raḥmān I.

How did Arabic calligraphy enter al-Andalus? The answer is: through coinage. The organisation of the new state, its economy and its trade required a single currency. Arabic writing was present from the moment of the conquest, all during the epoch of the *wālī*s (governors loyal to the Umayyad caliphate of Damascus), in the form of books, above all Qurans, but the overwhelming majority of the population remained Christian for decades until, with the passage of time, the arrival of a new generation and the economic advantages of conversion, the Arabic language spread, it being necessary not only to speak and read the language of the new rulers but to write it too. Calligraphy proper probably entered al-Andalus through the coinage, and only later through texts, especially the Quran. Whenever a cache of coins dating from the time of the *wālī*s and particularly the *amīr*s is examined, a coin is often found with writing on its rim affirming that the high-grade silver dirham was struck in the city of Wāsiṭ (in present-day Iraq). The beautiful kufic letters are neat and precise, proportionate each to another, and with an angular rhythm in their clear epigraphic design.

Trade, the pilgrimage to Mecca and contacts between the Near East and the Iberian Peninsula carried on uninterruptedly, as is attested by the discoveries of coins of the period. The Umayyad *amīr*s soon started to mint their own coins "in al-Andalus", which at this time meant that they were minted in Córdoba. The calligraphic inscriptions on the eastern dirhams from Wāsiṭ show much finer early kufic lettering than those on Andalusī coins, though with time these attained an acceptable quality. Numismatic evidence forms an invaluable historical record to document the introduction of Arabic calligraphy into the country.

The calligraphy of al-Andalus and its zone of influence in North Africa is divisible stylistically into four successive periods: 1) Emiro-Caliphal (92/711-422/1031); 2) the *ṭāʾifa*s (422/1031-478/1085); 3) Almoravid-Almohad (478/1085-541/1147, 541/1147-629/1232); and 4) Naṣrid (629/1232-897/1492). Each period has its own characteristics, and when the period is a long one, (as are 1 and 4), distinct evolutionary phases can be discerned. The calligraphy which began being used in religious texts ends up used for poetry, embellishing architecture and other artistic forms.

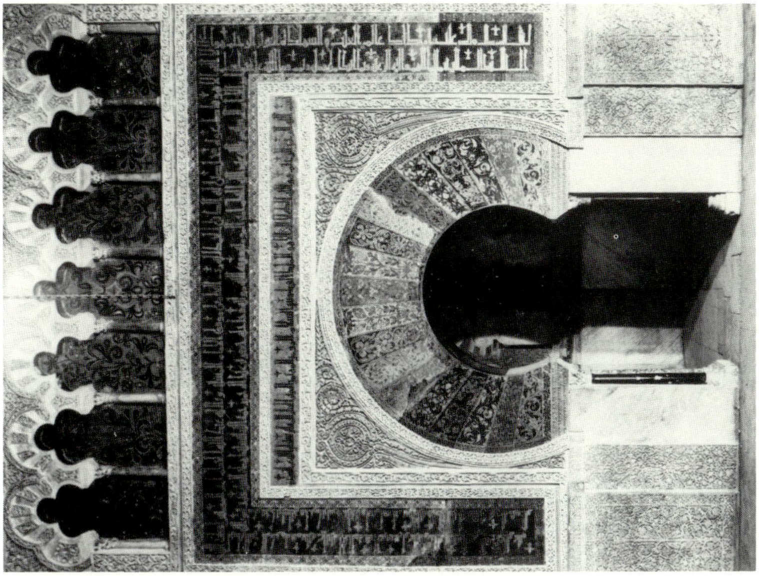

2

1

3

1. Córdoba Mosque: Inscription in the tympanum (241/855 – 6) of the Bāb al-Wuzarā'. Photo, Félix Hernández Giménez.
2. Córdoba Mosque: Façade of the *miḥrāb* (ca. 354/965). Photo, German Archaeological Institute, Madrid.
3. Córdoba Mosque: Façade of the *sābāṭ* (ca. 354/965). Photo, German Archaeological Institute, Madrid.

4

5

6

4. Saragossa, Aljafería: Oratory, façade of the *miḥrāb* (441/1049 – 474/1081). Photo, German Archaeological Institute, Madrid.
5. Toledo, Museum of Santa Cruz: Marble rim of the cistern well of the Great Mosque (423/1032). Photo, Museum of Santa Cruz.
6. Tlemcen (Algeria): Façade of the *miḥrāb* (529/1135). Photo, C. Ewert.

7

8

9

7. Málaga, Archaeological Museum: Funerary stone of the Almoravid princess Badr (496/1103). Photo, German Archaeological Institute, Madrid.
8. Toledo, Museum of Santa Cruz: Mudéjar tombstone (Latin-Arabic) of Miguel Semeno (1156). Photo, Museum of Santa Cruz.
9. Granada, Alhambra: Lantern-hall (Dos Hermanas) of the Main Qubba in the palace of the Riyāḍ (Lions). Verse of the *qaṣīda* of Ibn Zamrak (ca. 782/1380). Photo, Sadea-Albaycin.

12

10

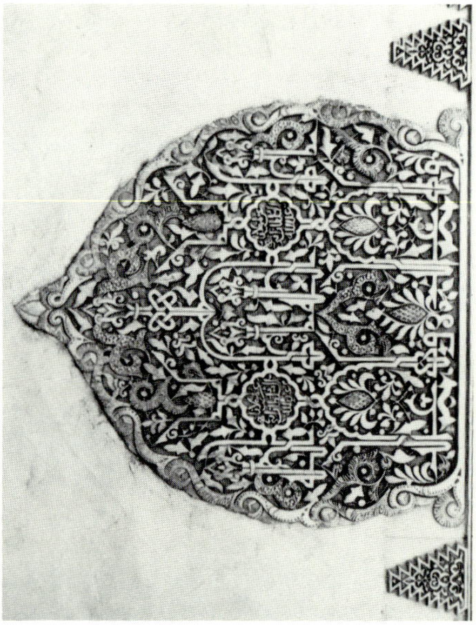

11

10. Granada, Alhambra: Hall of Comares, frieze in plaster (ca. 753/1352 – 755/1354). Photo, A. Fernández-Puertas.
11. Granada, Alhambra: N. Gallery of the Patio of Comares, floral-epigraphic arch (ca. 770/1368). Photo, A. Fernández-Puertas.
12. Granada, Alhambra: Mirador of the Main Qubba (today Lindaraja) (ca. 1380s). Photo, A. Fernández-Puertas.

I. The Emiro-Caliphal period (92/711-422/1031)

The first phase of calligraphy extends from the period of the *wālis* (92/711-138/756), through the independent emirate and Umayyad caliphate of Córdoba (138/756-422/1031), and covers al-Andalus and its area of political influence in the Maghrib. Within this period three distinct phases can be made out, from the evolving design of the characters on coins, monuments, architectural elements, stone slabs and other epigraphic materials. These are: (I.1) archaic kufic; (I.2) floriated kufic; and (I.3) ordinary kufic.[8]

I.1 *Archaic kufic calligraphy*

Archaic kufic calligraphy is found right up to the period of the *amīr* Muḥammad I (238/852-273/886), until the years 251/865-254/868. The letters are formed of simple straight strokes, and with the body of the letter thick and angular contrasting with the vertical strokes, though imperfectly shaped, with straight-line ligatures between the letters. To this period belongs the inscription incised on a grey-coloured column from the original Great Mosque of Seville dating from the 3rd/9th century (fig.1). It is the oldest architectural inscription in al-Andalus. The letters are primitive, neither well drawn nor well cut, although the hardness of the stone may have contributed to this. The inscription records that the mosque was built by the *amīr* ʿAbd al-Raḥmān [II] b. al-Ḥakam, and under the supervision of the *qāḍī* of Seville, ʿUmar b. ʿAdabbas, in 214/829-30, being the work of the calligrapher-epigraphist, or *kātib*, ʿAbd al-Barr b. Hārūn. It is a difficult text to decipher, and the chronicler of the Almohad epoch Ibn Ṣāḥib al-Ṣalāh was unable to record it correctly in his work.[9]

More elegant by far is the inscription on the Bāb al-Wuzarāʾ (plate I.1) of the Mosque of Córdoba, built by ʿAbd al-Raḥmān I in 169/785, and "consolidated" some 70 years later by Muḥammad I in 241/855-6 on account of the dilapidated state of the lintel and two windows.[10] The inscription, though with squat letters, is fluid and extends beyond the horizontal line of the script, and establishes a balance between round and angular letters, with finials tilted either left or right; the execution is fluent. Twenty-five years, almost a generation, separate this inscription in the Great Mosque of the capi-

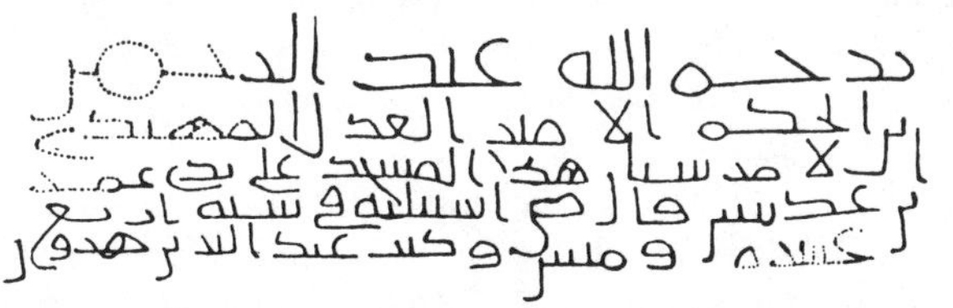

Figure 1. Seville: foundational inscription from the original Great Mosque (214/829-30). Drawing M. Ocaña Jiménez.

tal of the Emirate from the one in Ibn ʿAdabbas's mosque at Seville. Moreover, the inscription on the Bāb al-Wuzarāʾ was specially designed and carved on a series of slabs mortared into the stonework. The importance accorded this simple work of "consolidation" and "renovation" in the Mosque of Córdoba may be inferred from the text, which states that "the prince Muḥammad b. ʿAbd al-Raḥmān ordered the work of renovation and consolidation of this mosque ... and the work was finished in 241 [855-6] ... under the supervision of Masrūr, his *fatāʾ*."[11] This indicates that the work took place under an expert architect, a freedman of the emiral house since the time of the prince's father, the *amīr* ʿAbd al-Raḥmān II, who was serving him when the latter extended the mosque, according to al-Ḥasan b. Mufarrij and Muʿāwiya b. Hiṣhām, as reported by Ibn Ḥayyān in the section of his *Al-Muqtabis* dealing with the emirates of al-Ḥakam I and his son ʿAbd al-Raḥmān II.[12]

I.2 *Floriated kufic calligraphy*

Floriated kufic makes its appearance during the emirate of Muḥammad I and remains on the scene till the end of the reign of ʿAbd al-Raḥmān III (300/912-350/961). Vertical strokes terminate in bevelled finials, or, more frequently, in two or three palm leaves, one straight, another convoluted, and when there is a third it sprouts between them. This kind of floriated finial indifferently faces right or left. Some examples of the letter *nūn* are so rounded in shape as to form a swan's neck shape; and there is a series of semi-circular ligatures below the line. The letters are well drawn, with the proportion of length to width characteristic of Hispano-Islamic calligraphy, which establishes its own rules, such as: the superimposition of letters; representing the round body of the letters. The body of the script was broken by several specific letters that are standing free, both in the middle and at the end of the word.

The calligraphy of this second period plays a considerable ornamental role, marking the start of its decorative use in subsequent periods, culminating with the Naṣrids, under whom Hispano-Muslim calligraphy reaches its maximum development. As text and as ornament calligraphy will figure henceforward in all branches of art. On caliphal architecture it appears on bases, capitals, pilasters, the frames of arches, horizontal bands etc; likewise on coinage (which rivals Fāṭimid coinage for elegance), historico-commemorative and funerary slabs, ivory objects, ceramics and so on. Texts are either of a historical, religious or funerary nature.

An example can be seen in the basilical hall known as the Salón Rico, which ʿAbd al-Raḥmān III had built in Madīnat al-Zahrāʾ, where the epigraphy gives dates of construction of a base, an abacus of a capital, and the horizontal frieze above the arches, thus dating the different stages of construction of the pavement, the springing of the arches and the completion of the carved stone revetment, which extend through 341/952 to 346/957; and supplies the name of the reigning caliph, ʿAbd al-Raḥmān III.[13] The names of the artists and others responsible for the work on the hall are given on marble pilasters leading to the collateral chambers.[14]

In the Mosque at Córdoba the task of reinforcing the 2nd/8th century courtyard façade, which was collapsing, by means of buttresses or pillars joined by horseshoe arches supported on columns to form the new exterior façade of the patio, is recorded on a marble slab on the left of the entrance to the central nave. In beautiful floriated kufic it states that ʿAbd al-Raḥmān, Commander of the Faithful (for he had assumed the title of caliph in 316/929 for politico-religious reasons), gave orders for "the building of the façade and assuring its solidity", the work being completed "in the moon of *dh̲ū 'l-Ḥijja* of the year 346 [23 February-24 March 950], under the direction of his freedman vizier and *ṣāḥib* of his *madīna* ʿAbd Allāh b. Badr. Work of Saʿīd b. Ayyūb".[15]

This slab, along with the inscriptions in the hall at Madīnat al-Zahrāʾ, contains religious expressions and Quranic allusions, beginning with the *basmala*; in other words, as always with the Mālikis, the texts stress the divine omnipotence. In the caliphal period, calligraphy is a favourite mode of decoration painted on a slip in ceramics, with square or curved letters, the vertical strokes straight or bent, ending in a floriated finial. Such inscriptions are for the most part pious invocations such as *baraka* (blessing) or *mulk* (sovereignty or power), both with and without the article. Up to this time, Hispano-Muslim calligraphy has historico-documentary value and is an expression of religion in Andalusī life, but its use is limited as an aesthetic or decorative element.

I.3 *Simple kufic calligraphy*

The third and last phase of this first period is characterised by simple kufic, which reaches its climax with the reign of the second caliph al-Ḥakam II (350/961-366/976) and lasts into the beginning of the 5th/11th century as an archaic form with certain innovations during the course of that century. This script is known as simple kufic because the strokes and finials of the letters lack floriation, and it has a system of proportions between the body of the letters and the vertical strokes, which end obliquely bevelled, facing either right or left, to produce an impression of great elegance. The script is graceful, clearly drawn and executed, and the ligatures are semi-circular or straight.

Under al-Ḥakam II kufic assumes enormous decorative importance, occupying the most important and conspicuous places in any architectural ensemble, as can be seen in his enlargements of the Cordoban mosque, in the façades of the *miḥrāb*, the *sābāṭ* (the private passage which communicated the mosque with the caliphal palace) and the *bayt al-māl*.[16] and in the vaulted bay in front of the *miḥrāb* as well as in the *miḥrāb*'s own small, octagonal chamber (plate I.2, I.3).

Calligraphy also figures on the Quranic frieze which runs beneath the wooden ceiling of al-Ḥakam's extension of the central nave. The texts are still historico-religious in nature and furnish invaluable data on the history and architecture of the monument. In the *miḥrāb* façade and the vaulted bay preceding it there are beautiful inscriptions.

Within the *miḥrāb* octagonal chamber the border of the marble dado exhibits a masterly handling due to the beauty of the modelling of the letters cut in a hard material, as do the marble blocks of the imposts of the arch, faultlessly chiselled because they had been carefully planned and drawn before the craftsman started work.

This is worth mentioning, because the other inscriptions in the façade and bay of the *miḥrāb* are done in mosaic (plate I.2), working on larger surfaces and in material easier to handle, as the tiny cubic pieces of glass could be used to adjust the proportions of thick and thin in the lettering, insert free trefoil motifs between letters, and so on. Nonetheless, in the inscription framing the *miḥrāb* arch, the calligrapher (*kātib*) Muṭarrif b. ʿAbd al-Raḥmān—who is named in the inscriptions in the *maqṣūra*—was unable to solve the problem of turning the inscription at the corners of the frame. He made the vertical bands of the text intrude on the horizontal band.

On the façade of the *sābāṭ* (plate I.3) he superimposed lines of vertical and horizontal script, the vertical lines on the right reaching to the top of the upper corner, and the horizontal text extending to the left top corner. This is a solution which has at least the advantage of not confusing the eye, and will recur in later periods. The calligraphic defect in the frame of the *miḥrāb* arch is evident where two lines of script overlap (plate I.2). It is a fault that completely disrupts the beauty and harmony of the calligraphy. It is surprising to find such a fault in so conspicuous a position and important an inscription, because the problem of how to turn a corner with an inscription had already been solved in the four small arches of the *ṭāqāt* (niches) in the palatine residence in Madīnat al-Zahrāʾ belonging to the freedman and *ḥājib*, Jaʿfar b. ʿAbd al-Raḥmān, who was in charge of the work of al-Ḥakam II's expansion of the mosque.[17] These four small arches, executed during the last years of ʿAbd al-Raḥmān III's reign, in 349/960,[18] solve the problem by filling the corner with a stylised blossom, a device that will continue to be used into the Naṣrid period, together with the other solution of simply inserting a square at the corners.

It is odd that court calligraphers should have solved this problem five years earlier, yet those working on the mosque could not think of a solution. Was it an attempt at a new solution that failed to come off? Or were different calligraphers at work in the two places? I do not know, because the *ḥājib* Jaʿfar mentioned on the four arches also figures in the inscription on the Córdoba *maqṣūra* as the man in charge of the work of enlargement, though he died before the work was completed, according to the text on the first mosaic frame of the *sābāṭ* façade, where the mortuary formula, "May God have mercy on him", follows the mention of his name. Therefore the *sābāṭ* façade was done after the *miḥrāb* facade, and the *kātib* improved on his faulty *miḥrāb* solution in the later *sābāṭ* façade corners.

On all the inscriptions the caliph al-Ḥakam is mentioned only with his honorific caliphal title, al-Mustanṣir bi-Llāh, and in his twin functions as caliph: *Imām* and Commander of the Faithful. The texts on the imposts state that al-Ḥakam II ordered "his freedman and *ḥājib* ... to fix both these imposts". The mosaic text on the U-shaped band of the frame states, amongst Quranic verses and religious phrases, that al-Ḥakam II gave orders to "his freedman and *ḥājib* Jaʿfar b. ʿAbd al-Raḥmān for the building of this edifice ... completed ... under the inspection of Muḥammad b. Tamlīkh, Aḥmad b. Naṣr and Khālid b. Hāshim, his chiefs of police, and Muṭarrif b. ʿAbd al-Raḥmān, the *kātib*, his servitors".

The religious, historical and Quranic text on the dado of the octagonal chamber of the *miḥrāb* states that al-Ḥakam II ordered the chamber to be built and revetted in marble under the supervision of the same team of servitors. The inscriptions on the façade and niche of the *miḥrāb* bear the same date, the month of *dhū 'l-Ḥijja*, 354/November 28-December 27, 965.[19]

On the façade of the *sābāṭ*, the inner mosaic border of the horseshoe arch records that the caliph al-Ḥakam II ordered "this *fusayfisā'* [mosaic work] to be done in the venerable room, and it was completed in the year 3—[part of the date is missing]".[20] The frame consists of five consecutive borders, of which the second and fourth contain inscriptions, the latter being Quranic. The second states that "he [the caliph] ordered this access to his place of prayer", and mentions the deceased *ḥājib* Jaʿfar, along with the remaining servants of the crown already mentioned.

Islamic architecture is usually anonymous save for the name of the ruler, prince or magnate who commissioned the work, and even these may not figure. In the Near East, the Umayyads sometimes recorded their name and a date on an edifice. After the transfer of the dynasty to al-Andalus, inscriptions under both the Emirate and the Caliphate identify the person who, along with the *amīr* or caliph, had a hand in the construction, and specify their particular role, even if one had died in the course of the work, as also the exact date. Such wealth of historical data is uncommon in Islamic art, and least of all in epigraphy. Following the collapse of the Caliphate such inscriptions become briefer and almost disappear during the period of the Almohads in the second half of the 6th/12th century, to re-appear occasionally under the Naṣrids. Similar historical detail is to be found even on

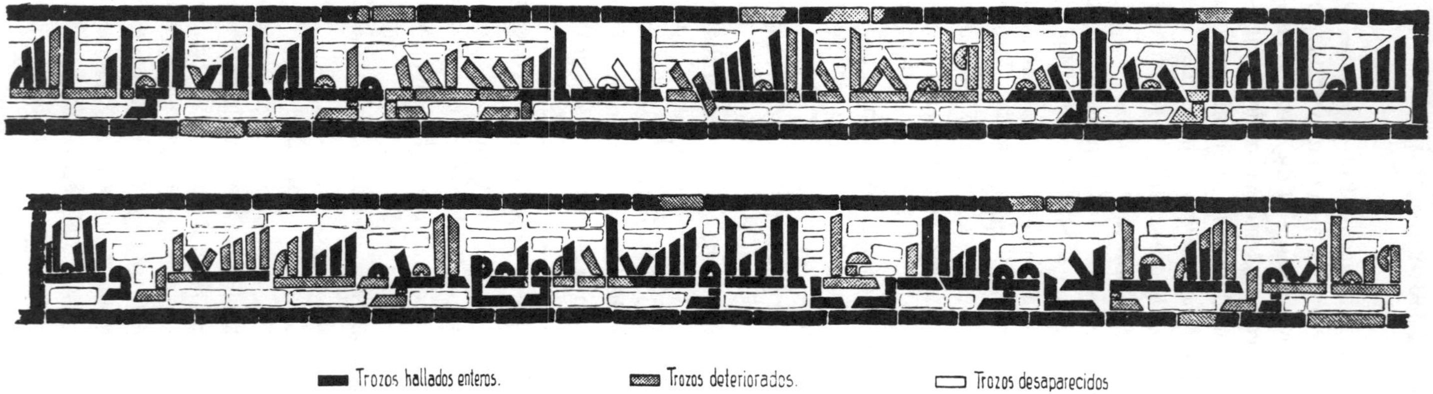

Figure 2. Toledo: Foundational inscription of Bāb al-Mardūm (390/999-1000), today Cristo de la Luz. Drawing M. Ocaña Jiménez.

less important foundations, such as a vanished minaret put up by a freedman of al-Ḥakam II called Durrī al-Ṣag̲h̲īr in what is today the province of Jaén, where the freedman owned a number of *al-munya*s (country estates), like that of Guadarromán, besides others in the vicinity.[21] Military architecture has the same sort of historical commemorative epigraphy, as is shown by the plaque of Baños de la Encina.[22]

Kufic calligraphy at this time adorns textiles, ceramics and metalwork, like the chest covered with sheets of silver preserved in Gerona Cathedral, which al-Ḥakam II had made for his son and appointed heir Prince His̲h̲ām.[23] Unique in Hispano-Muslim art, and belonging to this same period, are the ivory boxes and containers which usually identify the person who commissioned the work, the craftsman, and sometimes the recipient, besides recording the date. In coinage, the strokes are more stylised and it is standard practice to name, in the central space, the master of the mint for the year in which the coin was struck.

Under the government of the *ḥājib* al-Manṣūr, during the reign of His̲h̲ām II, calligraphy follows the same course as in the previous reign of al-Ḥakam II, as witness the coins, the *ṭirāz* of His̲h̲ām II, ivories, etc.[24] An exception is the piece of decorative carpentry on the back of the *minbar* in the Andalusiyyīn Mosque in Fez, which al-Manṣūr ordered to be restored, as the Fāṭimid work was in a state of disrepair.[25]

The proportioning of the letters in this first period of Hispano-Muslim calligraphy varies with the material on which the calligraphy is being applied. It is far harder to carve a text on marble, which can easily chip, than on hard ivory. But both are harder to work with than textiles or mosaic, and much harder than putting paint on ceramics, or laying mosaics. The proportion of width to height in the letters, the calligraphic arrangement, the ornamental flourishes, etc., all depend on the kind of material used. This is evident from the foundation inscription of the small Bāb al-Mardūm Mosque (known today as Cristo de la Luz), put up by a Toledan philanthropist "with his own money" in 390/999-1000, as stated in the text worked in brick, the angularity and flattened proportions of whose letters were imposed by the nature of the material (fig. 2).[26]

II. The *ṬĀʾIFA* Period (422/1031-478/1085)

The second phase of Hispano-Islamic calligraphy opens with the disintegration of the Cordoban caliphate in 422/1031, and the emergence of the *mulūk al-ṭawāʾif*, or regional kings, who mostly controlled city states. Four of these are important on account of their influence on subsequent stylistic developments: the Banū ʿAbbād of Seville; the Banū Hūd of Saragossa; the D̲h̲ū 'l-Nūn of Toledo; and the Banū Ṣumādiḥ of Almería.[27]

The period under review embraces little more than half a century, the briefest in our survey, but it was crucial on account of the different types of calligraphy which emerged in the various kingdoms. For the first time there is a rudimentary attempt at forming a geometrical pattern by prolonging the strokes of the letters, without the result being altogether satisfactory. Likewise calligraphy appears interlaced with independent geometric ribbons, and floriation is relegated to the tops of letters and used to fill space, without going so far as to form a grid. Its brevity notwithstanding, the period is thus important for the development of the calligraphic "ductus" and the ornamentation which will adorn the two subsequent periods of calligraphy in al-Andalus and its area of influence in the Maghrib.

II.1 *The Banū ʿAbbād*

In Seville, calligraphy is featured on foundation stones and gravestones, the border of ceramic lustre ware, gold dinars and silver dirhams. As a rule, this Sevillian calligraphy uses well-proportioned kufic adapted to the nature of the material used, the design being less rigid and geometric than in the previous period, with the base line less marked due to a series of curved strokes forming prolonged tails that descend until they almost touch the strokes of the line below. There is nonetheless a clear upward rhythm and greater slenderness to the characters, with strokes which terminate in widening bevelled finials. This may be seen from a foundation stone recording the restoration of a minaret by the king al-Muʿtamid dated 472/1079, on which, following caliphal precedent, the marble worker, one Ibrāhīm, is named, likewise the treasurer, Abū ʿUmar Aḥmad. The calligraphic composition is made up of very elegant letters innocent of any floral element.[28] In the borders of ceramic lustre ware in the Seville Archaeological Museum, and in another found in Palma del Río (Province of Córdoba),[29] the name of al-Muʿtamid appears in gold on a white ground, in well-traced letters, but with the strokes lacking elegance because of the confined space. As restored, the plate from Palma del Río shows a central area divided into four quadrants each with a blossom motif, all of them golden on a white glazed ground. The remaining text says "which al-Muʿtamid ordered to be made under [the supervision of ...]".

This raises the question whether al-Andalus in the 5th/11th century had kilns producing lustre ware or whether this crockery were commissioned in the Near East and then imported. The style of calligraphy induces me to postulate a Sevillian pottery workshop, a hypothesis reinforced by the discovery of two fragments of a plate rim on which the name of the Sevillian monarch appears similarly written. In ʿAbbādid coinage elegant, well executed letters fill the spaces, which inclines me to believe that artists from the caliphal mint in Córdoba emigrated to Seville to work for the ʿAbbādid rulers.

II.2 *The Banū Hūd*

Of the kings of this dynasty in Saragossa, important calligraphic remains survive in their palace of al-Jaʿfariyya (Aljafería), originally built *extra muros* close to the river Ebro. Other important remains have surfaced in the excavation of the palace-fortress of Balaguer (Province of Lérida).[30] Calligraphy in the Aljafería appears in various places: 1) bordering the alabaster dado in important rooms; 2) on capitals; on the convex moulding of a composite capital there figures the name of the sovereign, al-Muqtadir bi-Llāh, in whose reign the palace was built, along with a stylised blossom and ribbed palm leaves. The axial projections of the abacus of the capitals contain invocations composed of characters with interruptions and prolongation of the letters below the line of the script in addition to floral in-filling; 3) But it is in the remains of the calligraphic bands in the north transversal hall and in the Oratory where the great evolution of monumental calligraphy is quite remarkable (plate II.4). The letters in these bands have a rounded or somewhat pointed formation, the ligatures are curved, and the strokes tend to be tall and stylised with a width to height ratio of 1: 2.5 or 3. They terminate in wide concave finials. The lettering on these bands has, beneath the calligraphic composition, some curved stalks inexpertly drawn, with a sinuous spiral movement to which palm leaves, stylised blossoms and pine cones are attached. The most interesting feature in these calligraphic bands is another type of stroke that extends in form of a ribbon, where two of them form a cross with rounded arms, their ends terminating in ribbed palm leaves pointing in opposite directions. This is the first attempt at geometric kufic, not entirely successful, but a momentous innovation that opens up possibilities of future development. Together with this calligraphic composition where the geometric strokes do not cross over each other, but on meeting form rounded crosses, another design appears with geometric closed ribbons, centrally grooved, which form at the point of intersection of the cross a knot with five angular loops.

Here, therefore, in the *ṭāʾifa* period, there has emerged a calligraphy which has either a vegetal floral background, or is linked to an incipient geometric composition of the simplest form. Sometimes the ribbons of prolongation get mixed and link two strokes, leaving the upper parts of both to float free as a ribbon with loose ends, the kind of error a beginner would make. This type of calligraphic mistake in the tracing of kufic is found even in the supreme works of Hispano-Muslim calligraphy, as in the tympanum above the north window in the Mirador of Lindaraja in the Alhambra.

II.3 *The Dhū 'l-Nūn*

Under the Dhū 'l-Nūn dynasty of Toledo calligraphy is to be found on marble capitals and bases,[31] ivories worked in the ateliers of Cuenca (a dependency of Toledo at this time),[32] funeral *cippi*—marble or stone cylinders—the marble rims of cisterns wells, funerary bricks, coins, etc.[33] Two types of calligraphy stand out, clearly differentiated. One is angular in character, with vertical strokes ending in curved finials facing either right or left and perforated with an opening; rarely does the stroke curve, and the spaces between the letters are filled with stalks with gently undulating branches showing a central incision where the flower is attached. The other kind of calligraphy has its prototype in the bands which adorn the cylindrical rim of the cistern well of the Great Mosque of Toledo (plate II.5), where the mosque's construction by al-Ẓāfir b. dhī 'l-Nūn, the first *ṭā'ifa* king of Toledo, in 423/1032, is commemorated.[34] The rim exhibits three bands of script, the highest one so thin and squat that it has got worn away with use. The other two bands have their height proportioned in keeping with the calligraphic script, which has centrally incised letters, finials that expand with an oblique, somewhat curved stroke, and the strokes and terminal prolongations of letters bursting into flower and ending in palm leaves or blossoms, which tend to fill the spaces above such letters as do not have vertical strokes. Some final letters have a swan's neck silhouette with floral finial; floral ornamentation can appear individually or connected to a stalk. The calligraphic beauty of such inscriptions is in marked contrast to the coins, which are badly designed, difficult to decipher and with text running in concentric circles.

II.4 *The Banū Ṣumādih*

The calligraphy of the *Banū Ṣumādiḥ* is of an elegant sober and balanced kufic lettering, with proportioned strokes, with bevelled finials, with free vegetal decoration filling the empty spaces. Practically all the calligraphic texts known are either from gravestones or from coins. This high-quality type of calligraphy was to influence decisively the two succeeding periods, giving definitive form to the shape of certain letters such as the *hā'*, with two curls and a curving stroke above them. The proportioned calligraphy also appears in a frame or an arch, an innovation which will persist into later periods.

Of the four schools discussed here it is the elegance and stylisation of the Sevillian letter, the geometric-floral innovations of Saragossa, and the proportional shape in the body of the Almerian letters that calligraphers will take into account in the succeeding period, when al-Andalus once again reverts to a unified political command.

The all-important documentary-historical value of calligraphic texts at the time of the Umayyad Caliphate persists into other periods to some degree in the architectural remains or pieces which have survived, as the examples already quoted show.

III. THE ALMORAVID-ALMOHAD PERIOD (478/1085-629/1232)

The third period of calligraphy in al-Andalus begins when the Berber *amīr* of the North African Ṣanhāja tribe, Yūsuf b. Tās̲h̲fīn, came to the aid of the regional kings, who had panicked at the capture of Toledo by Alfonso VI, king of Castile. On observing the weakness of these petty rulers, he stripped them of their possessions, and unified al-Andalus politically, uniting it with his emirate in North Africa. The second phase of this period starts in 541/1147, when the Almohads took the Almoravid capital Marrakesh. After a brief interlude of instability, al-Andalus continued united under the Almohad caliphs, Berbers of the Maṣmūda tribe, till 629/1232.

III.1 *The Almoravids (478/1085-541/1147)*

The Almoravids were responsible for three important innovations in calligraphy: 1) the use of cursive script in architecture and ornamentation; 2) a kind of proportioned kufic that divides the body of the letter from the vertical prolongation of the stroke by means of a horizontal stem; 3) another kind of kufic characterised by an emphatic vertical development of the stroke, with an extended horizontal ligature enabling the second part of the invocation to be located above the first, all within lobed floral arches, with dense ribbed floral filling attached to stalks.

The Almoravids were prompt to introduce the cursive "ductus" *naskh̲ī*, unless the Zīrid *ṭā'ifa* kings merit the credit for its initial introduction, as the inscription, naming the Zīrid king Bādīs on a marble basin carved with lions and deers looted from one of al-Manṣūr's palaces and brought to Granada, would appear to indicate.[35] If future research should confirm the earlier date, this would mean that the *ṭā'ifa* period established all the basic types of calligraphy to appear in al-Andalus and North Africa during the later third and fourth periods. What is certain is that the Almoravids introduced the *naskh̲ī* "ductus" into ornamental calligraphy in architecture, as can be seen in the Qubba Barūdiyyīn at Marrakesh (ca. 513/1119),[36] the Mosque of Tlemcen (530/1135) and the Qarawiyyīn at Fez (531/1136-7).[37]

How can we account for the appearance of the *naskh̲ī* script at this particular point in time? The reasons are varied, and similar to those elsewhere in Islam: 1) there was a political need to propagandise the dynasty by making sure that texts were easily legible, at least by those able to read; 2) few even among educated people in the 6th/12th century could follow the kufic script, which because of its rigid shape does not admit the use of diacriticals (we have already noted the chronicler Ibn Ṣāḥib al-Ṣalāh's mistake in transcribing the Seville inscription); 3) the geometrisation of the kufic and its ornamentation rendered it even more difficult to decipher and grasp the propaganda message intended.

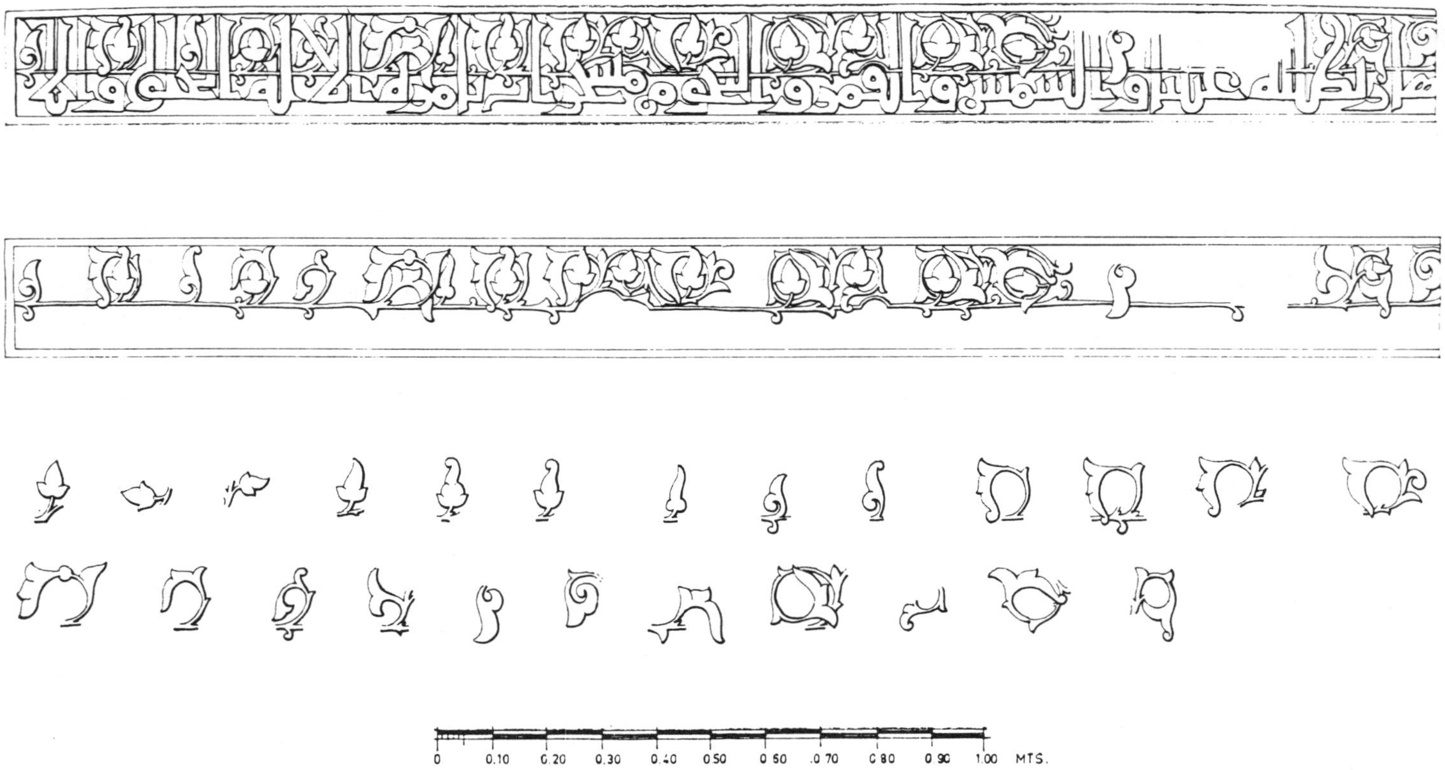

Figure 3. Granada: Almoravid wooden frieze (ca. 514/1120-534/1140). Drawing M. López Reche

Initially *naskhī* in architectural decoration lacks monumentality, though its letters are clear, and its future development can be foreseen, as it includes a background floral scheme based on spiralling stems. It assumes this particular form in the curved borders of the dome in front of the *miḥrāb* at the Qarawiyyīn, where the hands of at least two calligraphers are apparent from the way in which letters and vowels have been drawn and executed, one hand fluent with fine drafting, the other less skilful. The calligraphy in the Mosque of Tlemcen resembles that of the skilful one (plate II.6).

In al-Andalus, I assign to this period the Quranic text on the double horseshoe arch preserved at Játiva.[38] The remnants of a calligraphic band in *naskhī* which has surfaced, with some floral ornament, on the Mawrūr hill in Granada is also Almoravid but belongs later, probably to around 524/1130, during the reign of ʿAlī, the son of Yūsuf b. Tāshfīn, since below the text there is floral ornament with ribbed palm leaves.[39]

Almoravid kufic of either kind shows well-drawn letters, a clear line of script and uniform width of formation. Typical Almoravid kufic has the area of the body of the letter divided from that of the vertical stroke by the intrusion of a horizontal stem (fig. 3). This division establishes a clear proportion in the calligraphy, visible to the eye: two-fifths of the height of the band, panel, frieze, slab or surface to be decorated is taken up by the body of the letter; the other three-fifths are reserved for the development of the stroke and floral ornamentation based on palm leaves and blossoms, which sprout upward from the horizontal stem-line, or from serpentine stalks that issue from it, or float free in the background of the epigraphic composition. At a subsequent stage there appears above the stem-line a system of spiralling stems which carry the flower, but these horizontal stem-lines ultimately disappear (fig. 4). The vegetal element is confined to the upper area of the composition. The colouring of the letters also helped to distinguish them from the floral ornamentation, making the text easier to read. Decorative components were usually picked out in white edged with black, on a red or blue background; the flower was internally decorated with black lines.

This style of calligraphy, based on a canon of strict proportion, makes a brilliant appearance in the Qarawiyyīn mosque on borders and bands in the bay before the *miḥrāb* and the double bay in front of the *miḥrāb* belonging to the Almoravid rebuilding.[40] In al-Andalus it appears in wooden friezes discovered and preserved in Granada and Tarifa (figs. 3, 4), as well as on funerary slabs.[41] This style of proportioned kufic, free of horizontal stalks and floral decoration, appears on the narrow cartouches bordering the upper panels of the jambs of the *miḥrāb* façade in the Mosque of Tlemcen (plate II.6), and in an inscription of the Qarawiyyīn mosque which mentions the name of Salama b. Mufarrij, the artist who designed the circular vault of *mocárabes* work in the transverse nave.

Figure 4. Tarifa: Almoravid-Almohad wooden frieze, 6th/12th Century. Drawing E. Camps Cazorla.

Simultaneously with this kufic governed by a canon of proportions marked by the stem, another stemless kufic appears in other bands, with the upper part covered with a dense and complicated background pattern of spiral stalks to which palm leaves, pepper pods, segmented blossoms and fir cones are attached, as on the borders of the *miḥrāb* frame in the mosques of Tlemcen and the Qarawiyyīn, and on the frames of the arches in the latter mosque.

The problem of the corners in the frame bands is solved by the insertion of a square, inscribed with an eight-pointed star. Two kinds of star appear: either a star with eight 90 degree points, or one with four angular points separated by four semi-circular ones. This ingenious solution lasted throughout the Almohad period and into the Naṣrid one.

The other kind of letter used is calligraphically more developed. It appears in the Qarawiyyīn in the concave rectangular surface of the *adarajas* (carved prisms)[42] of the *mocárabes* vault in front of the *miḥrāb* and in the double bay vault preceding it in the central nave. The balanced calligraphic text, perfect in its proportions of width to height, sheltering beneath a lobed arch formed of palm leaves, exhibits a type of letter virtually indistinguishable from that of the later Almohads, who had taken up arms against the Almoravids by the time the mosque was undergoing extension and redecoration. The most frequent calligraphic compositions in these surfaces are invocations formed by the word *Allāh*, the *lām*s of which are separated by a long ligature. All the letters are of uniform width and with very slender strokes which turn obliquely to end in a concave finial, or a floriated one after the latest fashion. Both kinds pass on to the Almohads and thence to the Naṣrids. Above the long ligature referred to there is an interlaced version of the second word of the kufic invocation, the background being filled with ribbed floral decoration. Henceforth kufic comes associated with architecturo-floral forms (the arch of palm leaves), and a dense, highly developed background vegetal decoration that lends resonance to the text with its even surface and distinct colour. The elegance of these compositions is probably owing to Spanish Muslim artists working in North Africa for Yūsuf b. Tā<u>sh</u>fīn's son, ʿAlī. The door leaves are preserved in the Cloister of S. Fernando in the Monastery of Las Huelgas at Burgos (fig. 5), a work which, to judge from its ornamental motifs and simple phrases of invocation, I would date as Almoravid, and which, together with the *minbar*s, confirms the high grade of artistic refinement of Hispano-Muslim woodwork.[43] The *minbar* of the Kutubiyya, made in Córdoba between 519/1125 and 524/1130, is outstanding. Its exquisite workmanship shows three different kinds of kufic: one archaic, another transitional, and yet another which looks forward to the kufic of the 7th/13th century.

Almoravid kufic and *nas<u>kh</u>ī* inscriptions on architecture follow the model set by emiro-caliphal practice. Thus, in the Qarawiyyīn mosque there appear the names of the *amīr* ʿAlī b. Tā<u>sh</u>fīn, and of the *qāḍī* in charge of the alterations, Abū Muḥammad ʿAbd al-Ḥaqq b. ʿAbd Allāh b. Muʿī<u>sh</u>a al-Kinānī, on

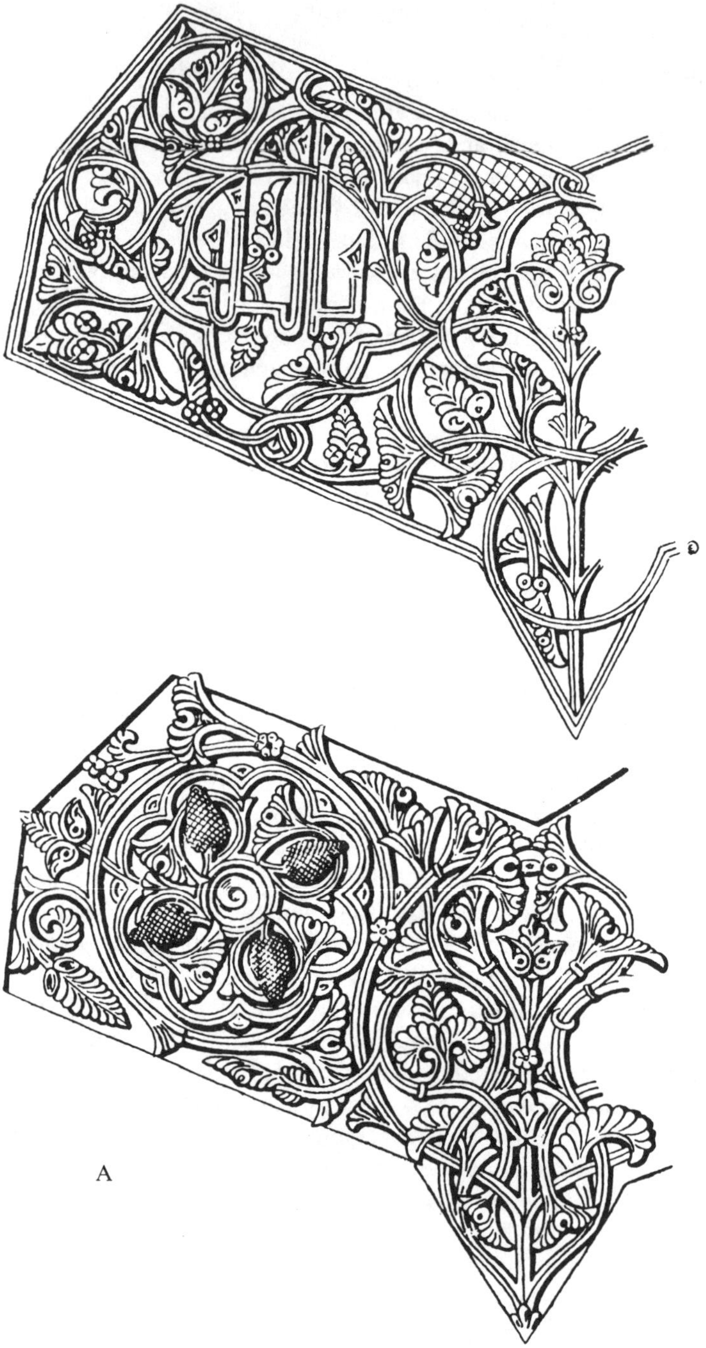

Figure 5. Burgos: Panels of the Almoravid door from the Monasterio de las Huelgas (first half of the 6th/12th Century). Drawing E. Camps Cazorla.

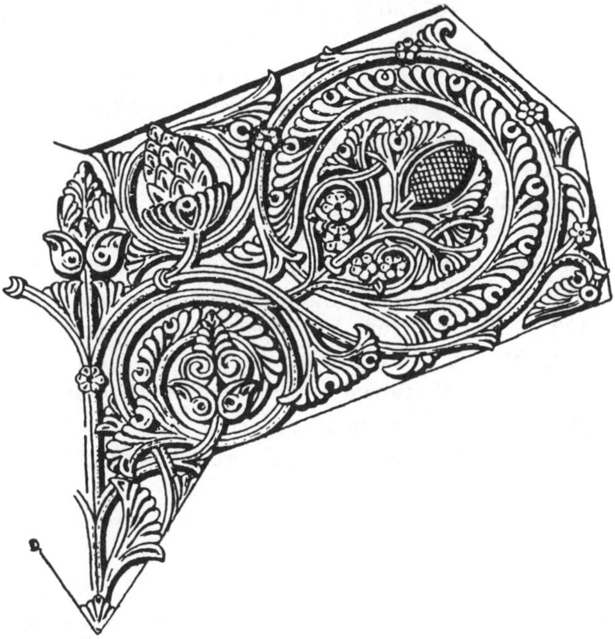

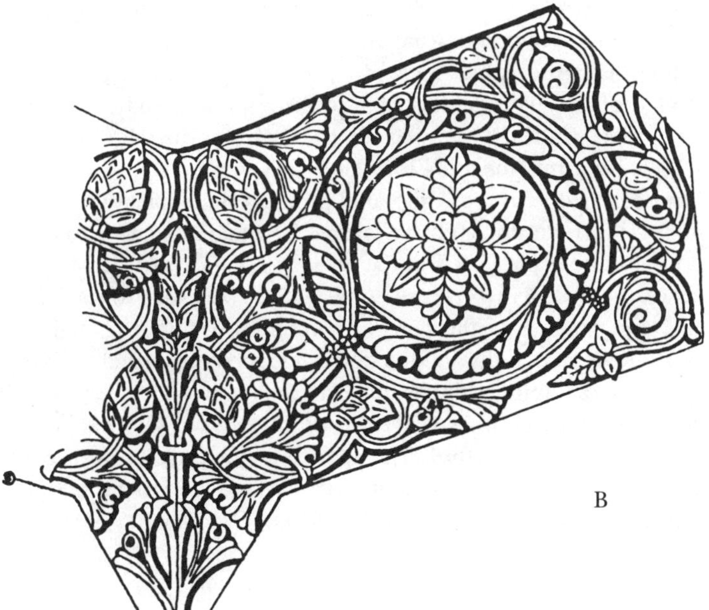

B

Figure 5. Burgos: Panels of the Almoravid door from the Monasterio de las Huelgas (first half of the 6th/12th Century). Drawing E. Camps Cazorla.

the *mocárabes* vaulting in front of the *miḥrāb* and in the double span preceding it in the central nave, stating that both vaults were finished "during the month of *Ramaḍān* ... in the year 531 [May 23-June 21, 1137]". In the double-span vault the name of the artist responsible, Ibrāhīm b. Muḥammad, is also mentioned. On the façade of the *miḥrāb* in a square there is an eight-pointed star with four sharp points and four semicircular ones, where (in lively stepped cursive on four lines), we read that this is the "work of ʿAbd Allāh b. Muḥammad, completed ... during the month of *Ramaḍān*, the year 531 [May 23-June 21, 1137]". By affiliation Ibn Muḥammad, he may have been the brother of the Ibrāhīm who designed the double-span vault; both were certainly Andalusis. This is confirmed in the chronicle *Rawḍ al-Qirṭās*, where, speaking of the Granadine *qāḍī* in charge of the restoration, Abū Muḥammad ʿAbd al-Ḥaqq, and quoting the inscriptions, the chronicler uses the word al-Gharnāṭī, i. e. the Granadine.[44]

Monumental inscriptions may not be so explicit about the holders of court appointment as in Umayyad times, but they nevertheless furnish all manner of detail: the reigning sovereign, the builder, the person legally responsible, the designer or designers, as well as the date, specifying both year and month. On coins Almoravid kufic evinces good design in the lettering (both in the strokes and in the slender body of the letter), which distinguishes the Almoravid period from any other in numismatics.

Owing to the calligraphic shape of Almoravid letters it is possible to date a series of bronzes, like candlesticks, incense burners and the magnificent gryphon of Pisa Cathedral, which all bear witness to the survival of the caliphal style right into the 6th/12th century.[45]

The funerary stone of the Almoravid princess Badr (plate III.7), daughter of the *amīr* Abū 'l-Ḥasan ʿAlī b. Taʿishshā 'l-Ṣanhājī, dated 496/1103, found in Córdoba but now preserved in the Málaga Archaeological Museum, follows the caliphal design of those *ṭāqāt* niches (referred to as *miḥrāb*s in chronicles and poems) in the house of Jaʿfar in Madīnat al-Zahrāʾ.[46] The funerary stone depicts a diminutive horseshoe arch supported on disproportionately squat columns with the imposts adorned with kufic calligraphy. The arch encloses seven lines of writing with the word for "hundred", *miʾa*, written over the previous word. The spandrels depict gadrooned palmettes, and the frame has a border with its vertical and horizontal scripts overlapping, as on the *sābāṭ* façade in the mosque of Córdoba.

III.2 *The Almohads (541/1147-629/1232)*

The second phase of this period is that of the Almohads, who were Berbers belonging to the Maṣmūda tribe. A radical change takes place in the field of aesthetics due to the ethic of purity and austerity preached by Ibn Tūmart from the 1120s on, and which is imposed after the capture of Marrakesh, the

Almoravid capital, in 541/1147. The first three rulers, who were undoubtedly not only the best politically but the most active builders, did not have their names inscribed on any mosque, monument, city gate or any edifice they had erected; in place of a name are either Quranic verses or pious phrases, attesting to the important role of religion.[47] The use of calligraphy on religious monuments is reduced to a minimum, without however disappearing altogether. The splendour and richness of ornamental calligraphy on architecture, which began in al-Andalus, especially with al-Ḥakam II's enlargement of the Mosque of Córdoba, and endures in the *ṭā'ifa* Oratory of the Aljafería and the Almoravid mosques of Tlemcen and Qarawiyyīn, is missing from the surviving Almohad mosques of the 6th/12th century: that of Tinmal (549/1154) and the second Kutubiyya (558/1162). Instead there is an emphasis on an aesthetic of simplicity, on the plain surfaces and lines of walls and arches rendered in white stucco, with the geometric element (or *lazo*) prominent, and architecturo-decorative and floral ornamentation either flat or in very shallow relief. Calligraphy vanishes from the façades and niches of *miḥrāb*s to reappear beneath the *mocárabes* vaults. Kufic letters are narrow and inordinately tall, with their strokes overlapping and the ligatures descending to the bottom of the panel, and with double palm leaves filling any empty spaces. In short, they follow the elegant calligraphic development of the Almoravids as found in the rectangular concave surfaces of the *mocárabes* vaults in the Qarawiyyīn mosque, that is to say, the second kind of kufic.[48] One is tempted to conclude that the sacred nature of Quranic script, its status as revealed truth, had induced the first Almohad rulers not to use calligraphy as mere ornament for fear of profaning the texts.

Notwithstanding the use of invocatory phrases in the springing lines of the *mocárabes* vaults at Tinmal, they recur in the coloured stucco decoration of the minaret of the Kutubiyya, which exhibits two very different types of kufic. One consists of well-proportioned, broad and flattened letters; the other of letters that are slender, proportioned and flowing to reach the limit of the architecturo-decorative art, tending to form symmetrical compositions.[49]

During the last twenty years of the 6th/12th century the Bāb al-Ruwāḥ, the gate of the *qaṣaba* of the 'Udāya in Rabat and the Bāb Aghnā' in Marrakesh were all built. The Quranic texts on the frames of all these gateways appear within angular cartouches, having their corner squares inscribed with a four-lobed figure. Letters cut in stone have a squat and thick body, albeit well designed, following Almoravid models, with the spaces above the vowels taken up with palm leaves and fruits either on their own or issuing from short stems. The calligraphic texts of these gateways do not give evidence of any artistic progress, in spite of the important place they occupy.

With the passing of time the initial austerity is relaxed and yields to the art of al-Andalus, as had happened in the case of the Almoravids, who had also at first reacted against *ṭā'ifa* art in all its forms.

Dating from the start of the decade 586/1190-596/1200 are the leaves of the main gate (today called the Gate of Perdon) of the great Almohad mosque of Seville. The leaves are plated on the outside with plaques of cast bronze alloy, forming a geometric composition of four-pointed stars and hexagons (*alfardones*), which alternate either with floral decoration or pious phrases in kufic against a floral background, the strokes of the letters almost touching the top of the frame, where they terminate in bent finials that fill the upper part of the composition, balancing the upper area with the line of the writing —so setting a precedent which would henceforth be followed.

The knockers of this gate are exceptional pieces in the art of Islam. They are formed of perforated palm leaves with a border composed of six solid double-leaved palms, bearing Quranic text in very beautiful *naskhī*, very advanced in the quality of writing, with highly evolved letters and long ligatures that pass underneath, extending below the neighbouring word. The letters are skilfully adapted to the concave and convex palm leaves that shape the rim of the knocker.[50]

An Almohad lamp of a tin and copper alloy, with overlapping plates decreasing in diameter, is preserved in the Almoravid mosque of the Qarawiyyīn in Fez. The surface of the plates is worked and pierced with kufic ornamentation wherein the strokes extend into ribbons forming lobed arches and geometric figures, constituting a kind of kufic which survives into the Naṣrid period under Muḥammad II (671/1272-701/1302) and his son Muḥammad III (701/1302-708/1309). The Qarawiyyīn lamp bears a *naskhī* inscription stating that it was made by order of the caliph Abū ʿAbd Allāh, son of the caliph al-Manṣūr Abū Yūsuf. This was the caliph Abū ʿAbd Allāh Muḥammad al-Nāṣir who was defeated in the battle of Las Navas de Tolosa in 609/1212, the son of Abū Yūsuf Yaʿqūb al-Manṣūr, who conquered the Christians at the battle of Alarcos in 591/1195. This lamp was executed under the supervision of the *kātib*, or calligrapher, Abū Muḥammad ʿAbd Allāh b. Mūsā, who was active between 599/1202 and 616/1219, using the kind of kufic that will be prevalent at the start of the Naṣrid period. It is interesting that the lamp should mention the "caliph" even when the dynasty was in irreversible decline, having been decisively defeated by the Christian kings at Las Navas.[51]

The kind of kufic seen in the frames of the great gates of Rabat and Marrakesh, with emphatic horizontal development of the body and no vertical development of the stroke, is the same kind as used for sura titles in Qurans dating from this century, where the characters are outlined in dark ink and their inner body is gilded, with floral pinnacles of a more or less circular shape at the sides. The floral element is based on stems with varied flora painted in blue, red or gold, and somehow manages to convey the impression that this floral cap to the sura title symbolises the crown of the Paradisial Tree, whose trunk is the calligraphic composition of the title of the sura.[52]

Calligraphy inscribed on gravestones assumes a variety of forms. In Toledo, the southernmost limit of the kingdom of Castile, the Mudejar phenomenon asserts itself on the bilingual (Latin-Arabic) tombstone of Miguel Semeno (d. 1156) (plate III.8). It carries the Latin text in the middle and the Arabic text as a frame round about, with the lines overlapping at the corners. It is interesting to note the anachronism perpetrated by the Mudejar calligrapher in using floriated finials on letters in final position, as in earlier caliphal and *ṭā'ifa* times.[53]

At Murcia was found a sepulchral slab of a *qā'id* of the Hispanic Islamic leader, Ibn Mardanīsh, who rose against the Almohads. It is dated 566/1171, and the upper part is missing. It has a palm-leaf arch with serpentine springers (as already seen in the rectangular surfaces of the *mocárabes* vaults in the Qarawiyyīn), and it presents its text enclosed within the arch, using a letter very close to the elegant Almerian script. The spandrels of the floral arch portray palm leaves and plain pepper pods of Almohad type. Two vertical borders frame the whole composition within another arch.[54]

The gravestone of the *shaykh* Abū Yaḥyā Bakr b. Dūnās, dated 587/1191, found and preserved in Córdoba, has an original composition based on an architectural scheme consisting of a double arch, floral ornamentation in the spandrels and calligraphy. The two very sharply pointed horseshoe arches enclose an inscription in kufic script, with some letters extending beneath others or prolonging their tails in swan-neck manner, the final tip of which is floriated or pointed. Final letters either describe an upward curved ending or terminate in a finial. The letters of the *lām-alif* "nexus" interlace and knot their strokes. The spandrels of the double arch portray flowers, with a border in *naskhī* script squaring off the slab. Its letters have a broad and flat body, and the lines of the script overlap at the corners. On both the vertical and the horizontal axes there are circles containing six-petalled rosettes.[55]

A new form of gravestone makes its appearance around this time, the *mqābriya*, formed like an elongated pyramidal prism. It was to stay in fashion for a long time in western Islam, with all four faces presenting ornament. In the Málaga Museum one such stone dated 618/1221 is inscribed in very elegant kufic, with slim characters, the finials of the letters split, and the curved body of the *nūn* prolonged as a vertical ribbon. The background is filled with loose curving stems attached to palm leaves and blossoms with carved incisions. The borders have a ribbon forming knots in the corners.[56]

One development in the Almohad period important for the Naṣrid epoch is how the strokes of kufic letters become more geometrical in the manner of ribbons in their prolongations, in such a way that in the corners of a composition they form a square knot with perforations at its corners shaped like drops of water, as may be seen on the slab from Jerez de la Frontera.[57] The use of *naskhī* is now on the increase as coins pass from hand to hand, on which there appears the innovation of inscribing a square inside the circle, thereby dividing both obverse and reverse into five sections, a square central section and four segments of a circle. At the same time a coin worth twice the dinar makes its appearance, whence the name *dobla* (English "dubloon"). This class of coinage continues to be minted during the Naṣrid period.

The pennant seized at Las Navas de Tolosa, which is preserved at the monastery of Las Huelgas in Burgos, is a very fine tapestry exhibiting a composition similar to the opening pages of the al-Andalus and Maghribi Qurans: a central circular space, four corner triangles with curved hypotenuses, four borders and a square in each corner, a scheme which the Naṣrid stuccoists reproduce in the Partal in the Alhambra, with the same sense of textile design.[58] The central circle contains a calligraphic composition of geometric kufic in the shape of a radiating design with a central eight-pointed star, formed by crossing the strokes of the word *al-mulk* (sovereignty, power) over each other sixteen times. *Al-mulk* is written twice in each of the eight points of the outer star. From the borders of the points to the central radiating design the geometric arrangement of the calligraphy is in a decreasing proportional relation of $\sqrt{2}$. Similar compositions occur in Naṣrid art in the stuccowork of the Palace of Riyāḍ (the so-called Palace of the Lions).

The calligrapher responsible for this composition was a consummate artist who not only knew kufic to perfection but how to lace together the ligatures and *kāfs* in final position, to compose an eight-pointed star that forms an inward radiating design (*lazo*), using a system of decreasing proportions —something truly extraordinary in calligraphy—and completing the ends with split finials. This is a masterpiece of calligraphy worked on a textile and is fit to compare with anything in the Islamic world. On the four bands framing the central composition there is a religious text in *naskhī* with the bodies of the letters flexed and contorted, with letters and vowels written above the prolongations of other letters or words, and with strokes that increase in girth as they ascend until they round off, standing upright or leaning to the left. Many letters show embroidered leaves in their interior. In two bands the text traced by the calligrapher spilled over the area reserved for it whilst it was being embroidered, and the embroiderer chose to move it on to the frame of the band. This very dynamic arrangement of cursive script, with words and letters internally adorned and superimposed one on another was possible only because the artist was working with fabric. The band adjacent to the pole has identical characteristics, albeit with letters of a different colour and outlined in white. The cursive script does not show great calligraphic evolution in comparison with these developments in kufic.

At the court of Castile, Almohad artists worked on and decorated the larger cloister, that of S. Ferdinand, in the monastery of Las Huelgas,[59] where in the stuccowork may be found elegantly executed invocations in Almohad kufic, the Arabic text whereof is Christian in content, praising Christ, the Holy Spirit and so on. No more Islamisation than this could be looked for in a monastery whither the Castilian monarchs were wont to repair on religious holidays and which served them as a place of sepulchre.[60]

The Castilian royal family and the higher nobility were buried in sumptuous silks and other textiles, examples of which have come to light in tombs in the monastery of Oña, in Las Huelgas, and Seville and Toledo Cathedrals, besides other places.[61] These textiles are adorned with borders containing calligraphed phrases alternately reading from right to left, and left to right, what is called the mirror effect, and, sometimes, with two lines of script, one normal and the other upside down, a veritable double mirror image. These examples are in ordinary kufic, proportioned and geometric, with the strokes ending in floriated finials.

IV. The Naṣrid Period (629/1232-897/1492)

IV.1 *Poetic* naskhī *calligraphy*

The fourth and last calligraphic period in al-Andalus coincides with the Naṣrid sultanate (629/1232-897/1492), when kufic and *naskhī* ornamentation was used in every type of art. During this time kufic script reached the peak of its development in Western Islam, and *naskhī* script was imprinted on the walls of Naṣrid palaces in poems written by the court poets, like a marvellous book with pages forever open on which the calligraphic texts speak in the first person, as if the halls, rooms and fountains were reciting poems and fragments of *qaṣīda*s explaining the real and symbolic significance of the place they adorned, using appropriate terminology and praising the reigning sovereign. These poetic texts also have a marvellously decorative quality, framed within rectangular and round cartouches, creating—as the texts themselves say—*ṭirāz*es, horizontal bands of precious "textile", in carved and moulded polychrome plaster, with the text in gold or silver on a turquoise background and a spiralling or free floral infill. There are four known poets of the Naṣrid *Dīwān al-Inshā'*, a kind of royal chancery, who left poems inscribed in the palaces of the Alhambra and Generalife: Ibn al-Jayyāb and his pupil Ibn al-Khaṭīb, his pupil Ibn Zamrak, and Ibn Furkūn, who was trained in the school of the last of these poets. The calligraphic poems by Ibn Furkūn inscribed in the Alhambra are only known to us now through his *Dīwān*.

Ibn Jayyāb entered the service of Muḥammad II, the second ruler of the dynasty, and continued without interruption to serve Muḥammad III, Naṣr, Ismāʿīl I, Muḥammad IV and Yūsuf I, dying at a great age in 749/1348, in his own home and not assassinated, a unique case among these poets.[62] Poems of his that have survived are found on the funeral slab of Muḥammad II, who died in 701/1302 (Museo Nacional de Arte Hispanomusulmán),[63] in the alfiz of the entrance portico to the north aisle in the Generalife, and in the *ṭāqāt*, niches, in its intrados; and in the main hall of Yūsuf I's al-Qalahurra 'l-Jadīda, where the poems describe the decoration of the floor, walls and ceiling of the room in great detail, using appropriate literary terms, perhaps with artistic and aesthetic significance.[64] The poems of Ibn al-Khaṭīb can be found in the niches of the intrados of the entry to the throne room in the Comares palace,[65] and perhaps also by him is the poem in the throne *qubba* which specifies the function of the "Seat of Power", or "Sovereignty", distinguishing this recessed *qubba* from the other eight recesses and giving it a unique character. Ibn Zamrak says specifically that he wrote the poems adorning the palaces of his sovereign Muḥammad V.[66] This sultan completed the building of the Comares palace in 772/1370, and so to this poet must be attributed the poems on the façade of the *al-qubba 'l-ulyā*, the only room of the *mashwar* still standing, those in the Sala de la Barca and in the niche of the entrance to it, in the north and south galleries of the Patio de Comares, and on the façade of the Comares palace.[67] The published part of his *Dīwān* includes poems for the palace which he calls "of the Riyāḍ" (now Leones).[68] The one on the Lion fountain describes with amazing precision the system of its water supply and drainage, the impression created by the white marble fountain and its water gliding along the runlets, etc.[69] The poems of Ibn Furkūn decorate the *al-dār al-kabīra* restored by the sultan Yūsuf III, himself a poet influenced by his contact with Ibn Zamrak.[70] The only surviving inscription by this poet is a brief eulogy in honour of Yūsuf III, in beautiful calligraphy executed in architectural ceramic tiles in the Museo Nacional de Arte Hispanomusulmán, and the unparalleled large ceramic tile known as the Fortuny tile in the Instituto Valencia de Don Juan, Madrid.

The poets of the Naṣrid court narrated not only the glorious memorable and martial deeds of their sovereigns but all kinds of events in their lives, especially the *iʿdhār*, the circumcision of the princes of the royal house. On the occasion of that of Abū ʿAbd Allāh Muḥammad, a son of Muḥammad V, Ibn Zamrak composed a long *qaṣīda* which he recited at the time and from which twenty-four verses, with some alterations (plate III.9), were inscribed into the architecture like a permanently open book, on a fine plaster *ṭirāz* in the lantern hall of the Main Qubba of the Riyāḍ palace (Sala de las Dos Hermanas), describing the palace, its courtyard, hall, mirador and garden, etc. with metaphors full of symbolism and allegory.[71] When I undertook the systematic study of the kufic and cursive alphabets of this calligraphy, in the Alhambra and Generalife, and drew them to scale, I found the development of a strict canon of proportion in the script, which appears to follow Pythagoras' ratios. For example, the incommensurable ratios between width and height of the letter *lām* as 1 to 2/3; 1 to 1/2; 1 to 1/3 etc. vary with different stylistic periods of Naṣrid art and different poets. This has revealed two aspects of calligraphy which have been totally disregarded: the chronological evolution of a canon of proportion, and the calligraphic evolution of successive schools of the *Dīwān al-Inshāʾ*, according to whoever was its head in each period.[72] These facts were previously unknown in relation to Naṣrid calligraphic poetry, a rare case in Islamic court art of any period.

The symbolic value of the position of the text painted on the high frieze of the throne room in the Comares palace, the 63rd sura, "the Sovereignty" or "the Power", which begins at the right-hand corner of the north wall facing the entrance, proves once again that in this hall aesthetic contemplation involved "reading" from right to left, as in the façades of *miḥrāb*s after that of Córdoba, and elsewhere. This Quranic text was appropriate to the throne room, whose wooden ceiling represented geometrically and symbolically the heavens of the Islamic paradise, the Throne of God, the trees of paradise in the four diagonals, etc. Another Quranic text is placed symbolically around the central window in the façade of the Comares palace. In the Main Qubba (Dos Hermanas) of the Riyāḍ palace, the twenty four verses of Ibn Zamrak's poem are also read by moving round the room from right to left (plate III.9).

The *naskhī* script acquired monumentality in the foundation stone of the Bāb al-Sharīʿa in the Alhambra, which consists of three marble slabs forming a great horizontal cartouche with lobed ends. It contains two lines of slender vocalised script with a floral background, all carved in relief. The background is inlaid with black slate to make the great inscription stand out so that it can be read without difficulty from ground level. The text says that Yūsuf I ordered the building of the gate of the "Esplanade" which was completed in *Rabīʿ* I, 749/June 1348. Ibn Jayyāb was at that time *raʾīs* of the *Dīwān al-Inshāʾ* and Ibn al-Khaṭīb was working under him.

The second monumental foundation stone which has survived intact is that of the Māristān, written in *naskhī* without foliage decoration (Museo Nacional de Arte Hispanomusulmán). It is carved on two slabs in the form of a pointed horseshoe arch, with jambs and impost lines, like a *miḥrāb*, a shape which originated in the caliphal *ṭāqāt,* niches, analysed above and was used for the headstone of the Almoravid princess Badr. This was placed over the lintel of the principal entrance, with vocalised *naskhī* letters gilded on a turquoise ground, well proportioned, drawn and carved, but it lacks the monumentality of the magnificent slab of the Bāb al-Sharīʿa and could only be read from the ground because it was at first-floor level. It says that Muḥammad V *al-Ghanī bi-Llāh* ("he who is content with the help of God") ordered the construction of the Māristān hospital, which took from the middle of *Muḥarram* 767 to the middle of *Shawwāl* 768 (26 September-9 October 1365 to 9-18 June 1367). The Māristān hospital, was therefore probably built by June 1367. But Muḥammad V only took the honorific title of *al-Ghanī bi-Llāh* at the end of that year, after his autumn campaigns of Jaén, Ubeda and the siege of Baeza. So the final decoration of the Māristān, on carving the marble foundation slab of its façade, occurred around the end of the year, possibly when the building was inaugurated by the victorious sovereign.[73]

IV.2 *Kufic calligraphy*

During this period kufic calligraphy was primarily decorative. At first it derived from Almohad patterns, forming a kind of large letters, "macroletra", in the first part of an inscription, very simple and elegant with palm finials and straight strokes, and completing the inscription in smaller letters, "microletra", which in the upper part of bands or cartouches formed a pattern of lobed arches deriving from the stylised strokes of the letters *alif* and *lām*. This is exemplified in the *Dār al-manjara al-kubrā* (Cuarto Real de Santo Domingo) of the time of Muḥammad II, and in the Partal, the work of his son Muḥammad III. Beginning in this period, the strokes of the letters were extended as ribbons to form a *sebca* or underlying rhomboid grid.

In the next stage, beginning under Ismāʿīl I and culminating under his son Yūsuf I, kufic calligraphy was used in framed vertical patterns tending to symmetrical design on either side of a central axis. In horizontal cartouches (plate IV.10) a compensation of volumes was sought between the line on which the body of the letter was written, the upper part of the cartouche and the intermediate zone by vertical development of the strokes, crossing them and forming knots and shapes with them, terminating them symmetrically with vertical, horizontal or descending finials. This is the period of the great calligrapher who worked in Yūsuf I's al-Qalahurra 'l-Jadīda (Cautiva) and the Comares throne room, first under the orders of Ibn al-Jayyāb and then of Ibn al-Khaṭīb.[74] Another, young, calligrapher appears beside him in the throne room towards the end of Yūsuf I's rule, who was to take the definitive step in Naṣrid calligraphy in designing calligraphic patterns that were completely symmetrical with respect to the centre, with every type of knot, ribbon, movement on the right of the axis being matched on the left. This is the calligraphy that was developed in the Riyāḍ palace. The older man was the better calligrapher, but his pupil was more inventive, with a different kind of elegance inspired in pure geometry and rhythmic symmetry, more decorative, with more grandiose patterns, but lacking a feeling for the aesthetic value of calligraphy. He worked under Ibn Zamrak during the reign of Muḥammad V.

His first work in the Comares hall was completing the patterns under the blind arches of the *mocárabes* cornice of the great wooden ceiling, and the ascending patterns of the intrados of the entrance to the hall;[75] between these came the cartouches above the dado of the transverse passage which precedes the hall. When Yūsuf I was assassinated in 755/1354 his son Muḥammad V completed the expansion that had been begun above the palace of Ismāʿīl I. This artist was responsible for some marvellous patterns such as the arches of palm leaves above the dados of the north and south galleries of the Patio de Comares (plate IV.11),[76] where, under pointed horseshoe arches (made of both plain and fringed leaves and pepper pods), the dynastic motto appears twice in kufic, the centre of each one on the base line and the other half above on the line of the diameter, the strokes of the letters forming arches and lobed circles and ending in different kinds of finials: bent, scrolled, and with palms. The background is filled with a grid of free stems with the typical flora of the time of Muḥammad V, whose name appears in *naskhī* in the lobed circles.

This calligrapher, already in his full maturity, reached the heights of the Hispanic kufic and *naskhī* calligraphies in the Riyāḍ palace, built in the 1380s, both in the Qubba of the Banū 'l-Sarrāj (Abencerrajes) and in the Main Qubba (Dos Hermanas). In the spandrels of the squinches and the *mocárabes* arches, the geometric kufic calligraphy evolves symmetrically mirrorwise at the angles of union of the spandrels (fig. 6).[77] In these, for once in calligraphy, the extended ribbons of the strokes are made to serve as the stems of five-leaved palmettes, independent of the rich floral background.

The greatest achievement lies in the patterns in the mirador of the Main Qubba (Lindaraja) (plate IV.12), in the timpana of its three blind *mocárabes* arches, which have symmetrical geometric patterns in ascending triangular design, as the lines of the writing ascend up the blind arches, in texts praising the ruler, Muḥammad V.[78] The most important and visible of these patterns, on the double arch of the north (plate IV.12), contains a spelling error made by the calligrapher[79] which confirms that kufic calligraphy, even when so well mastered and successful, remained the province of only a small élite. Beneath these patterns the calligraphers drew a marvellous infill of spiralling stems inhabited by elegant palm leaves which vary to fit the geometrical development of the letters.

The letters were gilt on red and blue grounds, and the floral ornamentation either had blue or red serrations painted in contrasted colour to the grounds, or else were plain with gilded or silvered surfaces. Few traces of this remain except in the backgrounds, so the present effect is completely different from the Islamic original, in which the painted colours were shaded and carefully combined, suggestive of textiles as well as of the Graeco-Roman tradition inherited by Islamic art. The calligraphy usually shows signs of having been covered with gold- or silver-leaf, or painted an intense white edged with black.

Naṣrid calligraphy under Yūsuf I and Muḥammad V created patterns proportionate to the site they occupied, with appropriate colouring and the necessary luminosity. In addition to these great calligraphic patterns, kufic script was also used for inscriptions with invocations in which the strokes extended in ribbons forming geometrical motifs, repeated to the top of ornamental panels. Calligraphic-epigraphic schemes were used in other decorative patterns in *sebca*, with a floral background.

Islamic kufic calligraphy in general had an enormous influence on the decorative and graphic aspects of Christian art. "The beauty of the kufic

Figure 6. Granada, Alhambra: Partial elevation of the lantern-hall (Dos Hermanas) from the Main Qubba in the palace of the Riyāḍ (Lions). Drawing Owen Jones and Jules Goury.

script, with a line that is sometimes impetuous and sometimes serene, apart from its astonishing potential for variation and its incomparable ornamental value, attracted the interest of Christian artists from the very beginning. It is possible to make an impressive list of works of the Romanesque period in which kufic writing, although in general not understood, was accepted as purely decorative. When the Emperor Frederick II introduced the Gothic "ductus" to his chancery, perhaps it was in the hope of giving the western world a decorative script as effective as the one he admired in the works that had reached him from the Arabs."[80]

Kufic and cursive inscriptions with invocations appear in medieval and Renaissance Christian decorative art in the Iberian Peninsula and even in northern Europe, on carpets, personal adornment, cloth, weapons, etc., and can be seen in paintings by the Valencian painter Yáñez de la Almedina and of Hans Holbein the Younger.[81]

1 J. D. Pearson, "Ḳur'an", *Encyclopaedia of Islam*, 2nd ed., Vol. V, Leiden, 1986, pp. 400-32, especially pp. 404-09.

2 F. Buhl, "Koran", *Encyclopaedia of Islam*, 1st ed., II, 1063-76, especially pp. 1068-71, 1073-74; Pearson, *op. cit.*, pp. 408, 409, 419, 421; Hichem Djaït, "al-Kūfa", *Encyclopaedia of Islam*, 2nd. ed., V, 345-51; J. Sourdel-Thomine and others, "Khaṭṭ", *ibid.*, Vol. IV, 1978, pp. 1113-30, especially pp. 1119, 1121, 1123.

3 K. A. C. Creswell, *Early Muslim Architecture*, I-1, Oxford, 1969, pp. 69-73; note 6, p. 69, note 1 p. 72, plates 6-22; A.. Grohmann, *Arabische Paläographie*, I-II, Teil, *Forschungen zur Islamischen Philologie und Kulturgeschichte*, Vienna, 1967, 1971, pp. 71-92, figs. 50, 51-67, plate XI.

4 Creswell, *op. cit.*, I-2., pp. 506-18, plates 85c-91, especially pp. 506-07, note 1, plate 85c.

5 I have pointed this out in my study of the Quṣayr ʿAmrā inscription painted on stucco on the upper W. window of the right hand N. vault of the great compartmented room of the frigidarium, or *bayt al-bārid*. The complete text is impossible to decipher, but in my reading it states "... [Ib]n ʿAbd al-Malik ...". As I have pointed out elsewhere, I reject the possibility that this refers to the reigning al-Walīd I, though built in his time; it was done by one of his brothers, namely a "Son of ʿAbd al-Malik".

6 On the portion removed to the National Museum in Damascus. See D. Schlumberger, *Qasr el-Heir el Gharbi*, Vol. 120 in collection of *Institut français d'archéologie du Proche-Orient, Beyrouth-Damas-Amman. Bibliothèque Archéologique et Historique*, Paris, 1986, p. 1, n.10, and pp. 26-28. In my own collection of photographs these texts are much more abundant than those published in this book and by other colleagues.

7 R. W. Hamilton, *Khirbat al Mafjar. An Arabian Mansion in the Jordan Valley*, Oxford, 1959, plates XCIV-XCV; *Walid and his friends. An Umayyad Tragedy*, Vol. 6 of *Oxford Studies in Islamic Art*, Oxford, 1988. Information on the chronology of Mshaṭṭa was first made public by Dr. Enderlein in a lecture given at the S.O.A.S.(London), and then confirmed recently by Professor K. Brisch, after reading an inscription on a brick.

8 M. Ocaña Jiménez, *El cúfico hispano y su evolución*, in collection of *Cuadernos de Historia, Economía y Derecho Hispanomusulmán*, Madrid, 1970, pp. 19-20.

9 The column is preserved in the Seville Archaeological Museum. See M. Ocaña Jiménez, "La inscripción fundacional de la Mezquita de *Ibn ʿAdabbas* de Sevilla", *Al-Andalus*, 12, 1947, pp. 145-51; L. Torres Balbás, "La primitiva mezquita mayor de Sevilla", *Al-Andalus*, 11, 1946, pp. 425-39, especially pp. 427-29.

10 A. Fernández-Puertas, "La decoración de las ventanas de la Bāb al-Uzarāʾ según dos dibujos de Don Félix Hernández Giménez", *Cuadernos de la Alhambra*, 15-17, 1979-1981, pp. 165-210, especially pp. 168, 169, 209, figs. 2, 3, plates I-III.

11 M. Ocaña Jiménez, "Documentos epigráficos de la Mezquita", in *Exposición La Mezquita de Córdoba: siglos VIII al XV*, Córdoba, 1986, pp. 16-17.

[12] E. Lévi-Provençal discovered this unpublished section of the work of Abū Marwān b. Ḥayyān, *Kitāb al-Muqtabis fī ta'rīkh rijāl al-Andalus.* Cf. "Documents et notules. I. Les citations du 'Muqtabis' de Ibn Ḥayyān rélatives aux agrandissements de la Grande-Mosquée de Cordoue au IXe siècle", *Arabica* (Leiden), 1, 1934, pp. 89-92. They were translated into French, with commentaries by E. Lambert, "Histoire de la Grande-Mosquée de Cordoue aux VIIe et IXe siècles d'après des textes inédits", *Annales de l'Institut d'Etudes Orientales de la Faculté de Lettres de l'Université d'Alger* (Paris), 2, 1936, pp. 165-79. Their Spanish translation and study was undertaken by L. Torres Balbás, "Nuevos datos documentales sobre la construcción de la mezquita de Córdoba en el reinado de 'Abd al-Raḥmān II", *Al-Andalus*, 6, 1941, pp. 411-22. See E. Lévi Provençal, *España musulmana. Hasta la caida del califato de Córdoba (711-1031 D. J.)*, Vol. IV of *Historia de España*, dirigida por R. Menéndez Pidal, 2nd. ed., Madrid, 1957, pp. 168-69, note 79; L. Torres Balbás, *Arte Hispanomusulmán hasta la caida del califato de Córdoba*, Vol. V of *Historia de España*, Madrid, 1965, p. 387, note 39.

[13] Ocaña Jiménez, *El cúfico*, p. 31; "Capiteles epigráficados de Madīnat al-Zahrā'", *Al-Andalus*, 4, 1936-1939, pp. 158-66; "Obras de al-Ḥakam II en Madīnat al-Zahrā'", *Al-Andalus*, 6, 1941, pp. 157-68.

[14] Ocaña Jiménez, *El cúfico*, pp. 34-35.

[15] Ocaña Jiménez, "Documentos epigráficos", pp. 18-19.

[16] This was completely rebuilt in 1915, using the *sābāṭ* wall as a model. See M. Ocaña Jiménez, "Las inscripciones en mosaico del *miḥrāb* de la gran mezquita de Córdoba y la incógnita de su data", in H. Stern (ed.), *Les mosaïques de la grande Mosquée de Cordoue*, Vol. 11 of *Madrider Forschungen*, Berlin, 1976, pp. 48-52, specially p. 50.

[17] M. Ocaña Jiménez, "Ŷa'far el eslavo", *Cuadernos de la Alhambra*, 12, 1976, pp. 217-23.

[18] Three were found truncated in the 1974 excavations, and the fourth is preserved in Tarragona Cathedral. See M. Gómez-Moreno, *El arte árabe español hasta los almohades*, Vol. 3 of *Ars Hispaniae*, Madrid, 1951, p. 90, fig. 124. I assume this small arch to belong to the same house because there are four spaces for these arches in the N. wall, and its calligraphic text is similar in text, dimensions and carving. It was probably taken to Tarragona in the 5th/11th century as part of the spoils from Madīnat al-Zahrā'.

[19] Ocaña Jiménez, "Documentos epigráficos", pp. 20-25.

[20] *Ibid.*, 26-27.

[21] A. Fernández-Puertas, "Dos lápidas aparecidas en la provincia de Jaén", *Al-Andalus*, 41, 1976, pp. 213-24.

[22] E. Lévi-Provençal, *Inscriptions arabes d'Espagne*, Leiden-Paris, 1931, pp. 134-35, No. 150.

[23] Gómez-Moreno, *op. cit.*, p. 337, fig. 399.

[24] Grohmann, *op. cit.*, p. 99; F. Spuhler in J. Sourdel-Thomine and B. Spuler (eds.), *Die Kunst des Islam*, Vol. 4 of *Propyläen Kunstgeschichte*, Berlin, 1973, p. 206, plate 108; J. Ferrandis, *Marfiles árabes de Occidente*, Vols. I-II, Madrid, 1935; *Marfiles y azabaches españoles*, volume in *Colección Labor*, Barcelona, 1928, pp. 50-113, especially pp. 51-82; J. de Navascués y de Palacio, "Una escuela de eboraria, en Córdoba, de fines del siglo IV de la hégira (XI de J.C.), o las inscripciones de la arqueta hispanomusulmana llamada de Leyre", *Al-Andalus*, 39, 1964, pp. 199-206; M. Gómez-Moreno, "Los marfiles cordobeses y sus derivaciones", *Archivo Español de Arte y Arqueología*, Madrid, 1927, pp. 233-43; *El arte árabe español*, pp. 297-310, figs. 355-370.

[25] H. Terrasse, *La Mosquée des Andalous a Fès*, Vol. 38 in collection of *Institut des Hautes-Etudes Marocaines*, Paris, 1942, p. 34 *et seq.*; Torres Balbás, *Arte Hispanomusulmán*, p. 299 *et seq.*; H. Terrasse, in *Die Kunst des Islam*, pp. 205-06, plate 107.

[26] M. Ocaña Jiménez, "La inscripción fundacional de la mezquita de Bīb al-Mardūm en Toledo", *Al-Andalus*, 14, 1949, pp. 175-83.

[27] A. Fernández-Puertas, *La escritura cúfica en los palacios de Comares y Leones*, Granada, 1974, pp. 29-33; Madrid, 1981, pp. 12-14.

[28] Lévi-Provençal, *Inscriptions*, I, 39-40, No. 31; II, plate Xa.

[29] It is exhibited in the Museo Arqueológico of Córdoba. J. Guerrero Lovillo drew it and published it, *Al-Qasr al-Mubarak. El Alcázar de la bendición* (lecture delivered on entering the Academia de Sevilla, 1970), Seville, 1974, p. 106, note 50, plate 1; "Andalucía I", in *Tierras de España*, Madrid, 1980, p. 291, plate 242.

[30] C. Ewert, *Islamische Funde in Balaguer und die Aljafería in Zaragoza*, Vol. 7 of *Madrider Forschungen*, Berlin, 1971, with a study by G. Kircher, "Epigraphische Studien zu Stuckfragmenten aus Balaguer", pp. 243-50; translated into Spanish as *Hallazgos islámnicos en Balaguer y la Aljafería de Zaragoza*, volume in *Excavaciones Arqueológicas de España*, Madrid, 1979; *Spanisch-islamische Systeme sich kreuzender Bögen. III. Die Aljafería in Zaragoza*, 1 and 2, Berlin, 1978, 1980, figs. 6, 7; plate 10.

[31] Klaus Brisch, "Zu einer Gruppe von islamischen Kapitellen und Basen des 11 Jahrhunderts in Toledo", *Madrider Mitteilungen*, 2, 1961, p. 205 *et seq.*; translated as "Sobre un grupo de capiteles y basas islámicas del siglo XI de Toledo", *Cuadernos de la Alhambra*, 15-17, 1979-1981, pp. 155-64, plates I-XVIII.

[32] Ferrandis, *Marfiles árabes*, I, 43-47, 86-100; II, plates XLV-LXI; P. Marinetto Sánchez, "La decoración vegetal del taller de marfil de Cuenca, I", in *Homenaje al Prof. Darío Cabanelas Rodríguez, ofm., con motivo de su LXX aniversario*, Vol. II, Granada, 1987, pp. 241-59, figs. 1-9, plates 1-3; "Plaquita y bote de marfil del taller de Cuenca", *Miscelánea de Estudios Arabes y Hebraicos*, 35, 1986, pp. 45-100, figs. 1-31, plates 1-8.

[33] Gómez-Moreno, *El arte árabe español*, p. 219, figs. 273, 274; Lévi-Provençal, *Inscriptions*, pp. 59-62. M. Ocaña Jiménez, "Tres epitafios musulmanes toledanos del siglo XI", *Al-Andalus*, 19, 1954, pp. 407-10; J. de Navascués y de Palacio, "Tres epitafios hispanoárabes del Museo Arqueológico de Toledo", *Al-Andalus*, 26, 1961, pp. 191-93; A. Fernández-Puertas, "Lápida del siglo XI e inscripción del tejido del siglo X del Monasterio de Oña", *Miscelánea de Estudios Arabes y Hebraicos*, 26, 1977, pp. 117-27.

[34] Lévi-Provençal, *Inscriptions*, I, 65-66, II, plate XVa, b.

[35] It reads thus in the epigraphic band that frames the front rectangular faces. The two vertical sections have a different type of letter from the horizontal one, though it is believed that they were incised in the Naṣrid period under Muḥammad III in 705/1305. The type of *naskhī* is, however, different; though I believe it is Naṣrid. See Gómez-Moreno, *El arte árabe español*, p. 188, figs. 246c, 247; A. Fernández-Puertas, "Un paseo por el Museo Nacional de Arte Hispanomusulmán", *Miscelánea de Estudios Arabes y Hebraicos*, 37, 1988, p. 106.

[36] Jacques Meunié and Henri Terrasse, *Nouvelles recherches archéologiques à Marrakesh*, Vol. 62 in collection of *Institut des Hautes-Etudes Marocaines*, Paris, 1957, pp. 21-30.

[37] G. Marçais, *Art musulman d'Algérie. Album de pierre, plâte et bois sculptés*, fasc. I, Algiers, 1909, pp. 17-31, figs. 13-15, plates V-X; *L'Architecture musulmane d'Occident*, Paris, 1954, pp. 192-97; L. Torres Balbás, *Artes almorávide y almohade*, volume in *Artes y Artistas*, Madrid, 1955, p. 39, plates 2 and 3; H. Terrasse, *La mosquée al-Qaraouiyin a Fès*, Vol. 3 of *Archéologie Méditerranéenne*, Paris, 1968, cf. the appendix of Deverdun, "Les inscriptions historiques", pp. 77-81, plates 9, 30, 32, 37, 39, 58, 60-63, 78, 87-89; A. Fernández-Puertas, *La fachada del palacio de Comares. The Façade of the Palace of Comares*, Vol. I, Granada, 1980, pp. 69-72, 240-241, figs. 27, 28, plates LIX, LXa.

[38] "Inscripciones cursivas del doble arco almorávide de Játiva" (forthcoming). M. J. Rubiera Mata ascribes it to the period of *Ibn Mardanīsh*; see "Las inscripciones árabes de Játiva: Una hipótesis y una propuesta sobre la denominación de un estilo", in *Homenaje al Prof. Darío Cabanelas Rodríguez*, II , 293-95.

[39] Gómez-Moreno, *El arte árabe español*, p. 265, fig. 317.

[40] Terrasse, *La mosquée al-Qaraouiyin*, plates 9, 30, 32, 48, 49-51, 63.

[41] M. Gómez-Moreno, *La ornamentación mudéjar toledana. Mudéjar Ornamental Work in Toledo*, in *Arquitectura Española*, Madrid, 1923-26, pp. 8, 10, fig. 14. A. Fernández-Puertas, "Tabla epigrafiada de época almorávide o comienzos de la almohade", *Miscelánea de Estudios Arabes y Hebraicos*, 20, 1971, pp. 109-12; "Tablas epigráficas de época almorávide y almohade", *Miscelánea de Estudios Arabes y Hebraicos*, 23, 1974, pp. 113-19.

[42] A. Fernández-Puertas, "Muḳarbaṣ", *Encyclopaedia of Islam*, 2nd. ed., Vol. VII, 1991, pp. 500-01, plate XLIV-6.

[43] Gómez-Moreno, *La ornamentación mudéjar*, pp. 8, 11-13, figs. 6, 17-19; Terrasse, in *Die Kunst des Islam*, pp. 285, 286, plates 230, 231.

[44] Terrasse, *La mosquée al-Qaraouiyin*, 18-19, 78-80, láms. 50, 51, 78 etc. A. Fernández-Puertas, "Las puertas chapadas hispanomusulmanas", *Miscelánea de Estudios Arabes y Hebraicos*, 29-30, 1980-81, pp. 164-65, n. 4.

45 A. S. Melikian Chirvani, in *Die Kunst des Islam*, p. 263, plate 194. A. Fernández-Puertas, "Candiles epigráficos de finales de siglo XI o comienzos del XII", *Miscelánea de Estudios Arabes y Hebraicos*, 24, 1975, pp. 107-14; "Incensario de época almorávide", *Miscelánea de Estudios Arabes y Hebraicos*, 25, 1976, pp. 115-22; "Las puertas chapadas", pp. 163-65, plates 1-4.

46 Lévi-Provençal, *Inscriptions*, I, 30-31, No. 24, II, lám. VIIIa; K. Brisch, in *Die Kunst des Islam*, p. 257, plate 185.

47 H. Basset et H. Terrasse, *Sanctuaires et forteresses almohades*, Vol. 5 in collection of *Institut des Hautes-Etudes Marocaines*, Paris, 1932, p. 65.

48 Fernández-Puertas, *La escritura cúfica*, 1974, p. 37; 1981, p. 16.

49 Basset and Terrasse, *Sanctuaires*, pp. 132-33.

50 Fernández-Puertas, "Las puertas chapadas", pp. 164-68, 172-75, fig. 2, plates V-VI.

51 Terrasse, *La mosquée al-Qaraouiyin*, pp. 57-59, 80, 81, plates 104-07.

52 M. Lings, *The Quranic Art of Calligraphy and Illumination*, World of Islam Festival Trust, London, 1976.

53 Lévi-Provençal, *Inscriptions*, I, 78, 79, No. 81; II, plate XVIIIa.

54 *Ibid.*, I, 99-100, No. 103, plate XXIVb.

55 *Ibid.*, I, 34-35, No. 28; II, plate IX.

56 M. Ocaña Jiménez, "Una mqabriya almohade malagueña del año 1221 J. C.", *Al-Andalus*, 11, 1946, pp. 224-30, 445-46; L. Torres Balbás, *Arte almohade*, Vol. 4 of *Ars Hispaniae*, Madrid, 1949, p. 51, fig. 41.

57 A. Fernández-Puertas, "Dos lápidas almohades. Mqabriya de Játiva y la lápida de la cerca de Jerez de la Frontera", *Miscelánea de Estudios Arabes y Hebraicos*, 27-28, 1978-1979, pp. 223-32.

58 Torres Balbás, *Arte almohade*, p. 61, fig. 47; *Arte almorávide y almohade*, 1955, p. 46, plate 47; A. Fernández-Puertas, "Un paño decorativo de la Torre de las Damas", *Cuadernos de la Alhambra*, 9, 1973, pp. 37-52, figs. 1-6, plates I-VI.

59 L. Torres Balbás, "Las yeserías descubiertas recientemente en las Huelgas de Burgos", *Al-Andalus*, 8, 1943, pp. 209-54, plates 1-8, especially 4. My study on this plasterwork, proposing these ideas, is still unpublished.

60 M. Gómez-Moreno, *El panteón Real de las Huelgas de Burgos*, Madrid, 1946; G. Menéndez Pidal, "Las Cantigas. La vida en el siglo XIII según la representación iconográfica (II). Traje, aderezo y afeites", in collaboration with Carmen Bernis, *Cuadernos de la Alhambra*, 15-17, 1979-1981, pp. 89-154, plates I-X; republished in *La España del siglo XIII leida en imágenes*, Madrid, 1986, chapter devoted to "Traje, aderezo y afeites", pp. 51-104.

61 M. Gómez-Moreno, "Preseas reales sevillanas", *Archivo Hispalense* (Seville), 2nd. period, Nos. 27-32, 1948, pp. 1-16; Fernández-Puertas, "Lápida del siglo XI e inscripción del tejido del siglo X del Monasterio de Oña", pp. 117-27.

62 M. J. Rubiera Mata, *Ibn al-ŷayyāb. El otro poeta de la Alhambra*, Granada, 1982.

63 Lévi-Provençal, *Inscriptions*, pp. 145-48. He gives a reading of the poem in Arabic, p. 146, but assumes it to be lost, when the slab exists and is in fact exhibited in this Museum.

64 M. J. Rubiera Mata, "Los poemas epigráficos de Ibn al-Ŷayyab en la Alhambra", *Al-Andalus*, 35, 1970, pp. 453-73; *Ibn al-Yayyab*, 125- poema XXIV, 127- LIII, 129- LXXI, 130 LXXXVI; 131 CII, CXIV; D. Cabanelas Rodríguez and A. Fernández-Puertas, "Las inscripciones poéticas del Generalife", *Cuadernos de la Alhambra*, 14, 1978, pp. 1-86; "Inscripciones poéticas del Partal y de la fachada de Comares", *Cuadernos de la Alhambra*, 10-11, 1974-1975, pp. 117-200; E. García Gómez, *Poemas árabes en los muros y fuentes de la Alhambra*, Madrid, 1985, pp. 137-43, 148-50.

65 Ibn al-Khaṭīb, *Dīwān al-ṣayyib wa 'l-jahām wa 'l-māḍī wa 'l-kahām*, ed. Muḥammad al-Sharīf Qāhir, Argel, 1973, p. 347, poems Nos. 112 and 113; M. J. Rubiera Mata, "De nuevo sobre los poemas epigráficos de la Alhambra", *Al-Andalus*, 41, 1976, pp. 207-11; E. García Gómez, *Poemas*, pp. 103-06. Both translators follow the text of the *Dīwān* and not the text epigraphed which has clearly marked diacritical points and vocalisation, and differs in at least one respect from the text of the *Dīwān*, while keeping perfect rhyme. For a study of the inscriptions, it is essential to start by reading the inscribed texts "in situ" and only then turning to the other sources. Moreover, one should never accept what has been read by other scholars, as their errors in reading are then maintained and the errors multiply.

66 E. García Gómez, "La etimología de 'Alixares'", *Al-Andalus*, 2, 1934, pp. 226-29; *Ibn*

Zamrak el poeta de la Alhambra (lecture delivered on entering the Real Academia de la Historia), Madrid, 1943, p. 70, note 2.

67 See notes 65, 66 above.

68 M. J. Rubiera Mata, "Ibn Zamrak, su biógrafo Ibn al-Aḥmar y los poemas epigráficos de la Alhambra", *Al-Andalus*, 42, 1977, pp. 447-51; graduation thesis of Tawfiq al-Nayfar, University of Tunis, 1971.

69 D. Cabanelas Rodríguez and A. Fernández-Puertas, "El poema de la fuente de los Leones", *Cuadernos de la Alhambra*, 15-16, 1979-1981, pp. 1-88; García Gómez, *Poemas*, pp. 111-14.

70 Ibn Furkūn, *Dīwān*, ed. Muhammed Bencherifa, Rabat, 1987; García Gómez, *Poemas*, pp. 251-63.

71 García Gómez, *Ibn Zamrak*, pp. 76-77; Rubiera Mata, "Ibn Zamrak, su biógrafo", pp. 449-50; *La arquitectura en la literatura árabe*, 2nd ed., Madrid, 1988, pp. 154-56, note 19. I discuss my interpretation of this poem at some length in a forthcoming book.

72 What I began in my own work in 1971-72, Ahmed Moustafa M. Hasan Ma has done in a different way in *The Scientific Foundation of Arabic Letter Shapes*, according to the Theory of "The Proportional Script" by Ibn Muqla (272/886-328/940) (thesis submitted for Ph D. degree, CNAA, 1989).

73 Fernández-Puertas, *La fachada*, I, 26, 215, note 3. For both inscriptions cf. pp. 116-17, 121-25, 263, 265-68, figs. 59, 62, 63, plates LXXXV, LXXXVIII-XCII.

74 The only existing work on this fourth period of Hispano-Muslim epigraphy is my book, *La escritura cúfica en los palacios de Comares y Leones*, Granada, 1974, pp. 1-547, alphabets 1-26, drawings 1-32, plates 1-433. I shall henceforth quote only the pages and figures of this 1974 text; pp. 286-95, alphabet 9, elevation 32, plates 180, 182, 184, 185; pp. 299-302, alphabet 13, plate 190.

75 Pp. 275-81, alphabet 8, plate 165; pp. 306-12, elevation 16, plates 181, 196-99; "Algunas consideraciones sobre la escritura cúfica en los palacios de Comares y Leones", *Actas XXIII Congreso Internacional de Historia del Arte, 1973,* II (Granada), 1976, pp. 89-94.

76 Pp. 239-42, alphabet 2, plate 132.

77 Pp. 435-37, 516-18, alphabet 24, plates 329, 330, 425, 426.

78 Pp. 459-75, alphabets 21-23, plates 355-60.

79 In the para-caliphal title, *al-Ghanī bi-Llāh*, he has made the calligraphic error of uniting the proposition *bi* to the name *Allāh*, without suppressing the initial *ʿalif*, *bi-Allāh*, which is entirely ungrammatical, but he may have needed it for a symmetrical composition, which would be excusable, whether he intended this or not. This has only been noticed typographically by E. Lafuente y Alcántara, *Inscripciones árabes de Granada*, Madrid, 1860, p. 142, No. 148, without his making any comment other than marking a separation in the arabic text. A constant re-reading and revision of the inscriptions continues to show up these errors and variants.

80 Ernest Kühnel, *Islamische Schriftkunst*, Berlin-Leipzig, n. d., pp. 20-22.

81 See, for example, his two paintings, the "Santa Catalina" in the Prado Museo (Registered No. 2.902) and "La Resurrección" in the Museum of Valencia. Cf. J. Ferrandis Torres, "Alfombras hispano-moriscas tipo Holbein", in *Archivo Español de Arte*, 1942, pp. 104-11; cf. Roberto Salvini, "La obra pictórica completa de Holbein el joven", *Clásicos del Arte*, Barcelona-Madrid, 1972, plates XIII, XXXI, XXXV, XXXIX and LXIII.

BIBLIOGRAPHY

Basset, H., and H. Terrasse, *Sanctuaires et forteresses almohades*, Vol. 5 in collection of *Institut des Hautes-Etudes Marocaines*, Paris, 1932.

Brisch, Klaus, "Una nota marginal a la epigrafía árabe de la Mezquita de Córdoba", *Al-Andalus*, 24, 1959, pp. 183-89.

——, "Zu einer Gruppe von islamischen Kapitellen und Basen des 11 Jahrhunderts in Toledo", *Madrider Mitteilungen*, 2, 1961, p. 205 *et seq.*; translated as "Sobre un grupo de capiteles y basas islámicas del siglo XI de Toledo", *Cuadernos de la Alhambra*, 15-17, 1979-1981, pp. 155-64, plates I-XVIII.

Buhl, F., "Koran", in *Encyclopaedia of Islam*, 1st ed., II, 1063-76.

Cabanelas Rodríguez, Darío, ofm., *El morisco Alonso del Castillo*, Granada, 1965.

——, "Valor documental de los poemas epigráficos de la Alhambra" (lecture on his reception into the Real Academia de Bellas Artes Nuestra Señora de las Angustias), Granada, 1984, pp. 7-40.

——, "Literatura, arte y religión en los palacios de la Alhambra" (inaugural lecture at Granada University on the opening of the 1984-1985 academic year), pp. 7-43.

Cabanelas Rodríguez, D, and A. Fernández-Puertas, "Inscripciones poéticas del Partal y de la fachada de Comares", *Cuadernos de la Alhambra*, 10-11, 1974-1975, pp. 117-200.

——, "Las inscripciones poéticas del Generalife", *Cuadernos de la Alhambra*, 14, 1978, pp. 1-86.

——, "El poema de la fuente de los Leones", *Cuadernos de la Alhambra*, 15-16, 1979-1981, pp. 1-88.

——, "Los poemas de las tacas del arco de acceso a la Sala de la Barca", *Cuadernos de la Alhambra*, 19-20, 1983-1984, pp. 61-152.

Caskel, Werner, *Arabic Inscriptions in the Collection of the Hispanic Society of America*, New York, 1936.

Creswell, K. A. C., *Early Muslim Architecture*, Oxford, 1969.

Djaït, Hichem, "al-Kūfa", *Encyclopaedia of Islam*, 2nd. ed., Vol. V, Leiden, 1986, pp. 345-51.

Ewert, C., *Spanisch-islamische Systeme sich kreuzender Bögen. III. Die Aljafería in Zaragoza*, 1 and 2, Berlin, 1978, 1980.

——, *Islamische Funde in Balaguer und die Aljafería in Zaragoza*, Vol. 7 of *Madrider Forschungen*, Berlin, 1971, with a study by G. Kircher, "Epigraphische Studien zu Stuckfragmenten aus Balaguer", pp. 243-50; translated into Spanish as *Hallazgos islámnicos en Balaguer y la Aljafería de Zaragoza*, in *Excavaciones Arqueológicas de España*, Madrid, 1979.

Fernández-Puertas, A., "Tabla epigrafiada de época almorávide o comienzos de la almohade", *Miscelánea de Estudios Arabes y Hebraicos*, 20, 1971, pp. 109-12.

——, "Tabla epigrafiada almohade", *Miscelánea de Estudios Arabes y Hebraicos*, 21, 1972, pp. 77-86.

——, "Dos lápidas hispanomusulmanas: La del castillo de Trujillo y una guardada en el Museo de Evora", *Miscelánea de Estudios Arabes y Hebraicos*, 22, 1973, pp. 145-52.

——, "Un paño decorativo de la Torre de las Damas", *Cuadernos de la Alhambra*, 9, 1973, pp. 37-52.

——, *La escritura cúfica en los palacios de Comares y Leones*, Granada, 1974.

——, "Tablas epigráficas de época almorávide y almohade", *Miscelánea de Estudios Arabes y Hebraicos*, 23, 1974, pp. 113-19.

——, "Candiles epigráficos de finales de siglo XI o comienzos del XII", *Miscelánea de Estudios Arabes y Hebraicos*, 24, 1975, pp. 107-14.

——, "Algunas consideraciones sobre la escritura cúfica en los palacios de Comares y Leones", *Actas XXIII Congreso Internacional de Historia del Arte, 1973*, II (Granada), 1976, pp. 89-94.

——, "Dos lápidas aparecidas en la provincia de Jaén", *Al-Andalus*, 41, 1976, pp. 213-24.

——, "Incensario de época almorávide", *Miscelánea de Estudios Arabes y Hebraicos*, 25, 1976, pp. 115-22.

——, "Dos ventanas decoradas en la mezquita de al-Hakim en el Cairo", *Al-Andalus*, 42, 1977, pp. 421-46.

——, "Lápida del siglo XI e inscripción del tejido del siglo X del Monasterio de Oña", *Miscelánea de Estudios Arabes y Hebraicos*, 26, 1977, pp. 117-27.

——, "Palacio del Partal. Composición ornamental con tres funciones distintas", *Cuadernos de la Alhambra*, 13, 1977, pp. 19-32.

——, "Dos lápidas almohades. Mqabriya de Játiva y la lápida de la cerca de Jerez de la Frontera", *Miscelánea de Estudios Arabes y Hebraicos*, 27-28, 1978-1979, pp. 223-32.

——, "La decoración de las ventanas de la Bāb al-Uzarā' según dos dibujos de Don Félix Hernández Giménez", *Cuadernos de la Alhambra*, 15-17, 1979-1981, pp. 165-210.

——, *La fachada del palacio de Comares. The Façade of the Palace of Comares*, Vol. I, Granada, 1980.

——, "Las puertas chapadas hispanomusulmanas", *Miscelánea de Estudios Arabes y Hebraicos*, 29-30, 1980-81, pp. 163-76.

——, "Catálogo de los fondos numismáticos hispanomusulmanes del Museo de Cuenca", *Cuadernos de la Alhambra*, 18, 1982, pp. 115-42.

——, "El fenómeno mudéjar en la decoración de yesería de sus edificios", *Miscelánea de Estudios Arabes y Hebraicos*, 33, 1984-85, pp. 189-202.
——, "Un paseo por el Museo Nacional de Arte Hispanomusulmán", *Miscelánea de Estudios Arabes y Hebraicos*, 37, 1988, pp. 105-09.
——, "Mukarbas", *Encyclopaedia of Islam*, 2nd. ed., Vol. VII, 1991, pp. 500-01, plate XLIV-6.
Ferrandis, J., *Marfiles árabes de Occidente*, Vols. I-II, Madrid, 1935.
——, *Marfiles y azabaches españoles*, in *Colección Labor*, Barcelona, 1928, 2 vols.
García Gómez, E., *Ibn Zamrak el poeta de la Alhambra* (lecture delivered on entering the Real Academia de la Historia), Madrid, 1943.
——, "La etimología de 'Alixares'", *Al-Andalus*, 2, 1934, pp. 226-29.
——, *Poemas árabes en los muros y fuentes de la Alhambra*, Madrid, 1985.
Gómez-Moreno, M., *La ornamentación mudéjar toledana. Mudéjar Ornamental Work in Toledo*, in *Arquitectura Española*, Madrid, 1923-26, 4 vols.
——, "Los marfiles cordobeses y sus derivaciones", *Archivo Español de Arte y Arqueología*, Madrid, 1927, pp. 233-43.
——, *El Panteón Real de las Huelgas de Burgos*, Madrid, 1946.
——, "Preseas reales sevillanas", *Archivo Hispalense*, 2nd. period, Nos. 27-32, Seville, 1948, pp. 1-16.
——, *El arte árabe español hasta los almohades*, Vol. 3 of *Ars Hispaniae*, Madrid, 1951.
Grohmann, A., *Arabische Paläographie*, I-II, Teil, *Forschungen zur Islamischen Philologie und Kulturgeschichte*, Vienna, 1967, 1971, 2 vols.
Guerrero Lovillo, J., *Al-Qasr al-Mubarak. El Alcázar de la bendición* (lecture delivered on entering the Academia de Sevilla, 1970), Seville, 1974.
Hamilton, R. W., *Khirbat al Mafjar. An Arabian Mansion in the Jordan Valley*, Oxford, 1959.
——, *Walid and his friends. An Umayyad Tragedy*, Vol. 6 of *Oxford Studies in Islamic Art*, Oxford, 1988.
Ibn Furkūn, *Dīwān*, ed. Muhammed Bencherifa, Rabat, 1987.
Ibn al-Khaṭīb, *Dīwān al-ṣayyib wa 'l-jahām wa 'l-māḍī wa 'l-kahām*, ed. Muḥammad al-Sharīf Qāhir, Argel, 1973.
Kühnel, Ernst, *Die Islamischen Elfenbeinskulpturen. VIII-XIII Jahrhundert*, Berlin, 1971.
——, *Islamische Schriftkunst*, Berlin-Leipzig, n. d.
Lafuente y Alcántara, E., *Inscripciones árabes de Granada*, Madrid, 1860.
Lambert, E., "Histoire de la Grande-Mosquée de Cordoue aux VIIe et IXe siècles d'après des textes inédits", *Annales de l'Institut d'Etudes Orientales de la Faculté de Lettres de l'Université d'Alger* (Paris), 2, 1936, pp. 165-79.
Lévi-Provençal, E., *Inscriptions arabes d'Espagne*, Leiden-Paris, 1931.
——, "Documents et notules. I. Les citations du 'Muqtabis' de Ibn Ḥayyān rélatives aux agrandissements de la Grande-Mosquée de Cordoue au IXe siècle", *Arabica* (Leiden), I, 1934, pp. 89-92.
——, *España musulmana. Hasta la caida del califato de Córdoba (711-1031 D. J.)*, Vol. IV of *Historia de España*, dirigida por R. Menéndez Pidal, 2nd. ed., Madrid, 1957.
Lings, M., *The Quranic Art of Calligraphy and Illumination*, World of Islam Festival Trust, London, 1976.
Marçais, G., *Art musulman d'Algérie. Album de pierre, plâte et bois sculptés*, fasc. I, Algiers, 1909.
Marinetto Sánchez, P., "Plaquita y bote de marfil del taller de Cuenca", *Miscelánea de Estudios Arabes y Hebraicos*, 35, 1986, pp. 45-100, figs. 1-31, plates 1-8.
——, "La decoración vegetal del taller de marfil de Cuenca, I", in *Homenaje al Prof. Darío Cabanelas Rodríguez, ofm., con motivo de su LXX aniversario*, Vol. II, Granada, 1987, pp. 241-59, figs. 1-9, plates 1-3.
Menéndez Pidal, G., "Las Cantigas. La vida en el siglo XIII según la representación iconográfica (II). Traje, aderezo y afeites", in collaboration with Carmen Bernis, *Cuadernos de la Alhambra*, 15-17, 1979-1981, pp. 89-154, plates I-X; republished in *La España del siglo XIII leida en imágenes*, Madrid, 1986, chapter devoted to "Traje, aderezo y afeites", pp. 51-104.
Meunié, Jacques, and Henri Terrasse, *Nouvelles recherches archéologiques à Marrakesh*, Vol. 62 in collection of *Institut des Hautes-Etudes Marocaines*, Paris, 1957.
Navascués y de Palacio, J. de, "Tres epitafios hispanoárabes del Museo Arqueológico de Toledo", *Al-Andalus*, 26, 1961, pp. 191-93.

——, "Una escuela de eboraria, en Córdoba, de fines del siglo IV de la hégira (XI de J.C.), o las inscripciones de la arqueta hispanomusulmana llamada de Leyre", *Al-Andalus*, 39, 1964, pp. 199-206.
Nykl, A. R., "Inscripciones árabes de la Alhambra y Generalife", *Al-Andalus*, 4, 1939, pp. 174-94.
Ocaña Jiménez, M., "Capiteles epigrafiados de Madinat al-Zahra'", *Al-Andalus*, 4, 1936-39, pp. 158-66.
——, "Obras de al-Ḥakam II en Madīnat al-Zahrā'", *Al-Andalus*, 6, 1941, pp. 157-68.
——, "Nuevos datos sobre la mqabriya almohade malagüeña del año 1221 J.C.", *Al-Andalus*, 11, 1946, pp. 445-46.
——, "Una mqabriya almohade malagueña del año 1221 J. C.", *Al-Andalus*, 11, 1946, pp. 224-30, 445-46.
——, "La inscripción fundacional de la Mezquita de *Ibn ʿAdabbas* de Sevilla", *Al-Andalus*, 12, 1947, pp. 145-51.
——, "La inscripción fundacional de la mezquita de Bīb al-Mardūm en Toledo", *Al-Andalus*, 14, 1949, pp. 175-83.
——, "Nuevas inscripciones árabes de Córdoba", *Al-Andalus*, 17, 1952, pp. 379-88.
——, "Tres epitafios musulmanes toledanos del siglo XI", *Al-Andalus*, 19, 1954, pp. 407-10.
——, *Repertorio de las Inscripciones árabes de Almería*, Madrid-Granada, 1964.
——, *El cúfico hispano y su evolución*, Vol. 1 in *Cuadernos de Historia, Economía y Derecho Hispanomusulmán*, Madrid, 1970, 2 vols.
——, "Las inscripciones en mosaico del *miḥrāb* de la gran mezquita de Córdoba y la incógnita de su data", in H. Stern (ed.), *Les mosaïques de la grande Mosquée de Cordoue*, Vol. 11 of *Madrider Forschungen*, Berlin, 1976, pp. 48-52.
——, "Ŷaʿfar el eslavo", *Cuadernos de la Alhambra*, 12, 1976, pp. 217-23.
——, "Documentos epigráficos de la Mezquita", in *Exposición La Mezquita de Córdoba: siglos VIII al XV*, Córdoba, 1986, pp. 16-28.
Pearson, J. D., "Ḳurʾan", *Encyclopedia of Islam*, 2nd ed., Vol. V, Leiden, 1986, pp. 400-32.
Rubiera Mata, M. J.,"Los poemas epigráficos de Ibn al-Ŷayyab en la Alhambra", *Al-Andalus*, 35, 1970, pp. 453-73.
——, "De nuevo sobre los poemas epigráficos de la Alhambra", *Al-Andalus*, 41, 1976, pp. 207-11.
——, "Ibn Zamrak, su biógrafo Ibn al-Aḥmar y los poemas epigráficos de la Alhambra", *Al-Andalus*, 42, 1977, pp. 447-51.
——, *Ibn al-Ŷayyāb. El otro poeta de la Alhambra*, Granada, 1982.
——, "Las inscripciones árabes de Játiva: Una hipótesis y una propuesta sobre la denominación de un estilo", in *Homenaje al Prof. Darío Cabanelas Rodríguez, ofm., con motivo de su LXX aniversario*, Vol. II, Granada, 1987, pp. 293-95.
——, *La arquitectura en la literatura árabe*, 2nd ed., Madrid, 1988.
Schlumberger, D., *Qasr el-Heir el Gharbi*, Vol. 120 in collection of *Institut français d'archéologie du proche-Orient, Beyrouth-Damas-Amman. Bibliothèque Archéologique et Historique*, Paris, 1986.
Sourdel-Thomine, J., and B. Spuler (eds.), *Die Kunst des Islam*, Vol. 4 of *Propyläen Kunstgeschichte*, Berlin, 1973.
Sourdel-Thomine, J., and others, "Khaṭṭ", *Encyclopaedia of Islam*, 2nd. ed., Vol. IV, 1978, pp. 1113-30.
Terrasse, H., *La Mosquée des Andalous a Fès*, Vol. 38 in collection of *Institut des Hautes-Etudes Marocaines*, Paris, 1942.
——, *La mosquée al-Qaraouiyin a Fès*, Vol. 3 of *Archéologie Méditerranéenne*, Paris, 1968.
Torres Balbás, L., "Nuevos datos documentales sobre la construcción de la mezquita de Córdoba en el reinado de ʿAbd al-Raḥmān II", *Al-Andalus*, 6, 1941, pp. 411-22.
——, "Las yeserías descubiertas recientemente en las Huelgas de Burgos", *Al-Andalus*, 8, 1943, pp. 209-54, plates 1-8.
——, "La primitiva mezquita mayor de Sevilla", *Al-Andalus*, 11, 1946, pp. 425-39.
——, *Arte almohade*, Vol. 4 of *Ars Hispaniae*, Madrid, 1949.
——, *Artes almorávide y almohade*, volume in *Artes y Artistas*, Madrid, 1955.
——, *Arte Hispanomusulmán hasta la caida del califato de Córdoba*, Vol. V of *Historia de España*, dirigida por R. Menéndez Pidal, Madrid, 1965.

SOCIAL HISTORY AND LIFESTYLE

THE SOCIAL HISTORY OF MUSLIM SPAIN FROM THE CONQUEST TO THE END OF THE ALMOHAD RÉGIME (EARLY 2ND/8TH-EARLY 7TH/13TH CENTURIES)

PIERRE GUICHARD

INTRODUCTION

The impact of the Arab conquest of Spain has, as is well known, been the subject of historiographical controversy. For a whole "traditionalist" trend, exemplified by such major figures of Hispanic medievalism as Ramón Menéndez Pidal and Claudio Sánchez Albornoz, the attachment of most of the Peninsula to the Muslim empire (*dār al-Islām*) had, in the initial stages at least, only limited effects on the social and even cultural life of its inhabitants. According to this interpretation, the conquerors, a few thousand Arabs and a slightly larger number of Berbers from the Maghrib, simply represented a dominant element without any profound influence on either the "vital structure" or the "idiosyncratic nature" of the Hispanics, who largely preserved their own customs and cultural traditions. Indeed, it was rather the case that these foreign elements, of Eastern and Maghribi descent, became hispanicised through inter-racial mixing with native Hispanic women. As such the process of Islamisation or Arabisation is to be seen as a superficial phenomenon, affecting only the "superstructure" of Muslim Spain, whose "underlying structures" remained fundamentally indigenous.

Two quotations perfectly sum up this thesis—a thesis which may be called "traditionalist" insofar as it places primary emphasis on the continuity of a Western and Hispanic tradition to the detriment of the eastern aspects of Hispano-Muslim civilisation. The first is taken from the Arabic scholar, Julián Ribera, writing in the 1920s. One could, he said, compare this Hispano-Muslim civilisation, deeply faithful to its local roots, but modified in appearance by an Arab-Islamic colouring brought from the outside, to the waters of a lake stained red by a small quantity of aniline; while the expanse of water appears changed to the observer, the chemical structure of the water itself is not truly altered by this foreign element.[1] The second quotation is one from Sánchez Albornoz, for whom "Arab influence on culture and customs was necessarily insignificant for many decades in a Spain whose race, life and culture were western ... Over whole centuries, the inhabitants of the Peninsula lived deeply rooted in their pre-Islamic past". It was only in the 5th/11th and 6th/12th centuries, with the "African invasions" of the Almoravids and Almohads, that the "Hispanic sap", which had, over four centuries, nourished a civilisation henceforth appropriately to be termed Hispano-Muslim, would run dry.[2]

It will be noted, however, that this does not accord with the way the actual Muslim inhabitants of the Peninsula referred to themselves during the Middle Ages; they rather used the sole term *Andalusī* to describe anything relating to the Islamised part of the former Roman and Visigothic Hispania, the Islamised zone itself being called, invariably, *al-Andalus*—a term generally assumed to have been handed down by the Vandals who occupied Hispano-Roman Baetica for a time during the era of the Germanic invasions. Regardless, however, of the exact origin of the toponym, it is certain that the Arab conquerors used it in preference to such names as *Hispania*, *Spania* or the Arabic *Ishbāniya*, with which they were perfectly familiar, and which they could have adopted as they did the term *Africa* (become *Ifrīqiya* in Arabic) to designate the Arabised part of the Maghrib. Moreover, the use of this new name—possibly borrowed from the local usage of the people living on the two shores of the Straits of Gibraltar, but representing in any case a shift from the name commonly used in the past—cannot even have sprung from a need to distinguish the Islamised zone from the Peninsula as a whole; for, while the northern part of the Peninsula did indeed rapidly escape the influence of the new religion and the power of Córdoba, the term *al-Andalus* appears very early as an exact synonym of *Hispania* with respect to the territory designated.

The Islamic coins minted in Spain in the very earliest years of the conquest—even before the dissidence of the Asturian Kingdom had become really marked, and when Muslim domination seemed certain to spread through virtually the whole of the Peninsula and even beyond it towards Gaul—were inscribed first in Latin (in the years 93/711-2 and 94/712-3), then bilingually (98/716), and finally in Arabic (from 102/720-1 onwards). In the bilingual series, the Latin legend *Spania* and the corresponding Arabic legend *al-Andalus* appear together, after which it is the latter which permanently prevails.

Consciously or not, then, the Arab-Berber leaders chose for this new entity, formed during the days following the conquest, a name marking a clear rupture with the past; and the fact that usage then hallowed this new name, while it obviously does not "prove" any lack of continuity between Romano-Visigothic Hispania and Arab-Islamic al-Andalus, is at least an indication of a radical break occurring, spontaneously, in the collective mentality of the citizens of what would subsequently be called Muslim Spain.

The past fifteen years or so have, however, witnessed a reaction against this "traditionalist" historiographical tendency, with a number of historians emphasising elements which do in fact reveal such a discontinuity—reflected not only in the language and religion brought to the Peninsula by the conquerors, but also in the deeper underlying structures of mental, social and "ethnological" organisation. I have myself contributed to this "anti-continuist" trend in a work devoted to such "Eastern" social structures, published in Spanish and French in 1976 and 1977 respectively; and as such it is necessary, before embarking on this treatment of Andalusī society, to forewarn the reader of my own historiographical leanings. Both the tone and the contents of this paper would no doubt be rather different had it been written by a historian upholding a more "traditionalist" viewpoint.

We are dealing here with a history where sources are relatively sparse, and where, as a result, interpretation often tends to take on a greater role than conclusions firmly supported by established documented data. Moreover, social life and structures represent a realm of Andalusī history which has, until recently, been the subject of few specific studies. The chronicles primarily used, up to now, by writers on the history of the different periods have only permitted the establishment of a political and event-related context, with scarcely a glimpse of the realities of the social background, while the literary or juridical texts that have been the subject of special study have allowed, at best, insights only into narrow and limited sections of Andalusī society, such as the class of secretaries and learned men very closely associated with the ruling power, and the class of jurists—with little information, moreover, provided on the economic bases of their existence. The nature of urban society can be glimpsed only through the descriptions (both very brief and too general) of geographers, while the study of rural life is only just beginning, using archaeological approaches which until recently seemed the only ones capable of shedding light in an area where the written sources studied provided almost no information at all. Now, however, we have also begun to make use of the rich documentary material contained in collections of *fatwas*, or legal judgements, delivered by Andalusī doctors of the 4th/10th-7th/13th centuries and preserved in large treatises of jurisprudence, the most important of these being that of the Moroccan jurist Aḥmad b. Yaḥyā al-Tilimsānī al-Wanṣharīsī (834/1430-914/1508). The initial data derived from material of this kind is extremely promising, and I shall be referring to it on a number of occasions, though it must be stressed that such work is still in its early stages.

I. Ethnic Composition of the Population

I.1 *Elements of Eastern and Maghribi origin*

This is one of the points most often examined, though the scarcity of sources on the subject, as on so many other subjects, firmly precludes any final conclusions. Any evaluation of the relative size of Eastern and Maghribi ethnic groups in the Peninsula would first require an approximate knowledge of the volume of the native population, which we by no means possess, any demographic figures for the Peninsula on the eve of the Muslim invasion being frankly tentative. José Orlandis, an expert on Visigothic Spain, cites assessments ranging from three to ten million inhabitants at the end of Antiquity, of which the former figure is probably closer to the real one, and uncertainty is still greater with regard to population figures around the end of the period of the Visigothic Kingdom—a period marked by extensive unrest and disasters of every kind, and which may indeed be regarded as one long crisis, ending in a Muslim invasion which, if not absolutely devastating, would still probably have contributed in the short term to making the character of these "dark age" centuries still more sombre.

To this no doubt broadly ruralised population, probably fairly scattered and still depressed and disorganised by the Arab-Muslim conquest, were now added Arab-Berber elements; and for these Arab sources do provide a few figures, in that they supply information on the armies taking part in the conquest and on the contingents of the various tribes or ethnic groupings engaged in the numerous civil wars between Arabs, or between Arabs and Berbers, which marked the first half-century of the Muslim occupation of the Peninsula. The second invading army, mainly composed of Arabs, entered Spain in 93/712 (the first one, almost entirely of Berbers, having entered the previous year), and, according to the sources, comprised ten to eighteen thousand men. Subsequently a contingent of some ten thousand warriors came from Syria to the Maghrib to combat the Great Berber Revolt of 123/740, and, following its defeat there, was forced to cross into Spain, where it settled permanently.

Traditions in connection with ʿAbd al-Raḥmān I's seizure of power in al-Andalus, in 138/756, give some specific idea as to the size of the contingents established in or around the largest cities of present-day Andalucía. The Umayyad claimant is said, for instance, to have recruited around a thousand Arab horsemen from Yemeni tribes in the province of Seville, and two thousand more in the neighbouring cities of Elvira, Rayyo and Sidonia. His main force comprised a group of some five hundred warriors linked to the Umayyad family by bonds of clientship and recorded as such in the *dīwān*, or register, of the army. Figures of this kind do not permit any really accurate calculation of the number of Easterners now settled in Spain, but we may infer a probable figure of several tens of thousands of warriors—some thirty thousand according to the lowest estimates, probably more if all textual data is taken into account.

"Traditionalist" authors saw settlement essentially in terms of men alone, cut off from all ties with their original society and therefore likely to be speedily assimilated into the local society through inter-racial breeding. This is a highly aprioristic way of seeing things, and hardly accords with the traditions and customs of Arab society at the time of the conquest, a society still close to its bedouin origins, in which warriors apparently still often travelled with their entire tribal or family group—such, at any rate, is the picture given by the Carolingian historian Paul the Deacon, as he describes the Muslims entering southern Gaul in about 101/720 "with their women and children, as if to settle there",[3] and we may suppose the same to have been true for a large proportion of the Arab warriors who arrived in the first invasion. It is certain, in any case, that these Arab elements, far from integrating with the native inhabitants as has so often been assumed, strongly affirmed their ethnic identity, within tightly-knit family and tribal groups, until at least the later part of the 3rd/9th century, and that the serious political unrest marking this latter period was primarily of ethnic origin. Arab authors refer to this era of unrest as the *fitna*, which, in the terminology of medieval Muslim chroniclers, designates a period of cleavage within the *Umma*, or Muslim community. The often very detailed accounts of the events in question clearly indicate the existence, in Andalucía and in the Upper Frontier lands or Ebro Valley, of relatively numerous and quite individualised Arab groups not in the least assimilated into the mass of the native population.

Numerous Arab families of Yemeni tribal origin, for example, lived in and around Seville, and these elements, having initially played a major part in raising the first Umayyad ʿAbd al-Raḥmān I to power in al-Andalus, revolted several times in the early days of the emirate, together with their clients throughout the western region, or Algarve. The revolts had died down by the end of the 2nd/8th century, and these groups did not lose their distinctive identity during the century following, although some of them contracted marriages with women of native origin, including some of very high social rank—the best known example being the marriages of the famous Sara the Goth (grand-daughter of the penultimate Visigoth King Witiza), who owned large holdings of land in the Seville region and successively married two Arab chiefs. A number of large Sevillian families came from such unions in the first centuries of the Muslim period, such as the Banū Ḥajjāj, who played a very important role in the Sevillian *fitna* of the end of the 3rd/9th and beginning of the 4th/10th century.

However, a local chronicle of the era, reproduced by later historians, provides exceptionally detailed information on the unrest surging through the Andalusī capital during the period in question, and this information in no way suggests an aristocracy "assimilated" into the native population. On the contrary, the Banū Ḥajjāj, together with another great family of Eastern descent, the Banū Khaldūn (ancestors of the great 8th/14th-century Maghribi historian Ibn Khaldūn) set themselves up as the heads of the Arabs in Seville, and bloody fights took place there against the native elements of the city. This Arab aristocracy was powerful enough to impose itself forcibly both on native neo-Muslims—a sort of urban "bourgeoisie" whose resistance had been broken by massacres—and on the Umayyad *amīr* in Córdoba, ʿAbd Allāh. The latter's power was similarly threatened by unrest breaking out in most of the provinces, and he was forced, in view of his limited scope for action, to allow a virtually autonomous Arab emirate to be established in Seville, headed first by the head of the Banū Ḥajjāj, Ibrāhīm, then by Ibrāhīm's son ʿAbd al-Raḥmān, this local emirate lasting from 285/899 to 300/913. In the latter year these two figures both died, and the new *amīr*, ʿAbd al-Raḥmān III, began to restore the authority of the central power. The Sevillians then put an end to political dissidence and once more submitted to him.

Arab elements settled in other parts of al-Andalus also intervened in the civil unrest surging through the whole country at the time; we have, for instance, fairly detailed information on the uprisings of those who lived in the Elvira province, i.e. the present region of Granada. Such revolts, less organised and apparently carried out in the face of more concerted resistance on the part of the native population, did not lead to any kind of stable local government and ended in turmoil and confusion. On the Upper Frontier, on the other hand, a powerful Arab family from the Tujīb tribe profited from events to establish a dominant role for itself, by offering to uphold the authority of the central power in Córdoba against the excessively independent policy of the great native Banū Qasī family, which had affirmed its power in the region during the 3rd/9th century. This preponderance of Arab elements seems to have been maintained, under the Caliphate, in both Seville and Saragossa, because when the latter collapsed at the beginning of the 5th/11th century it was families of Arab descent which succeeded in seizing the power left vacant by the downfall of the central authority: the Banū ʿAbbād at Seville, who belonged to the same Lakhm tribe as the Banū Ḥajjāj, and a branch of the Banū Tujīb at Saragossa, founded the ʿAbbādī and Tujībī *ṭāʾifa* dynasties in the two cities.

Comparable information may be deduced, from the same sources, with regard to the Berbers who became established in the Peninsula alongside the Arabs. While the texts concerning them are less numerous, the markedly higher figures mentioned nevertheless lead us to conclude that Berbers came from the near Maghrib in far greater numbers. Whereas, when the Umayyad ʿAbd al-Raḥmān arrived in 138/756, the combined Arab Yemeni tribes of Seville and the neighbouring areas brought him a contingent of a thousand horsemen, a single Berber clan or family of the Ronda region, the Banū Khalīʿ, brought him 400. With the army he thus gathered in Andalucía, he drove the Cordoban governor, Yūsuf al-Fihrī, from power and took his place; then, when the latter revolted against him shortly afterwards, he recruited from the districts of Seville, Mérida and Laqant (Fuente de Cantos) an army composed largely of Berbers and amounting to some twenty thousand men. A century and a half later, in 288/901, an agitator of Shiʿite inspiration, Ibn al-Qiṭṭ, raised, in the same central and central-west regions (between the Guadalquivir and Tagus valleys), an army (again Berber) which the—fairly reliable—sources relating the event estimate at sixty thousand men.

The texts concerning Ibn al-Qiṭṭ's revolt several times reflect a type of society, in these Berberised regions of the centre of the Peninsula, which is still marked by tribal and clan-type structures, while the geographer al-Ya'qūbī, who provides a brief description of al-Andalus around the same period (end of the 3rd/9th century), speaks of "Berber tribes" populating the Valencia region. A second proof of the relative extent of Berberisation in al-Andalus may specifically be found in the toponymic signs left by Berber tribal groups in the formerly Islamised part of the Peninsula, where numerous place names still attest to their presence: names of present-day towns or large villages, such as Mequinenza in Aragon, Adzaneta in the Valencia region and Azuaga in the south of the present province of Badajoz, still, for instance, recall the tribal names Miknāsa, Zanāta and Zuwāgha, of Maghribi origin. There were undoubtedly many other such cases in the geography of al-Andalus. In fact the geographer al-Iṣṭakhrī, from the first half of the 4th/10th century, indicates, along the stages of the road from Córdoba to the Lower Frontier, in regions on the two sides of the Guadiana between the Guadalquivir and Duero valleys, districts or localities bearing the names of the Miknāsa, Hawwāra and Nafza Berber tribes. In this case, toponymic information simply confirms textual reports of a sizeable presence of Berber groups. However, an abundant typonymy of the same kind may be identified in other regions for which our information is less extensive, such as the Valencia region, where relatively numerous place names preserve the memory of settlements by the Zanāta, Ṣinhāja, Hawwāra, etc., confirming the small number of texts which once again mention—albeit fleetingly—the presence of this Maghribi element.

The tendency noted earlier (in the case of Arabs) for the predominance of foreign elements to increase still further at the expense of the native population between the 2nd/8th and 5th/11th centuries, at least on the aristocratic level, also applies to the Berbers. During the *fitna* period at the end of the emirate, in the late 3rd/9th and early 4th/10th centuries, chroniclers several times speak of conflicts between population groups of local origin and groups of Maghribi origin; and this seems to occur especially in the vast regions of the centre of the Peninsula, where it was Berbers and not Arabs who clearly constituted the larger foreign ethnic element—for example, in the regions, already noted, of the present-day Extremadura, on either side of the Guadiana, or in the high regions stretching between Toledo and the sea. With respect to the latter, we have numerous references to the presence, from the conquest of the 2nd/8th century on, of a large Berber settlement in the mountains occupying the greater part of the present provinces of Cuenca and Teruel. In the 3rd/9th century, particularly during the crisis of the central power at the end of the emirate, chroniclers several times report armed conflicts between these Berbers and citizens of native origin, both Muslim and Christian, living in Toledo. In the 4th/10th century, the Caliphate fostered the progress, in these regions, of a powerful Berber military aristocracy, no doubt descended from ancient tribal chieftainships, granting them veritable "fiefs" in exchange for services rendered in the defence of the Upper Frontier against the Christians.

During the crisis of the Caliphate at the beginning of the 5th/11th century, the local power entrusted to a few quasi-seignorial families—the Banū G̲h̲azlūn at Teruel, the Banū Qāsim at Alpuente, the Banū Razīn at Albarracín and the Banū Zannūn, or D̲h̲ī 'l-Nūn, in the region of Uclés, Huete and Cuenca—became more or less naturally transformed into a larger political power, so giving rise to the small *ṭā'ifa* dynasties of this region. What is more surprising, however, is that the Toledans, unable to govern themselves in any satisfactory way following a rather unconvincing attempt to administer the city, apparently submitted of their own free will to one of these Berber chiefs, Ibrāhīm b. D̲h̲ī 'l-Nūn, under whom the Berber *ṭā'ifa* of Toledo was thus set under way. Still less is known about the process leading to the establishment of the *ṭā'ifa* adjacent to Badajoz, but here again a city which, at the end of the 3rd/9th century, had been a centre of resistance on the part of native elements submitted without evident difficulty to the authority of a dynasty of Berber origin, that of the Banū 'l-Afṭas. Thus, during the 5th/11th century of the *ṭā'ifa*s, the two cities in which native particularism had been expressed with the greatest force prior to the Caliphate were now placed under the authority of Berber dynasties, both of which, moreover, claimed to be of Arab origin.

I have so far considered only the first settlement of the Berbers in Spain, that which took place following the conquest of the 2nd/8th century; other Maghribi elements, as we shall see, arrived subsequently to settle in al-Andalus, first under the Caliphate, then during the period of Almoravid and Almohad domination. However, these first seem to have been the most important with respect to the composition of the Andalusī population. While preserving distinctive features over quite a long period, particularly with respect to their tribal and clan structures, they seem to have been fairly quickly Arabised on the linguistic level, and we have just noted how the most important families ended up effectively merging themselves with the Arab element by claiming to be of Eastern descent. This is why, all in all, they seem to me to be a fairly important factor in the process of easternisation.

Several references will also be made, in the course of this essay, to the Jewish element, which should not be omitted from any picture of the Andalusī population. Persecuted under the Visigoths, the Jewish seem to have returned to the Peninsula in large numbers, primarily as merchants, acting as middlemen between the Frankish world and Muslim Spain. They also, however, developed a brilliant Judaeo-Andalusī culture, although this belongs to a study of cultural rather than social life. The most conspicuous period of this Jewish presence in Muslim Spain was the era of the Banū Nag̲h̲rīlla, the extremely powerful Jewish ministers of the Zīrid kings of the *ṭā'ifa* of Granada towards the middle of the 5th/11th century. However, this predominance was fragile and vulnerable to swings of opinion, and the second minister of this name in fact perished in a riot by the people of Granada, who on this occasion massacred the Jews of the city. Yet, despite such occasional tensions, the Jews—who were, like the Arabs, of Semitic origin and culture —undoubtedly provided further impetus for the easternisation of Andalusī civilisation.

I.2 *Elements of native origin*

The predominance of the Arab-Berber aristocracy at the time the *ṭā'ifa*s were created, which seems to me to be fairly well established at least with respect to those groups holding power, obviously does not mean there were no longer any elements of native origin; it is simply that these latter do not occupy the front of the stage. They were, we know, divided into Muwallads, who had been converted to Islam, and Mozarabs, who had remained loyal to the Christian faith. There is an abundant literature on the second group, since the "traditionalist" authors of the 19th century—notably Francisco Javier Simonet, author of the magisterial *Historia de los mozárabes de España*—viewed them as preservers of the national religious tradition in face of "Muslim oppression" and accordingly marshalled all the learning of which the era was capable to find the slightest traces of their presence in Muslim Spain. They were aided, it must be said, by the sizeable collection of Latin texts on the doctrinal controversies agitating the Andalusī Mozarab community of the 3rd/9th century, particularly with respect to the dramatic episode of the "Córdoba martyrs" at the beginning of the second half of the century. It is evident that a large and socially diversified Mozarab society existed in Córdoba at this period, as it also did, no doubt, in other cities for which documentation is less extensive. In addition to numerous clerics, monks and nuns, we find, among the notable persons referred to in these texts, people of noble descent, traders, *kuttāb* (Arab-language secretaries), a servant at the *amīr*'s palace, persons in charge of the judicial and fiscal affairs of the Christian community, and so on.

The main problem posed with respect to the history of this Mozarab community is that of the rate of decline, caused by conversions, emigration towards the northern part of the Peninsula during the upheavals of the 3rd/9th century, and also, no doubt, by the ethno-religious conflicts of the same period. The American historian R. W. Bulliet, in a stimulating work based on the quantitative use of onomastic data as furnished by scholarly biographical dictionaries, concluded that it was only in the 4th/10th century, under the Caliphate, that the numerical ratio of Muslims and Christians in al-Andalus was reversed in favour of the former. He himself, nevertheless, regards his conclusions as fairly fragile, given that they rest on too narrow a foundation of information.[4] In fact, the impression given by chronicles concerning the revolts breaking out in all parts during the last decades of the 3rd/9th century, and the slow reduction of these revolts due to the persevering efforts of ʿAbd al-Raḥmān III, is that of a country already largely Islamised, including rural areas. In a very brief, but highly suggestive passage in his chapter on Spain, the geographer Ibn Ḥawqal, who visited the country in the middle of the 4th/10th century, does, it is true, speak of frequent revolts by Mozarab peasants employed on large estates, probably those of the ruling aristocracy; but we may feel that he is merely repeating information about a situation existing before the caliphal era, and therefore "out of date"—what he says is surprising for this period, though perfectly in accord with information conveyed to us in chronicles dealing with the end of the emirate.

Under the Caliphate, the impression is of Mozarab elements being more peacefully integrated within the political and social order, the best known example being that of Rabīʿ b. Zayd (Recemund), a palace official who wrote the famous *Calendar of Córdoba* for ʿAbd al-Raḥmān III, undertook various diplomatic missions (in Germania and Byzantium) and was rewarded with the Bishopric of Elvira. It should, however, be made clear that we have very little information on the Mozarabs of this period, the sources being in fact almost exclusively centred on those holding power and their entourages. Relatively large numbers of Mozarab communities did, however, continue to exist up to the end of the *ṭāʾifa* kingdoms: there were several parishes in Toledo when the Christians occupied the city in 478/1085, and abundant documentation in Arabic is preserved on the Mozarabs of this city (though solely with respect to the Christian period). An apparently still significant Mozarab group, which is the subject of a number of passages in the Arabic chronicles dealing with the Cid's dominion over Valencia, was also to be found there during this same period, while the memoirs of the *amīr* of Granada, ʿAbd Allāh, clearly indicate the existence of a relatively large rural Christian population in some parts of the Málaga region towards the end of the 5th/11th century. At the other end of the social scale, we know the names of a number of high-ranking Christian dignitaries in the service of the *ṭāʾifa* kings. They are not, however, very numerous and seem to be exceptions.

This Christian population was no doubt very badly affected by the hardening of relations between Christianity and Islam during the Almoravid period. We know, for example, that in 492/1099 the people of Granada, by order of the Almoravid *amīr* Yūsuf b. Tāshfīn acting on the advice of his *ʿulamāʾ*, symbolically destroyed the main Mozarab church of the Christian community. However, it was particularly after the King of Aragon, Alfonso the Warrior—answering an appeal from the Mozarabs of Granada, who were no doubt anxious about the increasingly precarious nature of their situation—

had undertaken a major expedition into Andalucía in 519/1125-520/1126 that drastic measures were taken by the Almoravid regime for the mass deportation of Mozarabs to Morocco. Not all, however, were forced to leave the country, since the same sources also subsequently report the existence of a Mozarab community in Granada. It was in fact apparently finally decimated in 557/1162, when the Almohads reoccupied the region after a bitter war against the *amīr* of Murcia, Ibn Mardanīsh (the latter having taken over the city with the support of Jewish Mozarab "tributaries" who feared a union with the power of Marrakesh). According to Ibn al-Ṣayrafī, who was a contemporary of these events, "only a small group, accustomed to contempt and humiliation" was afterwards left in Granada. One may suppose that a comparable situation applied in most of the other cities. In those reconquered after the middle of the 6th/12th century, particularly those of the Levant and Andalucía, the Mozarabs are not mentioned in scholarly sources, and, as such, no longer seem to represent significant minorities.

Problems concerning Muslims of native descent are naturally of a quite different kind. 2nd/8th-century sources concentrate especially on fighting between Arabs and Berbers, and then on the revolts of these same Eastern and Maghribi elements against the Umayyad emiral power, and have very little to say about this Islamised, or Muwallad, native element. The latter do, however, achieve prominent mention in chronicles from the time they begin rebelling against the political, social and economic domination of the Arab-Berber aristocracy established in the country with the conquest, and against the emirate of Córdoba, which was closely linked with this social class. The year 181/797 witnessed the famous "day of the grave pit", when the *amīr* al-Ḥakam I had very large numbers of prominent Toledan citizens massacred to forestall any uprising on their part. The city, whose population was very largely of native descent, did not, through the whole of the 3rd/9th century, neglect any opportunity to rise up against the emiral power. The chroniclers, however, provide little more than the bare facts of such revolts, so that it is not possible to study the Toledan society of the period, and the same may be said of the history of other cities under the emirate, such as Mérida. For the Upper Frontier, or Ebro Valley, more information is available on native aristocratic families like the Banū ʿAmrūs and Banū Shabrīt who converted to Islam, the most important such family being that of the Banū Qasī, who had originally held a kind of seignorial power over the Tudela region. So firm were the local roots of these families that we see them making matrimonial ties with their "cousins" from great families in those areas which had remained Christian. The most famous figure is Mūsā b. Qasī, whom the *amīr* Muḥammad I of Córdoba recognised as governor of Saragossa between 237/852 and 246/860, and who, according to one Christian chronicle, called himself "the third King of Spain".

II. Andalusī Society under the Caliphate

Over a long period the different ethnic and religious elements of which Andalusī society was composed formed a mosaic of groups living side by side rather than a "melting pot", within a social complex marked by antagonisms which, as we have several times noted, broke out with particular virulence in the disturbances of the *fitna* of the end of the emirate, during the last three decades of the 3rd/9th and the first two decades of the 4th/10th century. The weariness of the people, the increasing Islamisation, the growing sense of a need for unity in the Andalusī community, or *jamāʿa*, together, perhaps, with other factors of which we are unaware, favoured a return to civil peace and political order. The main architect of this restoration of central power over al-Andalus as a whole was the eighth Umayyad *amīr* of Córdoba, ʿAbd al-Raḥmān III, during the first fifteen years of his reign, which began in 300/912. With peace and unity restored and the power of the state strengthened, this sovereign had himself proclaimed caliph in 316/929, thus reviving, in the West, the title which his ancestors in Damascus had held from 41/661 to 132/750, prior to their overthrow by the Abbasids. It was under this "Córdoba Caliphate", for a little under a century, that Muslim Spain reached its political peak, characterised by the achievement of a social equilibrium within which the tensions so strongly marking the preceding period seem to have been resolved. As I have stated above, I believe this unification was accomplished in a social and cultural context of Arabisation, rather than one involving ethnic assimilation to the ways of a native element which, whether Mozarab or Muwallad, remained very unobtrusive during this period.

It is, in any case, rather difficult to offer an exact and concrete picture of Muslim Spain during the 4th/10th century, in that the sources for the period focus so exclusively on the life of the capital, the government and the court, which ʿAbd al-Raḥmān III established in the princely city of Madīnat al-Zahrāʾ, a vast palatine complex he had built a few kilometres downstream from Córdoba, on the foothills of the heights overlooking the right-hand bank of the Guadalquivir. We know little, for this period, about anyone beyond the dignitaries of the Caliph's entourage, who comprised a kind of microcosm of high-ranking people of various origins—such a diversity, at the service of the caliphal power, reflecting the evident unification of Andalusī society. At the head of the state were the prince's relatives, members of the Umayyad family and its clients from the Arab Quraysh family, while Arab families of more or less noble descent provided some of the high officials of the state, local governates and the army. The Banū Tujīb of Saragossa, for example, were largely successful in maintaining control of the Upper Frontier, or Ebro Valley. More influential and omnipresent at the helm of government were the large families of Umayyad clients of Eastern descent, such as the Banū Jahwar, the Banū Shuhayd and the Banū Bāsil, who formed veritable dynasties of high officials, ministers and generals —these had in fact already been the backbone of the Umayyad state during the emiral era. Berbers appear to have been fairly numerous at all levels of the social and political structure: "feudal lords" of the Frontiers, such as the Banū Razīn from the south of Aragon, or *ʿulamāʾ* assuming important posts, such as the chief *qāḍī* of Córdoba, Mundhir b. Saʿīd al-Ballūṭī, who came, as his name indicates, from the mountainous region of *Faḥṣ al-Ballūṭ*, situated to the north-west of Córdoba and known for its population of Maghribi origin. Also found here, in a less powerful and less centrally important entourage, were Jews, like the very learned physician, Ḥasday b. Shaprūt, and Mozarab Christians, such as Rabīʿ b. Zayd, the author, as noted above, of the *Calendar of Córdoba*. There were no doubt, in the palace and in the various branches of the government and administration, large numbers of Christian and Muslim officials of native origin. However, it is often rather difficult to be precise as to individuals, since their names do not, as in the case of Arabs and Berbers, imply a precise tribal—and therefore ethnic—origin. Moreover, they do not figure prominently, any more than they do in overall Andalusī society, of which they must, nevertheless, have comprised very much the majority element.

Towards the middle of the 4th/10th century, these elements of diverse origin seem, as far as high official posts are concerned, to co-exist in a way reflecting a fairly harmonious synthesis achieved by the Córdoba Caliphate; one gains the impression that, under the aegis of an Eastern dynasty and a predominantly Arab-Berber ruling class, a lasting equilibrium had been established between the political power and a society in the process of being Arabised and Islamised. Yet the success apparently achieved is in fact misleading. Very soon a gulf was to open between an increasingly artificial and alien ruling circle and Andalusī society as a whole—a situation which was to have dramatic consequences for the development of the caliphal regime. In line with a trend which seems to be specific to the Muslim political régimes of the Middle Ages, and which was later to be schematised, in the 8th/14th century, by the eminent philosopher of history and "sociologist" Ibn Khaldūn, the Umayyad power was gradually to cut itself off from local social realities, and to rely exclusively on foreign elements, principally Berbers recently arrived from the Maghrib and white slaves or former slaves imported from Western Europe, who were given the name *Ṣaqāliba*. The former were mercenaries, recruited in North Africa as part of the expansionist policy conducted by the Caliphate beyond the Mediterranean in the last third of the century, beginning with the reign of al-Ḥakam II (350/961-366/976), then, especially, under the autocratic rule of the great ʿĀmirid chief minister al-Manṣūr, from 370/980 to 392/1002. They constituted a light and very effective cavalry which the caliphal government employed both in Spain, against the Christians, and in the wars it conducted to take over Morocco.

They were not no doubt very numerous—probably a few thousand warriors only—but they remained in homogeneous corps within the structure of their clans and tribes, under their own chiefs. They did not integrate with Andalusī society and, as such, were detested by the Cordobans.

The case of the *Ṣaqāliba* is different. These formed only one category of the slaves found in al-Andalus, and in other medieval Muslim societies, at all levels of the social and political structure. Neither Christianity nor Islam eliminated slavery, which remained an obtrusive feature of the Mediterranean world in the early Middle Ages. The Muslim conquest was accompanied by the reduction to slavery of a part of the populations conquered, particularly in the Maghrib, but the Muslim world, where there was a large demand for slaves, had, subsequently, to satisfy this demand from beyond its borders. In the markets of big cities, particularly in Córdoba under the Caliphate, slaves of every origin were sold. Blacks, imported from West Africa through the Sahara, were found there, but Spain was especially known, from the 3rd/9th century on, for its export of white European slaves from Christian countries, who were given the name *Ṣaqāliba*, or "Slavs". Medieval Muslim geographers considered, not entirely wrongly, that the land of the Slavs comprised a vast territory of which one end (the western one for us) bordered on to the land of the Franks—which was itself in contact with the Muslims of Spain and Sicily—and the other, in the South-East, bordered on to the Muslim East, more specifically the lands of the Caspian and Khorassan. "Slavs" were, then, imported from both sides regardless of their actual origin. Many, no doubt, did initially come from the Slavic countries of Central Europe, having been captured in Carolingian wars against the pagans of these regions, then brought by merchants—who often seem to have been Jewish—to be sold to the Muslims of Spain. However, the same name was given to slaves from Christian Europe, many of these being people captured in the wars against the Northern Spanish states, or in the *razzias* undertaken by Andalusī pirates, in the 3rd/9th and 4th/10th centuries, off the coasts of southern Gaul and Italy and in the islands of the Mediterranean. Such "Slavs", or "Slavonians", were particularly highly valued in the Muslim world, and it was probably the exportation of these—possibly after castration had transformed them into eunuchs (required in view of their frequent use in harems)—that underlay the astonishing growth of a port like Almería. Originally a small commercial station founded by Andalusī merchants at the end of the 3rd/9th century, the city actually become one of the major commercial centres of the Mediterranean in the 4th/10th-5th/11th centuries, and a number of texts indicate that trafficking in slaves was one of the first activities to be organised there.

Many of these slaves were used as domestic servants in wealthy homes, while a more notable category was that of the *qiyān*, comprising female slaves used as concubines, dancers or singers; these were particularly prized in Eastern and Andalusī aristocratic circles, and were trained in veritable schools or institutions established for the purpose. The number of slaves in this latter category was certainly considerable. The great "polygraph" Ibn Ḥazm of Córdoba, who spent his youth and adolescence in the Cordoban aristocratic circles of the end of the Caliphate, several times mentions female slaves of this type in the anecdotes making up his famous "Dove's Neck-ring" (*Ṭawq al-ḥamāma*), or "Treatise on Love and Lovers". In the same period, that is, at the end of the Caliphate and the beginning of the *ṭā'ifa*s, there is reference to a vizier of the first sovereigns of Almería whose harem apparently comprised five hundred slaves. One well-known anecdote of the same period describes how a citizen of Elvira, near Granada, was misled in an amusing way about the quality of the goods: wishing to acquire a beautiful foreign woman, he had paid a high price in the Córdoba market for a supposedly Christian slave who, it seemed, understood not a word of Arabic, and had brought her back with him, in great state, as though she were nothing less than a princess from beyond the frontiers. The young woman was actually a prostitute and a native of the region, and, as they entered the town, could not hold herself back from greeting an old acquaintance they chanced to meet, thereby revealing the unscrupulous scheme she and the merchant had concocted together to cheat a naive customer.

Slaves in a domestic role are also found at the level of socio-political organisation. Eunuchs, originally recruited for the harems of the prince and aristocracy, were among the most intimate and influential servants of a hugely inflated palace (thousands of male and female slaves lived in the palace of Madīnat al-Zahrā'); they were given important civil and military posts as generals and governors, and there were entire army corps made up of Slavs, these, together with the Maghribi Berbers, making up the most solid and reliable permanent element of the caliphal army. We know little of the precise methods by which the great 'Āmirid *ḥājib* al-Manṣūr accomplished his major "military reform" in the last years of the 4th/10th century, but we do know that one of his goals was to break the traditional tribal framework of the Arab Andalusī *jund*, his army being ever more heavily made up of these non-Arab elements, primarily Berbers and Slavs, who seemed more docile and reliable to the Cordoban ruling power.

III. The Era of the *Ṭā'ifas*

The socio-political contradictions indicated above, due to the seizure of effective power by the 'Āmirid *ḥājib*, who left the Caliph with a purely symbolic role, and the overwhelmingly foreign character of the politico-administrative structure of the state, were undoubtedly part of the underlying reason for the grave crisis of the Caliphate in the years 399/1009-422/1031. This period of anarchy began with the "Córdoba revolution", which removed the

ʿĀmirid regime and deeply destabilised the Caliphate, and concluded with the actual disappearance of the Caliphate; after which the unitary political organisation al-Andalus had known up to then was splintered through the formation of the "*ṭā'ifa* kingdoms" characterising the 5th/11th century in the Muslim part of the Peninsula. Whereas the caliphal system had been centred on Córdoba, whose importance far eclipsed that of the provincial capitals, political power was now redefined on a regional basis, with each large provincial city becoming the capital of a small state. Nevertheless, the urban model with respect to the organisation of power was not questioned at the level of the individual state. The functions of each capital remained, albeit no doubt on a more modest level, those which the capital of the Caliphate had formerly fulfilled. There was no desire to deviate from this "caliphal model", which continued to serve as a reference point for the mode of socio-political organisation.

The period of the *ṭā'ifa*s should definitely not be considered (as has sometimes tended to be the case) an era of "feudalisation". In contrast to the situation in the 11th-century West, neither Andalusī society nor the Andalusī state gave structural precedence, in this period, to military elements, which merely comprised one branch of state organisation—important, certainly, and sometimes even predominant, but not effectively destroying the state itself, as occurred with the militarised aristocracy of post-Carolingian western Christianity. Nor do castles and fortresses seem to have been owned privately, or by landed lords; on the whole, they remained either straightforward rural fortified dwellings, many of these appearing during the turbulent period at the end of the emirate, or state fortifications for paid garrisons. When sources do refer to territorial and fiscal concessions made to the military, as, for example, at the end of the century in the memoirs of the *amīr* of Granada, ʿAbd Allāh, these do not appear to depart from the framework of a state organisation which continues to exercise control over it. When the military did in fact assume power in any particular state, within the political mosaic represented by Muslim Spain at this time, they simply placed themselves at the head of a state system which they ruled for their own personal gain, but whose nature they did not change.

At the head of each of the *ṭā'ifa* states, the ruling groups constituted an aristocracy whose ethnic origin was either Berber, as in the kingdom of the Zīrids of Granada referred to above, or Arab, as in Seville and Saragossa, or *Ṣaqāliba* as in Denia and Almería, where it was Slav leaders who managed to seize power. Around the princes was formed a governing aristocracy of ministers, learned secretaries and administrative and military heads, such people comprising the upper level of society, or *k͟hāṣṣa*—those, in other words, who received from the state, in contrast to the mass of taxpayers, the *ʿāmma*, or "plebeians", made up of subjects, or *raʿiyya*. Privileged social categories should be taken to include the *ʿulamā'*, or *fuqahā'*, doctors of

Islam expert in the juridical and religious sciences, who were one of the influential elements rulers must control if they were to retain a firm grip on the country. A person could not occupy a high rank in society without receiving an initial juridico-religious training which was the basis of medieval Muslim culture. Young men who were destined for administration or important state positions were then subsequently schooled in the arts, so enabling them to master the elegant diplomatic style indispensable for writing official documents, while those who chose to study the juridico-religious sciences in greater depth were rather destined for the posts of *qāḍī*, *muftī*, reader of the Quran, preacher in the mosques or leader of prayer. This religious and judicial hierarchy was technically separate from the administrative organisation of the state, but in actual practice there was no clear distinction between the two spheres.

The Spain of the *ṭā'ifa*s, proved to be incapable of defending itself against growing pressure from increasingly enterprising Christian sovereigns, based on Christian societies spurred on by their ever-greater integration with the feudal West. Governors of small Muslim states were forced to buy peace from their northern neighbours by making heavy tribute payments, or *parias*, in silver; this no doubt had its socio-economic effects, which are, however, difficult to judge in view of the lack of sufficiently specific documents. On the other hand, an especially interesting passage by Ibn Ḥazm of Córdoba, written towards the middle of the century, evokes a vivid picture of the system of relations established, within the framework of a state structure and a monetarised economy, between the various socio-professional categories. Attacking extra-Quranic taxation—an abuse, in his eyes, for that very reason—which the *ṭā'ifa* sovereigns imposed on their subjects, he protested against the "tyrant" who used the money received from taxes to pay soldiers who were the ultimate guarantee of his power. The soldiers (and the ruling classes) in turn used this money to purchase products (particularly manufactured goods) sold to them by traders and craftsmen in the cities—who in *their* turn "bought with this money what they needed from other subjects of the tyrant, so that monies in gold and silver were transformed ... into wheels which rolled in the middle of the fire of hell".[5]

A rigorous jurist of Ibn Ḥazm's stamp thus saw the entire social body as corrupted by the circulation of a money made impure by illegal fiscal practices. However, Ibn Ḥazm himself—a severe critic of his time, and thereby vulnerable to a hostility within official circles which forced him to spend the last days of his life in haughty retirement—also left us, especially in his youthful writings, a pleasanter picture of the society of his period. I have already referred to his "Dove's Neck-ring" (*Ṭawq al-ḥamāma*), written in 418/1027, three years before the downfall of the Cordoban Caliphate, and when the geography of the *ṭā'ifa*s was virtually established. The turmoil in Córdoba forced the author, who was the son of a minister of the Caliphate, to seek refuge in Eastern Spain, where he lived for several years in the medium-sized city of Játiva. This is his most famous work, and still, today, his most "popular" work in Spain. It treats of love and lovers in a style at once personal and anecdotal, succeeding, as the Arabist Juan Vernet has written, in "distilling from specific examples, and almost always identifying the real, flesh-and-blood people who experienced them, the real essence of love, unchangeable through centuries and civilisations".[6] However, the *Ṭawq* is also a most interesting sociological and psychological document, providing most interesting indications concerning the Andalusī mentality, and on the condition of women in aristocratic circles.

Ṭā'ifa literature and poetry, and particularly the work of Ibn Ḥazm, has led a number of writers to draw particular conclusions about the nature of Andalusī civilisation. Henri Pérès, for example, in his important work *La poésie andalouse en arabe classique*, considers that Andalusī woman enjoyed a more "liberal" way of life than their sisters in the eastern part of the Muslim world, and that this reflects deeply-set "western" roots with respect to the psychology and customs of the Andalusī people, who were only superficially Arabised and easternised. I believe, as I have already said, that such interpretations should be somewhat modified. With regard to the situation of women in particular, not enough attention has been given to the fact that the anecdotes apparently reflecting this "liberalism" usually concern women from the category of *qiyān* and *jawārī* described above, in other words slaves whose purpose was to entertain gatherings of men from aristocratic society with their dances and songs. Since they were also used as concubines by their masters, their "freedom of behaviour" was part and parcel of what might be termed their "socio-professional" situation, and did not go beyond the juridical limits applicable to their servile status. Apart from a few famous cases—such as that of the Umayyad princess Wallāda bint al-Mustakfī, who "hit the headlines" in the chronicle of *ṭā'ifa* Córdoba by maintaining a kind of literary salon—it seems that women of free status, or at any rate those of good birth, were, as elsewhere in the Arab-Muslim world, subject to strict obligations ensuring the preservation of family honour, and, as such, did not enjoy a very different condition from those in eastern urban circles of the same period.

IV. Al-Andalus under the Hispano-Maghribi Régimes

From the final years of the 5th/11th century on, the Andalusis were mostly subject to rulers of Maghribi origin: first the Almoravids, who intervened in the Peninsula in answer to an appeal from the sovereigns there, and with the aim of defending Islam on the Peninsula against the Christian threat, then the Almohads, who revolted against the Almoravids themselves, replacing them from the middle of the 6th/12th century on. During the post-Almoravid crisis, and again as the Almohads collapsed, Andalusī power was briefly restored, but it was generally fragile and short-lived, and its history is especially vague and obscure. The most important of these local emirates, which lasted from 542/1147 to 568/1172, was that of the *amīr* Ibn Mardanīsh of Murcia. This was established in the eastern region shortly after the fall of the Almoravids, and managed, by means of fierce fighting, to resist the extension of Almohad power for some twenty years, before finally being conquered. Yet we know virtually nothing of the internal history of this Eastern Spanish state. Scholarly bio-bibliographical dictionaries, which are a major source of information on the educated class and men of religion, seem only to indicate that the structure of this society, dominated by governing classes linked to the ruler and by men of learning and religion, experienced very little change during this "Mardanīshī" period.

The problems most clearly visible during this period are of a cultural rather than a social kind. The reforming movement of the Almoravids had succeeded in ensuring, in Morocco and Spain, a strict observance of the rules of Islam, in accordance with the tradition of the very conservative and legalistic Mālikī school which had, by and large, been firmly dominant in the Muslim West since the 3rd/9th century. On the intellectual level, the régime adhered to the strictest and most rigid religious tradition, immovably devoted to niggling practices and to the mechanical knowledge of juridical conclusions developed two or three centuries earlier by the great Eastern and Maghribi scholars who had founded the school. There was, moreover, an increasing tendency to base practice not so much on these founding texts themselves, but rather on compilations of lesser value, derived from the preceding ones and produced by commentators and abridgers of the second rank. Meanwhile, in the East, new intellectual and religious trends were appearing, trends which were leading to a renovation of Islam on the basis of a synthesis between, on the one hand, the ritualism and legalism advocated by tradition and, on the other, aspirations towards a more affective kind of religion, reflected in the numerous Sufi brotherhoods which were beginning to multiply throughout the Muslim world. The main name associated with this synthesis is that of the jurist and theologian al-Ghazālī (d. 505/1111, in Iran), whose works enjoyed immense and immediate success, and received the support of intellectuals and rulers alike.

On the cultural level, therefore, the rigid Mālikī standpoint of the Almoravids, while in accordance with a tradition to which most Andalusī *ʿulamāʾ* remained faithful, conflicted with the general trend towards a new religious sensibility. The latter was expressed, in al-Andalus as elsewhere, through the development of new, opposing movements of mystical tendency, giving rise to doctrines that attempted to find some alternative to the stultifying legalism of the official religion. This need for new thinking had been felt back in the 5th/11th century by such an independent spirit as Ibn Ḥazm, whose viewpoint, Ẓāhirī and anti-Mālikī, was to have its attractions for the intellectuals of the Almohad period. However, the first half of the 6th/12th century mainly saw the spread of Ghazālī's thought, and of a popular Sufism tinged with political messianism, whose development was discernible in several regions at the end of the Almoravid era, particularly in rural areas which were probably less closely controlled by the urban *fuqahā'* class. This was the case, for example, in Seville, around Almería and in the Algarve. Such observations suggest the existence of social oppositions between cities and countryside in al-Andalus, but this is, unfortunately, impossible to verify, due to the lack of adequate sources.

The best-known movement in al-Andalus, that of the Algarve, is not without analogies in Almohad practice. The preaching of an ascetic-mystical agitator, who seemed to focus his attention on the inhabitants of rural towns, began in 539/1144, with the revolt, in this region, of a sect called the *Murīdūn*—the leader of this sect, Ibn Qasī, proclaiming himself *imām*, that is, he claimed the religious and political leadership of the Muslim community. The Almoravid regime was by now exhausted, undermined in Morocco itself by the decisive successes of the Almohad movement, which was in revolt in the Atlas throughout the second quarter of the 6th/12th century. The Almoravid collapse was accompanied in al-Andalus by further movements of revolt in Córdoba, Valencia, Murcia, Almería and other cities, whose inhabitants often returned the power to the *qāḍī*s who were in office at the time. Our knowledge of the complex events of this exceptionally troubled period, in which Almoravid power collapsed and Almohad authority was, with difficulty, established, is too slight for us to discern much more than the main outlines of the social history involved; the most we can do is to attempt to paint a picture of the principal aspects of urban life and rural life in the period of the Hispano-Maghribi empires.

IV.1 *Urban society and its institutional framework in the 6th/12th century*

No synthetic study exists of the economic and social life of this period. No doubt we can use, and apply to the 5th/11th and 6th/12th centuries, the data provided by Lévi-Provençal in his classic *Histoire de l'Espagne musulmane*, but we should, nevertheless, be cautious of anachronisms. One of the main differences between the caliphal period and the centuries following is, as already stated, the relative decline of Córdoba, which stagnated in the 4th/10th century, and the rise of numerous provincial cities, favoured by their promotion to the status of capitals during the *ṭā'ifa* period. To a certain extent, these provincial capitals maintained their importance in the 6th/12th century, but some of them were reconquered early by the Christians, notably Toledo in 578/1085 and Saragossa in 512/1118. Córdoba itself was seriously weakened by the civil fighting which tore Andalucía apart in the middle of the

6th/12th century, and recovered only with difficulty from the destruction and depopulation suffered during these troubled periods. According to the chronicle of Ibn Ṣāḥib al-Ṣalāh (writing in the second half of the 6th/12th century, when Almohad authority had been re-established there following temporary occupation by the troops of the *amīr* of Murcia, Ibn Mardanīsh) the former capital of the Caliphate had a mere 82 inhabitants! The figure refers, presumably, to the families of leading citizens, but destruction does seem to have been considerable, since it was necessary to undertake repairs to the palaces and homes which had suffered from the war. The same was no doubt true in Almería which, following its occupation by the Castilians between 542/1147 and 551/1157, did not apparently regain the level of population and activity which had made it one of the main economic centres of the Peninsula under the Almoravids.

In the 6th/12th century, the question of the ethnic composition of the Andalusī population no longer, it should be stressed, assumed the importance it had had up to the caliphal period. The Andalusis appeared to exhibit no ethnic differences among themselves. There is no evidence of the Slav and Berber elements visible in the 5th/11th century, nor of any distinction, so marked under the emirate, between native Muwallads and the Arab-Berber population; many Muslims in the Peninsula, perhaps out of a kind of aristocratic vanity, bore Arabic *nisbas*, at least among the ruling classes and in *'ulamā'* circles. They considered themselves Arabs regardless of their actual origin, and, as such, viewed themselves as distinct from the Maghribi Berbers who comprised the governmental and military framework. Relations between Peninsular and African Muslims were not always harmonious, though we should not perhaps exaggerate Andalusī opposition to the Almoravid and Almohad regimes outside periods of acute crisis. One source of population renewal was still, no doubt, the practice of slavery, about which we have, however, less information than for the preceding period; one may suppose that the importing of slaves, particularly women, in earlier periods, had produced a degree of inter-racial mixing within the population. Christian documents concerning the capture of Minorca by the Catalonians in 686/1287, and the reduction of its population to slavery, seem to indicate that most of the island's inhabitants were regarded as black or of mixed race, but further primary evidence would be necessary to draw from these surprising figures—which in any case refer only to certain groups of slaves—figures which would be valid for the whole of al-Andalus.

Arab authors, as we have seen, traditionally distinguish two social categories within the Andalusī population. The first is the aristocracy, or *khāṣṣa*, comprising, primarily, the ruling circles within the government and administration, the court, the army and the general governing structure of Islam, namely all the viziers and high-ranking secretaries, heads of government departments and high-level personnel within the provincial administration, together with learned men within the entourage of the ruling circles and most of the class of *ʿulamāʾ*, or *fuqahāʾ*, who carried out religious and civil administrative functions (as *qāḍīs*, market supervisors, etc.). The second category is that of the *ʿāmma*, the common people (also often called the *raʿiyya*), made up of the mass of tax-payers—craftsmen, small- and medium-scale traders, and cultivators of varying socio-economic status, who lived in the city, or in the suburbs, or in the outlying rural areas which were directly dependent on the urban network, and were the setting for its gardens and its *faḥṣ*, i.e. the intensely cultivated surrounding plain. The *khāṣṣa* class was apparently largely made up of those supported by payments and pensions disbursed by the treasury, or *bayt al-māl*. It is certain, however, that these people also gained an income from landed revenues and that large properties were owned. The latter, except for the sovereign's possessions (and we do not really know whether these were in fact distinguished from those of the public treasury) are not very apparent in the sources. Almohad sources, and also the memoirs of the *amīr* ʿAbd Allāh, record land or fiscal concessions, whose precise nature is very unclear, but which were probably similar in principle to the *iqṭāʿ*s of the Muslim East. However, they did not apparently assume the same degree of importance in al-Andalus; and, similarly, there is no more sign than in earlier periods of the socio-political system, which continued to be strongly state-centred under the Almoravids and Almohads, being affected by any kind of "drift towards feudalism"—here, again, any such tendency was no doubt less evident than in the East.

It was the cities which were the important Andalusī organisms of the time, and an attempt has been made to assess the population of these by calculating a mean probable value based on the *intra muros* surface area. The most commonly accepted calculations are those of Leopoldo Torres Balbás, who proposed a figure of about 350 inhabitants per hectare. The figures roughly applicable to the 5th/11th-6th/12th centuries would be 37,000 inhabitants for Toledo (106 hectares), making it one of the largest cities, 27,000 (79 hectares) for Almería in its heyday, 26,000 for Granada (75 hectares), 17,000 for Saragossa (47 hectares) and 15,000 for Málaga (37 hectares). The area of Valencia contained 44 hectares, i.e. about 16,000 inhabitants, a figure supported by the count of houses given in the *repartimiento* of the city, carried out at the time of the reconquest. The most important city is Seville, which, in the 6th/12th century under the Almoravids and Almohads, attained an extent of about 200 hectares (estimates vary from author to author), which would correspond to some 70,000 inhabitants; it seems, however, that part of the area had not been built on. Given that these figures should be viewed with caution, it was still obviously a highly urbanised society. Each major city served as a centre for a region economically, politically and fiscally dependent on it, and it was around these provincial capitals (Valencia, Murcia, Almería, Málaga, Jaén, and more modest centres such as Silves) that first the *ṭā'ifa*s, then the great, fairly autonomous governments of the following periods were organised.

The appearance of the cities is relatively well-known through the geographers, the most important of these being al-Idrīsī, who died after 561/1166; it does not differ from what is known of traditional Islamic and, particularly, Maghribi cities. The city was often dominated by a *qaṣaba* (*alcazaba*), which might house a state garrison governed by a *qā'id* (as, for example, at Játiva, Orihuela and Badajoz); the *qaṣaba* of the major cities might be the residence of the *amīr* (Almería, Málaga), and the latter might also, in the cities of the plain, reside in the governmental *qaṣr* (*alcázar* or palace) (Córdoba, Valencia, Murcia, Seville). The focal points of urban life were the "public" areas: the great mosque (the largest being that built at Seville by the Almohads), baths, souks and caravanserais. Urban administration was in principle entrusted to functionaries, and we have a detailed description in this respect in the treatise on *ḥisba* or, "market supervision", by the Sevillian, Ibn ʿAbdūn, written around 500/1100, at the beginning of the Almoravid period. The person responsible for the *ḥisba*, the *ṣāḥib al-sūq*, was also concerned with municipal administration and public morals, monitoring, in particular, taverns, places of prostitution and, more unexpectedly, cemeteries, where women could go alone under the pretext of visiting family tombs, and which might thus serve as places of rendezvous. The other posts of urban authority were those of the chief of police (*ṣāḥib al-shurṭa*) and the chief civic official (*ṣāḥib al-madīna*), each of these public servants having his own agents (*aʿwān*), ten or so in each sector for a city such as Seville. According to Ibn ʿAbdūn, all these officials, who were appointed to office and removed from it by order of the ruling political power (*al- sulṭān*), were under the authority of the highest among them, the *qāḍī*, or Quranic judge, who had his own subordinates: a *ḥākim*, or judge for minor suits, and various other subordinates responsible for registering marriages, vacant successions, etc. One thing specific to al-Andalus was the importance of the council, or *shūra*, of *mufti*s (*fuqahā'* acting in an advisory capacity) who assisted the chief magistrate. Ibn ʿAbdūn considers it desirable that the *qāḍī* should entertain specially close relations with the vizier of the government. A similar type of organisation certainly existed in other cities, although the staff under the orders of these public officers was probably less numerous and possibly not all posts of authority existed in every case.

We are, it must be said, not very sure of the place held in this society, and in the economy supporting it, by a possible class of large-scale traders, and by long-distance exchange activities. "Bourgeois" categories, which are, as such, outside the world of poets and learned men, simply do not figure for an author like the anthologist, Ibn Saʿīd (who lived in the first half of the 7th/13th century); as far as he is concerned, men of letters can only be sovereigns, ministers, secretaries, *qāḍī*s or other public officers, or, possibly, generals—people, in other words, who are in one way or another part of the Islamic "state system". References to merchants are, in general, not very numerous, and are often extremely vague. The only specific ones are those from *Geniza* documents in Cairo, and refer to Almerian Jewish merchants of the Almoravid period. However, a number of Almerian funerary inscriptions dating back to the same period concern merchants, some of them from other Andalusī cities and one, even, from Alexandria. Geographers also mention the very important mercantile activity of Almería, which was, in this era, one of the most important ports of the Western Mediterranean. We also know that one of the main centres of economic life, in every large city, was the *qaysāriyya*, where luxury items were traded. *Ḥisba* treatises provide little specific information, however, beyond that on the petty trading of the souk which was carried on by large numbers of small craftsmen and traders involved in highly diversified activities, and seems primarily to have concerned urban classes of modest income. We may hope to derive new and more abundant data, on this point and on many others, from the collections of the *fatwa*s delivered by major jurists of the period, which are only now beginning to be examined.

As already stated, Jewish and Christian urban minorities, which still played a major role in the 5th/11th century under the *ṭā'ifa*s, saw their importance diminish in the 6th/12th, especially, it would seem, in the Almohad period. We must take into account the more or less spontaneous conversions, and also the emigrations and, sometimes, deportations and expulsions, which took place with the reciprocal hardening of relations between Christianity and Islam during the crusades and the reconquest. Gradually Andalusī society lost its often-stressed composite character as an ethnic, religious and to some extent cultural "mosaic", which had distinguished it over the first centuries, and rather became a society very markedly Islamised and Arabised. There is little evidence of the use of the native Romance language after the end of the 5th/11th century—a point clearly demonstrated, for example, by the American historian R. I. Burns, with respect to the region of Valencia and Murcia, where, in the period of the reconquest a little before the middle of the 7th/13th century, native Muslims seemed capable of communicating with the conquerors only through interpreters noted in Christian sources. This trend towards cultural uniformity applied to rural and urban areas alike, and it was upon such a culturally homogeneous society that the Christian conquerors of the 6th/12th and 7th/13th centuries advanced.

IV.2 *Rural society*

Relatively little work has so far been done in connection with the social structures obtaining in the Andalusī countryside, a lack of sources making the subject a difficult one to treat. A rather miserable picture is quite often painted of rural Hispano-Muslim society: workers in the countryside lived, it is said, under the economic, social and fiscal domination of cities which heavily exploited them, the instrument of such domination being large absentee properties. This view of things is no doubt based, primarily, on the clear demographic importance of the cities, and also on the frequency of share-cropping arrangements evidenced in notary formulae and collections of legal judgements, or *fatwa*s. However, on the basis of Christian documents concerning Muslims from the period of the reconquest, and also on the basis of archaeological data, a rather different view of this rural society has recently been put forward. In the Valencia region, for example, where contemporary Christian sources concerning the Catalonian-Aragonese seizure of the country are relatively abundant, we find reports of strong rural communities, or *aljamas*, which deal directly with the king or the new seignorial powers and often induce them to maintain the previously existing tax system. The oft-repeated notion of a "crushing taxation" weighing down on rural Muslims is not borne out; taxes seem in fact to have been moderate, and even basically compatible with the Islamic ideal of the Quranic tithe. Moreover, the evidence at our disposal makes reference only to state taxes, with no suggestion of any authority of a "feudal" or seignorial nature possessing private rights over land and men.

According to accounts of the conquest, notably the extraordinary autobiographical chronicle of the conqueror of Valencia, King Jaime I of Aragon, these rural Muslims apparently exercised their own control over a good many of the castles scattered through the countryside, since it was the communities themselves, on the advice of the elders or notables leading them, which turned these castles over to the Christian conquerors. Such a notion is confirmed by the examination of archaeological remains. Research carried out on these originally Muslim fortified sites, of which large numbers are still to be found in the Spanish countryside, has shown that their structure did not resemble that of the "feudal" castles of the West, which were used to shelter a seignorial group or a small garrison responsible for containing the population: they are rather either simple villages on high ground, providing protection for a permanent population, or else vast enclosures serving primarily as temporary refuges for the inhabitants of villages located in the vicinity. These, together with a number of other factors, indicate that the Andalusī countryside was largely populated by communities, or *jamāʿa*s, of landowning peasants, possessing a greater degree of cohesiveness and autonomy than is generally attributed to them. It may be added that a number of recently published *fatwa*s similarly indicate communal structures and castles being used as a refuge rather than as seignorial dwellings, thereby confirming what is already suggested by Christian texts and archaeological data.

We may also add, in support of this view of rural Andalusī society—and also for certain regions like the Balearic Islands, the Spanish Levant and some parts of Andalucía—the evidence of "gentilic" toponymy. In these areas of formerly Muslim Spain, the names of hamlets or villages were very often actual "family names", derived from the term *Banū*, meaning "sons of" and implying a group of descendants, together with the personal name of an eponymous ancestor (the hamlet called Beniali, for example, was inhabited by the Banū ʿAlī, an agnatic group descended from a personage of that name). Such toponyms suggest "Arab-Berber" types of structure, and the relatively durable co-occurrence of such family groups with a territory belonging to them. Here again, *fatwa*s studied only recently seem to confirm the existence of such rural micro-societies, marked by strong familial structures, and apparently fairly similar to those found in the Maghrib up to the present day. For example, a legal judgement tendered in the Almoravid period by the *qāḍī* of Córdoba, Ibn Rushd (the grandfather of the great jurist and philosopher of the same name, who lived during the Almohad period and was called Averroes by the Christians) concerns a suit among the inhabitants of "a rural locality [*qarya*] made up of different districts [*ḥawāʾir*], each bearing the name of a group [*qawm*, which here, as in various other Andalusī texts, seems to mean 'family group'] and known to be their heritage and that of their fathers". Another *fatwā* of the same jurist refers to a *qarya* inhabited by an agnatic group made up of "cousins", or *banū ʿamm* (literally "sons of a paternal uncle", i. e., relatives in a male line of descent), which claims collective use of an irrigation channel, or *sāqiya*, in the face of abuse on the part of one of their number, who, with the support of the authorities, had erected a mill that now diverted part of the water needed for irrigating the land of this rural community.

The role played by irrigation was in fact one of the most important aspects of the Andalusī rural society and economy. The *huertas* of the Andalusī coastal plains and valleys were not limited to the famous irrigated regions surrounding such large cities as Valencia, Murcia and Granada; very large numbers of rural communities were based on the use of a small *vega*, or surrounding plain, irrigated by means of diverting an often modest water course. On this point, too, archaeological study of the details of material life is updating our knowledge on the organisation of Andalusī rural societies. Studies conducted in Majorca, for example, have demonstrated the importance of the hydraulic developments undertaken by Muslim peasant communities, whether terraces irrigated through complex tank and channel systems, or underground water canalisation similar (if on a smaller scale) to that exemplified by the *qanāt*s of Iran or the Sahara. Here again, toponymy sometimes reveals a correspondence between irrigation systems based on each particular human group "taking turns" with the water and the fragmentation of society into small communities, whose familial nature may appear in onomastic data. This is the case, for example, in the plain of Gandía, on the East coast, where an extant Christian text immediately subsequent to the colonisation of the 1240s describes the water distribution system before the reconquest. According to this, the villages so taking "turns with water" in a manner fixed by tradition mostly bore gentilic names of the kind noted above, some of these, such as Beniarjó, Beniflá, Benieto, Benirruat, etc., corresponding to places still in existence today.

V. The Destruction of Andalusī Muslim Society: The Mudejar Epilogue

From the annexation of the Andalusī *ṭā'ifa*s by the Almoravid *amīr* Yūsuf b. Tāshfīn in the years 483/1091 to 487/1094 to the anti-Almohad revolt of 626/1228, the history of al-Andalus cannot really be separated from that of the Maghrib, insofar as the Andalusis were governed by a power ruling from Marrakesh and extending its authority through all or most of Muslim Spain, by the agency of Berber military forces and governmental personnel largely belonging to the dynastic group and settled in the Peninsula.

From the end of the 5th/11th century, however, another Islam existed in Spain: Mudejar Islam, that of the Muslims who, in large numbers, stayed on in the territories "reconquered" by the Christians. The Mudejars of the 6th/12th century have not been the subject of many studies, and their history is not very well known. It begins with the annexation of Toledo by Alfonso VI in 478/1085, and it seems that, initially, a large Muslim population remained in the city and in the region, no doubt on the basis of an agreement with Alfonso VI, who appointed the Mozarab Sisnando Davidiz as the first governor of the city, and continued to collect a tax called *alessor* (that is, *al-'ushr*, the Quranic tithe) from the Muslims. Arabic bio-bibliographical dictionaries mention a number of Muslim scholars who died in Toledo after the Christian conquest.

Nevertheless, we have very few sources concerning these Toledan Muslims, whose relative size seems to have diminished fairly quickly, whereas the Mozarab element continued to represent a substantial proportion of the population. It is probable that their situation quickly became precarious, if only because of the Almoravid threat which weighed on the city from 1086 onwards. We know that the great mosque was, despite promises to the contrary, quickly converted into a cathedral (thereby probably emptying the city centre of its Muslim population), apparently under pressure from the "Franco-Cluniac party" whose prominent figures were Queen Constance and the Archbishop of Toledo, Bernard de Sédirac. The same state of affairs no doubt existed in the former "Kingdom of Toledo", at least in the northern part, which remained in Christian hands after the Almoravid invasion.

No major Muslim communities appear to have remained in the north and centre of Portugal, which was reconquered between the end of the 5th/11th century and the middle of the 6th/12th. We know that serious massacres accompanied the taking over of Santarem and Lisbon, the cities of this region, and there are no apparent indications of a Muslim rural population existing subsequently. On the other hand, fairly large Muslim populations remained in Aragon and, to a lesser extent, in New Catalonia. We still have the texts for the surrender of two cities reconquered in the 6th/12th century: for Tudela in 513/1119 and Tortosa in 543/1148. In both cases the Muslims were to evacuate the *civitas* (the enclosed city) and go and live in the outlying areas; and, by virtue of this arrangement, they were to keep their belongings, their religion and their law and customs, and had only to pay the tithe to the king. Identical conditions were made with respect to rural communities, as is shown in another surviving text of surrender with regard to the Muslim inhabitants of several "castles" in the Ebro Valley above Tortosa. Similar conditions, as noted above, were to be agreed in the 7th/13th century, with respect to numerous communities in the Valencia region at the time of their reconquest by the Catalonians and Aragonese.

The social situation of the Aragonese Muslims seems to have changed, but to have remained, nevertheless, a relatively privileged one. Major urban communities continued to exist, although large numbers among the political, social and cultural élite had no doubt emigrated. Several families from this region are found to have settled in cities further south, such as Valencia, one known case being that of the great philosopher Ibn Bājja, who had been vizier to the Almoravid governor of Saragossa, Ibn Tifilwīt, between 504/1110 and 512/1118, and who left the city following the Christian conquest of 512/1118 and spent the rest of his life in Almoravid territory. The urban populations seem to have consisted largely of craftsmen. In the countryside of the Ebro Valley, which was largely characterised by irrigated agriculture, there appears to have been a growth in seignorial landholdings and forms of social and economic dependence, the best known being that of *exarico*, a word derived from Arabic *al-sharīk* and denoting a kind of share-cropping (a contract binding landowner and cultivator, according to various formulae). We may also, however, note the permanent existence of sizeable communities dependent on the king, on great Aragonese lords, or on the Church, but little is known of their specific situation in this earlier period (we have a much better grasp of the situation of the Valencian Mudejars of the 7th/13th century, thanks to the major studies of them by R. I. Burns).

It is beyond the scope of this brief synthesis to provide more detailed treatment of the situation of these Muslims under Christian domination—a subject which, in any case, involves significant regional disparities; my intention has simply been to note the context within which the history of this Andalusī Muslim society reached its conclusion. Despite the temporary coexistence of the two civilisations, and the reciprocal contacts and influences of which "Mudejar" art is a good example, there was no lasting synthesis; there was at most, to use the expression of R. I. Burns, a "symbiosis". These societies living side by side, within the context of overall political, social and economic domination of Christian over Muslim, were not, in my view, very compatible. Yet this did not prevent a certain "heritage" being transmitted from one civilisation to another, for example in the realm of irrigated agriculture, where the Christians had everything to learn from the Muslims. Whether because of the incompatibility of the respective mentalities and structures, or because of the unscrupulous character of the conquerors, promises made during the reconquest were often not kept, and Muslims very often found themselves subjected to a seignorial régime that reduced them to a harsh economic and social dependency vis-à-vis their Christian masters. Moreover, acceptance of Christian political authority was, in principle, difficult for Islamic orthodoxy, a situation which—after a more or less lengthy period characterised, often, by relatively harmonious coexistence, but more often, I feel, marked by open or covert conflict—led first to the forcible conversion, then to the final elimination of the Muslims.

[1] J. Ribera, *Disertaciones y opúsculos*, Madrid, 1928, I, 26.

[2] Claudio Sánchez Albornoz, "Espagne préislamique et Espagne musulmane", *Revue Historique*, 237, 1967, pp. 300-01.

[3] P. Guichard, *Structures sociales "orientales" et "occidentales" dans l'Espagne musulmane*, Paris-The Hague, 1977, pp. 140-41.

[4] Richard W. Bulliet, *Conversion to Islam in the Medieval Period. An Essay in Quantitative History*, Cambridge (Mass.)-London, 1979.

[5] Miguel Asín Palacios, "Un códice inexplorado del Cordobés Ibn Ḥazm", *Al-Andalus*, 2, 1934, p. 40.

[6] Juan Vernet, *Literatura árabe*, Barcelona, n. d., p. 115.

BIBLIOGRAPHY

Almagro, Antonio, "Planimetría de las ciudades hispanomusulmanas", *Al-Qanṭara*, 8, 1987, pp. 421-48.

Arié, Rachel, *España musulmana (siglos VIII-XV)*, Barcelona: Labor, 1982.

Avila, María Luisa, *La sociedad hispano-musulmana al final del califato (aproximación a un estudio demográfico)*, Madrid: C. S. I. C., 1985.

Barceló, Miquel, "El hiato en las acuñaciones de oro en al-Andalus, 127-316/744(5)-936(7)", *Moneda y Crédito* (Madrid), 132, March 1975, pp. 33-71.

Barceló, Miquel, María Antonia Carbonero and Ramón Marti, *Les aigües cercades (Els qanat/s de l'illa de Mallorca)*, Palma de Mallorca: Institut d'Estudis Balearics, 1986.

Barceló, Miquel, Helena Kirchner, Joseph M. Lluro *et al.*, *Arqueología medieval. En las afueras del "medievalismo"*, Barcelona: Crítica, 1988.

Bazzana, André, Patrice Cressier and Pierre Guichard, *Les châteaux ruraux d'al-Andalus: histoire et archéologie des ḥuṣūn du Sud-Est de l'Espagne*, Madrid, Casa de Velázquez, 1988.

Benassar, Bartolomé, *Histoire des Espagnols, I, VIe-XVIIe siècle*, Paris: Armand Colin, 1985.

Bolens, Lucie, *Agronomes andalous du Moyen Age*, Geneva: Droz, 1981.

Bosch Vilá, Jacinto, *Albarracín musulmán*, Teruel, 1959.

——, *Sevilla islámica, 712-1248*, 2nd ed., Seville: University of Seville, 1984.

——, *Los Almorávides* (facsimile of the Tétouan edition, 1956), Granada: University of Granada, 1990.

Bulliet, Richard W., *Conversion to Islam in the Medieval Period. An Essay in Quantitative History*, Cambridge: Harvard University Press, 1979.

Burns, Robert I., *Islam under the Crusaders: Colonial Survival in the Thirteenth-Century Kingdom of Valencia*, Princeton: Princeton University Press, 1973.

——, *Muslims, Christians, and Jews in the Crusader Kingdom of Valencia: Societies in Symbiosis*, Cambridge: Cambridge University Press, 1984.

Cagigas, Isidro de las, *Minorías étnico-religiosas de la Edad Media española*, I (*Los Mozárabes*) and II (*Los Mudéjares*), Madrid: Instituto de Estudios Africanos, 1947-49.

Casa hispano-musulmana, La, Aportaciones de la arqueología, Granada: Patronato de la Alhambra y Generalife, 1990.

Chalmeta, Pedro, "España musulmana", in *Historia General de España y América*, Vol. III, ed. Rialp, Madrid, 1988, pp. 459-543.

——, *El señor del zoco en España*, Madrid: Instituto Hispano-Arabe de Cultura, 1973.

Chalmeta, Pedro, Pierre Guichard, *et al.*, *Al-Andalus: musulmanes y cristianos (siglos VIII-XIII)*, Vol. III of *Historia de España*, ed. Antonio Domínguez Ortiz, Barcelona: Planeta, 1989.

Chejne, Anwar G., *Muslim Spain. Its History and Culture*, University of Minnesota, 1974.

Dozy, Reinhart, *Histoire des musulmans d'Espagne jusqu'à la conquête de l'Andalousie par les Almoravides*, new ed., ed. E. Lévi-Provençal, Leiden: E. J. Brill, 1932, 3 vols.

Glick, Thomas F., *Irrigation and Society in Medieval Valencia*, Cambridge: Harvard University Press, 1970.

——, *Islamic and Christian Spain in the Early Middle Ages: Comparative Perspectives on Social and Cultural Formation*, Princeton: Princeton University Press, 1979.

Guichard, Pierre, *Structures sociales "orientales" et "occidentales" dans l'Espagne musulmane*, Paris-The Hague: Mouton-Ecole des Hautes Etudes en Sciences Sociales, 1977.

——, *L'Espagne et la Sicile musulmanes aux XIe et XIIe siècles*, Lyon: Presses Universitaires, 1990.

——, *Les musulmans de Valence et la Reconquête (XIe-XIIIe siècles)*, Damascus: Institut Français de Damas, 1990-91.

Ibn Ḥazm, *El collar de la paloma, tratado sobre el amor y los amantes*, trans. E. García Gómez, 2nd ed., Madrid, 1967.

Khalis, Salah, *La vie littéraire à Séville au XIe siècle*, Algiers: S. N. E. D., 1966.

Lagardère, Vincent, "La tariqa et la révolte des Muridun en 539 H./1144 en Andalus", *Revue de l'Occident Musulman et de la Méditerranée*, 35, 1983, 1st Semester, pp. 157-70.

——, *Le Vendredi de Zallaqa: 23 octobre 1086*, Paris: L'Harmattan, 1989.

Lévi-Provençal, Evariste, *Histoire de l'Espagne musulmane*, Paris: Maisonneuve and Larose, 1950-67, 3 vols.

Lévi-Provençal, Evariste and Emilio García Gómez (trans.), *El siglo X en primera persona: las "memorias" de ʿAbd Allah, último rey ziri de Granada destronado por los Almorávides (1090)*, Madrid: Alianza Editorial, 1980.

Miles, George C., *The coinage of the Umayyads of Spain*, New York: The American Numismatic Society, 1950.

Pastor de Togneri, Reyna, *Del Islam al Cristianismo. En las fronteras de dos formaciones economico-sociales*, Barcelona: Peninsula, 1975.

Pérès, Henri, *La poésie andalouse en arabe classique au XIe siècle: ses aspects généraux et sa valeur documentaire*, Paris, 1937.

Sánchez Albornoz, Claudio, "Espagne préislamique et Espagne musulmane", *Revue Historique*, 237, 1967, pp. 295-338.

Simonet, Francisco Javier, *Historia de los Mozárabes de España*, Madrid, 1903.

Soufi, Khaled, *Los Banu Yahwar en Córdoba (1031-1070 d. J. C., 422-462 H).*, Córdoba: Real Academia de Córdoba, 1968.

Tibi, Amin T. (trans.), *The Tibyan. Memoirs of ʿAbd Allah b. Buluggin, last Ziri amir of Granada*, Leiden: E. J. Brill, 1986.

Torres Balbás, Leopoldo, *Ciudades hispano-musulmanas*, Madrid: Instituto Hispano-Arabe de Cultura, n. d.

Urvoy, Dominique, *Le monde des ulémas andalous du V/XIe au VII/XIIIe siècle. Etude sociologique*, Geneva: Droz, 1978.

Viguera, María J. (ed.), *La mujer en al-Andalus: reflejos históricos de su actividad y categorías sociales*, Madrid: Universidad Autónoma de Madrid, 1989.

Wasserstein, David, *The Rise and Fall of the Party-Kings: Politics and Society in Islamic Spain, 1002-1086*, Princeton: Princeton University Press, 1985.

AṢLUḤU LI 'L-MAʿĀLĪ
ON THE SOCIAL STATUS OF ANDALUSĪ WOMEN

MARÍA J. VIGUERA

I. *Women's poetry: the expression of love*

Verses composed by women poets in al-Andalus, or put into their mouths, reflect[1] a considerable degree of personal initiative on their part: they did not seem, on the evidence of these poems, to be restrained by any obvious barriers, and they show surprising freedom in the expression and fulfilment of their feelings of love. Probably the best-known verses of this kind are those of the Umayyad princess Wallāda, the daughter of the briefly reigning Caliph of Córdoba al-Mustakfī (reigned 416/1025). In the words of W. Hoenerbach: "Where Romanticism saw a distinguished lady, our realistic century discovered in her the emancipated woman."[2] Schack refers to "beautiful, discreet Wallāda",[3] while Cour, in 1920, approached matters from an entirely different perspective, finding in this woman poet "une émancipation quasi totale vis-à-vis du sexe fort ... elle se moquait des convenances ... L'amour pouvait-il être pour une 'garconne' comme elle autre chose qu'une performance physique?". Wallāda broke off her relationship with Ibn Zaydūn "pour rompre avec celui qui l'excédait"; and her verses, even more openly than her behaviour, proclaimed "la liberté qu'elle tenait à garder vis-à-vis du sexe fort".[4]

Let us consider some examples of Wallāda's verses, beginning with the poem that opens: *Anā wa 'Llāhi aṣluḥu li 'l-maʿālī*:[5]

> Worthy am I, by God, of the highest, and
> Proudly I walk, with head aloft.
> My cheek I give to my lover and, to those who wish them,
> I yield my kisses.

Challenging statements. Elsewhere she says:[6]

> Wait for my visit when darkness falls;
> night is the best concealer of secrets.
> Such passion I feel for you that, if they felt so,
> the sun would not shine, the moon not appear,
> the stars not move.

These are just a few samples of a poetry far from prudish. Nor was Wallāda the only case:[7] other, earlier women poets in al-Andalus had also frankly revealed their loves and spoken of them, like Mutʿa,[8] a slave of the poet Ziryāb, who came to al-Andalus from Baghdad in the 3rd/9th century. At a literary gathering she openly declared to *Amīr* 'Abd al-Raḥmān II (206/822-238/852) the passion she felt for him:

> Oh, you that hide your passion! Who can hide the day?
> I was owner of my heart, then love seized me and it fled away
> Was it mine, alas, or only borrowed? I love a Qura<u>sh</u>ī,
> and abandoned shame for his sake.

In the following century we have the case of Ḥafṣa of Guadalajara,[9] who shows no fear before her mother:

> I have a lover who does not bear my reproaches.
> If I leave him he says with with disdain:
> "Do you know one to compare with me?" And I say:
> "Do you know one who resembles me?"

On a similar occasion, Uns al-Qulūb, a slave of al-Manṣūr, suddenly revealed her love for Abū 'l-Mu<u>gh</u>īra b. Ḥazm, who was among those present:[10]

> Companions, wonder at an antelope, which, when close to me, is unjust
> to my love.
> Oh! if I could beat a path to him, and with his love fulfil my desires!

And in the same (5th/11th) century as Wallāda another princess, Umm al-Kirām, the daughter of al-Mu'taṣim, Petty King of Almería (443/1051-484/1091), sang of her love for a *fatā*, who will have been a servant in the palace:[11]

> Such is my love for him, if he left me,
> my heart would run after him.

And she says frankly:[12]

> Oh to be alone with him! The guardians' vigilance thwarts me.
> A wonder it is! I yearn to be alone with one already within my breast.

In the 6th/12th century the libertine poet (*mājina*) Nazhūn, moving easily and as a peer[13] in a circle of other poets of the kind, such as Ibn Quzmān, al-Kutandī and al-Ma<u>kh</u>zūmī, declared:

> I paid a poem with another: tell me, by my soul, who is the better poet?
> If woman be my nature, man is my poetry.

Not only was she conscious of her poetry's worth, but also used it to proclaim her love:[14]

> Precious are nights! How good they are!
> And the best is the night of Sunday!
> Had you been with us, when the eyes of the guardian closed,
> You would have seen the rising sun in the arms of the moon,
> Or <u>Kh</u>āzima's gazelle in the arms of a lion.

Such expressions of love are by no means unique. Let us take three more examples from the 6th/12th century. First, Qasmūna, from a cultured Jewish family:[15]

> I see a garden with ripe fruit; yet the gardener, it seems,
> will not stretch out his hands to it.
> How pitiful!, youth fleets by and is lost, and something I will not name remains lonely.

Then Ḥafṣa al-Rakūniyya, the most noteworthy Andalusī woman poet, who came from a rich noble family of Granada:[16]

> I praise that mouth, and, upon my word, I know what I say .
> I do it justice, I would not lie before God; it is sweeter than wine to the taste.

In another poem, she asks her beloved Abū Jaʿfar b. Saʿīd (d.560/1163):[17]

> Will you come to me or I to you? My heart will go where you wish.
> You will not thirst if you ask me to come, nor will the sun burn you .
> My lips are a clear, sweet spring; the branches of my hair cast deep shadow.
> Answer me at once; it is not just, oh Jamīl, to keep your Buthayna waiting!

Finally Zaynab of Almería, probably as late as the 7th/13th century:[18]

> Oh you who ride so fast, stop and hear how I suffer!
> No one, of all the others, has suffered such passion as I.
> I am content to see him happy;
> for his love and joy I will strive to the end of time.

II. *Proof of emancipation?*

As pointed out above, when considering Hoernerbach's remarks,[19] some experts regard the poetry of Andalusī women as evidence of the very high —and very unusual—level of freedom the women of the country enjoyed. Shack, in the 19th century, noted: "The position of women in Spain was freer than in other Muslim countries. Women took part in all the intellectual and cultural events of their time, and the number of those winning fame for their scientific works, or by their contending with men for the palm of poetry, was not small".[20]

20th-century critics have continued to follow this line. According to Henri Pérès: "... Andalusī women were not the prisoners Islamic rules would have us see in all Muslims ... the clearest example of female freedom in all Muslim Spain is that of Wallāda ... Her self-confident look, her disdain for the veil, her daring conversation and her sometimes eccentric attitudes show clearly that she had become free of many prejudices. She came under attack, naturally, but the very fact that she was allowed to lead such a life implies that Islam, so strict and rigid with regard to women, had singularly relaxed its rigour throughout al-Andalus, and we are compelled to admit that a more liberal concept of women's condition sprang from the atmosphere created by Christian customs. The level of female emancipation becomes still clearer when we add to the portrait of the "liberated woman", as seen in Wallāda, another portrait, that of the slave of male appearance (*ghulāmiyya*), already known in the East, but acquiring distinct features in al-Andalus."[21]

According to Shawqī Ḍayf: "If we read what is related of Wallāda's life in the *Dhakhīra* and in the *Nafḥ al-ṭīb*,, and note also what the *Nafḥ al-ṭīb* has to tell us about other noble women in al-Andalus, we will see that women in Andalusī literature played a similar role, in some respects, to that played by women in French literature in the 17th and 18th centuries."[22]

Finally, Mahmud Sobh notes: "The freedom Andalusī women enjoyed, not only in the expression of their feelings and opinions, but in the fulfilment of their wishes in matters of love, arouses simultaneous admiration and surprise. This was, I think, the result of Muslims and Christians living together in al-Andalus, in a relation different from that existing in other Arab countries, both with regard to mixture of lineage, and to culture, and to ways of natural behaviour. Does it not seem strange that, in Abbasid times, with their similarly rich difference in cultures and races, there were no female poets possessing the freedom of Andalusī women?". Dr. Sobh notes, in this connection, the comparative lack of sociological studies on the subject of al-Andalus,[23]

Re-examining the whole matter from such a sociological viewpoint, Pierre Guichard[24] begins by noting how these two aspects—the "freedom" of women and the original way in which women expressed their feelings of love—are used as basic arguments by those propounding the idea of "Occidentalism" in Andalusī society, but also notes how they conflict with the importance assumed by "Eastern" structures in Andalusī society—a contradiction he solved by pointing out "la dualité du milieu feminin qui caracterise la civilisation du Moyen Age musulman".[25] In this environment, he says, free women acted according to all the various requirements of Islamic family structures, while, on the other hand, slaves, singers and dancers "sont en effect au centre de la vie andalouse de la fin du 10e et du 11e siècle". After examining a number of literary references, especially Ibn Ḥazm's *Ring of the Dove*, he concludes: "les femmes libres ... sont, normalement, matériellement and moralement recluses; et les quelques exemples contradictoires que l'on peut invoquer à l'appui de cette assertion sont assez peu convaincants". He also mentions a very significant statement, made in a rather interesting overall context, by the Cordoban philosopher Ibn Rushd (d. 595/1198): "The competence of women is unknown, however, in these cities since they are only taken [in them] for procreation and hence are placed at the service of their husbands and confined to procreation, upbringing, and suckling. This nullifies their [other] activities. Since women in these cities are not prepared with respect to any of the human virtues, they frequently resemble plants in these cities. Their being a burden upon the men [in these cities is one of the causes of poverty of these cities. This is because they are to be found there in double the number of men, while not understanding through [their] upbringing any of the necessary actions except for the few actions —like the art of spinning and weaving—that they undertake mostly at a time when they have need of them to make up for their lack of spending [power]".[26] For Guichard, then, Andalusī civilisation does not extend far beyond its Eastern roots.

M.J. Rubiera, reviewing the question of women's poetry and social position in al-Andalus in the introduction to his book *Poesía femenina hispano-árabe,* mentioned above,[27] portrays domestic reclusion as being widespread for women of the upper social class; such women could only escape from their enclosed situation if they had no family patrimony, since then they had, to the best of their ability, to play their part in the working world as slaves did; there were "working" slaves just as there were "slaves for pleasure", and these were "the only women who had access to the gatherings where poetry was created and spread", being able, as such, to enjoy freedom of movement and feeling.[28]

With the aid of these various contributions, the true facts concerning women's poetry in al-Andalus can now, I think, be inferred; and it is clear, in the light of the remarks made by Guichard and Rubiera, that these facts do not admit the existence of genuine freedom for women in the country. The whole matter has not just interesting literary and historiographical implications, but historical, social, cultural and economic ones, which should be considered in the context of more wide-ranging studies about the position of women in al-Andalus. What follows is a brief attempt to set the subject within such a framework.

III. *Sources of information regarding women in al-Andalus*

Let us now supplement the poems quoted at the beginning of this article by considering more general sources of information relating to women in al-Andalus. What becomes immediately clear is that Andalusī sources refer, as a rule, to the central individuals within society, in other words, to men, with women appearing merely in connection with men, as either their relatives or their servants. These sources tend, moreover, to deal with women who undertake some kind of religious, intellectual or artistic activity,[29] although it should be pointed out, in this connection, that all the sources we know are the work of men (except for the verses of female poets, and such verses were in any case composed by men as well). The near total lack of directly relevant records deprives us of possibly essential sources, but we do, on the other hand, have many and varied written texts—chronicles, or works of a geographical, legal, bibliographical, artistic, scientific or technical kind—within which patient and systematic research may well yield interesting results.

The most useful among these, for our purpose, are legal texts—not simply theoretical legal sources, but, much more importantly, the factual ones: compilations of judicial decisions, of notarial deeds, and of all sorts of legal instances and behavioural patterns[30] which permit a more complete view of social reality because they set ideal norms of behaviour against actual facts. A systematic exploitation of such sources will notably increase our knowledge of Andalusī society, although much work still remains to be done before we can publish and analyse the huge amount of relevant material, even if we limit our reference to al-Andalus or the medieval Maghrib.[31]

Literature too—the particular case of Andalusī women's poetry has already been pointed out—can offer telling insights into the condition of women. The creative works in question may, indeed, be tinged by the author's particular mood and moulded into a certain aesthetic shape, may be conceived with the aim of instruction or amusement and be subject to cliché and fashion; nevertheless, they are, finally, a rich source of information about women. Among works in prose we may consider the miscellaneous genre of *adab*, collections of anecdotes and tales of belles lettres and good manners; we have, for example, the first Andalusī encyclopedia, *Al-ʿIqd al-farīd* of Ibn ʿAbd Rabbihī (d. Córdoba, 328/940), whose 21st book is dedicated to women, and, in later centuries, the *Bahjat al-majālis* of Ibn ʿAbd al-Barr al-Qurṭubī (d. Játiva, 463/1070), who devoted many chapters to women (*bāb maʿnā ʿishq al-nisāʾ* ; *bāb fī waṣf al-nisāʾ bi ʾl-ḥusn wa ʾl-riqqa* ; *bāb al-amthāl al-sāʾira fī ʾl-nisāʾ*, and so on), and we also have other Andalusī books of *adab*, such as the late *Kitāb alif bāʾ* of Yūsuf b. al-Shaykh al-Mālaqī.[32] These works all comprise almost exclusively arabo-oriental material; nevertheless their employment in al-Andalus is also proof of a generalised Andalusī-oriental literary mentality about women, with the extreme contrasted topics of misogyny and feminine idealisation clearly present.

The genre of *maqāma*s and *risāla*s, also cultivated in al-Andalus, supplies further data, sometimes more realistic than that found in books of *adab* —with respect to slaves, for instance. We may consider, on this latter subject, the *risāla* of the Andalusī writer Abū Bakr al-Rundī describing his visit to a slave market (*sūq al-raqīq*) in an Andalusī city, probably in the 7th/13th century: he finds a very beautiful female slave, who is described meticulously and with great sorrow (he was outbid in the auction). We also have the consolatory *risāla* of his friend Ibn Yazīd, which concerns further interesting references to the social status of slaves and to male attitudes towards them.[33]

Some of the 8th/14th century prose texts of the Naṣrid vizier and polymath Ibn al-Khaṭīb provide a realistic picture of Andalusī women, who, in Granada, "go to extremes in adornment and colourful clothing, competing so much in the use of embroideries and brocades, and in the ostentation of their various garments, that it becomes licentious". He also refers to women's abandonment of the veil in some Naṣrid cities, provoking discussion among modern scholars on how exactly the reference should be interpreted.[34]

Collections of proverbs[35] and of tales[36] should also be considered, though we must be careful here to distinguish between local and universal elements. We have, for example, the rich collections of Andalusī proverbs made by al-Zajjālī al-Qurṭubī, in the 7th/13th century,[37] where we find a direct portrayal of Andalusī women: the free woman, for example, who does almost no work (proverb 856: *ḥurra mukarrashat al-zayf*, "a free woman with her dress tucked up"!), or the same free woman benefiting from an exclusive social prestige (proverb 193: *lā tabqā 'l-dunyā bi-lā walad ḥurra,* "no world without a free woman's son"), or the problems of unmarried daughters (proverb 1965: *wayyā ʿalā man māt wa-khallā sabʿ banāt,* "woe to the one who dies leaving seven daughters"), or ridicule of unmarried women (proverb 1710: *ʿAzbat Bayyāna rāt qūl al-rajul wa-qālat: ish dhāk al-kināna!?*, "the unmarried woman of Baena, seeing the organ of a man, asked: What is that cartridge belt?"), or the possibility of sexual relations before marriage, with virginity nevertheless preserved (proverb 582: *būs wa-uqruṣ wa-khallī mawḍiʿ al-ʿarūs*, "kiss and pinch, but preserve the place [of virginity] of the bride"). There is certainly no lack of references—but further systematic analysis is necessary. Much work remains to be done with respect to all these various sources, notably in connection with the large number of legal documents still unexamined; there are, too, other sources—historical chronicles, bibliographical compilations, etc.—which have not yet been completely, or sufficiently, classified or evaluated in this particular connection.

IV. *General considerations*

Women in al-Andalus were differentiated according to their ethnic origins, religion, economic class and politico-economic level: we have, specifically, Arab women, Berber women, indigenous women, Muslim women, Mozarab women, Jewish women, upper-class women (*khāṣṣa*s) or common women (*ʿāmma*s), city women or country women, etc.—all aspects on which information needs to be gathered and classified.[38] Literary sources, in fact, occupy themselves almost exclusively with Arabo-Muslim women of the upper-class (*khāṣṣa*s), or with those connected with them in some way; information on other women is scarce, and is generally found only in very special circumstances, as in the case of Mozarab women martyrs.[39]

We must also consider that community values transcended all others in medieval Islam, and that representation of the community, in political, religious, economic and family matters, was, by explicit Islamic regulation,[40] the business of men, not women—this being based on the old concept of their "superiority". Thus, among the six natural qualities which must be possessed by an *imām*, the head of the political religious community, we find the condition that he must be a male (*dhukūriyya*), so that, as al-Ghazālī[41] pointed out, "women, weak beings by nature" remained barred from that function. As Abdel Majid Turki[42] notes (when drawing our attention to the exception represented by the 5th/11th century Cordoban polymath Ibn Ḥazm), this weakness was regularly brought up by medieval Muslim thinkers.

Women's role within Medieval Islam was in fact confined to the family environment, family lying, of course, at the heart of society and being, as Cahen notes, "ruled by men".[43] The traditional Andalusī family was essentially patriarchal, or, more precisely, agnatic,[44] but it should be noted that recent studies present a less monolithic view of the Islamic family structure in general and of the Andalusī family, in particular;[45] possible modifications and changes in this respect should be viewed in the light of scattered but representative data—as, for instance, that found in the *Iḥāṭa* of Ibn al-Khaṭīb, which, as far back as the 7th/13th century at the very least, indicates a wish for monogamy of the kind expressed by the wife of the *amīr* Ibn Hūd, who rebelled against the Almohads in al-Andalus, and who, "as some people mentioned, had promised his wife not to take any other wife in his lifetime, but, as soon as he was in power, he fell in love with a Christian woman, who had responded to him among the captives ..."[46] An analysis of family structures is essential for determining the position of women, and these can be established from legal documents, especially from the rich collections of Andalusī *fatwa*s which provide wide-ranging evidence concerning marriages, divorces and economic aspects.[47]

V. *The "best-known" Andalusī women*

Concrete information about the position and activities of Andalusī women becomes greater in proportion to their connection with men of social relevance; we hear, therefore, of women belonging to the families of kings or distinguished men, of women who were their servants (including slaves), and of those women figuring, in however restricted a fashion, in intellectual and/or artistic activities.

Women of the Court[48] are mentioned in Chronicles in connection with various distinguished persons; we know, by name at least, wives, concubines, mothers, daughters, and sometimes, grandmothers, grand-daughters and sisters of Umayyads in Córdoba, petty *ṭā'ifa* rulers, Almoravids, Almohads and Naṣrids.[49] Thus Ibn Ḥazm, for instance, in his *Naqṭ al-ʿarūs fī tawārīkh al-khulafā'*,[50] merely mentions "women who were related to caliphs", "those who were the mothers of two caliphs", "the mothers of two presumptive heirs", "the mother of a caliph, remarried after his son's caliphate", "extraordinary cases or royal marriages". True to his logic, he does not even mention the name of a Ḥammūdī princess, "the daughter of Idrīs b. ʿAlī married to Ḥasan b. Yaḥyā b. ʿAlī b. Ḥammūd, the sister of Muḥammad b. Idrīs ...", even though this lady was the main character in a family revenge—"when another of her brothers, Yaḥyā b. Idrīs, known as 'Ḥayyūh', was killed by her husband [Ḥasan], she killed her husband by poisoning him. This lady had seen her father [Idrīs, as Caliph of Málaga], her grandfather [ʿAlī b. Ḥammūd, as Caliph of Córdoba], her brother [Muḥammad, as Caliph of Málaga] and her husband [Ḥasan, also as Caliph of Málaga], all of them caliphs."[51] Chronicles also make mention of other upper-class women, both in the state capital and in different regions.[52]

As a rule we know very little of them beyond their names unless some "extraordinary" circumstance attaches to them: if, for example, one of these Court women played a leading part in crucial events on the political scene, perhaps through significant influence over her husband's actions, as was the case of Iʿtimād with the king of Seville, al-Muʿtamid, whom she "dominated", according to Ibn al-Abbār; enumerating al-Muʿtamid's more illustrious sons, the latter concludes that all these were sons "of his slave (*jāriya*) Iʿtimād, his favourite and the woman with all ascendancy over him (*al-ghāliba ʿalay-hi*) ... she was formerly named "Rumaykiyya" by her owner Rumayk b. Ḥajjāj, from whom al-Muʿtamid acquired her ... and he, in exaggerated affection for her, adopted the title of "al-Muʿtamid" in order to adjust his name to the letters of her name. She induced him to kill Ibn ʿAmmār for his censorious verses".[53] We also find the case of al-Mustakfī, Caliph of Córdoba, who, according to Ibn Ḥayyān, was criticised because he "consented to be ruled by a depraved woman" named Bint al-Marwaziyya —this domination being all we know of her.[54] Alternatively, we may hear of the outstanding influence of some king's mother, as in the case of the petty king of Granada, ʿAbd Allāh, whose mother was omnipresent, notably in the final episode of the sovereign's overthrow by the Almoravids; when the Almoravid *amīr* asked ʿAbd Allāh for all his possessions, the latter replied: "... 'if the *amīr* will let me go in person to the palace, I will bring him everything. Otherwise, my mother can do this together with a number of his trusted followers, so that he will not lose a single thread'. On leaving, I was so apprehensive of being arrested that I was afraid I should be parted from my mother if I left her in the palace. I therefore left together with her, and paid no attention to anything else".[55] According to Rachel Arié, the activities of some Naṣrid princesses were also very notorious:

> En dehors des dons de l'esprit, les femmes acquéraient du prestige dans l'appareil social grâce à l'influence qu'elles exercaient dans leur milieu familial, lorsqu'elles occupaient le rang d'épouse favorite du sultan ou de concubine choyée entre toutes. On se rappelle la conspiration ourdie par la mère d'Ismāʿīl, Maryam, qui avait été la concubine préférée de Yūsuf I, en 760/1359, contre le souverain légitime Muḥammad V. Non moins important fut le rôle que joua Fāṭima, épouse légitime d'Abū 'l-Ḥasan ʿAlī et mère de Boabdil, pour obtenir la libération de son fils, après la défaite de Lucena.[56]

However, such participation in political events, being counter to the Law which removed women from politics, was usually censured and labelled as "court intrigue"—the standard term for any political activity undertaken by women.

Court women were expected to limit themselves to a decorative or strategic role within the entourage of the king or other important person in question, officially accompanying him in wars[57] or at celebrations,[58] and doing so in an ostentatious way, since luxury—as Ibn Khaldūn observed—"increases the strength of a dynasty".[59] These women had property,[60] which they sometimes used to endow public foundations,[61] thereby contributing to the future prestige of their family; this underlying political aim being, again, noted by Ibn Khaldūn.[62]

Andalusī chronicles also occasionally mention the servants and slaves who supplemented the domestic surrounding of important persons, and more data about slaves is available from legal and medical sources.[63] Andalusī Kings often married slaves,[64] with the result that history has at least preserved their names, which usually give some indication of the ornamental and pleasing role they played: for example, Laymā ("Sweet lime"), Raḍiyya ("Delight"), Shams ("Sun") or Murjān ("Coral").[65] The number of servants and slaves was a symbolic indication of power and wealth: there were in fact 6,314 women in Madīnat al-Zahrā', including wives, concubines, relations and servants. Slaves fall into two categories, being devoted either to serving (*jawārī 'l-khadam*) or to pleasure (*jawārī 'l-ladhdha*).[66] As refined and highly cultivated[67] hetairas, they took part in literary gatherings[68] and served their masters, who usually demonstrated an outstanding predilection for them—there are numerous references to the way *ṭā'ifa* kings competed in acquiring the most and the best slave singers.[69] They also accompanied their masters in adversity: when Ibn 'Abd al-Jabbār, for example, fled his home and was subsequently pursued in Córdoba, he kept thirteen slaves (*jawārī*) at his side until they were finally taken from him and brought to the new caliph.[70]

Bio-bibliographical compilations—a more specific kind of source material—and also literary anthologies refer to women who have carried out intellectual and/or artistic activities; these sources have been skilfully exploited in recent scholarly work.[71] 116 well-educated Andalusī women are recorded in bio-bibliographical dictionaries between the 2nd/8th and 8th/14th centuries, of whom just two are designated as "scholars" (*'ālima*)—the *faqīha* Fāṭima 'l-Maghāmī and Ḥafṣa bint Ḥamdūn—and three distinguished as cultivators of knowledge (*'ilm*), while others are merely included by virtue of their connection with some outstanding family. Their principal activity is poetry (44 cases), while 22 are literary persons (*adība*), 11 secretaries (*kātiba*), 4 copyists, 3 lexicographers and 2 grammarians; 16 know or read the Quran, 6 have devoted themselves to Tradition (*ḥadīth*) and 8 to asceticism; 6 know jurisprudence (*fiqh*), 4 history (*tā'rīkh* / *akhbār*), 1 arithmetic (*ḥisāb*), 1 scholastic theology (*kalām*) and 1 the law of descent (*farā'iḍ*), together with many of her father's *fatwas*). One woman, the wife of a *qāḍī* of Loja (Granada) in perhaps the 8th/14th century, was outstanding for her juridical knowledge—according to Ibn al-Khaṭīb she knew juridical sources better than her husband;[72] others had medical knowledge,[73] and even practised medicine, though only, as legal documents show, with women patients.[74] Further examination of such documents, which still remain largely unexploited, would permit a clearer view of the reality of Andalusī women's social position, far beyond the "taboos laid on women in traditional Arab society",[75] which at present, no doubt, form a barrier between our knowledge and that reality.

1 Three recent books have appeared on the subject: Mahmud Sobh, *Poetisas arábigo-andaluzas*, Granada, 1985; Teresa Garulo, *Diwan de las poetisas de al-Andalus*, Madrid, 1986; María Jesús Rubiera Mata, *Poesía femenina hispanoárabe*, Madrid, 1989. See also: J. M. Nichols, "Arabic women poets in al-Andalus", *Maghreb Review*, 4, Sept.-Dec. 1981, pp. 85-88; 'Abd al-Kareem al-Heitty, "The collection and criticism of the work of early Arab women singers and poetesses", *Al-Masāq*, 2 ,1989, pp. 43-47.

2 "Notas para una caracterización de Wallāda", *Al-Andalus*, 36, 1971, pp. 467-73; "Zur Charakteristik Wallādas der Geliebten Ibn Zaidūn", *Die Welt des Islams*, 13, 1971, pp. 20-25.

3 A. F. von Schack, *Poesie und Kunst der Araber in Spanien und Sizilien*, Spanish trans. by J. Valera, *Poesía y arte de los árabes en España y Sicilia*, reprint Madrid, 1988, p. 300.

4 Quoted in Henri Pérès, *La poésie andalouse en arabe classique au XIe siècle*, 2nd ed., Paris, 1953; Spanish trans. by M. García-Arenal, *Esplendor de al-Andalus. La poesía andaluza en árabe clásico en el siglo XI*, Madrid, 1983, II, 249, n.3.

5 Al-Maqqarī, *Nafḥ al-ṭīb fī g͟huṣn al-Andalus al-raṭīb*, ed. I. 'Abbās, Beirut, 1968, IV, 205; Sobh, *op. cit.*, pp. 40-57; Garulo, *op. cit.*, pp. 141-46; Rubiera Mata, *op. cit.*, pp. 101-05.

6 *Nafḥ al-ṭīb*, IV, 206.

7 Also J. M. Nichols, "Wallāda, the Andalusian lyric and the questions of influence", *Literature East and West*, 21, 1977, pp. 286-91.

8 *Nafḥ al-ṭīb*,, III, 131; Garulo, *op. cit.*, pp. 108-09.

9 *Nafḥ al-ṭīb*,, IV, 285-86; Ibn Sa'īd, *Al-Mug͟hrib fī ḥulā 'l-Mag͟hrib*, ed. S͟hawqī Ḍayf, 2nd. ed., Cairo, 1955, II, 37-38; Sobh, *op. cit.*, pp. 20-27; Garulo, *op. cit.*, pp. 69-70; Rubiera Mata, *op. cit.*, pp. 81-84.

10 *Nafḥ al-ṭīb*, I, 616-18; Garulo, *op. cit.*, pp. 138-40.

11 *Nafḥ al-ṭīb*,, IV, 170; Sobh, *op. cit.*, pp. 66-71; Garulo, *op. cit.*, pp. 133-34; Rubiera Mata, *op. cit.*, pp. 115-17.

12 *Al-Mug͟hrib*, II, 202-03.

13 *Nafḥ al-ṭīb*,, I, 192-93; Sobh, *op. cit.*, pp. 78-93; Garulo, *op. cit.*, pp. 110-18; Rubiera Mata, *op. cit.*, pp.127-29.

14 *Nafḥ al-ṭīb*,, IV, 298.

15 *Nafḥ al-ṭīb*,, III, 530; Sobh, *op. cit.*, pp. 124-47; Garulo, *op. cit.*, pp. 121-23; Rubiera Mata, *op. cit.*, pp. 149-51; J. M. Nichols, "The Arabic verses of Qasmūna bint Ismā'īl ibn Bagdāla", *IJMES*, 13, 1981, pp. 155-58.

16 *Nafḥ al-ṭīb*, IV, 171-78; L. di Giacomo, "Une poétesse andalouse du temps des Almohades: Ḥafṣa bint al-Ḥājj ar-Rakūniyya", *Hespéris*, 34, 1947, pp. 9-101; Sobh, *op. cit.*, pp. 94-115; Garulo, *op. cit.*, pp. 71-85; Rubiera Mata, *op. cit.*, pp. 139-47.

17 *Nafḥ al-ṭīb*,, IV, 178; W. Hoenerbach, "Los Banū Sa'īd de Alcalá la Real y sus allegados: Su poesía según la antología *al-Mugrib*", *Revista del Centro de Estudios Históricos de Granada y su Reino*, 2, 1989, pp. 81-102; "Die andalus-arabische Dichtung im Allgemeinen und die Dichtung der Banū Sa'īd im Besonderen", *Zeitschrift der Deutschen Morgenländischen Gesellschaft*, 140, 1990, pp. 260-89.

18 *Nafḥ al-ṭīb*,, IV, 286; Sobh, *op. cit.*, pp. 116-19; Garulo, *op. cit.*, p. 149; Rubiera Mata, *op. cit.*, pp. 157-59.

19 See above, n. 2.

20 *Poesie und Kunst*, p. 65.

21 *La poésie andalouse*, pp. 400-02.

22 *Al-Fann wa-mad͟hāhibu-hū fi 'l-s͟hi'r al-'Arabī*, Cairo, 1965, p. 440.

[23] Sobh, *op. cit.*, p. 136; see also his "La poesía amorosa arábigo-andaluza", *Revista del Instituto (Egipcio) de Estudios Islámicos en Madrid*, 16, 1971, pp. 71-109.

[24] *Structures sociales "orientales" et "occidentales" dans l'Espagne musulmane*, Paris, 1977: "condition féminine et sentiments amoureux en al-Andalus", pp. 164-74.

[25] *Structures*, p. 166.

[26] *Averroes on Plato's "Republic"*, trans. with an introduction by R. Lerner, Cornell University Press, 1974, p. 59.

[27] *Op. cit.*, p. 7.

[28] *Ibid.*, p. 14.

[29] As defined later, in the section entitled "The "best-known" Andalusī women".

[30] M. J. Viguera, "La censura de costumbres en el "Tanbīh al-Ḥukkām" de Ibn al-Munāṣif", *Actas II Jornadas de Cultura Árabe e Islámica*, Madrid, 1985, pp. 591-611.

[31] See the significant references in Emilio Molina, "Preliminar" to the reprint of Jacinto Bosch, *Los almorávides*, Granada, 1990, pp. LXII-LXIV.

[32] M. J. Viguera, "Preliminar" to *La mujer en al-Andalus. Reflejos históricos de su actividad y categorías sociales*, Madrid-Seville, 1989, pp. 28-29.

[33] F. de la Granja, "La venta de la esclava en el mercado en la obra de Abū l-Baqā' de Ronda", in *Maqamas y risalas andaluzas*, Madrid, 1976, pp. 139-71.

[34] W. Hoenerbach, "La granadina", *Andalucía Islámica. Textos y Estudios*, II-III, 1981-1982, pp. 9-31; J. Bosch Vila and W. Hoenerbach, "Un viaje oficial de la corte granadina. (Año 1347)", *ibid.*, p. 41, n. 27.

[35] M. Ben Sharīfa, *Amthāl al-ʿawām fī 'l-Andalus. Proverbes andalous de Abū Yaḥyā 'l-Zajjālī, 1220-1294*, Fez, 1975, I, 242.

[36] See Nadia Lachiri's doctoral dissertation on "Literary sources concerning Andalusī women" at the Complutense University, Madrid, under the supervision of Dr. del Moral and Dr. Viguera. In contrast see, for example: H. Zotenberg, "L'histoire de Galʿād et Schimas", *Journal Asiatique*, 1896, pp. 25-31; A. Llinarès, "Deux versions mediévales espagnoles de la laitère et le pot au lait", *Revue de Littérature Comparée*, 33, 1959, pp. 230-34. Or the transfer of a subject, as in the literary fiction about "the Moorish woman of Antequera": F. López Estrada, "La leyenda de la morica garrida de Antequera en la poesía y en la Historia", *Archivo Hispalense*, 88-89, 1958, pp. 141-231; S.G. Armistead and J.T. Monroe, "A new version of *La morica de Antequera*", *La Corónica*, 12, 1984, pp. 228-40.

[37] See the work by al-Zajjālī mentioned above (n. 33), I, 242 and II, proverbs 856, 193, 1965, 1710, 582.

[38] On *khāṣṣa* /*ʿāmma* perspectives, see: Manuela Marín, "Las mujeres de las clases sociales superiores", in Viguera (ed.), *La mujer en al-Andalus*, pp. 105-27; Aḥmad al-Ṭāhirī, *ʿĀmmat Qurṭuba fī ʿaṣr al-khilāfa*, Rabat, 1971.

[39] K.B. Wolf, *Christian Martyrs in Muslim Spain*, Cambridge, 1988; Gloria López de la Plaza, *Ámbitos de la religiosidad femenina andalusí: la dinámica público-privado y sus correlaciones sociales*, Magister Dissertation, under the supervision of Dr. C. Segura, Complutense University, Madrid, 1990.

[40] 'Abdul Raḥmān I. Doy, *Woman in Shariʿah (Islamic Law)*, London, 1989.

[41] E. Laoust, *La politique de Gazālī*, Paris, 1970, p. 314.

[42] "Femmes privilégiées et privilèges féminins dans le système théologique et juridique d'Ibn Ḥazm", in *Théologiens et juristes de l'Espagne musulmane. Aspects polémiques*, Paris, 1982, pp. 101-58.

[43] *El Islam.I. Desde los orígenes hasta el cominzo del imperio otomano*, Spanish trans., Madrid, 1972, pp. 122-23.

[44] Viguera, "Preliminar" to *La mujer en al-Andalus*, pp. 25-26, n. 56, 56 and 57.

[45] Zuhayr Khaṭīb, *Taṭawwur binā' al-usra 'l-ʿArabiyya*, 3th. ed., Beirut, 1983; Angela Degand, *Geschlechterrollen und familiale Strukturen im Islam*, Frankfurt am Main, 1988; Pierre Guichard, "De la Antigüedad a la Edad Media: familia amplia y familia estricta", *Estudios sobre Historia Medieval*, Valencia, 1987, pp. 7-25; M.T. Bianquis, "La familia en el islam árabe", *Historia de la familia*, dir. A. Burguière and others, Spanish transl., Madrid, 1988, pp. 583-631. A complementary view may be obtained from the study of families notorious in the aristocratic or cultural sphere: on this subject, see Luis Molina, "Familias Andalusíes: los datos del Ta'rij 'ulamā' al-Andalus de Ibn al-Faraḍi", *Estudios Onomástico-Biográficos de al-Anda-*

lus, II, ed. M. L. Avila, Granada, 1989, p. 19, n. 1. On another crucial perspective, see: *Hériter en pays musulman. Habus, lait vivant, manyahuli*, dir. by M. Gast, Paris, 1987.

46 *Al-Iḥāṭa fī akhbār Gharnāṭa*, ed. 'A. A. 'Inān, Cairo, II, 1974, p. 132.

47 Amalia Zomeño is at present preparing a doctoral dissertation on the subject of Andalusī *fatwas* at the Complutense University, Madrid, under the supervision of Dr. Viguera. H. R. Idris has opened the way, with a number of articles on the subject: see, for example, "Le mariage en Occident musulman. Analyse de *fatwas* médiévales extraites du *Mi'yār* d'al-Wanšarīšī", *Revue de l'Occident musulman*, 12, 1972, pp. 45-62.

48 See above, n. 37.

49 Viguera, "Preliminar" to *La mujer en al-Andalus*, pp. 30-31, n. 80-84.

50 *Rasā'il Ibn Ḥazm*, ed. I. 'Abbās, Beirut, 1981, II, 43-116, especially pp. 65-67.

51 *Ibid.*, p. 67.

52 On Banū Qasī women, on the northern frontier, see: M. J. Viguera, *Aragón musulmán*, 2nd. ed., Saragossa, 1988, pp. 84 and 94.

53 *Al-Ḥulla al-siyarā'*, ed. H. Mu'nis, Cairo, 1963, II, 62.

54 *Apud* Ibn 'Idhārī, *Al-Bayān al-mughrib*, ed. E. Lévi-Provençal, Paris, 1930, III, 141.

55 G. Martínez Gros, "Femmes et pouvoir dans les Mémoires d' 'Abd Allāh", *La condición de la mujer en la Edad Media*, Coloquio Hispano-Francés, Casa de Velázquez, Madrid, 1984; A.T. Ṭibi, *The Tibyān, Memoirs of 'Abd Allāh b. Buluggīn, last Zīrid amīr of Granada*, Leiden, 1986, p. 156.

56 Rachel Arié, *L'Espagne musulmane au temps des Nasrides*, Paris, 1973 (2nd. ed., 1990), pp. 148-57, and 368.

57 Seventy women accompanied the *ḥājib* Sanchuelo in a military campaign (Ibn 'Idhārī, *Bayān*, III, 72).

58 Viguera, "Preliminar" to *La mujer en al-Andalus*, p. 31, n. 93.

59 *Al-Muqaddima*, French trans. by V. Monteil, Beirut, 1968, p. 341.

60 Joaquina Albarracín, "Un documento granadino sobre los bienes de la mujer de Boabdil en Mondújar", *Actas I Congreso Historia de Andalucía*, 2nd ed., Córdoba, 1982, pp. 341-42.

61 R. Valencia, "Presencia de la mujer en la corte de al-Mu'tamid b.'Abbād de Sevilla", in Viguera (ed.), *La mujer en al-Andalus*, p. 136, n. 46; M. Marín, in *ibid.*, p. 112; Viguera, in *ibid.*, p. 32, n. 96.

62 *Muqaddima*, p. 345.

63 P. Coello, "Las actividades de las esclavas según Ibn Buṭlān y al-Saqaṭī de Málaga", in Viguera (ed.), *La mujer en al-Andalus*, pp. 201-10.

64 Some cases in Ibn 'Idhārī, *Bayān*, III, 140 and 145; Fatima Mernisi, *Sultanes oubliées. Femmes chefs d'Etat en Islam*, Paris-Casablanca, 1990, pp. 17-113: "sultanes et courtisanes".

65 Viguera, "Preliminar" to *La mujer en al-Andalus*, p. 32, n. 99-102; M. Marín, "Notas sobre onomástica y denominaciones femeninas en al-Andalus (siglos VIII-XI)", in *Homenaje al prof. Darío Cabanelas*, Granada, 1987, pp. 37-52.

66 Viguera, "Preliminar" to *La mujer en al-Andalus*, p. 32, n. 104.

67 *Ibid.*, n. 107. Ibn 'Idhārī, *Bayān*, III, 56, 92 and 142 refers to slaves in the 5th/11th century, and we can find also many references in Ibn Bassām, *Al-Dhakhīra fī maḥāsin ahl al-Jazīra*; these need classification for the purposes of coherent interpretation, as in S. 'Abd al-Wahhāb al-Furayḥ, *Al-Jawārī wa 'l-shi'r fī 'l-'aṣr al-'Abbāsī 'l-awwal*, Kuwait, 1981.

68 Rubiera, *op. cit.*, 14.

69 The king of Seville, al-Mu'taḍid, had numerous concubines and boasted of them (see Ibn Bassām, *Dhakhīra*, 2nd. section, Cairo, 1975, pp. 19-20).

70 Ibn 'Idhārī, *Bayān*, III, 92.

71 M. L. Avila, "Las mujeres 'sabias' en al-Andalus", in Viguera (ed.), *La mujer en al-Andalus*, pp. 139-84; R. Valencia, "Tres maestras sevillanas de la época del Califato Omeya", in *ibid.*, pp. 185-90; M. I. Fierro, "Mujeres hispano-árabes en tres repertorios biográficos. Ŷadwa, Ṣila y Bughya, s. X-XII", in *Las mujeres medievales y su ámbito jurídico*, Madrid, 1982, pp. 177-82. And some contributions to *Estudios Onomástico-Biográficos de al-Andalus*, I-IV, Madrid and Granada, 1988-1990; and I. Goldziher, "Women in the hadith literature", in *Muslim Studies*, ed. S. M. Stern, London, 1971, II, 366-68.

72 Al-Maqqarī, *Nafḥ al-ṭīb*,, IV, 294.

73 Ibn al-Khaṭīb, *Iḥāṭa*, I, 438-39.

[74] L. F. Aguirre de Cárcer, "Sobre el ejercicio de la medicina en al-Andalus: Una fetua de Ibn Sahl", *Anaquel de Estudios Arabes*, II, 1991.

[75] As observed by S.K. Jayyusi, "Two Types of Hero in Contemporary Arabic Literature", *Mundus Artium*, 10/1,1977, p. 46.

BIBLIOGRAPHY

Arabic texts

ʿAbd Allāh, *The Tibyān, Memoirs of ʿAbd Allāh b. Buluggīn, last Zīrid amīr of Granada*, translated, with notes by A. T. Ṭibi, Leiden, 1986.

Ibn al-Abbār, *Al-Ḥulla al-siyarāʾ*, ed Ḥ. Muʾnis, Cairo, 1963, 2 vols.

Ibn Bassām, *Al-Dhakhīra fī maḥāsin ahl al-Jazīra*, ed. I. ʿAbbās, Beirut, 1979.

Ibn Ḥazm, *Rasāʾil*, ed. I. ʿAbbās, Beirut, 1981.

Ibn ʿIdhārī, *Al-Bayān al-mughrib*, ed. E. Lévi-Provençal, Paris, 1930, Vol. III.

Ibn Khaldūn, *Al-Muqaddima*, French trans. by V. Monteil, Beirut, 1968.

Ibn al-Khaṭīb, *Al-Iḥāṭa fī akhbār Gharnāṭa*, ed. M. ʿA. A. ʿInān, Cairo, 1974, Vol. II.

Ibn Rushd, *Averroes on Plato's "Republic"*, trans. with introduction by R. Lerner, Cornell University Press, 1974.

Ibn Saʿīd, *Al-Mughrib fī ḥulā 'l-Maghrib*, ed. S. Ḍayf, 2nd ed., Cairo, 1955, Vol. II.

Al-Maqqarī, *Nafḥ al-ṭīb min ghuṣn al-Andalus al-raṭīb* ed. I. ʿAbbās, Beirut, 1968, 8 vols.

Al-Zajjālī, *Amthāl al-ʿawām fī 'l-Andalus*, ed. M. Bensharīfa, Fez, 1975, 2 vols.

Scholarly works

Albarracín, Joaquina, "Un documento granadino sobre los bienes de la mujer de Boabdil en Mondújar", *Actas I Congreso Historia de Andalucía*, 2nd ed., Córdoba, 1982.

Aguirre de Cárcer, Luisa F., "Sobre el ejercicio de la medicina en al-Andalus: Una fetua de Ibn Sahl", *Anaquel de Estudios Arabes*, II, 1991.

Arié, Rachel, *L'Espagne musulmane au temps des Nasrides*, Paris, 1973 (2nd ed. 1990).

Armistead, S. G., and James T. Monroe, "A new version of *La morica de Antequera*", *La Corónica*, 12, 1984, pp. 228-40.

Avila, María Luisa, "Las mujeres 'sabias' en al-Andalus", in Viguera (ed.), *La mujer en al-Andalus*, pp. 139-84.

Bianquis, M. T., "La familia en el Islam árabe", in *Historia de la familia*, directed A. Burguière and others, Spanish trans., Madrid, 1988, pp. 583-631.

Bosch, Jacinto, *Los almorávides*, 2nd ed. by E. Molina, Granada, 1990.

Bosch, Jacinto, and Wilhelm Hoenerbach, "Un viaje oficial de la corte granadina. (Año 1347)", *Andalucía islámica*, 2-3, 1981-82, pp. 9-31.

Cahen, Claude, *El Islam. I: Desde los orígines hasta el comienzo del imperio otomano* (Spanish trans.), Madrid, 1972.

Coello, Pilar, "Las actividades de las esclavas según Ibn Butlan y al-Saqati de Málaga", in Viguera (ed.), *La mujer en al-Andalus*, pp. 201-10.

Ḍayf, Shawqī, *Al-Fann wa-madhāhibu-hu fī 'l-shiʿr al-ʿArabī*, Cairo, 1965.

Degand, Angela, *Geschlechterrollen und familiale Strukturen in Islam*, Frankfurt-am-Main, 1988.

Doy, ʿAbdul Rahman I., *Woman in Shariʿah*, London, 1989.

Fierro, María Isabel, "Mujeres hispano-árabes en tres repertorios biográficos. *Ŷadwa, Ṣila* y *Bugya*,s X-XII", in *Las mujeres medievales y su ámbito jurídico*, Madrid, 1982, pp. 177-82.

Al-Furayḥ, S. ʿAbd al-Wahhāb, *Al-Jawārī wa 'l-shiʿr fī 'l-ʿaṣr al-ʿabbāsī 'l-awwal*, Kuwait, 1981.

Garulo, Teresa, *Diwan de las poetisas de al-Andalus*, Madrid, 1986.

Gast, H., (dir.), *Hériter en pays musulman. Habus, lait vivant, manyahuli*, Paris, 1987.

Giacomo, L. di, "Une poétesse andalouse du temps des Almohades: Ḥafṣa bint al-Ḥājj ar-Rakūniyya", *Hesperis*, 34, 1947, pp. 9-101.

Goldziher, Ignaz, "Women in the hadith literature", in *Muslim Studies*, ed. S. M. Stern, London, 1971, II, 366-68.

Granja, Fernando de la, "La venta de la esclava en el mercado en obra de Abū 'l-Baqā' de Ronda", in *Maqāmas y risālas andaluzas*, Madrid, 1976, pp. 139-71.

Guichard, Pierre, "De la Antigüedad a la Edad Media: familia amplia y familia estrica", in *Estudios de Historia Medieval*, Valencia, 1987, pp. 7-25.

——, *Structures sociales "orientales" et "occidentales" dans l'Espagne musulmane*, Paris, 1977.

Al-Heitty, 'Abd al-Kareem, "The collection and criticism of the work of early Arab women singers and poetesses", *Al-Masāq*, 2, 1989, pp. 43-47.

Hoenerbach, Wilhelm, "Los Banū Sa'īd de Alcalá la real y sus allegados: Su poesía según la antología *al-Mugrib*", *Revista del Centro de Estudios Históricos de Granada y su Reino*, 2, 1989, pp. 81-102.

——, "Die andalus-arabische Dichtung im Allgemeinen und die Dichtung der Banū Sa'īd im Besonderen", *Zeitschrift der Deutschen Morgenländischen Gesellschaft*, 140, 1990, pp. 260-89.

——, "Notas para una caracterización de Wallāda", *Al-Andalus*, 36, 1971, pp. 467-73.

——, "Zur Characteristik Wallādas der Geliebten Ibn Zaidūn", *Die Welt des Islams*, 13, 1971, pp. 20-25.

——, "La granadina", *Andalucía Islámica*, 2-3, 1981-82, pp. 9-31.

Idris, H. R., "Le mariage en Occident musulman. Analyse de fatwās médiévales du *Mi'yār* d'al-Wanšarīsī", *Revue de l'Occident Musulman*, 12, 1972, pp. 45-62.

Jayyusi, Salma Khadra, "Two types of Hero in Contemporary Arabic Literature", *Mundus Artium*, 10/1, 1977, p. 46.

Khaṭīb, Zuhayr, *Taṭawwur binā' al-usra al-'Arabiyya*, 3rd ed., Beirut, 1983.

Laoust, E., *La politique de Gazālī*, Paris, 1970.

Llinarès, A., "Deux versions médiévales espagnoles de la laitère et le pot au lait", *Revue de Littérature Comparée*, 33, 1959, pp. 230-34.

López Estrada, Francisco, "La leyenda de la morica garrida de Antequera en la poesía y en la Historia", *Archivo Hispalense*, 88-89, 1958, pp. 141-231.

López de la Plaza, Gloria, *Ambitos de la religiosidad femenina andalusí: la dinámica público-privado y sus correlaciones sociales*, Magister Dissertation, Universidad Complutense, Madrid, 1990.

Marín, Manuela, "Las mujeres de las clases sociales superiores", in Viguera (ed.), *La mujer en al-Andalus*, pp. 105-27.

——, "Notas sobre onomástica y denominaciones femeninas en al-Andalus (siglos VIII-XI)", in *Homenaje al prof. Darío Cabanelas*, Granada, 1987, pp. 37-52.

Marín, Manuela, M. L. Avila and L. Molina, (eds.), *Estudios Onomástico-Biográficos de al-Andalus*, Madrid-Granada, 1988-90, 4 vols.

Martínez Gros, Gabriel, "Femmes et pouvoir dans les Mémoires d''Abd Allāh", *La condición de la mujer en la Edad Media*, Coloquio, Casa de Velázquez, Madrid, 1984.

Mernisi, Fatima, *Sultanes oubliées. Femmes chefs d'Etat en Islam*, Paris-Casablanca, 1990.

Molina, Luis, "Familias andalusíes: los datos del *Ta'rīj 'ulamā' al-Andalus* de Ibn al-Faraḍī", *Estudios Onomástico-Biográficos*, II, 19-99.

Nichols, J. M., "Arabic women poets in al-Andalus", *Maghrib Review*, 4, September-December 1981, pp. 85-88.

——, "The Arabic verses of Qasmūna", *IJMES*, 13, 1981, pp. 155-58.

——, "Wallāda, the Andalusian lyric and the questions of influence", *Literature East and West*, 21, 1977, pp. 286-91.

Pérès, Henri, *La poésie andalouse en arabe classique au XIe siècle*, 2nd ed., Paris, 1953; Spanish trans. (*Esplendor de al-Andalus*), Madrid, 1983.

Rubiera Mata, María Jesús, *Poesía femenina hispanoárabe*, Madrid, 1989.

Von Schack, Adolf F., *Poesie und Kunst der Araber in Spanien und Sizilien*, Spanish trans. (*Poesía y arte de los árabes en España y Sicilia*), 3rd ed., Seville, 1981, reprinted Madrid 1988.

Sobh, Mahmud, "La poesía amorosa arábigo-andaluza", *Revista del Instituto Egipcio de Estudios Islámicos en Madrid*, 16, 1971, pp. 71-109.

——, *Poetisas arábigo-andaluzas*, Granada, 1985.

Al-Ṭāhirī, Aḥmad, *'Āmmat Qurṭuba fī 'aṣr al-khilāfa*, Rabat, 1989.

Turki, A. M., "Femmes privilégiées et privilèges feminins dans le système théologique et juridique d'Ibn Ḥazm", in *Théologiens et juristes de l'Espagne musulmane. Aspects polémiques*, Paris, 1982, pp. 101-58.
Valencia, Rafael, "Presencia de la mujer en la corte de al-Mu'tamid b. 'Abbād de Sevilla", in Viguera (ed.), *La mujer en al-Andalus*, pp. 185-90.
——, "Tres maestras sevillanas de la epoca del Califato omeya", in Viguera (ed.), *La mujer en al-Andalus*, pp. 129-37.
Viguera, María Jesús, *Aragón musulmán*, 2nd ed., Saragossa, 1988.
——, "La censura de costumbres en el *Tanbīh al-ḥukkām de Ibn al-Munāṣif*", *Actas II Jornadas de Cultura Arabe e Islámica*, Madrid, 1985, pp. 591-611.
—— (ed.), *La mujer en al-Andalus. Reflejos históricos de su actividad y categorías sociales*, Madrid-Seville, 1989.
Wolf, K. B., *Christian Martyrs in Muslim Spain*, Cambridge University Press, 1988.
Zotenberg, H., "L'Histoire de Gal'ād et Schimas", *Journal Asiatique*, 1896, pp. 25-31.

THE CULINARY CULTURE OF AL-ANDALUS

DAVID WAINES

Introduction

Around the middle of the 7th/13th century, on the western edge of the Islamic dominions, there appeared two cookbooks.[1] They described, in hundreds of preparations, the Arab-Islamic bourgeois urban culinary tradition of the Maghrib and the Iberian Peninsula.

Cooking traditions, whether high or low, are by their very nature conservative; it is therefore probable that these culinary manuals reflect not only the tastes and cooking techniques of 7th/13th century North Africa and al-Andalus but also of an earlier period, commencing perhaps with the 3rd/9th and 4th/10th centuries. They also clearly reflect influences from the East; the Abbasid political capital of Baghdad had also been the imperial cultural centre, where, among other developments, an *haute cuisine* had begun to emerge around the time of the reign of Hārūn al-Rashīd (d. 194/809).[2] The influence of this culinary high tradition subsequently spread westward.[3]

Culinary manuals are not, of course, the only source material from which information may be extracted concerning medieval tastes and attitudes towards food.[4] Within the medical field, in addition to sections on dietetics and hygiene included in the large medical compendia, specialist works were written on diet; these describe, together with their properties, the benefit and harm of various foodstuffs and cooked dishes, and often recommend ways of recovering from their ill effects. Such works dealt with the individual's personal régime and implied a domestic context of food preparation and consumption; in this sense, the dietetic guides are the converse of the culinary manuals, which express, as well, a familiarity with the views on food current among the doctors. Certain *adab* works, such as the *Al-ʿIqd al-farīd* of Ibn ʿAbd Rabbihī (d. 328/940) also reflect the later food lore of the urban and urbane population. Belonging to yet a different genre are works on the *ḥisba*, the market inspectors' manuals which record, among other matters, the way food in public market places ought to be prepared and sold. While this is not always explicitly stated, the *ḥisba* manuals strongly hint at the undesirability of eating prepared food in the market, owing to the endless dodges of producers to cheat their customers. Home cooking was not only better, but safer.

Yet for all the range of materials available (limited though these might appear to be), it is the culinary manuals alone which provide an insight into an aspect of medieval domestic life which has only begun to be explored.[5] From the recipe collections it is possible to construct a picture not only of the cuisine itself, but also of the many activities undertaken in the domestic kitchen, and of its place within the household and the neighbourhood community. Moreover, they implicitly point to the central role which food played in the social order of values, showing that the hospitality of the table, whether with family, friends, political allies or others, was a matter of the private, not the public domain.[6] On these particular issues there is considerable uniformity across the medieval Arab/Islamic world, and cooking styles and techniques were not in fact distinctly different in urban al-Andalus and Iraq. Differences in food preference, however, are a matter of regional choice and speciality, and these may be illustrated from the culinary manuals themselves. In the discussion which follows, two aspects of the Andalusī food tradition will be treated: the kitchen as the locus of food preparation and the major characteristics of the cuisine.

I. *The kitchen*

The dishes described in the culinary manuals were prepared in the kitchens of homes belonging to urban families of "middle class" standing; they reflect neither the exclusive milieu of the courts of the period nor the hearths of the urban poor or country folk. Thus, a variation of the common dish *tharīd*, called *al-kāmil*, comprising many meats and fowl, well spiced, with sausages, meatballs, eggs and olives all neatly arranged and served on a large platter, stands in such contrast to ordinary dishes that it is noted as being "one of the plates of kings and wazirs".[7] Overall the culinary manuals implicitly represent the cooking customs of the broader-based artisan-scholar-bureaucratic segments of urban Andalusī society.[8] Ibn Khaldūn is certainly correct in observing that the two main dietary characteristics of (presumably comfortable) urban dwellers was meat and fine wheat, although his generalised attribution of the Andalusis' good health to a spartan diet of the cereal sorghum and olive oil is not reflected in these culinary manuals. It is worth recalling in this context that al-Andalus experienced, in the 4th/10th and 5th/11th centuries, a rapid expansion of towns in which a leisure class enjoyed food for its own sake. Moreover the development of irrigation agriculture, the introduction and acclimatisation of new crops[9] and the integration of the economy of al-Andalus into the Islamic Mediterranean trade network ensured ready access to the raw materials of the urban cuisine.

Kitchen activities and the *batterie de cuisine* are well depicted in the recipes. The picture is one of labour intensive preparation of daily meals, and of condiments and conserves stored for future use, the range of utensils used indicating the complexity of these labours.

There were two major appliances in the kitchen, the hearth (*al-nār*)[10] and the oven (*al-tannūr*).[11] The former provided heat directly to the bottom of pots in which the ingredients of a dish were combined, while the latter provided dry heat for baking and roasting. The heat of both appliances could be regulated to some extent. A recipe for roasting a whole animal in the *tannūr* describes how the prepared carcass is placed on a spit (*al-safūd*) and inserted through the open top of the oven with the spit end resting on a pan to catch the dripping fat. The oven top is then covered with a lid and both it and the other apertures sealed with clay to enclose the heat until the animal is thoroughly cooked.[12] In another, similar preparation, the embers of the fire are removed from the *tannūr* when it has heated and water is sprinkled on it before the meat is placed inside; the top is then again sealed but the bottom apertures left open.[13] The recipe adds in conclusion that the dish could also be cooked in the neighbourhood or communal oven (*al-furn*).

Mention of the *furn* is common in the cookbooks. It was resorted to for a number of reasons: lack of adequate kitchen space or equipment for the preparation of large dishes, such as the one just mentioned, or for special occasions. It was perhaps most frequently used to bake the daily household bread, although certain types (e.g. *al-malla*, using an unglazed earthenware or metal utensil) were made at home. Some dishes, however, were half cooked in the home and then finished off in the neighbourhood oven, a combination of hearth cooking and baking.[14] In another case, a recipe gives a home-cooked and *furn*-cooked option.[15]

The cooking pot (*al-qidr*) came in several sizes and materials. The most common was fired clay or earthenware (*al-fakhkhār*), glazed (*al-muzajjaj* or *al-muḥantam*) or unglazed, but tinned copper (*al-qidr min al-nuḥās al-muqaṣdara*) or other metal was also used. Vessels of gold and silver were highly regarded,[16] but it is unlikely that they were employed in households where the recipes of these cookbooks were prepared. Pots containing cooked food were covered, while still hot, with lids with tiny holes to allow vapours to escape; the belief was that if such vapours were not released, a toxic force would develop in the food.

Matters of cleanliness in the kitchen are addressed in almost all cookbooks, and the Andalusī ones are no exception. It seemed to be a common complaint that servants either did not wash pots at all or did not wash them thoroughly enough after use; the problem led to the advice that a new earthenware pot should be used every day, and a glazed pot replaced every five days.[17] These somewhat drastic measures were probably not always adopted, as pots could be adequately cleaned, under proper supervision of the domestics, with hot water and bran. Nevertheless, such circumstances explain the opening expression found in not a few recipes to "take a new pot". In one preparation the cooking pot was deliberately broken when it returned from the communal oven, and the dough seal was removed by knocking it, which may have resulted in the pot's cracking.[18]

The cooking pots, or casseroles, just described were the vessels in which meat and poultry dishes were prepared. Fish however, was generally cooked in a pan (*al-ṭājin*) or fried in oil in a frying pan (*al-miqlāh*), although *qudūr* were used when the fish was sent to the communal oven (to acquire a crisp coating). Instructions state that fish must, before cooking, be descaled, scalded slightly, washed and then left to dry; depending on the size of the fish, it is prepared either in pieces or whole. One unusual home method was to place the fish in one pan and cover it with another, placing both over a hot fire which dried up the sauce in which it cooked. Fish were also barbecued over the fire on a skewer propped up on a stone and then turned by hand.

In all these operations involving the preparation of substantial dishes for the table, it is evident that the kitchen staff were working with fresh produce of meat, fowl and fish. For example, a recipe for a chicken dish opens with the words, "Take a fat castrated bird, slaughter it, scald it, open its belly to remove the innards, then joint it". Lamb was treated in the same manner, and recipes note how all parts of the animal could be used if the entire carcass is not to be cooked intact. With beef dishes, on the other hand, the specific parts of the calf or mature animal to be cooked are mentioned, or else the more general phrase "Take the best portions of the animal" is used. The meat for these latter dishes was obtained fresh from the market, although in the case of larger households the slaughter of a calf could as easily have taken place in the kitchen courtyard. The daily preparation of fresh meat, "on the hoof" as it were, and of poultry and fish, also indicates that the seasonings employed in cooking were not, as has often been claimed, used solely to conceal the odour of fetid meat. It is true that the essential oils of cinnamon and pepper (both common favourites in Andalusī dishes) were known for their antiseptic and preservative properties; yet culinary aesthetics were also acknowledged as important in producing dishes of balanced bouquet and flavour. The preservative function of the spices mentioned would have been useful if leftovers were served the following day.

The kitchen was also the scene of operations other than those directly related to the preparation of the daily meals. Butter and cheese were made by first preparing the starter, *al-ʿaqīd* in the case of cheese, using the rennet (*al-infaḥa*) from the stomach of a lamb or goat, and *al-rāʾib* in the case of butter. Cheese-making appears to have been a seasonal activity, the cheese being initially prepared in March-April, then left outside until May to cure in the shade. Hints are given as how to keep milk from souring too quickly and for restoring butter which has become rancid.

Common to all regions of the medieval Arab world from which culinary manuals are extant is a range of various prepared seasonings or condiments called *kawāmikh*, used both in the cooking process itself and alone as an accompaniment to other dishes. For example, olives, limes, capers, eggplant and fish were prepared in similar fashion for storage in large jars until they were needed. Olives, harvested in October or November, were placed in a *khābiya* along with small twigs of the olive tree, lime shrub and thyme, then filled with water and left for several days, salt being added if required.[19]

A prepared seasoning common to all Arab cooking of this period was *murrī*. It required a long and complicated process, which took some ninety days from the end of March when preparation commenced. Shorter processes lasting only two days also existed, and these could be used the year round, although connoisseurs may not have regarded them as the real thing. There were two kinds of *murrī*, the more usual made from barley flour, the other from fish.[20] The fast method of preparing *murrī* was to make a "loaf" from two *raṭl*s of barley flour and half a *raṭl* of salt; this was baked hard in the *furn*, pounded to crumbs and then soaked in water for a day and a night. The resulting mixture was then strained, this being called the first *murrī*. Next raisins, carobs, seasonings of *rāziyānaj* (Anethum foeniculum), *s̲h̲ūnīz* (Nigella sativa),[21] sesame, anis, mace, citron leaf and pine seed milk were covered with water and boiled, then strained. This second *murrī* was mixed with the first in a pot and the mixture boiled until it thickened. *Murrī*, used in small quantities, appears in every kind of substantial dish throughout the cuisine. Its flavour must have been distinctive, acting rather like salt in ordinary use; a suggested substitute mentioned in one of the eastern cookbooks was the rather acidic-tasting spice, *summāq*.

The medieval Arab cookbook was not merely concerned with food for pleasure but also with matters of bodily equipoise. Recipes for main dishes, as discussed above, frequently add a brief note on the particular advantage of a dish for a person's régime and hygiene. One preparation may "stimulate the appetite and strengthen the stomach"; another, a summer dish, was useful "for cooling the body"; yet another was suitable for the "elderly and those of moist temperaments"; another, a winter dish, was for those suffering from "cold ailments"; and so on. In addition to such helpful advice, a number of specific preparations are included in the cookbooks which deal more directly with the consequences of consumption, over-indulgence for instance, and also with other bodily functions and desires. These include recipes for *jawāris̲h̲*, *maʿjūn*, *sufūf*, *rubb*, *s̲h̲arāb* and *us̲h̲nān*. For example, *maʿjūn*, an electuary, was made by combining a particular ingredient (e.g., carrot or green walnut) with honey and seasonings, such as cinnamon, clove and ginger, and boiling the mixture until a thick consistency was acquired which would then set. Eaten in walnut-sized portions with food or afterward, the benefits ranged from stimulating the digestion to warming the kidneys and increasing the sexual appetite and semen. *S̲h̲arāb* was made from a number of basic ingredients such as mint, citron leaf, sandal, unripe grapes (*ḥiṣrim*) and carrots. The process involved boiling the main ingredient to extract its "strength", straining and then adding to sugar or honey with seasonings and boiling further until the consistency of *s̲h̲arāb* was obtained. The substance was evidently like syrup, as the instructions note that it should be diluted with two to three parts water and then drunk. The benefits of these beverages also varied but refreshment and the quenching of thirst were clearly intended.[22] Finally, a powdered substance, *u<u>sh</u>nān* (or *<u>gh</u>āsūl*), was used for cleansing the hands, the body and the mouth and gums, and dispelling the odours of greasy food. One preparation, containing thc valuable ingredient camphor and musk, is described as what "kings and great personages wash their hands with after a meal".[23] A more modest preparation, powdered *ḥummuṣ*, was employed by the common man for the purpose. A third, "middle class" variety was made from the fruit of the *nābiq* bush,[24] dried oregano, rose petals, dried citron leaf, mace and sandal.

Some attention has been given here to these non-mealtime activities, because they further indicate the kitchen's central importance in the household. Not only were daily meals for the family, and special meals for friends and other guests, prepared here, but the kitchen appears at other times as a veritable atelier for the production and processing of a variety of ingestibles associated with family health, bodily welfare and future food consumption. The activities imply careful organisation and an organiser to oversee the smooth running of the enterprise, possibly a steward responsible to the head of the household, or of course, the household head herself. Our sources do not, unfortunately, permit us to make more precise observations on the nature of the household personnel.[25]

It remains only to note briefly, in concluding this section, some of the other kitchen utensils not yet mentioned and cited in the cookbooks. The list is by no means exhaustive, but is rather intended to show the considerable refinement of the cooking processes. There were several types of vessel or container, apart from the ordinary *qidr*, the purposes of which appear to be associated with particular kinds of preparation; or else a particular one may be described by its main characteristic or in terms of an equivalent. The *qaṣriyya* was used in cooking fish. The *ṭanjīr*, used in a chicken preparation, was a shallow dish "with a wide mouth". The *<u>gh</u>iḍāra* appears to have been a vessel in which cooked food was placed, possibly for serving at the table. The *miʿjana* was, as its name implies, a container in which dough was allowed to rise before kneading, but it was also used in the preparation of mint vinegar. Other implements included a rolling pin (*shawbaq*) and a marble slab (*ṣalāya*) used in pastry making; a utensil for stirring (*qaṣaba*); a rod-like instrument used for beating meat (*qaḍīb*); a basket-like container (*al-quffa*) made from rushes (*ḥalfā*) used for draining the whey in cheese making; a fan (*mirwaḥa*) also made from rushes for the fire in the hearth or oven; various sizes and shapes of spoons (*mi<u>gh</u>rafa*) for measuring, stirring and, in one case, easing an omelette away from the sides of a pan; a sieve (*<u>gh</u>urbāl*), which could be made of different materials depending upon the degree of fineness required; a *<u>kh</u>irqa,* used in the same manner as bouquet garnis in the modern kitchen; a thread used for slicing hard-boiled eggs in halves in the preparation of stuffed eggs; and the mortar (*al-mihrās*), made of white marble or wood (metal was not recommended) and used for crushing herbs and other foods such as hard cheese. Finally, the kitchen had one utensil not found in the eastern kitchen (so far as we know), the couscousière which will be treated below as we turn now to a description of the chief characteristics of the Andalusī cuisine.

II. *The cuisine of al-Andalus*

Many were the dishes, tastes and techniques which the people of al-Andalus shared with others throughout the Arab world. We have already noted that the Andalusī cookbooks included recipes called "eastern" (*Mashriqī*). Names and types of dishes, familiar in the eastern cookbooks, are found also in the Andalusī-Maghribi tradition. We have already noted above the pickled preparations called *kawāmikh*. Similarly popular in all regions were the numerous dishes with meat which went by the name of *tharīd*; the common feature of these was the addition of crushed bread (from the verb *tharada*, meaning "crumble") to the stock in the pot at the last stage of cooking. The substitution of one meat for another, chicken for mutton for example, was another practice familiar in both eastern and western culinary traditions; recipes often note that a particular dish could be made with, for example, either chicken, lamb or veal. A close comparison of the dishes, eastern and western, is not, however, very rewarding, as multiple recipes for a dish of the same name can be found in the same cookbook.[26] Nevertheless, it is likely, as in other cuisines, that dishes were transformed as they moved from one region to another, very much as peasant fare was transformed when it appeared on the merchant's table.

One needs, therefore, to look for regional dishes peculiar to the Andalusī-Maghribi cooking tradition, or at least perceived by the compilers of recipes as being of local character. Al-Tujībī, for example, states in the introduction to his work that he has included many *al-andalusiyyāt*, one being a pastry preparation named after the city of Toledo (*al-Ṭulayṭuliyya*).[27] Made from fine wheat flour, the half-moon shaped pieces were filled with a mixture of fresh cheese and aniseed, together with mint and fresh coriander water, baked on a *milla* over the hearth, then, when ready, coated with honey, butter and cinnamon sugar. Another dish, a kind of gruel, was known both by its Andalusī names (*zabzīn* or *zbīnā*) and its Moroccan name (*barkūs*).[28] The anonymous work mentions the proper manner for preparing fish, which was the way followed by the people in Seville and Córdoba: first the fish was scaled and dipped briefly in boiling water, then cut up and cooked in the communal oven.[29] One dish, apparently known throughout al-Andalus as the "seven stomachs" (*sabʿa buṭūn*), was also known as *al-fayjāṭa*. This rather complicated formula required visits to the communal oven on three separate occasions during its preparation; it consisted of layers of thin bread and cheese, baked with milk added at the second stage, and finally topped with honey or spiced sugar.

Berber influence is explicitly noted in two recipes called *al-Ṣinhājī*, after the name of the tribe of Berbers who brought the Almoravid dynasty of the Maghrib to power in the Peninsula. One, a "plain dish enjoyed by the [tribal] élite",[30] was a well-seasoned stew preparation of lean beef, lamb, chicken, pigeon, partridge and small birds with types of sausage and meatballs topped with almonds. The inclusion of beef in this and other recipes is interesting, forming as it does a feature of the cooking of al-Andalus which was virtually absent in the East, at least as far as the evidence of cookbooks permits us to judge. It is not possible to tell whether an appreciation of beef was actually a Berber introduction or whether it was enjoyed in al-Andalus before their arrival. Al-Tujībī devotes a section of his work to recipes with beef, and there are scattered references to it in the anonymous work. However, mutton and lamb—again on al-Tujībī's evidence—were still by far the most popular meats consumed, followed by poultry and fowl of various kinds. This is true, too, of eastern recipes where a meat dish is indicated simply by the use of the word *laḥm*, which implied mutton, while beef (*al-baqar*) is rarely mentioned explicitly. Thus, the inclusion of beef in the Andalusī cookbooks suggests a different taste preference.[31]

A dish of particular interest is the one called *tafāyā*, which has survived to this day in Morocco.[32] Both al-Tujībī and the anonymous work have more than one version of the preparation, and it could be made with chicken, fish or, more usually, with mutton. It came in two basic varieties, "white" and "green". In the former type dried coriander[33] is called for among other seasonings, while in the latter fresh coriander water is used, the purpose being to colour the stock green. The compiler of the anonymous work notes the particular benefits of the dish, as being of "balanced nutrition, appropriate for a weak stomach, producing good blood, and suitable for both healthy and convalescent persons. It is an element basic to all types of cooking".[34] The compiler, however, also calls the simple "white" version of *tafāyā* by a name well known in the East, namely *isfīdbāja*, whose healthy properties are similarly acknowledged.[35] This name was not the one by which it was apparently widely and popularly known in al-Andalus.[36]

The same compiler notes *al-tafāyā* as being one of several types of dish common to the cooking tradition in al-Andalus.[37] Another was a substantial preparation called *al-muthallath*. It could be made from beef or mutton, and its special feature appears to have been the amount of saffron employed—a feature which might have passed unremarked by a modern reader of the recipes, but for the words of a poet who expressed his detestation of *al-muthallath* because of the saffron, but his fondness for *al-tafāyā* on account of its green colour.[38]

Al-mujabbana was clearly a favourite throughout al-Andalus. The anonymous compiler mentions its being made in Toledo, Seville, Córdoba and Jerez as well as in the Maghrib, and the word survives in Spanish as *almojá-*

bana.[39] It was a pastry filled with fried cheese and eaten coated with cinnamon-sugar, honey or *sharāb* of roses. It was advised to use cheeses made from both sheeps' and cows' milk, mixed together in the proportion of three quarters to one quarter respectively. This mixture would hold the filling together during cooking and prevent it from seeping out.[40] As the pastry was judged difficult to digest, it was recommended that one take *sharāb* or *maʿjūn* after eating them.[41]

A preparation known in eastern cookbooks as *laqāniq*, appears in the Andalusī tradition as *al-mirqās*, a kind of sausage made of spiced mutton and fat.[42] *Laqāniq* was known to al-Tujībī but, although he describes its preparation in the same terms as that for *mirqās*, it was seasoned not with *murrī* but with onion and fresh coriander, and a larger and wider intestine was used to contain the filling. A flat meatball was known as *al-aḥrash* (called in Marrakesh, *isfiriyyā*).[43] Round ones were called *banādiq*, and were included, pre-cooked (sometimes along with *mirqās*), as part of other meat dishes, a feature more common to the cooking tradition of al-Andalus than to that of the East.

A striking feature of dishes included in the two Andalusī cookbooks we possess, and thus evidently representative of that culinary tradition, is the frequent use of eggs in a wide range of substantial dishes. One method was to cover the cooked dish with a layer of beaten egg (sometimes mixed with flour), with seasonings sprinkled on top.[44] This must have been a popular way of finishing off a dish, for in one of the Andalusī *ḥisba* manuals of the period the market cooks (*al-ṭabbākhūn*) are expressly forbidden to cover the top of the cooked dishes with an egg layer because this concealed what was underneath.[45] Sometimes the egg, beaten, was stirred into a cooking dish as a kind of binding agent. Another method was to allow eggs to set whole on top of a dish as a decoration (*yunajjam bil-bayḍ*).[46]

Modern specialist cookbooks on the Middle East mention *kuskusū* as a characteristic part of North African cuisine; and that it was a very traditional and widely known dish in al-Andalus as well is evident from the cookbooks. The compiler of the anonymous work considered the dish so common that he mentions only a version of it, called *al-fityānī*, made in Marrakesh. Al-Tujībī, on the other hand, provides five recipes, four variations on one basic preparation:

> Joints of beef are cooked in a large pot in seasoned water together with whatever vegetables are available at the time; these could be, for example, cabbage, turnip, carrot, lettuce (*al-khass*) and eggplant. The couscous (*al-samīd al-raṭb*) is prepared beforehand by placing it in a bowl, sprinkling water and a little salt on top and then moving the grains between the finger tips so they stick together; then the grains are rubbed between the palms of the hand until they become the size of ants' heads. The *couscousière*, with holes in the bottom, is filled and placed on top of the large cooking pot, and any space between them is sealed with dough; the top of the *couscousière* is covered with a thick cloth to keep the vapours in

> and to cook the couscous. The indication that the couscous is done is the strength of the vapours rising to the top, and, when the pot is struck with the hand, one hears it hiss. The couscous is then rubbed with clarified butter, cinnamon, mastic and spikenard, and placed in a serving dish over which the sauce of the meat and vegetables is poured, sufficient for it to be absorbed. The meat and vegetables are then placed over the couscous and more cinnamon, and some pepper and ginger, are sprinkled on top.

More of a paraphrase than a translation of the recipe, the passage nevertheless reveals the degree of detail and explanatory comment common in medieval Arab culinary manuals. Quantities are seldom mentioned, although the process of preparation is clearly laid out and the cook can judge the proper proportions of ingredients to suit the family taste.

Finally, a point of interest in the anonymous work is the appearance in it of four dishes described as Jewish preparations,[47] two being dishes of partridge, one of chicken and the last of mutton. There is nothing in the ingredients used, or in the methods of cooking, which sets these apart from other dishes, but their inclusion (unique, I believe, in Arab culinary collections) is interesting in view of the considerable presence of Jewish communities in Muslim Spain.[48]

A broad survey such as this cannot hope to deal with all the points of interest which might have been raised. Implicit in the argument presented here is a degree of special pleading for cookbook sources to be taken more seriously by scholars of medieval Arab culture than has been the case up till now. What has been attempted here is to describe some of the practices of the urban high cooking tradition which al-Andalus (and the Maghrib) shared with other regions of the Arab world, while, at the same time, illustrating some of the features peculiar to the region itself. If the attempt has been successful, then further interest may be kindled in two of the most fascinating culinary works in the vast treasury of Arab recipes, and in their relation to broader aspects of the culture of al-Andalus.

[1] The two works are Ibn Razīn al-Tujībī, *Faḍālat al-khiwān fī ṭayyibāt al-ṭaʿām wa 'l-alwān*, ed. Muḥammad Benchekroun, Beirut, 1984, and the anonymous work edited by Ambrosio Huici Miranda, *La Cocina Hispano-Magrebi en la Epoca Almohade*, Madrid, 1965. Al-Tujībī was an Andalusī author, originally from Murcia, and he compiled his book sometime between 636/1238 and 640/1242, the latter being the year Murcia fell under Christian control. Huici Miranda suggests that the anonymous author too was Andalusī, and lived before the fall of large cities such as Seville (646/1248).

[2] An account of these developments will be found in David Waines, *In a Caliph's Kitchen*, London, 1989.

[3] Al-Tujībī includes in his book a number of recipes which he calls *Mashriqī*, while the anonymous work contains a section dedicated to the memory of the Abbasid prince and erstwhile caliph Ibrāhīm b. al-Mahdī, who had most likely compiled the first cookbook in the Arabic language. See Waines, *op. cit.*, pp. 11-15.

[4] A good general treatment of the source material is to be found in Expiración García Sánchez, "Fuentes para el estudio de la alimentación en la Andalucía Islámica", in *Actas del XII Congreso de la U.E.A.I.*, Málaga, 1985, Madrid, 1986, pp. 269-88.

[5] Peter Heine has made an important contribution to these studies in his book *Kulinarische Studien*, Wiesbaden, 1988.

[6] Arab customs of entertainment contrasted with those of another major contemporary culture, China, where the practice of eating together in public places such as restaurants and tea houses was well established. See the excellent treatment of Chinese food traditions in K. C. Chang (ed.), *Food in Chinese Culture*, New Haven, 1977.

[7] Huici Miranda, *La Cocina*, pp. 179-80. In his stimulating work on *Cooking, Cuisine and Class*, Cambridge, 1982, p. 129, Jack Goody writes of the medieval Arabic cookbooks that they "referred to the cuisine of the court, a court that had developed patterns of conspicuous consumption, based upon their Roman, Greek and Persian predecessors. They were composed not by cooks, but by great personages who concentrated upon their favourite recipes, omitting any reference to ordinary dishes". While there is much of value in Goody's notion of hierarchical cooking traditions, he has misunderstood the nature of Arabic cookbooks. In the case of the two works considered in the present article, neither—as can be judged from internal evidence alone—was compiled by a "great personage". They do include "ordinary dishes", of a kind familiar within the milieu of an urban leisure class outside the court or ruling circles.

[8] I am not proposing that the society of al-Andalus was rigidly class based. There is greater explanatory potential in the view of social stratification based upon groups where membership was ascribed on some basis other than strictly economic, for example, ethnicity, religion and kinship. Nevertheless, since we must assume these dishes were not confined to one ethnic or religious group (Arab, Berber or other; Muslim, Jew or Christian), the cookbooks do in fact strongly reflect the prosperous economic standing of households participating in this cooking culture, indicating a co-existence of class and status structures. Evidence from the cookbooks with respect to the political sphere would suggest, interestingly, that the view attributing the cause of the collapse of the Caliphate to "the absence of a middle class interested in maintaining a strong central government" (W.M. Watt, *A History of Islamic Spain*, Edinburgh, 1965, p. 87) is much oversimplified. See Thomas Glick, *Islam and Christian Spain in the Early Middle Ages*, Princeton, 1979, chapters four and five on social structure and ethnic relations.

[9] Glick, *op. cit.*, p. 77, gives a list of the edible crops introduced into the peninsula by the Arabs. They are the olive [*sic*!], apricot, artichoke, carob, rice, saffron, sugar, jujube, eggplant, parsnip, lemon, orange, grapefruit and carrot. On the complicated question of the diffusion of food crops in the medieval Middle East see Andrew Watson, *Agricultural Innovation in the Early Islamic World*, Cambridge, 1983.

[10] This is the word used almost exclusively in the texts. From one passage in al-Tujībī, *Faḍāla*, p. 71; however, it is likely that this was a shortened form of the expression *kānūn al-nār*, or used for the *kānūn*, whether of the moveable or stationary variety, upon which cooking pots and pans were placed over the heat.

[11] The word and appliance are of ancient Mesopotamian origin. Cylindrical, bee-hive shaped, it gave the appearance of a large inverted earthenware pot, from which it had probably evolved. Fuel, preferably good charcoal, was inserted through a bottom side opening, and then ignited. The top of the oven was open, and bread was placed through this opening to bake on the inner walls, or meat, and sometimes pots, lowered to bake.

[12] Another roasting method, probably less usual, was to dig a hole in the ground, place the meat inside and cover with a large pan (*al-ṭājin*), sealing the sides with mud so heat could not escape. Firewood placed on top of the pan was lit and the meat was first cooked on one side and then turned over on the other, in a rather slow and lengthy process. Only after the meat was ready was it seasoned with salt and pepper. See al-Tujībī , *Faḍāla*, p. 125.

[13] Huici Miranda, *La Cocina*, p. 103.

[14] Al-Tujībī, *Faḍāla*, p. 168. In this instance the mouth of the pot was sealed with a plate and dough. The reason for the use of the *furn* in cases like this could have been the absence, in the home, of a *tannūr* with a sufficiently wide opening for an awkward shaped pot to be inserted. The *furn*, being a much larger apparatus, could also cook dishes at different temperatures depending on the proximity of the pot to the source of the heat (see *ibid.*, p. 51).

[15] *Ibid.*, p. 212, recipe No. 5.

[16] *Ibid.*, p. 31. Al-Tujībī adds that gold and silver pans were best for frying, but not copper, which reacted to dishes cooked in a lot of oil. The same view is expressed in the anonymous work. See Huici Miranda, *La Cocina*, p. 83.

17 Al-Tujībī, *Faḍāla*, p. 31, and Huici Miranda, *La Cocina*, p. 84.

18 In a preparation for khabīṣ, the vessel in which the doughy substance is made is sent to the communal oven for slow baking, and when returned to the kitchen it is gently broken to preserve the shape of the contents. See Huici Miranda, *La Cocina*, p. 99.

19 Al-Tujībī, *Faḍāla*, p. 255.

20 There has been much confusion over the exact nature of *murrī*, the prevalent view being that it derived from the Roman *garum*, a fish preparation. In fact the most common form to which the recipes refer is *murrī naqī'* made from cereal grain.

21 These are the identifications found in H. P. J. Renaud and G. S. Colin's edition of the *Tuḥfat al-aḥbāb*, Paris, 1934, Nos. 358 and 454 respectively.

22 E. Lévi-Provençal rather underestimates the variety of beverages available when he states of Andalusīs that "no bebían más que agua, perfumada a veces con esencias de azahar o de rosa". See *España musulmana*, volume V of the *Historia de España*, ed. Ramón Menéndez Pidal, Madrid, 1957, p. 274. For the *sharāb* recipes, see Huici Miranda, *La Cocina*, pp. 236-40.

23 Al-Tujībī, *Faḍāla*, p. 279.

24 Jujube or "fruit de *sidr*", as identified in Renaud and Colin, *Tuḥfat*, No. 293.

25 In a recent work on the subject of women in al-Andalus, the lack of data on the activities of persons outside the ambience of the ruler's court is acknowledged. Even of women in the upper classes (not those involved in the kitchen activities of the cookbooks) Manuela Marín states: "Aunque ... los datos sobre las mujeres de la corte son relativamente numerosos, ello no quiere decir que nos permitan construir una visión más o menos completa del tema que nos ocupa." See "Las mujeres de las clases sociales superiores", in *La mujer en al-Andalus*, ed. María J. Viguera, Madrid, 1989, p. 105. Again, there is no textual evidence for Lévi-Provençal's observation that "En los familias de las clases baja y *media* era la dueña de la casa quien guisada las comidas" (italics mine). See *España musulmana*, p. 272.

26 An exception, the dish *zīrbāj*, tends to underline the general point. In both the Andalusī cookbooks and the earliest extant culinary manual, the *Kitāb al-ṭabīkh* of Ibn Sayyār al-Warrāq, edited by K. Ohrnberg and S. Mroueh, Helsinki, 1987, p. 152, the basic ingredients and procedure of cooking are the same. It is a chicken dish, with almonds, and cooked in a sweet-sour combination of vinegar and sugar. See also al-Tujībī, *Faḍāla*, p. 155 and Huici Miranda, *La Cocina*, p. 39.

27 *Faḍāla*, p. 85. A similar recipe appears in the anonymous work; Huici Miranda, *La Cocina*, p. 201.

28 Al-Tujībī, *Faḍāla*, p. 60.

29 For example, Huici Miranda, *La Cocina*, p. 173.

30 Huici Miranda, *La Cocina*, p. 24. There had, of course, been *Ṣinhājis* in al-Andalus long before the Almoravids became the rulers of the whole territory; for example, the Zīrids of Granada. There is no way, therefore, of knowing when Berber influence on the eating habits of Andalusīs actually began.

31 Indirect support for this conclusion comes from the nutritional work of Ibn Zuhr, who notes that beef is slow and difficult to digest, although the meat of a suckling calf would be easier than that of a mature animal. But the custom of eating beef at the table was, he states, a matter outside medical opinion, implying thereby that its consumption was popular. I have consulted the typescript of this work edited by Expiración García Sánchez, which she has re-edited for publication, using additional manuscript sources, and which is in press.

32 See R. Dozy, *Supplément aux Dictionnaires Arabes*, Paris, 1927, *s .v. tafāyā*. The actual recipes in the cookbooks are, however, more complex than Dozy's simple description of the dish.

33 In the medieval culinary manuals it is unclear whether dried coriander, a frequently mentioned ingredient, means the dried seeds of the plant or the dried leaf. In modern adaptations of these recipes, I have, for convenience, always used the dried seed.

34 Huici Miranda, *La Cocina*, p. 85. In a recipe for a dish called *al-lamtūniyya* (*ibid*., p. 187), obviously also of Berber origin, which was made from almost any kind of fowl, the instruction says the dish should be prepared half-way as though one were cooking *tafāyā*. The dish itself was said to have been prepared in *al-Andalus wa 'l-gharb*, i.e., both in al-Andalus and in North Africa.

35 Two recipes for a "green *isfīdbāja*" appear in al-Warrāq's early cookbook and each contains the water of fresh coriander (*Kitāb al-ṭabīkh*, p. 159-60). The introduction of *tafāyā* into al-Andalus is attributed to a Baghdadi, Ziryāb.

[36] In his treatise on food and health, Ibn Zuhr also comments on the value of chicken cooked in the manner of *tafāyā*. In his treatise on foodstuffs, al-Arbūlī notes that the greater the amount of coriander in the dish, the more it would tend towards the nature of "coldness", as understood in humoural theory, while if less were used it would be more in "balance". The Hippocratic-Galenic terms used by the physicians were, as this case illustrates, well known to the compilers of culinary manuals. On al-Arbūlī, see Amador Diaz García, "Un tradado nazari sobre alimentos: *Al-Kalām ʿalā ʾl-agdhiya de al-Arbūlī*. Edición, traducción y estudio, con glosarios (II)", *Cuadernos de Estudios Medievales*, 1973, pp. 5-91.

[37] Huici Miranda, *La Cocina*, p. 85, where seven types of dish are mentioned. The passage is obscure, as one type of dish (*al-muʿassal*) is mentioned twice and it is unclear from the recipes of the various types of dish what their special characteristics were. They could, however, possibly be divided into three groups: main, or substantial dishes, which include *al-tafāyā*, *al-muthallath* and *al-jumlī*; pickles and condiments; and sweetbreads.

[38] Confusion as to the nature of the dish arises because there are preparations called *al-muthallath* which do not contain saffron. Two, however, which do emphasise its use are found in al-Tujībī, *Faḍāla*, p. 97, and Huici Miranda, *La Cocina*, p. 222. The poet's comment is to be found in Henri Pérès, *La poésie andalouse en arabe classique au XIe siècle*, Paris, 1953, p. 315.

[39] The modern preparation is sweet pastry, but not, however, made with cheese.

[40] Huici Miranda, *La Cocina*, pp. 199-200. See also Pérès, *op. cit.*, p. 316.

[41] Al-Arbūlī, in "Un tradado nazari", p. 33.

[42] This was possibly the forerunner of the modern Spanish *salchichón* and *chorizo*, although pork meat was naturally not used in the Muslim cooking of al-Andalus. Of the pig, *khanzīr*, Ibn Zuhr states laconically in his book on nourishment that "according to our law, we should not mention anything about it". Nor does he. Recipes for *mirqās* can be found in al-Tujībī, *Faḍāla*, pp. 144-45 and Huici Miranda, *La Cocina*, p. 21, where it is spelled *mirkās*. Emilio García Gómez notes that the word *mirkās* is attested to in the Iberian Peninsula from antiquity, and probably derives from the "romance hispánico". See his translation of Ibn ʿAbdūn, *Sevilla a comienzos del siglo XII*, Madrid, 1948, p. 140, n.1.

[43] A version of *isfīriyya* which was made in the market is found in the anonymous work, Huici Miranda, *La Cocina*, p. 137, and another home-made preparation with eggplant, p. 169.

[44] An example of this method will be found in al-Tujībī, *Faḍāla*, p. 114; see Huici Miranda, *La Cocina*, p. 127. Ibn Zuhr expresses the opinion in his work on nutrition that the combination of egg and fish was poisonous, yet the anonymous compiler includes dishes with just this combination. See, *ibid.*, p. 136.

[45] E. Lévi-Provençal (ed.), *Documents arabes inédits, Trois traités hispaniques de ḥisba*, Cairo, 1955, p. 97, in the treatise of Aḥmad b. ʿAbdallāh b. ʿAbd al-Raʾūf.

[46] One is tempted to see in this widespread use of eggs an early attestation of the modern Spanish dishes known as *revuelto*.

[47] See recipes in Huici Miranda, *La Cocina*, pp. 67, 70, 71, 74.

[48] There is just one reference in the Andalusī manuals to the cooking traditions of Christians (*bilād al-rūm*); the only other reference to Christian eating customs appears in the early eastern cookbook of al-Warrāq, concerning dishes prepared by Christians for the fast.

BIBLIOGRAPHY

Anonymous, *Kitāb fī tartīb awqāt al-ghirāsah wa ʾl Maghrūsāt*, ed. and trans. Angel C. López y López, Granada, 1991.

Arié, R., "Remarques sur l'alimentation des musulmanes d'Espagne au cours du Bas Moyen Age", *Cuadernos de Estudios Medievales*, 2-3, 1974-75, pp. 299-321.

Bolens, L., "Pain quotidien et pains de disette dans l'Espagne musulmane", *Annales E.S.C.*, 25, 1980, pp. 462-76.

Chang, K. C. (ed.), *Food in Chinese Culture*, New Haven, 1977.

Diaz García, Amador, "Un tratado nazari sobre alimentos: *Al-Kalām ʿalā ʾl-Agdhiya de al-Arbūlī*. Edición, traducción y estudio, con glosarios (II)", *Cuadernos de Estudios Medievales*, 1973, pp. 5-91.

Dozy, R., *Supplément aux Dictionnaires Arabes*, Paris, 1927.
García Sánchez, Expiración, "Fuentes para el estudio de la alimentación en la Andalucía Islámica", in *Actas del XII Congreso de la U.E.A.I.*, Málaga, 1984, Madrid, 1986, pp. 269-88.
García Gómez, Emilio, and E. Lévi-Provençal, *Sevilla a comienzos del Siglo XII: El tratado de Ibn ʿAbdūn*, Madrid, 1986.
Glick, Thomas, *Islam and Christian Spain in the Early Middle Ages*, Princeton, 1979.
Goody, Jack, *Cooking, Cuisine and Class*, Cambridge, 1982.
Heine, Peter, *Kulinarische Studien*, Wiesbaden, 1988.
Huici Miranda, Ambrosio, *La Cocina Hispano-Magrebi en la Epoca Almohade*, Madrid, 1965.
Ibn al-Khaṭīb, Muḥammad b. ʿAbd Allāh, *Kitāb al-wuṣūl li-ḥifẓ al-ṣiḥḥa fī 'l-fuṣūl*, ed. and trans. María de la Concepción Vázquez de Benito, Salamanca, 1984.
Lévi-Provençal, E., *España musulmana*, Volume V of *Historia de España*, ed. Ramón Menéndez Pidal, Madrid, 1957.
——, *Trois traités hispaniques de ḥisba*, Cairo, 1955.
Marín, Manuela, "Las mujeres de las clases sociales superiores", in *La mujer en al-Andalus*, ed. María J. Viguera, Madrid, 1989.
Pérès, Henri, *La poésie andalouse en arabe classique au XIe siècle*, Paris, 1953.
Al-Rāzī, Abū Bakr Muḥammad b. Zakariyya, *Kitāb al-madkhal fī ṣināʿat al-ṭibb*, ed. María de la Concepción Vázquez de Benito, Salamanca, 1979.
Renaud, H. P. J., and Colin, G. S. (eds.), *Tuḥfat al-aḥbāb*, Paris, 1934.
Al-Tujībī, Ibn Razīn, *Faḍālāt al-khiwān fī ṭayyibāt al-ṭaʿām wa 'l alwān*, ed. Muḥammad Benchekroun, Beirut, 1984.
Al-Warrāq, Ibn Sayyār, *Kitāb al-ṭabīkh*, ed. K. Ohrnberg and S. Mroueh, Helsinki, 1987.
Watt, W. M., *A History of Islamic Spain*, Edinburgh, 1965.
Waines, David, *In a Caliph's Kitchen*, London, 1989.

ECONOMIC HISTORY

AN APPROXIMATE PICTURE OF THE ECONOMY OF AL-ANDALUS

PEDRO CHALMETA

Introduction

The study of this aspect of al-Andalus—an entity which vanished several centuries ago—constitutes a chapter of medieval economic history, and this means that we must, as a preliminary, precisely limit the geographical area and period under consideration and define what we mean by economic history. There can perhaps be a degree of pedantry in insisting too strongly on the definition of concepts, but we must, nevertheless, know what we are speaking about, and it is therefore as well to indicate the precise scope of the terms used, so as not to vitiate the study, from the beginning, with fundamental ambiguities.

I. *Concepts*

Al-Andalus, as everyone knows, was the Arabic term referring to Muslim Spain. It is, however, too often forgotten that the precise signification of this name varied over the centuries. Around 102/720-112/730 it implied the whole Iberian Peninsula, together with a good part of Languedoc-Rousillon, while in 885/1480 it corresponded to no more than than the present provinces of Málaga, Granada and Almería. Between these two extreme points there was a particular period of more than two centuries when conditions were fairly stable, and in which a correspondingly fixed geographical area was in evidence. In this period al-Andalus referred, strictly speaking, to the part of the Peninsula south of the Duero, together with the Ebro Valley.

The period under review (that following the phases of the Conquest, the recognition of Islamic politico-military superiority and the setting up of an Islamic administrative structure) corresponds with this geographical area, and stretches from the fall of Barcelona and Tarragona at the hands of the Franks (185/801-192/808) to the abolition of the Córdoba Caliphate in 422/1031. This particular time span has been chosen because it corresponds to the existence of a coherent overall picture, from the political, administrative, economic, institutional and cultural viewpoint alike. It was followed by the upheaval of the *mulūk al-ṭawā'if,* which led to the establishment of ephemeral regional units emphasising local differences already present; and none of the attempts at "re-establishment", Almoravid, Almohad or Naṣrid, was to prove capable of reconstructing an entity coherent and self-sufficient from every point of view.

The term "economics" will be used to imply the study, over a certain period, of events, norms and institutions which are properly speaking economic; those, in other words, connected with the production, circulation, apportioning and consumption of goods and services where these elements are geared to satisfying the needs of society through the joint efforts of its members.[1] It is a known fact that the exercise of such efforts follows a certain "model", which the society in question fixes as its goal and attempts to realise; the model thus depends on this society and is subordinate to it. As such, production, circulation, apportioning and consumption will vary in their organisation according to whether the needs to be met are those of all the members of the society or those of a group. From the model adopted by a society will stem the priorities and aims this society fixes for itself, and, therefore, the way it is organised.

We need, therefore, to study the volume of agricultural or industrial production and its forms of organisation: whether an undertaking is carried out by individuals or by co-producers, whether it is directed, in a particular case, by the individual producer, by co-producers, by non-producing owners or by the State. Auto-consumption, though essential for the vast majority of the population (for the mass of agricultural producers and even for a good many owners living in towns) has a merely negative effect on economic analysis, for the latter can only be carried out by evaluating the relative importance of such auto-consumption, its fluctuations vis-à-vis that part of goods produced which enters into circulation. Circulation and redistribution occur on the basis of provision forced on the producer, of immediate bilateral exchanges between producers, and of movement from producers to intermediaries and from producers or intermediaries to consumers. Such relationships are shaped within the context of institutions: the fiscal system, the various regulations concerning property, the ways the item produced is apportioned between producers and owners, contracts of sale and purchase, and, finally, the market. On the other hand, exchange can be carried out between intermediaries: exchanges of things produced, of means of production, of tokens of exchange. From this spring such institutions as associations of traders, and means of circulation like transfers of debt, cheques, promissory notes, etc. Finally, distribution with a view to consumption can also be achieved by furnishing or by exchange, by direct or indirect sale or by furnishing without payment.

This enumeration is far from complete. It will allow us, nevertheless, to grasp the complexity and enormous extent of the field covered—or influenced—by economic factors within a given society. The analysis of any one of these aspects would require, as a preliminary step, the preparation of a whole series of monographs—a task which is still, unfortunately, far from being completed.

II. *Approach*

Given the limitations of space, this study will confine itself to a presentation of the broad outlines of the economy of al-Andalus, with a much greater use of macro-analysis than of micro-analysis. I shall in fact be attempting a strictly economic analysis here, without becoming entangled in the kind of geographico-enumerative studies which have been almost exclusively produced up to now. While there is no wish to ignore the efforts—meritorious for their time—of C. Dubler[2] and E. Lévi-Provençal,[3] this study will be undertaken on a different level, with the aim of making advances in conceptual analysis and going beyond the stage of simple, straightforward enumeration. Rather than merely establishing an exhaustive list of commodities and original appellations, the main effort will be devoted to an attempt to explain, rationally, the overall way a particular society functions. Three essential aspects will be studied with a view to attaining this: (a) the production of goods; (b) the furnishing of services; and (c) the apportioning of the surplus obtained.

To this end, and given that the selected frame of reference is economic history, it will be necessary: (1) to describe the sources utilised; (2) to demonstrate the representative nature of the materials used; (3) to set out the limits of a statistical analysis applied to the period and area under study; and (4) to verify the relative exactness of the figures obtained, by setting them against descriptive sources capable of furnishing "judgements and estimates".

III. *Sources*

There is little point here in detailing sources to be used in providing an economic study of al-Andalus, since there is already a published treatment of the subject to which the reader may be referred.[4] The same also applies to study of the society.[5]

Let us simply note, to ensure the clarity of the economic treatment, that al-Andalus embodied a pre-capitalist structure based on the exploitation of the rural community. We are dealing, essentially, with an agrarian society, in which the vast majority of income derived from the tilling of the soil. Given that the appropriation and transfer of the surplus produced took place through the levying of various taxes, al-Andalus must be classed, in economic terms, as a fiscally based society.

IV. *Representative nature of the materials*

To venture on a numerical analysis of a collective economic phenomenon —albeit a medieval one—presupposes the use of statistics. The first question, therefore, must be whether these existed in al-Andalus. The answer is: yes. Of course the "lists" in question are not, for all the administrative curiosity of al-Manṣūr, as complete and ubiquitous as the statistics of our present-day world. Nevertheless, they did exist, and in fact formed the basis of administrative efficiency in every area of organisation. There were: (a) censuses of adult males in the subject population—these were indeed made from the beginning, under the governorships of ʿAbd al-ʿAzīz (95/713-97/715), ʿUqba (116/734-123/740) and Yūsuf al-Fihrī (129/746-138/756), together with updates (that of Hostegesis for the diocese of Málaga being compiled in 248/862); (b) registries of lands created for fiscal purposes, to establish whether a property was liable to *kharāj* or *ʿushr* (al-Samḥ, 100/718-103/720); (c) lists of urban taxpayers (under al-Manṣūr); (d) lists of fiscal levies by province (such as the one partially preserved by al-ʿUdhrī for the various *iqlīm*s of the *kūra* of Córdoba; (e) a statement of revenues (partly recopied by Ibn ʿIdhārī and Ibn Ḥawqal); (f) an overall register of lands made to establish the basis of taxation *pro exercito* (*Amīr* ʿAbd Allāh, al-Ṭurṭūshī).

The second question is: have these statistics come down to us? And here we have to admit that we know only fragments of them. It should, nevertheless, be possible—with a reasonable margin of error and allowing for a degree of approximation—to *reconstruct* the amount of certain net receipts. The figures set out below stem from such a hypothetical reconstruction of total sums, carried out on the basis of such details of component sums as have come down to us. While they do not actually drift into the realm of "created and invented" statistics (as described by W. Kula), it must be admitted that the results obtained are far more speculative and problematical in their nature than is scientifically desirable. The difficulties of the undertaking are undoubtedly considerable; S. D. Goitein declared, bluntly, that "the study of prices ... let alone in Arabic literary sources is like attempting to solve an equation with four unknowns,"[6] and this opinion is shared by W. Kula.[7] Yet it seems preferable, in spite of everything, to follow the principle *meglio fare e pentirsi che stare e pentirsi* ("it is better to act and repent than to stand back and repent") so dear to Machiavelli.

The data reproduced by geographers allows us, at the very most, to prepare embryonic lists, with names of products, regional specialities, a few large centres, etc.—data which, however useful it may be for giving us an idea of the diversification of production, cannot in any way be used to establish its volume. We must therefore adopt an approach other than the piling up of data which is in any case misleading because so many elements are lacking; an approach which allows us to reconstruct the overall picture. Since the fiscal system is based on the collection, by the State, of a percentage of production, it becomes possible to calculate the latter; it is merely necessary to have the following data available: the amount of tax paid, the means of imposing taxation and the official accounting procedures. This should provide us, *a priori*, with an approximate figure for the population, the amount of agricultural production and the total volume of money corresponding to the annual budget.

V. *Fiscal system*

As far as the fiscal system is concerned, al-Andalus was a "classic" Muslim country, in that taxation was imposed on the basis of religious faith. As such, there was one kind of tax (*ʿushr*) imposed with respect to the Muslim, and another, different one for the "protected" non-Muslim (*dhimmī*), this latter being divided into a poll tax (*jizya*) and a territorial tax (*kharāj*). Grafted on to this basic scheme were: (a) extracanonical levies made up of indirect taxes (*mukūs*, *ḍarāʾib*, *maghārim*, etc.), which affected the whole population; (b) payments for release (*fidāʾ*) from military or other obligations (applying only to Muslims); and (c) the census tax (*ṭabl*, *ṭasq*), which had, in principle, to be paid only by the Muwallads, or neo-Muslims.[8]

This fiscal system employed different kinds of collector according to the object of the taxation and the individual liable. The tithe, or *ʿushr*, levied in kind, was handed over to the *qābiḍ*, or *ʿashshār*. The *kharāj* and the *ṭabl* —after estimation of the *ʿibra* by the *khāriṣ*—were levied in money by the agents of the *ʿāmil*. The *jizya* was gathered either by a tax collector or by the head of the local community (the bishop, or the *qūmis*).[9] The indirect taxes were gathered by the *makkās* or *mutaqabbil*. Fiscal liability was either individual (for large properties, or *ḍayʿa*s) or collective (for members of village communities, or *qarya*s). These last represented the basic lower administrative unit. This description, summary though it is, will perhaps give an idea of the complexity of the Andalusī fiscal system and the variety of agents responsible for collection, and will make it clear that there had, by force of circumstances, to be several accounting procedures.

VI. *Accounting procedures*

Let us, before going any further, note the precise extent of the documentation preserved. The data reproduced by the geographers (al-Bakrī, al-ʿUdhrī, Ibn Ḥawqal) or the historians (Ibn ʿIdhārī, Ibn al-Khaṭīb, al-Maqqarī) all demonstrate the same particular characteristic, which forms a kind of common denominator: they are taken from works written by Muslims for Muslims, and are thus concerned only with subjects (*raʿāyā*) who are Muslims, exhibiting no data that does not affect their co-religionists. References found in a text to the *jibāyat al-Andalus* only, therefore, apply to Muslims; the authors have nothing whatever to say about *dhimmī* taxation. It would seem, then, that we must, for the latter, *add* the appropriate quantity (an extremely difficult one to evaluate) to the amount of the *jibāya*. If we fail to do so, we shall see only the total taxes paid by Muslims, not the true revenues of the Andalusī Umayyad State.

VII. *Basic data*

Al-ʿUdhrī has preserved for us details of rural taxation (the number of *qarya*s, taxes in kind and taxes in money) for the province (*kūra*) of Córdoba around 206/822. Unfortunately, the list is incomplete due to the disappearance of the *iqlīm*s of Awliyya, al-Wādī and A... Maryam. The *Dhikr* gives the figure for the *qarya*s and that for the total fiscal revenues. Al-Maqqarī has preserved the amount of taxation in kind and in money. Using the data provided by these authors and the geographer al-Bakrī, we shall attempt, through cross-checking and comparison, to define the characteristics of the *kūra* of Córdoba. Then, proceeding with the utmost caution (we are dealing with an exceptional province, in that its proximity and relationship to the capital made it islamicised, large, taxed and superintended to an unusual degree), we shall attempt to calculate, by reference to the Cordoban receipts, what the overall Andalusī receipts might have been.

The statistics of al-ʿUdhrī note 773 *qarya*s for the *kūra*.[10] This figure must be supplemented by the list of the *Dhikr*, giving us a total of between 1,079 and 1,083. The *qarya*s are not all homogeneous. Some were subject to the *ʿushr* ((1080 × 560) : 773 = 782). The figure for this *ʿushr* was 3,336 *mudis* of wheat and 4,734 of barley (making a total of 8,070 *mudis* of cereals) for the 12 *iqlīm*s noted by al-ʿUdhrī. This would give, for the 15 *iqlīm*s of the province, cereal taxation of 11,275 *mudis*. Ibn Ghālib, in al-Maqqarī, gives 4,600 m.[11] of wheat and 7,646 of barley, making a total of 12,246 to 12,600 m. There is thus a divergence of about one-tenth—by default— between our calculations and the results from the sources—a reasonable discrepancy, but one which emphasises the extreme prudence with which hypotheses must be advanced. This *waẓīfa* in kind would represent a monetary value of 31,344.5 to 34,043 D., according to whether we base ourselves on our own calculations or on the figures given by al-Maqqarī (which must correspond to the 53,000 m. and 73,000 m.—to be divided by 10—of al-Bakrī).

Al-ʿUdhrī's statistics next note the monetary revenues:

— The *naḍḍ lil-ḥashd*, or discharge from military obligations (for Muslims) amounts to 21,267 D., which would suppose a sum of 29,713 D. for the province as a whole. This pecuniary substitution constitutes the *ḍarībat al-ḥushūd wa 'l-buʿūth*, also known as *waẓīfat al-nafīr*.[12] It appears to have been established around 184/800 by the *amīr* al-Ḥakam, and to have been sufficiently burdensome for the *amīr* Muḥammad to make its suppression, in 238/852, his accession gift to the inhabitants of the capital. The economic importance of this "ransom" (*fidāʾ*) was considerable, involving probably something like the amount collected by means of the *ʿushr* and *ṭabl*.

— The *naḍḍ lil-ḥashd* is followed by the *ṭabl*, which amounts to 13,782 D., giving 19,255 D. for the province as a whole. This *ṭabl* is none other than the former territorial tax which the indigenous cultivator paid—a tax which received a new appellation on the owner's conversion to Islam without the actual amount paid undergoing any change. It was thus the *kharāj* by another name[13] and was a tax for neo-Muslims (Muwallads), while the *ʿushr* constituted the taxation proper of Arabo-Muslims.

The fiscal scheme of al-Andalus was therefore as follows: (a) The Arabo-Muslim paid only the *zakāt* / *ʿushr* on what he produced; (b) the *dhimmī* had to pay the *kharāj* (calculated according to cultivable land area) and the *jizya*; (c) the neo-Muslim ceased to pay the *jizya*, but continued, in al-Andalus, to make payment in respect of cultivable land area—a tax (*ṭabl*), the amount of which was identical to that of the former *kharāj*. It seems unlikely, in fact, that the fiscal authorities would expect the Muwallad to add commercial definition of his crop (so as to be able to hand over the *ṭabl*/*ṭasq*) to the collection of the tithe on lands. This would suppose the incredible complexity of a measurement of fields, plus a calculation of the crop, carried out by two teams of agents belonging to different "administrations". It seems equally hard, on social and political grounds, for the ideologico-juridico-fiscal change arising out of his conversion to be seen as representing anything more than a simple substitution of names: *kharāj* becoming *ṭabl* and *jizya* being transformed into *ʿushr*. It is probable, therefore, that the neo-Muslim assumed the moral duty of disbursing the *zakāt* (which he could fulfil through direct almsgiving to the poor and to travellers), but not the fiscal obligation to pay it—this situation, whereby discharge of the *zakāt* was entrusted to people's good faith (*kāna 'l-nās muʾminīn ʿalā mā yuʿṭūnahu min zakāt amwālihim ilā 'l-masākīn*), being exactly that described by the *Tibyān* (p. 17) with respect to the end of the Caliphate.

The relative importance of the *ushr* and the *ṭabl* within a region would thus correspond to the relative importance of the properties in the hands of descendants of the conquerors or descendants of early converts (i.e., the heirs of Witiza, of the *comes* Fortun b. Casius, etc., whose conversion predated the land survey of al-Andalus carried out by al-Samḥ in 100/718-102/720), as against those owned by neo-Muslims. As such it provides an index for the extent and chronology of islamicisation within a particular region. Unfortunately, we still lack numbers for the *dhimmis*.

The *ṣadaqa* is reckoned in terms of money—an abnormal procedure, since it was payable in kind. This may, however, reflect a conversion to money values subsequently carried out by the fiscal authorities for the creation of reserves, rather than the actual collection. This fiscal income amounts to only a tiny sum, which would indicate the small extent of animal husbandry in the province (or else the extreme fragmentation and dispersion of property).

The total revenues of the *kūra* come to 110,020 D. (Maqqarī), 112,000, 120,000, 142,000 D. (Bakrī), 133,023 D. (*Dhikr*). The sums collected in cash (50,955 D.) are very much lower than these figures, there being a "gap" ranging from 59,065 D. to 91,045 D., according to the overall figure taken. Such a proportion (between 53.6% and 64%) is far too high to be taken as representing simple "supplementary entries" (*mukūs*, *maghārim*); clearly we are lacking one of the key elements of the Andalusī fiscal system.

This element can only be the *kharāj*, which is not reflected in our sources since it was levied on non-Muslims and could not therefore be included in the *jibāya*, but which would be included within the overall provincial revenues. If we attempt to relate the "gap" to the sums collected with respect to the *ṭabl*, we obtain a ratio between 3 and 4.7—a figure which (supposing, as posited above, an identical fiscal levy for lands subject to *ṭabl* and those subject to *kharāj*) would indicate that, in the province of Córdoba around 206/822 *dhimmī* properties were somewhere between three times and five times more numerous than those of the Muwallads.

To round off this summary of Cordoban taxation, let us note that, around 238/852, "Serbandus ... in centum milia solidos daris sibi postulavit a rege" —the *jizya* of the Christians.

VIII. *Overall revenues of al-Andalus*

There is no text available which has preserved the amount of the overall Andalusī yield. We are, therefore, obliged to *deduce* it, in the hope that errors arising from gaps in our information will not distort the results too much. We shall attempt, in other words, to move on from the non-existent to the theoretical and approximate.

The problem is the following one: if we know the revenue of a province, is an equation available through which we can obtain a coefficient of multiplication that will give the overall volume for al-Andalus? I believe it is. Let us therefore proceed to determine this coefficient. Al-ʿUdhrī notes revenues in money from the provinces of Moron, Niebla, Siduna, Seville, Algeciras and Ilbira as totalling 250,802 D., whereas Córdoba paid 120,000 D. Thus the taxation from this province was equivalent to a little more than double that of another. The *Dhikr* records 13,950 *qarya*s for 11 *kūra*s. Since al-Andalus was divided into 33 *kūra*s,[14] this will give (33 : 11) × (13,950 : 3,000) = 13.95, following the enumeration of the *Dhikr*. If we follow al-ʿUdhrī, on the other hand, we have (33 : 6) × (250,802 : 120,000) = 11.49. Let us take the average of these coefficients, namely 12.72.

Basing ourselves on revenues of 120,000 D. for the Province of Córdoba, the Muslim Andalusī total will be 120,000 × 12.72 = 1,526,400 D.

Any attempt to posit the number of non-Muslims living in al-Andalus is extremely hazardous. They appear to have been especially densely concentrated in Córdoba, Málaga, Ilbira, Ronda, Cabra, Jaén, Moron, Carmona and Ecija, and, very probably, far more scattered in the Borderlands (*thughūr*). Proceeding with the most extreme prudence, and as a simple hypothesis, we may put forward a coefficient of 10 (it should be stressed that we are acting solely on the basis of "impression" here). This will give 100,000 × 10 = 1,000,000 D. as the amount of *jizya* paid out by the *dhimmis* of the whole of al-Andalus.

IX. *Net agricultural product*

Agricultural production can be established only on the basis of calculating the amount collected with respect to the *ʿushr*. The tariff for this was, as everyone knows, 5% for artificially irrigated lands and 10% on those which were not. Yet it is too often forgotten that there was a minimum rate payable (*niṣāb*) of 5 *wasq*—in other words 252.34 × 5 = 1,261.7 l., or the equivalent of 194.3 × 5 = 971.5 kgs. Thus all calculations based on the tithe necessarily "forget" small undertakings with a production below this quantity (which is sufficient for the annual consumption of 7 persons at 140 kgs. per head).

The revenues are recorded in *mudis*. From the palaeographic point of view, it is difficult to decide whether we should read *mudd* (which would be preferable from the point of view of *sharīʿa*) or *mudī* (the measure normally used in al-Andalus). The *mudd nabawī* had a capacity of 1.05 l., or 0.812 kgs. The capacity of the *mudī*, on the other hand, poses serious problems on account of its extreme variability. Al-Nuwayrī makes it the equivalent of 2.5 *qafīz* of Qayrawān (504 kgs.), while for Ibn Ghālib it represented 12 *qafīz* and a weight of 8 *qinṭārs*. Since al-Saqaṭī gives the weight of the *qinṭār* as 100 *riṭls*, a *mudī* would represent between 368.6 and 384 kgs. (we shall return to this figure later).

Taking as our basis the collection of the *ʿushr*, we can calculate the value of *Hispano-Muslim* cereal production (the *dhimmis* did not pay in kind). Let us use the figure of 7.5% as an average one between the rates payable on irrigated and non-irrigated lands, and regard wheat and barley as homologous. The Cordoban *waẓīfa* (the only one we know) is thus equivalent to 7.5% of the gross old-Muslim agricultural product, in other words (12,446 × 100) : 7.5 = 163,280 m. This is a figure below the real one, to which we must add the appropriate figure for undertakings with a yield inferior to the *niṣāb*. It is also virtually certain (though not demonstrable) that property in mortmain (*waqf-ḥabīs*), that of State Lands (*ṣawāfī*, *ṣafāyā*), and that of the "private sphere" (*māl al-khāṣṣa*) were regarded as exempt from payment of the *ʿushr*. Their economic importance was quite considerable, since the returns from the *mustakhlaṣ* (not counted in the *jibāya*) and from commercial transactions amounted to 765,000 D. at the time of al-Nāṣir. The multiplication of this volume by the coefficient proposed above gives 163,280 × 12.72 = 2,076,921 m. (between 768,453 and 797,539 tons)—a quantity sufficient to feed between 5,123,020 and 5,316,864 persons per year.[15]

The *kharāj* quota varied between 20% and 50% of the value of the crop (the lower figure will be adopted here). This allows us to estimate Muwallad and *dhimmī* production. It could attain a maximum of (*ṭabl* + *kharāj*) : commercial value = 28,172 to 39,676 m. This would make, for Córdoba, a production of (28,172 to 39,676) × 5 = 140,860 to 198,381 m. The volume for the whole of al-Andalus would be 12.72 times greater, amounting, therefore, to between 1,791,739 and 2,523,406 m. (between 674,000 and 950,000 tons), a quantity sufficient to feed between 4,500,000 and 6,333,000 persons. This supposes (between *ʿushr* lands and *kharāj* properties) the possibility of sustaining a population of around 10,600,000. This is, however, a theoretical maximum which takes no account of the need to reserve one-fifth of the crop for the following year's seed (and small expenses for repair and replacement of materials), plus one-sixth (average yield was 6 to 1) so as to be able to carry out the sowing and keep going for 24 months in the event of loss of the crop anticipated. It would seem, therefore, that the actual population cannot have exceeded 7,000,000.

X. *Economic growth*

The historical significance of this production should be stressed. Around 206/822 about half the area under cultivation in al-Andalus seems to have been made up of *ʿushr* lands; that is to say, they belonged either to those "collaborating" with the Occupation (the heirs of Witiza with their 3,000 properties, the descendants of the former Visigothic aristocracy, etc,) or to Arabo-Muslims of the first wave (the Syrians received no lands). There are several possible interpretations, all of them interlinked, to account for the fact that such a system of division of landed property could be established without provoking any notable reaction. The number of the new occupants was relatively low. The progress from the Visigothic to the Arabo-Muslim system was effected fairly smoothly, with a good proportion of people remaining in place and integrating into the new structures. The settlement of the invaders took place in a context of deep demographic recession and of contraction of the level of production. In such circumstances the former peasants, if they should in fact be dispossessed, could resettle without too much difficulty by undertaking tillage of some of the abundant uncultivated lands. In this respect the Berbero-Arab invasion checked the process of Visigothic decline and then set in train a new forward movement for agricultural production and the Hispanic economy.

Clearly a *jibāya* of 5,480,000 D. such as that attributed to al-Nāṣir by Ibn ʿIdhārī 125 years later represents a considerable increase—3.6 times compared with fiscal revenues recorded at the time of al-Ḥakam I. Such a rise can only be accounted for by a growth in population (after 339/950 there are 3,000 Cordoban *qarya*s compared to 1,080 earlier) and a considerable increase in the amount of land under cultivation, with these two factors leading to a raising of overall production, and the whole situation occurring against a background of economic and social acceleration and a more efficient system of taxation. Yet the really interesting thing is not so much the growth of fiscal revenue as the basis of taxation: between 206/822 and 339/950 al-Andalus underwent significant evolutionary change on the qualitative and quantitative level alike.

In fact the fiscal system of the 3rd/9th century involved, in decreasing order of importance, first agricultural taxes levied in kind, then "dispensations from military duties", and finally the *ṭabl*. Revenues under the Caliphate, though, were no longer so exclusively based on agriculture as under the Emirate. According to Ibn ʿIdhārī, they derived first and foremost from "[income] from the provinces and from the villages", but to these had to be added "[income] from royal lands [*mustakhlaṣ*] and [taxes on] commercial transactions".[16] And in fact this new factor, involving 765,000 D., amounted to one-seventh of the first-named in terms of revenue.

Let us now attempt to determine the importance of the *mustakhlaṣ*. If customs duties (which, according to Ḥasday b. Shaprūt, amounted to 100,000 D.) are taken as "commercial transactions", we are thinking of property (*khāṣṣ*) yielding 500,000 D.; this would be equivalent to the market value of 180,000 m. of cereals, i.e. 11.3% of the total produce from *ʿushr* lands in the Province of Córdoba. We are thus led to conclude that the *mustakhlaṣ* must have been very greatly enlarged if, in the 4th/10th century, it amounted to 150% of the *jibāya* of the *kūra* a century earlier. The accumulation of land as a result of acquisitions and "recoveries/confiscations" (*muṣādarāt*) was clearly of considerable proportions.

The description given by Ibn Ḥawqal[17] serves to supplement the picture presented above, and bears witness to the existence of revenues known to al-ʿUdhrī but not explicitly treated by him, and also to the appearance of new sources of taxation which had been either non-existent or regarded as negligible in the earlier period. Their existence, and, above all, the actual amount imposed, is an indication of the importance now assumed by commercially-based transactions, and also of the increased control exercised by the State with respect to the economy of the country. "... The resources [*marāfiq*] and tax revenues [*jibāyāt*] available [to the Andalusī caliph], the abundance of his treasures and goods. One indication of this abundant wealth is that annual payments for the right to mint money came to 200,000 D. To this we must add the *ṣadaqa* [on livestock] of the country, its taxes [*jibāyāt*], territorial levies [*kharājāt*], agricultural tithes [*aʿshār*], proceeds from tax farming [*ḍamānāt*], tolls [*marāṣid*], levies on the individual [*jawālī*], customs duties [*amwāl*] gathered on merchandise imported or exported by sea, and rights over commercial sales [*rusūm al-buyūʿ*]."

The socio-economic and political evolution of al-Andalus brought certain changes in its wake. Besides regions directly administered by the Caliphate (taxed on a *qarya* basis), there were others governed by local powers recognising the hegemonic sovereignty of Córdoba. It is probably to the latter that Ibn ʿId̲h̲ārī is referring when he speaks of *al-jibāya min al-kuwar;* this, for example, would be the status of the Upper Frontier. While the fiscal system did indeed continue to be based on agricultural production and the rearing of livestock, the amount derived from these must have increased considerably as a consequence of new land cleared for cultivation and improvements in farming techniques.[18] The increase in agricultural production implies a proportional increase in the *zakāt*. On the other hand, the accelerating process of conversion within the indigenous population—under the caliphate of al-Nāṣir a little more than half the population was already Muslim—together with the emigration of local Christians,[19] must have reduced collections of the *jizya-jawālī* by 50 to 60 per cent. It is symptomatic, in this respect, that the enumeration of Ibn Ḥawqal places them after proceeds from tax farming and tolls (which automatically implies their lesser importance relative to these) and just before customs duties—which amounted to only 100,000 D.—and rights over (urban) transactions, which must have been worth 150,000 D. The importance assumed by these commercial elements can be seen from the fact that the amount imposed was greater than that of the overall revenues for the Province of Córdoba around 206/822. There is, unfortunately, no evidence available as to the extent of taxes on the transit of merchandise (*marāṣid*).

XI. *Monetary movement*

Ibn Ḥawqal treated "the annual amount payable for the right of the Mint to strike money as the significant index of the wealth and opulence of the Cordoban Caliphate", and set it at 200,000 D. This was a considerable sum, equivalent to double the income derived from the customs of the time and to 166% of the revenue of the Cordoban *kūra* under the Emirate. The figure for this *ḍamān*, which must necessarily be lower than the overall figure anticipated by the tax farmer, will allow us to calculate the volume of money struck under the Caliphate and to deduce, from this, the total amount of taxation anticipated by the State.

The charge for minting was 1.75% for silver and 3% for gold, with a rate of 17 dirhams to 1 D.[20] The number of dirhams issued must have been around 20 times the number of dinars. The anticipated minting was thus greater than a figure from 6,666,666 to 11,428,571, according to the metal used in striking. There was obviously no need to mint this amount in order to collect 6,250,000 D.; the amount issued must be seen in relation to far greater fiscal revenues. Ibn Ḥawqal does indeed state that he has "heard from several collectors [*muḥaṣṣils*] worthy of belief and possessing an intimate knowledge of the taxes of the country and the [liquid assets] [*ḥāṣil*] of ʿAbd al-Raḥmān b. Muḥammad that this wealth, around the year 340/951, amounted to a little under 20,000,000 D". Let us attempt to establish the precise amount of this income, which seems to vary, between Ibn 'Idhārī's account and that of Ibn Ḥawqal, in the proportion of one to three.

The *Dhikr*, which postulates a continuity of fiscal resources throughout the Caliphate and the 'Āmirid dictatorship, states that "the taxes of Córdoba and its dependencies [*jibāyāt ... wa aḥwāzihā*] amounted to 3,000,000 D" (p. 27). If we suppose the taxation in the capital to have been equal to that of the provinces, we will have, as a figure for al-Andalus, 3,000,000 × 6.36 = 19,000,000 D. Various writers claim that the budget was divided into three, with one-third being destined for the army. It would seem, according to Ibn Ḥayyān,[21] that military expenses could be in excess of 4,000,000 D. (giving us, therefore, a total of 12,000,000 D.), and that there were always supplementary sums. According to al-Maqqarī, "the emoluments of each vizier (there were always more than ten of them) amounted to 40,000 D. per year"[22]—and viziers' salaries of 440,000 D. would equal 8% of the Andalusī *jibāya*. Such a disproportion is unacceptable, unless we accept the following:

(1) The *jibāya* represented only a fraction of the State's income. Such a notion—difficult to accept by our modern criteria for taxation—is supported by the following points: (a) al-'Udhrī did not enter the *jizya* in the *jibāya*; (b) Ibn 'Idhārī noted the *mustakhlaṣ* and duties on commercial transactions in addition to the amount given for the *jibāya*; (c) for Ibn Ḥawqal the *jibāya* represented just one component out of nine within the taxation system under the Caliphate; (d) Ibn Ḥayyān,[23] writing of the situation under al-Manṣūr, states that "to the amount of taxes [*mablagh al-jibāya*] we must add [sums arising from] property where no one inherits, and proceeds from the sales of captives and spoils of war, proceeds from confiscations, and other similar [sources] *which do not fit into normal [fiscal] categories* [*mimmā lā yarji'u ilā qānūn*]".[24] This effectively recognises the existence, on the edge of the official fiscal system regularly recorded and quoted, of another, parallel system which was ignored by *sharī'a* because it was "outside the law", and which was swept under the carpet in the official statistics.

This was undoubtedly the case with the 'Āmirid fiscal system, where the same text, which calculated its *jibāya* at 4,000,000 (73% of the "official" total for the Caliphate), omitted to mention the supplementary taxation levied for military purposes—a "voluntary" form of taxation which made the Andalusī fiscal load significantly heavier—for which we have the double testimony of the *amīr* 'Abd Allāh and al-Ṭurṭūshī. For all the self-justifying view of things put forward by the *amīr* 'Abd Allāh, not only did the 'Āmirid dictatorship see a very clear increase in the burden of taxation imposed on the *ra'āyā* (subjects), but, also, it is clear that there was nothing spontaneous about what was paid. We are no longer dealing with some people electing for a voluntary "redemption" in respect of a fixed sum, but rather with a percentage of the produce of the lands of the whole population, designed to pay the army: "He levied a charge [*iqṭā'*] on them, and had all of people's property entered in the fiscal registers [*ḥaṣṣala fī 'l-dawāwīn jamī' amwāl al-nās*]. Dividing up this [charge] among [those liable to pay], he fixed a rate appropriate for the maintenance of the army." This was, in plain language, a compulsory extension of the option to buy off one's military obligations, with the *naḍḍ lil-ḥushūd* now become a fixed source of income for the Treasury. And for all attempts to convince us that such income "was not related to landed property or profits [*min gayri uṣūlihim wa lā iktisābihim*]", it is perfectly clear that it represented the major source of revenue, since there was an army of Maghribi mercenaries to be paid, an army so numerous as to be thoroughly burdensome.[25] Thus, even when they speak of totals, authors are generally setting out only part of the sums collected by the Cordoban state.

(2) According to normal administrative procedure, the provinces, instead of sending the entire sum levied to the Treasury, settled initial local expenses by means of sums obtained on the spot and remitted the outstanding sum [*fā'id*] thereafter. A question therefore poses itself: do the amounts set out by the various authors correspond to the total sums levied, or only to the effective returns in the *khizānat al-māl*? Indeed, it seems physically impossible that al-Manṣūr, with an annual budget of a mere 4,000,000 D., and the constant drain on resources of expensive military campaigns, should have been able to construct (in two years) a palace for which the cost of materials amounted to 5,500,000 D. and from which 1,500,000 D. in coin was excavated[26]—unless the sums embezzled by al-Nāṣir's officials, from a budget of 5,480,000 D., were so enormous that they led to a recovery/confiscation of 20,000,000 D. by al-Ḥakam II.[27]

Let us, in the light of the points noted above, attempt to establish the volume of money in circulation. This should in principle correspond to the total amount of taxation, plus the quantity necessary to maintain continuous market operations, the appropriate sum in respect of imports and losses from destruction and breakage, and sums held and kept by individuals. We should also note that it was not necessary to mint the same quantity every year, for once the system had been set in motion, an amount equal to the internal expenses of the State would be returned to circulation (supplemented by the amount which individuals in need of liquidity caused to be minted). Since the State, in theory, held a third of its revenues in its coffers, it had to issue only a quantity equal to its savings, plus withdrawals due to imports, amounts saved by individuals, destruction, etc. The injection of new specie necessary to maintain a fluid economy did not need to exceed a third of fiscal revenues. These latter should have been around 18,000,000 D. annually[28], and we will take this sum as corresponding to the total amount collected by the Cordoban Caliphate. This gives us a gross revenue for the country as a whole of between 36,000,000 and 54,000,000 D. These figures, together with figures for size of population, will enable us to calculate the mean per capita income and the mean per capita fiscal charge.

XII. *Population*

Recent studies of the Hispano-Roman period tend to indicate a considerable fall in numbers as against the censuses of the Augustan era, which, by Beloch's estimates, gave a total of 60,000,000 inhabitants for the Empire as a whole and 7,000,000 for Hispania. Estimates for the population of the Iberian Peninsula around the year 700 now stand at between 3,000,000 and 5,000,000, while our calculations concerning the number of persons Andalusī agricultural production was probably capable of feeding around 206/822 gave a figure of about 7,000,000—which should be increased to accommodate production from gathering, hunting and fishing, rearing of livestock and arboriculture (probably 10%), plus all those things which escaped taxation. This would give a population of between 7,000,000 and 7,700,000. The *Dhikr*, for the period 206/822-339/950 (a span of six generations), appears to indicate strong demographic growth, with the number of *qarya*s in the Province of Córdoba possibly tripling. Thus, the population of al-Andalus under the Caliphate will have exceeded 10,000,000. Let us attempt to verify the accuracy of these figures by other means.

In 300/913, the town of Evora contained 4,730 inhabitants, and thirty or so population centres of comparable importance may be identified under the Caliphate; this gives us 4,000 × 30 = 120,000. The archaeologico-demographic studies of L. Torres Balbás, based on urban perimeters and areas under habitation, have calculated the population of ten other towns at 310,000. The length of the walls of Córdoba was 10 miles according to al-Bakrī, 14 miles according to Ibn Ghālib and 15.83 miles according to Ibn al-Khaṭīb, which would give population figures of 220,000, 294,000 and 330,000 respectively. The city had 21 outlying districts. Al-Bakrī (followed by the *Dhikr*) states that a census of the whole agglomeration [*wa bi-arbāḍihā*] ordered by al-Manṣūr showed 213,077 households of ordinary citizens (=852,308 inhabitants), plus 60,300 houses belonging to notables, officials and others. I myself will adopt, for Córdoba, the mean between these figures: (850,000 + 220,000) : 2 = 500,000 inhabitants approximately. The urban population of al-Andalus would, therefore, be 120,000 + 310,000 + 500,000 = 930,000. Taking a proportion of ten rural dwellers for one urban dweller, the rural population would be 9,300,000 and the population of al-Andalus 9,300,000 + 930,000 = 10,230,000.

XIII. *Mean fiscal charge*

The fiscal charge per head of family or household (not per capita) may be obtained by dividing the total charge by the number of those liable to payment—the latter being itself derived by dividing the population figure by that of the number of persons making up the household, which may be assessed at between four and five. For between 2,000,000 and 2,500,000 taxpayers, then, we have a per capita levy of between 9 and 11.25 D. In the knowledge that the earnings of a worker varied between 1 and 1.5 d. per day (20.6 to 31 D.) and those of a military colonist were 2 D. monthly, this will give us, according to the figure taken for number of taxpayers, percentages varying between 45.7% and 54.6% in the first case, and between 29% and 36.3% in the second.

XIV. *Mean income*

Working still on a household basis, the mean income may be derived through dividing the total amount coming in[29] by the number of taxpayers. According then, to the values assigned to these:

(1) The State collects half the product of the taxpayer's work, giving us figures of 36,000,000 : 2,000,000 = 18 D., or 36,000,000 : 2,500,000 = 14.4 D.

(2) The State gathers in only a third of the product of the taxpayers' work, i.e. 54,000,000 : 2,000,000 = 27 D., or 54,000,000 : 2,500,000 = 21.6 D.

This gives us sums ranging from 14.4 D. to 27 D., figures which do in fact correspond to data given by al-Saqaṭī and al-Maqqarī on workers' earnings.

Conclusion

For purposes of conclusion—and of verification—it is sufficient to re-read the travellers' impressions and geographers' descriptions so beautifully summarised by Ibn Ḥawqal: "The cities vie with one another in their situations, and by [the amount of] their taxes and their incomes ... There is no town which is not well populated and surrounded by a huge rural district, by a whole province rather, with numerous villages and labourers living in prosperity, owning large and small livestock, good equipment, beasts of burden and fields... The price of goods is pretty much that of a region with a good reputation for commerce, prosperous and rich in resources, where life is easy ..."[30]

For the inhabitants of the Christian kingdoms in the north of the Iberian Peninsula, al-Andalus represented a kind of El Dorado, or Promised Land. Very soon these feelings gave birth to predatory, covetous ones, which became so widespread as to give rise to a policy of systematic oppression geared to economic ends. The subsequent conquest and exploitation of al-Andalus was the avowed aim of the upper classes of Hispano-Christian society, which, rather than developing its own internal resources, preferred to bend all its efforts to a "protection/extortion" policy towards its neighbours, aiming, essentially, at obtaining *botín y las parias*. If we really wish to understand the importance and wealth of al-Andalus, we must remember that its economy was self-sufficient and enjoyed continuous growth over three centuries. For 75 years from 400/1009 al-Andalus was also capable of sustaining and (involuntarily) financing the development of another, external and parasitical social entity: the Christian kingdoms of the North. It would be difficult to provide a better indication of the economic situation and importance of al-Andalus from its establishment up to the Almoravids' seizure of power.[31]

1 See M. Rodinson, "Histoire économique et histoire des classes sociales dans le monde musulman", in *Studies in the Economic History of the Middle East*, ed. M. A. Cook, Oxford, 1970.

2 "Über das Wirtschaftsleben auf der Iberischen Halbinsel vom XI zum XIII Jahrhundert", *Romana Helvetica*, 22, 1943, pp. 1-185.

3 *Histoire de l'Espagne musulmane*, III, 233-324.

4 See P. Chalmeta, "Sources pour l'histoire socio-économique d'al-Andalus: essai de systématisation et de bibliographie", *Annales Islamologiques*, 20, 1984, pp. 1-14.

5 See P. Chalmeta, "Al-Andalus: société féodale?", in *Le cuisinier et le philosophe. Hommage à Maxime Rodinson*, Paris, 1982; "La sociedad andalusí", in *Historia General de España y America*, III, Madrid, 1988.

6 S. D. Goitein, *A Mediterranean Society*, Berkeley, 1967, I, 217.

7 *Problemas y metodos de la historia económica*, Barcelona, 1973, p. 271.

8 See P. Chalmeta, *Encyclopédie de l'Islam, s. v.*

9 *Ibid.*

10 M. Barceló, "Un estudio sobre la estructura fiscal y procedimientos contables del emirato omeya de Córdoba (138-300/755-912) y del califato (300-366/912-976)", *Acta Historica et Archaeologica Mediaevalia*, 1984-85, was the first to provide an extended analysis of this. Even so, his conclusions will not be totally followed here.

11 This should probably read 5,427-5,517, following the figures of al-ʿUdhrī and al-Bakrī.

12 Ibn ʿIdhārī, *Al-Bayān al-mughrib fī akhbār al-Andalus wa 'l-Maghrib*, Vol. II, ed. G. S. Colin and E. Lévi-Provençal, 1951, p. 109; Ibn Ḥayyān, *Al-Muqtabas min anbāʾ ahl al-Andalus*, Vol. II, ed. M. ʿA. Makkī, Beirut, 1973, p. 271.

13 P. Chalmeta, "Au sujet du *ṭabl*", in preparation.

14 J. Vallvé, *La división territorial de la España musulmana*, Madrid, 1986.

15 This supposes an average ration of 150 kg. per person—a quantity which must exceed the real one, since the Muslim diet, although cereal-based, involved heavy consumption of fresh and dried vegetables, greenstuff, fresh and dried fruit and olive oil. This diet is confirmed by the taunts, criticisms and descriptions of the Christians with respect to Mudejar and Morisco foodstuffs. To give an example, in 324/936, the provisions sent by al-Nāṣir to Mūsā b. Abī 'l-ʿĀfiya comprised 1,000 m. of wheat and barley, 50 m. of beans, 10 of chick peas, 300 *qafīz* of figs, 30 *qisṭs* of honey, 30 of *samn* and 100 of oil (*Muqtabas*, V, 263). Non-cereal items form around 19% of the total, with a very high calorific value.

16 *Bayān*, II, 231-32.

17 *Ṣūrat al-arḍ*, ed. J. H. Kramers, Leiden, 1938, I, 108.

18 L. Bolens, *Agronomes andalous du Moyen Age*, Geneva, 1981.

19 Chalmeta, *Encyclopédie de l'Islam, s. v.* "Mozarabe".

20 P. Chalmeta, "El dirham *arbaʿīnī, dukhl, Qurṭubī, Andalusī*: su valor", *Acta Numismática*, 1986; "Monnaie réelle, monnaie fiscale, monnaie de compte", *Annales Islamologiques*, 1980.

21 *Apud* Ibn al-Khaṭīb, *Aʿmāl al-aʿlām fī man būyiʿa qabl al-iḥtilām min mulūk al-Islām*, ed. E. Lévi-Provençal, Beirut, 1956 p. 98.

22 *Nafḥ al-ṭīb min ghuṣn al-Andalus al-raṭīb*, ed. I. ʿAbbās, Beirut, 1968, I, 356.

23 *Apud* Ibn al-Khaṭīb, *Aʿmāl*, p. 98.

24 This passage should be considered in conjunction with one in Ibn Sāʿid (see al-Maqqarī, *Nafḥ al-ṭīb*, I, 146), which is grammatically incorrect, but whose sense is clear: "in the past the sum of taxes levied annually by the Umayyads, *in the normal run of things* [*qawānīn*], was 300,000 dinars of Andalusī dirhams."

25 According to Ibn al-Khaṭīb, *Aʿmal*, p. 99, it amounted to 46,000 horsemen and 26,000 footsoldiers.

26 Ibn ʿIdhārī, *Bayān*, III, 61; Ibn al-Khaṭīb, *Aʿmal*, p. 111.

27 Ibn Ḥawqal, *Ṣūrat al-arḍ*, I, 112.

28 See above, pp. 13-14.
29 See above, p. 15.
30 *Ṣūrat al-arḍ*, I, 114-16.
31 P. Chalmeta, "*Murābiṭun*", in *Encyclopédie de l'Islam*.

BIBLIOGRAPHY

Amīr ʿAbd Allāh, *Kitāb al-tibyān*, ed. E. Lévi-Provençal, Cairo, 1955.

Al-Bakrī, *Jugrāfiyat al-Andalus wa Urūbba min kitāb al-masālik ilā 'l-mamālik*, ed. M. al-Hajjī, Beirut, 1968.

Dhikr bilād al-Andalus, ed. L. Molina, Madrid, 1983.

Goitein, S. D., *A Mediterranean Society*, Berkeley, 1967.

Ibn Ḥawqal, *Ṣūrat al-arḍ*, ed. J. H. Kramers, Leiden, 1938.

Ibn Ḥayyān, *Al-Muqtabas min anbā' ahl al-Andalus*, Vol. II, ed. M. ʿA. Makkī, Beirut, 1973.

Ibn ʿIdhārī, *Al-Bayān al-mughrib fī akhbār al-Andalus wa 'l-Maghrib*, Vol. II, ed. G. S. Colin and E. Lévi-Provençal, Leiden, 1951.

Ibn al-Khaṭīb, *Aʿmāl al-aʿlām fī man būyiʿa qabl al-iḥtilām min mulūk al-Islām*, ed. E. Lévi-Provençal, Beirut, 1956.

Kula, W., *Problemas y metodos de la historia económica*, Barcelona, 1973.

Lévi-Provençal, E., *Histoire de l'Espagne musulmane*, Paris, 1950.

Al-Maqqarī, *Nafḥ al-ṭīb min ghuṣn al-Andalus al-raṭīb*, ed. I. ʿAbbās, Beirut, 1968.

Al-Saqaṭī, *Un manuel hispanique de ḥisba*, ed. G. S. Colin and E. Lévi-Provençal, Paris, 1931.

Al-ʿUdhrī, *Fragmentos geográfico-históricos de al-Masālik ilā ğamīʿ al-mamālik*, ed. ʿA. ʿA. al-Ahwānī, Madrid, 1965.

MUSLIM MERCHANTS IN ANDALUSĪ INTERNATIONAL TRADE

OLIVIA REMIE CONSTABLE

During the medieval period, the cities of Muslim Spain (al-Andalus) were important economic centres for merchants and commodities from all regions of the Mediterranean world. They provided markets where Andalusī and foreign merchants could transact the business of long-distance, or "international", trade. Throughout most of the period of Muslim rule, from the central Umayyad period, in the 4th/10th century, until the main victories of the Christian *reconquista* in the middle of the 7th/13th century, Andalusī commerce remained closely tied to other regions of the Islamic Mediterranean. Goods and merchants moved freely along the land- and sea-routes linking Andalusī markets to those of the Maghrib and the Near East.

Cities such as Almería, Seville and Málaga functioned as commercial clearing-houses where imports and exports were handled by Muslim, Jewish and Christian traders. An Andalusī Muslim trader might have purchased indigo, wool or grain from a North African colleague, and sold Spanish silk, timber or singing girls (captured from the Christian north) in return. Likewise, a Jewish trader from Egypt might have arrived with a cargo of flax, pearls and brazilwood (a red dye), with perhaps a packet of eastern medicines as a gift for his Spanish partner's family; on the homeward journey, he may have carried Andalusī saffron, qirmiz (another red dye) and paper back to Alexandria. By the 7th/13th century, Italian merchants came to trade in Andalusī markets, seeking local products such as Cordoban leather, textiles, ceramics and olive oil.

The organisation of the merchant population into religious groupings reflected the composition of Andalusī society as a whole. Significant changes are evident in the relative status of these three merchant groups, and commercial shifts went hand in hand with more general political and social changes in the balance of power in medieval Iberia. During the years of Muslim hegemony, the Muslim merchants formed the dominant group —economically, politically and socially—in Andalusī trade. At the same time, however, Jewish traders from Spain and the eastern Mediterranean were also an important element in the Andalusī commercial world. This situation had changed by the middle of the 7th/13th century, when much of the Iberian Peninsula became part of the Christian political and commercial sphere. Whereas Iberian international trade had once been controlled by Muslim and Jewish traders, economic power now shifted into the hands of Christian merchants.

Information on the activities of Muslim merchants in Andalusī international trade is scarce, in part because these businessmen were rarely of sufficient importance to merit inclusion in chronicles and most other non-economic sources. Nevertheless, existing documentation provides information on two fronts. First, the sources tell something about the different types of Muslim trader active in Andalusī commerce, in terms both of their professional operations and of their group affiliations. Second, and more important to this paper, the distribution of references to Muslim merchants suggests clear chronological patterns, even if the limited availability of information indicates the need for caution in making quantitative estimates for any given period. It is particularly striking that references to Muslim merchants engaged in long-distance trade become rare after the shift from Muslim to Christian rule in the south of Spain. While it is possible that their activities continued in the later 7th/13th century, Muslim merchants no longer appear in the sources of that time, when they would have been in competition with increasingly powerful Christian merchants who had the advantage of support from the new Christian rulers.

Among the materials that are available to document Muslim trade, Arabic biographical dictionaries (*tarājim*) provide valuable data on Muslim merchants working in al-Andalus during the Islamic period. However, these books focus on a single type of businessman, namely the merchant-scholar. Since biographical records were concerned with scholarly rather than commercial credentials, they provide details on names, dates and itineraries, but give little information on trade specialisation, associates or social class.[1] Other Arabic sources, including handbooks for market inspectors (*ḥisba* manuals) and collections of legal opinions (*fatwa*s), also yield scattered information, as do geographies, travel narratives and other literary materials. Some further details of Muslim mercantile activities can also be gleaned, though sometimes only through extrapolation, from non-Islamic sources such as the Judaeo-Arabic letters from the Cairo *Geniza* and Latin Christian documents.

According to the sources, several different types of merchant were active in medieval Andalusī trade, and these men were differentiated by their business activities as well as by their religious and regional affiliations. The focus here is on long-distance traders, the "international" merchants who travelled and carried goods between Andalusī markets and other regions of the Mediterranean world and who maintained a far-flung network of business communications and partnership ties.[2] These international traders cannot be studied in isolation, however, since every merchant in Andalusī trade must have had dealings with other types of merchant. A sedentary importer, for example, would have acquired goods through a travelling partner (either in a long-term arrangement or for an individual commercial voyage), while international traders needed to maintain relations with local merchants (probably wholesalers) in order to buy and sell their wares in particular markets.

International traders were described as *tujjār* (sing. *tājir*), which is the most common Arabic term for a merchant. The word could signify men engaged in a variety of commercial dealings, including simple local trade, but it most frequently applied to merchants involved in large-scale, long-distance commerce. In one description of different merchant types in the medieval Islamic world, the eastern writer Abū 'l-Faḍl al-Dimashqī cited three basic categories of *tujjār*. His first category was the *khazzān*, or stapler, a sedentary merchant who stocked goods when their price was low for later resale when the price rose. Next came the *rakkāḍ*, who travelled on business for himself or in the employ of a third variety of merchant, the *mujahhiz*, a sedentary importer/exporter.[3] Of the three, the *mujahhiz* seems to have operated on the largest scale, frequently acting as the central organiser for a wide network of travelling and sedentary partners abroad.

Most data on Muslim merchants active in Andalusī international commerce describes men conforming to the category of the *rakkāḍ*, or travelling merchant. However, this picture is distorted because it was often the very fact of their travels that earned these traders a place in the historical record. It is likely that the travelling merchants mentioned in the documents operated within a larger Andalusī mercantile network roughly following the pattern of al-Dimashqī's description.[4]

Mercantile interaction and partnerships did not mean that the businessmen trading to and from al-Andalus formed an open community. On the contrary, by their choice of associates the merchants separated themselves into groups based on geographical origin and, more importantly, on religion. The ties of allegiance and identity apparent in the merchant community were in line with more general trends in Andalusī society, since economic collaboration often grew out of social and religious collaboration. To some degree, it appears that Andalusis—merchants and otherwise—were bound together by their common geographical identity.[5] Nevertheless, strong divisive forces were also present in Andalusī society. While there may have been a bond of Andalusī affiliation, religious and ethnic diversity tended to override any regional identity.

One example of this tendency can be found in a letter written by Moses Maimonides cautioning his son Abraham to beware of strangers on his travels and not to "befriend intimately any group except our own loving brethren of Spain, who are known as Andalusians". By this, Maimonides intended that Abraham should be friendly with Andalusī Jews, not necessarily with Andalusī Muslims or Christians.[6] It is probable that Muslim Andalusis subscribed to similar sentiments. Thus, although geographical origin was important, causing merchants and other travellers to seek out the company of their compatriots, they particularly identified themselves with their own religious communities.

This pattern of religious segregation was true of society throughout the Islamic world, and shows up clearly in the differentiation of sources. It is rare, for instance, to find a genre or individual source which contains general information on merchants of different religions. Further evidence for religious segregation is provided by data on routes of travel and commodity specialisation.[7] Christian shipping routes were not necessarily the same as those followed by Muslims and Jews. In general, Christian merchant ships tended to prefer routes along the northern Mediterranean littoral, bordering Christian territories, while merchants from the *dār al-Islām* favoured more southerly itineraries.[8] Nor did merchant groups carry identical cargos, although most medieval merchants dealt in a wide spectrum of goods. For example, both Christians and Muslims—but not Jews—traded in timber, even in the face of religious prohibitions against trading shipping materials to "the enemy". Similarly, merchants did not sell or transport slaves of their own religion: Muslims bought and sold Christian slaves, while Christians did the same with Muslims.

Separate identification on the grounds of religion and geographical origin remained the norm, in spite of strongly similar traits that inevitably existed between the individual merchant groups. Businessmen of different religions certainly had contact with one another, particularly in exchanging commercial information, acquiring goods and organising marine transportation. Likewise, these merchants engaged in individual commercial transactions, but they never—or very rarely—formed lasting interfaith partnerships. By and large, they preferred commercial dealings and partnerships with their co-religionists.

Thus, Muslim merchants active in Andalusī commerce formed a distinct, though not an isolated or homogeneous, group. Sources show that these men pursued a variety of commercial interests and traded in many different goods, including textiles, foodstuffs, spices, precious stones, furs, animals, books and slaves. Some travelled to and from al-Andalus as merchant-scholars, while others came for more exclusively commercial purposes. Some merchants were of Iberian origin, seeking economic and spiritual gains abroad, while others arrived in Andalusī markets from homelands in North Africa and the Near East. Overall, however, the Muslim merchant population in Islamic Spain followed a common chronological pattern of success and decline over the period from the late 3rd/9th to the middle of the 7th/13th centuries.

The documentation on Muslim merchants shows commercial traffic between al-Andalus and other regions of the *dār al-Islām* for most of this period, although there may have been some fluctuation in merchant business under different Muslim regimes. Differences also appear, at times, between the activities of Andalusis and non-Andalusis. Both of these perceived trends, however, may result from the nature of the source materials. In contrast, the sudden drop in data after about 650/1250 is much more striking and potentially informative.

Arabic sources show that the final century of Umayyad rule in Córdoba was a fertile period for mercantile activity. During the 4th/10th century, the geographer Ibn Ḥawqal referred to Andalusis trading in Tabarca and noted a Spanish merchant colony in Tripoli.[9] By 361/972, the historian al-Rāzī had noted another Muslim merchant, Muḥammad b. Sulaymān, plying similar routes between al-Andalus and Ifrīqiya.[10] At about the same time, Andalusī merchants were trading with the eastern Mediterranean, and a large merchant ship is known to have been dispatched to Egypt in 344/955 and to have returned to Spain from Alexandria loaded with goods.[11]

Muslim Spanish merchants also travelled farther afield—even if only in legend. According to one 4th/10th-century tale, a ship sailing from Sīrāf with "a crowd of merchants ... from every country" foundered in the China Sea and was brought to safety through the wisdom of "an old Muslim from Cádiz".[12] Indeed, history could match imagination, as in the case of a merchant-scholar, Abū Muḥammad b. Muʿāwiya al-Marwānī, who left his native Córdoba to go eastward on pilgrimage in 295/908. Having completed the *ḥājj*, he travelled on commercial business to Baghdad, Kufa, Basra and India, whence, after amassing 30,000 dinars, he set out for home with his profits, only to be shipwrecked in the Indian Ocean or Red Sea. After thirty years he returned, penniless, to teach in Córdoba.[13]

Compilers of biographical dictionaries, including Ibn al-Faraḍī, al-Ḍabbī, Ibn Bashkuwāl and Ibn al-Abbār, mentioned several Cordoban merchant-scholars who traded in the Mashriq during the late 3rd/9th and 4th/10th century. Of these, two traders lived during the 3rd/9th century, and the rest were active in the mid-to-late 300s/900s. Two of the latter died in 378/988, after travelling extensively in Syria, Egypt and Iraq, and a couple of their close contemporaries (both dying near the turn of the Christian millennium) traded less widely in Egypt and the Near East.[14] As with many figures in Islamic history, the best-known facts about Andalusī Muslim merchants are their deaths—which are recorded in their biographies and occasionally on their tombstones. Among two hundred and fifty epitaphs inscribed on Muslim tombs in Qayrawān, only five of the dead were noted as being Andalusis. One merchant, who died in 249/862, is found among them.[15]

Biographical dictionaries include only a few references to eastern merchants arriving in Islamic Spain at this period. Ibn al-Abbār noted one early merchant, Muḥammad b. Mūsā (d. 273/886), who worked in al-Andalus. Later, Ibn al-Faraḍī mentioned a 4th/10th-century trader from Ceuta who, after wide travels through the Maghrib and Mashriq, lived for a period on the Andalusī frontier as a merchant and soldier.[16] Likewise, Ibn Bashkuwāl cited a Baghdadi merchant-scholar who arrived in al-Andalus in 356/966 and two more who came from Egypt and Qayrawān early in the next century.

The latter scholar was particularly known for his excellent grasp of commercial matters (*kāna min ahl ... al-nafādh fī ummūr al-tijāra*).[17]

Ordinary merchants also arrived from the East to trade in the markets of Umayyad Spain, even during periods of political tension between the Umayyads and other Islamic rulers. Writing during the reign of the caliph ʿAbd al-Raḥmān III (300/912-350/961), the Jewish official Ḥasday b. Shaprūt extolled the natural wealth of Spain, and listed the merchants who flocked to the Peninsula for trade. Among these, he particularly noted Egyptians (who brought perfumes, precious stones and other luxuries) and the "merchant-envoys of Khurāsān".[18] At about the same time, Ismāʿīlis were also coming to Spain to spread Shiʿism, although according to the 5th/11th-century Cordoban jurist, Ibn Sahl (d. 486/1093), they hid "their true purpose under the pretext of legitimate activities such as commerce, or science, or itinerant Sufism..."[19] Towards the end of the Umayyad period, under the *ḥājib* al-Muẓaffar (392/1002-398/1007), Ibn Ḥayyān also recorded the appearance in Spain of foreign merchants from Egypt, Iraq and elsewhere.[20]

During the 5th/11th century, it is not uncommon to find evidence of Muslim Spanish businessmen involved in commerce with Maghribi ports, as well as with more distant destinations.[21] The geographer al-Bakrī mentioned the presence of Andalusī traders in al-Mahdiyya, and provided detailed and varied itineraries for their maritime crossings of the channel between North Africa and al-Andalus.[22] Many other more general indications of Andalusī commerce with the Maghrib also exist, both in legal documents and in geographical descriptions of this period. We often learn in passing of travelling merchants when their absence caused family members or acquaintances to take cases to court. Ibn Sahl recorded several suits of this type. In one, dated 458/1066, a merchant was seeking a partner missing in Fez. A later *fatwā*, collected by al-Wansharīsī, concerned the case of a servant girl in Granada whose merchant master had been long absent in Tunis.[23]

The number of references to native Andalusī merchant-scholars travelling abroad decreased during the *ṭāʾifa* and Almoravid regimes, even in biographical works largely devoted to scholars living in these periods. Ibn al-Abbār noted a Cordoban merchant who died in Valencia in 419/1028, and Ibn Bashkuwāl cited two further Andalusī merchant-scholars, both from Seville, who were active in the early 5th/11th century. One, clearly of Arab origin (bearing the name al-Qaysī), was reported to have "wandered for a time through the lands of Ifrīqiya and al-Andalus, searching for knowledge and trading" before his death in 424/1033. The other Sevillian, possibly of Berber heritage, also traded in Ifrīqiya.[24]

In contrast to this paucity of references to Andalusī merchant-scholars travelling eastward in the early 5th/11th century, there is a relative abundance of biographical information on merchant-scholars arriving in Islamic Spain between the years 414/1023 and 432/1041. Ibn Bashkuwāl recorded the names of twenty-two merchant-scholars active during this short period (while he noted only two further foreign merchants for the century following). The Muslim traders whom he cited came from all over the Islamic World. A few had origins as far away as Yemen and Iraq, some came from North Africa, while the majority had travelled to Spain from Syria and Egypt.[25]

The time frame is intriguing, because these twenty years span the gap between the final years of the Umayyad dynasty and the emergence of the early *ṭāʾifa* states, an era thought to have been troubled by unrest and civil war. One would expect to see a decrease in merchant activity in this period, as is suggested by the data on native Andalusī traders.[26] In contrast, although the sample is small, *tarājim* references indicate that foreign merchants continued to arrive in Andalusī markets during this period of political turmoil and weak government control in Islamic Spain.

After this brief heyday of abundant references, biographical information on eastern merchant-scholars suddenly becomes scarce after the middle of the 5th/11th century. As noted above, Ibn Ba<u>sh</u>kuwāl cited only two more examples, a Syrian trader and a Baghdadi, who came to Spain in 466/1073-4 and 483/1090 respectively, and Ibn al-Abbār remarked on a merchant-scholar from Qalʿat Banī Ḥammād who visited al-Andalus, then died in Fez in 567/1172.[27] Information on Andalusī scholars shows a similar trend. Ibn Ba<u>sh</u>kuwāl recorded only one 6th/12th-century merchant, who lived in Almería until his death in 531/1136, while Ibn al-Abbār mentioned a single merchant from Denia who died in 547/1152.[28]

This apparent decrease in the activities of merchant-scholars should probably be attributed to non-commercial causes—perhaps the arrival in Spain of the Almoravids and Almohads—since it was not reflected in sources pertaining to the rest of the merchant population. Outside the sphere of the *tarājim*, a *fatwā* recorded by the jurist al-Māzarī (d. 536/1141) concerned a Maghribi merchant selling goods in Spain earlier in the century, and *Geniza* letters from 1138 and 1140 reported that Muslim merchants had arrived in Spain from Alexandria and Libya.[29] Three epitaphs from Almería, dated 519/1125, 527/1133, and 540/1145, also attest to the mercantile presence in the first half of the 6th/12th century. Their accompanying Quranic quotations show that the deceased were all Muslim, and one was certainly of Spanish origin, as shown by his *nisba*, al-<u>Sh</u>ātibī (from Játiva). Another, named Ibn Ḥalīf, was a merchant from Alexandria who presumably died in Spain while on a voyage.[30]

Information on Andalusī Muslim merchant activity increases slightly in the Almohad period, which began in the middle of the 6th/12th century and continued into the 7th/13th century. The geographer al-Idrīsī reported that Andalusis were trading with Salé and other Moroccan ports around 550 A. H. (the 1150s A. D.), bringing Andalusī oil to the Maghrib in exchange for local grain. Meanwhile, merchants from western Muslim lands, including al-Andalus, were seen in the markets of Alexandria by the Spanish Jewish traveller Benjamin of Tudela in about 560/1165.[31] Perhaps one of these Andalusis was the merchant-scholar Aḥmad b. Marwān who, according to the biographer al-Silafī, travelled to Alexandria, Isfahan, and Iraq at roughly this period.[32] Ibn al-Abbār provided information on five more merchant-scholars, all probably of Andalusī Arab heritage, who died between 580/1184 and 642/1245.[33] Eastern traffic with Spain also continued to operate through the 6th/12th century, as indicated by al-S͟haqundī (writing 595/1199-609/1212) when he casually mentioned Muslim commercial shipping in Málaga.[34] Somewhat later, we learn in passing of another merchant, the brother of a Murcian scholar Abū 'l-ʿAbbās, who travelled to the East on pilgrimage with his family in 640/1242. Shipwrecked off Bône, only Abū 'l-ʿAbbās himself and his elder brother, the merchant, survived from the family. The brothers went to Tunisia, where the older one continued to work in commerce, and the younger opened a Quran school.[35]

Thus far, we have looked at Muslim traders trafficking within the borders of the *dār al-Islām*, but Muslim merchants from al-Andalus also traded with the Christian Spanish kingdoms to the north. In this respect, Andalusī merchants differed from their eastern counterparts. Given the common border between Islamic and Christian Spain, the opportunities for Muslim Spanish merchants to trade in Christian lands were greater than in most other areas of the Islamic World. Despite Muslim religious sanctions against commercial traffic to non-Muslim lands, northern Spanish sources show Muslim Andalusī merchants trading in Christian markets during the 5th/11th, 6th/12th, and early 7th/13th centuries.[36]

A number of 12th-century Castilian and Aragonese town charters (*fueros*) included tariff lists that cited people and goods coming "from the land of the Moors". The 1166 Fuero of Evora, for example, listed "Christian, Jewish, as well as Moorish, merchants and travellers" among those people affected by its rulings.[37] Likewise, another late 12th-century *fuero*, from Santa María de Cortes, promised that "free Saracens will be secure if they come to this town for the purpose of trading in animals".[38] In the next century, the 1231 *fuero* of Cáceres permitted Christians, Jews and Muslims to come to an annual fair, whether from Christian or Muslim territories.[39]

Little is known of Muslim Spanish trading ventures north of the Pyrenees. Probably most of Christian Europe lay outside of the direct Andalusī Muslim trading sphere during the medieval period. This apparent lack of interest in commercial expeditions to Europe fits into more general patterns of Islamic commerce. It was characteristic throughout the medieval Mediterranean world to find Jews and Christians trading freely with all regions, whereas Muslim merchants generally restricted their sphere of operation to the *dār al-Islām*. For some reason, Muslim traffic with Christian Spain appears to have been an exception to this rule.

The lack of data on Muslim merchants after the middle of the 7th/13th century does not necessarily indicate their absence from Andalusī markets. Nevertheless, the concurrent appearance of Christian mercantile traffic in the region when important port cities came under Christian political control strongly suggests that the earlier mercantile hierarchy had been overturned. Although some of the most important Andalusī ports, notably Almería and Málaga, remained in Muslim hands for another two and a half centuries, much of the western Mediterranean, including the strategic Balearic channel and the Straits of Gibraltar, was now patrolled by Christian shipping. At the same time, Ferdinand III of Castile and James I of Aragon granted special concessions to Christian merchants operating within their domains. These privileges extended not only to their own subjects, but often to foreign merchants as well. The Genoese, for example, were awarded extensive liberties in the newly-Christian regions of southern Castile, and in 1264 Alfonso X of Castile went so far as to put a Genoese admiral in command of his kingdom's navy.

Thus, the relative power and prominence of different merchant groups in Andalusī commerce underwent a distinct change between the 4th/10th and the 7th/13th centuries. During the Umayyad, *ṭā'ifa*, Almoravid and Almohad periods, Andalusī international trade was dominated by Muslim and Jewish merchants, both from Spain and from other regions of the Islamic world. These men travelled between east and west either overland or by southern Mediterranean shipping routes, and they often maintained close commercial networks with their co-religionists throughout the Maghrib and the Near East.

While Muslim rule remained firm in al-Andalus, the southern Spanish markets in which these Jewish and Muslim merchants traded functioned as international emporia, handling a wide range of goods from all over the Mediterranean world and beyond. Through the 5th/11th and first half of the 6th/12th century, al-Andalus played the role of a mediator and distributor in western Mediterranean trade. Merchants brought goods from the East (such as textiles, indigo, pepper and other spices) to Muslim Spain for local sale and redistribution to the Christian north; they carried away Andalusī products (silk, saffron, olive oil, leather, dye-stuffs and other items) and goods of more northerly origin (mainly furs and slaves) which had come south into Andalusī markets.

Thus, a 5th/11th century merchant might have arrived in Almería from Cairo or Tunis, bringing a cargo containing cinnamon, pearls, wheat or flax. Having sold these goods, he would return eastward, taking a load of—perhaps—raw silk, cumin, paper and coral (all products of the western Mediterranean). Since merchants rarely specialised in particular goods, it is likely that this merchant's Spanish purchases were dictated by his perception of favourable prices and his knowledge of demand for these items elsewhere. The goods which he had brought from the East and sold in Almería may have been disposed of locally, or they may have been traded (or sent as tribute) to Christian Spain, or shipped further on to markets in southern France or Italy.

This commercial situation began to change in the middle of the 6th/12th century, when increasing numbers of Christian merchants began to enter the Andalusī trading sphere. These traders came to dominate western Mediterranean commercial routes by the early 7th/13th century. With the expansion of Christian naval power in the era of the Crusades, Christian shipping acquired a monopoly over the safest and fastest Mediterranean routes (those running along the northern shores). References to Muslim merchants in Andalusī trade decline in this period, so that by the later 7th/13th century Iberian international trade seems to have been largely in the hands of a new set of merchants. In Naṣrid Granada and southern Castile, Genoese traders controlled most commercial activity. In northern Castile a nascent Castilian merchant class dominated trade through Atlantic ports. At the same time, Catalan merchants were building a Mediterranean trading empire to rival that of the Italians.[40]

The development of Christian sea routes and shipping in the later 6th/12th century lent support to rapidly growing southern European ports and to their merchant communities. New routes also began to spring up between Italy and North Africa, and with them, the southern Iberian coast lost its preeminence as a shipping channel linking the markets of the northern and southern Mediterranean. In consequence, by the 7th/13th century, Andalusī ports had ceased to be distribution points for goods travelling between the eastern and western Islamic world, or between the markets of the northern and southern Mediterranean. In their place, Genoa and other Christian cities took over as the new international emporia and entrepots. The same goods which might once have come to southern Europe by way of Andalusī markets, now began to come to Spain on Italian ships.

By the 7th/13th century, we begin to see changes in the commodities of western Mediterranean trade, including those coming to and from southern Spanish ports. The appearance of new goods in Andalusī markets, together with the southward progress of the Christian *reconquista,* effected the internal Andalusī economy. For instance, cloth from the nascent textile industries of the Low Countries, Italy and France began to be sold in the Mediterranean world, and must have had an effect on Spanish textile production. During this period, there were dramatic changes in Iberian commercial industries, and a decline in production of some of the region's staple exports. Earlier, al-Andalus had been an important source of raw silk and woven silk textiles to Mediterranean trade, and silk cultivation and weaving had been the dominant industry in many of the towns and rural areas along the southern Andalusī coast. In contrast, Christian Spain (particularly Castile) began producing wool in the late 13th century, so that, by 1350, the Peninsula competed with England in exporting wool for European looms. Meanwhile silk production dropped sharply, and Spanish silk was replaced by Italian silk in Mediterranean markets. At the same time, other new Iberian exports—including iron and alum—also appeared on the scene, replacing earlier Andalusī products such as copper. In only a few instances, as with Cordoban leather and Játiva paper, was continuity of production and export maintained through the transition from Muslim to Christian rule. It is noteworthy that these particular items—leather and paper—were not faced with the same kind of external competition as in other industries.

The role of Iberian markets changed in the 7th/13th century, just as the merchant population had changed. By the time Spanish trade was in the control of Christian merchants, the Peninsula had lost the commercial importance which it had enjoyed in earlier times. Once, at the edge of the Islamic West, al-Andalus had played a vital role within the Islamic trading sphere, producing, consuming and redistributing goods. Later, Spanish markets—on the southern frontier of the Christian West—became an appendage to the European commercial orbit. Spain continued to be a consumer of imported goods—from both the Islamic world and from Europe—and it increasingly became a source of raw materials for European markets and industries. However, it was no longer a major international entrepot.

The Mediterranean commercial world had been turned upside-down, and Muslim merchants now found it difficult to operate in the Iberian markets which they had once controlled. By the middle of the 7th/13th century, it appears that most Muslim merchants had abandoned the newly-Christian markets of southern Spain, and transferred their commercial attention to the more economically promising ports of North Africa, the eastern Mediterranean and the Indian Ocean.

[1] It should be remembered that biographical dictionaries were written for the purpose of recording the lives and scholarly connections of learned men in order to verify the transmission of religious knowledge. These books were not intended to record individual professions aside from those connected to scholarship. Other problems also arise with their use. First of all, a person with *al-tājir* ("the merchant") as part of his name was probably, but not necessarily, a merchant. Instead, it may have been a family profession. Only in cases where he is described as "making his living as a merchant" or coming to a place "as a merchant" (*tājiran*), is his trade certain. I have only included examples of the latter type in this survey. Secondly, one finds a high percentage of people coming to Spain "as merchants" from the East, but relatively few Andalusis going East for the same purpose. The reasons for this are obvious: trade was a reasonable explanation for a journey to Spain, but biographers preferred to cite pilgrimage as the motivation for Andalusis venturing to the East. If these Andalusis were also trading on the side, it was not necessarily mentioned.

The primary biographies used in this study are the *Kitāb taʾrīkh ʿulamāʾ al-Andalus* of Ibn al-Faraḍī (d. 403/1013) ed. F. Codera, *Bibliotheca Arabico-Hispana* (*BAH*) Madrid, 1890; *Al-*

Ṣila fī ta'rīkh a'immat al-Andalus by Ibn Bashkuwāl (d. 578/1183), Cairo, 1955; *Bughyat al-multamis fī ta'rīkh rijāl ahl al-Andalus* by Aḥmad al-Ḍabbī (d. 598/1202), ed. F. Codera, *BAH*, Madrid, 1885; and the *Takmila* of Ibn al-Abbār (7th/13th c.), ed. F. Codera, *BAH*, Madrid, 1886. The *Ṣilat al-ṣila* by Ibn al-Zubayr (d. 708/1308), ed. E. Lévi-Provençal, Rabat, 1938, contains no merchant interlopers among the scholarly ranks. One further source is the *Akhbār wa-tarājim Andalusiyya* of al-Silafī (d. 576/1180), of which the section on Andalusis travelling in the East has been edited separately by I. 'Abbās, Beirut, 1963.

Merchant-scholars were by no means unique to al-Andalus. In a study of the professional affiliations of Eastern scholars through the 5th/11th century, H. J. Cohen has found that 4,200 out of 14,000 entries describing scholars in biographical dictionaries contained information on their trade. Among these, 22% were employed as merchants or artisans in the textile industry, 13% in foods, 4% in jewels, 4% in perfumes, 4% in leather-work, 4% in books, 3% in metals, 2% in wood, 2% in general commerce and 9% in other commodities. Besides these straight traders, 3% acted as bankers and 2% were middlemen or commercial agents. See "The Economic Background and Secular Occupations of Muslim Jurisprudents and Traditionists in the Classical Period of Islam", *Journal of the Economic and Social History of the Orient*, 13, 1970, pp. 26-31.

2 This paper will not consider purely local merchants (shopkeepers and the like), for although their volume of business could have been reasonably large, their sphere of action was limited. Only in the Iberian frontier regions (*thughūr*) were they engaged in anything approximating international trade. Local merchants, markets and trade in al-Andalus have been extensively treated by P. Chalmeta in his *El señor del zoco en España*, Madrid, 1973.

3 Abū 'l-Faḍl Ja'far al-Dimashqī, *Kitāb al-ishāra ilā maḥāsin al-tijāra*, Cairo, 1318/1900, pp. 48-52. The dates of this author are disputed. He may have lived as early as the 3rd/9th century, but he is more generally believed to have been a 5th/11th-century figure.

4 Documents from the Cairo *Geniza* show Jewish merchants of all three types active in Andalusī trade, and it is likely that their activities were paralleled in the Muslim commercial sphere.

5 The issue of Andalusī identity has been much debated. See, for example, D. Wasserstein, *The Rise and Fall of the Party-Kings; Politics and Society in Islamic Spain 1002-1086*, Princeton, 1985, p. 165; and N. Roth, "Some Aspects of Muslim-Jewish Relations in Spain", *Estudios en homenaje a D. Claudio Sánchez-Albornoz*, II, Buenos Aires, 1983, p. 203. Also: M. Benaboud, "'Asabiyya and Social Relations in al-Andalus during the Period of the Taifa States", *Hespéris-Tamuda* 19, 1980-81, pp. 5-45; M. Shatzmiller, "The Legacy of the Andalusian Berbers in the 14th-century Maghreb", *Relaciones de la Península Ibérica con el Magreb*, ed. M. García-Arenal and M. J. Viguera, Madrid, 1988, pp. 205-36; P. Guichard, *Structures sociales "orientales" et "occidentales" dans l'Espagne musulmane*, Paris, 1977.

6 *Letters of Maimonides*, trans. Leon D. Stitskin, New York, 1977, p. 157. This tendency to associate with religious compatriots is abundantly demonstrated in letters from the Cairo *Geniza*, which show partnership networks of Andalusī Jewish merchants operating in the eastern Mediterranean.

7 For more on the professional specialisation of different religious and ethnic groups in Andalusī society (although not relating to international merchants), see M. Shatzmiller, "Professions and Ethnic Origins of Urban Labourers in Muslim Spain", *Awrāq*, 5-6, 1982-83, pp. 149-59.

8 On shipping routes, see J. Pryor, *Geography, Technology, and War*, Cambridge, 1988.

9 Ibn Ḥawqal, *Kitāb ṣūrat al-arḍ*, ed. J. H. Kramers, Leiden, 1938, p. 78, and in *Journal asiatique*, 1942, p. 168. See also C. Courtois, "Remarques sur le commerce maritime en Afrique au XIe siècle", *Mélanges d'histoire et d'archéologie de l'occident musulman: Hommage à Georges Marçais*, Algiers, 1957, p. 54.

10 E. García Gómez, *Anales palatinos del califa de Córdoba al-Hakam II, por 'Isā b. Aḥmad al-Rāzī*, Madrid, 1967, pp. 110-11.

11 Ibn al-Athīr, *Al-Kāmil fī 'l-ta'rīkh*, ed. C.J. Tornberg, Leiden, 1851-76, VIII, 384-85. French trans. by E. Fagnan, *Annales du Maghreb et de l'Espagne*, Algiers, 1898, pp. 358-59.

12 Buzurg b. Shahriyār, *The Book of the Wonders of India*, trans. G. S. P. Freeman-Grenville, London, 1981, pp. 13-18. The story is fiction, yet there is no reason to believe that the mention of Spaniards was part of the wonder related. The storm, not the unfortunate travellers, was the subject of the tale. As in the *Arabian Nights*, the genre of *'ajā'ib* literature usually contains enough of daily life properly to set off the wonders described.

13 Al-Marwānī was known as a transmitter of the *Kitāb nasab Quraysh* of al-Zubayrī; cf. E. Lévi-Provençal, "Le 'Kitāb nasab Quraysh' de Muṣ'ab al-Zubayrī," *Arabica* 1, 1954, p. 95. Un-

like the names of most merchants, al-Marwānī's name may tell us something of his class, since it suggests that he was a member of the Umayyad family.

14 Ibn al-Faraḍī, pp. 51-52, #181; p. 53, #184; pp. 68-69, #235; pp. 130-31, #453; pp. 179-81, #650; Ibn Bashkuwāl, p. 31, #43; p. 456, #1042 (no date!); al-Ḍabbī, pp. 186-87, #455; Ibn al-Abbār, I, 96, #320. Ibn Bashkuwāl mentioned a further Cordoban, probably of this period, whom I have not included among these seven since the author provided no dates and listed his name, though not necessarily his profession, as *al-tājir* (p. 492, #1135). Since the source of most of these 4th/10th-century examples, Ibn al-Faraḍī, died in 403/1012-3, the trend towards early dates is not surprising.

15 B. Roy & P. Poinssot, *Inscriptions arabes de Kairouan*, Paris, 1950, I, 114.

16 Ibn al-Abbār, I, 366, #1048; Ibn al-Faraḍī, II, 61, #1604. No dates are given for this second man, Yaḥyā b. Khalaf al-Sadafī, but it is reasonable to assume that he lived during the 4th/10th century, as did the majority of scholars described by Ibn al-Faraḍī.

17 ʿAbd al-ʿAzīz b. Jaʿfar ... al-Baghdādī, Ibn Bashkuwāl, pp. 356-57, #802; ʿAbd al-Raḥmān b. Muḥammad ... al-Miṣrī arrived in Spain from Egypt in 394/1003-4 where he made his living through commerce [*kāna maʿāshuhu min al-tijāra*] (*ibid.* p. 337, #756); Muḥammad b. al-Qāsim ... al-Qarawī, came to Spain ca. 400/1009-10 (*ibid.* pp. 564-65, #1309).

18 Egyptians: W. Heyd, *Histoire du commerce du Levant au moyen âge*, Leipzig, 1885, I, 49. Khurāsānis: D. M. Dunlop, *The History of the Jewish Khazars,* Princeton, 1954, pp. 134-35. There has been considerable debate concerning the authenticity of Ḥasday's correspondence. Dunlop considered that the letters written by Ḥasday himself were genuine, although the replies may be later fabrications (p. 120 *et seq.*).

19 Ibn Sahl, *Thalāth wathā'iq fī muḥārabat al-ahwā' wa 'l-bidaʿ fī 'l-Andalus*, ed. M. A. Khallāf, Cairo, 1981, p. 44.

20 Ibn Bassām, *Al-Dhakhīra fī maḥāsin ahl al-jazīra*, Cairo, 1364/1945, IV/1, 65. Ibn Bassām attributed his information to Ibn Ḥayyān.

21 There is some evidence, though it is not specifically commercial, that Andalusī scholars began travelling abroad more frequently in the early 5th/11th century. M. L. Avila, *La sociedad hispano-musulmana al final del califato*, Madrid, 1985, p. 83, has determined the percentage of scholars journeying abroad (for pilgrimage and other reasons) from biographical evidence: 350/961 (29%); 360/970 (34%); 370/980 (38.4%); 380/990 (35.5%); 390/999 (38.4%); 400/1009 (37.6%); 410/1019 (36.5%); 420/1029 (34.6%); 430/1038 (23.4%); 440/1048 (24.1%). High figures may be due to political turmoil in al-Andalus in the early 400s/1000s.

22 Al-Bakrī, *Description de l'Afrique septentrionale*, ed. & trans. M. de Slane, Paris, 1911, p. 67.

23 Ibn Sahl, *Al-Aḥkām al-kubrā*, General Library, Rabat, MS 838Q, fols.180, 183-86, 189-90; Al-Wansharīsī, *Al-Miʿyār al-muʿrib wa 'l-jāmiʿ al-mughrib*, Rabat, 1981, V, 281. The latter case was brought before the *Qāḍī* of Granada, Abū 'l-Qāsim b. Muḥammad b. Sirāj.

24 Ibn al-Abbār mentioned Khalīl al-Qurṭubī as being "by profession a merchant" [*muḥtarifan bi 'l-tijāra*] (I, 59, #187); Ibn Bashkuwāl referred to Niẓār b. Muḥammad b. ʿAbd Allāh al-Qaysī (who *jāla fī bilād Ifrīqiya wa 'l-Andalus zamānan ṭāliban lil-ʿilm wa tājiran*) (p. 606, #1407), and Marwān b. Sulaymān b. Ibrāhīm b. Mūrqāṭ al-Ghāfiqī (d. 418/1027) (*ibid.*, p. 581, #1347). These two only partially qualify as belonging to the 5th/11th century, but they were active in the early 400s/1000s, and belong to a later generation than the late 4th/10th-century merchants.

25 See Ibn Bashkuwāl, entries 779, 652, 528, 674, 1314, 1406, 285, 957, 1311, 948, 1313, 1402, 1312, 269, 1366, 654, 960, 1400, 247, 1316, 1338, 1445. These are arranged chronologically by the date when the traveller arrived in al-Andalus, and origins are based on *nisba*. The phrasing which Ibn Bashkuwāl generally uses reads: "he came to al-Andalus as a merchant in the year ... " [*qadima 'l-Andalus tājiran sanat ...*]. Also on Ibn Bashkuwāl and his references to merchant-scholars, see M. A. Khallāf, *Qurṭuba 'l-Islāmiyya*, Tunis, 1984, pp. 98-100.

26 It should be noted, however, that evidence provided by M. L. Avila (see note 21 above) shows many Andalusī scholars travelling abroad in this period, although we do not know whether these men were also merchants.

27 Ibn Bashkuwāl: Naṣr b. al-Ḥasan ... al-Shāmī, p. 602, #1399, and Mubārak b. Saʿīd ... al-Baghdādī, p. 599, #1391. Ibn Bashkuwāl also recorded two further non-Andalusis arriving in Spain (p. 113, #264; p. 409, #924] but included no dates. Ibn al-Abbār, I, 370, #1054.

28 Ibn Bashkuwāl, p. 410, #927. The Denian, Muḥammad b. al-Ḥasan al-Maqqarī, was cited by Ibn al-Abbār (pp.193-95, #669).

29 Al-Māzarī: H. R. Idris, *La Berbérie orientale sous les Zirides*, Paris, 1962, p. 678. *Geniza*: Bodl. D74.41; TS 16.54.

30 E. Lévi-Provençal, *Inscriptions arabes d'Espagne*, Paris, 1931, pp. 116, 121, 127. The origin of the third merchant was not noted, but it seems likely that he was Andalusī.

31 Al-Idrīsī, *Opus geographicum*. Vol. III, Naples, 1972, p. 239; and Benjamin of Tudela, "The Itinerary of Benjamin of Tudela", trans. M. N. Adler, *Jewish Quarterly Review* 18, 1906, p. 686. It is clear from the context of this latter passage that the author is referring to non-Jewish merchants.

32 Al-Silafī, *Akhbār wa tarājim*, p. 21, #5. It is possible that Aḥmad travelled in the East during an earlier period, but since al-Silafī (d. 576/1180) does not provide a date for his death, he was probably a contemporary of the biographer.

33 Ibn al-Abbār: Three of these merchants bore the name "al-Anṣārī", but do not appear otherwise related; the other two were "al-Undī" and "al-Bāhilī". The three Anṣāris were from Seville (d. 580/1184) (p. 249, #803); Valencia (d. 598/1201-2) (p. 274, #864); Baeza & Jaén (d. 630/1232-3) (p. 340, #993); the others were respectively from Valencia (d. 622/1225) (p. 650, #1810) and Málaga (d. 642/1244-5) (p. 519, #1456).

34 Al-Shaqundī: Arabic text in al-Maqqarī, *Analectes*, ed. R. Dozy, Leiden, 1855-60, II, 148. Because these Muslim merchants were mentioned together with Christian (Italian) merchants and the context of their shipping appears international, I am assuming that al-Shaqundī is here referring to foreigners rather than Andalusis.

35 G. Elshayyal, "The Cultural Relations between Alexandria and the Islamic West in al-Andalus and Morocco", *Maʿhad al-dirasāt al-Islamiyya*, Madrid, 36, 1971, p. 65.

36 Although travel to and trade with non-Islamic lands was discouraged [*makrūh*], it was not usually reckoned among things forbidden [*ḥarām*] by Islamic law (see B. Lewis, *The Muslim Discovery of Europe*, New York, 1982, p. 61). However, perhaps as a consequence of the geographical proximity between Christian regions and al-Andalus (and, to a lesser extent, North Africa), western Mālikī jurists tended to adopt a more rigid stance against travel and trade to the *dār al-ḥarb* (non-Islamic lands) than did other schools of Islamic law. The early jurist Saḥnūn (3rd/9th-century) cited Mālik as having a "strong repugnance" [*karāhiya shadīda*] for Muslim commercial activity in non-Muslim territories, and later Andalusī legal scholars, including Ibn Ḥazm (a Ẓāhirī, d. 456/1064) and Ibn Rushd (d. 595/1198), also ruled against trade to *ḥarbī* lands (Saḥnūn, *Al-Mudawwana al-kubrā*, Cairo, 1323/1905, X, 102; Ibn Ḥazm, *Al-Muḥallā*, Cairo, 1347/1928-29, VII, 349-50; Ibn Rushd, *Muqaddimāt al-mumahhidāt*, Cairo, 1325/1907, II, 285. A later Maghribi scholar, Ibn Juzayy (d. 741/1340) was also strict on this matter, ruling that "it is not permitted to trade to the *dār al-ḥarb*" (*Qawānīn aḥkām al-sharīʿa*, Beirut, 1968, p. 319).

As with most legal evidence, however, there seems to have been a considerable disparity between judicial theory and commercial reality. For more on this topic, see also M. Khadduri, *War and Peace in the Law of Islam*, Baltimore, 1955; J. Yarrison, *Force as an Instrument of Policy*, Ph.D Dissertation, Princeton University, 1982, p. 269 *et seq.*

37 *Mercatores vel viatores christianos iudeos sive mauros*; see *Portugaliae monumenta historica: Leges et consuetudines*. I, Lisbon, 1856, p. 393. The *Fuero* of Mós (1162) referred to Moorish textiles [*rouba de terra de mauros*] (*ibid.*, p. 391).

38 *Saraceni liberi, si cum pro recua mercaturam venerint ad eandem villam sint securi*; see A. Ballesteros y Beretta, *Historia de España*, Barcelona, 1920, II, 529.

39 *... omnes qui ad istam feriam voluerint venire, tam Christiani, quam Judei, quam Sarraceni ... tam de tierra Sarracenorum quam de tierra Christianorum ...* See T. González, *Colección de privilegios, franquezas, exenciones, y fueros*, IV, Madrid, 1833, p. 94.

40 On Genoese activity in southern Castile, see J. Heers, "Les hommes d'affaires italiens en Espagne au moyen âge: le marché monétaire", in *Fremde Kaufleute auf der iberischen Halbinsel*, ed. H. Kellenbenz, Cologne-Vienna, 1970, pp. 74-83; R.S. López, "Alfonso el Sabio y el primer almirante de Castilla genovés", *Cuadernos de Historia de España*, 14, 1950, pp. 5-16; and "Il predominio economico dei Genovesi nella monarchia spagnola", *Giornale storico e letterario della Liguria*, 11, 1936, pp. 65-74. On northern Castile, see T.F. Ruiz, "Burgos y el comercio castellano en la baja Edad Media", in *La ciudad de Burgos. Actas del congreso de historia de Burgos*, Madrid, 1985, pp. 37-55. On Catalonia, see C.E. Dufourcq, *L'Espagne catalane et le Maghrib aux XIIIe et XIVe siècles*, Paris, 1966, and other works by the same author.

BIBLIOGRAPHY

Primary works

Al-Ḍabbī, Aḥmad, *Bughyat al-multamis fī ta'rīkh rijāl ahl al-Andalus*, ed. F. Codera, *Bibliotheca arábigo-hispana*, Madrid, 1885.

Al-Dimashqī, Abū 'l-Faḍl Ja'far, *Kitāb al-ishāra ilā maḥāsin al-tijāra*, Cairo, 1318/1900.

Ibn al-Abbār, *Takmila*, ed. F. Codera, *Bibliotheca Arabico-Hispana*, Madrid, 1886.

Ibn Bashkuwāl, *Al-Ṣila fī ta'rīkh a'immat al-Andalus*, Cairo, 1955.

Ibn al-Faraḍī, *Kitāb ta'rīkh 'ulamā' al-Andalus*, ed. F. Codera, *Bibliotheca Arabico-Hispana*, Madrid, 1890.

Ibn Sahl, *Al-Aḥkām al-kubrā*, General Library, Rabat, MS 838Q.

Lévi-Provençal, E., *Inscriptions arabes d'Espagne*, Paris, 1931.

Roy, B., and P. Poinssot, *Inscriptions arabes de Kairouan*, Paris, 1950.

Al-Silafī, *Akhbār wa-tarājim Andalusiyya*, sections edited by I. 'Abbās, Beirut, 1963.

Al-Wansharīsī, *Al-Mi'yār al-mu'rib wa 'l-jāmi' al-mughrib*, Rabat, 1981, 8 vols.

Secondary works

Avila, M. L., *La sociedad hispano-musulmana al final del califato*, Madrid, 1985.

Benaboud, M., "'Asabiyya and Social Relations in al-Andalus during the Period of the Taifa States", *Hespéris-Tamuda*, 19, 1980-81, pp. 5-45.

Chalmeta, P., *El señor del zoco en España*, Madrid, 1973.

Cohen, H. J., "The Economic Background and Secular Occupations of Muslim Jurisprudents and Traditionists in the Classical Period of Islam", *Journal of the Economic and Social History of the Orient*, 13, 1970, pp. 16-61.

Courtois, C. "Remarques sur le commerce maritime en Afrique au XIe siècle", in *Mélanges d'histoire et d'archéologie de l'occident musulman: Hommage à Georges Marçais*, Algiers, 1957, pp. 51-59.

Dufourcq, C. E., *L'Espagne catalane et le Maghrib aux XIIIe et XIVe siècles*, Paris, 1966.

Guichard, P., *Structures sociales "orientales" et "occidentales" dans l'Espagne musulmane*, Paris, 1977.

Heers, J., "Les hommes d'affaires italiens en Espagne au moyen âge: le marché monétaire", in *Fremde Kaufleute auf der iberischen Halbinsel*, ed. H. Kellenbenz, Cologne-Vienna, 1970, pp. 74-83.

Heyd, W., *Histoire du commerce du Levant au moyen âge*, Leipzig, 1885.

Idris, H. R., *La Berbérie orientale sous les Zirides*, Paris, 1962.

Khallāf, M. A., *Qurṭuba 'l-Islāmiyya*, Tunis, 1984.

López, R. S., "Alfonso el Sabio y el primer almirante de Castilla genovese", *Cuadernos de Historia de España*, 14, 1950, pp. 5-16.

——, "Il predominio economico dei Genovesi nella monarchia spagnola", *Giornale storico e letterario della Ligurgia*, 11, 1936, pp. 65-74.

Pryor, J., *Geography, Technology, and War*, Cambridge, 1988.

Ruiz, T. F., "Burgos y el comercio castellano en la baja Edad Media", in *La ciudad de Burgos. Actas del congreso de historia de Burgos*, Madrid, 1985, pp. 37-55.

Shatzmiller, M., "The Legacy of the Andalusian Berbers in the 14th century Maghreb", in *Relaciones de la Península Ibérica con el Magreb*, ed. M. García-Arenal and M. J. Viguera, Madrid, 1988, pp. 205-36.

——, "Professions and Ethnic Origins of Urban Labourers in Muslim Spain", *Awrāq*, 5-6, 1982-83, pp. 149-59.

Wasserstein, D. *The Rise and Fall of the Party-Kings; Politics and Society in Islamic Spain 1002-1086*, Princeton, 1985.

PHILOSOPHY

ISLAMIC THOUGHT IN THE IBERIAN PENINSULA

MIGUEL CRUZ HERNÁNDEZ

I. *Origins of Ibero-Islamic thought*

I.1 *The Eastern sources of Andalusī thought*

Islam established itself in the Iberian Peninsula between 92/711 and 139/756. However, while the Umayyad prince ʿAbd al-Raḥmān b. Muʿāwiya's persevering campaign to gain mastery over different social groups (*baladī* Arabs, Berbers, Syrians, Mozarabs and Jews), and structure them within an Arab Islamic monarchy, established the political and social bases of Islam in al-Andalus, the antagonism between the Umayyads of Córdoba and the Abbasids of Baghdad ensured that the former would always view with suspicion anything coming from the East. The fourth Umayyad monarch, ʿAbd al-Raḥmān II, was obliged, nevertheless, to restructure his "administration" in accord with the Baghdadi model, which was none other than that inherited from the Sassanids, and commercial relations, together with journeys made in accordance with the precept of pilgrimage (*ḥajj*) to the Islamic holy places, encouraged the arrival of Eastern "novelties" in al-Andalus.

Learning was introduced into al-Andalus through five cultural vehicles: (1) Islamic law (*fiqh*), first of the Awzāʿī school and later of the Mālikī school, which was the official one of the Umayyad monarchy and in subsequent periods; (2) ascetic and mystical spirituality (*taṣawwuf*), which is recorded early; (3) esoterism (*bāṭiniyya*), of which examples are found from 271/851; (4) Muʿtazilī theology, with which the Cordoban physician Abū Bakr Faraj b. Sallām was familiar as early as the beginning of the 3rd/9th century; and (5) the sciences (astronomy, mathematics and medicine). It was only later, as we shall see, that philosophy in the strict sense (*falsafa*) became established.

I.2 *The Masarrī school*

Muḥammad b. Masarra (7 *Shawwāl* 269/19 April 883-8 *Ramaḍān* 319/October 20 931) was responsible for the first structuring of Andalusī thought. His father, ʿAbd Allāh b. Masarra (who died in Mecca in 266/899), had initiated him into the Bāṭinī, Muʿtazilī and spiritual doctrines he had acquired in the East, and he himself founded a small retreat for friends and companions in the caves of the Sierra de Córdoba, where prayer and penitence were practised. However, the group awakened the suspicions of the official establishment, and Ibn Masarra was, as a result, obliged to spend several years in North Africa and the East, probably returning at the end of the *fitna* (civil war) of the reign of the *amīr* ʿAbd Allāh. Thereupon he summoned a group of followers to his new retreat. We know that he wrote at least two books: *Kitāb al-tabṣira* ("The Book of Discerning Explanation") and *Kitāb al-ḥurūf* ("The Book of [the esoteric meaning of] Lctters"), of which we have only the titles. His thought has been reconstructed by Asín Palacios, thanks, above all, to the evidence of Ṣā'id of Toledo, Ibn Ḥazm and Ibn 'Arabī.

The thought of Ibn Masarra is a synthesis of Mu'tazilī doctrines concerning the unity of God, divine justice and free will, and of Sufi theory and practice as expounded by Dhū 'l-Nūn al-Miṣrī and al-Nahrajūrī. However, he articulated these ideas, if we are to believe the accounts that have come down to us, in an original and personal way. God is that essence to which unity pertains *per se*; and, as there is no analogy whatever for such a sublime mode of being, the divine essence can only be known though ecstatic union with God. In order to make some kind of reference, Ibn Masarra compares the cosmos to a cubic building: its roof is the Divine One; the walls are created beings; five columns symbolise the five basic substances; an interior room, lacking doors and windows, is the unknowable Divine Essence, the implication being that reason can find no orifice to penetrate and know it. Outside the building, however, leaning against the walls, is another column of the same essence as that of the five interior ones; and if man clings to this, it serves as an intermediary (*farzāj*) enabling him to attain the ecstatic union which leads to God.

The cosmos has its origin in prime matter, symbolised by the Throne, from which all creatures proceed—none can be created directly by God because of His essential sublimity. All creatures have a twin reality: the apparent, or perceptible, and the inner essence. Apparent reality is maintained by Adam, Abraham and Muḥammad. Intimate reality is displayed by the angels Gabriel, Isrāfil, and Michael; Mālik governs the inferno, and Riḍwān paradise. Four kinds of phenomenon occur in the cosmos: the creation of the material world; the creation of the spiritual world; the preservation and providence of creation; and the last judgment, which rewards or punishes.

Prime matter, or the Throne, is structured as a reflection of the divine light which produces the celestial forms, luminous bodies capable of receiving angelic spirits. The first is the universal intellect in which God instils infinite and universal knowledge; this is the divine Pen, whose writing is the universal soul, which gives rise to pure nature. The superabundance of being which springs from God through the intermediary of pure nature finally covers the ontological hollowness of darkness itself, and this is the origin of secondary matter, which constitutes the universal body out of which the world of generation and corruption proceeds. Upon this world God again sheds His light, engendering in each one of its forms an immaterial, indivisible spirit, each one of these being distinguished by its relative capacity to receive the divine light. Its conservation is due to its sustaining principles, which are reason and illumination for the spirit, and food and drink for the body. Finally, God has created for all beings four kinds of happiness: distributive, according to the intention of the subject; commutative, according to its constitution; essential, in accord with the perfection of being; and legal, according to obedience to positive law. God knows everything universally and eternally, but does not on this account determine human acts, since, in his omnipotence, he wished to create men free and responsible for their acts.

The human condition, free and responsible, means that man requires a rule of life to cleanse the soul of imperfections inherent in the carnal condition of our life here and now. This rule includes the ascetic practices of mortification, penitence, fasting, patience, poverty, silence, humility, prayer, service, brotherly love, faith in God and the conscientious examination of positive acts, this last practice being the most highly prized, since it permits us to discover the progress of the spiritual intent of our acts. Thus, the spiritual rule provides the human spirit with a perfection similar to, but not equal to, that of the prophetic spirit. This gift is the apex of spiritual life, permitting the human soul to reflect, like a well-polished mirror, the image of divine wisdom, in preparation for the definitive joy of union with God.

I.3 *The disciples of Ibn Masarra*

For all the fears aroused by the Masarris, Muḥammad b. Masarra's teachings were highly successful. Mistrust of the thinker had probably emerged by the time of the *amīr* ʿAbd Allāh, grandfather of ʿAbd al-Raḥmān III, and the *faqīh* al-Zajjālī (d. 301/914) later promulgated an "edict" of harsh condemnation which the caliph ʿAbd al-Raḥmān III ordered to be updated and published after Ibn Masarra's death, the Masarris being then condemned and their persecution ordered. These Masarris can be grouped into two circles, that of Córdoba and that of Pechina. To the first belonged, among others, three members of the distinguished Muwallad family of the Banū Ballūṭī, namely the physician al-Ḥakam (d. 420/1029), Saʿīd (d. 404/1013) and ʿAbd al-Malik (d. 436/1044), while members of the second group included Ismāʿīl b. ʿAbd Allāh al-Ruʿaynī (ca. 339/950-432/1040), his son Abū Hārūn, a daughter whose name has not survived, her husband Aḥmad, and a grandson of al-Ruʿaynī named Yaḥyā.

The Cordoban group involved few notable divergences from the thought of Muḥammad b. Masarra. On the contrary, al-Ruʿaynī was regarded as the *imām* of the group, receiving the *zakāt*, or canonical tithe, and proclaiming that only he knew the authentic esoteric significance of Masarrī thought, which he interpreted in a communistic sense, not only with reference to the ownership of goods, but also with respect to sexual relations: "All the things which are owned in this world are illicit ... the only thing which a Muslim is permitted to possess is his daily sustenance, whatever means he might employ to procure it."[1] According to Ibn Ḥazm, "Ismāʿīl approved marriage or sexual unions contracted for a [specified] period of time as licit".[2]

I.4 *Influence and significance of the Masarrī school*

Masarrī ideology became the principal root of the dialectical thought of the Sufis of al-Andalus, and was highly influential within what Asín Palacios called the "School of Almería", whose central members acquired such power that the *fuqahā'* of Almería, led by al-Barjī, were the only ones of their time who dared to condemn the burning of al-Ghazālī's writings ordered by the chief *qāḍī* of Córdoba, Ibn Ḥamdīn. The principal figure of the group was Abū 'l-ʿAbbās Aḥmad b. Muḥammad b. Mūsā b. ʿAṭā' Allāh b. al-ʿArīf, who was born in Almería in 485/1088 and died in Marrakesh in 361/1141 after eating a poisoned eggplant. Leaving aside his strictly Sufi doctrines, which will be discussed in the appropriate section, I will here simply point out his use of Masarrī neo-Platonism, as it appears in his book, *Maḥāsin al-majālis*. His main disciples were Abū Bakr Muḥammad b. al-Ḥusayn of Majorca, Abū 'l-Ḥakam b. Barrajān (d. ca. 536/1141) and Abū 'l-Qāsim b. Qasī (d. 546/1151), author of a book called *Khālʿ al-naʿlayn*, which was used by Ibn ʿArabī.

Acquaintance with the Masarrī school is fundamental for understanding the history of Andalusī thought, its continuation in the Almería School, and the latter's influence on Ibn ʿArabī, giving it a basic role in Andalusī Sufism as a vehicle of the neo-Platonic ideology which structures its dialectical formalisation. Nevertheless, neither the ideological constructs that we will call "encyclopaedic" nor Andalusī philosophy were receptive to its ideology. Ibn Ḥazm, the best authority on Masarrī thought, rejected it, and the Andalusī philosophers were ignorant of it. Asín Palacios pointed out certain parallels between Masarrī ideology and the thought of Ramon Llull, but these are insignificant coincidences and did not in any case come directly from Ibn Masarra, but rather from the ideas of popular Sufi circles at the beginning of the 7th/13th century, more or less contemporaneous with Ibn ʿArabī.

II. *The period of the encyclopaedias*

The first half of the 5th/11th century witnessed a second formulation of Andalusī thought, one which was both removed from esoterism and Sufi mysticism and also very difficult to fit into the traditional parameters of Islamic thought, whether in the realm of philosophy, theology, esoterism or mysticism. The nature of these works leads me to name this era "the period of the encyclopedias", and it involves, in particular, three important figures, Ibn Ḥazm of Córdoba, Ṣāʿid of Toledo and Ibn al-Sīd of Badajoz.

II.1 *Ibn Ḥazm of Córdoba*

II.1.1 *Life and work*

The eminent polymath Abū Muḥammad ʿAlī b. Aḥmad b. Saʿīd b. Ḥazm (Ibn Ḥazm) was born in Córdoba, probably of Muwallad ancestry, on 7 *Ramaḍān* 384/November 7 994. His grandfather and father were palatine functionaries of the Andalusī Umayyads, and had been steadfastly loyal to their cause, this leading to his imprisonment and exile during the *fitna*, or civil war, that followed the death of the second son and successor of al-Manṣūr. His character, perhaps forged in his childhood years among the women of the house, led him into precocious and more or less unfortunate love affairs, and also provided him with an accusingly polemical cast of mind, aggravated by his adherence to the Ẓāhirī (literalist) juridical school. Finally weary of polemics he retired to an ancestral residence called Casa Montija, near Huelva, where he died on 28 *Shaʿbān* 455/July 15 1063. His written production was extraordinary, the following (leaving aside his historical and juridical works) being central to an understanding of his thought:

— *Kitāb al-fiṣal fī 'l-milal* ("Book of Divine Solutions") [about religions, sects and schools].
— *Kitāb al-akhlāq wa 'l-siyar* ("Book of customs and characters")
— *Kitāb al-iḥkām fī uṣūl al-aḥkām* ("Book of the principles of juridical foundations")
— *Ṭawq al-ḥamāma* ("The dove's neck-ring") [about love and lovers]
— *Kitāb fī marātib al-ʿulūm* ("Book of the classification of the sciences")
— *Faṣl fī maʿrifat al-nafs bi-ghayrihā wa jahlihā bi-dhātihā* ("Article about the knowledge that the soul has of things different from it and of the ignorance it has of itself")
— *Risālat al-tawqīf ʿalā shārat al-najāt bi-ikhtiṣār al-ṭarīq* ("Epistle about divine aid in finding the road to salvation by an exhaustive method")
— *Faṣl hal li 'l-mawt alam, aw lā* ("Chapter about whether or not death is painful")
— *Kitāb al-taqrīb li-ḥudūd al-kalām* ("Introduction to theological definitions")
— *Kitāb al-taḥqīq* ("Book of certification [against the metaphysics of Muḥammad b. Zakariyya al-Rāzī]")
— *Kitāb al-naṣāʾiḥ* ("Book of sincere advice [against Muʿtazilis, Murjiʾis, Khārijis, and Shiʿites]")

II.1.2 *Classes and classification of the sciences*

Ibn Ḥazm was an extraordinary historian, an excellent jurist and a great writer, but a notable acquaintance with philosophy, in the ancient sense of the term, is also a feature of his "encyclopaedic" mind. Thus he wrote: "The following are the sciences of the ancients: (1) philosophy and the laws of logic, about which Plato, his disciple Aristotle, Alexander of Aphrodisia and those who followed in their steps wrote. This science is good and of lofty status, because upon it is based the intuitive knowledge of the entire world and all that is in it, its kinds and species, substances and accidents; and in addition it sets out conditions which apodictic demonstrations must display, without which one could not ascertain the truth or error of anything. Thus this science is most useful in discerning the real essences of beings and in eliminating what is irrelevant to them. (2) The science of numbers. ... It is also a good, true and apodictic science; but its usefulness extends only to life on earth because it is only worthwhile for dividing up wealth ... (3) The science of geometry, which the compiler of the Book of Euclid and those who followed his lead discussed. This is also a good, apodictic science. Its basic principle is the intuitive knowledge of the proportional relation that lines and figures have with one another. This knowledge is applied to two things: first, to understanding the description of the exterior form of the heavenly spheres and of the Earth; second, to the lifting of weights, to architecture and surveying. ... (4) Astronomy, which Ptolemy, Hipparchus and, later, those who followed in the path of both of them, discussed, as well as those who followed the path of other [astronomers] who preceded them both, Indians, Nabataeans, and Copts. It is an apodictic science [based in] sense experience and is morally good. Its objective is to know the celestial spheres, their circular motion, their intersections, their poles and distances; and to know as well the stars, their movement of translation, their magnitudes, their distances, and the orbits of their revolutions. The usefulness of this science consists solely in that by means of it one attains knowledge of the perfection [of the cosmos] and the great wisdom of the Creator. (5) Medicine, as treated by Hippocrates, Galen, Dioscorides and those who followed them. It teaches how to heal bodies of their illnesses. ... It is a good, apodictic science, but useful only for the present life. Moreover it is not a general art, inasmuch as we frequently see that the inhabitants of deserted places ... are cured of their diseases without any physician and their bodies enjoy good health without any treatment, as good as those who use medicines and even better."[3] All the sciences can be classified according to whether they be generic or peculiar to certain peoples.

II.1.3 *Attitude towards knowledge*

For Ibn Ḥazm men are divided into two dichotomous groups with respect to knowledge. Some renounce all scientific knowledge and are content with religious knowledge, while others overvalue strictly rational thought. Most people entertain the first attitude, as he himself did until he learned "the methods of logical demonstration which, thank God, I mastered, but they did not increase at all the certainty of my previous faith".[4] By contrast the *fuqahā'* continued secure in their rutinary method, "repeating the letter of the texts mechanically without understanding their meaning and not bothering themselves to understand it; or else they devoted themselves to casuistry, but without recurring to the textual sources ... , because their only preoccupation is to maintain their prestige and their social position ... This school, moreover, despises all apodictic demonstration, and to justify their hate they merely say, 'Dialectics is forbidden us'. But I would like to know who prohibited it."[5] Nevertheless, the study of revealed truth itself requires the education undertaken by the philosophers, who "devoted the first-fruits of their intelligence to mathematics ..., passing on gradually to study the position of the stars ... and all the other physical and atmospheric phenomena and accidents. To this they add the reading of some of the books of the Greeks in which the laws that regulate discursive reasoning are determined."[6] Therefore, "philosophy, considered in its constitutive foundation, in its meaning, its effects and the end to which its study leads, is none other than the correction or improvement of the human spirit, whether by means of the practice of moral virtues and of good conduct in this life in order to achieve salvation in the next, or by means of good social organisation, not only domestic but political."[7]

Having explained the need for revelation and clarified certain physical and metaphysical doctrines (such as the formal distinction between essence and being), together with the concepts of body and its accidents, Ibn Ḥazm goes on to study divine attributes, creation and divine knowledge in its relation to human freedom.

II.1.4 *Social behaviour*

In his treatise entitled *The Characters and Conduct Concerning the Medicine of Souls*, a work quite similar in intent to the *Tahdhīb al-akhlāq* of the Persian Ibn Miskawayh, Ibn Ḥazm traces the principles of human moral behaviour, which should be based upon the equilibrium of action. The end of all ethical conduct consists in attaining a life that balances and calms the soul. But these generic principles, which are as old as Socrates, are particularised in Ibn Ḥazm through the framework of his own experience: "In this book," he writes, "I have gathered together many ideas which the Author of the light of reason inspired in me as the days of my life passed and the vicissitudes of my existence succeeded one another. God granted me the favour of being a man who has always been concerned with the vagaries of fortune ... so much so that I have spent the greater part of my life in this kind of meditation."[8] Adding stoic imperturbability to the Aristotelian principle ("Virtue lies between excess and deficiency. The extremes are hateful. That virtue which lies between both is praiseworthy."), Ibn Ḥazm holds that the rule of life which leads to happiness is temperance in all things.

The foregoing ethical concept could lead to a degree of moral rigorism, but Ibn Ḥazm softens it through balance, not only in the book just mentioned, but, even more, in the *Dove's Neck-ring*. Here, love is seen as the union of souls which are divided and which are also attracted to one another, such an impulse explaining not only the supreme love of God but also human love. In the latter love is excited by "some accidents of bodily attraction and visual approval which do not extend more than to physical appearance".[9] But in this attraction there appear a number of gradations: sweetness, harmony, beauty and grace, with beauty defined as a "thin gauze which adorns the face with a certain splendour and fleeting glow towards which hearts are attracted".[10] Personal, concrete love begins with sympathy (*istiḥsān*), proceeds through fancy (*iʿjāb*), produces love (*ulfa*), reaches adulation (*kalāf*) or passion (*ʿishq*) and culminates in amorous obsession (*shaghaf*), "which neither sleep, nor food, nor drink can conciliate, except very little, and one can even grow sick or fall into swoons and ecstatic states, speaking to oneself like a madman, or reaching the extreme of dying of love".[11]

As for the political dimension of social behaviour, Ibn Ḥazm is a decided partisan of traditional Islamic monarchy and of Umayyad legitimism. Nevertheless, his political experience leads him to put aside historical legitimacy and accept a *de facto* version in order to avoid the dangers of civil war which he himself had experienced.

II.2 *Ṣāʿid of Toledo*

The *qāḍī* Abū 'l-Qāsim b. Ṣāʿid, known as Ṣāʿid of Toledo, was born in Almería in 419/1049, and was the author of the *Ṭabaqāt al-umam*, a work of great value for understanding Andalusī culture of the 3rd/9th century and first half of the 4th/10th. Part of its originality lies in its inclusion of Jewish thinkers, notably Ibn Gabirol. The sections referring to Antiquity and the East have their origin in eastern sources, but those referring to al-Andalus are from local sources, and include personal observation. Al-Kindī is the only "philosopher" he seems to know of. He holds that no Andalusī, up to his own time, had cultivated physics or metaphysics with true zeal, but does note various authors who were interested in logic (Saʿīd b. Fatḥūn of Saragossa, Aḥmad b. Ḥakam b. Ḥafṣūn, Ismāʿīl b. Badr, who was known as the Andalusī Euclid, Ibn Ba<u>gh</u>ūnī<u>sh</u> of Toledo, and others). Four authors are mentioned as students of physics (Ibn al-Fawwāl of Saragossa, Abū 'l-Faḍl Ḥasday, who studied the treatise *De Coelo*, Ibn al-Nabbā<u>sh</u> of Pechina and Abū ʿĀmir). He says of the physician and mathematician al-Kirmānī that "when he returned to al-Andalus he brought with him the treatises known as the *Rasāʾil i<u>kh</u>wān al-Ṣafāʾ* and we know of no one before who had introduced them in al-Andalus ... [Even though] he was poorly acquainted with scientific astronomy and logic ... he had no rival in al-Andalus in the theoretical sciences (*al-ʿulūm al-naẓariyya*)".[12]

II.3 *Ibn al-Sīd of Badajoz*

Ibn al-Sīd was born in Badajoz in 444/1052, lived in Albarracín (Teruel), Toledo and Saragossa, and died in Valencia in 521/1127. His philosophical education depended above all on the *Rasāʾil I<u>kh</u>wān al-Ṣafāʾ* mentioned above, but he is also the first Andalusī to cite al-Fārābī, revealing his acquaintance with the logic of that author, since he wrote on a question "concerning whether al-Fārābī had erred when enumerating the first three Aristotelian categories or not".[13] Among his works were "The Book of Improvisation, by way of commenting on the 'Secretaries' Guide' of Ibn Qutayba", "The Book of Equanimous Advice concerning the Causes that Engender Discrepancies of Opinion in Islam", "The Book of Questions" (*Kitāb al-masāʾil*), and, above all, "The Book of Walls" (*Kitāb al-ḥadāʾiq*).

As in the case of Ibn Ḥazm, he had some notion of philosophy, which is conceived as a love of learning, increased by his partial knowledge of al-Fārābī. His philosophical and theological concordism owes a good deal to the *Rasāʾil*, but he is clearer than Ibn Ḥazm in his analysis of the existence of God, divine science, the procession of created beings, and the gradations of the soul and the intellect. Thus he holds that happiness is attained "when one achieves the acquisition of intellect, inasmuch as man only possesses natural dispositions and aptitude for the attainment of happiness; if in fact he understands his own essence and the status in the cosmos which pertains to him, he is saved and is happy".[14]

II.4 *The development of logic*

Ṣāʿid of Toledo has left us the names of some of the first Andalusī logicians, Ibn Ḥazm demonstrates knowledge of the field and Ibn al-Sīd has left some logical questions in his treatises. Nevertheless, the first Andalusī book of logic seems to be the "Rectification of the Mind" (*Taqwīm al-dhihn*) of Abū Ṣalt Umayya, who was born in Denia in 406/1067, resided in Seville, Cairo and Alexandria, and died in al-Mahdiyya, in Tunisia, in 529/1134. The title avoids the term logic (*manṭiq*), which was distasteful to the Mālikī *fuqahāʾ* of al-Andalus, and is a calque on *Taqwīm al-ṣiḥḥa* ("Rectification of Health") by the physician Abū 'l-Ḥasan b. Buṭlān. In the prologue to his work, Abū Ṣalt explains its contents: "In the first place, I have included a concise summary of the treatise *On the Five Universal Ideas*; after, in chapter two, I study the contents of the treatise *On the Ten Categories*; in chapter three, the treatise *On Interpretation*; in the fourth, the treatise *On Syllogisms* and in the fifth the treatise *On Demonstration*. I have put in the form of schematic tables the kinds of the three figures of syllogism, pure and combined, which will help the student understand them."[15] Except for these synoptic tables, twelve in number, there is nothing new here as against the classical Eastern manuals.

III. *Ibn Bājja (Avempace)*

III.1 *Life and works*

Abū Bakr Muḥammad b. Yaḥyā b. al-Ṣāʾigh b. Bājja (Ibn Bājja), known in the West as Avempace, was born in Saragossa around 462/1070 and died in Fez in 523/1138. He resided in Saragossa, Almería, Granada, Seville (where he was imprisoned and later released thanks to the intervention of Ibn Rushd al-Jadd, grandfather of the philosopher Averroes), Jaén and Fez. His death is said to have been caused by eating an eggplant poisoned by his enemies, the court literati and physicians.

He wrote numerous works, thirty-seven of which survive. Among them should be cited his paraphrastic commentaries on various works of Aristotle,

Euclid, Galen and al-Fārābī, together with three of his most original works: "Letter of Farewell" (*Risālat al-wadā'*); "Treatise on the Union of Intellect with Man" (*Risāla fī ittiṣāl al-'aql bi 'l-insān*) and, the most famous, the "Rule of the Solitary" (*Tadbīr al-mutawaḥḥid*).

III.2 *Human knowledge*

The problem of knowledge is at the heart of Ibn Bājja's thought. Intellection depends instrumentally on sensible forms, but its final attainment requires the cooperation of the active intellective, which is something extrinsic, celestial, eternal and immortal. The speculative knowledge obtained is the basis for directing man to his ultimate end.

Ibn Bājja was strongly influenced by al-Fārābī, with whose works he was well acquainted, and it is on the basis of this scholar's idea that he develops his ideal of a utopian society governed by the righteous. For all the diversity of human functions and actions, man constitutes a radical unity governed by the rational power of the soul which presides over natural, artificial and spiritual instruments. The first of these is the vegetative soul with which man is endowed from the very moment of conception, and whose powers are the cause of the foetus and its development. These activities "also are found in plants from the beginning of their existence. ... When the foetus has left its mother's womb and makes use of its senses, it is then similar to the irrational animal which moves locally and has desires and appetites".[16] That is, one receives sensible powers upon birth, but these are dominated by rational powers which lead to the process of abstraction.

Abstract reasoning is achieved through three essential moments: (1) knowledge of spiritual forms of the imagination; (2) knowledge, by means of these forms, of things intelligible in the act; and (3) union with the active intellect. In the first moment knowledge is linked to sense data; in the second, it pertains to the materiality inherent in the imaginative faculty; and in the the third the object and subject are converted into a single thing, of a strictly intellectual nature, representing the highest level of human perfection. Thus the knowledge common to mankind is like the idea held by a man located in the darkness of the Platonic cave, and the knowledge of experts like that of those located on the threshold of the cave. Only the wise have the knowledge proper to those who can gaze directly into the Sun and are converted into sunlight.

The operations proper to man and relevant to the acquisition of intelligible forms can give rise to four kinds of action: (1) those which have the objective of acquiring pure bodily form, such as drinking, eating and so forth; (2) those whose objective is the perfection of that corporeality and which can be based on common tastes (like elegance in dress), on imagination (like games and honest pleasures), and on cognition (like study and apprenticeship); (3) those which are directed to the acquisition of knowledge, which are strictly intellectual; and (4) those which seek only pure spirituality or definitive union with the active intellect, which are proper to the authentic scholar. Ibn Bājja reduces the role of the passive intellect, which is included in the intellect-in-habit, and also that of the intellect-in-act, which is almost wholly incorporated within the active intellect. In reality his intellectual operation seems to resolve itself into two kinds of intellect, the speculative and the agential. The first is engendered, corruptible, unique and individual. The second is eternal, immaterial, universal and common to all. All intellectual activity is directed towards the union of the two kinds of understanding, which is the most important act of human life, and also its goal.

III.3 *Ethics, the road to perfection*

To reach the highest goal of human life, man must follow a straight path, equidistant between two harmful extremes. In accordance with the use of his natural faculties, mankind is divided into three groups: (1) the vice-ridden who, through their lack of moderation, are limited to the excessive exercise of their faculties; (2) cowards and indecisive people who, because they do not use all their faculties, or use them too little,allow their powers to wane; and (3) the balanced, who make wise use of their powers and risk health, mental faculties and life only in cases of strict necessity. With respect to the utilisation of artificial means, mankind can likewise be classified into three groups: (1) the prodigal, who waste whatever they have; (2) the miserly, who hoard their means with such attachment as to render them useless; and (3) the moderate, who save them in order to use them at the proper moment. In any case, human actions are always complex, and in order to establish their real end one most know their intention. One of the ways to establish intent is to relate it to the concept of pleasure. If one takes pleasure only from sentient joys, then human operations have a merely egoistical intent and lead to vice; if the intent is for glory and honour, then, even though these actions are worthier than those of the previous group, they do not reach the ideal of the wise man; only the intent to seek wisdom for the simple enjoyment of the truth, found in union with the active intellect, is a sign of the highest virtue.

III.4 *Ideal society*

The supreme ideal of the scholar presents serious difficulties at the moment of its realisation, but the greatest of all these is the real situation of man in the midst of a society inadequate to such an objective. Ibn Bājja, who knew and used the works of al-Fārābī on the model or virtuous society, and at the same time encountered social problems in the society of his own time, treated this difficult problem in his *Rule of the Solitary*, in which he analyses social structure, human social behaviour and the means of achieving the ultimate end and happiness of mankind in spite of all these problems. Inasmuch as he doubted the possibility of any imminent regeneration of society, Ibn Bājja refers repeatedly to the notion of solitary people who must live within an imperfect society, but without letting themselves become corrupted by its vices. These he calls "shoots", not only because of their rare and sporadic appearance, but also because they represent hope for the future flowering of a better society. The work just cited is devoted to their study, formation and virtues, and, as such, constitutes a spiritual medicine (*tadbīr* means "medicinal régime") which might make possible a utopian model society in the future. This would be so constituted that none of the three kinds of "physicians" present in an imperfect society would be necessary. There would be no need for physicians of the body, because the absence of vice would put an end to illness; nor for "physicians of order", that is, judges, because social relations would always be just; and there would be no "spiritual doctors", because citizens of the perfect society would seek only supreme perfection and would never fall into sin or be carried away by egoistical passions.

III.5 *Evaluation and influence*

If we go by strict chronology, the thought of Ibn Bājja represents a late reception of eastern *falsafa* and especially of that of al-Fārābī. Nevertheless, he adds two elements which enrich the doctrines of his remote Eastern master: one is his concept of the theoretical life of the scholar; the other his way of understanding ideal society and the status of its present aspirants within a real, but imperfect, society. The analysis of imperfect societies carried out by al-Fārābī was clear, critical and realistic, but his model of the virtuous city still seemed possible. Ibn Bājja follows him in the harshness of his denunciation of current society, but does not, at bottom, believe that an ideal society will be possible in the foreseeable future.

The thought of Ibn Bājja was reflected in Ibn Ṭufayl, Ibn Rushd and Maimonides, although the first two, especially Ibn Rushd, display some reserve towards Ibn Bājja's philosophy (in some cases, in fact, Ibn Rushd's interpretations appear to be simply incorrect). Maimonides' position, on the other hand, is very close to that of Ibn Bājja, and the latter seems, next to al-Fārābī, to have been the Jewish thinker's principal philosophical source. Although there were few Latin translations of Ibn Bājja, Latin thinkers also made use of his philosophy. St. Thomas Aquinas, for example, incorporated some of Ibn Bājja's ideas into his theology, generally conjoined with those of Maimonides, when he agreed with them.

IV. *Ibn Ṭufayl*

IV.1 *Life and works*

Abū Bakr Muḥammad b. ʿAbd al-Malik b. Ṭufayl (Ibn Ṭufayl) was born in Guadix (Granada) some time before 504/1110. We know he practised medicine in Granada, serving as physician to that city's governor, and his fame led to his occupying the same position, and also that of secretary, with Abū Saʿīd, son of the first Almohad sultan, ʿAbd al-Mu'min, while he was governor of Ceuta. Around 559/1163 he was named court physician and vizier to the second sultan, Abū Yaʿqūb Yūsuf, and in 565/1169 he presented Ibn Rushd, who was to succeed him as physician in 578/1182, to the Almohad court, while himself keeping the post of vizier until his death in 581/1189. Such was his fame, and the esteem in which he was held, that the third Almohad sultan, al-Manṣūr Yūsuf b. Yaʿqūb, attended his funeral. He wrote various astronomical and medical works. A manuscript of his commentary on Ibn Sīnā, the *Urjūza fī 'l-ṭibb* ("Medical conspectus in verse") is preserved in Fez, but it is his *Risālat Ḥayy b. Yaqẓān*, known in the West as *The Autodidactic Philosopher*, to which he owes his universal fame.

IV.2 *Education and orientation of his thought*

Ibn Ṭufayl was well acquainted with the evolution of Andalusī thought, of which he wrote: "Don't believe that Andalusis have written nothing of value on this subject. Those men of cultivated spirit who lived in al-Andalus before logic and philosophy were known here worked only on mathematics, in which they reached a very high level, but they did not study the other [sciences]. After these there followed another generation [that of Ibn Ḥazm] which immersed itself somewhat more in the study of logic; they already studied that science ... After them came another generation of men who were much more adept at speculation ... Among all of them none possessed a sharper wit, a firmer mind and more authentic vision that Abū Bakr b. al-Ṣā'igh [Ibn Bājja], although I did not know him personally."[17]

Ibn Ṭufayl was the first Andalusī thinker who knew and used Ibn Sīnā: the *Shifā'*, the prologue at least of the *Manṭiq al-Mashriqiyyīn*, the *risāla*s of *Ḥayy b. Yaqẓān*, *Salāmān wa-Absāl* and *Al-Ṭayr*. From the first two he took names for personages in his work, and some of the ideas, but not Ibn Sīnā's actual stories. Moreover, Ibn Ṭufayl is one of those indicating the existence of an esoteric work by Ibn Sīnā entitled *Al-Ḥikma al-Mashriqiyya*: "With regard to the writings of Aristotle, the master Abū ʿAlī [Ibn Sīnā] endeavoured to explain its contents to us and he follows the methods of his philosophy in the *Kitāb al-shifā'*. In the beginning [=prologue] of this work he says that, in his opinion, [absolute] truth is somewhat different from the way it is discussed in the book, which has been composed solely according to the doctrine of the peripatetics. As such, whoever wishes to learn the Pure Truth should consult his *Kitāb al-ḥikma al-Mashriqiyya*."[18]

IV.3 *The "History" of Ḥayy b. Yaqẓān*

Ibn Ṭufayl resorts to Ibn Sīnā's system of "symbolic" writings in accordance with the Almohad policy of upholding traditional religion among the people, without any concession, and of maintaining intellectual freedom for the scholar, so long as he does not propagate his ideas among the people or cause any scandal; but he does so also because it accords with the tradition of philosophical esoterism. Thus he writes: "The secrets which we have divulged in these few pages we have left covered with a tenuous veil, which the initiates will see through quickly, but which will remain opaque and almost impenetrable for those who are not worthy of penetrating it."[19] The story he uses is the following:

Ḥayy b. Yaqẓān appears, alone, on an island deserted of human beings —being either born by spontaneous generation or the love child of a princess who placed him in a container and abandoned him to the waters. The child's cry attracts a gazelle who has lost her doe, and who accordingly suckles and adopts him. Though receiving no language or any kind of knowledge from any human being, his unaided reason slowly leads him to learn whatever is necessary for living, and to explain the cosmos and life itself, until he arrives at the idea of a Supreme Being, creator of all and giver of life, to whom he should lift his thought. On a neighbouring island, where a religion preached by a prophet inspired by God is practised, live Salāmān and Absāl. The latter "was a partisan of allegorical interpretation, whereas Salāmān preferred the literal sense".[20] When Absāl arrives on Ḥayy's island, meets him and teaches him to speak, they discover that their ideas coincide, but when Ḥayy visits the other island, of which Salāmān is ruler, its inhabitants do not wish to accept the true sense of Absolute Knowledge. Earlier two points had caused Ḥayy to marvel, "one, because that prophet had used allegories to speak to men ... and he had abstained from discovering the truth clearly ...; another was because he limited himself to some ritual precepts and prescriptions, permitting the acquisition of riches."[21] The moral is obvious: Absolute Truth is for wise men only; the people should follow "traditional precept and outward practices rigorously and involve themselves little in things that don't concern them, to believe the mysteries easily, shun dissent and passion, to imitate virtuous predecessors and avoid novelties".[22] There is basic agreement only between reason and the spirit of revelation, not between revelation and popular religion.

IV.4 *"Scientific" and philosophical knowledge*

The story of the autodidact permits Ibn Ṭufayl to expound his "scientific", particularly his biological, theories: the possibility of spontaneous generation and the origin and development of the human embryo, beginning with a fine, homogeneous matter which "upon being agitated produces by its viscosity a very small bubble divided into two parts by a very fine membrane and filled with a subtle material, like air, constituted exactly according to the proportions required"[23] by a living being. Upon receiving animation, "there is formed another bubble divided into three compartments separated by a very thin membrane, communicating through openings and filled with a gaseous material similar to that which filled the first, but even more diluted".[24] Thereafter a third bubble appears and on the basis of the three bubbles, and following this curious mitosis, he describes the origin and differentiation of the organs in the embryo. Then he applies a developmental mechanism to explain the development of the human psyche and the progressive unfolding of the faculties of the spirit.

The first knowledge attained by Ḥayy—and therefore by man—is that of practices originating from experience; then the physical or natural; and finally the strictly metaphysical. Thus he arrives at the notion of a soul with three successive stages: vegetative, sentient, and rational. This latter is capable of attaining the idea of being, of the cosmos and of God as the agent, prime mover and final cause of everything, by analysing the principal divine attributes.

IV.5 *Knowledge as union with Absolute Truth*

Having attained the concept of God, Ḥayy "realised that he knew Him by means of his own essence and that knowledge of Him was engraved on his soul. He saw too that evidently his own essence, by means of which he had known Him, was something incorporeal, with no corporeal quality and that everything external and corporeal which he himself perceived was not the reality of his essence, inasmuch as his essence consisted in that by whose mediation he had learned of that Being whose existence was necessary."[25] From that moment he chose the solitary life, limiting all necessary vital acts to what was indispensable.

IV.6 *Meaning and influence*

The thought of Ibn Ṭufayl represents a late continuation of the philosophy of Ibn Sīnā and a third way between the radically esoteric interpretation of al-Suhrawardī and the more Aristotelian line which would later be represented by Latin scholasticism. While historical facts demonstrate the relationship between Ibn Ṭufayl and Ibn Rushd, the latter's thought did not follow the same direction as Ibn Ṭufayl's—though Ibn Rushd, in criticising Ibn Sīnā, did not include Ibn Ṭufayl in that criticism. Only in his conception of the relations between rational and revealed truth did Ibn Rushd build upon the stance of Ibn Ṭufayl. In any case, the "philosophical novel" of Ibn Ṭufayl represents a dialectical expression of confidence in experience and reason rarely expressed up to that point in the history of Islamic philosophy.

Ibn Ṭufayl's work was not directly known to medieval Latin scholastics. Translated into Hebrew in 1349 by Moses of Narbonne, it was edited in 1671 by E. Pococke, accompanied by a Latin version with the title *Philosophus Autodidactus*, and met with surprising success in the western world. In 1672 it was translated into Dutch, then into English (1673, 1674, 1678) and German (1726, 1783). In 1900 Gauthier's critical edition was published with a French translation, which was reprinted several times; in 1920 it was translated into Russian, in 1955 into Urdu, and in 1956 into Persian. It has twice been translated into Spanish (1890 and 1936). Some authors have pointed out the parallelism between Ibn Ṭufayl's story and the *Robinson*

Crusoe of Daniel Defoe, and also with the beginning of *El Criticón* by Baltasar Gracián.

V. *Ibn Rushd (Averroes)*

V.1 *Life and works*

Andalusī thought and even the whole of Islamic philosophy culminates with Averroes, the Latinisation of the Arab name Ibn Rushd, by way of the Hispano-Arab pronunciation *Abén Rochd*. The family of Banū Rushd, probably of Muwallad origin, is documented over at least five generations. Its first figure was Abū 'l-Walīd Muḥammad b. Aḥmad b. Muḥammad b. Rushd, nicknamed al-Jadd, "the grandfather" (to distinguish him from his grandson Averroes, who had the same name), who lived between 450/1058 and 520/1126. He was an important *faqīh*, writing several books on Mālikī law which have been preserved, was chief *qāḍī* (*qāḍī al-jamāʿa*) of Córdoba, and enjoyed the esteem of the Almoravid court, which, on more than one occasion, he advised efficaciously and with great critical boldness. His son Abū 'l-Qāsim Aḥmad b. Muḥammad b. Rushd (487/1094-564/1168), father of the philosopher, was also chief *qāḍī* of Córdoba, and this man's son, known as Averroes in the West, was born in Córdoba in 520/1126 and died in Marrakesh Thursday the 9 *Ṣafar* 595 (December 10 1198), possibly owing to chronic arthritis, known to us through his own diagnosis. He received an excellent education in the Quran, Arabic humanities, law, philosophy, medicine and theology. Ibn Ṭufayl presented him to the Almohad court, probably in 568/1168, and almost immediately he was named chief *qāḍī* of Seville. Upon the death of Ibn Ṭufayl he was appointed chief physician to the Sultan's household and *qāḍī* of Córdoba, enjoying the confidence of the Almohad sultans Abū Yaʿqūb Yūsuf and his successor Abū Yūsuf Yaʿqūb al-Manṣūr. In 591/1195 the Sultan, under pressure from the *fuqahā'*, exiled Ibn Rushd, confining him to the town of Lucena for two years. Then, in 594/1198, a few months before his death, the Sultan rescinded his exile and took him with him to his court in Marrakesh, where he died. Several months later his body was brought to Córdoba, where he was buried in the cemetery of the Banū ʿAbbād.

The writings of Ibn Rushd are very extensive and extremely important, up to 125 titles being attributed to him, of which, however, only 83 are actually his (others being errors or repetitions, or else written by his grandfather, or one of his sons, or by other authors). Several of his works are extant in more than one recension. For all that is sometimes said in histories of philosophy, it is not certain that he commented on the work of Aristotle three times. The ill-named "minor commentaries" (four works, comprising twenty-one books) are loose compendia (*jawāmiʿ*), while the so-called "middle commentaries" (ten works containing seventeen books) are free paraphrastic expositions (*talkhīṣāt*), among which stand out the paraphrase of the *Physics*, the *De Anima*, the *Metaphysics*, the *Nicomachaean Ethics* and Plato's *Republic*, all of them fundamental to Ibn Rushd's thought. The only strict "commentaries" are the five called "best" or "literal" (*tafsīrāt*): those on the *Second Analytics*, *Physics*, *De Coelo et Mundo*, *De Anima*, and the *Metaphysics*, all fundamental for the exposition of his ideas. To these one must add the famous *Tahāfut al-tahāfut* (Destruction of the "Destruction of the Philosophers" of al-Ghazālī); the *De Substantia Orbis* (*Maqāla fī jawhar al-falak*) and the two theological works *Faṣl al-maqāl* ("Decisive doctrine about the concordance between revelation of wisdom"), and the *Kashf ʿan manāhij al-adilla* ("Exposition of the paths that lead to the demonstration of the articles of faith"). He also wrote a juridical work, *Bidāyat al-mujtahid*, and thirteen medical works, among which the *Kitāb al-kulliyyāt fī 'l-ṭibb* ("Book of the general principles of medicine") is the most famous.

V.2 *Basic principles of his thought*

For Ibn Rushd, Aristotle was not only the philosopher by antonomasia, but also the author of the most complete and exact doctrinal corpus of wisdom; to be a *faylasuf* meant to read, assimilate and then develop the Aristotelian corpus. But submission to this method did not imply the renunciation of one's own mental acuity, or the empirical observation of natural and social phenomena, or the mastery of the cultural ambience of his time or his own personality. If Ibn Rushd adds commentary to compendious reading and paraphrastic exposition, which had not been done in philosophy up to that time, it is because he wanted to go further. Ibn Sīnā had implicitly accepted the need for a synthesis of the Islamic world view and, utilising a neo-Platonic framework had fashioned a "marvellous order of being" which was later to be useful for Latin scholasticism. Ibn Rushd was critical of such a viewpoint, accepting the Islamic concept of the cosmos, but granting to God what is God's (theology) and to temporal wisdom what corresponds to it (philosophy).

The thought of Ibn Rushd is marked by three exceptional milestones: the conscious, reasoned break with the neo-Platonic synthesis; the emphasis on his naturalistic education and his personal and empirical observations; and his break with philosophical-religious reductionism, involving the recognition of two levels of wisdom: one religious and the other exclusively scientific. The break with the neo-Platonic synthesis was fully conscious, explicitly reasoned and consubstantial with his peculiar mode of thought. He repeatedly notes his lack of agreement with the synthesis, refuting the thinkers (notably Ibn Sīnā) who upheld it in spite of the problems and sometimes serious conflicts this led to, such as those concerning the creation as described in the Quran. Against neo-Platonism, Ibn Rushd used two principal groups of arguments, which certainly sat none too comfortably in those times: first, the synthesis betrays the very modality of Aristotelian thought; and, moreover, it is the result of supplementing the Stagyrite, or viewing his thought, from the standpoint of the suppositions of Muslim theology.

There exist, in fact, two levels of wisdom, one religious, the other philosophical. Ibn Rushd was a sincere believer; while Ibn Sīnā finally took refuge in the famous "Eastern wisdom", writing no work of strict scholastic theology (although he did write symbolic commentaries), Ibn Rushd himself was the author of the *Faṣl* and the *Kashf*, both theological works. Might this not lead to a genuine confrontation, to the germ of the well-known doctrine of two truths? It might have done, but in fact the formal unity of Ibn Rushd's thought was never broken.

V.3 *Philosophy and theology*

If one admits the possibility of a formal duality of thought, on the one hand religious, on the other philosophical, the conclusion would be scepticism, as had occurred (in his view) in the case of the *mutakallimūn* and al-Ghazālī. What we today would call scientific validity is supported, as Ibn Rushd observed many centuries before Kant, by the universal value of the general principal of causality. This principle is not a postulate, but rests on the reiterated observation of experience. It deals with creation, generation, transformation or motivation. In order for knowledge to be such, it is necessary to accept the real necessity of a cause; without this there can be no science. Evidently, for Ibn Rushd, a sole cause is to be found at the end of any causal chain, namely God, the one, universal and eternal being, whose natural law rules the cosmos, just as His revelation enlightens humanity. As such, the philosophy attained by the wise on the one hand, and revelation on the other, both exhibit the law promulgated by God physically and ethically; in other words, the whole world of being has a rational structure, with two formal levels whose intentionality is distinguishable by reason: the theological and the philosophical.

The "first level"—the term is Ibn Rushd's—is investigated in four works of very different length, but which conform to a certain plan: *Tahāfut*, *Faṣl*, *Kashf*, and *Ḍamīma*. The first aims to destroy the dangerous and sceptical dialectic of al-Ghazālī, who had doubted the ability of the human mind to comprehend the world and praise its Creator. As for the second, the principle of the *Faṣl* appears from the following: "The intent of this essay is to inquire, from the point of view of revealed religion, whether by chance speculation about philosophy and logical science is permitted according to revealed religion, or if it is prohibited; and if it is recommended, whether by way of mere invitation or by way of a rigorous precept."[26]

The second level is represented by various readings of the *Corpus aristotelicum arabum*. This other task is strictly philosophical, within the meaning of that term in *falsafa*, the most important thing being the purpose of the

Cordoban thinker: to find the truth. Thus, in spite of his attacks on al-Ghazālī, he presents himself as a true reviver of theology and as a defender of free philosophical work; and, for all his criticism of Ibn Sīnā, he will say that the *falāsifa* were correct rather than the Eastern theologian. Not even the pre-eminence of Aristotle can restrain him: he will not extend the consequences of the Stagyrite's thought to his theology, nor will he accept them if they conflict with his personal observations.

V.4 *Knowledge and being*

For Ibn Rushd knowledge is supported in reality. Knowledge is founded on the principles of being, and the root of science is planted in the ontological structure of reality. What permits the formal reality of nature to be converted into the formal reality of understanding is the basic relationship of consubstantiation which exists between the ontological and gnosological worlds. Man's being comprehends the being of things. Concrete living beings are also necessary. The Necessary Being *per se* (God) is always necessary; but concrete, caused beings become necessary only after being created, and are not merely possible, as Ibn Sīnā had maintained. Physics precedes metaphysics, and from it one can see the hylemorphic composition of the concrete being and the relationship between potential and act. Even the "philosophical" proof of the existence of God is physical; to complete it one need only recur to the "theological" proof, as he does.

The entire cosmos has a causal structure and order. This relates to the celestial bodies, to distinct astral intelligences, to the terrestrial world, livings beings and man himself. What distinguishes mankind from the rest of terrestrial beings is not the generic mode of vital motors (the soul), but the higher or rational part: understanding. This is sustained by two elements: something engendered (our understanding) and something not engendered (the agential understanding). Therefore material or human understanding is unique for the entire species, and is also capable of universal knowledge. What is particular and personal for each person is his possible understanding. This conception, when it was acquired by Latin scholastics, gave rise to the theory of the unity of understanding, which was viewed as a negation of the individuality and eternity of each concrete human soul. No doubt Ibn Rushd did not intend to make such an affirmation, inasmuch as he negated it on many occasions. What he surely wished to say is that the mind of all men functions in the same way. The personal perspective of "our truth" will die with our bodies; its truth will last forever and is that which is united with the Divine Light. Clearly all this was stated in accordance with the terminology, beliefs and problematic of the thought of the times.

V.5 *Individual and social ethical concepts*

Knowledge is the most vital and human aspect of mankind. Man has been created to know, he develops in knowledge, he makes progress through knowledge and perfects himself in it. Ultimate happiness can only be attained through wisdom. Moral order is a consequence of ontological order and is structured in accordance with metaphysical categories. Within it man acts freely but this does not imply a voluntaristic autarchy but rather a free compass within the necessary general order. Freedom is the human remedy for the physical fact of natural contingency. There can be no pure, unconditional exercise of freedom, but rather an adjustment to the laws of logic and physics. Only those who act accordingly acquire legitimate moral authority and can exercise it freely. Most men, who generally do not achieve self-control and freedom, achieve ethical behaviour through the permitted use of concrete goods. On the other hand, scholars achieve moral authority and practice in the act of freedom, and this authority should be projected upon society, which is conceived by Ibn Rushd as humanity's educative structure. Therefore the art of politics and the exercise of moral authority or prudence are the same thing.

In his *Exposition of the Republic*, Ibn Rushd analyses the social life of the Islamic societies of his times in a realistic manner. The Islamic *umma* is a model society, but in fact this has not been realised (even in the times of the Prophet and his first four successors, the *rāshidūn* caliphs). All that came into existence subsequently were timocracies, ending up as plutocracies and degenerating into demagogy and tyranny. Ibn Rushd does not hesitate to list examples of this, including the Umayyad and Almoravid monarchies, and even the Almohad system in which he lived—which took more than a little courage. Still, compared to Ibn Bājja and Ibn Ṭufayl, he was not an absolute pessimist, since he believed in the possibility of political transformation, so long as scholars became governors—though this seemed almost totally impossible to him—or else when monarchs took scholars as advisers, which was also neither easy nor common.

V.6 *Significance and influence*

Ibn Rushd was the most important thinker of al-Andalus and the culmination of medieval Aristotelianism. An original spirit, he was an impassioned observer of nature and even an enthusiast of empirical verification, and he so praised his native country that, in today's language, he could be termed an Andalusī chauvinist. He was a complete scholar, standing out as a physician—and not only as a theorist, for his works give evidence of practice. On the other hand, his determination to break with the Aristotelian/neo-Platonic synthesis of Ibn Sīnā underlines his sense of philosophy as an independent enterprise. He is, as he made clear in his writings on more than one occasion, firm in his rejection of the supposedly philosophical interpretations of "theologians of the three religions".

The presentation of Ibn Rushd (when his works were translated into medieval Latin) as the Commentator of Aristotle had both positive and negative aspects. The positive side consisted in an appreciation of the quality, quantity and depth of his hermeneutics; as soon as St. Thomas Aquinas learned of the literal commentaries of Ibn Rus̲h̲d, he abandoned the paraphrastic method and imposed that very model of literal exegesis on the Latin world. The negative side was to view him as a simple commentator, albeit an inspired one. St. Thomas appropriated many of Ibn Rus̲h̲d's ideas, in philosophy as well as in theology, but he modified his idea of a strict philosophy and converted what in Ibn Rus̲h̲d was a parallelism between philosophy and revelation into a full agreement between reason and faith. The Latin Averroists, on the other hand, not only developed the theory of the unity of the intellect, but also maintained the idea of a strict philosophy independent of theology and applicable not only to physics, gnosology and metaphysics, but also to ethics and politics. Hence Ibn Rus̲h̲d was doubly present in the Renaissance: negatively, insofar as the Averroists of the 15th to early 17th centuries were the most rigid scholastics, and positively insofar as his ideas about a strictly rational philosophy and a theology based on scriptures were typical ideas of the Renaissance and the Reformation respectively.

The famous Andalusī poet Ibn Quzmān dedicated a *zajal* to Ibn Rus̲h̲d; Dante remembered him in the *Divine Comedy* as "Averrois, che il gran commento feo". The anti-Averroist polemics, a plastic reflection of the "triumphs" of St. Thomas Aquinas, presented a cleaned-up, idealised figure of Ibn Rus̲h̲d, to be painted by the artists of the Quattrocento, as in the fresco, "The Triumph of St. Thomas" in Santa Maria Novella, Florence.

In the Islamic world all trace of Ibn Rus̲h̲d faded from the 8th/14th century on. In the West, except for a curious citation in the 18th-century polemic between Lessing and Herder, with which Kant was familiar, Ibn Rus̲h̲d was just another scholastic, until E. Renan, in 1852, published his study of the Cordoban thinker, and so returned him to the living history of philosophy. When Faraḥ Anṭūn (1277/1860-1341/1922) translated part of Renan's work into Arabic, Ibn Rus̲h̲d's reputation in the Islamic world was restored to its legitimate place.

VI. *The crisis of Islamic philosophy*

VI.1 *The "refuge" of the neo-Platonic synthesis*

After Ibn Rus̲h̲d *falsafa* disappeared from al-Andalus, and with it all philosophical thought in the western Islamic world. The reasons for this eclipse are to be sought not only in the juridical and political status of medieval Islamic society, but also in the critical, dynamic and strongly rationalist nature of *falsafa* itself, characteristics which were taken to their limits by Ibn Rus̲h̲d and which could not be digested by Sunni Islamic society of the 7th/13th and following centuries. It is no accident that the only Andalusī philosophical work which might be considered *falsafa*, the *Introduction to the*

Art of Logic, by Ibn Ṭumlūs of Alcira (ca. 522/1175-620/1223) does not even mention the name of Ibn Rushd, who was the author's teacher. The Islamic thought of al-Andalus continued its development by other routes, producing figures of exceptional quality, such as Ibn ʿArabī and Ibn Khaldūn, but the ideological bases or instruments of both thinkers, and of others too, relate to the "refuge" of the Islamic neo-Platonic synthesis. In the case of Ibn ʿArabī (17 *Ramaḍān* 560/July 20 1165-28 *Rabīʿ* II 638/November 16 1240), the internal armature of this synthesis supports his grandiose work and mystical conception, which is studied elsewhere in this volume.

VI.1.1 *Ibn Sabʿīn of Murcia*

Something similar occurs, *mutatis mutandis*, in the case of Ibn Sabʿīn, who was born in the Valley of Ricote, near Cieza, Murcia, in 613/1216, and died in Mecca in 668/1270. As a youth he moved to Ceuta, where the governor of that city, Ibn Khalāṣ, charged him with responding to a letter sent by the emperor Frederick II of Sicily to the Almohad sultan Abū Muḥammad ʿAbd al-Wāḥid al-Rashīd. This reply, *Ajwiba Yamaniyya ʿan asʾila Ṣiqiliyya*, made him famous in the West (in the Islamic world he was famed as a Sufi). Apart from this work, he was also the author of the "Book of the Baggage of the Gnostic" (*Kitāb budd al-ʿārif*) and the "Book of the Right Path" (*Kitāb al-daraj*).

Leaving aside the mystical aspects of Ibn Sabʿīn's thought, his philosophical stance is reminiscent of that of the *Rasāʾil Ikhwān al-Ṣafāʾ*. To it he adds a reference to the supposed *Al-Ḥikma al-Mashriqiyya* of Ibn Sīnā, of which he remarks: "This science which I mentioned to you is that called *Al-Ḥikma al-Mashriqiyya*. I do not want to imply that you should cultivate it by accepting it unconditionally, but rather because it is closer to the truth than the rest."[27] Although he does not specify further, his ideas are more easily relatable to the interpretation of al-Suhrawardī than to the thought of Ibn Sīnā. He even added several personal experiences to al-Ḥallāj's doctrine of mystical identification with God.

VI.1.2 *Ibn al-Khaṭīb*

That the recourse to refuge in the neo-Platonic synthesis was a typical posture in Andalusī thought of the 7th/13th and 8th/14th centuries can be observed not only in the Sufi thought of the *Shādhiliyya* but also in a curious and difficult work written by the Granadan polymath Lisān al-Dīn b. al-Khaṭīb, who was also famous as a historian and as one of the three Arab poets whose verses appear in the decorative calligraphy adorning the Alhambra. He was born in Loja, Granada, on 25 *Rajāb* 713/November 15 1333, and was executed in Fez at the end of 776/May-June 1375 at the instigation of his former lord and friend king Muḥammad V of Granada, whom he had served as chief vizier. His accuser was his former disciple the poet Ibn Zamrak, the best of the three whose poems are embodied in the Alhambra arabesques. He was accused of impiety, although the ultimate reasons were in fact political, the pretext being the doctrines expounded in his book, "The Garden of Gnostic Knowledge of Divine Love" (*Rawḍat al-taʿrīf bi 'l-ḥubb al-sharīf*).

The work in question is written in the typical symbolic form of a tree, in this case, a tree of love—an old tradition in the Islamic world which was later popularised in the West by Ramon Llull's *Arbre de filosofia d'amor* (1298). The roots of the tree of love are anchored in the soil of the human soul, which has four layers: soul, understanding, spirit and heart. Its roots, not only the esoteric ones but the exoteric and intermediate ones (*barzakh*), are irrigated by the four waters of generative dust, measure, revelation and reason. The stump of the trunk is formed by explanations, sojourns, intellections and definitions. Its bark is the word, praise its sap. The branches are the categories of love: lovers, loved ones, signs and notices of love. The twigs are mystical phenomena; the leaves, manifestations of love; the flowers, purified human spirits; the fruit, union with God. Possibly Ibn al-Khaṭīb hides his debt to Ibn ʿArabī, and, in turn, cites Ibn Sīnā and the *ishrāqīyyūn*. His relation to *shādhīliyya* is evident. There is no authentic echo of Ibn Sīnā in him, but rather signs of *ishrāqī* interpenetration. The only recognisable texts of Ibn Sīnā found in the work are one from the *Ithbāt al-nubuwwa* and another from the *Risālat al-ḥudūd*, which he confuses with the *Kitāb al-burhān*. Perhaps the most curious aspect of Ibn al-Khaṭīb's book is the large number of expressions taken from Shiʿite thought, such as the theory of "Muḥammadan light" (*al-nūr al-muḥammadī*) or that of the angelic *malakūt* and *jabarūt*.

VI.2 *Ibn Khaldūn*

VI.2.1 *Life and works*

The family of the Banū Khaldūn resided in Seville until the times of the grandfather of ʿAbd al-Raḥmān b. Khaldūn (Ibn Khaldūn), and when the latter came to live in Seville as ambassador of the king of Granada at the court of Pedro I of Castile, the king offered to return all his goods if he would agree to enter his service. The author was born in Tunis on 1 *Ramaḍān* 732/ May 27 1332, and served the Marīnid and Ḥafṣid sultans, residing, Tunis and Seville apart, in Fez, Granada, Bougie and Tiaret. Later he emigrated to Egypt, where he lived till his death on 16 *Ramaḍān* 808/March 17 1406, but not before having endured imprisonment at the hands of Tamerlane (803/1400), who eventually freed him, having been impressed by his historical knowledge. As a young man he wrote a theological/philosophical primer entitled *Lubāb al-muḥaṣṣal fī uṣūl al-Dīn* ("Synthesis of the principles of religion"). During his stay in Egypt he wrote the *Shifāʾ al-sāʾil li tahdhīb al-masāʾil* ("The cure for those who seek to resolve questions"). But his great work was the *Kitāb al-ʿibar*, a universal history whose long introduction, or *Muqaddima*, made him famous. The book also contains an autobiography which, although sometimes published separately, is, like the introduction, part of *Al-ʿibar*.

VI.2.2 *Philosophical education*

Ibn Khaldūn is basically a historian, particularly well informed on the history of the Berbers. His philosophical training was, nevertheless, considerable. He knew about the origins of *falsafa*, the reasons why the Arabs received and developed it, and the names of the principal *falāsifa*. Moreover, he uses them more in his works than one might deduce from quotations alone, and one may suppose that he used Ibn Rushd's *Exposition of the Republic* without citing it, either directly, or through what he learned from his teachers, notably al-Abīlī.

It may well have been his good cultural and philosophical education, together with his keen spirit of observation, which made him (without either knowing or intending such a thing) the remote founder of positive sociology and of the philosophy of history, which were not to be developed in the West until the 19th century.

VI.2.3 *The limits of historical positivism*

Ibn Khaldūn deduced, from his analysis of historical facts, a series of principles which he considered absolutely original, the spontaneous fruit of his research. These principles are: (1) History must be founded on the analysis of concrete facts. (2) The objective of history is eminently sociological, inasmuch as history "has as its own objective to know the social situation of man, that is, civilisation, and to inform us about concomitant phenomena such as the savage life, sweetening customs, family and tribal spirit, the differences in power between some peoples and others which account for the birth of empires and dynasties, the distinct kinds of rank, the occupations to which men devote their work and efforts, such as the professions, and so forth."[28] (3) All historical events have a causal explanation, whether sociological, economic, political, ethnological, or whatever. (4) Real historical cities, that is, political actions and bodies, are based on the principle of the origin and evolution of sovereignty. (5) All historical phenomena, however trivial and mundane they may appear, must have a sociologically sufficient reason (in the light of this principle, Ibn Khaldūn is never content with pointing out events, but always attempts to explain them). (6) Historical facts can originate from current sociological distinctions but also from an original distinction (Ibn Khaldūn, who was acquainted with the Muslim kingdoms of Tunis, Fez, Bougie, and Granada, was well apprised of such facts). (7) One must establish a positive or negative link between material and cultural progress and political power. (8) To explain historical facts one must know three kinds of phenomena: (a) psychological characteristics of human groups; (b) economic characteristics of the life of human groups and their relationship to geographical conditions; (c) political phenomena which condition the historical process. (9) Insofar as is possible, the historian should refer only to purely natural causes to explain historical events. (10) Individuals and nations do not form a historical unit of analysis; it is rather homogeneous and social groups which do so. The concrete and individual protagonists of history are not individual leaders of the masses, but a "product" engendered by those groups. (11) It is the social environment (as Ibn Khaldūn observed long before Marx), and not inheritance, which conditions the individual and social groups.

VI.2.4 *The sociological bases of history*

Along with material bases like climate, lifestyle, tribal organisation, modes of production and settlement, Ibn Khaldūn also analyses important elements of social psychology, such as the sense of imitation, the attraction of authority, sympathy and antipathy, and bellicose practices. He locates the origins of sovereignty in the force of tribal power, but the legitimacy of power resides not in its origin but in the force of social cohesion (*ʿaṣabiyya*), whose pressure accounts for the only authentic nobility. The traditional Arab concept of aristocracy leads "to the disappearance of any force of social cohesion among them and to this change is owing ... the ruin of Arab power in this country and ... of the dynasty which founded it. Freed of the dominion of the Berbers ..., these Arabs have lost the force of social cohesion and of mutual aid which carried them to power and preserve nothing more than their genealogies ...; they imagine that with their birth alone and a job with the government they can conquer a kingdom and govern man ..."[29] Ibn Khaldūn also criticises the opinion of Ibn Rushd, which is similar to that of the Spanish Muslims: "Ibn Rushd says that a family is noble when it has been established in a city for a long time ... I would like to know what advantage a family can derive from a long stay in a city if its does not possess that force of social cohesion which assures it respect and obedience."[30]

Ibn Khaldūn grounds the evolution of social classes in this "force of social cohesion". When that spirit and the conditions that gave rise to it disappear, then social groups atrophy, and if its members are able to stabilise themselves in power, their descendants will live a tranquil life and their energy will dissipate until they are completely demoralised: "Nobility and enlightenment, which are accidents of human life ... reach their end after four successive generations."[31] And he goes on to explain, in a mathematical, way how *ʿaṣabiyya* diminishes: it survives intact in the founder of political power, is weakened in the sons' generation, and is effaced completely in that of the great grandson, who believes in his superiority as an individual and not in *ʿaṣabiyya*, and finds himself incapable of maintaining his privileged situation. In four generations, therefore, the whole historical cycle is completed, from the founder of the empire, full of moral and physical vigour, up to the kingdom's liquidator, who, due to his life of comfort, is lacking in any virtue.

VI.2.5 *Significance and influence*

When, in the mid-19th century (1865), Ibn Khaldūn began to be read in the West there began a wave of admiration which has lasted to this day. Though already known as a historian, he had not till then been appreciated in the Islamic world as a sociologist and philosopher of history; when he was so recognised, his exceptional calibre kindled limitless fervour and enthusiasm. However, Ibn Khaldūn cannot be regarded as the pioneer of positive history, since he did not apply the methodology of the *Muqaddima* to the rest of his work, nor is he the precursor of Hegel, Nietzsche, or Comte, nor the antecedent of historical materialism, as has been asserted. Ibn Khaldūn's empiricism has very concrete limits; in fact, many of the expositors and students of Ibn Khaldūn have been too impregnated by their own positivism to notice that he applied his theories within a very limited experiential framework, namely the Arabs and Berbers of the Maghrib. As Taha Husain observed, Ibn Khaldūn did not take advantage of his later life in Cairo to moderate his pessimism with regard to urban civilisations. Neither had he taken the best advantage of his earlier time at the Christian court of Seville. Moreover, his attitude towards al-Andalus is filled with resentment. Ibn Rushd said that al-Andalus civilised Arabs and Berbers and had made them better men; Ibn Khaldūn, by contrast, asserted that it made them bourgeois and effeminate and deprived them of *ʿaṣabiyya*. His critique of the urban, agrarian, artisanal and commercial civilisation of al-Andalus, and his silence regarding Egypt, constitutes an *a priori* attitude and not a sociological deduction.

Yet, even if we restrict his great work within its proper limits, the analysis of historical and social reality carried out by Ibn Khaldūn was, for all the antecedent analyses of al-Fārābī and Ibn Rushd, an extraordinary achievement. Moreover, his appropriation by modern Islamic thinkers, following his rediscovery, has served to set in motion the modern, positive sociology and philosophy of history in the Islamic world.

1 Ibn Ḥazm, *Kitāb al-fiṣal*, Cairo, 1317/1899, II, 199-200.

2 *Ibid*., II, 226.

3 Ibn Ḥazm, *Epistola del auxilio divino*, part. trans. M. Asín Palacios, "Un códice inexplorado de Ibn Ḥazm", *Al-Andalus*, 4, 1936-39, pp. 9-11.

4 *Kitāb al-fiṣal*, II, 39.

5 *Ibid*., II, 91-92.

6 *Ibid*., II, 96-97.

7 *Ibid*., II, 94.

8 *Los carácteres y la conducta*, ed. and trans. M. Asín Palacios, Madrid, 1916, pp. 7-8; trans., pp. 1-2.

9 *El collar de la paloma*, trans. E. García Gómez, Madrid, 1957, p. 80.

10 *Los carácteres y la conducta*, p. 58; trans., p. 89.

11 *Ibid*., p. 56; trans., p. 85.

12 Cf. M. Cruz Hernández, *La recepción de los "falāsifa" en al-Andalus: problemas críticos* (in press).

13 Cf. M. Cruz Hernández, *Filosofía hispano-musulmana*, Madrid, 1957, I, 310.

[14] M. Asín Palacios, "Ibn al-Sīd de Badajoz", *Al-Andalus*, 5, 1940, p. 528.
[15] *Introducción al arte de la lógica*, ed. and trans. M. Asín Palacios, Madrid, 1916, pp. 5-6; trans., pp. 57-58.
[16] *El régimen del solitario*, ed. and trans. M. Asín Palacios, Granada, 1946, p. 50; trans., p. 85.
[17] *Hayy ibn Yaqdhan, roman philosophique d'Ibn Thofail*, ed. and trans. L. Gauthier, 2nd ed., Beirut, 1936, pp. 5-6.
[18] *Ibid.*, p. 17.
[19] *Ibid.*, p. 118.
[20] *Ibid.*, p. 105.
[21] *Ibid.*, p. 115.
[22] *Ibid.*, p. 117.
[23] *Ibid.*, p. 22.
[24] *Ibid.*
[25] *Ibid.*, p. 68.
[26] *Faṣl al-Maqāl*, trans. M. Alonso, *La teología de Averroes*, Madrid, 1947, p. 150.
[27] Cf. Cruz Hernández, *Filosofía hispano-musulmana*, II, 308.
[28] *Ibid.*, II, 323.
[29] *Ibid.*, II, 331-32.
[30] *Ibid.*, II, 332.
[31] *Ibid.*

BIBLIOGRAPHY

In view of the fact that many readers of this chapter may be neither Arabists nor Arabic-speaking, and that the essay itself is of a general and synthetic nature, this bibliography is restricted to general works. Broader and more specific bibliographies may be found in many of the works here cited.

Alonso, M., *La teología de Averroes*, Madrid, 1947.
Ammar, A., *Ibn Khaldun's Prolegomena to History*, Cambridge, 1941.
Asín Palacios, M., *El islam cristianizado*, Madrid, 1931 (new ed., 1981).
——, *La escatología musulmana en la Divina Comedia*, 2nd ed., Madrid, 1943.
——, *Obras escogidas*, Vol. I, Madrid, 1948.
Badawi, A., *Histoire de la philosophie en Islam*, Vol. II, Paris, 1972.
Corbin, H., *Histoire de la philosophie islamique*, Vol. I, Paris, 1966.
Cruz Hernández, M., *Filosofía hispano-musulmana*, Madrid, 1957, 2 vols.
——, *Historia del pensamiento en el mundo islámico*, Vol. II, Madrid, 1981.
——, *Abu-l-Walid Ibn Rušd, Averroes: vida, obra, pensamiento, influencia*, Córdoba, 1986.
Fakhri, M., *Islamic Occasionalism and its Critique by Averroes and Thomas Aquinas*, London, 1958.
——, *A History of Islamic Philosophy*, London-New York, 1983.
Husain, Taha, *La philosophie sociale d'Ibn Khaldun*, Paris, 1918.
Ibn al-ʿArīf, *Maḥāsin al-majālis*, trans. W. Elliot and S. K. Abdulla, Amsterdam, 1980.
Ibn Bājja, *El régimen del solitario*, ed. and trans. M. Asín Palacios, Madrid, 1946.
Ibn Ḥazm, *Los carácteres y la conducta*, trans. M. Asín Palacios, Madrid, 1916.
Ibn K͟haldūn, *The Muqaddimah*, trans. F. Rosenthal, New York-London, 1967, 3 vols.
Ibn Ṭufayl, *Hayy ibn Yaqdhan, roman philosophique d'Ibn Thofail*, ed. and trans. L. Gauthier, Algiers, 1900 (2nd ed., Beirut, 1936).
Landau, R., *The Philosophy of Ibn ʿArabī*, London, 1959.
Mahdi, M., *Ibn Khaldun's Philosophy of History*, London, 1957.
Rabic, M., *The Political Theory of Ibn Khaldun*, Leiden, 1967.
Schmidt, N., *Ibn Khaldun, Historian, Sociologist and Philosopher*, New York, 1937.
Sharif, M., *A History of Muslim Philosophy*, Wiesbaden, 1969.
Various authors, *Multiple Averroès*, Paris, 1978.
——, *Mahrajan Ibn Rushd*, Algiers, 1400/1978.

THE PHILOSOPHY OF IBN RUSHD

THE EVOLUTION OF THE PROBLEM OF THE INTELLECT IN THE WORKS OF IBN RUSHD: FROM PHILOLOGICAL EXAMINATION TO PHILOSOPHICAL ANALYSIS

JAMAL AL-DIN AL-ʿALAWI

Introduction

Scholarly study has failed, as yet, to explore the full range and significance of Ibn Rushd's philosophy, and this adds to the difficulties of providing a precise and satisfactory treatment of the subject within such a brief paper as this. I have therefore felt it appropriate to focus on a single theme in Ibn Rushd's writings, and to attempt to establish, around this, the preliminary outlines of a new strategy for studying the Rushdī corpus and the philosophical system contained within it.

Several aspects of Ibn Rushd's thought might have served as such a focus. Of particular interest, for example, would be an examination of his metaphysical writings in the light of his evolving perspectives on any one of the philosophical problems in these works; or a consideration of his works on logic with respect to the development of a theory of knowledge and demonstrative proof. This paper, however, is concerned with the evolution of the problem of the intellect, a subject selected on account of its prominence in the history of medieval philosophy, and also because of the increasing interest now also felt by present-day writers in a subject clearly likely to give rise to fruitful research. This will further permit us to evaluate other related types of philosophical questions which have hitherto escaped the attention of ancient and modern scholars.

The question of the intellect occupies an obviously important place both in the general history of philosophy and in the particular context of the historical study of Ibn Rushd. No other aspect of the Rushdī discourse, indeed, has such a unique and distinguished history behind it; and while other aspects have failed to leave lasting reverberations, this one led on to the crucially important intellectual current subsequently known as Latin Averroism.

I should like, from the very outset, to stress this twofold aspect: we have to consider, on the one hand, the intrinsic question of the problem of the intellect in the Rushdī corpus; and, on the other, the place this question assumes within the history of medieval philosophy among the Latins. The latter aspect should not, however, lead us to overestimate the significance of the problem itself, nor should one stretch the problem beyond its own natural context by seeing it exclusively in terms of its role as an axis of Averroism. Still more importantly, the problem should not be seen as the defining element for comparing Ibn Rushd's philosophy with other philosophical systems; to do so would be to give the reader the impression that other Rushdī topics and questions are insignificant, and that Averroism in its entirety can, in the final analysis, be reduced to a theory of the intellect. No doubt the problem of the intellect was a central feature, if still not the most important one, of Latin Averroism, but it was not a key element within Ibn Rushd's original Arabic writings, or within the historical context in which he lived. As such I believe we must first develop a reading of the problem of the intellect as embedded in the Rushdī corpus itself. I do not intend, here, to undertake a critical review of work carried out in this area, but rather to establish a different framework for considering Ibn Rushd's heritage, focusing, to this end, on a single theme in his psychological writings.

In a previous work[1] I set out a general strategy for the reading of the Rushdī corpus based on a comparative survey of Ibn Rushd's writings, particularly those in the original Arabic. It was maintained that there exist different yet correlating levels in the corpus, these correlations involving aspects of the following selected writings: *Al-Mukhtaṣarāt* (the Epitomes), *Al-Jawāmiʿ* (the Short Commentaries), *Al-Talākhīṣ* (the Middle Commentaries) and various other commentaries and treatises. At this point I should like to re-examine[2] this thesis, in order to analyse how far the development of the definition of the intellect in Ibn Rushd's writings can in fact be determined.

Before presenting brief conclusions on the subject, derived from discussions and from my own research,[3] I should like to draw attention to a centrally important principle which is often overlooked: namely, that the foundations of the Rushdī corpus have to be properly established before we are in a position to analyse Ibn Rushd's thought. An appreciation of this will set the present study on a proper footing, and will also shed critical light on the current state of Rushdī scholarship. Present-day students of Ibn Rushd are all too ready to apply the "synthetic approach" (*al-naẓar al-tarkībī*) to his writings, or to probe his philosophical depth and ideological intention, without realising that much more fundamental textual work still needs to be done. While not wishing to curb the legitimate aspirations of such scholars, I feel that their work is really premature; that the present state of Rushdī studies firmly precludes systematic analysis of this kind.[4]

Clearly, then, several difficulties have to be met. First, there is the particular difficulty of determining what, in the writings of Ibn Rushd, the problem of the intellect actually is, the barrier here being a linguistic obscurity which at times makes the author's intended meaning impossible to discover —all the more so when we are working with the translation of a lost original text, as is the case with the main textual fragment forming the basis of the theory of the intellect in his writings, i.e., *Al-Sharḥ al-kabīr* (the Long Commentary) of the *De Anima* (*Kitāb al-nafs*). Still more problematic is the fact that the surviving primary sources, Ibn Rushd's psychological writings themselves, exist in manuscripts which still remain unedited by recognised standards of editing[5]—a discipline which requires the researcher first to undertake the work of the philologist. To this end the text and its manuscripts must be compared with the aim, on the one hand, of establishing a sound text and, on the other, of critically analysing the variants between the manuscripts. Such work is a prerequisite both for a general study of Ibn Rushd and for a specific examination of the problem of the intellect.

This, then, must be our starting point for any serious study of the question; and until this first phase is accomplished, none of our efforts will achieve fully satisfactory results, if indeed they achieve any worthwhile results at all. While it is no inalienable rule that philological and historical examination should precede philosophical examination, it is nonetheless our task, as students of the history of philosophy, to lay the proper groundwork for the study of philosophy and philosophical theory; and this will only be possible if we first focus on improving and correcting the primary tools of research. It is essential, in this case, that we assemble all the manuscripts at our disposal and verify their authenticity.

This first section of the paper will investigate a group of texts which form the basis of Ibn Rushd's psychological studies, and will attempt to clarify long-standing obscurities and confusions surrounding it. The examination will be restricted to those texts preserved in the original Arabic, namely, *Al-Mukhtaṣar* (the Epitome) and *Al-Talkhīṣ* (the Middle Commentary) (*Al-Sharḥ al-kabīr* (the Long Commentary) will be examined in a subsequent section, where an attempt will be made to assess the influence of Averroism on the subject). Only the relevant chapters in the texts, namely those concerned with the question of the intellect, will be considered, and these will be examined as if with a view to publication according to the scientifically recognised principles of editing. In the second section I shall attempt to assess what developments, if any, may be discerned between the positions advocated by Ibn Rushd in *Al-Mukhtaṣar* and *Al-Talkhīṣ* and those in *Al-Sharḥ al-kabīr*. Our re-reading of the original texts in the first section will, therefore, prepare us for the analysis provided in the second; and it is for this reason that the subtitle "from philological examination to philosophical analysis" has been chosen for this paper.

I

I.1 Al-Mukhtaṣar *on psychology*

Al-Mukhtaṣar (the Epitome) on psychology has a special significance as against the other *Al-Mukhtaṣarāt* (Epitomes) and *Al-Jawāmiʿ* (Short Commentaries). In addition to being an analysis of Aristotle's *De Anima*, it examines the entire peripatetic heritage on psychology, thus also introducing themes present in *Al-Jawāmiʿ*;[6] for Ibn Rushd had intended the latter to be an inventory of Aristotle's scientific statements as extracted from the dialectical arguments dispersed through the latter's writings. However, this *Mukhtaṣar* does not endeavour to deduce demonstrative proofs from *De Anima*: the prime motive behind the text is not, as is the case in *Al-Jawāmiʿ al-ṭabīʿiyya*, to provide an abstract of Aristotle's opinions, but rather to defend his position concerning the problem of the intellect.[7] This intention is reiterated at several points in the text and will become more evident in the course of our analysis. Yet, having established the thematic relationship of this text to *Al-Jawāmiʿ*, we are now precluded from seeing it as part of the *Mukhtaṣarāt*; for the *Mukhtaṣarāt* were all written prior to Ibn Rushd's study of Aristotle and thus the text—contrary to what I previously affirmed in my study *Al-Matn al-Rushdī*—is an anomaly.

With this established, we should now be in a better position to approach the work; and I hope, indeed, to return to the whole question in another study of the "Problematic of the Rushdī Text". What I wish to do here is to point out the difficulties involved in the reading of the text.

Two problems seem to me to be of central importance. The first of these will be briefly summarised and the second elaborated in greater detail thereafter.

The first difficulty concerns the actual wording of the text. Ibn Rushd covers a wide range of ideas, leading the reader on from discussions of the theoretical intellect (*al-ʿaql al-naẓarī*) to a consideration of theoretical intelligibles (*al-maʿqūlāt al-naẓariyya*), then shifting to an exposé on the matter and the form of these intelligibles, and also examining the role of imaginary representations (*al-maʿānī 'l-khayāliyya*) in the process of intellection (*ʿamaliyyat al-taʿaqqul*) and the problem of conjunction (*ittiṣāl*) in the light of what had been affirmed by Ibn Bājja in his famous epistle on the subject. The course of the discussion may be summed up as follows: he begins with the theoretical intellect, then moves on to the theoretical intelligibles which serve as the pivot of the problem, and this subject is studied in depth, before he next moves on to a discussion of the active intellect (*al-ʿaql al-faʿʿāl*), which is defined and examined in relation to the material intellect (*al-ʿaql al-hayūlānī*); he then concludes by defining the problem of conjunction within the context of the rational faculty (*al-quwwa 'l-nāṭiqa*).

It is important to note that the order of subjects followed by Ibn Rushd in this text differs from that established by Aristotle in his investigation of the rational faculty in *De Anima*—this indicating that Ibn Rushd was not examining the book of the First Teacher (Aristotle) as he had done in the *Jawāmiʿ* texts and in both the *Talkhīṣ* of *De Anima* and *Al-Sharḥ al-kabīr* (Long Commentary) on it. For this reason the text is unique when set against the other types of Rushdī commentary.

The second difficulty in reading this text arises from the presence of several manuscripts,[8] together with different printed editions of the text.[9] A comparative analysis of the manuscripts yields its own peculiar difficulties, which will be examined in detail later, but first I should like to point out the related difficulties associated with the printed editions. For example, the Egyptian edition has prepared a text from a synthesis of two very different manuscripts (Cairo and Madrid).[10] Yet the difference between these manuscripts is substantial enough to have warranted treating them separately; it would have been more appropriate to choose and print one manuscript, with the text of the other being reproduced in the margins. Preserving the distinctiveness of each manuscript would allow us to differentiate between what was written first and the later additions; and it is in fact these later additions that have convoluted the meaning of the text, thereby further confusing and misguiding the reader in his attempts at interpretation.

It is obvious, then, that the text should be studied in the light of all the different manuscripts at our disposal—only so can we claim to have met the requirements of scientific research and reliability. Moreover, familiarity with the manuscripts brings to the surface differing interpretations which cannot be reduced merely to a matter of identifying common differences; the only way, in fact, to make sense of these differences is to assume that the text, subsequent to its composition, has been subject to revision, modification and augmentation. It is regrettable that the present state of Rus̲h̲dī studies makes reiterations of this kind necessary. Such matters could simply have been dispensed with had the editors prepared the groundwork properly, and so provided the researcher with accurate and academically verified material.

We may surmise, therefore, that the manuscripts, collectively or individually, do not lend themselves to amalgamation into one, coherent text; attempts to do so will in fact only further remove us from an understanding of the content and aims of the work, and may also distort and exaggerate the force of the questions raised by Ibn Rus̲h̲d. The only sure way of proceeding is, as indicated earlier, to make a scrupulous distinction between the earliest version and later accretions; and the manuscripts should then be read in the light of *Al-Talk̲h̲īṣ* and, in particular, of *Al-S̲h̲arḥ al-kabīr*.

Thus there definitely exists, I believe—especially with regard to those chapters dealing with the problem of the intellect—a first version of the book, in which Ibn Rus̲h̲d drafted his initial thoughts, and within which a set of specific amendments and additions was later incorporated in the light of his subsequent writings, particularly *Al-S̲h̲arḥ al-kabīr*. This would appear to provide the most probable explanation for the differences, in spite of Ibn Rus̲h̲d's own assertion, in one of the Madrid manuscript copies, that he had not deleted anything he had originally written about the material intellect—a statement made in the context of certain other changes he had made in that manuscript on the subject of the rational faculty. I believe that the amendments in question were indeed made, but went unacknowledged, possibly because they were incorporated long after the time of the work's initial composition. An examination of the extant manuscripts yields specific clues enabling us to differentiate between the first version and the later additions.[11] Some editors have been aware of variants among the manuscripts, and of the distinction between an earlier and a later version, but they have not fully grasped the intellectual significance of these variants, with the result that the latter have hitherto remained unanalysed.

A careful comparative study of the manuscripts leads me to conclude that specific additions stem from his subsequent intellectual development, which saw a profound change in his position on the problem of the intellect; a change that involved a reformulation of his position on the nature of the theoretical intellect, and represented, too, a shift in his position on the nature of the material intellect and its relationship to imaginative forms. Ibn Rushd's psychological theory constitutes a very well defined structure, to the extent that a change in any one of the constituent elements will radically alter the structure as a whole; as such, his shifting positions constitute a reformulation of the entire system, and a careful effort has therefore been made to differentiate those elements within the manuscripts which are traceable to the first version and those which represent later amendments. Let us now consider the distinctiveness of this text vis-à-vis the other psychological writings of Ibn Rushd.

The major distinctive differences between the two versions can best be summed up[12] by saying that the first constitutes a coherent and well organised text, while the second contains additions to the first which create uncertainties over the actual meaning. Moreover, such uncertainties and dissonances manifest themselves throughout the text, so that it is in fact unintelligible in more than one place. The second part of this study will demonstrate in detail how sense may be made of these incongruities in the light of a perceived evolution in Ibn Rushd's own perspectives.

The differences between the two versions may be treated with respect to six specific factors, two of these involving the first version and the others the second.

The peculiar features of the first version are as follows:

(1) The analogy of the tablet is used to define the capacity of the imaginative faculty (*al-quwwa 'l-khayāliyya*) to accept intelligibles, which are represented by the writing on the tablet,[13] while the subjective self (*al-nafs al-mawḍūʿa*) of this capacity is represented by the tablet itself. It is clear that parts of this analogy reflect certain perspectives on the material intellect, imaginary representations and the theoretical intellect different from those set out in *Al-Talkhīṣ*, and significantly different from the conclusions reached in *Al-Sharḥ al-kabīr*.[14] Interestingly, these perspectives are similar to those held by Ibn Bājja. The absence or omission of this analogy from the other manuscript copies is the first indication of Ibn Rushd's changing position on the structure of the material intellect (I am not postulating this evolution simply on the basis of one passage in one manuscript, which would be clear-

ly unacceptable: the hypothesis is further supported by another version of the analogy in *Al-Talkhīṣ* and a third version in *Al-Sharḥ al-kabīr*).[15]

(2) The long chapter discussing the rational faculty is divided into two parts: in the first part Ibn Rushd summarises a portion of Ibn Bājja's *Risālat al-ittiṣāl,* while in the second he sets out what appears to be a summary of Ibn Bājja's method—in such a way as to suggest support for it. The conspicuous absence or omission of these passages from later versions can be interpreted as a disavowal, by Ibn Rushd, of Ibn Bājja's theory of conjunction. A probable explanation for this is to be found not in *Al-Talkhīṣ* but in relevant sections within *Al-Sharḥ al-kabīr* of *De Anima*,[16] with further evidence also to be found in the *Sharḥ mā baʿd al-ṭabīʿa* (Commentary on the Metaphysics) under the heading *Al-Ṭāʾ* and *Al-Lām*.[17]

If we now turn our attention to the later manuscript, we find additions and amendments characterised by four features. The first of these is well known, because it is explicitly dealt with in the manuscripts, while the remaining three have been deduced by comparing the text not simply with the manuscript copies, but also with *Al-Talkhīṣ* and *Al-Sharḥ al-kabīr*.

The first feature is the amendment with which he concludes the chapter on the rational faculty,[18] replacing the sections summarising portions of Ibn Bājja's *Risālat al-ittiṣāl.* In this amendment Ibn Rushd clearly states that his earlier position on the material intellect, as set out in *Al-Mukhtaṣar*, was incorrect, and that his revised opinion can be found in *Al-Sharḥ al-kabīr* of *De Anima*—the implication being that Ibn Bājja had been responsible for leading him into error. Although this amendment is so well known, it has not been sufficiently considered by scholars, who have thus failed to conclude that Ibn Rushd, having initially upheld Ibn Bājja's position, later relinquished it.

It has already been pointed out that Ibn Rushd's psychological theory is framed within a highly integrated structure, so that tampering with any one of its elements will affect all the other elements of the system; and, as such, the amendments to Ibn Rushd's positions on the theoretical intellect and theoretical intelligibles, and also on the subject of the material intellect and imaginary representations, must be seen as embodying a reformulation of his whole psychological theory. The amendments cited thus far are not in themselves sufficient basis for postulating such a reformulation, but it is hoped that the ensuing analysis of the remaining features will provide further evidence to this end.

Perhaps the most important of these is the twofold amendment relating to the material intellect and theoretical intelligibles. The first version, reflecting Ibn Bājja's influence, defines the material intellect as being that potentiality in imaginative forms through which intelligibles are received. In his amendment, however, he sets out, in the form of an overall summary, a viewpoint similar to that which he had demonstrated in *Al-Sharḥ al-kabīr*, stating that he no longer considers the material intellect to be a capacity within imaginative forms, but rather a substance which represents, *in potentia*, all intelligibles, but which in itself is not anything. Had he still been in agreement with Ibn Bājja, these differences would not have existed. He further confirms the amendments by linking theoretical intelligibles with two objects: one of them the material intellect, which he regards as eternal, and the other the imaginative forms, which are viewed as a corruptible entity. An examination of *Al-Sharḥ al-kabīr* reveals a contradiction with the position taken in the earlier version, where he had concluded that these intelligibles were material, contingent, generating, corrupting, multiple and changeable. The fourth amendment focuses on the conception of Man as possessor of a capacity linked to imaginative forms, which enables Man alone, and no animal, to accept intelligibles. This amendment, though less valuable than the preceding one, is nonetheless important because it indicates a change in Ibn Rushd's position, if only in connection, apparently, with the role played by imaginative forms. The gist of his argument is that imaginative forms are not stationary but in motion, and this leads on to the formulation of what is effectively a new and specific position, in which he proclaims his disagreement with two major schools within the history of Aristotelianism,[19] and further states that commenting on these two schools and judging between them will require far more extensive analysis than is possible within the confines of the *Mukhtaṣar*. This new position is developed in two successive stages, the first represented in *Al-Talkhīṣ*, and the second transmitted through *Al-Sharḥ al-kabīr*, which will be examined in the second part of this study.

These, very briefly, are the most important deductions from my reading of this unique work, the general conclusion being that it would be an error to regard *Al-Mukhtaṣar* as a single well-ordered text, or as a reliable source for establishing Ibn Rushd's position on the problem of the intellect. We may further conclude that, with regard to the problem of the intellect, and in particular to the question of the material intellect, he was influenced by Ibn Bājja and other commentators on Aristotle—such a position being incompatible with what he writes later in *Al-Talkhīṣ* and *Al-Sharḥ al-kabīr*, where he returns to reading the original texts of Aristotle (although, it should be noted that his position in *Al-Talkhīṣ* is closer to *Al-Mukhtaṣar* than to *Al-Sharḥ*).

The parameters of the work will now become clearer to us, and we shall be forced to choose between two alternatives: we can either, when examining the problem of the intellect, focus solely on *Al-Sharḥ* and use *Al-Mukhtaṣar* and *Al-Talkhīṣ* as supplementary works; or, on the other hand, *Al-Mukhtaṣar* may be viewed as an initial, fundamental fragment permitting us to examine the evolution of the problem of the intellect in the writings of Ibn Rushd—in which case the three texts will be treated initially as of equal value for our research, with preference given to *Al-Sharḥ al-kabīr*, as the most important, at a subsequent stage.

We might, also, examine the evolution of Ibn Rushd's position, or try to demonstrate the structure of the Rushdī system. In this case we would have to rely on *Al-Mukhtaṣar* as a primary text, or use it in conjunction with other texts containing similar passages and perhaps even addressing similar questions. I do not, however, believe that such an approach would be warranted by the texts.

I.2 *The* Talkhīṣ *(Middle Commentary) of* De Anima

This *Talkhīṣ* occupies an intermediate position between *Al-Mukhtaṣar* and *Al-Sharḥ*, exhibiting similarities and differences, vis-à-vis these texts, in both form and content. With respect to form, *Al-Talkhīṣ* is a commentary on Aristotle's *De Anima*, being in fact Ibn Rushd's first commentary on this work,[20] and its structure differs from that of *Al-Mukhtaṣar*, while bearing some similarities to that of *Al-Sharḥ*. With respect to content, particularly in its conceptualisation of the problem of the intellect, *Al-Talkhīṣ* is closer to *Al-Mukhtaṣar* and differs from *Al-Sharḥ*.[21]

It is immediately clear that the various positions of *Al-Talkhīṣ*, particularly in its first version, may reasonably be regarded as an extension of those adopted in the minor *Mukhtaṣar*. The text is of crucial importance, not only because it records a shift in Ibn Rushd's position, but also on account of the distinctive style in which it is written. However, the primary consideration of this study is to identify the problems and difficulties the text places before the reader; and these are similar to the ones encountered in the preceding analysis of *Al-Mukhtaṣar*.

Al-Talkhīṣ does indeed differ from *Al-Mukhtaṣar* in two significant ways: in the varying number of extant manuscripts,[22] and by the fact that *Al-Talkhīṣ* still only exists in manuscript form. Nevertheless, the difficulties involved in reconstructing the two texts are similar in principle, although they are less evident in *Al-Talkhīṣ*. It should be pointed out at the outset that, whereas our analysis and conclusions concerning *Al-Mukhtaṣar* were based on significant variants among the manuscript copies, the two important manuscripts of *Al-Talkhīṣ* agree more closely with each other. Yet I have concluded that the *Talkhīṣ* manuscripts represent two different versions, with one manuscript, particularly in respect of those chapters relevant to this study, representing an earlier version, and the other containing additions and amendments made to the text at a later date. The differences between the two manuscripts will be discussed later in this paper.

The distinction between earlier and later version is indicated in the first and third chapters of the text, where it becomes evident that revision has taken place following the completion of *Al-Sharḥ al-kabīr*. However, this cannot in itself be taken as sufficient confirmation of the differences: we must undertake a detailed examination of the text, particularly of those passages devoted to the problem of the intellect.

I have concluded that *Al-Talkhīṣ* advances two mutually contradictory positions on the nature of the material intellect, which can only be reasonably explained as reflecting a later revision. In his first position one can trace the influence of the Alexandrian school of commentators, which claimed that the material intellect was a potentiality in which nothing exists. Yet it does not appear that Ibn Rushd adopted the position of the Alexandrian school in its totality: rather, he simply adopted some of the well-known conclusions of Alexander, the ancient commentator himself. His position can thus be seen as shifting from that of *Al-Mukhtaṣar*, in which he follows the school of Ibn Bājja, to that of *Al-Talkhīṣ*, where he inclines towards the Alexandrian school.

As for the second position, this emerges in an important subsequent amendment in *Al-Takhhīṣ*, which represents a break from his previous view that the material intellect is solely a potentiality. Here, for the first time, he postulates the material intellect to be a separate substance in and of itself, and, in addition, he advocates a doctrine of reconciliation between the opinions of Alexander and those of Themistius. This doctrine, which he refers to as *madhhab al-jamʿ* ("doctrine of synthesis"), will be examined later when considering the amendments from *Al-Mukhtaṣar* and *Al-Sharḥ*.

These amendments and additions, which I take as evidence of a new position, change the meaning of the text as preserved in the first version. Moreover, they change the definition of important concepts in such a way as to align them with definitions advanced in *Al-Sharḥ*. Two additions in particular reflect the influence of the latter.

The first of these, cited in the first chapter, concerns the theoretical intellect and the habituated intellect (*al-ʿaql bi 'l-malaka*).[23] The amendment concisely summarises the positions found in *Al-Sharḥ*, namely that the theoretical intellect is neither generating nor corrupting, but is rather a corruptible entity due to the matter (*mawḍūʿ*) which acts within it. The second addition, of less significance than the first, clarifies Themistius' stand on "the intellect which is within us".[24]

There are two other amendments relating to the material intellect and, to some extent, to the active intellect, although no reference, explicit or implicit, is made to *Al-Sharḥ*. The likelihood that they were composed at the same period is heightened by the fact that the second amendment refers to the first[25] and that they both convey his new position on the material intellect. The later amendment summarises arguments that the intellect is potential, and is other than a faculty or a capacity, this being clearly contrary to the position expressed more than once in the first version of *Al-Talkhīṣ*.

All this would suggest that the revision of the text was completed at different periods, the first amendment being added before the completion of *Al-Sharḥ* and the second thereafter, and it heralds an enormous change in Ibn Rushd's conception of the material intellect. The new position cannot, it is true, be readily equated with that found in *Al-Sharḥ al-kabīr*; nonetheless, it represents a decisive break with the position advanced in the first version of *Al-Talkhīṣ*, and also with that of *Al-Mukhtaṣar*.

Al-Talkhīṣ is, therefore, a text of basic importance for understanding the developing treatment of the problem of the intellect in the writings of Ibn Rushd. *Al-Talkhīṣ* and *Al-Mukhtaṣar*, in all their versions, are to be seen as embodying preliminary perspectives which were later superseded by the final version set out in *Al-Sharḥ al-kabīr*. This is the main conclusion to be reached through an examination of his psychological writings as a whole.[26]

Let us now, in the light of this conclusion, briefly review the positions articulated in the three texts in question, with a view to laying the foundations (as suggested above) of a new strategy for approaching the Rushdī corpus.

II

Introduction

From the above analysis, we can deduce two different stages in the evolution of Ibn Rushd's view of the intellect. The first, which may be referred to as the Ibn Bājja-Alexandrian phase, can be traced back to the two original versions of *Al-Mukhtaṣar* and *Al-Talkhīṣ*, i.e., those versions containing no amendments or additions; the second is that embodied in *Al-Sharḥ*, and may be called the Rushdī stage. Given that these two stages involve radically different and contradictory conceptions, our study may now proceed in one of two directions. One alternative would be to trace the evolution in Ibn Rushd's writings; this would involve an examination of all three texts, and our analysis would proceed on the assumption that there are two discernible stages, and that the amendments in *Al-Talkhīṣ* represent the middle ground between them. The other would be to attempt an analysis of Ibn Rushd's psychological system, or, more specifically, of his conception of the problem of the intellect. In this case we would no longer need to examine *Al-Mukhtaṣar* and *Al-Talkhīṣ* or, indeed, refer to them.

Since the differences between the texts are clearly the result of a developing process, an examination focusing on all three texts would be awkward and misguided. We are, in effect, postulating the existence of two possible approaches towards the problem of the intellect, stemming from what is not merely an evolution but an enormous change in Ibn Rushd's position, with two distinct stages being divided by a weak intermediate link (this link will be more fully considered later). Let us therefore now examine these stages more closely, confining ourselves, in our review, to those elements involving the material and theoretical intellect.

II.1. *The Ibn Bājja-Alexandrian stage or the Ibn Bājja-Alexandrian Ibn Rushd*

This stage, as noted above, combines two phases, contained in *Al-Mukhtaṣar* and *Al-Talkhīṣ*. The rationale for combining these into one single stage springs from important perceived similarities between the two texts in question; nonetheless, there are also differences between them, particularly, as mentioned earlier, with respect to the respective strategies employed. The significant similarities stem from the fact that Ibn Rushd compiled both these texts in the light of others' viewpoints; he was, at this stage, much more dependent on the opinions and analyses of previous commentators, effectively seeing and hearing Aristotle through the eyes and ears of others rather than cultivating his own independent perceptions. At the beginning he was primarily influenced by Ibn Bājja, then, later, by Alexander, and he only freed himself of these influences, finally, when he composed *Al-Sharḥ al-kabīr*; it is in this text that we are offered a new image of Ibn Rushd, which best captures the independence and uniqueness of his thought. *Al-Sharḥ's* originality gives a sense of personal satisfaction, making all our arduous and painstaking efforts appear worthwhile in the end. As we follow Ibn Rushd's argument, we are struck by the insightful way he criticises the positions of earlier writers, positions which he himself had earlier upheld in *Al-Mukhtaṣar* and *Al-Talkhīṣ*; and, as such, his arguments might be interpreted as a form of self-criticism and self-revision. This is why I have combined *Al-Mukhtaṣar and Al-Talkhīṣ* as representing a single stage, with the second stage represented by *Al-Sharḥ*. Let us begin by examining the two phases of the first stage as articulated in the original texts.

For all the difficulties associated with reading *Al-Mukhtaṣar*, its analysis can reasonably be seen as centring around the theoretical intellect or theoretical intelligibles. He regards these intelligibles as the most important structural element in his theory of the intellect, other elements having importance only in so far as they elucidate the nature of the intelligibles themselves—this applying, also, to the material and active intellect, which he considers to constitute the matter and form of the intelligibles (there will be an opportunity to examine this structure in more detail later in the paper). It is this conception of intelligibles which distinguishes *Al-Mukhtaṣar* from *Al-Talkhīṣ*. Yet despite these differences—which become still more marked when we compare *Al-Talkhīṣ* with *Al-Sharḥ*—the two works do in fact share a common approach.

In the first stage of his analysis Ibn Rushd concludes that intelligibles are subject to alteration. They therefore necessarily possess matter and have in the first place a potential existence and in the second place an actual existence. They are contingent, corruptible and plural with regard to the plurality of objects and they are numerous in the range of their numbers. This is significant when it is considered that their conjunction with imaginative forms is spontaneous. The analysis shows Ibn Rushd following Ibn Bājja's conclusions as set out in *Risālat al-ittiṣāl*, although he never in fact mentions Ibn Bājja by name.[27] It must be emphasised that this position is very different from the one adopted in *Al-Sharḥ*, where he asserts that the theoretical intellect is eternal with respect to its substance and a corruptible entity with respect to its action—intelligibles being, in other words, linked with two objects: the material intellect which is eternal and imaginative forms which are a corruptible entity.[28] This analysis is equally relevant for understanding the positions found in *Al-Mukhtaṣar*, particularly his concept of the material intellect or the matter of intelligibles. When Ibn Rushd distinguishes between the form and the matter of intelligibles he states quite clearly that their form, which is the active intellect, remains unchanged, being neither generating nor corrupting. When considering the matter of intelligibles, however, he shows awareness of disagreements between the earlier commentators, and, by adopting the stand of Ibn Bājja, he rejects the other positions, particularly the view that the material intellect is an eternal substance; this rejection stemming from the contradiction inherent in the proposition that the intellect is eternal while the intelligibles found in it are contingent. Contingency, Ibn Rushd says, is incompatible with an eternal substance; and if intelligibles were in fact contingent, then the material intellect would also have to be contingent, because the material intellect is merely the capacity giving rise to the formation of intelligibles. This capacity is irreducible, and it is thus necessarily a special object, which is neither body nor intellect, but rather a soul. The conception of the soul is seen as being the object of intelligibles and is represented by imaginative forms—hence, the capacity found in imaginative forms capable of accepting intelligibles is the material intellect. The habituated or theoretical intellect can best be explained as the actualisation of intelligibles which had previously existed *in potentia*. Ibn Rushd buttresses his interpretation by citing examples used by Aristotle, especially when attempting to define the passivity of the intellect by comparing it to the passivity of the tablet which is merely disposed to writing. He states that the capacity of the imaginative faculty to accept intelligibles is similar to the corresponding relationship between the tablet and writing; the soul, subject to this capacity, being in the position of the tablet. Yet this capacity is not an actual thing in and of itself; thus the concept of passivity cannot really be applied to it. This analysis is no more than an interpretation of Ibn Bājja's propositions.[29] By the admission of Ibn Rushd himself, Ibn Bājja was the first commentator to state that the material intellect is merely a capacity found in imaginative forms; a capacity able to accept intelligibles. This interpretation endeavours to surmount some of the absurdities put forth by Alexander. The conclusion in *Al-Sharḥ* is that the material intellect is neither an actual thing nor an explicitly eternal thing or separate substance. It is evident that a considerable interval separated the two stages as reflected in the two positions in question. Some of the reasons which led Ibn Rushd, subsequently, to revise and amend *Al-Mukhtaṣar* have already been pointed out.

Such, then, is the basic nature of the first phase of this stage. The important points to bear in mind include the way Ibn Rushd deals with the problem of conjunction as set out in Ibn Bājja's famous treatise on the subject and the way he adopts Ibn Bājja's interpretation of the problem of the intellect, and his arguments should also be examined in the light of the selected themes and subsequent amendments in *Al-Mukhtaṣar*. Let us now examine the second phase of this stage, as represented in the text of *Al-Talkhīṣ*.

Whereas the argument of *Al-Mukhtaṣar* revolved around the theoretical intellect or intelligibles, the analytical thrust of *Al-Talkhīṣ* is primarily directed towards the material intellect and its role in the process of intellection.[30] This thematic difference between the two texts is both marked and significant.[31]

The change reflects the evolving position of Ibn Rushd on the problem of the intellect and, in particular, on the question of the material intellect, and it can, as mentioned earlier, be generally explained in terms of Ibn Rushd's transition from an echoing of Ibn Bājja's stand to his subsequent inclination towards the views of Alexander (though the two commentators do, we should remember, share the view that the material intellect is only a capacity and not a separate substance). Let us therefore consider further the full significance of the differences between *Al-Talkhīṣ* and *Al-Mukhtaṣar*, and let us focus on the amendments incorporated in *Al-Talkhīṣ*, especially those relating to the nature of the material intellect, which mark a revolution in Ibn Rushd's view of the subject and, indeed, on the entire question of the intellect—a revolution which later becomes fully articulated in *Al-Sharḥ*.

Ibn Rushd begins, in accordance with the text of Aristotle, by stating that the faculty capable of accepting intelligibles is neither passive nor subject to change. If there is indeed any question of passivity, this is merely confined to the acceptance of the intelligibles and does not imply mixing with any of the material forms. By this, Ibn Rushd means that the material intellect is the accepting faculty, accepting and comprehending all forms and all things. However, if it were to accept any forms, we would have to uphold one of the two following explanations: either it does not comprehend the other forms, only the form with which it is mixed; or it would be a mixed form which would change what it comprehends through the intellect, and it would thus be unable to comprehend fully the essence of things as they really are.

The material intellect is unable to mix with anything and is hence only a capacity; this implying, too, that the potential intellect is merely a capacity, containing nothing. However, although it is an object ultimately incapable of mixing, it is not to be classified as a subject of the potential intellect. On the whole the intellect carries a sense of passivity which is not confined to the process of acceptance only, and the subject of this acceptance is not a thing but a capacity able to accept intelligibles; there can be no notion of an independently existing capacity. This, as is well known, represents a summary of Alexander's position on the material intellect, and it is this position which is incorporated within *Al-Talkhīṣ*, or at least in the passage from *Al-Talkhīṣ* noted above.

Among the many features of *Al-Talkhīṣ* which help to clarify Ibn Rushd's concept of the material intellect, the most prominent is the passage in which he compares the capacity in the intellect with the potentiality in the tablet to accept writing. He emphasises that, just as the capacity found on the surface of the tablet does not mix with the tablet itself, so this is the case, also, with the intellect and the intelligibles. The acceptance of the tablet does not signify passivity, and, analogously, the acceptance of the intellect is neither passive nor active. This interpretation differs from the one given in *Al-Mukhtaṣar*, where the capacity is represented by the ability of imaginative forms to accept intelligibles—a capacity, that is, whose object is embodied in the imaginary processes of the soul. However, in this case the capacity is not conceived as being similar to the blank tablet, and this is because the intellect as such is perceived as being a capacity and not an actual thing. As for the written tablet it resembles the perfected intellect while the actual intelligibles represent another type of intellect.

The analogy of the tablet helps us to understand the evolution in Ibn Rushd's position on the material intellect, not only in connection with the transition from *Al-Mukhtaṣar* to *Al-Talkhīṣ* but also with respect to its final version as found in *Al-Sharḥ al-kabīr*. In this final version Ibn Rushd traces the different positions back to their original authors,[32] and it is in this context that he severely criticises Alexander's comparison of the intellect with the potentiality found in the tablet. His other criticisms will be examined later.

Other themes connected with Ibn Rushd's discussion of the active intellect should also be briefly noted: the first of these concerns the ontological nature of the active intellect, and the second its role in the process of intellection and cognition (*maʿrifa*).

He begins his first discussion in *Al-Talkhīṣ* by citing an Aristotelian proposition that establishes a correspondence between the intellect and material things. Aristotle asserts that there exist, in all categories of natural matter, two things in opposition: that which has the capacity to receive and that which is the agent; the receptive capacity is potential in all things that exist, while the agent acts in everything within these categories. Ibn Rushd applies this notion of Aristotelian opposition to his concept of the intellect, thereby postulating the existence of an active and passive intellect;[33] and, despite the difference between this and what he later concludes in *Al-Sharḥ*, he continues to maintain that the active intellect is a transcendent substance, not a corruptible entity, comprehending its own essence when it is separated from humanity and comprehending the material affairs of the world when it is linked to humanity. As such, the intellect and intelligibles, contrary to Ibn Rushd's later conception of the material intellect, are one and the same.

The second discussion in *Al-Talkhīṣ* focuses on the process of intellection, with analysis centring on the active intellect to the exclusion of others. Like Aristotle, Ibn Rushd compares the role of this intellect with light; more precisely, it is a light which translates colours from potentiality to actuality, thus enabling the eye to see and experience them. Similarly, the active intellect provides the material intellect with the capacity for accepting intelligibles, and this capacity further changes the imaginary representations of the intelligibles until they are no longer potential but actualised. Though this description is very similar to what is contained in *Al-Sharḥ*, the passage still leaves us with some difficulties and questions.

The preceding discussion touches upon the most important points contained in *Al-Talkhīṣ*. There is, however, another dimension to this text which in effect makes it an intermediate link between the first and second stages of Ibn Rushd's thought. It is possible to examine this text from two different angles: on the one hand, it can be viewed, along with *Al-Mukhtaṣar*, as constituting the first stage in the evolution of Ibn Rushd's psychological system; on the other, it can be seen as representing a bridge by means of which he was able to construct another version or form of the problem of the intellect. This dual viewpoint is made possible by the very nature of the amendments in *Al-Talkhīṣ*; for these not only help us to distinguish the differences between *Al-Talkhīṣ* and *Al-Mukhtaṣar*, but also allow us to evaluate *Al-Talkhīṣ* vis-à-vis *Al-Sharḥ*. The amendment to the analogy of the tablet marks the first transition from the former position, with the material intellect, regardless of the arguments put forth by Ibn Bājja or the Alexandrian school, now viewed simply as a capacity. As noted earlier, this change does not completely crystallise into a new position, but rather foreshadows the new developments that eventually took place in *Al-Sharḥ*. Let us now, as an introduction to the changes occurring in the second stage of Ibn Rushd's thought, examine the context from which the amendment emerged, confining our examination, for the moment, to a discussion of the nature of the material intellect and leaving till later a more general consideration of the intellect as a whole.

It is immediately apparent that the amendment reflects Ibn Rushd's struggle with the difficulties and absurdities inherent in Alexander's position (which, it will be recalled, he had earlier upheld, together with corresponding positions attributed to Themistius and other ancient commentators); he is attempting to formulate a conciliatory viewpoint through which to establish an appropriate interpretation of the viewpoints of the Alexandrian school.

He maintains, as Alexander had also done, that the material intellect is a capacity independent of material forms, but claims that it is also a transcendent substance invested with this capacity. In other words, this capacity is found in Man, and yet it is solely an object connected to a transcendent substance. It is not, as claimed by earlier commentators, a capacity existing, as it were, by the very nature of this transcendent substance; nor is it, as Alexander had claimed, a mere capacity.

The material intellect is a product of the conjunction between a transcendent substance and the capacity existing in Man. It can also be viewed as a compound of the capacity and its connection with the intellect. We must, therefore, seek to understand the nature of this compound and of the capacity inherent in it, and, also, to understand the link between the transcendent substance and its corresponding capacity. As for the transcendent substance, what is meant by it here is clearly the active intellect, the implication being that this intellect becomes a potential intellect in the state of conjunction. The substance of the active intellect is transformed when it is invested with a certain type of capacity, the character of which is best understood as the continuous movement from potentiality to actuality. In this movement the action of the intellect is transformed from one state to another; in other words the active intellect is eventually transformed into a material intellect, while the material intellect is, in its turn, eventually transformed into an active intellect. Ibn Rushd's rationale for this analysis is that he views the intellect as being one thing which yet contains two functions with respect to the soul: the first being the action of intelligibles, and the second that of accepting intelligibles.

While the identity and meaning of the separate substance has now been clarified, the notion of "capacity found in Man" remains somewhat obscure: we do not, for example, know whether this capacity is an intellect or a soul, or, moreover, whether it is capable of mixing with any of the faculties in the body. This obscurity can be attributed to the fact that Ibn Rushd did not himself define the nature of this capacity and its contents—which means that we also do not know the meaning of his statement that the material intellect is a compound of the capacity and that the intellect is linked with this capacity. A possible explanation can be found if we assume that the material intellect is not in itself a separate substance. Such an assertion would, however, run contrary to Ibn Rushd's later conclusion in *Al-Sharḥ*, where he makes a clear distinction between the active and the material intellect, considering them both to be transcendent substances, neither generating nor corrupting. We do not, though, know whether this amendment in *Al-Talkhīṣ* refers to the material or the active intellect.[34]

Ibn Rushd is advancing, through this amendment, a new interpretation which he believes accurately reflects the original view of Aristotle, and he refers to this interpretation as the "school of synthesis", implying, by the latter term, a middle road between the views of Alexander and those of other commentators on the nature of the material intellect. According to Ibn Rushd, the synthesis enables him to go beyond the absurdities inherent in these, the avowed aim being to free himself from the necessity to debase a transcendent thing in whose substance some capacity exists, merely because this transcendent thing happens to exist in conjunction with Man rather than by virtue of its own nature. He further notes that the synthesis frees him from the necessity of limiting the potential intellect to being solely a capacity, merely on the basis that there is, somehow, a separate thing to which this capacity accidentally clings.

For all his claims, Ibn Rushd ultimately fails to construct a genuine synthesis; its falsity and incoherence soon, indeed, become clear to him, leading him to embark on a revision of his views in *Al-Sharḥ al-kabīr*, where he does not refer to the doctrine of synthesis, but laboriously examines, one by one, the views of the schools of Ibn Bājja, Alexander and Themistius, then criticises them by comparison with the original Aristotelian text. And from the springboard which this critical strategy provides he simultaneously articulates and justifies his own new interpretation. Ibn Rushd's influence on the development of philosophy among the Latins, from the middle of the 13th century onwards, can be traced back to the legacy of this critical method.

Such, then, are the main characteristics of Ibn Rushd's new position—a position which, as noted earlier, represents both the end of the first stage of his thought and a link or bridge, with respect to postulations about the material intellect, to the subsequent stage. It now remains to demonstrate how the analytical strands of this new position culminated in the creation of a new, second stage in his writings.

II.2. *The Rushdī stage; or the Rushdī Ibn Rushd*

This final stage was the fruit of more than thirty years of study and ceaseless probing. In retrospect, his writings can best be interpreted as a quest for both an original and an authentic interpretation of Aristotle's philosophical system—a quest sustained, as it were, both through a persistent dialogue with Aristotle's writings and through a concurrent critical engagement with major thinkers within the Aristotelian heritage.

Ibn Rushd's commentary on *De Anima* is, as I have noted in an earlier work,[35] the most important text among his psychological writings. Let us now examine it in detail, in order to analyse the evolution of his thought, and, more importantly, to assess the originality of his philosophical contribution.

The preceding analysis of *Al-Mukhtaṣar* and *Al-Talkhīṣ* revealed the gradual processes whereby Ibn Rushd critically rejected the views of Alexander and, subsequently, those of Ibn Bājja, thereby exorcising the Alexandrian-Ibn Bājja influences in his own earlier writings. A similar transition had also in fact occurred with respect to Abū Naṣr al-Fārābī: his earlier writings on logic had been deeply influenced by al-Fārābī's views, but in a later commentary on the *Analytica Posteriora* (*Al-Burhān*) he severely criticised al-

Fārābī on account of views which he himself had specifically upheld earlier in *Mukhtaṣar al-Burhān* (Epitome of *Analytica Posteriora*).[36] Ibn Rushd's revisionist inclinations aptly demonstrate the degree of rigour and seriousness with which he pursued his philosophical vocation; and there is no better example of this rigour than *Al-Sharḥ al-kabīr*, which formulates a completely different psychological system and a completely different approach to the problem of the intellect, whose force almost annuls much of what he had previously written in *Al-Mukhtaṣar* and *Al-Talkhīṣ*.

The analysis of *Al-Sharḥ* will be conducted somewhat differently from those made of *Al-Mukhtaṣar* and *Al-Talkhīs*, the reason being that the original Arabic text of the work is lost; the earliest authoritative version is in fact preserved in a Latin translation. For the purposes of this paper I shall be basing myself on sections of the text which have been translated into French from the Latin version,[37] and on portions of the text which have been recorded in the margins of the manuscript copies of *Al-Talkhīṣ* found in the Modena library. Let us begin by briefly reviewing the central strands of this text, which sufficiently indicate the complete transformation in Ibn Rushd's thought.

The transformation appears not only in the new views advanced but in the very style in which *Al-Sharḥ* is written. There is a conscious attempt, on Ibn Rushd's part, to articulate processes of thought which have now led him to confront hitherto unexplored questions and unexamined obscurities. The conclusions reached in the work are advanced in a manner which implicitly suggests a new set of perspectives.

Ibn Rushd immediately makes it clear that the material intellect[38] constitutes the central theme of this text,[39] but he also clearly indicates, thereafter, that the examination of the material intellect in isolation from the other faculties would be impractical and misguided. As such, the scope of changes in *Al-Sharḥ* affects not only the conception of the material intellect, as previously articulated in *Al-Mukhtaṣar* and *Al-Talkhīṣ*, but his entire psychological structure, involving all the major elements from the intellect, theoretical intelligibles and the active intellect to imaginary representations. The implications of these structural changes are examined from the perspective both of epistemological states and of the different ontological states in question; his discussion of the material intellect is thus constantly linked up with all the other aspects of the intellect. With regard to the relationship between the material intellect and the senses, Ibn Rushd states that, while the material intellect is not affected by a passivity similar to that of the senses, and does not experience change analogous to what the senses undergo, there does nonetheless exist within it a concept of passivity whose meaning is subsumed within its function of acceptance. The material intellect is regarded as belonging among the genus of passive faculties, and is thus rightfully distinguished from the active intellect, yet it is neither a body nor a faculty within a body; it is, in effect, a substance which accepts all forms without itself being one of the forms it accepts. This is because the material forms are not separate, whereas the material intellect is simple and separate. The material intellect is devoid of a specific nature, except in so far as it exists *in potentia*. It contains, potentially, all universal material intelligibles, but in actuality it is not a thing prior to its being endowed with the faculty of reason.[40] Hence it differs from the irrational prime matter which accepts particular forms, and, similarly, differs from the form, the matter and the compound of both. It is a part of a particular mode of existence. To assert that the material intellect exists *in potentia* does not mean that it is not a definite thing or a substance; what is implied is that, whatever the substrate bears, it cannot exist in actuality and thus cannot be taken in an absolute sense, but should rather be approached in a qualified manner. However, the substrate need not be a definite thing in actuality; rather, what the substrate bears should not be found in it in actuality.

The first obstacle to understanding the nature of this intellect is the question of how it can be from the genus of the passive faculties, while at the same time being simple, separate and not mixed in with the body. If we say that it is separate and simple, does this mean that the intellect and the intelligibles within it are one, as is the case with the active and separate intellects? This is a second difficulty.

The solution to the first difficulty lies in defining the concept of passivity in the context of the material intellect; for passivity, here, has a specialised meaning, implying a form of changeless potentiality, analogous to the disposition in the tablet to receive writing without being affected by passivity or change. Just as the tablet does not bear any writing either in actuality or *in potentia* approaching actuality, so the material intellect does not embrace any of the intelligible forms which it accepts, either in actuality or *in potentia* approaching actuality. It would be wrong to say, with Alexander, that the material intellect is similar to the disposition that exists in the tablet, rather than to the tablet itself inasmuch as it is disposed.[41] This is because we must first know the nature of the thing that is disposed before we can completely know the nature of the disposition—this because the material intellect is not only a disposition. Here, clearly, Ibn Rushd is not only criticising the views of Alexander, but also laying aside his own positions in *Al-Talkhīṣ* and *Al-Mukhtaṣar*. He emphasises for the first time that the capacity within the intellect is different from all other capacities, since it does not bear any intelligibles, either in actuality or *in potentia*, and is neither a body nor a faculty within a body. Nor is it a capacity existing within imaginative forms; for, among the many other absurdities enumerated,[42] this would make it a faculty within a body and therefore accepting the intellect itself.

As for the second difficulty, he asserts that the material intellect is closer to the other faculties of intellection than to separate intellects. There is, however, an important distinction, namely that it is, in its essence, an intellect existing in actuality, while the other intellects exist *in potentia*. He further states, however, that the material intellect ranks lowest among the separate intellects, in that the action of the material intellect is less powerful than that of the separate intellects. Furthermore, the material intellect is marked more by passivity than by activity, and in this respect it differs from the active intellect.[43]

In *Al-Sharḥ* the material intellect is not simply discussed for the elementary purposes of formulating a new definition, but is also analysed for its philosophical significance. Ibn Rushd daringly asserts that the material intellect is eternal and unitary with respect to mankind, and it is this which underlines the radical transformation in his thought and the revolt against his own earlier positions and those of his predecessors. It is not possible, here, to analyse the significance of this assertion in detail; this paper will rather content itself with a brief review of the changes arising out of the new position. To this end, we must analyse the text with reference to general approach, content of the dialogue, criticism and the final conclusions embodied in the text, as against those reached in his earlier writings.

Ibn Rushd has finally broken away from Alexander's position on the material intellect, which he himself had earlier upheld, and, just as he had attacked Ibn Bājja's writings, so he criticises the school of Themistius and others for their views on the theoretical intellect and the active intellect.[44] The main criticism is directed against Themistius' view that the theoretical intellect springs from the conjunction of the active and material intellect within us, and is therefore external. Since the first two intellects are external, Ibn Rushd asserts that Themistius' viewpoint has departed from that of Aristotle and is in opposition to truth itself. Ibn Rushd had already criticised this position earlier, in *Al-Mukhtaṣar*, but there his criticism reflects his adoption of the Ibn Bājja or Alexandrian school, whereas now it springs from a new position and a new conception of the system of relations required by the process of intellection. The criticism is equally determined by the ontological position of the material and active intellect, together with the role played by imaginary representations. All this is in contrast to the viewpoint of earlier schools, which had concluded the theoretical intellect to be eternal. It is this belief, in Ibn Rushd's view, that will eventually lead to absurdities undermining the process of intellection and the intellect itself.

The intellect is indeed the offspring of the material and active intellect, yet different from both. The compound of two things which are eternal, as the material and active intellect are, must itself necessarily be eternal and one. There is, however, another important element neglected by Themistius and his followers, namely the decisive role played by imaginative forms in the process of intellection. In this respect, the connection of the theoretical intellect to its activity regarding imaginary representations in particular is corrupting and multiple, due to the corruption and multiplicity of the imaginary representations themselves. This necessary connection is similar to the connection existing between the senses and sensibles. Just as the senses do not perceive anything without the presence of sensibles, so, similarly, the rational faculty does not conceptualise without imagination. Hence the intellect and intelligibles are not to be seen as contingent, generating and corrupting.

Yet it cannot be conceived that intelligibles are contingent while the intellect is eternal; for this would not correspond with the proposition that the material intellect is eternal and one. In other words, if the material intellect is the first perfection of Man and the theoretical intellect is the second perfection, then both these categories should be functioning under the same conditions. For example, if Man is generating and corrupting, this would apply equally to the first and second perfection within Man—a viewpoint which contradicts earlier conclusions and leads to absurdities and ambiguities concerning the material intellect. The assertion, for example, that the material intellect is a body or a faculty within a body could not possibly be upheld, since it has already been postulated that the intellect is not generating or corrupting. When we say that the first perfection is one and not multiple in relation to the human race, then inescapable ambiguities emerge, which can only be resolved if we assert that the first perfection is an individual concept embedded in matter, which is corruptible and multiple in relation to the multiplicity of individuals. We are then left with several questions: can we resolve this problem, and what exactly is the nature of the theoretical intellect and theoretical intelligibles if we are to assume that the material intellect is one and eternal?

Alexander resolves the problem by stating that the material intellect is generating and corrupting, and is at the same time a faculty. This Ibn Rushd rejects, just as he rejected Ibn Bājja's position, which, in his view, did not satisfactorily resolve Alexander's inconsistencies. All earlier views are in fact judged inadequate, the only way out being through the assertion that theoretical intelligibles have two elements, the first contingent and the second eternal. The first element makes them contingent and the second element makes them one of the existents. Imaginative forms are the first element and the material intellect is the second element. Imaginary representations or forms set the intellect into motion, this motion arising out of the process whereby the active intellect has transformed imaginary representations from potential intelligibles into active intelligibles.

I conclude, with Ibn Rushd, that there are two separate aspects to intelligibles: with respect to the subject which makes them contingent they are generating and corrupting, while with respect to the material intellect which makes them one of the existents of the world they are eternal; from this perspective they can be viewed as simultaneously generating, corrupting and eternal. The theoretical intellect is, in other words, eternal with respect to its activity. This solution bypasses the difficulties and absurdities found in the previous schools of commentators, and Ibn Rushd takes evident pride in his significant discovery, which enables him to uphold and further fortify his central thesis about the intellect and its eternity.[45]

Conclusion

These, then, are some of the major points it has been possible to derive from Ibn Rushd's key psychological texts. It has not been the aim of this study to analyse the points in full critical detail, but rather to explore the transformation in approaches to the problem of the intellect up to the writing of *Al-Sharḥ*. If the paper has shed some light on this area, then any oversights apparent in the analysis may perhaps be excused.

There are, I am convinced, two distinct phases in the evolution of Ibn Rushd's psychological system—this is indeed the claim from which the study begins—and the recognition of an evolution in his thought provides further encouragement for taking a more chronologically systematic approach to the Rushdī corpus. The discovery of amendments, as in the case of *Al-Mukhtaṣar* and *Al-Talkhīṣ*, will inevitably lead us to label Ibn Rushd's earlier writings as obsolete, yet such an approach will, nevertheless, ultimately provide us with deeper and richer insights. It would in any case be mere obstinacy to ignore such established differences between texts as occur in the various versions of *Al-Mukhtaṣar* and *Al-Talkhīṣ*.[46]

What must now be investigated is the nature and philosophical significance of the evolution in Ibn Rushd's thought. Was it, for example, an evolution born of successive and laborious interpretations of the Aristotelian text, or did it rather reflect a philosophical curiosity in search of new horizons beyond the limits of the original text? In either case what is the scope and depth of this evolution? Is it possible to speak of an evolution or a change within the context of an interpretative philosophy? These and other such questions represent a whole new and vital area of study. For the moment I shall rest content merely with raising them, in the hope of tackling them in a future study.

[1] *Al-Matn al-Rushdī, madkhal li-qirā'a jadīda*, Casablanca, 1986.

[2] Another examination of the evolution of the theory of demonstration according to Ibn Rushd was made in a paper contributed to *Al-Ḥalqa al-Rushdiyya. Symposium Ibn Rushd I*, which took place in Fez in March 1989.

[3] In its original format this study was a critical review of the book *Ishkāliyyat al-'aql 'ind Ibn Rushd* by Muḥammad al-Miṣbāḥī, Casablanca, 1988.

[4] A commendable effort has been under way for some years now to publish the works of Ibn Rushd in their original language, as well as in their Hebrew and Latin translations. Hopefully this work will soon be completed, and the major basic impediment to contemporary Rushdī studies removed.

[5] Ibn Rushd left behind nearly ten treatises on the soul (*nafs*), the intellect (*'aql*) and conjunction (*ittiṣāl*), all of which are lost in the original Arabic, with the exception of an addendum

to the doctrine of the rational faculty within an Epitome (*Mukhtaṣar*) of the *De Anima* in the Cairo manuscript; this addendum being, apparently, a commentary or part of a commentary on the *Risālat al-ittiṣāl* of Ibn Bājja. Most of it is in Hebrew and Latin translations. He also composed three texts which represent, I believe, the kernel of the Rushdī study of the subject, these being, in order: (a) the Epitome (*Al-Mukhtaṣar*) on the soul, which is extant in the original Arabic and has several printed editions (which might rather mislead the reader than guide him), foremost among these being the Egyptian edition; (b) The *Talkhīṣ* of *De Anima*, which is also extant in the original Arabic, although transcribed in Hebrew characters, but remains for the moment in manuscript. A published edition by Professor Alfred Ivry is expected shortly; (c) The commentary on *De Anima* , whose original is of course lost, although fragments are to be found in the marginal notes of the Modena manuscript of the *Talkhīṣ* of *De Anima*, transcribed in Hebrew characters. Some years ago, also, Kalmen P. Bland published Ibn Rushd's *Risāla fī imkān al-ittiṣāl bi 'l-ʿaql al-faʿʿāl* (New York, 1982) with a commentary by Moses of Narbonne, which will not, however, be discussed in this study.

[6] See my book *Al-Matn al-Rushdī*, where the commentaries of Ibn Rushd are discussed in detail and the position of each of the texts is explained. Although a viewpoint was adopted there concerning the abridged *Mukhtaṣar* of *De Anima*, I feel this is now in need of further careful examination and revision.

[7] I am referring to the short commentaries (*jawāmiʿ*) on *Al-Samāʿ al-ṭabīʿī* (*De Physico Auditu*), *Al-Samāʾ wa 'l-ʿālam* (*De Coelo et Mundo*) (ed. Jamāl al-Dīn al-ʿAlawī, Fez, 1984), *Al-Kawn wa 'l-fasād* (*De Generatione et Corruptione*) and *Al-Āthār al-ʿulwiyya* (*Meteorologica*). We may add to these the synthesis (*jawāmīʿ*) of *Mā baʿd al-ṭabīʿa* (*Metaphysica*).

[8] There are six known manuscripts today: two in Cairo and one each in Madrid, Teheran, the Chester Beatty Library and Hyderabad.

[9] There are three printed editions: *Rasāʾil Ibn Rushd*, Hyderabad, 1947; *Talkhīṣ kitāb al-nafs*, ed. F. al-Ahwānī, Cairo, 1950; and *Epitome de Anima*, ed. Salvador Gómez Nogales, Madrid, 1985.

[10] The other two printed editions are in no better state.

[11] Perhaps the latest editor to indicate this is Gómez Nogales in his edition of this *Mukhtaṣar*,which he calls a "*Talkhīṣ*", as al-Ahwānī had done. He states that the Madrid manuscript is the most recent copy and that he will be basing himself upon it. His edition of the book is no less bad than the previous two, despite his having new manuscript copies at his disposal.

[12] It is possible, by and large, to say that the second version has been transmitted to us in the Madrid manuscript and the first version by the others—although differences between the latter are such that we may in fact consider there is an intermediate link represented by the Hyderabad manuscript. However, let us, for practical convenience, consider what we have as two versions until at least part of the book has been edited in an accurate and scientific fashion.

[13] We do not find this analogy in the Madrid manuscript copy , or in the printed Hyderabad edition, which relied on another manuscript, being taken from the Cairo manuscript copy. Whether it is recorded in the other copies I do not know, as I have as yet had no opportunity to study them.

[14] Possibly he deleted it for this reason when he revised the text of *Al-Mukhtaṣar* some time after its composition.

[15] In *Al-Sharḥ al-kabīr* he mentions Ibn Bājja as comparing the imaginative faculty's capacity to accept intelligibles with the tablet's retention of writing, the created self (*al-nafs al-mawḍūʿa*) of this capacity being compared to the tablet. In other words, this analogy follows the school of Ibn Bājja entirely.

[16] See particularly section 36 of chapter III of the commentary on *De Anima*, Latin translation, edited by Crawford.

[17] *Tafsīr mā bāʿd al-ṭabīʿa*, ed. Maurice Bouyges, Bibliotheca Arabica Scholasticorum, Série Arabe, Beirut, 1938-52, II, 1230 and III, 1489-90.

[18] The Madrid manuscript copy is the only one with this amendment, just as the Cairo manuscript copy is the only one with the *Talkhīṣ* of the *Risālat al-ittiṣāl* of Ibn Bājja. The Hyderabad edition does not contain either the amendment or the summary.

[19] I.e., with the school of Alexander (together with Ibn Bājja) and the school of Theophrastus and Themistius. It will be seen how he reconciles the viewpoints of the two schools in *Al-Talkhīṣ*, and we shall further see how, in *Al-Sharḥ*, he goes beyond both these schools to establish a new school which won him great fame among the Latins.

20 It is the first if we consider as commentaries other treatises which he composed on questions treated in the *De Anima* of Aristotle; otherwise it would be one of two, namely *Al-Talkhīṣ* and *Al-Sharḥ al-kabīr.*

21 This definition of *Al-Talkhīṣ* is verified in the first version. If, however, we consider the additions to it, then we may say that it forms an intermediate link between *Al-Mukhtaṣar* and *Al-Sharḥ.*

22 There are two manuscript copies of the *Talkhīṣ* of *De Anima*, transcribed in Hebrew characters: those of Paris and Modena (Italy).

23 See folio 114, recto, of the Paris MS.

24 See folio 147, recto, of the Paris MS. The text does, however, lend itself to two readings, the first ("as we have shown in our *sharḥ* of Aristotle's words") clearly suggesting, as said, a reference to the *Sharḥ*, and the second ("as he has shown in his *sharḥ* on the words of Aristotle") embodying a reference to the *sharḥ* of Themistius. What makes the first reading more probable, however, is that Ibn Rushd calls the work of Themistius "*Talkhīṣ*" and not "*Sharḥ*".

25 On the first amendment, see folio 144, recto (second column), and 141, verso, in the Paris MS. On the second amendment, see folio 148, recto, in the same manuscript.

26 It will be seen from the preceding and following argument that I do not share the viewpoint of Professor Alfred Ivry, editor of the *Talkhīṣ* of *De Anima*, who claims that this *Talkhīṣ* abrogates opinions expressed by Ibn Rushd in *Al-Sharḥ al-kabīr* etc. See his study "On the commentaries of Ibn Rushd on Aristotle's book on Psychology" contributed to the Rushdī Symposium I in Fez, March, 1989. This will be published shortly in the proceedings of the symposium.

27 The really strange thing is that Ibn Bājja is not mentioned in *Al-Mukhtaṣar*, either explicitly or implicitly. As for the mention of him at the end of the discussion on the rational faculty in the Madrid manuscript copy, this is, as noted earlier, merely an amendment made by Ibn Rushd after composing *Al-Sharḥ al-kabīr.*

28 This viewpoint is magisterially summarised in his revision of *Al-Mukhtaṣar.*

29 See my classified list of the later writings of Ibn Bājja, notably *Tadbīr al-mutawaḥḥid, Risālat al-wadā'* and *Risālat al-ittiṣāl*, the last being the most important in this connection (*Rasā'il Ibn Bājja 'l-ilāhiyya*, Beirut, 1968).

30 I mean that Ibn Rushd's preoccupation with the material intellect in *Al-Talkhīṣ* exceeds his preoccupation with the other kinds. We should remember, in this connection, that the *Talkhīṣ* —unlike *Al-Mukhtaṣar*—follows the text of Aristotle and respects the order of its discussions.

31 Foremost among these reasons is that *Al-Talkhīṣ* is a commentary on the meaning of Aristotle's text. As such, Ibn Rushd had to submit to the logic and order of the original text.

32 In the light of what is written in *Al-Sharḥ,* we may say that the analogy as it appears in *Al-Mukhtaṣar* is taken from Ibn Bājja, but that that in *Al-Talkhīṣ* derives from Alexander. Ibn Rushd states, in *Al-Sharḥ,* that he held the opinions of Ibn Bājja when writing *Al-Mukhtaṣar* and leaned towards the standpoint of Alexander when writing *Al-Talkhīṣ.*

33 The designation of the material intellect as the passive intellect, together with the twofold designation active and passive, should be stressed, and should be borne in mind later when we compare what he has to say in *Al-Sharḥ al-kabīr.*

34 His discussion, in the final analysis, concerns the active intellect. As for the material intellect, it is the conjunction of the active intellect with the capacity existing in Man. Hence the active intellect is not only a capacity, nor is it only a transcendent substance.

35 See *Al-Matn al-Rushdī*, referred to above.

36 See my article "*Taṭawwur naẓariyyat al-burhān 'ind Ibn Rushd*", contributed to the symposium *Al-Ḥalqa al-Rushdiyya al-ūlā*, Fez, March 1989, to be published shortly in the proceedings of the symposium.

37 This translation was made by Alain Griffaton, in collaboration with Muḥammad al-Miṣbāḥī, and was published in instalments in *Majallat kulliyyat al-ādāb,* Fez, Nos. 4-5 (1981-1982) and No. 6 (1982-1983), covering Crawford's edition, pp. 379-454.

38 There is also a particular interest in the active intellect and in the ambiguity of the conjunction with the active intellect.

39 I am referring to sections 5 to 20 and section 36 of Chapter III of *Al-Sharḥ al-kabīr* of *De Anima* (ed. Crawford). See also the translation referred to above.

40 See section 4 of Chapter III of *Al-Sharḥ*, ed. Crawford. See also section 5.

41 The view attributed here to Alexander is, as noted earlier, the one he himself upheld in *Al-Talkhīṣ*.
42 See sections 4, 5, 14 and 19.
43 See sections 13, 15 and 16. I have also, in this brief synopsis, relied on the first twenty sections of the commentary on Chapter III of *De Anima*, ed. Crawford.
44 See section 5 of Chapter III. See also section 20.
45 In *Al-Sharḥ al-kabīr* of the *Metaphysics*, he has summarised, in chapter *Al-Lām*, some of the conclusions emerging from his commentary on *De Anima*, ending this short commentary by referring to the synopsis indicated. See pp. 1487-1490, ed. Maurice Bouyges.
46 Mention must be made here of two important studies published in recent years by Professor H. A. Davidson, the first on Ibn Rushd's view of the material intellect and the second on the active intellect. See, respectively, "Averroes on the Material Intellect", *Viator*, 17, 1986, and "Averroes on the Active Intellect as a Course of Existence", *Viator*, 18, 1987.

BIBLIOGRAPHY

Al-ʿAlawī, Jamāl al-Dīn, *Al-Matn al-Rushdī, madkhal li-qirāʾa jadīda*, Casablanca: Dār Tūqbal li 'l nashr, 1986.

——, "Taṭawwur naẓariyyat al-burhān ʿind Ibn Rushd", paper contributed to the symposium *Al-Ḥalqa al-Rushdiyya 'l-ūlā*, Fez, March 1989, to be published shortly in the proceedings of the symposium.

Davidson, H. A., "Averroes on the Material Intellect", *Viator*, 17, 1986.

——, "Averroes on the Active Intellect as a Course of Existence", *Viator*, 18, 1987.

Ibn Rushd, *Epitome de Anima*, ed. Salvador Gómez Nogales, Madrid: Instituto Hispano-Arabe de Cultura, 1985.

——, *Rasāʾil Ibn Rushd*, Hyderabad, 1947.

——, *Risāla fī imkān al-ittiṣāl bi 'l-ʿaql al-faʿʿāl*, ed. Kalman P. Bland, New York: Hebrew Theological Seminary, 1982.

——, *Al-Samāʾ wa 'l-ʿālam* (*De Coelo et Mundo*), ed. Jamāl al-Dīn al-ʿAlawī, Fez: Faculté des Lettres, 1984.

——, *Tafsīr mā baʿda 'l-ṭabīʿa*, ed. Maurice Bouyges, Bibliotheca Arabica Scholasticorum, Série Arabe, Beirut: Imprimerie Catholique, 1938-52, 4 vols.

——,*Talkhīṣ kitāb al-nafs*, ed. F. al-Ahwānī, Cairo: Nahḍat Miṣr, 1950.

Al-Misbāḥī, Muḥammad, *Ishkāliyyat al-ʿaql ʿind Ibn Rushd*, Casablanca: al-Markaz al-Thaqāfī, 1986.

IBN ṬUFAYL AND HIS *ḤAYY IBN YAQẒĀN*: A TURNING POINT IN ARABIC PHILOSOPHICAL WRITING

J. C. BÜRGEL

I

Ibn Ṭufayl was born near the beginning of the 6th/12th century at Guadix, about 50 miles north-east of Granada, and died in 581/1185. He earned his living mainly as a physician, serving several members of the Almohad dynasty, among them his last patron, Sultan Abū Ya'qūb Yūsuf (reigned 558/1163-580/1184), who was a learned man and a fervent promoter of the rational sciences. Ibn Ṭufayl was last but one in the line of six great Arabic Aristotelians: al-Kindī (d. after 257/870), al-Fārābī (d. 339/950), Ibn Sīnā (d. 428/1037), Ibn Bājja (d. 533/1138), himself and Ibn Rushd (d. 595/1198),[1] and one of his works, his philosophical tale *Ḥayy ibn Yaqẓān* ("The Living, Son of the Awake"), brought him great fame.

Although this novel is one of a long series of philosophical allegories and edifying tales (the Arabic term for the genre being *tamthīl*), it stands out as unique not only in Arab Andalusia but within medieval Arabic literature as a whole. Medieval Arabic fiction was either popular, or of foreign origin, or both. Of the famous tales belonging to high literature, *Kalīla wa-Dimna*, translated into Arabic by Ibn al-Muqaffa' (d. 139/757), one of the pioneers of Arabic prose writing,[2] and *Bilawhar wa-Budhasaf*, also known as Barlaam and Yoasaph, a version of the Buddha legend,[3] are of Indian origin, whereas the delightful long tale "Man and Animal Before the King of the Genii", inserted in the Encyclopaedia of the Brethren of Purity, is evidently of Persian stock.[4] The tales of the *Thousand and One Nights* sprang from various sources, but were regarded as old wives' tales (*khurāfāt*)[5] rather than serious literature. The allegorical tales devised by Ibn Sīnā (370/980-428/1037)[6] and Shihāb al-Dīn al-Suhrawardī (550/1155-587/1191)[7] were much shorter and full of dreamlike fantasies. On the other hand, Arabic narrative which was non-fictional (or pretended to be so) usually consisted of brief anecdotes or short reports, hardly ever stretching over more than a few pages.[8] As for *maqāmāt*, the only fictional genre apart from the *tamthīl* that was acknowledged as serious literature by the *udabā'*, this again involved anecdotes, developed into small stories and revolving around a picaresque hero.[9] Notwithstanding their comic surface, the *maqāmāt* of al-Hamadhānī (d. 398/ 1008) and al-Ḥarīrī (d. 516/1122) contain sharp social criticism, notably an attack on the misuse of religious language, the legitimisation of immoral goals by sacred speech being viewed as one of the central sins of a decayed religion-based society.[10]

Ibn Ṭufayl's novel thus differs from most of the works noted above by its length and rigid structure, by its realistic vein and by its being of authentic Arabic origin. Moreover, this tale, a mixture of narrative and philosophical reflection, is not only a rare achievement of Arabic literary art, but also a precious document of the struggle between philosophy and orthodoxy, and of the complex relationship between *falsafa* and Islamic mysticism. It will now be discussed in more detail under the following headings:

- The narrative and its structure
- The conflict between philosophy and orthodoxy
- Philosophy and mysticism

II

Ḥayy ibn Yaqẓān[11] is the tale of a man who grows up on an uninhabited island and attains the highest degree of insight, both philosophical and religious, by dint of his inborn capacities, by his experiences, perceptions and reflections. Having reached this highest possible state of development, he is visited by a man named Asal,[12] who comes from another island. Asal first teaches him human speech, then tells him of his religion, whereupon the two discover that their persuasions are in principle the same. Ḥayy then visits Asal's island and its people, whom he finds to be superficial believers, concerned with the pleasures of the body; he tries to open their eyes to the higher realities of the other world, but in vain. He and Asal thereupon leave them and decide to retire to the lonely island and spend the rest of their lives in devotions there.

The tale is thus divided into two parts with quite different contents. In the first section, we have a straightforward, uninterrupted development involving a gradual, continuous ascent on the ladder of human cognisance; the ascent itself is divided into seven stages of seven years each, this number having no doubt been chosen on account of its cosmological and religious connotations.[13] By its very structure this development is represented as an ideal one, which could hardly take place in any real human existence, at least not in this perfect, unhampered manner—to say nothing of the beginning, involving Ḥayy's rearing by a gazelle, which could, at best, produce a mental cripple like Kaspar Hauser. Goodman is probably right, therefore, when he states that Ibn Ṭufayl makes Ḥayy's ontogeny recapitulate human phylogeny: "His Adam-like position alone on an island, his Promethean role as discoverer of fire ... show that he is intended to symbolise mankind ..."[14] Nevertheless, the development of Ibn Ṭufayl's hero is not devoid of realistic detail capable of application to a real individual's life.

Ḥayy's life begins with what resembles either legend or fairy-tale. He is born by spontaneous generation from the mud of the shore, or—in another version offered for those who do not believe in spontaneous generation—he is the offspring of an illicit union between a noblewoman and her lover on a neighbouring island, and was sent out by his mother in an ark, a remote allusion to the early fate of Moses (Exodus, II, 1-10; Quran XX, 37-40a).

He is brought up, nurtured and protected by a female gazelle—a picture which, for the Arabic reader, must have aroused all the associations of the "Lady Gazelle and her Murderous Glances", the standard metaphor for the beloved girl or woman with her dangerous semi-magic power over the lover.[15] Here, however, the power of the gazelle is limited to nurturing, and she dies before the youngster has reached puberty. The island is, as Fedwa Malti-Douglas called it, "a male utopy", where the female element is eliminated or reduced to its non-erotic aspects.[16] It is Ḥayy who gains power over the gazelle: when she dies he opens her chest, discovers her heart and concludes from the emptiness of the cavities within that an invisible life principle, the human soul, must have escaped from it at the moment of death. Thus—and this is an aspect overlooked in the somewhat feminist approach of Malti-Douglas—it is the only female being in the story which enables Ḥayy first to survive and, finally, to form an idea of the human soul.

Ḥayy imitates the animals, clothing himself and chasing other animals. He even imitates them in his burial of his foster-mother, having watched ravens burying one of their number which had been killed—another Quranic allusion this, for Cain learned to bury his dead brother from a raven (V, 31). If these two references are not merely accidental, they would mean that Ḥayy was born with all the faculties of a prophet, in other words of a perfect man; but that, deprived of the protection of his innocent nurse, he has now become a man capable of sinning, even though the problem of sin does not emerge in practice in the further course of Ḥayy's personal history, he being, as it were, totally immune to the temptations of human flesh.

Instead he spends his time studying nature, discerning the differences between animals, plants and minerals, and arriving at the notions of matter and form, and of species and genus. Having realised the importance of form as the principle instilling life and individual actions into matter, he considers the body of minor importance and places all his emphasis on the further investigation of the soul, the principle of form. Furthermore, he soon infers the necessity of there being an originator of the inborn particularities that recur in every individual representative of a given species. Remarkably, the author here refers to a Quranic verse and a *ḥadīth* which in fact belong to totally different realms of argumentation. The Quranic verse "You did not slay them, but God slew them, and when thou threwest, it was not thyself that threw, but God threw ..." (VIII, 17) is one of the cornerstones of Ash'arī theology, being its main argument for the doctrine of predestination and the denial of free will. On the other hand, the prophetic saying "I am His ear, through which He hears, and His eye, through which He sees" stems from the stock of *ḥadīth*s current in mystical circles. One gains the impression that the author wanted to satisfy both mystical and Ash'arī readers in choosing these quotations. Their common denominator, at any rate, is the direct link between the divine and the human, the participation of man in God's power.[17]

Ḥayy has reached the age of twenty-eight, and he now turns to pondering on this supreme being, spending the next heptad of his life over this problem and being persuaded, finally, that this necessary being is "the Cause of all things", "the Maker"; "He is being, perfection and wholeness. He is goodness, beauty, power, and knowledge. He is He"; "all things perish except His face."[18]

There is no further differentiation between the next two heptads, but the first of them appears to be devoted to solving the problem of how man can acquire knowledge of God and how he can approach Him. Ḥayy realises that he is evidently the only created being on the island aware of God's existence and longing to know Him, and he discovers that it is by virtue of his own self, i.e. the incorporeal, eternal part of his existence, that he will be able to apprehend the Necessarily Existent Being. He further perceives the necessity of imitating the three categories of beings whom he resembles: animal, in order to preserve his physical existence; the celestial bodies, because they are the purest created beings; and the Supreme Being itself. He also discovers that it is through the contemplation of God that man attains happiness.

The last heptad is devoted to practice. It has become apparent to Ḥayy that he must imitate the celestial bodies in three respects: in their care for the world of creation; in their circular movements; and in their constant contemplation of the Creator. He accordingly starts, first, to practice the life of an ascetic and a whirling dervish, totally devoted to ecstasy and contemplation. It is worth mentioning that, in the course of this development, he takes on an attitude that can only be called "environmentalist". He realises that, in nourishing himself from plants and animals, he destroys these created beings and thus prevents them from attaining perfection—or, in Aristotelian terms, fulfilling their entelechy; he therefore decides to do them as little harm as possible. Pondering, further, on the imitation of the celestial bodies, he comes to recognise their constant care for the world of generation and decay, "giving warmth, essentially, and *per accidens* cooling, radiation of light, thickening and thinning and all the other things they do to prepare the world for the outpouring of spirit-forms upon it from the Necessarily Existent Being".[19] He therefore "imitated their action by never allowing himself to see any plant or animal hurt, sick, encumbered, or in need without helping it if he could".[20]

This ecological alertness, praiseworthy though it seems to us, is not, nevertheless, a goal in itself for Ibn Ṭufayl. It is only a passing stage in the development of Ḥayy, who soon comes to feel that this kind of care is still too much involved with the physical world and therefore holds him back from the pure contemplation of God in a state of ecstasy. He abandons whirling for the same reason, and withdraws to a cave where he devotes himself exclusively to the contemplation of God.

> So Ḥayy undertook to expel all this from himself, for none of these things was conducive to the ecstasy he now sought. He would stay in his cave, sitting on the stone floor, head bent, eyes shut, oblivious to all objects of the senses and urges of the body, his thoughts and all his devotion focused on the Being Whose Existence is Necessity, alone and without rival. When any alien thought sprang to his imagination, Ḥayy would resist it with all his might and drive it out of his mind.[21]

This way of life continues until, when Ḥayy has reached the fiftieth year of his life, it is interrupted by the appearance of Asal.

III

Ibn Ṭufayl shows us a man who, without any outside help, without any teacher or book, attains the highest degree of knowledge, or gnosis, by dint of his inborn intelligence. The possibility of such a development is not in itself a tenet of Greek philosophy. Nevertheless, and despite the mystical tinge of this treatise, Ibn Ṭufayl does defend a much disputed tenet of the *falāsifa*, the Arabic philosophers of the Aristotelian school: the possibility of knowing God and reaching a state of perfection through one's own intelligence, without a prophet or holy book. It is true that Ḥayy's development does not represent the normal curriculum of a philosopher, which would consist of listening to the lectures of a teacher, participating in scholarly discussions, reading books and writing dissertations. Yet the fact that Ḥayy has no teacher only underscores the enormous power attributed in this tale to human reason. What Ibn Ṭufayl is here affirming, without expressly saying so, is what Arabic philosophers before him had always contended, namely that philosophy can dispense with religious training, since it conveys the same truth, only on another level of language which is inaccessible to the untrained mind.

A statement in one of Fārābī's lesser-known treatises is of particular importance in this context:

> Upon realising that this religion is a parabolic version of the message of philosophy, the philosophers will not oppose the religion; but the exponents of the religion will oppose the philosophers. Philosophy and philosophers, rather than playing (as they should) a leading part in administering the religion and its followers, will be rejected. Religion will not receive much support from philosophy, while great harm may come to philosophy and philosophers from the religion and its followers. In the face of this threat philosophers may be compelled to oppose the religious, in quest of safety for themselves. They will take care not to oppose the religion itself. What they oppose is the idea of the religious that their religion is contrary to philosophy. They endeavor to eradicate this idea, trying to make the

> religious understand that the message of their religion is [a] parabolic [representation of philosophy].[22]

There can thus be no doubt that Ibn Ṭufayl's text, for all its apparent harmony with orthodox views, must have sounded provocative to the ears of orthodox people, and would have done so even had he limited himself to the first part of his story. No doubt Ibn Ṭufayl is eager to soothe such potential readers as far as possible, without, however (none of the great Arabic Aristotelian philosophers would, it seems, ever have deigned to do so) abandoning any of the Aristotelian tenets. An example in our text is Ḥayy's reflection on the question of whether the world is eternal or created. As is well known, the eternity of the world is one of the three Aristotelian doctrines which al-Ghazālī (d. 505/1111) judged to be heretical in his great attack on Greek philosophy, "The Incoherence of the Philosophers" (*Tahāfut al-falāsifa*).[23] Now, Ibn Ṭufayl makes his hero ponder long over the question of "whether all this had come to be from nothing, or in no respect emerged from nothingness but always existed".[24] The answer Ḥayy—and with him the author—finally arrives at is in between: the things on earth are, of course, finite, but the motion of the heavens is eternal. Thus, after years of pondering this problem, Ḥayy "was no longer troubled by the dilemmas of creation versus eternity, for either way the existence of a non-corporeal Author of the universe remained unscathed ..."[25] The answer aims at reconciling the two tenets, but the orthodox party would, one imagines, hardly have accepted it as satisfying.

Similarly, the frequent quotations from the Quran aim to give the impression of being in line with the "Law-giver". On the other hand, Ibn Ṭufayl does not suppress his criticisms of this law when it comes to social realities. There can be little doubt that the island inhabitants sketched in the second part of his story are intended to typify a Muslim society and the *sharīʿa* aspects of Islam. Even though Ibn Ṭufayl leaves the identity of the islanders' religion vague—calling them "followers of a certain true religion, based on the teachings of a certain ancient prophet"[26]—it is obvious from the religious duties observed by this community, which are those of Islam, namely prayer, alms tax, fasting and pilgrimage. The two other monotheistic religions are, however, not expressly excluded.

From this it follows that the criticisms directed at this religion through the mouth of Ḥayy are criticisms that the author himself wished to launch against certain aspects of exoteric Islam. Here again, surely, Ibn Ṭufayl makes an effort to win over his readers before turning to his critical remarks. The description of the first encounter between Ḥayy and Asal is not without a certain humour or self-irony, if we take Ḥayy to be a projection of the author himself; at any rate it may be understood as a symbolic scene betraying the difficulties of the encounter between reason and religious tradition.

When Ḥayy sees Asal, who is wearing a long black cloak of wool and goat hair, he wants to meet him, but Asal is afraid of him and runs away:

> Ḥayy ran after him, and with the power and vigor God had given him, not just mentally, but physically as well, he caught up with him and seized him in a grip from which he could not escape. When he got a good look at his captor, clothed in hides still bristling with fur, his hair so overgrown that it hung down over a good part of his body, when he saw how fast he could run and how fiercely he could grapple, Asal was terrified and began to beg for mercy. Ḥayy could not understand a word he said. But he could make out the signs of fright and did his best to put the other at ease with a variety of animal cries he knew. Ḥayy also patted his head, rubbed his sides, and spoke soothingly to him. Eventually Asal's trepidation died down and he realised that Ḥayy did not mean him any harm.[27]

The difficulties of mutual approach are further highlighted by Ḥayy's hesitation to eat from the food Asal offers him. But ultimately both men overcome their mistrust. Ḥayy learns human speech from Asal, and then the two tell each other of their religious experiences, which turn out to be, in principle, identical:

> Hearing Ḥayy's description of the beings which are divorced from the sense-world and conscious of the Truth—glory be to Him—his description of the Truth Himself, by all his lovely attributes, and his description, as best he could, of the joys of those who reach Him and the agonies of those veiled from Him, Asal had no doubt that all the traditions of his religion about God, His angels, books[28] and prophets, Judgement Day, Heaven and Hell were symbolic representations of those things that Ḥayy ibn Yaqẓān had seen for himself. The eyes of his heart were unclosed. His mind caught fire. Reason and tradition [*al-maʿqūl wa 'l-manqūl*] were at one within him. All the paths of exegesis lay open before him. All his old religious puzzlings were solved; all the obscurities clear. Now, he had "a heart to understand."[29]

This is the usual way the *falāsifa* would indicate their readiness to cooperate with the believers, stressing the identity of religious and philosophical truth. However, the orthodox reader must have noticed the barely veiled hitch: so far Asal, who had a traditional religious training, has been puzzling over the obscurities of his religion, but as soon as he encounters a philosopher, all these problems are solved by means of exegesis. We are reminded of Fārābī's remarks in his *Enumeration of the Sciences*, where, dealing with religious law (*fiqh*) and scholastic theology (*kalām*), he mentions the difficulties arising from the fact that certain religious tenets contradict human reason, and how the theologians try to cope with this problem by various stratagems ranging from exegesis to violence.[30] It also reminds us of Ibn Sīnā's introductory remarks to his *Treatise on the Confirmation of Prophetic Missions*, in which he addresses an unnamed friend, saying that he wants to dispel his doubts arising from the fact that prophets assert things which are merely possible, as necessary, without having a logical argument, be it apodictical or dialectical, in support of them, and [that they claim] even impossible things, resembling old wives' tales.[31] What Ibn Sīnā does in this treatise is to interpret certain verses of the Quran allegorically; in other words, teach how to read the Quran as a philosopher.

The attitude of the philosopher towards revelation is thus very often one of superiority and condescension, most palpable in the famous saying of the Brethren of Purity, that the religious law is medicine for the sick, whereas philosophy is medicine for the healthy.[32] Here again, Ibn Ṭufayl is eager to soothe potential suspicions. When Ḥayy has learned about Asal's religion, he is persuaded that its founder must have been "a messenger sent by God". And when Asal has described to him prayer, alms tax, fasting, pilgrimage, "and other such outward practices", he "held himself responsible to practice these things in obedience to the command of one whose truthfulness he could not doubt".[33] The statement is, perhaps, not without hidden irony; for to whom, on this lonely island, should Ḥayy pay alms tax, and in what kind, having no money or possession, and where should he perform the pilgrimage? All this seems to be said for the sake of gaining inclined ears for what follows:

> Still there were two things that surprised him and the wisdom of which he could not see. First, why did this prophet rely for the most part on symbols to portray the divine world, allowing mankind to fall into the grave error of conceiving the Truth corporeally and ascribing to Him things which He transcends and is totally free of (and similarly with reward and punishment) instead of simply revealing the truth? Second, why did he confine himself to these particular rituals and duties and allow the amassing of wealth and over-indulgence in eating, leaving men idle to busy themselves with inane pastimes and neglect the Truth? Ḥayy's own idea was that no one should eat the least bit more than would keep him on the brink of survival. Property meant nothing to him, and when he saw all the provisions of the Law to do with money, such as the regulations regarding the collection and distribution of welfare or those regulating sales and interest, with all their statutory and discretionary penalties, he was dumbfounded. All this seemed superfluous. If people understood things as they really are, Ḥayy said, they would forget these inanities and seek the Truth. They would not need all these laws. No one would have any property of his own to be demanded as charity or for which human beings might struggle and risk amputations. What made him think so was his naive belief that all men had outstanding character, brilliant minds and resolute spirits. He had no idea how stupid, inadequate, thoughtless, and weak-willed they are, "they are but as the cattle, nay, further astray from the way!"[34]

In other words, Ḥayy criticises the following aspects: the anthropomorphic descriptions of God in the Quran, the stress on legalistic aspects combined with a certain laissez-faire attitude in matters of moral discipline, and the lack of a higher ethical code that would equal in standard the philosophical ethics of Plato or Aristotle. However, Ibn Ṭufayl then immediately goes on to criticise his hero for making these criticisms, which, he says, proceed from an illusory image of man.

In fact, this point is developed further. Ḥayy's illusions about the true character of human society make him hope "that it might be through him that they would be saved",[35] and he and his friend accordingly wait for a ship to take them to the other island. There Ḥayy starts preaching his wisdom to the inhabitants, but in vain. It is only because he is a friend of Asal, who is himself the friend of the ruler of the island, Salamān, that they respect him as a person; and "the moment he rose the slightest bit above the literal [sense of the scripture] or began to portray things against which they were prejudiced, they recoiled in horror from his ideas and closed their minds".[36]

> Thus Ḥayy now understood the human condition [*fahima aḥwāl al-nās*].[37] He saw that most men are no better than unreasoning animals, and realised that all wisdom and guidance, all that could possibly help them was contained already in the words of the prophets and the religious traditions.[38]

Taking his leave of Salamān and his friends, he "apologised, dissociating himself from what he had said", and "urged them to hold fast to their observance of all the statutes regulating outward behavior and not delve into things that did not concern them, submissively to accept all the most problematical elements of the tradition and shun originality and innovation, follow in the footsteps of their righteous forbears and leave behind everything modern".[39]

Ḥayy and Asal then return to the lonely island and spend the rest of their lives in devotion.

This retreat from society is a time-honoured attitude of philosophers. Plato talks of it in his *Republic*;[40] Fārābī mentions it in his political writings;[41] Ibn Bājja, the immediate predecessor of Ibn Ṭufayl, wrote a treatise on the subject entitled *On the Conduct of the Solitary*;[42] and Ibn Rushd speaks of the desperate situation of philosophers in non-philosophical societies in his commentary on Plato's *Republic*.[43]

What gives a particular pointedness to Ibn Ṭufayl's handling of the topic is the high degree of ambiguity involved; for he intersperses his text with Quranic quotations, and even proves the rotten state of this Muslim society by means of a Quranic verse which was, however, not meant to describe Muslims at all, but unbelievers, who here, as elsewhere in the Holy Book, are equated with animals.

He justifies the character of the book and the law of this religion by the "human condition", and has his hero apologise and revoke his criticisms in an almost cynical way, revealing his total disillusion and resignation vis-à-vis the community in question. Goodman compares this act of revocation with the concealment of one's true conviction in communist states.[44]

We should, however, be cautious how far we suspect Ibn Ṭufayl of crypto-heresy. Certainly the possibility exists. He was in the fortunate situation of having a generous, open-minded patron, the Almohad sultan Abū Yaʿqūb Yūsuf (reigned 558/1163-580/1184), who would not refrain from discussing with him such "hot" topics as the question of the eternity of the world. There is a famous tradition that, when the young Ibn Rushd came to his court and the Sultan asked him "What do they [the philosophers] believe about the heavens? Are they eternal or created?", Ibn Rushd was very upset, not knowing how to answer and apparently fearing a trap; until the Sultan "turned to Ibn Ṭufayl and began to discuss the question with him, referring to the positions of Aristotle and Plato and all the other philosophers, and citing the arguments of the Muslims against them".[45]

The historian ʿAbd al-Wāḥid al-Marrākushī characterises Ibn Ṭufayl as a man who "was eager to reconcile religion and philosophy and gave great weight to revelation, not only at the literal, but also at the more profound level. Besides this he was tremendously learned in Islamic studies".[46] However, this characterisation might, again, spring from a desire to show the philosopher in a light that would make him more acceptable to orthodox readers.

More importantly, Ibn Ṭufayl himself makes the point that religion has, as it were, two levels: "In the Law were certain statements proposing a life of solitude and isolation and suggesting that by these means salvation and spiritual triumph could be won. Other statements, however, favoured life in a community and involvement in society".[47] Asal clings to the first, Salamān to the second way. But at the same time, Asal is described as searching after the inner (*bāṭin*), the spiritual meaning (*al-maʿāni ar-rūḥāniyya*) and allegorical interpretation, whereas Salamān is qualified as "anxious to preserve the literal [*ẓāhir*]" and "refraining from thought and independent decisions due to his cowardous nature".[48]

Although most people wish to restrict themselves to its literal (*ẓāhir*) meaning, the scripture itself does thus lend itself to allegorical exegesis; it does have deeper, spiritual meanings, which, however, the majority of believers are unable or unwilling to grasp.

Ibn Ṭufayl's verdict on Muslim society anticipates the situation soon to come into being in al-Andalus: an intolerant orthodox climate drawing its growing vigour from the onslaught of the Christian *reconquista*. Yet the bases of this attitude had been laid in the East, mainly by al-Ghazālī's *Tahāfut al-falāsifa*, which may be said to have dealt a lethal blow to the Peripatetic school in the Arabic and Islamic world.[49]

Ibn Rushd (d. 595/1198) was the last of a series of Arabic *falāsifa* to attempt to prove the compatibility of philosophy and the Law, reason and revelation [*al-maʿqūl wa 'l-manqūl*], particularly in his famous *Faṣl al-maqāl wa-taqrīb mā bain al-sharīʿa wa 'l-ḥikma min al-ittiṣāl* ("Decisive Discourse on the Compatibility of Religion and Philosophy"). These efforts of his, however, no longer made any impact in the Islamic world, and, with Ibn Rushd, Arabic Aristotelianism came to an end, though certain elements of Aristotle's philosophy were incorporated in later systems. In its place another star was soon to rise in Spain, and another doctrine to radiate from there to many parts of the Islamic world: namely, the Andalusī mystic Ibn al-ʿArabī (d. 638/1240) and his doctrine of *waḥdat al-wujūd*, or pantheism.[50]

If Ibn Rushd may be regarded as the pinnacle of Arabic Aristotelian philosophy, Ibn Ṭufayl is rather a pivot linking that school with Islamic mysticism, although his influence seems to have been limited in his own time due to the ever-increasing orthodox animosity towards the *falāsifa*, whose very name, according to Ibn al-ʿArabī, had become a matter for suspicion in his time.[51]

IV

If genuine Aristotelian thought was alien to mysticism, this was not the case with Arabic Aristotelianism, due to the influence of the so-called "Theology of Aristotle"; this was a paraphrase of the *Enneads* of Plotinus (d. 270 A.D.), which lent a neo-Platonic tinge to most of the works of Arab *falāsifa*. Three elements are paramount: the so-called emanation which consists in spherical beings ruling the stars and linking the One with the many; the interpretation of created beauty as a reflection of divine beauty; and the possibility of reaching union with the universal reason, the Active Intellect, which is at the same time the tenth and lowest of the intelligences emanating from God and linking the world with the Creator. Of these neo-Platonic elements it was the union with the Active Intellect which particularly appealed to the Arabic philosophers. Fārābī speaks of it in his political philosophy and his prophetology: the perfect man, fitted to be the ideal leader of the community, must unite within himself the faculties of the statesman, the philosopher and the prophet, and this can only be attained through a contact with the Active Intellect.[52] Ibn Bājja devotes a treatise to the subject under the title of "Man's Union with the Active Intellect".[53]

In Ibn Ṭufayl's novel there is a clear shift from this kind of neo-Platonic idea to what we might call philosophical mysticism. He undertook the novel with the intention of speaking of something beyond reason, though not contradicting it. He is aware that he is not the first to make a bridge between philosophy and mysticism; although he does not mention his "Theology", he mentions the "Oriental Wisdom" of Ibn Sīnā—which seems, incidentally, to refer to Ibn Sīnā's so-called "Visionary Accounts" rather than to his lost philosophical compendium. In any case, Ibn Ṭufayl states that the three heroes of his novel, Ḥayy ibn Yaqẓān, Salamān and Asal take their names from Ibn Sīnā, which is a clear reference to two of the three accounts, but also an indication that Ibn Ṭufayl does not seem to know them directly, for his heroes have little or nothing in common with their namesakes in Ibn Sīnā's tales. On the other hand, the journey of the soul related by Ibn Sīnā's Ḥayy ibn Yaqẓān, who, in his tale, is a personification of the Active Intellect, culminates in the contemplation of God's enrapturing beauty, and the same is true of his *Treatise of the Birds*.[54]

Ibn Ṭufayl announces that he intends to talk of experiences hardly expressible in human speech, capable only of being enjoyed or beheld in ecstasy and contemplation; and this is what his hero finally arrives at after long training. The reader will remember that Ḥayy attempted to approach the

Creator by imitating the celestial bodies in three respects, in their care for nature, their circular motions and their contemplation of God. In doing so Ḥayy adopted various attitudes familiar in mystical life patterns. His care for animals and plants reminds one of certain mystical saints, and also of Christian anchorites; the legendary Arabic poet Majnūn, who lived in the desert in close friendship with the wild animals, would approximate closely to this type.[55] His whirling is, of course, as mentioned above, to be interpreted as the whirling of mystics, already a long established practice at that time, at least in the East, where it seems to have started in the second half of the 3rd/9th century.[56] But ultimately Ḥayy leaves all this behind him, withdraws into a cave and devotes himself exclusively to ecstasy and contemplation. "Drowned in ecstasy, he witnessed 'what no eye has ever seen or ear heard nor has it entered into the heart of man to conceive' ". It is remarkable that Ibn Ṭufayl should use this Biblical quotation,[57] and not a Quranic verse, to describe the highest degree of mystical vision. It is true that mystics knew a similar saying in the form of a *ḥadīth qudsi*,[58] but, since Ibn Ṭufayl does not say this, we may surmise that he either did not know its origin, which is unlikely, or wished his readers to recognise it as a Biblical quotation (and many readers in the Andalusī milieu must have known the Bible); in other words, he deemed nothing more appropriate, in his search for words to express the inexpressible, than this extra-Quranic saying. In fact Ibn Ṭufayl uses this quotation several times in the course of the following descriptions of Ḥayy's visions, also pointing, here again, to the linguistic problem involved: the ineffableness of Ḥayy's—and therewith his own—experiences.[59] Yet Ibn Ṭufayl has found a way, and an admirable one at that, of putting at least one of his visions into speech, using a most evocative image which opens a cosmic vista before the inner eye of the reader. Although somewhat long, the whole passage should be quoted:

> Passing through a deep trance to the complete death-of-self and real contact with the divine, he saw a being corresponding to the highest sphere, beyond which there is no body, a subject free of matter, and neither identical with the Truth and the One nor with the sphere itself, not distinct from either—as the form of the sun appearing in a polished mirror is neither sun nor mirror, and yet distinct from neither. The splendor, perfection, and beauty he saw in the essence of that sphere were too magnificent to describe and too delicate to be clothed in written or spoken words. But he saw it to be at the pinnacle of joy, delight and rapture, in blissful vision of the being of the Truth, glorious be His Majesty.
>
> Just below this, at the sphere of the fixed stars, Ḥayy saw another non-material being. This again was neither identical with the Truth and the One, nor with the highest sphere, nor even with itself, yet distinct from none of these. It was like the form of the sun appearing in one mirror, reflected from a second which faced the sun. Here too were glory, beauty and joy as in the highest. Lying just below he saw the identity of the sphere of Saturn, again divorced from matter and neither the same as nor different from the beings he had seen—as it were, the reflection of the reflection of the reflection of the sun; and here too he saw splendor and rapture as before.

> Thus for each sphere he witnessed a transcendent immaterial subject, neither identical nor distinct from those above, like the form of the sun reflected from mirror to mirror with the descending order of spheres. In each one Ḥayy sensed goodness, beauty, joy, and bliss that 'no eye has seen, or ear heard, nor has it entered the heart of man to conceive', until finally he reached the world of generation and decay, the bowels of the sphere of the moon.
>
> Here too was an essence free of matter, not one with those he had seen—but none other. Only this being had seventy thousand faces. In every face were seventy thousand mouths; in every mouth, seventy thousand tongues, with which it ceaselessly praised, glorified, and sanctified the being of the One who is the Truth.
>
> In this being, which he took to be many although it is not, Ḥayy saw joy and perfection as before. It was as though the form of the sun were shining in rippling water from the last mirror in the sequence, reflected down the series from the first, which faced directly into the sun. Suddenly he caught sight of himself as an unembodied subject. If it were permissible to single out individuals from the identity of the seventy thousand faces, I would say that he was one of them. Were it not that his being was created originally, I would say that they were he. And had this self of his not been individuated by a body on its creation I would have said that it had not come to be.
>
> From this height he saw other selves like his own, that had belonged to bodies which had come to be and perished or to bodies with which they still coexisted. There were so many (if one may speak of them as many) that they reached infinity. Or, if one may call them one, then all were one. In himself and in the other beings of his rank, Ḥayy saw goodness, beauty, joy without end, the like of which eyes cannot see, ears hear, or human hearts conceive.[60]

This gorgeous vision, so reminiscent of Dante's Paradise,[61] is the pinnacle not only in Ḥayy's life, but also in Ibn Ṭufayl's story. Structurally it adds the vertical or space dimension, divided into the seven spheres, to the horizontal or time dimension of Ḥayy's life, divided into the seven heptads. The two dimensions are linked, and the seven is multiplied in the sublunar being with its seventy thousand faces, which are many and yet one at the same time. This vision is almost exclusively neo-Platonic in its content, although the notion of the mirror, so dominant in this scene, also became central in Islamic mystical thinking and was often used, as it is here, to illustrate the close relationship between the Creator and His creation.[62]

A prominent question, interlaced with this vision, is also one of the central questions that preoccupied the neo-Platonists: how does the multiplicity of the world emerge from the One? For Ibn Ṭufayl, this problem takes on a somewhat different shape, namely: is the Creator One or All and thus many, are the created beings many or One? During the description of the vision Ibn Ṭufayl leaves the answer in suspense, or rather as an unsolved paradox. Later, however, he adds a clarifying remark: as far as God is concerned, the question is inadequate, since the categories of number belong to the world of bodies and can thus not be applied to what is beyond it.

For the rest, the text leaves no doubt that, in his moments of ecstasy, Ḥayy experiences identity with God. "His true self was the Truth."[63] In this respect Ibn Ṭufayl differs from all the other Arabic Aristotelians, although

Fārābī, Ibn Sīnā and Ibn Bājja do have their mystical dimension. But neither does the union with the Active Intellect, for all the ecstatic joy it conveys, equal mystical self-effacement and identity with the Creator, the "Truth" or "Reality" as Ibn Ṭufayl usually calls Him, nor do Ibn Sīnā's two allegories dealing with the soul's journey envisage anything like mystical union; they simply lead on to, and end with, the vision of eternal beauty. This demonstrates the closeness of Ibn Ṭufayl's mysticism to the Unity of Being (*waḥdat al-wujūd*) of Ibn ʿArabī.

There remains the question of how Ibn Ṭufayl's attitude towards orthodoxy ties in with his mystical strain. It seems to me that, of the three or four usual means of escape from the dry lowland of orthodoxy—hedonism, the fine arts, philosophy and mysticism—Ibn Ṭufayl's preference was for the last two, but that he apparently saw little prospect for a further development of Aristotelianism in view of the growing rigidity of the orthodox party. In other words, he seems to have anticipated that the only way successfully to transcend the Law in an Islamic environment lay in mysticism, rather than philosophy. Ibn Rushd's efforts to revive the authentic Aristotle remained unsuccessful as far as the Islamic East was concerned, and the same was true of his ardent endeavours to prove the compatibility of philosophy and revelation. Under the pressure of the approaching *reconquista* his patron had to yield to the pressure of the *fuqahāʾ* by banning the philosopher from his court and forbidding the reading and propagation of works of philosophy. Ibn Ṭufayl thus appears as a logical link between Ibn Sīnā's foundations of "Oriental Wisdom",[64] marginal as these were within the huge body of his philosophical and medical works, and the near ascent of both the "Wisdom of Illumination" (*ḥikmat al-ishrāq*) of Suhrawardī and the "Unity of Being" of Ibn ʿArabī. Both, however, were hardly less "heretical" than Ibn Ṭufayl, even though they far outdid him, and Ibn Rushd, in filling their texts with Islamic quotations. Suhrawardī was, in fact, condemned to death by an orthodox law-court, while Ibn ʿArabī spent most of his life as an emigrant in the East. The parable of two men, a believing philosopher and a philosophising believer, who leave the religious community to which they belong because they want to say what they think and practice what they believe, is unfortunately not outdated. Such things still happen, *mutatis mutandis*, in many a real life of today.

[1] For Aristotelian philosophy in Islam cf. A. Badawi, *Histoire de la philosophie en Islam*, Paris, 1972.

[2] Cf. C. Brockelmann, "Kalīla wa-Dimna", in *Encyclopaedia of Islam*, new ed., Leiden, 1960-.

[3] Cf. D. M. Lang, "Bilawhar wa-Yudasaf", in *Encyclopaedia of Islam*, new ed.

[4] *Rasāʾil Ikhwān al-Ṣafā*, Beirut, 1376/1957, II, 203-377; L. E. Goodman, *The Case of the Animals versus Man Before the King of the Jinn*, Boston, 1978.

[5] Cf. Ibn al-Nadim, *Kitāb al-fihrist*, ed. G. Flügel, Leipzig, 1871-72, p. 304.

[6] Cf. H. Corbin, *Avicenne et le récit visionnaire*, Vol. I, Teheran-Paris, 1954.

[7] Cf. H. Corbin (ed.), *L'archange empourpré. Quinze traités et récits mystiques traduits du persan et de l'arabe*, Paris, 1976.

[8] Cf. H. Waardenburg-Kilpatrick, "Selection and Presentation as Distinctive Characteristics of Medieval Arabic Courtly Prose Literature", in *Courtly Literature-Culture and Context*, ed. Keith Busby and Erik Kooper, Amsterdam-Philadelphia, 1990, pp. 337-53. The use of the adjective "courtly" in this article seems debatable to me.

[9] Cf.J. T. Monroe, *The Art of Badiʿ az-zaman al-Hamadhani as Picaresque Narrative*, Beirut, 1983.

[10] On the misuse of religious language cf. the chapter "Profanisierung sakraler Sprache" in my forthcoming book *Allmacht und Mächtigkeit*, Munich, 1991.

[11] Arabic edition by ʿAbd al-Ḥalīm Maḥmūd: *Falsafat Ibn Ṭufayl wa-risālatuhu: Ḥayy ibn Yaqẓān (Silsilat ad-dirāsāt al-falsafiyya wa 'l-akhlāqiyya)*, Cairo, n.d.; English version by L. E. Goodman: *Ḥayy Ibn Yaqẓān*, New York, 1972.

[12] Goodman uses the form Absal in his translation, which is, however, the form of the name used by Ibn Sīnā in his allegory "Salamān and Absal". Ibn Ṭufayl seems to have changed the name of his hero by intention, in order to emphasise the difference between him and Ibn Sīnā's hero.

[13] Cf. F. C. Endres and A. Schimmel, *Das Mysterium der Zahl. Zahlensymbolik im Kulturvergleich*, Cologne, 1984, pp. 142-71.

[14] Goodman, *Ḥayy*, p. 9.

[15] Cf. my "The Lady Gazelle and Her Murderous Glances", *Journal of Arabic Literature*, 20, 1989, pp.1-11.

[16] Cf. F. Malti-Douglas, "A Male Utopia", in *The World of Ibn Ṭufayl: Interdisciplinary Perspectives on Ḥayy ibn Yaqẓān*, ed. L. Conrad, Oxford, forthcoming.

[17] On the aspect of "mightiness", cf. the introductory chapter of my *Allmacht und Mächtigkeit*, (see note 10 above).

[18] Sura 28, 88; Goodman, *Ḥayy*, p. 134.

[19] Goodman, *Ḥayy*, p. 145.

[20] *Ibid.*, p. 146.

[21] *Ibid.*, p. 148.

[22] This passage, which is from al-Fārābī's *Kitāb al-ḥurūf*, is quoted by F. Zimmermann, in *Al-Fārābī's Commentary and Short Treatise on Aristotle's De Interpretatione*, London, 1981, Introduction CXIV, note 1.

[23] Cf. I. A. Bello, *The Medieval Islamic Controversy Between Philosophy and Orthodoxy. Ijmāʿ and Taʾwīl in the conflict between al-Ghazālī and Ibn Rushd*, Leiden, 1989, p. 84 *et seq.*

[24] Goodman, *Ḥayy*, p. 130.

[25] *Ibid.*, p. 133.

[26] *Ibid.*, p. 156.

[27] *Ibid.*, pp. 158-59.

[28] Goodman translates "bibles", which evokes a wrong impression.

[29] Sura 50, 36; Goodman, *Ḥayy*, p. 160.

[30] Al-Fārābī, *Iḥṣāʾ al-ʿulūm*, xxxx, 132-37.

[31] Ibn Sīnā, *Fī ithbāt al-nubuwwāt* ("Proof of Prophecies"), ed., with introduction and notes, Michael Marmura, Beirut, 1968, p. 41.

[32] Joel L. Kraemer, *Humanism in the Renaissance of Islam. The Cultural Revival during the Buyid Age*, Leiden, 1986, p. 171.

[33] Goodman, *Ḥayy*, p. 161.

[34] Sura 25, 46 (in a translation diverging from Goodwin's less exact one); Goodwin, *Ḥayy*, p. 161 *et seq.*

[35] *Goodwin, Ḥayy*, p. 162.

[36] *Ibid.*, p. 163.

[37] Arabic text, p. 149.

[38] Goodwin, *Ḥayy*, p. 164.

[39] *Ibid.*, pp. 164-65.

[40] *Republic.*, VI, 10.

[41] *Al-Madīna 'l-fāḍila*, Beirut, 1959, p. 109 *et seq.*

[42] *Fī tadbīr al-mutawaḥḥid*; cf. M. Fakhri, *A History of Islamic Philosophy*, London-New York, p. 261 *et seq.*

[43] *Averroes' Commentary on Plato's Republic*, ed., with an introduction, translation and notes, E. I. J. Rosenthal, Cambridge, 1966, p. 183.
[44] Goodman, *Ḥayy*, p. 236, n. 282.
[45] *Ibid.*, p. 4 *et seq.*
[46] *Ibid*, p. 4.
[47] *Ibid.*, pp. 156-57.
[48] Arabic text, p. 141; Goodman, *Ḥayy*, p. 156.
[49] Cf. Bello, *The Medieval Islamic Controversy.*
[50] On Ibn al-ʿArabī, cf. H. Corbin, *L'imagination créatrice dans le soufisme d'Ibn ʿArabī*, Paris, 1958.
[51] F. Rosenthal, "Ibn ʿArabī Between 'Philosophy' and 'Mysticism'", *Oriens*, 31, 1988, p. 15 *et seq.*
[52] Cf. R. Walzer, "Al-Fārābī's Theory of Prophecy and Divination", in *Greek into Arabic*, Oxford, 1963, pp. 206-19.
[53] Cf. D. M. Dunlop, "Ibn Bājja", in *Encyclopaedia of Islam*, new ed.
[54] Cf. above, note 6.
[55] Cf. A. Khairallah, *Love, Madness, and Poetry. An interpretation of the Magnun legend*, Beirut-Wiesbaden, 1980, p. 117 *et seq.*
[56] A. Schimmel, *Mystical Dimensions of Islam*, Chapel Hill, 1975, p. 181.
[57] I Corinthians, II, 9; cf. Isaiah, LXIV, 4.
[58] Cf. Goodman, *Ḥayy*, note 205.
[59] Cf. my "'Symbols and Hints'. Some Considerations Concerning the Meaning of Ibn Ṭufayl's Ḥayy ibn Yaqẓān", in Conrad (ed.), *The World of Ibn Ṭufayl.*
[60] Goodman, *Ḥayy*, pp. 152-53.
[61] On the possible influence of Ibn Ṭufayl's novel on the *Divina Commedia* via a Hebrew translation, cf. G. Strohmaier, "Chaj ben Mekitz-die unbekannte Quelle der *Divina Commedia*", *Deutsches Dante Jahrbuch*, 55-56, 1980-81, pp. 191-207.
[62] Cf. the passage on the mirror concept in J. C. Bürgel, *The Feather of Simurgh. The "Licit Magic" of the Arts in Medieval Islam*, New York, 1988, pp. 138-41.
[63] Goodman, *Ḥayy*, p. 150. The Arabic text is as follows: *k͟haṭara bi-bālihī annahū lā d͟hāta lahū yug͟hayyiru bihā d͟hāta 'l-haqqi taʿālā wa-anna ḥaqīqata d͟hātihī hiya d͟hātu 'l-ḥaqq* (Maḥmūd, *op.cit.*, p. 133).
[64] Cf. H. Corbin, *Histoire de la philosophie islamique*, Paris, 1964, p. 237 *et seq.*

BIBLIOGRAPHY

Badawi, A., *Histoire de la philosophie en Islam* (Etudes de Philosophie LX), Paris, 1972.

Bello, I. A., *The Medieval Islamic Controversy Between Philosophy and Orthodoxy. Ijmāʿ and Taʾwīl in the conflict between al-G͟hazālī and Ibn Rus͟hd* (Islamic Philosophy and Theology Texts and Studies, Vol. III), Leiden: E. J. Brill, 1989.

Brockelmann, C., "Kalīla wa-Dimna", in *Encyclopaedia of Islam*, new ed., Leiden: E. J. Brill, 1960-.

Bürgel, J. C., *The Feather of Simurgh. The "Licit Magic" of the Arts in Medieval Islam*, New York, 1988.

——, *Allmacht und Mächtigkeit*, Munich: Beck, 1991.

——, "The Lady Gazelle and Her Murderous Glances", *Journal of Arabic Literature*, 20, 1989, pp. 1-11.

——, "'Symbols and Hints'. Some Considerations Concerning the Meaning of Ibn Ṭufayl's Ḥayy ibn Yaqẓān", in *The World of Ibn Ṭufayl: Interdisciplinary Perspectives on Ḥayy ibn Yaqẓān*, ed. L. Conrad, Oxford: Oxford University Press, forthcoming.

Corbin, H., *Avicenne et le récit visionnaire, Tome Ier. Etude sur le cycle des récits avicenniens*, Teheran-Paris: Bibliothèque iranienne, 1954.

——, *L'archange empourpré. Quinze traités et récits mystiques traduits du persan et de l'arabe par H. Corbin*, Paris: Fayard, 1976.

——, *L'imagination créatrice dans le soufisme d'Ibn ʿArabī*, Paris: Flammarion, 1958.

——, *Histoire de la philosophie islamique*, Paris: Gallimard, 1964.

Dunlop, F. D. M., "Ibn Bājja", in *Encyclopaedia of Islam*, new ed., Leiden: E. J. Brill, 1960-.
Endres, F. C., and A. Schimmel, *Das Mysterium der Zahl. Zahlensymbolik im Kulturvergleich* (Diederichs Gelbe Reihe 52), Cologne: Diedrichs, 1984.
Al-Fārābi, *Al-Fārābi's Commentary A Short Treatise on Aristotle's De Interpretatione*, trans., with an introduction and notes, F. Zimmermann, London, 1981.
——, *al-Madīna 'l-fāḍila*, Beirut, 1959.
——, *Iḥṣā' al-'ulūm*, xxxx.
Goodman, L. E., *The Case of the Animals versus Man Before the King of the Jinn. A tenth-Century Ecological Fable of the Pure Brethren of Basra, Translated from the Arabic with introduction, a commentary, and notes*, Boston: Twain Publications, 1978.
Ibn al-Nadīm, *Kitāb al-fihrist*, ed. G. Flügel, Leipzig, 1871-72.
Ibn Rushd, *Faṣl al-maqāl wa-taqrīb mā bain al-sharī'a wa 'l-ḥikma min al-ittiṣāl.*
——, *Averroes' Commentary on Plato's Republic*, ed., with an introduction, translation and notes, E. I. J. Rosenthal, Cambridge, 1966.
Ibn Sīnā, *Fī ithbāt al-nubuwwāt* ("Proof of Prophecies"), ed., with introduction and notes, Michael Marmura, Philosophical Texts and Studies, II, Beirut: Dār al-Nahr, 1968.
Ibn Ṭufayl, *Falsafat Ibn Ṭufayl wa-risalātuhu Ḥayy ibn Yaqẓān (Silsilat al-dirāsāt al-falsafiyya wa 'l-akhlāqiyya)*, ed. 'Abd al-Ḥalīm Maḥmūd, Cairo, n. d.; English version by L. E. Goodman: *Ḥayy Ibn Yaqẓān*, translated from the twelfth-century Arabic, Library of Classical Arabic Literature, New York, 1972.
Rasā'il Ikhwān al-Ṣafā, Beirut: Dār Ṣādir, 1376/1957.
Khairallah, A., *Love, Madness, and Poetry. An interpretation of the Magnun legend*, Beiruter Texte und Studien, Vol. 25, Beirut-Wiesbaden, 1980.
Kraemer, Joel L., *Humanism in the Renaissance of Islam. The Cultural Revival during the Buyid Age*, Leiden: E. J. Brill, 1986.
Maḥmūd, 'Abd al-Ḥalīm, see *Ibn Ṭufayl.*
Malti-Douglas, F., "A Male Utopia", in *The World of Ibn Ṭufayl: Interdisciplinary Perspectives on Ḥayy ibn Yaqẓān*, ed. L. Conrad, Oxford: Oxford University Press, forthcoming.
Monroe, J. T., *The Art of Badī' az-zaman al-Hamadhani as Picaresque Narrative*, Beirut: the American University, 1983.
Rosenthal, F., "Ibn 'Arabī between 'Philosophy' and 'Mysticism'", *Oriens*, 31,1988, p. 15 *et seq.*
Schimmel, A., *Mystical Dimensions of Islam*, Chapel Hill, 1975.
Strohmaier, G., "Chaj ben Mekitz-die unbekannte Quelle der Divina Commedia", *Deutsches Dante Jahrbuch*, 55-56, 1980-81, pp. 191-207.
Waardenburg-Kilpatrick, H., "Selection and Presentation as Distinctive Characteristics of Medieval Arabic Courtly Prose Literature", in *Courtly Literature-Culture and Context*, ed. Keith Busby and Erik Kooper, Amsterdam-Philadelphia, 1990, pp. 337-53.
Walzer, R., "Al-Fārābī's Theory of Prophecy and Divination", in *Greek into Arabic. Essays on Islamic Philosophy* (Oriental Studies, Vol. 1), Oxford: Cassirier, 1963, pp. 206-19.

RELIGIOUS STUDIES

THE *ʿULAMĀʾ* OF AL-ANDALUS

DOMINIQUE URVOY

The notion of *ʿilm* is a very complex one, which has, over the ages, been used to describe very different forms of "knowledge". It remains, nevertheless, strongly affected by the use made of it in the Quran, where it implies the knowledge of God and of religious matters, as opposed to other forms of knowledge arising out of experience and reflection. The idea of "transmission" (*naql*) is also central to the concept: the transmission of revelation through the prophets; the transmission, through those close to him, of the acts, words or "approving silences" of the Prophet Muḥammad; and the transmission of the doctrinal development of these carried out by the great doctors.

There was a remarkable convergence of viewpoints, on this score, among the various elements making up Muslim Spain. Within the indigenous population the Visigothic Christian Church had fostered a highly traditional brand of religion based on the Bible and the liturgy, with the Fathers figuring, essentially, as "authorities"; while even the Jewish community there (unlike that of Qayrawān, which nevertheless served as a point of contact with the East) was not to become open to speculative thought for some time yet, so that, for them, the establishment of Muslim power meant in effect a strengthening of ties with the Talmudic centres of Iraq. The Christians and Jews of Spain, therefore, caused traditional factors to predominate within Islam itself on their conversion; and from this springs that "deliberately conservative, even archaising" character which Lévi-Provençal regards as the characteristic quality of Andalusī Islam[1]—though "deliberately" should be taken to imply an outcome collectively arrived at rather than consciously selected.

Two further factors came into play: first, the conquered country was largely broken up; and second, the social base was predominantly urban, as opposed to the situation in the Maghrib, where the old tribal structures were still fully intact. Given these factors, the legalism of the new religion provided almost the sole force for integration between the indigenous populations (Spanish and Jewish) and the occupying populations (Arab and Berber) who mingled there.

In fact the ruling power favoured such an outcome, and the beginnings of Law in al-Andalus, in so far as we can reconstruct them, demonstrate a noteworthy development. The first *qāḍī* whose method is known was Mahdī b. Muslim, who was appointed in 121/738. He referred to the Quran and the *Sunna*, and also made use of his own personal opinion (*raʾy*) placed alongside that of other learned men. The most important figure of this period, however, was Muʿāwiya b. Ṣāliḥ al-S̲h̲āmī (the Syrian), who arrived in 123/740; he was noted for his knowledge of *ḥadīt̲h̲*, and, without allying himself with any particular school, judged in accordance with his own independent criteria using a rudimentary form of analogical reasoning (*qiyās*).[2] The narrow scope for personal action which these jurists permitted themselves—considerably less than that exercised by the Ḥanafī School of Iraq—was subsequently to be reduced still further, and al-S̲h̲āmī, who enjoyed great fame in the East, came under censure in the West.

It was another Syrian tendency which came to predominate, whose approach was more narrowly based: Ṣaʿṣaʿa b. Sallām al-S̲h̲āmī, Mufti of Córdoba, spread the doctrine of al-Awzāʿī (d. 157/774, without having left Syria), who rejected *ra'y* and referred solely to *ḥadīt̲h̲* and the custom of the Companions of the Prophet, regarding the uninterrupted practice of Muslims since the Prophet, maintained by the first caliphs and most of the Umayyad dynasty and legitimised by scholars, as "living tradition". This determinedly archaic viewpoint kept alive "the most ancient solutions adopted by Islamic jurisprudence,"[3] and, if its systematic reasoning was elementary, it did have the merit of being explicit, and, as such, susceptible to teaching and transmission. The importance attached by this doctrine to military problems must have favoured its adoption in the period immediately following the conquest, but it made it less attractive to the Andalusis as peace became firmly established.

The doctrine of al-Awzāʿī did in fact give way to another doctrine where the traditional aspect was still more marked. Mālikism, which became the sole official school from the 3rd/9th century onwards, may be viewed as a combination of two aspects.

The better known of the two is Mālik's allegiance to Medina, the "city of the Prophet". Even more than the "living tradition" of al-Awzāʿī, whose Umayyad character is a two-edged sword (since the patriotic aspect can also be viewed as alienating in its particularity), the tradition of Medina supplied an element of reassurance for the faithful who were both geographically distanced and devoid of any tradition of judicial reflection. *Ḥadīt̲h̲*, generally speaking, allowed the intangible text to be linked to a chain of transmitters—in other words, it established a system of relations giving the appearance of a social structure within which one simply needed to take one's place—and the *ḥadīt̲h̲* of Medina defined this structure still more closely, avoiding the effect of over-rapid dispersal associated with the spread of Islam. Mālikism met the tension arising from the fact of being on the extreme frontier of the *dār al-Islām* by imposing a centripetal viewpoint of the latter.

The second aspect, which has often been neglected, concerns the authority of the great doctors of the school, such as Mālik and Saḥnūn, as reflected in the respect paid to their *ra'y*. While this last notion is normally regarded as characteristic of the Ḥanafism of Iraq, where each jurist could make his own judgements, it was also not absent from Mālikism, where it was reserved solely for the great names whose competence was beyond dispute. The opinions of the great doctors thus became material to be memorised (*ḥifẓ al-ra'y*) and transmitted (*'ilm al-ra'y*; *kutub al-ra'y*; *masā'il al-ra'y*).[4] In a few rare instances, however, less important individuals might be regarded as "having a good individual judgement" (*ḥasan al-ra'y*; *jazīl fī ra'yihī*) or, indeed, as having formulated an opinion which "contained validity as judgement" (*dhālika 'an ra'y al-qāḍī*). But it was largely through a substitution of terms that Mālikism reintroduced this element of individual evaluation: where Ḥanafism spoke of "approbation" and of a "search for the best solution" (*istiḥsān*), Mālikism laid stress on considerations of what was useful to the community (*istiṣlāḥ*). An objectivity of reference was indeed sought, but it was always an individual who must appraise this reference.

It is from the diverse ways in which one can attempt to reconcile or, alternatively, oppose these two factors—collective integration and individual authority—that the history of the activity of the *'ulamā'* of al-Andalus springs. This history is recounted to us through the chronicles, but these must be supplemented and corrected through the testimony of biographical compilations, not only with respect to details of events, but, still more, for what such compilations are able to tell us with regard to the overall collective memory, which causes them to transcend the individual perspective of their compilers. Such information may be obtained through a quantitative consideration of the notes, which, by their stereotyped character, lend themselves particularly well to such treatment.[5] These compilations are, furthermore, characterised by a remarkable homogeneity. It is true that there were specialised compilations in al-Andalus dealing with, for example, "scholars" in the modern sense of the term (such as the *Ṭabaqāt al-aṭibbā' wa 'l-ḥukamā'* of Ibn Juljul in the 4th/10th century, which were, in any case, only concerned to a minor extent with Spain), but the great majority of "national" collections were the product of traditionists who were clearly concerned above all with their own discipline, even if they included intellectuals who had not treated it. Authors who are known to us more particularly from other fields (such as Ibn Rushd, whom we know more particularly as a philosopher and physician) figured above all in connection with those things which interested contemporaries, i.e. as practitioners of the religious sciences (*fiqh* in the case of Ibn Rushd). In exceptional cases people might be included even if they were not mentioned in connection with any religious discipline in the strict sense of the term, provided they had attained distinction in an area which could be referred back to religion: for example, mathematics as it affected the calculation of successions (*farā'iḍ*) or even simple reckoning (*ḥisāb*). On the other hand, certain intellectuals who had become famous in other areas did not figure there because the biographer failed to find any means of incorporating them, however tenuously, within a religious perspective (examples of this being Ibn Bājja and Ibn Ṭufayl).

This homogeneity of perspective is considerably reinforced by the fact that the principal compilations are presented as linked with one another. Thus we have: the "History of the *ʿulamāʾ* of al-Andalus" (*Tārīkh ʿulamāʾ al-Andalus*) of Ibn al-Faraḍī (351/962-403/1013);[6] the "Continuation of the History of the Imams of al-Andalus" (*Al-Ṣila fī tārīkh aʾimmat al-Andalus*) of Ibn Bashkuwāl (494/1101-578/1183);[7] the "Supplement to the Continuation" (*Al-Takmila li-kitāb al-ṣila*) of Ibn al-Abbār (595/1199-658/1260);[8] the "Continuation of the Continuation" (*Ṣilat al-ṣila*) of Ibn al-Zubayr (627/1230-708/1308);[9] the "Continuation and Supplement" (*Al-Dhayl wa 'l-takmila*) of Ibn ʿAbd al-Malik al-Marrākushī (634/1237-703/1303-04).[10]

I. The Hierarchical Universe of the Period of the *Amīrs* and Caliphs

As long as central power was maintained in al-Andalus, the world of the *ʿulamāʾ* was centred on Córdoba; it was here, or in the surrounding areas, that the principal shifts and developments took place, not only in terms of official doctrine, but, also, in terms of autonomous, even heterodox tendencies. This was particularly the case during the reigns of *Amīr* Muḥammad I (238/852-273/886) and Caliph al-Ḥakam II (350/961-365/976), who found fit to show favour to other juridical schools in order to release the ruling power from the grip of the Mālikī hierarchy, whereas other sovereigns or effective rulers had preferred to solicit this hierarchy's support.

The official adoption of Mālikism was due to the *amīr*s Hishām I (172/788-180/796) and his son al-Ḥakam I (180/796-206/822). The former, whose reign was a peaceful one, and who left behind him the image of a very pious man, was notable for a number of religious foundations. He took an interest in the Islamic sciences, encouraged the training of *ʿulamāʾ* in the East and kept in touch with the development of religious disciplines there. As such he allowed the men of religion to take a place around him which his predecessors would have been too jealous of their power to permit. His son, whose reign was far more disturbed, and whose autocratic ways left an unpleasant memory behind them, very quickly made it clear to the members of the hierarchy around him that they should give their juridical opinions (*fatwa*s) and their judgements solely according to the school of Mālik.

Several direct disciples of Mālik b. Anas (d. 179/795-6), notably Yaḥyā b. Yaḥyā al-Laythī (d. 234/848), a Cordoban of Berber origin, disseminated their doctrine in this way. In the space of thirty years or so a privileged class—as was also the case in Qayrawān during the same period—came to be established, imposing a very rigorous inquisition both on the actions of the sovereign, when he showed signs of ceasing to consult his scholars, and on the faithful in their daily lives and their respect for practices. As for tributaries, those with an official role found themselves being harassed, and the *ʿulamāʾ* hunted down anything which might be considered hostile to Islam, acting repressively towards sovereigns who were often anxious to appease them in any case, and so pushing those who were desperate to acts of provocation, as in the episode of the "Córdoba Martyrs" in the middle of the 3rd/9th century.

Initially, in fact, Mālikism was established in al-Andalus in a thoroughly backward form. The use of *ḥadīth*, which was after all at the basis of Mālik's approach, was neglected in favour of simply transmitting codifications of special rulings (*furūʿ*) worked out by the first great successors of the master. The idea of submission (*taqlīd*) to the authority of the competent man capable of "personal effort" (*ijtihād*) was blindly and mechanically repeated, whereas the whole idea of *ijtihād* itself was proscribed. Not only was Mālik made the object of great veneration on account of his sanctity, but the devotional literature (*manāqib*) concerning him often assumed greater proportions than his actual teaching; the oldest known witness to this literature, which was to be in evidence throughout the history of al-Andalus, was the Cordoban Ibn Ḥabīb (d. 238/852), who wrote a book on his merits (*faḍāʾil*). Ibn Ḥabīb and another Cordoban, al-ʿUtbī (d. 255/868) codified the master's teaching in the form of responsa (*masāʾil*), and their manuals became the basis for successive commentaries, leading, also, to the very noteworthy development of a literature concerning procedure in the notarial and judiciary fields. A major subsequent witness to this cult of Mālik, the *qāḍī* ʿIyāḍ (6th/12th century), was to attest that al-Laythī and Ibn Ḥabīb were totally ignorant of the traditions.[11] Similarly all methodological reflection, such as that advocated in the East by al-Shāfiʿī, was rejected. On the other hand, an honourable place was accorded, for obvious practical reasons, to local "practice" (*ʿamal*). Some analysts claim that this favour was shown not only to the practice of the capital, but to that of the principal cities on the central frontier with the Christian kingdoms (Talavera, Talamanca and Toledo).

It would appear, in this process, that it was the Muslims of Spanish or Berber origins, rather than those of Arab stock, who were most attached to "maintaining a fixed order of things". On the other hand, it was also among the Muwallads, as we shall see later, that very specific attitudes arose aimed at counteracting this absence of reflection. It should also be noted that there were, in Muslim Spain, a number of cases of more or less profound adherence to Shiʿism. They remained, however, sporadic,[12] representing a posture of defiance rather than any positive position conducive to the integration of Andalusī Muslims.

Four relatively autonomous movements may be distinguished. Of these the first two were juridical schools: Shāfiʿism and Ẓāhirism. Shāfiʿism was discreetly favoured by Muḥammad I, possibly from a wish to assert his authority over the caste of jurists, but was forced to exercise discretion under ʿAbd al-Raḥmān III, who established the Western Caliphate in 316/929, and still more so in the reign of the *ḥājib* al-Manṣūr (370/981-392/1002). It was introduced by Qāsim b. Muḥammad b. Siyār (d. 277-8/890-1), who was protected by Muḥammad I against the attacks of the Mālikis by being made his personal notary (*wakīl*) for life. The school was also supported by ʿAbd Allāh, who was the son and heir of the caliph al-Nāṣir, but was put to death by the latter for conspiracy in 338/950.

It is not clear whether or not one of the greatest names of the age should be added here: that of Baqī b. Makhlad (d. 276/886 or 280/890). He made a visit to the East where he followed, among others, the teachings of Ibn Ḥanbal. He wished to accord an honourable place to the study of traditions, and, as such, received the protection of the sovereign Muḥammad I. He wrote a commentary on the Quran which was to be highly admired by Ibn Ḥazm—perhaps because there were considerable links between his approach and that of the founder of the "literalist" or "Ẓāhirī" school, the Easterner Dāwūd. More generally, however, he constructed, like the older doctors, works of independent *ijtihād* based solely on the Quran and the *Sunna*, and through his descendants, who formed a whole dynasty of Cordoban jurists up to 622/1225, he introduced a breath of reform from which Mālikism itself was eventually to benefit. This element of reform was also discernible in the case of his contemporary, Ibn Waḍḍāḥ (d.289/900).

Other authors were quite clearly Ẓāhirī. The earliest of these was ʿAbd Allāh b. Muḥammad b. Qāsim, a pupil of Dāwūd, who lived under Muḥammad I. But this school, which remained very sporadic, could above all boast within its ranks another disciple of Dāwūd, the chief *qāḍī* Mundhir b. Saʿīd al-Ballūṭī (d. 355/966), who, while showing the highest respect for the Mālikī norm, also introduced his own *ijtihād* along literalist lines.

The third movement was of a theological kind. Ibn Ḥazm speaks of Spanish Muʿtazila, and modern historians (Asín Palacios[13] and Lévi-Provençal) believe it possible to group together several members of an apparent "school", within which the influence of the famous literary figure Jāḥiẓ, who was also a theologian, was crucial in Spain. In fact little more can be put forward in this connection than a belief in free will proclaimed by certain *ʿulamāʾ* or supposed by their opponents. In any case, those works of Jāḥiẓ known in the Peninsula were by no means of a theological nature. Moreover, the individuals in question remained respected jurists among their compatriots, and the most famous of them, Khalīl b. ʿAbd al-Malik b. Kulayb, called Khalīl al-Ghafla, was the object of nothing more than a ransacking of his house and books after his death by the *fuqahāʾ*.

The last movement was also the one which has aroused the greatest interest. Asín Palacios has clearly demonstrated that, before the final crisis of the Caliphate, the only outlet the rigorism of the country allowed was into ascetic retreat. Several individuals were in fact noted for their rejection of the world, which won them great prestige in the eyes of the ruling power, the jurists and the common people alike. Conspicuous among them was Muḥammad b. ʿAbd Allāh b. Masarra, who was most certainly a man of Spanish stock, and who lived in a mountain hermitage near Córdoba, although his stay there was interrupted by a journey to the East to protect himself against those who failed to appreciate the fact of his dispensing esoteric teaching. He died in 319/931, at under fifty years of age, and it was after his death that the jurists, who had respected his prestige among the people, carried out a veritable persecution (recounted in detail in the fifth book of Ibn Ḥayyān's *Muqtabas*) of all his real or supposed disciples. The movement thereupon left the Córdoba region for Almería, where it was transformed into an esoteric sect led by a kind of guru. Scraps of the master's teaching were, however, still to be found reflected in the 5th/11th century in Ibn Ḥazm's compilation of religious ideas, and in the 7th/13th century with Ibn ʿArabī, who was a thorough-going collector of "initiation secrets".

A very brief note by the historian of ideas Ṣāʿid of Toledo (5th/11th century) links Ibn Masarra with the philosophical tradition of Empedocles[14]—as the latter is known, that is, in the Arabic recension, which is very different from what modern criticism has to tell us. On the basis of this, Asín Palacios has attempted to attribute to the Andalusī writer several doctrines of esoteric philosophy which Eastern historians derive from the Greek thinker. S. M. Stern, however, has shown in his turn[15] that Ṣāʿid's note was based on a misunderstanding of an Eastern text which simply stated that the philosophy of Empedocles had been taken up by the *Bāṭini*s (Muslim esoterics); Ibn Masarra having given esoteric teaching of his own, Ṣāʿid believed it possible to make an amalgam first of this and the teaching of Eastern figures —although there is no proof whatever on this score—and, following on from this, with Empedocles. Thus the image of Ibn Masarra as the first representative of philosophy (*ḥikma*) in al-Andalus breaks down. But this does not mean, for all that, that his thought was lacking in substance. Other testimonies, including that of the historian Ibn Ḥayyān published only in 1979,[16] gives us the picture of a very original *ʿālim*, but one whose approach was also typically Spanish and firmly rooted in the context of his times.

He was the pupil of Ibn Waḍḍāḥ, who was the author of an important "Treatise on Innovations" (*Kitāb al-bidaʿ*),[17] but who can himself be linked with the independent *mujtahid* Baqī b. Ma<u>kh</u>lad mentioned above. Even his opponents recognised that he had a certain gift of expression, and Ibn Ḥayyān says that he made a highly respected abstract of one of the great Mālikī works, the *Mudawwana*. According to this historian, his success sprang from two causes: first a pedagogy which moved on progressively from an abstract of texts to a setting out of difficulties and to argumentation; and second the union of a charismatic personality and skill in controversy on the one hand with wide knowledge on the other. As for the actual doctrine indicted by the jurists, this was essentially ethical, being characterised by a severe attitude towards the acquisition of material goods and the stigmatising, as unlawful, of things considered lawful by the jurists themselves. To this accusation of an élitism which leads on, in his work, to hermeticism and the discipline of the arcane, the chronicler adds just a single theological ground for complaint: his claim to go beyond Promise and Threat, his view of the *ḥadīths* concerning intercession as weak and his demand that people should abjure things that are in fact mercifully permitted to them by God.

The work of Ibn Masarra thus emerges as an exact counterpart, in the context of 4th/10th century Islam, of the attitude demonstrated by Priscilian in Christian Spain: an ascetic opposition to the clergy, who are accused of making compromises with the world. It is the asceticism which leads on to the Gnostic elaboration, and not the reverse, since Ibn Masarra's knowledge of Mālikī law allows him to draw up religious difficulties from the very heart of ritual practice and to move on to a search for hidden meaning (*ta'wīl*). He advocates the examination of conscience in order to reach purity of intention, and he believes that the gift of prophecy is necessary if a person is to move even halfway towards a total purification of the soul. All this results in a purely spiritual eschatology, without reward or punishment.

This moral approach is given theological support. Like the Muʿtazila, Ibn Masarra rejects the notion that the divine attributes are distinct from its essence. He safeguards human freedom by affirming that the Knowledge and Power of God are two created temporal attributes, and that there are two types of divine knowledge, one which God created entire and at once and which is that of universals, in other words of the hidden, and the other relating to particular existents, that is the apparent, which has being only as long as these existents themselves remain in being.

From this basis Ibn Masarra may well have pushed forward in a philosophical way, but we have no certain explicit indication of this. On the other hand we do have mystical developments with respect to the "Throne" (*ʿarsh*) of God, that is to say of the Being which rules the world, for God is too exalted for it to be possible to attribute to Him an action *ad extra*. This throne is the creation, whose four aspects (the origin and form of bodies; those of minds; that which perpetuates the soul; good or ill fortune) each have an evident meaning and a hidden meaning, themselves represented by an angel or a prophet. We know of this not only from Ibn ʿArabī but from the texts of Ibn Masarra himself, which were believed lost but have recently been discovered; these texts simply contain common neo-Platonic themes.[18] Ibn Ḥayyān stresses that Ibn Masarra's approach was one of bringing his disciples progressively to his viewpoint, not through a demonstration, but through piling up difficulties so as to leave them no other solution.[19]

If there was no essential link between Masarrism and Muʿtazilism on the doctrinal level, it would seem that the practice of the former prolonged that of the latter on the sociological level: there were two attempts at liberalisation in this respect, following a period of relaxation under al-Ḥakam II, which nevertheless showed that, all questions of legalism apart, spiritual integration could not yet be achieved by a fully rational, as opposed to a somewhat emotional adherence. It is this which explains the development, from the 3rd/9th century on, of groupings of jurist-ascetics (*zāhids*), who sometimes took on the role of "deviants" by embodying those possibilities which society perceived but was incapable of accepting by virtue of its fundamental chosen principles. There was, however, also an approach towards the idea that religious knowledge and more interior practices could exist together, this being manifested in the school founded at Córdoba by Yaḥyā b. Mujāhid of Elvira (d. 366/977), and, above all, in that of Ibn Abī Zamanīn (d. 399/1009), who, though trained in the capital, gathered his disciples at Elvira.

Thus, in the course of the 3rd/9th century, the world of the *'ulamā'*, while keeping the hierarchical, centralised structure which circumstances provided for it and which the ruling power deliberately reinforced, diversified on two levels: first on that of the individuals involved, through new independent and even isolationist attitudes; and second on that of approaches, involving a return, against the tendencies of the first generations of Andalusī Mālikis, towards the freer context within which the work of Mālik himself had been undertaken. Shocking though it was to the jurists initially, the return to *ḥadīth* was quickly seen to be indispensable for resolving new cases and preventing the fixed framework from cracking, while also preserving the same type of psychological process. An extra effort of memory did indeed become necessary, but it was still a matter of relying on a ready-formed system, with the possibility, even, of bringing together the respective lines of those transmitting tradition and those transmitting a specific juridical approach; indeed, the first Spanish traditionists were content to study Mālik as a *muḥaddith* and no longer as a jurist. A division of functions was thus established, with the *shaykh al-'ilm* (holder of the tradition) and the *shaykh al-fiqh* (specialist in ruling on disputes) sharing the tasks.

The establishment of the Caliphate was, nevertheless, a negative factor, in that it diverted a good many students towards administration and therefore transferred to the Caliph—who was the successor of the Prophet—a part of the authority of the people of the *'ilm*. Each person devoting himself to study found a post thrust on him and was subject to a policy of continual changing of office-holders, culminating in the monopolising by Córdoba of anyone who had distinguished himself in the regions. Thus the liberalisation noted above, which sprang from the *'ulamā'* themselves, was restricted by the action of the ruling power: the specialists in *'ilm*, who had gained authority over the people, were pushed back; Mālikism once again became obligatory in matters of practice, all other approaches having only speculative value; the study of *ḥadīth* finally came to be seen as a superfluous luxury.[20] In this struggle the jurists made compromises with the State, and there came into being a kind of court *qāḍī*, this situation culminating, under al-Manṣūr, in an unstable balance: the jurists had the advantage of the Caliph's being pushed into the background and the State was forced to make concessions to them; but, since they had discredited themselves in the eyes of the people, the State could if need be react by attacking them on the grounds of fanaticism.

II. The Crisis in the Caliphate and the Formation of Provincial Foci

It is generally considered that, following a long period of development, the period of the caliphs constituted a kind of plateau (from 319/929 to the death of the second *ḥājib*, al-Muẓaffar, in 399/1008), in which a balanced society was in evidence. But if this balance swiftly crumbled, subsequently, on the social and political levels, it was nevertheless the point of departure for an outstandingly brilliant cultural flowering. This is particularly well known with respect to the production of poetry, but it also involved the production of religious works. On the other hand, the splitting up of power into a multitude of small kingdoms (*mulūk al-ṭawā'if*), each cultivating its poets, had little effect on the major groupings in the spiritual field. What in fact emerged was certain localised sets of tendencies, as the civil war (*fitna*) broke the spell of Córdoba, and the provinces, by force of circumstances at first but later on their own initiative, set themselves to developing their own potentialities. These potentialities had always in fact been present but had been reined back; from the account given in the compilation of Ibn al-Faraḍī (who died during the *fitna*) we can distinguish—following the scattered, tentative nature of the initial proceedings—the struggle of the regions on the periphery, particularly in the upper borderlands, to maintain a degree of cultural autonomy in the face of the increasing pull, supported by the ruling power, that was exerted by Córdoba.

With these potentialities now released, a varied picture emerges. As far as the Peninsula is concerned, the classification of religious and intellectual disciplines is well enough known. There is a very clear dominance of juridical disciplines, followed by *ḥadīth*, the Quranic sciences and, for profane studies, *adab*. After this come poetry and the study of the Arabic language, and finally history and mathematics (basically applied). Among those subjects requiring (in some cases) the action of *'aql* (reason), and no longer *naql* alone, the religious disciplines of the methodology of Law (*uṣūl al-fiqh*), apologetic theology (*kalām*) and Quranic commentary (*tafsīr*) take precedence over the profane disciplines of medicine and pure mathematics, while Sufism and philosophy are quite simply set aside. On the level of practice, asceticism is well represented, including that involving the writing of exhortatory poetry.

The picture becomes somewhat different, however, when we take account of other factors. Let us first take the time factor. The policy of appropriation of talent on the part of the ruling power, from the end of the 4th/10th century, brought disaffection in its wake, and the *'ulamā'* were not to regain their full numerical strength till the end of the following century, with the establishment of the Almoravids. Next let us consider the orientation of disciplines. A study of the correlation between the disciplines studied by each *'ālim* shows that—on the inevitable basis of the study of tradition—scholars were divided into specialists in the practice of Law and specialists in the Book. The former, naturally, possessed a virtual monopoly of socio-cultural influence, but the latter, refraining almost wilfully from all attempts at gaining influence, developed purely intellectual activities such as *adab* and the study of the Arabic language, fields through which theology was progressively able to infiltrate. Sufism, on the other hand, was normally only in evidence outside these traditional disciplines. In fact, *kalām* and Sufism shared the speculative area equally with philosophy (*ḥikma*), which, in the 5th/11th century, remained a strictly lay matter having no link with religious disciplines.

The final factor was that of place. While the Córdoba region was losing its importance, it retained the same intellectual orientation and appears to have reacted to the disturbances by electing for a further development of the traditional sciences. The Seville region did not, as has been thought, come to devote itself exclusively to poetry; no doubt poetry was qualitatively better represented here than elsewhere, but not quantitatively. Nor was Seville a city of Sufis, at least not yet. The central region (Toledo) began by assuming the mantle of the Andalusī cultural heritage, not only in religious subjects, but also in *adab* and the study of language. Its conquest by the Christians in 478/1085 interrupted a rather fine flowering, characterised by positive reflective elements, but also by the according of a greater importance than elsewhere to the occult sciences—two aspects which were to be apparent in the so-called "Toledo" school of translation from Arabic into Latin. The upper borderlands (Saragossa) were much more violently subject to the vicissitudes of history, whether from repercussions of the internal crisis or from the effects of external pressure. It did not draw many people to the *fitna*, but knew how to use its people on the spot, and was to demonstrate, in relation to the Christians, a superior culture which, here too, was to put its mark on a school of translators, known as the Ebro Valley school. It was, nevertheless, political rather than religious circumstances which allowed the reforming work of al-Bājī (which will be referred to later) to be set forward there. The other regions were less marked by distinctive characteristics, except for the Spanish Levant (Valencia), which was strongly conservative and largely devoted to evaluation, as with the school of Quranic readings at Denia. The Levant was only gradually to advance to its position, in the 6th/12th century, as the second intellectual and religious focus of al-Andalus over against the Córdoba-Seville region.

The social structure of teaching reflects the repercussions of these variations in time and space. At the end of the period of the caliphs the teaching body emerges as strongly hierarchical and centred on Córdoba, with links with Seville and Toledo. At its head were a number of teachers mainly with the qualification of *faqīh* or, sometimes, *ḥāfiẓ* (memoriser) or *zāhid* (ascetic). These masters were recognised by most pupils, who followed one another under the instruction of each. In the next generation, on the other hand, a disintegration was under way, with just two teachers, Yūnus b. ʿAbd Allāh, known as Ibn al-Ṣaffār, and Abū ʾl-Muṭarrif al-Qanāziʿī gathering the main body of disciples round them, and other teachers having a limited and even specialised audience. There were even, on the fringe of this large group still centred on Córdoba, small groupings of masters in Toledo and Almería. Still more significantly, this generation did not associate itself with the great masters of the previous generation, but rather with authorities which had at that time been marginal, notably Ibn Abī Zamanīn, the jurist-ascetic and centre of a mysticising movement. Andalusī Islam was, therefore, taking a new direction around the beginning of the 5th/11th century.

In the period of the *ṭāʾifa* kingdoms, this body of teachers was subject to further restructuring. Initially a small number of important teachers came to the fore, with a secondary but numerous group sharing the audience of pupils about equally with them. Also, specialisation was developing in some degree and those concerned with Quranic readings (*muqrīʾ*s) became markedly more numerous. The people in question were no longer purely Cordoban, and the capital rather represented one stage of an overall circuit of the Peninsula to disseminate their knowledge. There were even some who only practised outside the city. This generation of *ʿulamāʾ* associated itself clearly with the previous one, especially with its most eminent representative, Yūnus b. al-Ṣaffār, although this did not prevent a further recourse to other teachers, including those in the centres of Toledo and Almería. However, this reintegration did not affect the Peninsula as a whole. There was still a place for separate initiatives.

It was also the most diversified generation, a fact which can be simply indicated by three cases. The first is that of the scholar who had the largest audience at that time, Abū ʿUmar b. Lubb (Spanish "Lope") al-Ṭalamankī (d. 428/1036). He was a native of the central region (Talamanca), who had followed the normal pattern of the period of the caliphs: the inevitable time spent in Córdoba, studies in the East, various polemics in Spain, and then return, finally, to end his life in the city of his birth. He demonstrated a particular interest in the methodology of Law (*uṣūl*) and even ventured to attack, if not Mālikism itself, at least the official orthodoxy. This caused him to be declared a k͟hārijī by several jurists in Saragossa, and he had, in this town, to submit to the judgement of his peers, being ultimately exculpated.[21]

The third master, in descending order with respect to the number of pupils cited by the biographical compilations, was the famous Quranic reader Abū

'Amr of Denia, who codified the seven canonical "readings". He was in fact only the most prominent of a whole group of Quranic specialists trained by the wish of the Prince of Denia and the Balearics, the Slav Mujāhid, who had himself been initiated into this discipline by order of al-Manṣūr.

Finally, another member of this generation was the greatest representative of the *'ulamā'*, and also the most original, Ibn Ḥazm (384/994-456/1064), whose works will be considered later. This originality, and the fact that he was of the Ẓāhirī school, did not prevent him from being the tenth master in order of influence.

If we take into account additionally that two of the principal authorities, Makkī b. Abī Ṭālib and Abū 'Amr al-Safāqusī, were Easterners, it is a quite exceptional moment in intellectual history which we are now contemplating; one in which a deliberately monolithic system was reconstituting itself following a crisis, but was attempting to do so on a highly diversified foundation.

This new state of affairs became still more evident with the following generation. There were indeed some traditional Cordoban *faqīh* figures, but, outside these, the system of teaching brought together all the regions of Spain and, from Almería to Saragossa, advanced the position of those areas (like Badajoz and the Levant) which had till then been neglected. All of this was sustained by the prestige of the great masters, who either attracted people to them or themselves made the tour of the great cities. The most influential of these was Abū 'Umar b. 'Abd al-Barr, who had been attracted by Shāfi'ism, before returning to Mālikism to develop it from within. The fourth after him, Abū 'l-Walīd al-Bājī, while remaining a convinced Mālikī, had interested himself in the East in the search for "basic principles" both in Law (*uṣūl al-fiqh*) and in theology (*uṣūl al-dīn*). Ibn 'Abd al-Barr had, in his youth, been the friend of Ibn Ḥazm, when the latter had also been attracted by Shāfi'ism, before moving on to embrace the literalist approach; al-Bājī was his main opponent in a contest held in Majorca, which was to have clear repercussions for the orientation of this marginal area by moulding a double theological tradition taking the sole point of agreement from those two inimical doctrines, Ẓāhirism and Ash'arism, namely a demand for rationality; this was to inform the philosophical apologetics of the Majorcan Ramon Llull in the 13th century, which themselves lay at the origin of the use of the combinatory method in the West.[22]

The end of the period of the *ṭā'ifa*s was marked by a split between the broad mass of teachers, whose activities were scattered, and a small number of great names with a considerable audience. Córdoba began once more to play a pre-eminent role, with the Levant acting as something of a counterbalance, the former being devoted especially to Law, the latter to Quranic readings and to traditions. The non-Andalusī masters once again became marginal, but there was a revival of travels to the East "in search of knowledge".

III. The Specific Contribution of the Andalusis of the Period of the *Ṭā'ifas* to the Islamic Sciences

The context described above explains the contrast between the poverty of work produced in the first centuries on the one hand and, on the other, the quantitative richness, and, still more, the substance and sometimes extreme originality of that produced in the 5th/11th century. To this we may add the pre-eminent role now restored to the *'ulamā'*—including pre-eminence on the political level—due to the disappearance of a strong ruling power and the people's mistrust of petty local potentates.

Nevertheless, we must here make a qualitative distinction. It has been stated that the *'ulamā'* "had deep popular roots in al-Andalus, and were generally of middle and lower class origins",[23] but, quite apart from the fact that this has not been proved with respect to the majority of the masters of the first rank, this has no bearing on the quality of what was produced. A famous anecdote demonstrates the ambiguous character of this problem of social status: al-Bājī told Ibn Ḥazm that the latter could not claim any merit for having studied because he was from a rich noble background, whereas he, al-Bājī, had had to work with his hands in the East, as a gold-beater, to pay for his lessons; to which Ibn Ḥazm proudly retorted that this showed that he, for his part, was disinterested whereas his opponent was aiming at social advancement. What is actually more important is that, as the historian al-Maqqarī was to note, there were no schools run by the State (*madrasa*s) until a late date, and paying for the teaching given in the mosques supposed a considerable motivation on the part of candidates.[24]

In fact the goals pursued by the most prominent authors were very diverse, even contradictory, but they joined to favour creation: Ibn Ḥazm was at once devoted to the pursuit of certainty and passionately attached to the notion of Umayyad legitimacy, which, for him, was the sole guarantee of continuity with the original Islam he sought to rediscover through his literalist method. Ibn 'Abd al-Barr, on the other hand, was more discreet, with the result that, although older than Ibn Ḥazm, he was nevertheless slower to influence disciples. He seemed anxious above all to conserve what had already been acquired, distinguishing himself as a traditionist, and returning to Mālikism after incursions into Ẓāhirism and Shāfi'ism, moving about a great deal within the Peninsula, pursuing a correspondence with Eastern masters and maintaining contact with independent figures. If Abū 'Amr's school of Quranic readings was developed in the Levant, it was, apparently, because it was well motivated by the need to establish the text and so counter criticisms made by the Christians concerning the diverse ways of reading the Quran; Ibn Ḥazm himself testifies to this when he states that these "readings" had all been revealed in the same fashion and transmitted by tradition worthy of belief. Al-Bājī also agonised over the loss of Muslim power brought about by the Christian thrust, and his development of *kalām* was undertaken above all with a polemical aim in mind, and in the hope—more or less vain except in Saragossa—of mobilising goodwill for a surge of effective resistance.

It is true that many works born in this way are valuable only as prolonging tendencies which had long been in existence. This is true of those works of Ibn al-Barr devoted to traditional techniques of religious knowledge (notably *Jāmiʿ bayān al-ʿilm wa faḍlihī wa mā yanbaghī fī riwāyatihī wa ḥamlih*),[25] or of Quranic readings of Abū ʿAmr (of which the most used was the *Kitāb al-taysīr*), and even of most of al-Bājī's books. With the last-named it is most often a matter either of condensing a piece of knowledge (e.g., *Risāla fī 'l-ḥudūd*)[26] or of a purely *ad hominem* discussion of little doctrinal substance (e.g., the reply to the "Monk of France").[27] But he is also able to introduce a personal tone in his "Testament" (*Waṣiyya li waladayhi*).[28] He is of particular interest for having re-established the art of the polemic within the principles of jurisprudence, and for having even introduced it into Spain. In *Al-Minhāj fī tartīb al-ḥijāj*[29] he envisages not only juridical solutions proposed by supporters of his particular method, but also those proposed by other schools, notably Shāfiʿism, which is treated with a degree of sympathy. His plan is to make dialectic (*jadal*) not something erratic and hesitant, or even shameful, but a matter of consciously reasoned practice, and to this end he examines all the subdivisions of the subject-matter and their ramifications. After an introduction which is a self-justification and a setting out of the proper procedure to be observed, he defines the technical terms, then successively examines the proofs arising from the different sources of Law, possible preliminary questions before discussion can take place, possible objections to arguments which are claimed to be based on the Quran, the *Sunna* or on consensus (*ijmāʿ*), the technique of analogical reasoning (*qiyās*) and possible challenges to it, the validation or invalidation of cause (*ʿilla*), the various other modes of argumentation (*istidlāl*), and finally the various modes of preference (*tarjīḥāt*). The work is noteworthy for the clarity with which it is put together and the care with which arguments of all kinds are set out.

Although al-Bājī (403/1012-474/1081) was younger than Ibn Ḥazm, his book sets the latter's work in perspective and also demonstrates its originality. Like his Mālikī opponent, Ibn Ḥazm seeks, in his various books, to make a proper statement of the question, to be exhaustive, to be clear, and to introduce a logical dimension. But if he stands out, this is not simply because he refers to a different juridical school, but because this latter implies a different methodology, which is, in its turn, as R. Arnaldez has very well demonstrated, amplified by this thinker into a veritable philosophy of language.[30]

His methodology is set out in his great work "On the perfect knowledge of juridical bases" (*Al-Iḥkām fī uṣūl al-aḥkām*).[31] Claiming to rely only on the "natural" rules of the Arabic language, which he manipulates, it must be said, with great virtuosity, Ibn Ḥazm shows now the general character of a

Quranic verse of apparently limited application, and now the limited character of a verse of apparently general application. His critical treatment of *ḥadīth* is extremely rigorous, leading him to reject many cases as apocryphal, while, at the same time, admitting a certain number of *ḥadīth aḥad* (those transmitted by a single person). His main attack, however, is reserved for the various "procedures" of the jurists, which he recapitulates in the very title of his *Mulakhkhaṣ ibṭāl al-qiyās wa 'l-ra'y wa 'l-istiḥsān wa 'l-taqlīd wa 'l-taʿlīl.*[32] In fact his basic target is the *qiyās*, developed by Shāfiʿism to "channel" the *ra'y* and finally accepted by Mālikism as renewed by such a man as al-Bājī; this is judged to be vague and arbitrary in its very essence, and is attacked each time it can be invoked on a practical point with a demonstration that there is no more reason to apply the analogy to one aspect of this point than to another.

Ibn Ḥazm thus undertakes a veritable "demythologising" of religious tradition subsequent to the period of the Prophet and his companions. He arrives, finally, at an ahistorical vision of matters and his compendium on Law (*Kitāb al-muḥallā*)[33] rejects everything which has been added since this period. This conception is untenable in practice and explains why, for all his intellectual stature and the real audience he had, his school was only able to exist, after him, as representing an approach that was above all "speculative" and taken up by isolated individuals. On the level of thought, on the other hand, this thoroughly austere intellectual approach proved to be very fruitful, as the rest of Ibn Ḥazm's own works shows. In fact it was this deliberately limited approach which led him to construct the first history of religious ideas, arising from a wish to attack, in his "Chapters on religions, sects and passions" (*Al-Fiṣal fī 'l-milal wa 'l-nihal wa 'l-ahwā*),[34] erroneous notions of men about God and everything concerning His works. The plan is, needless to say, methodical rather than historical. First the author attacks Judaism, then Christianity. Next he considers, subject by subject, all the known opinions within Islam itself, in order to refute them in sole favour of Ẓāhirī doctrine. Taking as his criterion the actual materiality of Revelation, he proceeds to examine every subject which can be raised in connection with it. Thus, the book devoted to Christianity does not simply provide a highly detailed comparison between the Gospels, so as to destroy their credibility as testimony by emphasising incompatibilities, but also raises the problem of the spherical nature of the earth by means of the Quranic text "He rolls the night on to the day and rolls the day on to the night" (XXXIX, 7)—this forming part of a stock of arguments proving the authenticity of the Quran, and which the author uses to oppose Christian objections.

This work illustrates, in condensed form, both the richness of Ibn Ḥazm's mind and its contradictions: a rejection of history leading to a gathering of historical material; an immense erudition which gives prime of place to what is distant and curiously neglects what is near;[35] a depth of perspective contrasted with the trivial nature of many analyses of detail; a sincere wish to convince others coupled with an appalling violence of expression and a total lack of respect for his interlocutor.

The works of Ibn Ḥazm go far beyond the field of *'ilm* to embrace the whole of Arab culture, including such specific lay aspects as genealogy. but it is noteworthy that efforts to build bridges between the various fields are not only clearly present, but are also, in their turn, the starting point for new and original experiments; this is the case, for example, in his treatise on logic (*Al-Taqrīb li-ḥadd al-manṭiq*),[36] which aims to blend the juridical categories of ordinary life with logical categories. It is even possible, in the Platonising literary conception of "The Ring of the Dove" (*Ṭawq al-ḥamāma*), to find a starting point for what is the opposite of this, namely the literalist methodology which excludes all "mythologising" formulation, in that literature may be considered the sole field in which man could legitimately consider himself as a creating god-figure.[37]

IV. The Political Synthesis of the Almoravids

The seizure of power by the Almoravids, who had been called on by the men of religion against the existing princes, and the territorial reduction of al-Andalus despite all their best efforts, had a restabilising effect for the body of *'ulamā'*, who had at once to drum up support within the (reduced) territory of the country to ensure its cohesion in the face of the threat from the North, and establish a solid position of their own with respect to the new rulers. The Almoravids were to disappear in the face of a politico-ideological challenge, that of the Almohads, their memory sullied by the effects of their adversaries' propaganda. We must, however, judge the facts themselves, according to all available sources of information. It will then be seen that the two goals noted above were in fact achieved.

Let us consider this first with respect to the structure of teaching. The hierarchical reconstruction begun during the period of the *ṭā'ifa*s reached its extreme point in the early decades of the 6th/12th century with the rise to prominence of a number of eminent masters who drew off the vast majority of pupils. Thereafter teachings came to be very much complementary to one another, from one master to the next. At the same time not only did the great peripheral cities of Spain become badly served, but a number of small cities which had formerly been "off the beaten track" became seats of teachings worthy of mention in the biographical compilations. This is remarkable given the upheavals of the times: upheavals which, if they particularly disturbed the frontier regions, also affected interior districts like Málaga and Murcia; which encouraged rivalries between Seville and Córdoba on the one hand and between these two and the Levant on the other; and which, finally, gave a quite new importance to the Maghrib, sometimes as a source of political support, sometimes even as a place of refuge.

Those disciplines which came to predominate were the study of the Quran on the religious level and that of the Arabic language on the profane level. The two were of course linked, but we should not, nevertheless, exaggerate the strength of this link, since one of the main authorities of the time, the chief *qāḍī* Abū Bakr b. al-ʿArabī, whose testimony has been preserved for us by Ibn Khaldūn, states that the teaching of language in al-Andalus was not normally based primarily on the Quran, as it was in the rest of the Muslim world. The essential emphasis was on poetry, which was the true memory (*dīwān*, i.e. archives) of the people. In this way misunderstanding of the sacred text on the part of children was avoided (although Ibn al-ʿArabī does in fact stigmatise a number of his compatriots who acted like other Muslims by putting the Quran directly into the hands of children), and the Arabic remained relatively closer to the spoken language. This is very typical of Andalusī Islam, which was evidently conservative in itself, but was susceptible to remarkable innovation in comparison with the rest of the *dār al-Islām*. On the other hand, it henceforth allowed itself to be conquered by a phenomenon which was becoming increasingly ubiquitous, namely Sufism.

As for the statement of autonomy with respect to the ruling power, it manifested itself not through a conflict between the two parties but through a kind of sharing of tasks. The ruling power, with the active help of the mass of "middle" *ʿulamāʾ*, sought to maintain ideological cohesion, keep al-Andalus anchored within the Muslim framework and eliminate anything liable to cause disturbance; while the élite men of religion, for their part, kept up the demand for a further development of studies which had been kindled within Mālikism at the time of al-Bājī. If this no longer led to the production of original work like that of Ibn Ḥazm, and if there were even, now, virtually no representatives of other schools, the situation was still a very far cry from the caricature, fostered by the Almohads, of a narrow juridicism centred solely on the transmission of rulings on specific disputes (*furūʿ*).

Rather than examining the whole of the work produced in this period, we may perhaps focus on one particularly enlightening phenomenon: the extent and limits of the influence of the great Eastern doctor al-Ghazālī, regarded as the "reviver of the sciences of religion" from the name of his most famous work. Almohad propaganda has made great play of the action taken by the Almoravid *amīr*s to prevent the circulation of his works, and has presented the chief *qāḍī* Ibn al-ʿArabī, who was his disciple, as a victim of these *amīr*s. Things were actually quite different, and, if Ibn al-ʿArabī did in fact experience imprisonment, it was at the hands of the Almohads themselves, following their seizure of power.

In contrast to the construction of Ibn Ḥazm, grandiose but lacking in historical grasp, Ghazālī's model was very attractive to the Andalusis by reason of its syncretic character, encompassing as it did the whole spiritual history of Islam, with the exception of forms which were totally marginal. Indeed, the attractions of this actually extended beyond Muslims to the Jews.[38] The influence was, however, felt in very different ways, and one of these aroused a reaction in certain *'ulamā'*, mostly of the second rank with the exception of Ibn Ḥamdīn of Córdoba, who, between 500/1106 and 510/1116, persuaded the *amīr* to order an auto-da-fé of Ghazālī's works. The majority remained silent, only a few men of religion from Almería opposing it, notably Abū 'l-Ḥasan al-Barjī (d. 509/1115).

Al-Andalus had in fact already known a form of union between juridicism and asceticism, that of the *ṭarīqa* of Ibn Abī Zamanīn. During the period with which we are concerned, it was subject to the influence of another master who developed a similar perspective, Abū Bakr al-Ṭurṭūshī, an Andalusī settled in Alexandria, who retained a large audience in his country through his letters and disciples. Though very severe towards Ghazālī on other points, he was nevertheless very close in what concerns us here. On the other hand a tendency began to emerge which used mysticism as a means of mounting a challenge. Thus Ibn Barrajān of Seville was to claim the imamate for himself, being executed in 536/1141. His disciple Ibn al-'Arīf was, however, pardoned after making formal submission. His treatise "on the most beautiful dwellings" (*Kitāb maḥāsin al-majālis*)[39] is devoted to describing the stages leading to union with God and, if a Gnostic element is clearly present, it is above all a practical work, taking up Eastern teaching. The heritage of Ibn al-'Arīf was also to be easily combined with that of Ghazālī. As for al-Barjī, he had been the master of Ibn al-'Arīf, but was himself dependent on highly traditional masters, and it appears that—in the wake of Ghazālī's syncretism—it was this ambiguous character of some Andalusī *'ulamā'*, who were neither completely traditional nor totally innovating, which was condemned.[40]

Insofar, on the other hand, as it bore on the development of already established Islamic sciences, Ghazālī's teaching was fully taken up. This may be seen in the work of his disciple Abū Bakr b. al-'Arabī (468/1076-543/1148), who devotes as much attention to *uṣūl al-Dīn* (in his book *Al-'Awāṣim min al-qawāṣim*)[41] as to *uṣūl al-fiqh* (this latter being treated particularly in his treatise on divergences—*khilāfiyyāt*—between jurists, the *Kitāb al-talkhīṣ*, which Ibn Khaldūn cites as being one of the major works in the genre, together, in fact, with a work by Ghazālī).[42] It was within these two areas, moreover, that opposition was focused, particularly in Córdoba, with a series of juridico-theological refutations of the Eastern scholar: a lost work by the *qāḍī* Ibn Ḥamdīn (d. 508/1114), another still in manuscript by Muḥammad al-Ilbirī (d. 537/1142-3) and further works up to the 8th/14th century at least. The very existence of al-Ilbirī, a jurist and traditionist who was also a theologian and a commentator on a mystical work, proves that we are dealing with a constructive opposition and not mere blindness.

The Almoravids had instituted the procedure of appointing judges, but retained the fiction of delegation. Themselves receiving delegations from the Abbasid caliph to whom they paid allegiance, they considered the *qāḍī*s merely as their own delegates and "reserved to themselves the prerogative of making appointments to important judiciary posts".[43] When contrasted with this kind of appointment, which tied the person in question to the centre and district relevant to his post, the scope allowed to a man like Ibn al-ʿArabī was remarkable, going far beyond that accorded to his predecessors during the Umayyad period, even in its best moments. But this freedom was accompanied by an almost total lack of originality. The noteworthy men of the Almoravid period were imitators of the East, either worthy pupils of far-distant masters, like Ibn al-ʿArabī, or else worthy followers-on from old Andalusī masters, like the chief *qāḍī* Ibn Rushd (the grandfather of the philosopher Averroes) or the *qāḍī* ʿIyāḍ. There was no creative figure. ʿIyāḍ's *Tartīb al-madārik wa taqrīb al-masālik bi maʿrifat aʿlām madhhab Mālik*[44] was a biographical compilation set apart from those of the line of Ibn al-Faraḍī not only by the more specifically focused and therefore more detailed nature of its notes, but above all by the apologetic tone of its preamble; it harks back, in fact, to the *manāqib* of the Umayyad period.

V. The Attempted Reforms of the Almohads

The Almohad movement was a phenomenon with its own logic, linked to its Maghribi context. The thought of its founder, Ibn Tūmart, originating as it did in a Berber milieu islamicised by the Khārijis, had no doubt been filled out through contact with the teachings of Córdoba and the East, but cannot be confined to them. This would be to make a mere syncretism of it, as was done in the analyses of ancient authors, uncritically followed by modern ones, which associate this thought with different and even antagonistic movements: Muʿtazilism, Ashʿarism, Ẓāhirism, *Falsafa*, Shiʿism, etc. It is in fact perfectly coherent and represents a radical attempt to provide a rational basis for belief: the elements of dogma (the existence of a creating God, different absolutely from His creatures, Whose attributes are only designations, and Who predestines men) are developed solely according to the dictates of reason, which, after the event, declares their conformity with Islamic Revelation refined by *ta'wīl* (interpretation), the Revelation thus established then serving as a base for the development of Law according to exclusively positive procedures.[45] Within the Maghribi context, the sole opponents of this vision of things were, on the one hand, those who rejected the notion of the refinement of Revelation by *ta'wīl* and, on the other, those who had no time for methodological reflection on Law. This situation underlies the two principal themes of Almohad propaganda: the accusation of anthropomorphism against those who took the Quranic text exactly as it stood, and the accusation of being concerned only with specific applications of Law (*furūʿ*).

These criticisms may not have been a matter of any particular concern to the Almoravids, even in the Maghrib. However, the Almohad reform had assumed a violence which brought it into direct confrontation with the ruling power, and an amalgam developed between the de facto situation within Morocco and the ideology ascribed to the established power. On moving into al-Andalus the Almohad revolt ran into further complications, for this country, significantly, practised the science of *uṣūl* in its two forms, theological and juridical. Propaganda thus had to encompass these two phenomena which contradicted its own version of events, and it was at this point that it seized on "the problem of Ghazālī". A meeting was invoked (whether real or imaginary is not clear) between the Eastern doctor and the future *mahdī*, with the latter being presented as a defender, against the Almoravids, of the former's work. Where necessary, as we have seen, history was rewritten so as to impute to the Almoravids persecutions which were in fact carried out by the propagandists themselves.[46]

The fact is that the meeting between Ghazālī and Ibn Tūmart, even if it really did take place, was without significance, for there was nothing in common between the mysticising syncretism of the one and the unyielding rationalism of the other. This is a source of pronounced ambiguity regarding the Almohads in al-Andalus: some confine themselves to the facts and stress this opposition between the two intellectual orientations, while others place their trust in the version provided by propaganda and put forward a hybrid version which retains only those aspects of Almohadism capable of assimilation by Andalusī tradition, i.e. elements close to the Ashʿarī *kalām* and juridical theses close to Ẓāhirism; in short, what could be called "practical" propaganda.

Initially the "drumming up of support" carried out by the Almoravids provided effective resistance. The new ruling power demanded of the *'ulamā'*, as of the dignitaries, recognition of their formulation of *tawḥīd*, but it would seem that this formality did not lead to many dismissals, and even if a particular major figure was affected, his less important disciples remained at their posts. The Almohads were thus compelled to await the disappearance of the generation already in place, which only occurred twenty years or so after the seizure of political power. However, they were preparing their offensive from the beginning, with intellectual propaganda as the dominant element. This latter achieved some results, but met with the passive resistance of the *'ulamā'* body—a passivity which was transformed into reclamations when the threat from outside forced the rulers to conciliate the people. The princes then opted for practical propaganda, which was more successful. However, the increasingly powerful thrust of their enemies (Christian in the North and challengers from within in such places as Morocco and the Balearics) led first to the suppression, then to the re-establishment, then to the final suppression of Almohad doctrine. Only the Almohad *fiqh* was to survive for some time yet in North Africa, as one juridical school among others.

The masters dominating the first Almohad period maintained a certain transitional connection with the Almoravid generation, notably with Ibn al-

ʿArabī, but were closer to a master who had then been somewhat marginalised, namely Ibn al-Dabbāgh. He had been the fifth in order of importance with respect to audiences, but his pupils had been scattered figures and his teaching had given him only a minor place within the hierarchy of teachers triumphantly dominated by Ibn al-ʿArabī, Shurayḥ and Ibn ʿAttāb. Almohadism was, then, attempting to win over semi-marginal figures, and it established what was effectively a new form of synthesis with respect to teaching, lacking the numerical strength of that of the previous generation, but covering the whole territory and all the disciplines, including, even, exponents in fields which had hitherto been rejected: mysticism and philosophy.

Remarkably, a man of the stamp of Ibn Rushd (520/1126-595/1198, the Averroes of the Latins) appears as fourteenth in order of influence; in other words, just after the important masters and ahead of the masters of second rank. The son and grandson of Cordoban *qāḍis* who had played important parts under the Almoravids, he openly supported the Almohads and was to be very close to them, both as physician to the Sultan and as the person officially responsible for making known the works of Aristotle. It is obvious, however, that any audience he was able to establish within the framework of al-Andalus derived above all from his capacity as an *ʿālim*. In fact, at the same time that he was preparing his first scientific and philosophical approaches, he was writing a treatise on Law, *Bidāyat al-mujtahid wa nihāyat al-muqtaṣid* ("The beginning for the one demonstrating *ijtihād* and the end for the one who is satisfied [i.e. with the teaching he has received]").[47] This treatise is doubly important.

On the intellectual level, it embodies Almohadism's ideal of rationality. It is a work of *ikhtilāf*, in which all the schools are examined, including the small and non-canonical ones. The author is at pains to demonstrate the mechanisms of the reasoning which has led—or which might have led—to the solutions proposed. Sometimes, even, he proposes a line of reasoning better than that which has effectively been given. The order is perfectly logical and the subject-matter is classified—as far as possible—in order of generality; the major classical divisions are respected, but the work pushes sub-divisions very far. As such the work represents the culmination of the Andalusī contribution to *uṣūl al-fiqh*; while naturally giving special weight to the school of his own country, he is not, for all that, slavish—he contests the adherence to the practice of Medina, while treating traditions in a Shāfiʿī spirit and coming close to Ibn Ḥazm in his sensitivity both to the precise meaning of language and to logic.

This treatise, of which the essential part was published in 564/1168, and whose introduction clearly indicates that the work was conceived with a practical personal aim in mind, led to Ibn Rushd being appointed, in the following year, *qāḍī* of Seville, a city especially favoured by the new rulers. Next he was appointed in Córdoba, then again in Seville, and finally in

Córdoba, this time as chief *qāḍī*, while being, at the same time, physician to the Sultan and living alongside him most of the time. He had, therefore, an evident wish to take part in the life of the community, and, as such, Ibn Rushd is a unique case in *Falsafa:* other of its exponents had been ministers and close to princes, but he alone undertook what he did within the framework of *fiqh*, the only truly stable framework, and made himself known in the field.

This was supplemented, on the theological level, by an original interpretation of Almohad dogma. Besides a (lost) commentary on Ibn Tūmart's Profession of Faith (*'aqīda*), Ibn Rushd wrote three philosophico-religious works, *Faṣl al-maqāl*,[48] *Kashf 'an manāhij al-adilla*[49] and *Tahāfut al-tahāfut*.[50] All three were written in connection with a stay in Seville in 575-6/1179-80. There was also a small treatise, *Al-Ḍamīma*, on a particular point of theology. These are the only cases where Ibn Rushd speaks in his own person. In them he develops both Almohad theses (religious rationalism, role and method of *ta'wīl*, etc.) and continuations specific to the situation in al-Andalus, making a particular point of attacking Ghazālī, who is regarded as the author of a bastard syncretism. He is concerned, on the one hand, to show the agreement of true wisdom (*ḥikma*) of a religious kind with a philosophy derived from Aristotle, and, on the other, the agreement of this élitist perspective with that of the mass of people whose approach to Revelation is an essentially practical one. All intermediate speculation (*kalām*, Sufism, etc.) is regarded merely as a source of disturbance.[51]

From 586/1190 onwards, in the face of the Portuguese threat and the rising discontent which this excited among the *fuqahā'*, the ruling power was forced to dissociate itself from Ibn Rushd, allow him to suffer a humiliating inquisition in 592/1196, and subject him to two years or more of disgrace, rehabilitating him only a few months before his death in 595/1198. It was "practical" propaganda and its half-measures which then prevailed. It is evident, however, that the *'ulamā'* charged with this work carried only a section of the Andalusī people. The majority, set apart from these, gathered around a position more in keeping with Andalusī tradition, and one in which mysticism was henceforth to play a prominent part. The foundations for this last had already been laid at the time of Ibn Rushd, since, still better placed than him in the matter of audiences was Ibn al-Mujāhid, the founder of the main mystical school of al-Andalus. The main feature at the end of the 6th/12th century is that it is henceforth "possible to discern a relatively unified pattern, involving a large part of the ascetics, a large part of the Sufis and several major names from *fiqh*, the science of traditions and those of the Quran, who act as intermediaries either between other mystics, or between the Eastern contribution and Spain, or who are heirs to this complex heritage".[52] The school of Ibn al-Mujāhid at Seville comprised only one fifth of this whole population, but it was the best structured nucleus, taking up the heritage of

Ibn al-ʿArīf and the Eastern heritage of Ghazālī and al-Ṭurṭūshī, which could be brought together in a number of cases, despite the hostility of the latter towards the former. It is within this shifting pattern that the famous theosophist Ibn ʿArabī (560/1165-638/1240) takes his place, while another group formed around Ibn Sabʿīn (613-14/1217-18-668-69/1269-71) was marginalised and even persecuted on account of its somewhat "philosophising" position.

VI. Evaluation and Prospects in the Naṣrid enclave

The brutal advance of the Christians in the 7th/13th century, the subordination of numerous populations who, under the name of Mudejars, were permitted to keep their religion, but with inferior status, the shrinking of the territory of al-Andalus to the Kingdom of Granada, itself politically subjugated and subject to a continual flow of people fleeing the regions conquered—all these are factors throwing the data into confusion. No systematic study has, unfortunately, as yet been made of the *ʿulamāʾ* body from this period on, either in the area still relatively independent, or, for clear enough reasons, in the conquered area. All we have is compilations of names, titles of works and surviving notes on minor, albeit sometimes significant points[53]

The status of the *ʿālim* hardly changed in Muslim territory, but sources are more explicit about the diversity of material circumstances. Although not officially remunerated, judges could live from landed revenues or from their teaching. Nevertheless, the precarious nature of their status led to their being offered, should the need arise, payment (*murattab*) whose exact value is not known, but which was unlikely to have been high, and which some refused, either on principle or because they were already rich. In Granada a number of *faqīr*s ("poor men") from Iran or India settled and engaged in petty trade; we know of these from the Maghribi traveller Ibn Baṭṭūṭa, but not from local sources. The latter, on the other hand, allude to hermitages and even quasi-monastic foundations (*rābiṭa*s) established in the capital and the area immediately round about; at least thirty-seven of these can be counted from historical records from the period of the Christian conquest. Attempts begun during the Almohad period to forbid Muslims to take part in foreign festivals, especially Christian ones, and to introduce new festivals such as that for the birth of the Prophet, finally led to a veritable "cult" of the Prophet, with ceremonial poetry and songs. Finally al-Andalus became open—at last—to the system of officially organised teaching. The first *madrasa* was founded in Granada by Yūsuf I in 750/1349, and assembled not only local scholars but also Maghribis, such as the famous Ibn Marzūq, who came in 754/1353.

This context of physical and mental withdrawal caused scholarly work to move in three separate directions. The first of these took the form of summaries, which could be of a bookish type. Thus there was, as in the rest of the

Arab world, a multiplication of verse works with a mnemonic purpose, the most famous example of these being the *Tuḥfat al-ḥukkām fī nukat al-ʿuqūd wa 'l-aḥkām*, known as *Al-ʿĀṣimiyya*, of Abū Bakr b. ʿĀṣim al-G̲h̲arnāṭī.⁵⁴ This was a work of around 1,700 lines in *rajaz*, the easiest and most frequently used meter. It was very extensively diffused and became one of the standard works of the Mālikī school, the subject of frequent commentaries up to our own century. The summary could also take the form of a historical recapitulation, the best exponent of this being the famous Ibn al-K̲h̲aṭīb (713/1313-776/1375), known as *Lisān al-Dīn* ("the tongue of religion"), a brilliant and equivocal figure, who was twice a minister, but was executed —no doubt wrongly—for heterodoxy. It is worth noting that, quite apart from the numerous notes on the history of the Andalusī *ʿulamāʾ* scattered throughout his historical works, particularly *Al-Iḥāṭa fī ta'rīk̲h̲ G̲h̲arnāṭa*, he devoted a special work to them: *Al-Katība 'l-kāmina*.⁵⁵ Above all, however, this man of distinctly unmystical cast took it upon himself to synthesise Sufi teaching in his *Rawḍat al-taʿrīf bi 'l-ḥubb al-S̲h̲arīf*.⁵⁶ This work takes a form which, if already known, was not widely used, at least in the Muslim West, that of the symbolism of the tree. It is also interesting for the classification it uses, before Ibn K̲h̲aldūn, with respect to Andalusī Sufi tendencies, distinguishing between the school of *tajallī*, or "irradiation" and the school of "absolute union".

A second orientation emerging within Andalusī scholarly work is that which may be termed the "critical evaluation". A still unpublished work with no known title, by Abū Isḥāq Ibrāhīm b. ʿAbd al-Raḥmān al-G̲h̲arnāṭī (8th/14th century)⁵⁷ falls within the framework of the renaissance of *fiqh* which can be observed throughout the Muslim world. Reacting against the plethora of literature concerned with notary formulae, the author reminds readers that the aim of Law is not formulae, but the "fear of God". Ibn al-K̲h̲aṭīb, meanwhile, goes so far as to compose a satire against the whole body of notaries.⁵⁸ Abū Isḥāq, for his part, sets out a historical vision with regard to Andalusī Law: beginning from Mālik's principle known as "*al-maṣāliḥ al-mursala*" (i.e. free application, or permitted equivalence—the idea being that legal principles may, if the *faqīh* considers it advisable, be applied in such a way as to take questions of public interest into account), he shows how his compatriots have in fact frequently gone against theoretical Mālikism. We know, independently of Abu Isḥāq, of a number of *fatwa*s which apply a "casuistical ruse" to circumvent difficulties of the strict law and adapt it to circumstances, so as, for example, to allow Muslims now under Christian control to buy back lands which had been taken from them as spoils of war.⁵⁹

The third orientation comprises a radical renewal of juridical methodology. Ibrāhīm b. Mūsā b. Muḥammad al-Lak̲h̲mī 'l-G̲h̲arnāṭī 'l-S̲h̲āṭibī (d. 790/1388) proposed that the traditional types of *uṣūl al-fiqh* should be replaced by a new science called "goals of legislation" (*maqāṣid al-sharīʿa*). This new science, whose way had been paved by the rationalisation gaining impetus from al-Bājī to Ibn Rushd, aimed at an absolute certainty based on general principles and leaving no room for conjecture. Al-Shāṭibī's work, *Al-Muwāfaqāt fī uṣūl al-sharīʿa*,[60] demonstrates those general principles (*kulliyāt*) of Law (such as "no injury or harmful effect" or "He has placed no constraint within religion") which are the foundation of its final aim: the safeguarding by God of the interests (*maṣāliḥ*) of men within the normal framework of their lives. In the light of this, absolute juridical indications—that is texts from the Quran or from *ḥadīth* which impose some kind of obligation or prohibition—are seen in terms of rational principles (justice, charity, pardon, endurance, etc.) which are the grounds of human reason itself, or, on the other side, in terms of iniquity, turpitude, etc.; while conditional indications—Quranic or *ḥadīth* texts involving recommendations—are seen in terms of devotional principles which reason perceives as external to itself.

This highly novel perspective was not, however, developed as it deserved to be; the teaching of al-Shāṭibī was lost in the practical popularisation of his pupil Ibn ʿĀṣim.

VII. The Survival of the Islamic Sciences under Christian Rule

The juridical question as to whether Muslims could remain in territory lost to Islamic rule was often resolved, as far as the mass of people was concerned, through compromise arrangements. The *ʿulamāʾ*, however, almost always followed the letter of the law. Very few remained to direct those among the population who were unable to emigrate; even some of those living in the Granada region were moved to flee to the Maghrib, or even to the East, decades, indeed centuries, before the final offensive. It is worth noting that such flight was particularly conspicuous among the Sufis! It was necessary, initially, for men of religion from North Africa to make visits to Spain to help the Mudejars (those who had remained Muslims under Christian rule). It was only later that the people of the Granadan enclave were once more to turn their gaze towards the North. Thus Abū Isḥāq al-Gharnāṭī was to be *qāḍī* of Majorca.

Nevertheless, the Christians were not necessarily ill-disposed, and Alfonso X, after taking Murcia in 1266, asked Muḥammad al-Riqūṭī to remain as a teacher at a college he had expressly founded, bringing together adepts of the three monotheistic religions. The experiment did not last, however, and al-Riqūṭī finally decided to settle in Granada, where, so we are told, he became embroiled (victoriously!) in a number of controversies—a sign, perhaps, that he had failed to fit in there. Another example of peaceful co-existence was provided by "Don Içe de Gebir", Chief *Qāḍī* and Mufti of Segovia, who, in 1462, left behind him a treatise on Law in *aljamiado*,[61] and who collaborated with the Franciscan Juan of Segovia in his work on the Quran.

As for Muslim activity properly speaking, only scattered landmarks stand out from now on. The most important author, undoubtedly, was the Castilian who styled himself "Mancebo ['young man'] of Arévalo" (late 15th/early 16th centuries). His texts—which are at present being published—still contain echoes of Ghazālī, this being due, perhaps, to his stay in Granada, whose religious life remained richer, but he mainly refers to a current popular mystic called "La Mora de Ubeda".[62] The writing of mnemonic verse appears once more in a *Breve compendio*, in which a certain Muḥammad Rabadan collaborated. Baray de Reminyo, *Qāḍī* of Cadrete in Aragon, was the disciple and friend of the Mancebo and also participated in this *Breve compendio de nuestra santa ley y sunna.*

Following the forced conversion (around 1501 in Castile, some thirty years later in the Crown of Aragon), a split took place. One branch, which soon faded out, attempted to associate itself with the Protestant influence and absorbed several anti-Catholic arguments from this source.[63] But it was in North Africa that writers referring back to al-Andalus were, up to the middle of the 17th century, to continue writing in honour of Islam, in Spanish if this was necessary for them to be understood by the exiles.[64]

1 *Histoire de l'Espagne musulmane*, III, Paris, 1967, p. 455.

2 M. 'A. Makki, *Ensayo sobre las aportaciones orientales en la España musulmana*, Madrid, 1968, pp. 61, 63.

3 J. Schacht, in *Encyclopédie de l'Islam*, 2nd ed., II, 796.

4 This is particularly evident in the biographical compilations. See D. Urvoy, *Le monde des ulémas andalous du Ve/XIe au VIIe/XIIIe siècle*, Geneva, 1978, pp. 209-14 ("La notion de *ra'y* dans l'Espagne musulmane").

5 Cf. *Le monde des ulémas*, pp. 7-25.

6 Ed. F. Codera, Madrid, 1892, 2 vols. New ed. Cairo, 1966.

7 Ed. F. Codera, Madrid, 1883, 2 vols. New ed. 'I. 'A. al-Ḥusaynī, Cairo, 1955, 2 vols.

8 Ed. F. Codera, Madrid, 1887-89, 2 vols. Beginning of the work, ed. A. Bel and M. Ben Cheneb, Algiers, 1920. Supplements, variants and index, ed. A. Alarcón and A. González-Palencia, *Miscelánea de estudios y textos árabes*, Madrid, 1915, pp. 147-690. New ed. 'I. al-Ḥusaynī, Cairo, 1963, 2 vols.

9 Part ed. E. Lévi-Provençal, Rabat, 1938.

10 Ed. Beirut, under publication.

11 Cf. A. Turki, "La vénération pour Mālik et la physionomie du mâlikisme andalou", *Studia Islamica*, 33, 1971, p. 45. Reprinted in *Théologiens et juristes de l'Espagne musulmane, polemical aspects*, Paris, 1982.

12 These are recorded in M. 'A. Makkī, "Al-tashayyu' fī 'l-Andalus", *Revista del Instituto Egipcio de Estudios Islámicos en Madrid*, 1954, pp. 93-149.

13 *Abenmasarra y su escuela: orígenes de la filosofía hispano-musulmana*, Madrid, 1917. New ed. in *Obras escogidas*, Madrid, 1946, I, 1-216.

14 *Ṭabaqāt al-umam*, ed. L. Cheikho, Beirut, 1912, p. 21.

15 "Ibn Masarra, Follower of Pseudo-Empedocles-An Illusion", *Actas do IV Congresso de Estudos Arabes e Islámicos*, Leiden, 1971, pp. 325-27.

16 Ibn Ḥayyān, *Al-Muqtabas*, Vol. V, ed. P. Chalmeta, F. Corriente and M. Subh, Madrid, 1979.

[17] Ed. and trans. M. I. Fierro, Madrid, 1988.

[18] Cf. K. I. Jaʿfar, "Min muʾallafāt Ibn Masarra ʾl-mafqūda", *Majallat Kulliyat al-tarbiya*, III, 1972, pp. 27-63.

[19] Cf. D. Urvoy, "Sur les débuts de la pensée spéculative en Andalus", *Mélanges de l'Université Saint Joseph*, 50, 1984, pp. 707-17.

[20] Cf. H. Monès, "Le rôle des hommes de religion dans l'histoire de l'Espagne musulmane jusqu'à la fin du califat", *Studia Islamica*, 20, 1964, p. 63 *et seq.*

[21] Al-Ḍabbī, *Bughyat al multamis fī taʾrīkh rijāl ahl al-Andalus*, ed. F. Codera, Madrid, 1886, No. 347; Ibn Bashkuwāl, *Ṣila*, No. 90; Ibn al-Abbār, *Takmila*, Nos. 420, 421, 425, 1292.

[22] Cf. D. Urvoy, "La vie intellectuelle et spirituelle dans les Baléares musulmanes", *Al-Andalus*, 37/1, 1972, pp. 87-132, and *Penser l'Islam; les présupposés islamiques de l' "Art" de Lull*, Paris, 1980.

[23] M. Benaboud, "The socio-political role of the Andalusian ulama during the 5th/11th century", *Islamic Studies*, 23/2, 1984, pp. 103-141, 106. Cf. the same author's *Al-tārīkh al-siyāsī wa 'l-ijtimaʿī li Ishbīliya fī ʿahd duwal al-ṭawāʾif*, Tétouan, 1983.

[24] *Nafḥ al-ṭīb min ghuṣn al-Andalus al-raṭīb*, ed. I. ʿAbbās, Beirut, 1968, I, 220-21.

[25] Ed. Cairo, 1346/1927.

[26] Ed. J. Hilal, *Revista del Instituto Egipcio de Estudios Islámicos en Madrid*, 1954, pp. 1-37.

[27] Ed. A. Turki, *Al-Andalus*, 31, 1966, pp. 73-153.

[28] Ed. J. Hilal, *Revista del Instituto Egipcio de Estudios Islámicos en Madrid*, 1955, pp. 17-46.

[29] Ed. A. Turki, Paris, 1978.

[30] *Grammaire et théologie chez Ibn Ḥazm de Cordoue. Essai sur la structure et les conditions de la pensée musulmane*, Paris, 1956.

[31] Ed. Cairo, 1345-47/1926-28, 8 books in 2 vols.

[32] Ed. S. al-Afghānī, Damascus, 1379/1960.

[33] Ed. Cairo, 1347/1928, 11 vols.

[34] Ed. Cairo, 1317/1899, 5 books in 2 vols. Abridged translation M. Asín Palacios, *Abenhazam de Córdoba y su historia crítica de las ideas religiosas*, Madrid, 1927, 5 vols.

[35] For example heterodox Christian elements within Muslim Spain itself. Cf. D. Urvoy, "La pensée religieuse des Mozarabes face à l'Islam", *Traditio*, 39, 1983, pp. 419-32.

[36] Ed. I. ʿAbbās, Beirut, 1959.

[37] Cf. D. Urvoy, "La *perception imaginative* chez Ibn Ḥazm", *Miscelánea de Estudios Arabes y Hebraicos*, in press.

[38] Cf. D. Urvoy, *Pensers d'al-Andalus. La vie intellectuelle à Cordoue et Séville au temps des empires berbères*, Toulouse, 1990, p. 159 *et seq.* ("La tentation ghazalienne").

[39] Ed. and trans. M. Asín Palacios, Paris, 1933.

[40] Cf. the detailed analysis of this in *Le monde des ulémas andalous*, pp. 129-31, and *Pensers d'al-Andalus*, pp. 83-85 and 161-62,

[41] Ed. ʿA. Ṭalbī, *Arāʾ Abī Bakr b. al-ʿArabī al-kalāmiyya wa naqduhu li 'l-falsafa al-yunāniyya*, Algiers, 1981, Vol. II.

[42] Cf. his bibliography in V. Lagardère, "Abū Bakr b. al-ʿArabī grand cadi de Séville", *Revue de l'Occident Musulman et de la Méditerranée*, 40, 1985/2, pp. 91-102.

[43] V. Lagardère, "La haute judicature à l'époque almoravide en al-Andalus", *Al-Qanṭara*, 7, 1986, pp. 135-228.

[44] Ed. A. B. Maḥmūd, Beirut and Tripoli (Libya), 1387/1967, 3 vols.

[45] Cf. D. Urvoy, "La pensée d'Ibn Tumart", *Bulletin d'Etudes Orientales*, 27, 1974, pp. 19-44.

[46] This is the version given around 600/1203 by Ibn Ṭumlūs of Alcira in the historical introduction to his treatise on logic (M. Asín, *Introduccion al arte de la logica por Abentomlus de Alcira*, Madrid, 1916).

[47] Found in numerous editions, e.g., Damascus: Dār al-Fikr, n. d.

[48] Ed. M. ʿAmāra, Beirut, 1981. Trans. G. Hourani, *Averroes on the Harmony of Religion and Philosophy*, London, 1961.

[49] Ed. M. Qāsim, Cairo, 1964. Partial translation by J. W. Sweetman, *Islam and Christian Theology*, London, 1965, Part I, Vol. II, pp. 82-189.

[50] Ed. M. Bouyges, Beirut, 1930. Trans. S. van den Bergh, London, 1969, 2 vols.

[51] On all of this see D. Urvoy, *Ibn Rushd (Averroès)*, London, Routledge, forthcoming, notably chapter II, paragraph 4, "la participation à la cité musulmane", and chapter II, paragraph 1, "la théologie rushdienne".

[52] *Le monde des ulémas*, p. 189.

[53] Cf., essentially, R. Arié, *L'Espagne musulmane au temps des Nasrides (1232-1492)*, Paris, 1973, notably pp. 277-99, "L'organisation judiciaire", and pp. 417-27, on bibliographical production.

[54] Ed. and trans. L. Bercher, Algiers, 1958.

[55] Ed. I. 'Abbās, Beirut, 1963.

[56] Ed. M. al-Kettani, Casablanca and Beirut, 1970, 2 vols.

[57] Cf. J. Aguilera Pleguezuelo, "Manuscrito No. 1077 en lengua árabe de la Biblioteca del Real Monasterio de El Escorial", *Miscelánea de Estudios Arabes y Hebraicos*, 36/1, 1987, pp. 7-20.

[58] Cf. Turki, *Thelogiens et juristes*, pp. 295-332.

[59] Cf. Arié, *Nasrides*, p. 419.

[60] Ed. 'A. Draz, Cairo, n. d., 3 vols.

[61] Ed. P. Gayangos, *Tratados de legislación musulmana*, Madrid, 1853.

[62] Cf. L. López Baralt and M. T. Narváez, "Estudio sobre la espiritualidad popular en la literatura aljamiado-morisca", *Revista de Dialectología y Tradiciones Populares*, 36, 1981, pp. 17-51.

[63] Cf. L. Cardaillac, "Morisques et Protestants", *Al-Andalus*, 36, 1971, pp. 29-61.

[64] Cf. L. Bernabé Pons, *El cántico islámico del Morisco hispanotunecino Taybili*, Saragossa, 1988.

BIBLIOGRAPHY

Asín Palacios, Miguel, "Abenmasarra y su escuela: orígenes de la filosofía hispano-musulmana", in *Obras escogidas*, Madrid, 1946, I, 1-216.

Benaboud, M., "The socio-political role of the Andalusian ulama during the 5th/11th century", *Islamic Studies*, 23/2, 1984, pp. 103-41.

Al-Ḍabbī, *Bughyat al-multamis fī ta'rīkh rijāl ahl al-Andalus*, ed. F. Codera, Madrid, 1886.

Fierro, M. I., "The Introduction of *ḥadīth* in al-Andalus (2nd/8th-3rd/9th centuries)", *Der Islam*, 66/1, 1989, pp. 68-93.

Ibn al-Abbār, *Al-Takmila li-kitāb al-ṣila*, ed. F. Codera, Madrid, 1887; new ed., 'I. al-Ḥusaynī, Cairo, 1963.

Ibn Bashkuwāl, *Kitāb al-ṣila fī ta'rīkh a'immat al-Andalus*, ed. F. Codera and J. Ribera, Madrid, 1883; new ed. 'I. al-Ḥasanī, Cairo, 1955.

Ibn al-Faraḍī, *Ta'rīkh 'ulamā' al-Andalus*, ed. F. Codera, Madrid, 1891-92; new ed., Cairo, 1966.

Ibn Ḥayyān, *Al-Muqtabas*, V, ed. P. Chalmeta, F. Corriente and M. Sobh, Madrid, 1979.

Ibn al-Khaṭīb, *Al-Iḥāṭa fī ta'rīkh Gharnāṭa*, ed. 'A. 'Inān, Cairo, 1955.

——, *Al-Katība al-kāmina*, ed. I. 'Abbās, Beirut, 1963.

Lagardère, V., "La haute judicature à l'époque almoravide en al-Andalus", *Al-Qanṭara*, 7, 1986, pp. 135-228.

Makki, M. A., *Ensayo sobre las aportaciones orientales en la España musulmana*, Madrid, 1968.

Al-Marrākushī, Muḥammad b. Muḥammad b. al-Anṣārī al-Awsī, *Kitāb al-dhayl wa 'l-takmila li-kitābay al-mawṣūl wa 'l-ṣila*, ed. I. 'Abbās, Beirut, 1973-.

Al-Maqqarī, *Nafḥ al-ṭīb min ghuṣn al-Andalus al-raṭīb*, ed. I. 'Abbās, Beirut, 1968.

Monès, H., "Le rôle des hommes de religion dans l'histoire de l'Espagne musulmane jusqu'à la fin du califat", *Studia Islamica*, 20, 1964, pp. 63-83.

Turki, R., *Théologiens et juristes de l'Espagne musulmane, aspects polémiques*, Paris, 1982.

Urvoy, D., *Le monde des ulémas andalous du Ve/XIe au VIIe/XIIIe siècle. Etude sociologique*, Geneva, 1978.

——, *Pensers d'al-Andalus. La vie intellectuelle à Cordoue et Sévilleau temps des empires berbères (fin XIe-début XIIIe siècles)*, Toulouse, 1990.

——, "Sur les débuts de la pensée spéculative en Andalus", *Mélanges de l'"Université Saint-Joseph*, 50, 1984, pp. 707-17.

MUSLIM RELIGIOUS PRACTICES IN AL-ANDALUS (2ND/8TH–4TH/10TH CENTURIES)

MANUELA MARÍN

INTRODUCTION

Andalusī Muslims, as an emerging community, have not received the attention given to other minority groups such as Christians and Jews; far more studies have been devoted, for example, to the Mozarabic "resistance" movement in 3rd/9th century Córdoba than to the religious usages and beliefs of their Muslim fellow-countrymen during the same historical period. The process of conversion to Islam in the Iberian Peninsula, following the conquest of 93/711, is not very well known, but an estimate locates the "midpoint of Spanish conversion" in 961 A.D.;[1] and, although the material on which this statement is based is scanty and relies only on biographical and onomastic data, it may be accepted as well-founded hypothesis. We can assume, then, that by the middle of the 4th/10th century, the greater part of the population of al-Andalus was practising Islam.[2]

In al-Andalus, as in other regions, conversion to Islam did not mean a total erasure of previous beliefs and social practices,[3] and it is impossible to deny the existence of cultural connections and influences between Islam and Christianity. But the field of religion was always a very sensitive one, and Muslims in al-Andalus—as everywhere—were conscious of the need not to adopt any Christian or Jewish practice. In the early period of their history especially, Andalusī Muslims, living on the edge of the Islamic world and coexisting with a substantial majority of Christians, tried to establish a clear set of rules of behaviour in order to protect the purity of their faith and their religious activity. It is not surprising, then, to find one of the earliest leading *ʿulamāʾ*, Muḥammad b. Waḍḍāḥ (d. 287/900), writing a book on "innovations" (*bidaʿ*)[4] which is devoted mainly to ritual deviations. Of one of his contemporaries, Yaḥyā b. Ḥajjāj (d. 263/878-7), it was said that he never entered a house which might contain an image or a dog. Nor are these isolated examples; throughout the 3rd/9th century we have evidence of a strong tendency to define and delimit the corpus of belief, together with its implications for the daily life of the Muslim community.

My purpose here is to deal with Andalusis as practising Muslims. They shared, of course, a common creed and ritual with the rest of the *umma*, an orthopraxis[5] that embraced individual and social life in a way few other religions have done. Again we find that much more research has been dedicated to what is called "popular Islam" than to the "orthodox" manner of practising it; and if this is particularly true of countries like Morocco, al-Andalus is no exception to this general trend. However, historical and biographical sources provide us with a considerable amount of information on the religious life of al-Andalus Through these texts (very different in their intent from the theoretical treatises written by the *fuqahā'*) we can observe Andalusī Muslims in their daily practice of religious ritual. Moreover, these sources, in the absence of hagiographical materials, allow us to know the beginning and early development of asceticism in al-Andalus, before the appearance of the great Sufi figures of later periods.

A basic problem posed by the use of these sources should be noted. With a few exceptions, they deal with only two social groups: first, the entourage of the court and the administrative apparatus; and second, the milieu of the *'ulamā'* and *fuqahā'*. This naturally gives a restricted view of Andalusī society, barely compensated for by the scant information found in some legal sources, such as *ḥisba* (market regulations) treatises and collections of *nawāzil* (legal cases). With this limitation in mind, we shall proceed to examine—in a necessarily cursory manner—the information available to us, arranging it under two main headings: 1) religious ritual and devotional practices; and 2) ascetic and pious manifestations.

I. Religious Ritual and Devotional Practices

I.1 *Prayer*

Of the five pillars of Islam, prayer is undoubtedly the central pivot of religious life,[6] a fact implicitly reflected in our sources, which are much richer in information on prayer than on any other aspect of religious practice. Evolution and changes in prayer ritual may be observed in al-Andalus, where two main questions related to it were discussed: the raising of hands during certain parts of the prayer and the recitation of the *qunūt* (invocations included in the *ṣalāt*). Traditionists of great prestige, like Baqī b. Ma<u>kh</u>lad (d. 276/889)[7] or Muḥammad b. 'Abd al-Salām al-<u>Kh</u>u<u>sh</u>anī (d. 286/899)[8] used to raise their hands, a gesture strongly disapproved of by Mālikī *fuqahā'*.[9] However, if this dissension reflects divergences between traditionists and *fuqahā'* in this period,[10] these same *fuqahā'* were themselves divided on the matter of the *qunūt*. This special part of the prayer, recalling one occasion on which the Prophet asked God to punish his enemies and bless his followers, had not been unanimously accepted in the Islamic East, and in al-Andalus, the great *faqīh* Yaḥyā b. Yaḥyā 'l-Lay<u>th</u>ī (d. 234/848), the leading Mālikī of his day, was totally opposed to this practice, in spite of Mālik b. Anas' own approval of it. Yaḥyā's descendants followed his opinion, which is duly recorded by the sources, and his family exercised a kind of monopoly over the recension of the *Muwaṭṭa'* which he had transmitted, and which became the most favoured recension in the Islamic West. As was the case with the *Muwaṭṭa'*, any *riwāya* originating from Yaḥyā was of great prestige, and in the second part of the 4th/10th century another member of the family, Abū ʿĪsā Yaḥyā b. ʿAbd Allāh (d. 367/977) still discouraged the *qunūt*, recalling Yaḥyā b. Yaḥyā's opinion. What is interesting in this case is that, despite the enormous prestige of Yaḥyā and his family,[11] the *qunūt* was a common practice in Andalusī mosques, surviving even in the prayers of the Mudejars.[12]

These discussions of the *fuqahā'* probably had only limited influence on the general practice of Muslims, although they helped to establish an acknowledged and accepted ritual. Here one should emphasise that, quite apart from the observance of ritual, Islamic prayer has a double significance, both collective and individual: through prayer a Muslim felt, on the one hand, that he was a member of the communal congregation assembled in the mosque during the Friday ceremonies, and, on the other, that communication with God was obtained in a personal way. In Córdoba the post of *ṣāḥib al-ṣalāt* was held by the most respected *ʿālim*, on the appointment of the *amīr* (or the caliph), and he usually also held the responsibilities of *khaṭīb* and judge. The implications of the *khuṭba* are well-known: Muslims are joined together, at the same hour, to express both their religious and their political allegiances. During the reign of the *amīr* ʿAbd Allāh (275/888-300/912), al-Naḍar b. Salama, judge of Córdoba, was appointed also as *ṣāḥib al-ṣalāt* and *khaṭīb*; and the *amīr* liked al-Naḍar's *khuṭba* so much that he ordered him not to change it, so that the judge repeated the same words for years. The assembled faithful came to know this famous homily by heart, and it became a model for other judges,[13] reflecting, obviously, the continuing legitimacy of the Umayyad power. But it was at this same period, filled with rebellions menacing the very existence of this power, that the *khuṭba* was pronounced in some places under the name of the Abbasid caliph, thus giving a totally different intent to the Friday prayer.

People attending the communal prayer were stern critics of the quality of the *khuṭba*, which was considered sacred oratory. Because of his ability and knowledge, and despite its constant repetition, al-Naḍar's *khuṭba* was very much appreciated by Cordoban Muslims, while another judge, ʿĀmir b. Muʿāwiya (d. 277/890), used to imbue his *khuṭba* with a "delicacy which won all the hearts".[14] Alongside the political implications and religious function, the Friday homily appears, too, as a way of moving the spirit of listeners through the use of language.

Prayers have marked the life of the Muslim community in a way unlike that of any other religion, with daily and weekly prayers establishing a pattern of time totally different from that of the Christian or Jew. Only exceptionally did the need arise for gathering the community outside this well-established rhythm, namely on occasions directly linked with natural catastrophes. Our sources give examples of prayers at the time of eclipses: the first instance is recorded in 218/833, when the terrorised population of Córdoba sheltered in the Great Mosque and the then judge, Yaḥyā b. Maʿmar, prayed and asked for God's mercy.[15] Earthquakes also provoked meetings and prayers in mosques, as occurred in 332/943;[16] but the most common reason for these exceptional communal prayers was drought.

The Iberian Peninsula, like the greater part of the central Islamic lands, is a semi-arid region, subject to periodic catastrophes when the rains fail to arrive in time. When faced with inclement natural conditions, Andalusī Muslims turned to God, following the ritual established in the East and known as *istisqāʾ*. According to the sources, the first *ʿālim* to adopt Eastern uses with regard to this kind of prayer was Ziyād b. ʿAbd al-Raḥmān, known as Shabṭūn (d. between 196/811-12 and 204/819-20). The main innovation introduced by Shabṭūn was the turning up of the mantle during the invocation, a gesture whose origin is attributed to ʿUmar b. al-Khattab.[17] The *istisqāʾ* was normally conducted by the *ṣāḥib al-ṣalāt* or the judge, but in some cases—due to the peculiar character of this prayer, which is intended not only as praise of God, but also as an appeal to His mercy—it was felt that someone different, of a more exalted piety, was necessary if a positive answer was to be obtained.

The sources record two cases of this kind, where two ascetics, Ayyūb al-Ballūṭī and Abū Naṣr al-Ṣadfūrī, were asked to preside at the *istisqāʾ*. The pattern of the events in which they appear is the same. During the prayer, the *imām* asked them to move forward and make the invocation; they tried at first to resist this invitation, but finally agreed, and obtained an immediate answer from Heaven. Then, shortly after this, they disappeared without trace.[18] These two short accounts, which are paralleled in Eastern pious literature, have a clear edifying intent, that of showing how genuine ascetics are the only ones God may answer and, also, how they conceal themselves from public applause and recognition.

The *istisqāʾ* sometimes appears in the sources as a kind of spontaneous gathering of believers, but this was probably more often the case in the sudden event of certain natural phenomena, like eclipses and earthquakes. The prayer for rain was a well-organised affair, ordered by the *amīr* or caliph when drought persisted; in 317/929, for example, Caliph ʿAbd al-Raḥmān III issued a letter to the governors of the provinces, ordering them to organise *istisqāʾ* in the main mosques, as he himself had done in Córdoba.[19] There was another place, besides the mosque, where this kind of prayer was said, namely the *muṣallā*. Here, on the outskirts of the city and in an open space, it was easier to gather crowds for the purpose—or for happier occasions, such as the end of the *Ramaḍān* festival or military parades (*burūz*).

Two *muṣallā*s existed in Córdoba,[20] their use alternating according to the needs of the populace. For a while the one favoured was the *muṣallā 'l-*

Rabaḍ, because it was a shorter distance from the *amīr*'s palace than the *muṣallā 'l-Muṣāra*; however, a number of accidents occurred on the way to the former, because it was necessary to cross the Guadalquivir bridge and many tried to cross the river by boat to avoid the crowds on it and were drowned. It was the renowned scholar ʿAbd al-Malik b. Ḥabīb (d. 238/852)[21] who asked the *amīr* to organise religious and social events, once more, in the *muṣallā 'l-Muṣāra*.[22] There people gathered to ask for rain, presided over, as we have seen, by the *ṣāḥib al-ṣalāt*, whose place was simply marked by a prayer carpet or a javelin stuck on the floor. As in the case of the Friday *khuṭba*, the invocation in the *istisqāʾ* was expected to be of a moving character, and to be ornamented with rhetorical devices. It was mainly a combination of Quranic texts and pious expressions,[23] arranged in such a way as to provoke a collective response from the crowd. The emotional ambience created—and the anticipated criticism of the public—could overwhelm the *khaṭīb*, as happened with Saʿīd b. Sulaymān, who, on one such occasion, could do nothing but repeat a number of pious formulae.[24]

To these communal prayers other examples might be added, such as the funeral prayer, in which it seems that the most important point was the personality of the *imām*; the biographical sources very frequently mention the name of the person in charge of the funeral service when giving information about deaths of *ʿulamāʾ* and *fuqahāʾ*. We may reasonably assume that presiding over this ceremony was a matter of prestige in the scholars' milieu; indeed, some disputes about precedence are recorded in this connection.[25]

However, prayer was not only a community celebration; it was also an expression of personal piety, of the direct relationship between God and man. The most intense manifestations of piety through prayer will be mentioned later; here I shall examine only the ordinary individual Muslim practice of addressing God.

Personal communication with God was obtained both through *ṣalāt* and through *duʿāʾ*, or supplication, but the latter is not, like the *ṣalāt*, framed by a ritual of gestures and recitations, nor is there any fixed time for its pronouncement. While the *ṣalāt* is, above all, performed in praise of God, as an act of adoration, the *duʿāʾ* allows the believer to express personal feelings, to seek forgiveness or assistance and to establish a closer link with God.[26] This does not imply, however, that the *duʿāʾ* is an open conversation between a man's soul and God. Already, in the second half of the 3rd/9th century, Muḥammad b. Fuṭays b. Wāṣil (d. 319/931) composed a book (now lost) entitled *Kitāb al-duʿāʾ wa 'l-dhikr*, which probably contained a number of texts designed to be recited during this kind of prayer. A later work, presumably of the same kind, has been preserved; entitled *Al-Duʿāʾ al-maʾthūr wa ādabu-hu*, it was written by Abū Bakr al-Ṭurṭūshī (451/1050-520/1126), and is a collection of supplications for a wide variety of occasions, which al-Ṭurṭūshī recorded in the following sequence: entering or leaving an uninhabited place; performing the ablutions for the communal prayer; listening to the call for prayer;

leaving the house; entering the mosque; performing the prayer; listening to the cock crow; going to bed; rising during the night to pray; facing a difficult circumstance; visiting a powerful person; wearing something for the first time; eating and drinking; travelling; saying farewell to somebody; riding a mount; sailing; falling ill; going to war; having a nightmare; suffering in a tempest; concluding one's business; going to the *istisqāʾ*; marrying; learning of someone's death; being lost; and going to the market.

For each of the occasions recorded, Abū Bakr al-Ṭurṭū<u>sh</u>ī provides one or more texts appropriate for the *duʿāʾ*, and in this list (reproduced in the same order as the occurrences) there are three kinds of situations: those related to daily life; those which follow religious practices; and, finally, those in which the individual is exposed to some danger. The first group emphasises a well-known feature of any Islamic society, that is, the utterance of a pious formula in social intercourse.[27] The second to some extent reflects the ritualisation of the *duʿāʾ*, which was gradually incorporated into the *ṣalāt* itself, a good example of the process being found in the biography of Aḥmad b. Baqī (d. 324/935-6),[28] son of the famous Baqī b. Ma<u>kh</u>lad, who was appointed judge and *ṣāḥib al-ṣalāt* in Córdoba in 314/926. The biographer records how, on one occasion, Aḥmad b. Baqī was uttering a *duʿāʾ*—presumably in the mosque—and when he arrived at the sentence "offer sincerely to God your invocation", he remained silent for a long while, until he considered that people had completed their own invocations. The text then continues:

> He said: 'Oh God! These are Your servants who invoke You in search of Your recompense. They are gathered before You, afraid of Your punishment, desiring Your recompense and trusting in Your praise. Accept them with their sins which You already know and have computed. Turn to them in this situation in which they find themselves with the mercy indispensable for them to enter Your paradise and let them be removed from Your punishment. Amen! Oh You, the most Merciful of the Merciful! Oh You, the Omnipotent!' Many preachers in al-Andalus have, up to the present day, followed Aḥmad b. Baqī's example in remaining silent at the end of the second homily during the *duʿāʾ*.[29]

The final set of situations presented by al-Ṭurṭū<u>sh</u>ī has a common character. These are the dangers which might menace the life and possessions of any Muslim when—as was the case with drought—the only possible help was of a supernatural nature. It is not, therefore, surprising to find some *duʿāʾ* texts especially praised as being able to produce an immediate answer, such texts being known as *duʿāʾ mustajāb*. Many of the accounts in which they appear are of a miraculous nature and will be examined later.

I.2 *The giving of alms*

While information on *zakāt* is rather scarce, the practice of almsgiving (*ṣadaqa*) is widely attested. Charity is seen as a means of expressing a communal solidarity, especially during times of difficulty. The historical sources emphasise the distribution of money and food by the *amīr*s and caliphs in periods of famine, but also on specific occasions, such as the end of *Ramaḍān*. One of these distributions, in 365/975, is vividly recorded by Ibn Ḥayyān: the caliph al-Ḥakam II, accompanied by his son, presided over the ceremony, in which slaves circulated among the crowd with open bags full of money.[30] As in other, similar cases, the intention of the chronicler here is to present the prince as a model of Islamic virtues and an embodiment of public piety. In the biographical sources the *ʿulamāʾ* practise charity in the same exemplary way, but there are also cases where special stress is laid on the hidden ways of giving alms.[31]

It is not infrequent to find, in the biographies of *ʿulamāʾ*, references to their distribution of money or food to people in need, even when they themselves were in straitened circumstances. Many of them held the post of *wālī/ṣāḥib tafrīq al-ṣadaqa*,and here again we may see how religious practices and piety could have an institutional dimension directly linked to the exercise of power. Before the end of the 3rd/9th century, judges used to order the distribution of *ṣadaqāt* once a year; they determined, too, who were to be the beneficiaries of charity. It was the judge Aslam b. ʿAbd al-ʿAzīz, who introduced some changes in this procedure: since, in his time, the sums of money collected were very high, he decided to make two distributions per year, and, moreover, he was the first judge to ask the *ʿulamāʾ* and the professional witnesses to be present when money was distributed. He also established appointed times for the distribution, having previously made a public appeal to poor people to attend it.[32]

One of the motifs concerning charity in Andalusī sources is that of assistance to people of noble ancestry who had lost their wealth; these were poor, but were too ashamed or too proud to beg or attend official distributions. Al-Ḥakam II was apparently very concerned about their situation, because in *Ramaḍān* 362/June 973 he gave special orders to search for such persons in Córdoba and made them the main beneficiaries of a distribution of alms.[33] A son of Yaḥyā b. Yaḥyā, ʿUbayd Allāh (d. 297/909 or 298/910),[34] is the central figure of an edifying story along the same lines. He had a neighbour, a man of Qurayshī descent, with whom he was on friendly terms. In a year of drought, the Qurayshī was reduced to extreme poverty, to the point where he and his family were without food for three days, so that his family asked him to look for help. Leaving the house, he met ʿUbayd Allāh b. Yaḥyā, who, on his own initiative, had brought him 10 dinars and some flour and oil.[35]

The account is interesting in that the same narrative scheme is used in stories of a miraculous nature, when help arrives in a similar way, but after the utterance of a *duʿāʾ*. In the present case, the narrator simply seeks to emphasise the charity of ʿUbayd Allāh, a man of great wealth of whom it was said that he once gave half his possessions as alms; and, to this end, the anonymous author of the story recorded by ʿIyāḍ has had recourse to an already known story framework, probably circulating in works of a pious nature. Stress is also laid, here as in other anecdotes of the same nature, not only on the act of charity itself, but on the generosity of the donor. A descendant of the above-mentioned Shabṭūn, Aḥmad b. Muḥammad b. Ziyād (d. 312/924) is described as *kathīr al-ṣadaqāt* ("donor of many alms");[36] at the same time we are informed that he had a good economic position and that he enjoyed entertaining guests: he scarcely ever ate alone and used to invite ten other *fuqahā'* every night. So in this case—and possibly in others—it is not easy to differentiate between charity as a religious practice and generosity as a social virtue.

I.3 *Fasting*

Fasting is not a feature exclusive to Islam, but the peculiarities of Muslim fast involved a series of collective and private manifestations. In Córdoba, during the *Ramaḍān*, the Great Mosque remained open throughout the night, fully illuminated—the amount spent on lamp oil during this month comprised half the annual expense—and *Laylat al-qadr* was signalled in this mosque by the burning of great quantities of expensive perfume, such as aloe and amber.[37] The fasting month was a period marked by the expression of intense religious feeling: by night people would gather in mosques, special prayers were pronounced and alms were distributed. The recitation of the Quran was increased and cases are recorded of pious men who completed the recitation of the holy text in a single night. Muḥammad b. 'Umar b. Lubāba (d. 314/926), for example, read the entire Quran 60 times during *Ramaḍān*, according to his biographer.[38]

The period of fasting was also regarded as a time of penitence by some; for example, Hārūn b. Sālim (d. 236/850) used to sleep on the floor, without a mattress.[39] Others retired from ordinary social activities in order to preserve the purity of their piety, such withdrawal occurring even within the cities. The same Aḥmad b. Muḥammad b. Ziyād whose generosity is so praised used to spend the fast of *Ramaḍān* in a house he owned, near the Great Mosque of Córdoba,[40] while Muḥammad b. 'Umar b. Lubāba did not leave his residence during the fast, except to attend prayers in the mosque,[41] There were also people who left the cities during *Ramaḍān* and stayed in castles, practising the *ribāṭ*; the first specific record we have to this effect comes from a slightly later time, from the first half of the 5th/11th century,[42] but the use of the *ribāṭ* as a place for retirement and devotional life was already common in the earlier period, and, as such, we may reasonably assume that spending *Ramaḍān* in a *ribāṭ* was, if not a common practice, at least already a possibility open to some.

The sources provide information about the festivities that marked the end of *Ramaḍān* (especially the ones organised in the royal palace of Córdoba), but it is difficult to find anything concerning the daily practices of the *ifṭār*, or breaking of the fast. Probably festive meals were prepared; from later culinary sources we know of the existence of dishes especially associated with *Ramaḍān*.

A curious episode, however, is mentioned in connection with the burial ceremony of ʿUbayd Allāh b. Yaḥyā, whose death had occurred during *Ramaḍān* of 298 (May 911). It was a very hot day and the crowd was so numerous that ʿUbayd Allāh's son and many others had to break the fast so as to be able to take part in the funeral service.[43]

I.4 *The* ḥajj, *or pilgrimage*

To round off this short survey of the orthopraxis of Andalusī Muslims, something must be said about the *ḥajj*, or pilgrimage. Living as they did a great distance from Mecca, it is amazing for the modern observer to note how many made this long journey, which could last months, and even years. Most of our information on this point comes from biographical sources, with the result that the religious aspect of the *ḥajj* is obscured by the particular interests of the *ʿulamāʾ*; in other words, we learn more about the teachers with whom they studied than about their religious experiences.[44] Only in a later period do we have testimonies of this latter kind,[45] which allow us to follow an Andalusī Muslim throughout his journey and gain an idea of the feelings experienced in the pilgrimage ceremonies.

As for the period under study, what is known is mainly related to the material difficulties of the journey. As sea routes were the ones most commonly taken, shipwrecks were not infrequent, and pilgrims were faced by other dangers as well, such as attacks by pirates and highwaymen, or by enemies of Muslims. This last was experienced by Salama b. Umayya b. Wadīʿ, who travelled to the East in 383/993: on his return to al-Andalus he was captured by Byzantines and spent some years in captivity.[46] Notwithstanding these dangers, there were *ʿulamāʾ* who made more than one journey during their lifetime; the reason for this could be an intention to repeat the *ḥajj*, as a sign of strong personal piety, or, in other cases, the desire to meet renowned Eastern scholars. ʿUṯmān b. Saʿīd b. ʿUṯmān (d. 372/983) travelled to the Hijaz while a boy, accompanying his father; then, years later, he repeated the journey in order to study with the Meccan scholars, something he had been unable to do during his first trip.[47]

From this last example we can infer that the *ḥajj* was also a family affair. The sources give many other instances of fathers and sons travelling together to the East and even some female names occasionally appear: Ṣawwāb, wife of Ibrāhīm b. Ismāʿīl al-Qabrī (d. 366/976), made the journey with her husband, as did Rāḍiya, a former slave of ʿAbd al-Raḥmān III, married to Labīb *al-fatā*.[48] But the most prominent case is that of the women of the Berber family of the Banū Wansūs: six of these, whose names have been preserved in biographical literature, performed the pilgrimage, and the most renowned of all, Umm al-Ḥasan bint Abī Liwā' Sulaymān b. Aṣbagh, made the journey to Mecca twice.[49] This was certainly an exceptional case, however, and we must bear in mind the high social position of this Berber family, whose fortune allowed many of its members to undertake what was an expensive affair. In other cases, *'ulamā'* of lower social standing had to employ themselves in various jobs during the journey, or seek the financial help of richer colleagues.

Up to this point, I have dealt with the "ordinary" expressions of religion, that is, with the performance of the basic rules of Islamic rituals. No doubt there were many other celebrations of private and daily life related to religion, such as births, circumcision or weddings, a complete study of which is still needed. My intention now, however, is to move to the field of personal religious attitudes, as they were experienced by men whom the sources call *zuhhād* or *'ubbād*.

II. Ascetic and Pious Manifestations

Many of the biographies of Andalusī *'ulamā'* use such descriptive epithets as *zāhid*, *'ābid*, *wari'*, *nāsik*, *mutabattil*, *khāshi'*, *munqabiḍ* or *mujāb al-da'wa*, the first two being the most common. These terms are usually translated as "ascetic", "worshipper", "pious", "humble", etc., while *munqabiḍ* is used in a more specific sense, referring to a person who leads a secluded life or who avoids contact with those in high position. The term *mujāb al-da'wa* is applied only in certain cases, of persons who are able to obtain an answer from God to a supplication addressed to Him.

From the biographies of these *'ulamā'* it is clear that many of those termed *zāhid* were simply good Muslims who abstained from anything illicit in their daily lives.[50] At the same time, it is possible to detect, from a very early period, the appearance of some forms of piety which clearly went beyond these narrow limits, and which may be called ascetic to say the least.

These extraordinary manifestations of devotion are based on the performance of the usual ritual obligations, the *zāhid* distinguishing himself from the ordinary Muslim in that his practice is more frequent. In the 3rd/9th century, for example, we find instances of *zuhhād* who prayed continuously, such as Yaḥyā b. Qāsim b. Hilāl (d. 272/885 or 297/909-10), who only left the mosque to sleep at home.[51] The continuous reciting of the Quran and the performance of *dhikr* was a common practice among pious scholars like Ibrāhīm b. Muḥammad b. Bāz (d. 274/887), who used to recite the sacred text on any occasion, "while walking, sitting or working. He made a complete recitation twice every day ... while he was in bed, he was always reciting the Quran."[52] The central role of prayer in Islamic piety (together with the recitation of the Quran) is more emphasised in the activities of the ascetic, and such behaviour continues into the following century.

Fasting outside the prescribed times of *Ramaḍān* was another honoured practice among ascetic persons. Abū 'l-Ajannas (who lived under al-Ḥakam I, 180/796-206/822) used to have only three meals every seven days during this month,[53] and it was not uncommon, among pious *ʿulamāʾ*, to perform similar fasts to that of *Ramaḍān* during other periods of the year. A person doing this was called a *ṣawwām*. Cases are recorded, too, of exceptional acts of charity, such as the one performed by Saʿīd b. ʿImrān b. Mushrif (d. ca. 275/888), who was the son of a wealthy merchant and distributed the greater part of his property among the poor before leaving for Mecca.[54]

Intensity of religious feeling was not, however, restricted to ritual practices. Emotions experienced while praying or listening to the recitation of the Quran were often expressed through weeping, and a bearing of extreme humility was a characteristic common to many *zuhhād*, a frequent case of the latter being that of an *ʿālim* who brings his own bread to the public oven, a task usually performed by servants. ʿAbd Allāh b. Ḥusayn b. ʿĀṣim (d. after 238/852), who was not a poor man, never rode a mount, preferring to walk barefoot in the dirty alleys of the market.[55]

The *mujāb al-daʿwa* appears in the biographical and historical sources as somewhat different from the cases just mentioned. His capacity for receiving an answer from God sets him apart from devout and pious men who dedicate themselves to the religious life; he is, of course, one of them, but his piety transforms him into an intermediary or mediator between God and man and, hence, a worker of wonders or miracles.

Andalusī sources do not abound in cases of miracles (*karāmāt*). In the earliest period, before the 4th/10th century, narratives containing this kind of material concern only a handful of very prominent *ʿulamāʾ*, such as Ibn Bāz, Yaḥyā b. Qāsim b. Hilāl, Baqī b. Makhlad and Muḥammad b. Waḍḍāḥ, already mentioned.[56] The stories in which they appear have clear parallels in the Islamic East, and the topoi were probably imported and applied to Andalusis at a later period. During this same century, traditions related to Eastern ascetics were introduced into al-Andalus; Muḥammad b. Waḍḍāḥ, in fact, made his first journey to the East in search of this kind of material.[57] But there existed, too, a local tradition within al-Andalus, preserved in a tenuous way in sources more concerned with other kinds of information. This tradition appears in short biographical entries, such as those dedicated to ascetic men who presided over the *istisqāʾ*, as noted above.[58] Another interesting case relates to the activity of the *mujāb al-daʿwa* as a redresser of injustice. In these examples the ascetic is portrayed as someone to whom people in distress, more specifically those oppressed by the powerful, could turn.

During the reign of al-Ḥakam I, the governors of the Upper Frontier of al-Andalus, the Banū Salama, made their subjects suffer all manner of vexations, and a *mujāb al-daʿwa*, ʿAbd Allāh b. al-Mughallis, was asked to invoke God against them. He refused to do so for a time, but then, after witnessing a particularly revolting act of injustice,[59] he implored God to put an end to this state of affairs. The appearance of rebels who destroyed the Banū Salama was considered the answer to his appeal.[60]

A case recorded in a later source[61] involves another form of injustice. Here the oppressors were not holders of political power, but rather *fuqahā'*. The hero of the story, one Ibn Ṣayqal, was threatened by Ibrāhīm b. ʿĪsā b. Ḥayyawayh, a member of a learned Cordoban family who wanted to buy Ibn Ṣayqal's house. Ibn Ṣayqal refused, and then went to seek the help of an ascetic living nearby, called Shaybān. Together with another pious man, Ḥassān, Shaybān spent a night praying and invoking the name of God. The next day, Ibn Ḥayyawayh was found dead in his residence.

In these two narratives, the moral is evident: evil should be opposed by exemplary behaviour. Evil is, too, equated with worldly concerns. It is not surprising to find in many ascetics an attitude of retirement (*inqibāḍ*) which leads them to avoid any contact with officials and persons related to political power; this is indeed a recurrent motif in many biographies.

All those narratives pertain to a well-established Islamic tradition from which many Eastern parallels could be drawn; it is, in fact, a literature of the exemplar, intended to set forth moral models and to insist on the virtues of religious practice. The spiritual model provided by these texts has a social value too, as the *ʿābid* could play the role of mediator with God and also help to establish the ideal order of things when there is menace from injustice. On the other hand, some of these ascetic men presented, in their way of living and their extreme piety, a challenge to those who practised Islam in a more casual way, or who were—as was the case with many *fuqahā'*—deeply involved in worldly pursuits. When piety reached certain extremes, the community of "men of religion" was liable to react against it, setting rules and establishing limits for such exaggerated expressions.[62]

An early instance of this mistrust may be observed in the biographical texts related to Yumn b. Rizq, an ascetic from Tudela, in the Upper Frontier.[63] He led a life of privation, yet, when he wished to give alms, he simply put his hand under the plain mat upon which he slept and took from what seemed to be an inexhaustible source of money. To this miraculous note is added the narration of a dream he had in early youth; he saw himself with a copper padlock on his heart holding a golden key in his hand, and with this key he opened his heart.

The narrative of this dream is exceptional for the early period; and, although no more is said on its possible meaning, it suggests a kind of mystical initiation into the mysteries of religion. Yumn b. Rizq wrote a book entitled *Kitāb al-zuhd*, which was fiercely condemned by both Andalusī and Qayrawānī scholars on the grounds that the author was a man of wicked thoughts. The book is lost, but we know that it was transmitted in Madrid, during the first half of the 4th/10th century, by a North African ascetic called Jassās.[64]

It is difficult, with so little data, to establish the reasons behind the disapproval of Yumn's book, although we may suppose that they were not related to his ascetic practices as recorded in his biography. Mystical initiation, on the other hand, was a novelty in this period, and was probably regarded, even by pious scholars, as something dangerous. The first occurrence of the term "Sufi" is in the biography of ʿAbd Allāh b. Naṣr, who died in 315/927.[65] A few years later (in 319/931) the death occurred of Muḥammad b. ʿAbd Allāh b. Masarra,[66] a crucial figure in the development of Andalusī religious thought. Ibn Masarra's ideas were condemned too—after his death—and, although they are not very well known, due to the loss of almost all his writings, it is easy to discern a strong mystical component in the traces we have.

It was, we may assume, in the period from the final years of the 3rd/9th century to the second half of the 4th/10th century that mysticism began to flourish in al-Andalus. For all the disparate nature of the materials, some common points may be observed. There is, first of all, a kind of reserve in the sources when dealing with facts of a miraculous nature; very few details are given about the performance of *karāmāt*, and, when narratives of this kind are reproduced, they are frequently of Eastern origin—the main characters may be Eastern themselves, or, if they are Andalusī, miraculous things happen to them while they are living in Eastern countries. All this suggests that, as happened in other fields of intellectual life, Andalusī religious practice accepted and adapted a tradition imported from the main centres of Islamic thought. This process of adaptation did not take place without difficulties and opposition, but it finally produced, from the second half of the 4th/10th century onwards, its own, original form. The development may be exemplified, in the case of the mystic, in the figure of Abū Wahb al-Zāhid (d. 344/955).[67]

Of obscure Eastern origins, Abū Wahb established himself in Córdoba, where he dedicated himself to a life of extreme piety. He was considered a madman at first, and was even attacked physically by passers-by. Gradually, however, he became accepted and revered, so much so in fact that great crowds attended his burial. The sources record verses of an ascetic character attributed to him; but three of them sound a mystical note:

> Oh you who censure me; you do not know Him. Leave me with Him; I am not deluded.
> Do you not always see me enraptured by Him, as if I were bewitched and seduced?
> Nothing better I heard of His love than to be described myself as mad and disturbed.

Conclusion

The object of this paper has been to show the ordinary religious practices of Andalusī Muslims, together with some of the ascetic trends which began to spread from an early date. We tend, in our agnostic age, to forget how central religion was for the life of people in earlier historical periods, and how embedded it was in their cultural identity. In the case of al-Andalus, the study of Islam as a "lived" religion is all the more important, in that it was a predominantly Muslim society located on the frontier with Christianity.

[1] R. W. Bulliet, *Conversion to Islam in the Medieval Period*, Cambridge (Mass.), 1979, p. 114 *et seq.*

[2] The study of minorities in Islamic countries has held appeal for modern scholarship—a fact which perhaps betrays the uneasy attitudes of Western scholars towards their own minority groups in medieval and modern times. In Spain this trend in scholarship has historical roots and is fused, in certain cases, with the ideological assumption that Islamic civilisation (with its religion) was a mere accident—and an unfortunate accident at that—in the history of the Iberian Peninsula. Thus, much effort was devoted to demonstrating the impact of Christian culture, and pre-Islamic culture in general, on the life and practices of the Muslim "invaders", thus emphasising the continuity of a so-called Spanish "essence" throughout the ages (there are and have been, of course, exceptions to this position; on the different attitudes of Spanish Arabists and intellectuals, see J. T. Monroe, *Islam and the Arabs in Spanish Scholarship (Sixteenth Century to the Present)*, Leiden, 1970, especially Chapter X).

[3] See, for instance, the studies by F. de la Granja, "Fiestas cristianas en al-Andalus", *Al-Andalus*, 34, 1969, and 35, 1970, pp. 1-53 and 119-42 respectively.

[4] Ed. and trans. M. I. Fierro, Madrid, 1988.

[5] See, on this matter, W. A. Graham, "Islam in the Mirror of Ritual", in *Islam's Understanding of Itself*, ed. R. G. Hovannisian and S. Vryonis, Malibu, 1983, pp. 53-71.

[6] See M. Ayoub, "Thanksgiving and Praise in the Qur'ān and in Muslim Piety", *Islamochristiana*, 15, 1989, pp. 1-10.

[7] On this Cordoban traditionist, see M. L. Avila, "Nuevos datos para la biografía de Baqī b. Majlad", *Al-Qanṭara*, 6, 1985, pp. 321-67, and M. Marín, "Baqī b. Majlad y la introducción del estudio del ḥadīṯ en al-Andalus", *Al-Qanṭara*, 1, 1980, pp. 165-208.

[8] See his bio-bibliographical references in M. Marín, "Nómina de sabios de al-Andalus (93-350/711-961)", in *Estudios Onomástico-Biográficos de al-Andalus*, I, Madrid, 1988, No. 1225.

[9] For a detailed study of the different doctrinal aspects of this matter, see M. I. Fierro, "La polémique à propos de *raf' al-yadayn fī 'l-ṣalāt* dans al-Andalus", *Studia Islamica*, 65, 1988, pp. 68-93. A later *'ālim* who followed this practice was Ahmad b. 'Umar b. Manṣūr (d. 312/924) (see 'Iyāḍ, *Tartīb al-madārik wa-taqrīb al-masālik li-ma'rifat a'lām madhhab Mālik*, n. d.-1983, V, 215-16).

[10] Well reflected in the process suffered by Baqī b. Makhlad; see M. Marín, "Baqī b. Majlad", and M. I. Fierro, "The Introduction of *ḥadīth* in al-Andalus (2nd/8th-3rd/9th centuries)", *Der Islam*, 65, 1987, pp. 69-90.

[11] See M. Marín, "Una familia de ulemas cordobeses: los Banū Abī 'Īsà", *Al-Qanṭara*, 6, 1985, pp. 292-320.

[12] M. Makki, *Ensayo sobre las aportaciones orientales en la España musulmana*, Madrid, 1968, pp. 166-67. The number of *rak'a*s during the prayer was also subject to some discussion: see the biographies of the *qāḍī* Yaḥyā b. Ma'mar, in Ibn Ḥārith al-Khushanī, *Quḍāt Qurṭuba*, ed. and trans. J. Ribera, 82/101, and of Isḥāq b. Yaḥyā b. Yaḥyā, in 'Iyāḍ, *Tartīb al-madārik*, IV, 424.

[13] Ibn Ḥārith al Khushanī, *Quḍāt Qurṭuba*, 158/196.

[14] 'Iyāḍ, *Tartīb al-madārik*, IV, 450.

[15] Ibn al-Qūṭiyya, *Ta'rīkh iftitāḥ al-Andalus*, ed. and trans. J. Ribera, Madrid, 1926, 66/52; Ibn Ḥayyān, *Al-Muqtabis min anbā' ahl al-Andalus*, ed. M. 'A. Makkī, Beirut, 1973, p. 57; Ibn Ḥārith al-Khushanī, *Quḍāt Qurṭuba*, 81/100.

[16] Ibn 'Idhārī, *Al-Bayān al-mughrib fī akhbār al-Andalus wa 'l-Maghrib*, II, ed. G. Colin and E. Lévi-Provençal, Paris, 1951, p. 211.

[17] See *Encyclopaedia of Islam*, new ed., Leiden, 1960-, *s. v. du'ā'*.

[18] Both stories are recorded by Ibn Bashkuwāl, *Kitāb al-mustaghīthīn bi-llāh*, ed. M. Marín, Madrid, 1991, Nos. 149 and 150; see my introduction to the edition of the Arabic text, where other sources are mentioned.

[19] Ibn Ḥayyān, *Al-Muqtabis V*, ed. P. Chalmeta, F. Corriente and M. Sobh, Madrid, 1979, trans. M. J. Viguera and F. Corriente, Saragossa, 1981, 165/190-1.

[20] On the Cordoban (and other) *muṣallās* in al-Andalus, see L. Torres Balbás, "'*Muṣallà*' y '*šarī'a*' en las ciudades hispanomusulmanas", *Al-Andalus*, 13, 1948, pp. 167-80.

[21] On him see the introduction to the edition of his *Ta'rīkh* by J. Aguadé, Madrid, 1991.

[22] Ibn Ḥayyān, *Muqtabis* (ed. Makkī), pp. 46-47.

[23] See an example in al-Ḥimyarī, *Kitāb al-rawḍ al-mi'ṭār fī khabar al-aqṭār*, ed. and trans. E. Lévi-Provençal, Leiden, 1938, 141/169.

[24] Ibn Ḥayyān, *Muqtabis* (ed. Makkī), p. 51.

[25] Ibn Ḥārith al-Khushanī, *Quḍāt Qurṭuba*, 100/122.

[26] See T. Izutsu, *God and Man in the Koran*, Tokyo, 1964, pp. 147-48.

[27] See M. Piamenta, *Islam in Everyday Speech*, Leiden, 1979.

[28] 'Iyāḍ, *Tartīb al-madārik*, V, 200-09.

[29] *Ibid.*, p. 209.

[30] Ibn Ḥayyān, *Muqtabis V* (trans. Viguera and Corriente), p.92; also in Ibn 'Idhārī, *Bayān*, II, 114.

[31] See the case of Muḥammad b. 'Īsā al-A'shā, in M. Marín, "The Early Development of *zuhd* in al-Andalus", *Proceedings of the 15th Conference of the U. E. A. I.*, Utrecht (in press).

[32] 'Iyāḍ, *Tartīb al-madārik*, V, 197.

[33] Ibn Ḥayyān, *Al-Muqtabis fī akhbār bilād al-Andalus*, ed. 'A. 'A. al-Ḥajjī, Beirut, 1965, Spanish translation by E. García Gómez, *Anales palatinos del califa de Córdoba al-Ḥakam II*, Madrid, 1967, p. 141.

[34] On 'Ubayd Allāh b. Yaḥyā, see my article "Una familia de ulemas cordobeses", pp. 296-302.

[35] 'Iyāḍ, *Tartīb al-madārik*, IV, 423.

[36] *Ibid.*, V, 190.

[37] Ibn 'Idhārī, *Al-Bayān al-mughrib*, II, 287; the text refers to the second half of the 4th/10th century.

[38] 'Iyāḍ, *Tartīb al-madārik*, V, 154.

[39] *Ibid.*, IV, 142.

[40] *Ibid.*, V, 190.

[41] *Ibid.*, V, 156.

[42] An example in Ibn Bashkuwāl, *Ṣila*, No. 591.

[43] 'Iyāḍ, *Tartīb al-madārik*, IV, 423.

[44] See L. Molina, "Lugares de destino de los viajeros andalusíes en el *Ta'rīj* de Ibn al-Faraḍī", in *Estudios Onomástico-Biográficos de al-Andalus*, I, Madrid, 1988, pp. 585-610, and M. Marín, "Los ulemas de al-Andalus y sus maestros orientales" in *ibid.*, III, Granada, 1990, pp. 257-306.

[45] See the *Riḥla* of Ibn Jubayr (d. 614/1217), ed. W. Wright and J. De Goeje, Leiden, 1907.

[46] Ibn Bashkuwāl, *Ṣila*, No. 515.

[47] Ibn al-Faraḍī, *Ta'rīkh 'ulamā' al-Andalus*, Cairo, 1966, No. 906.

[48] Ibn al-Abbār, *Al-Takmila li-kitāb al-ṣila*, ed. 'I. al-Ḥusaynī, Cairo, 1955, No. 338, and Ibn Bashkuwāl, *Ṣila*, No. 1534.

[49] M. L. Avila, "Las mujeres sabias de al-Andalus", in *La mujer en al-Andalus*, ed. M. J. Viguera, Madrid, 1989, No. 92.

[50] See L. Kinberg, "What is Meant by *zuhd*?" and M. Marin, "The Early Development of *zuhd* in al-Andalus".

[51] 'Iyāḍ, *Tartīb al-madārik*, IV, 428.

[52] *Ibid.*, IV, 446.

[53] Ibn al-Faraḍī, *Ta'rīkh*, No. 909.

[54] Marín, "Nómina", No. 558.

[55] *Ibid.*, No. 763.

[56] See a study of these miracles in my introduction to Ibn Bashkuwāl's *Kitāb al-mustaghīthīn bi-llāh*.

[57] See the introductory study of M. I. Fierro in her edition of Ibn Waḍḍāḥ's *Kitāb al-bida'*, Madrid, 1988, p. 15.

[58] See section II.1 above.

59 Walking along a river, he saw one of the Banū Salama accompanied by a servant who carried a falcon. The servant was ordered to throw the falcon against a woman who was bathing her child in the river. Mother and son perished.

60 See M. Marín, *Individuo y sociedad en al-Andalus*, Madrid (in press), paragraph 2.2.1.

61 Ibn Bashkuwāl, *Kitāb al-mustaghīthīn*, No. 77.

62 I have studied the different opinions of *fuqahā'* on the case of a man accused of disturbing his neighbours with his nightly prayers in "Law and Piety: a Cordovan *fatwā*", *British Society for Middle Eastern Studies Bulletin*, 17, 1990, pp. 129-36.

63 The date of his death is unknown. He probably lived at the end of the 3th/9th century. See Makki, *Ensayo*, p. 157.

64 M. Marín, "Núcleos urbanos y actividad cultural en la Marca Media", in *Actas del Coloquio "La Fundación de Madrid"*, Madrid (in press), p. 12.

65 Marín, "Nómina", No. 838.

66 See M. Asín Palacios, *Abenmasarra y su escuela*, Madrid, 1914, and M. I. Fierro, *La heterodoxia en al-Andalus durante el periodo omeya*, Madrid, 1987, pp. 113-18.

67 M. Marín, "Un nuevo texto de Ibn Baškuwāl", *Al-Qanṭara*, 10, 1989, pp. 385-403.

BIBLIOGRAPHY

Abū Bakr al-Ṭurṭūshī, *Al-Duʿā' al-ma'thūr wa ādābu-hu*, ed. M. R. al-Dāya, Beirut, 1988.

Asín Palacios, M., *Abenmasarra y su escuela*, Madrid, 1914.

Avila, M. L., "Las mujeres sabias en al-Andalus", in *La mujer en al-Andalus*, ed. M. J. Viguera, Madrid, 1989, pp. 139-84).

——, "Nuevos datos para la biografía de Baqī b. Majlad", *Al-Qanṭara*, 6, 1985, pp. 321-67.

Ayoub, M., "Thanksgiving and Praise in the Qur'ān and in Muslim Piety", *Islamochristiana*, 15, 1989, pp. 1-10.

Bulliet, R. W., *Conversion to Islam in the Medieval Period*, Cambridge, Mass., 1979.

Fierro, M. I., *La heterodoxia en al-Andalus durante el periodo omeya*, Madrid, 1987.

——, "The Introduction of *ḥadīth* in al-Andalus (2nd/8th-3rd/9th centuries)", *Der Islam*, 66, 1988, pp. 68-93.

——, "La polémique à propos de *rafʿ al-yadayn fī l-ṣalāt* dans al-Andalus", *Studia Islamica*, 65, 1987, pp. 69-90.

Graham, W. A., "Islam in the Mirror of Ritual", in *Islam's Understanding of Itself*, ed. R. G. Hovannisian and S. Vryonis, Malibu, 1983, pp. 53-71.

Granja, F. de la, "Fiestas cristianas en al-Andalus (Materiales para su estudio). I: *al-Durr al-munazzam de al-ʿAzafī*", *Al-Andalus*, 34, 1969, pp. 1-53.

——, "Fiestas cristianas en al-Andalus (Materiales para su estudio). II: Textos de al-Ṭurṭušī, el cadi ʿIyāḍ y Wanšarīsī", *Al-Andalus*, 35, 1970, pp. 119-42.

Al-Ḥimyarī, *Kitāb al-rawḍ al-miʿṭār fī khabar al-aqṭār*, ed. and trans. E. Lévi-Provençal, Leiden, 1938.

Ibn al-Abbār, *Al-Takmila li-kitāb al-ṣila*, ed. ʿI. al-Ḥusaynī, Cairo, 1955.

Ibn Bashkuwāl, *Kitāb al-mustaghīthīn bi-llāh*, ed. M. Marín, Madrid, 1991.

——, *Kitāb al-ṣila*, ed. ʿI. al-ʿAṭṭār, Cairo, 1955.

Ibn al-Faraḍī, *Ta'rīkh ʿulamā' al-Andalus*, Cairo, 1966.

Ibn Ḥārith al-Khushanī, *Quḍāt Qurṭuba*, ed. and trans. J. Ribera, Madrid, 1914.

Ibn Ḥayyān, *Al-Muqtabis fī akhbar balad al-Andalus*, ed. ʿA. ʿA. al-Ḥajjī, Beirut, 1965; Spanish trans. by E. García Gómez, *Anales palatinos del califa de Córdoba al-Ḥakam II*, Madrid, 1967.

——, *Al-Muqtabis min anbā' ahl al-Andalus*, ed. M. ʿA. Makkī, Beirut, 1973.

——, *Al-Muqtabas V*, ed. P. Chalmeta, F. Corriente and M. Sobh, Madrid, 1979; trans. M. J. Viguera and F. Corriente, Saragossa, 1981.

Ibn ʿIdhārī, *Al-Bayān al-mughrib fī akhbar al-Andalus wa 'l-Maghrib*, I-II, ed. G. Colin and E. Lévi-Provençal, Paris, 1948-51; III, ed. E. Lévi-Provençal, Paris, 1930.

Ibn al-Qūṭiyya, *Ta'rīkh iftitāḥ al-Andalus*, ed. and trans. J. Ribera, Madrid, 1926.

ʿIyāḍ, al-Qāḍī, *Tartīb al-madārik wa-taqrīb al-masālik li-maʿrifat aʿlām madhhab Mālik*, Rabat, n. d.-1983.

Izutsu, T., *God and Man in the Koran*, Tokyo, 1964.
Kinberg, L., "What is Meant by *zuhd*?", *Studia Islamica*, 61, 1985, pp. 27-44.
Makki, M. A., *Ensayo sobre las aportaciones orientales en la España musulmana*, Madrid, 1968.
Marín, M., "Baqī b. Majlad y la introducción del estudio del *ḥadīṯ* en al-Andalus", *Al-Qanṭara*, 1, 1980, pp. 165-208.
——, "The Early Development of *zuhd* in al-Andalus", *Proceedings of the 15th Conference of the U.E.A.I.*, Utrecht (in press).
——, *Individuo y sociedad en al-Andalus*, Madrid (in press).
——, "Law and Piety: a Cordovan *fatwà*", *British Society for Middle Eastern Studies Bulletin*, 17, 1990, pp. 129-36.
——, "Los ulemas de al-Andalus y sus maestros orientales", in *Estudios Onomástico-Biográficos de al-Andalus*, III, Granada, 1990, pp. 257-306.
——, "Nómina de sabios de al-Andalus (93-350/711-961)", in *Estudios Onomástico-Biográficos de al-Andalus*, I, Madrid, 1988, pp. 23-182.
——, "Núcleos urbanos y actividad cultural en la Marca Media", in *Actas del Coloquio "La fundación de Madrid"*, Madrid (in press).
——, "Un nuevo texto de Ibn Baškuwāl: *Ajbār Abī Wahb*", *Al-Qanṭara*, 10, 1989, pp. 385-403.
——, "Una familia de ulemas cordobeses: los Banū Abī ʿĪsà", *Al-Qanṭara*, 6, 1985, pp. 292-320.
Molina, L., "Lugares de destino de los viajeros andalusíes en el *Taʾrīj* de Ibn al-Faraḍī", in *Estudios Onomástico-Biográficos de al-Andalus*, I, Madrid, 1988, pp. 585-610.
Monroe, J. T., *Islam and the Arabs in Spanish Scholarship (Sixteenth Century to the Present)*, Leiden, 1970.
Muḥammad b. Waḍḍāḥ, *Kitāb al-bidaʿ (Tratado contra las innovaciones)*, new ed. and trans. by M. I. Fierro, Madrid, 1988.
Piamenta, M., *Islam in Everyday Arabic Speech*, Leiden, 1979.
Torres Balbás, L., "Muṣallà" y "šarīʿa" en las ciudades hispanomusulmanas", *Al-Andalus*, 13, 1948, pp. 167-80.

HERESY IN AL-ANDALUS

MARÍA ISABEL FIERRO

I. Al-Andalus without Heretics: the Image

An 8th/14th century text[1] on the virtues of al-Andalus counts among them the fact that a heretical sect (*ṭāʾifa mubtadiʿa*) or sectarian group (*firqa mutashayyiʿa*) had appeared only rarely and briefly; and the author of the text, the Andalusī al-Fakhkhār (d. 723/1323), remarks that when a person belonging to these groups appeared, God saved al-Andalus from his influence by destroying and annihilating him, as, for instance, in the case of Ibn Aḥlā in Lorca, al-Fazārī in Málaga and al-Ṣaffār in Almería. Quoting al-Ḥumaydī (d. 488/1095), al-Fakhkhār adds that the names of the Prophet's Companions were always mentioned from the *minbar*s with due respect; in other words, al-Andalus had also been kept free of Shiʿism.[2]

Earlier al-Ḥumaydī's teacher, Ibn Ḥazm (d. 456/1064), had stated in his *Risāla fī faḍāʾil ahl al-Andalus*, written before 246/1035, that controversies were mild in al-Andalus and that there was no division into sects (*lam tatajādhab fīhā 'l-khuṣūm wa lā khtalafat fīhā 'l-niḥal*).[3] When writing this *Risāla*, Ibn Ḥazm could not foresee that he himself would be considered a scholar deviating from orthodoxy. However, Ibn Ḥazm gives a rather different picture of al-Andalus in a later work, his *Kitāb al-fiṣal fī 'l-milal wa 'l-ahwāʾ wa 'l-niḥal*, where he mentions the presence in al-Andalus of Khārijis, Muʿtazilis, Murjis (Ashʿaris) and Sufis, the last two being the sects within Islam that he wished most vigorously to refute. He also notes the presence of sceptics who denied the existence of God and prophecy, or who believed in *takāfuʾ al-adilla*, "the equivalence of proofs", i.e., the impossibility of proving the truth of God, the prophets or any religion.[4]

The Eastern author al-Muqaddasī had earlier, in the 4th/10th century, given a very orthodox image of al-Andalus. Referring to its *madhāhib*, he says that al-Andalus follows the doctrines of Mālik alone, and the Quranic reading (*qirāʾa*) of Nāfiʿ, and that Andalusis claim to know only the Quran and the *Muwaṭṭaʾ* of Mālik. If they seized a Ḥanafī or a Shāfiʿī, they expelled him from the country, and if they discovered a Muʿtazilī or a Shiʿite, they sometimes killed him.[5]

Al-Muqaddasī's text introduces an element that has been considered of vital importance in constructing the image of the "orthodoxy" of al-Andalus, namely that it is a stronghold of Mālikism, which, according to this Eastern geographer, forestalled any rivalry from the other legal schools by expelling their followers, while guarding against possible sectarian doctrines by eliminating anyone propagating these.

Mālikism was, indeed, the predominant trend within Andalusī Islam. The story of its introduction and rise to hegemony in the Peninsula has been told several times,[6] the main stages being as follows. The school of the Syrian al-Awzāʿī (d. 157/774) was the first to be followed in al-Andalus, due to the strong presence of Syrians, before Andalusī students who travelled to Medina during the lifetime of Mālik b. Anas (d. 179/795) brought back his teachings. The most important of Mālik's Andalusī disciples was Yaḥyā b. Yaḥyā al-Laythī (d. 234/848), whose *riwāya* of the *Muwaṭṭaʾ* attained the highest authority in Western Islam; succeeding generations of scholars then studied with the Egyptian and Medinese disciples of Mālik, and their teachings were collected in such compilations of Mālikī *fiqh* as the *Wāḍiḥa* of ʿAbd al-Malik b. Ḥabīb (d. 238/852) and the *Mustakhraja* of al-ʿUtbī (d. 255/869), these compilations, together with the *Mudawwana* of Saḥnūn,[7] becoming the fundamental works of Andalusī Mālikism. The reception of Mālikism was accompanied by the veneration of Mālik,[8] although Andalusis were not in fact strict followers of his teachings, based on his legal reasoning (*raʾy*), as compiled in the *Muwaṭṭaʾ*. As a matter of fact, they often gave preference to the teachings of his pupils, and especially to the *raʾy* of Ibn al-Qāsim.[9] Mālikis are in fact described in Andalusī sources as *ahl/aṣḥāb al-raʾy*,[10] who refused to have anything to do with *ḥadīth*.

There are different interpretations of the success of Mālikism,[11] but the most convincing of these seems to point to a geographical reason: when performing the *riḥla fī ṭalab al-ʿilm* and the pilgrimage during the 2nd/8th-3rd/9th centuries, Andalusis travelled and studied in places such as *Ifrīqiya* and Egypt where Mālikism had already spread from Medina, Medina itself also being a city much visited by them; on the other hand, they hardly every visited Iraq,[12] where Ḥanafism was predominant. If, however, this factor was instrumental in the introduction and spread of Mālikism in al-Andalus, its hegemony was mainly due to political reasons. In 189/805 and 202/818 there were rebellions by the people of Córdoba against al-Ḥakam I (180/796-206/822), in which some Mālikī *fuqahāʾ* took part; and, although the Umayyad *amīr* was able to defeat the rebels, he realised that he could not, from then onwards, do without the support of the *fuqahāʾ* in controlling further outbreaks of discontent against his policies. The lesson was well learned by his successor ʿAbd al-Raḥmān II (206/822-238/852), who sought, and obtained, the collaboration of the *fuqahāʾ*. As generally occurred with the *fuqahāʾ* of the different *madhāhib* in other regions of the Islamic world,[13] Mālikis in al-Andalus opted for quietism in exchange for their becoming custodians of the religious law (*sharīʿa*). During the reign of ʿAbd al-Raḥmān II's successor, Muḥammad (238/852-273/886), the hegemony or *ahl al-raʾy* achieved by the Mālikis was challenged by the growing importance of the *ahl al-ḥadīth* and the influence of Shāfiʿism.

ʿAbd al-Malik b. Ḥabīb, mentioned above as one of the *fuqahāʾ* responsible for the introduction of Mālikī teachings, is also credited with having been the first to introduce *ḥadīth* into al-Andalus (attribution of the same role to Ṣaʿṣaʿa b. Sallām and Muʿāwiya b. Ṣāliḥ, who both died towards the end of the 2nd/8th century, is not supported by available evidence).[14] Prophetic traditions introduced by Ibn Ḥabīb correspond to the so-called "early *ḥadīth*"; and, as the material was far from meeting the requirements of classical *ʿilm al-ḥadīth* (see below), his transmissions were criticised and rejected by later traditionists.

Two scholars, both of whom died at the end of the 3rd/9th century, were the protagonists of the second phase of the reception of *ḥadīth*: these were Baqī b. Makhlad (d. 276/889) and Muḥammad b. Waḍḍāḥ (d. 287/900),[15] who, trained by Iraqi teachers, introduced into al-Andalus not only new *ḥadīth* material, but also the science of *ḥadīth* (*ʿilm al-ḥadīth*). Until their time, *fiqh* (introduced, as noted above, in the second half of the 2nd/8th century) and *ḥadīth* were seen as separate and different entities, and the scholars who introduced *fiqh* (mainly Mālikī *fiqh*) are not mentioned in the sources as traditionists. The reception of *ḥadīth* as a structured corpus of legal material, over and above the limited amount of *ḥadīth* embedded in Mālikī works, aroused the opposition of Andalusī Mālikis because of the threat this represented to their established doctrinal teachings and to existing legal practice in al-Andalus—an opposition which led to the accusation of *zandaqa* against Baqī b. Makhlad, who was, like Ibn Waḍḍāḥ, a traditionist, but was also the introducer of Shāfiʿī's works and an opponent of the *ahl al-raʾy*, whereas Ibn Waḍḍāḥ was and remained a Mālikī who tried to reconcile the positions of the *ahl al-raʾy* and the *ahl al-ḥadīth*. The *amīr* Muḥammad, however, supported Baqī, and, thanks to his intervention, the persecution of Baqī did not lead to his execution. The *amīr* thus played the role of umpire between the *ahl al-raʾy* and the *ahl al-ḥadīth*, without, though, replacing the former by the latter, probably because he found it useful for his own policy to have the scholars divided. Between the end of the 3rd/9th century and the first half of the 4th/10th century, the Shāfiʿis had a certain weight in the intellectual milieu; nevertheless, they succeeded neither in establishing their doctrine nor in displacing the Mālikis. In the year 338/950, ʿAbd Allāh, a son of the caliph ʿAbd al-Raḥmān III, was accused of plotting against his father and his brother (the future al-Ḥakam II), and was executed. He was a Shāfiʿī and his failure is linked to the failure of Shāfiʿism in al-Andalus. Its followers had always been, and now continued to be, a minority, and a few years after ʿAbd Allāh's death, ʿAbd al-Raḥmān III openly proclaimed Mālikism as the "official" doctrine of his reign, the caliph al-Ḥakam II subsequently thinking it worthwhile to do the same.[16] During the 4th/10th century, however, the Mālikis could not avoid the intellectual pressure of the traditionists and of al-Shāfiʿī's doctrine of the *uṣūl al-fiqh*; and, as such, they were forced to pay more attention to *ḥadīth*, although they did so without introducing any substantial change in their doctrine and practice.[17] From the end of the 4th/10th century onwards we have evidence of Mālikī activity in the field of the *uṣūl al-fiqh*, this trend reaching its peak with the work of the Mālikī-As͟hʿarī Abū 'l-Walīd al-Bājī (d. 474/1081), the author of a book entitled *Iḥkām al-fuṣūl fī aḥkām al-uṣūl*, which he probably wrote after the famous polemic in which he engaged with Ibn Ḥazm.[18] Al-Bājī's education and training took place mainly in the East, where he studied the art of polemics (*jadal*), As͟hʿarī theology and the Eastern Mālikī tradition of *uṣūl al-fiqh*, and he was respected and sought after for his knowledge when he returned to al-Andalus. In connection with his reliance on Prophetic tradition, al-Bājī transmitted the *ḥadīt͟h* according to which the Prophet wrote (*kataba*) on the day of Ḥudaybiyya (*ḥadīt͟h al-muqāḍāt*), and openly maintained that he did so, despite his being *ummī*. Although the hostility he met on this account did not lead to his being placed on trial, he was accused of infidelity (*kufr*), heresy (*zandaqa*) and of introducing innovations (*tabdīʿ*).[19]

Similar accusations had, as we shall see in the next section, been brought against Andalusis before al-Bājī; and the material collected there will show how the authors quoted at the beginning of this paper tended to play down the presence of heresy in al-Andalus.

II. The Heretics of al-Andalus

One of the terms commonly used in Islam to define a concept similar to "heresy" is *bidʿa* (pl. *bidaʿ*), or "innovation". An author as early as the Cordoban Muḥammad b. Waḍḍāḥ wrote a treatise devoted to the reprobation of innovations, where the cases he mentions, however, pertained to the sphere of ritual practices (*ʿibādāt*) and not of dogma. Although he makes no explicit reference to al-Andalus, all the practices he condemns were known in the Peninsula by his time, some of them also being condemned by authors in the following centuries, while others, such as the use of the rosary, were forgotten because other wide diffusion had secured their legitimacy.[20] This process can be checked thanks to the continuity of *kutub al-bidaʿ* written by Andalusī Mālikis.[21]

Numerous Andalusis are described in the biographical dictionaries as being "severe against innovators" (*s͟hadīd ʿalā ahl al-bidaʿ*), and dedicated to putting an end to reprehensible behaviour (*tag͟hyīr al-munkar*). The sources do not, however, always specify who the innovators were, or what was considered reprehensible and required changing. A diachronic study of the material preserved in the *kutub al-bidaʿ* and other sources shows that the concept of the "innovator", or of what was deemed reprehensible from a Mālikī point of view, was not always the same over the centuries: practice did not always correspond to what was established in the doctrine, and the doctrine in turn was able partly to adapt to the changing practice.[22]

The *fatāwā* on the subject of innovators and innovations[23] reveal the reluctance of the *fuqahā'* to commit themselves to an uncompromising attitude on a matter so elusive and difficult to define. The Andalusī Ibn Sahl (d. 486/1093) has preserved, in his collection of *nawāzil* entitled *al-Aḥkām al-kubrā*, a question posed to the Cordoban *muftī* Muḥammad b. ʿAttāb (d. 462/1070) on the difference between the *ahl al-bidaʿ* and grave sinners (*ahl al-kabā'ir*). Ibn ʿAttāb begins his *fatwā* by indicating his deep dislike of dealing with such a polemical issue, on which there were so many different opinions both within the Mālikī school itself and outside it, and his final statement is that the destiny of both groups depends upon the will of God. The same reluctance to state a clear judgement appears also in the case of al-Aṣīlī (d. 392/1001) and Ibn al-Makwī (d. 401/1010), who were asked whether innovators should be declared infidels (*al-takfīr*): they too responded without committing themselves. Ibn Sahl, however, dared to give a more specific answer. According to him, there were two kinds of innovator: the first kind, such as extremist Shiʿites who believed in the divinity of ʿAlī or in his being a prophet, undoubtedly lapsed into infidelity (*kufr*); while the second kind, such as those Shiʿites who limited themselves to exalting the imamate of ʿAlī and his descendants, and stating that ʿAlī was the most excellent Muslim, were judged only to be straying from the right path, deviating from the truth and abandoning tradition and the community (*ḍalāl wa-zaygh ʿan al-ḥaqq wa ʿudūl ʿan al-sunna wa 'l-jamāʿa*).[24]

As for the accusation of *zandaqa*, Mālik b. Anas mentions it in his *Muwaṭṭa'* under the heading devoted to *ridda* or apostasy, a crime punished in Islamic law by the death penalty. According to Mālik's view, the *zindīq* is an apostate who has secretly fallen away from Islam under the cloak of outward conformity, and he must be beheaded just like the apostate who does not hide his apostasy. However, Mālik grants the latter the opportunity of repentance (*al-istitāba*) and reconversion while denying the same opportunity to the former. The main characteristic of the *zindīq* is in fact his hypocrisy and concealment of his true beliefs; there is thus no way to be certain of the truth of his statements, and especially of the sincerity of his repentance. This doctrine was adopted by such Maghribi and Andalusī Mālikī scholars as ʿAbd al-Mālik b. Ḥabīb, Ibn Abī Zayd al-Qayrawānī (d. 386/996), Ibn ʿAbd al-Barr (d. 463/1070) and Ibn Farḥūn (d. 799/1397). When Mālik included mention of the *zindīq* in the *Muwaṭṭa'*, he must have had in mind the Manichaeans of his own times, who were secretly unfaithful while openly professing Islam, and whom he considered the most representative example of apostates who concealed their apostasy. In fact Mālik did not consider every "cloaked" apostate a *zindīq*, but this nuance is lost in later Mālikī works, where the word is applied to every Muslim considered to have become apostate while failing to admit his new belief or lack of belief. This Mālikī doctrine obviously opens the door to the legal possibility of eliminating doctrinal opponents under the accusation of *zandaqa*, by giving them no chance of avoiding the death penalty.[25]

The heretics cited by al-Fakhkhār in the text mentioned at the beginning of this essay belong to the 7th/13th century, and their careers, influence and eventual defeat have yet to be studied. The Andalusī Mālikī-Ashʿarī Abū Bakr b. Al-ʿArabī (d. 543/1148) informs us of two other Andalusī heretics whose names he gives to illustrate people who have gone astray (*qawm min al-ḍullāl*), namely Muḥammad b. Masarra (d. 319/931) and Maslama b. Qāsim (d. 353/964),[26] their deviation taking the form of suspected Bāṭinism.

Muḥammad b. Masarra (d. 319/931) is one of eight Andalusis charged with *zandaqa* between the 2nd/8th and the 5th/11th century,[27] and in his case, and in that of ʿAbd al-Aʿlā b. Wahb (d. 261/874), the accusation sprang from their adherence to Muʿtazilī views.[28] No trial took place, however, and their lives were not under threat; nor were the other Muʿtazilis recorded by the sources persecuted or charged with heresy. It must also be pointed out that Ibn Masarra's followers were not specifically accused of *zandaqa*—or at least this word is not recorded in the edicts promulgated against them by ʿAbd al-Raḥmān III, where the words *bidʿa*, *hawa*, *fitna*, *zaygh*, *ḍalāl* and *ilḥād* are used. Their books were burned and we are told that they were given the opportunity of repentance,[29] which, as we have seen, was not granted to those accused of *zandaqa*.

The accusation of *zandaqa* against al-Bājī, already mentioned, forced him to write a *Risāla* defending his interpretation of the *ḥadīth al-muqāḍāt*. Although there seem to have been certain attempts to prosecute him, there was no trial.

Two accusations of *zandaqa* did lead to trials, but not to capital punishment. Baqī b. Makhlad[30] was prosecuted for his membership of the *ahl al-ḥadīth* and his independence of the Mālikī school; and, if we recall that none of his Muʿtazilī contemporaries were prosecuted, we may conclude that the Mālikis felt a greater threat from the doctrines of the traditionists than from those of the Muʿtazilis. In the case of Baqī, they did not succeed in obtaining the *amīr*'s support against him, and thus failed in their attempt to rid themselves of a doctrinal opponent who was not perceived as a threat to the State. The other trial took place in the times of al-Manṣūr b. Abī ʿĀmir, under the caliphate of Hishām II.[31] The accused were scholars and poets interested in theology, philosophy and logic, such as Ibn al-Iflīlī (d. 441/1050), Saʿīd b. Fatḥūn al-Saraqusṭī, and also an Umayyad prince. The accusation of *zandaqa* and the resulting trial may have been one of the steps taken by al-Manṣūr to secure the support of the Mālikis, some of whom regarded an interest in non-Islamic sciences with suspicion, but it can also be assumed that al-Manṣūr feared these scholars might, during their meetings, be hatching a plot to end his power and replace the caliph Hishām II by an Umayyad pretender. At the trial, the Umayyad prince narrowly escaped the death penalty, while Ibn al-Iflīlī was imprisoned for a period and Saʿīd b. Faṭḥūn left al-Andalus.

In three cases accusations of *zandaqa* led to the execution of the accused: these were the cases of Muṭarrif, the son of the Umayyad *amīr* ʿAbd Allāh (275/888-300/912), of Abū 'l-Khayr in the reign of al-Ḥakam II (350/961-366-976),[32] and of Ibn Ḥātim al-Ṭulayṭulī during the reign of the party-king of Toledo al-Ma'mūn.[33] The first two were suspected of plotting against the existing rulers, Muṭarrif being merely an unsuccessful pretender, but Abū 'l-Khayr being, apparently, both a political plotter and a sectarian, more specifically a Shiʿite agent of the Fāṭimids. In the case of Ibn Ḥātim, political and religious motives for his trial are again intermingled: he seems to have been the scapegoat in the struggle between the two parties competing for political power in Toledo. I assume that he belonged to the party of the Banū 'l-Ḥadīdī, a family of notables connected with a group of scholars who had received a traditional education in Islamic sciences, but who, at the same time, had become interested and involved in studying the non-Islamic sciences. The most striking accusation against Ibn Ḥātim was his denial of the asceticism of the Prophet, a feature of Muḥammad's biography that was being increasingly stressed in al-Andalus in the context of the rising current of asceticism and mysticism, but also as a result of the polemics engaged by Muslims with Jews and Christians. Ibn Ḥātim's trial took place one year after the Muslim town of Barbastro had fallen into Christian hands (in 456/1064), an event that shocked the Muslims of al-Andalus, as it was the first major town to be lost (Coimbra was also conquered by the Christians in the same year). An ascetic of Toledo, Ibn Labīd, who is defined by the sources as *murābiṭ* and *muḥtasib*, showed extreme zeal in pursuing Ibn Ḥātim. He may have been an agent of the party struggling against the Banū 'l-Ḥadīdī, but more probably he acted out of a concern not to allow a heretic, who might contaminate the rest of the community, to go unpunished. His concern shows how Andalusī Islam of the 5th/11th century was on its guard against anything that might be seen as helping the Christians in their political and ideological offensive.[34]

Apart from the cases described above, there were people whose religious beliefs were suspect, but who were not accused of *zandaqa*—or, at least, that accusation is not recorded in the sources. The case of Ibn Ḥazm has already been mentioned: although his Ẓāhirism was seen as deviating from orthodoxy, he was never brought to trial; and, while it is true that his books were burned in Seville, it seems that the main reason was not his legal doctrines, but the fact that he had denounced as an impostor the Umayyad caliph proclaimed by the ʿAbbādids.[35] One of Ibn Ḥazm's teachers, Abū 'l-Walīd Hishām b. Aḥmad al-Waqqashī (408/1017-489/1095), and his contemporary al-Ḥannāṭ al-Kafīf (d. 437/1045) were regarded as suspect in their religion because of their interest in logic,[36] but, as in the case of the Muʿtazilīs, this did not put their lives in danger.

A special case is the trial of Abū ʿUmar al-Ṭalamankī (d. 428/1036 or 429/1037), a scholar whose works and activities aimed at the spiritual renovation of Islam by ascetic/mystical means. He was accused of having doctrines similar to those of the Khārijis, and of *khilāf al-sunna*, that is, innovation; the *qāḍī* in charge of his trial (in 425/1034) acquitted him. Although the sources give very little insight into the motives behind the trial, it is possible that the issue at stake was the doctrine of the imamate held by al-Ṭalamankī, which seems to have been that the *imām* should be the best Muslim, regardless of his genealogy. There is some evidence too that al-Ṭalamankī himself was considered a leader of the community by some of his followers, a path that was later followed by the mystic Ibn Qasī (d. 546/1151), who proclaimed himself *imām*.

There were even Andalusis who went so far as to proclaim themselves prophets.[37] Abū ʿUbayd al-Bakrī mentions that Yūnus al-Barghawāṭī made the *riḥla* to the East together with other North Africans and Andalusis, of whom three claimed to be prophets, including Yūnus himself.[38] This *riḥla* took place in the first half of the 3rd/9th century.

In the year 237/851 a teacher (*muʿallim*) who claimed to be a prophet rebelled in the east of al-Andalus. He made a peculiar interpretation (*ta'wīl*) of the Quran, preaching that it was forbidden to cut the moustache and the nails, or to depilate the body, his slogan being *lā taghyīr li-khalqi 'llāh*. He was crucified, and while on the cross he pronounced the Quranic verse XL, 29: "Would you kill a man who says 'My lord is God'?".[39]

In the year 288/901 the rebellion of Ibn al-Qiṭṭ took place. He was member of the Umayyad family, who initially managed to attract the support of Berber tribes by means of predictions and a call for *jihād* against the Christians; soon he presented himself as the Mahdī and came to be considered a prophet by his followers, capable of performing miracles. He was eventually defeated and killed in his campaign against the Christians.[40]

In the year 333/944 a man in Lisbon, who claimed to be a descendant of ʿAbd al-Muṭṭalib and of Fāṭima (probably not the daughter of the Prophet, but ʿAbd al-Muṭṭalib's wife of the same name, and the grandmother of ʿAlī b. Abī Ṭālib), stated that he was a prophet and that the angel Jibrīl had visited him with a revelation. He gave his followers a set of traditions and laws, among them that they should shave their heads, a practice common among Khārijis. He suddenly disappeared.[41]

The head of the Masarrī group of Pechina (Almería), Ismāʿīl b. ʿAbd Allāh al-Ruʿaynī (alive in the first half of the 5th/11th century), held that it was possible to acquire prophecy, and Ibn Masarra himself was accused by those writers refuting his doctrines of having claimed to be a prophet.[42] None of them lost his life because of such a doctrine.

If we compare al-Andalus with other regions of Islam, there are few examples of sectarian mobilisation. Khārijism, already defeated in the 2nd/8th century,[43] was restricted to the Berbers, who appear to have been the only group among the population of the Peninsula to express their discontent in sectarian terms; the followers of the "al-Fāṭimī", who rebelled during the reign of ʿAbd al-Raḥmān I, were Berbers,[44] as were the followers of the Mahdī Ibn al-Qiṭṭ, both these movements being influenced by Shiʿism. In other words, social, political and economic tensions in al-Andalus hardly every gave rise to sectarian movements.

III. Conclusions

The comments of Al-Fakhkhār and Ibn Ḥazm cited at the beginning of this article are to be expected from the genre of *faḍāʾil*. The point they wished to make was not that al-Andalus was completely safe from heretics, but rather that heretics were few and successfully eliminated, and this viewpoint has helped to build an image of al-Andalus as the land of monolithic Mālikism, which not only refused to allow any other legal school to prosper, but was itself free of changes and developments, regarding with suspicion any novelty in terms of legal, theological and ascetic/mystical doctrines. This is the impression given, for example, by Abū Bakr b. al-ʿArabī: "Imitation became their [i.e. the Mālikis'] religion and emulation their conviction. Whenever someone came from the East with [new] knowledge, they prevented him from spreading it and humiliated him, unless he went into hiding among them, acting as a Mālikī and putting his knowledge in a position of subordination".[45] One of the methods available to Andalusī Mālikis to rid the region of new doctrines was to dismiss them as innovations and heresies; and this they did. The accusation of *zandaqa*, moreover, could lead to the death penalty, although Mālikis appear to have been reluctant to formulate it: the cases we have examined show that when the accusation was in fact formulated, and led to the execution of the accused, it was because the alleged *zindīq* was seen mainly as a political threat, or as a plotter against the existing ruler. Among the "false prophets" recorded by the sources, only those who accompanied their claim to prophecy with a rebellion put their lives in danger.

Contrary to what al-Muqaddasī suggests, the maintenance and success of Mālikism should be looked for not in the physical elimination of its enemies, but in its capacity to survive the challenge of the new doctrines by adapting to them; in other words, in its capacity to change while preserving its identity.[46] This is a story yet to be told in detail, though there exists a highly ironical text written by an Andalusī logician that points in this direction.

Ibn Ṭumlūs (d. 620/1223), in the introduction to his treatise on logic,[47] tells how those who devoted themselves to the study of logic in his time were accused of committing innovations (*bidaʿ*) and heresy (*zandaqa*). He was even on the verge of abandoning his interest in logic, when he realised two things: first, that the accusers were people with no idea what logic was and why it should be condemned, and thus followed the "certitude of the weak" (*yaqīn al-ḍuʿafāʾ*)—that is, they accepted things out of imitation of a previous authority (*al-taqlīd*) without checking for themselves, a phenomenon frequent in every religion (*milla*); and second, he realised that al-Andalus had been conquered by people who lacked any knowledge except that of *fiqh*, so that they ended up by regarding *fiqh* as the only science and everything that contradicted it as infidelity and heresy (*al-kufr wa 'l-zandaqa*). They brought their accusations against Baqī b. Makhlad because of his introduction of *ḥadīth*, but afterwards became accustomed to the new doctrines, with the result that what had once been considered reprehensible turned out to be considered good, and what had been considered infidelity and heresy was later embraced in faith and religion (*fa-ʿāda mā kāna munkaran ʿindahum maʿrūfan wa-mā ʿtaqadūhu kufran wa-zandaqa īmānan wa-dīnan ḥaqqan*). When the science of *uṣūl al-dīn* was introduced later on, the same process took place: first condemnation, then, in the end, acceptance (although with more reservations than in the case of *ḥadīth*). Then the books of al-Ghazālī were introduced into al-Andalus, and again the new doctrines were considered infidelity and heresy, until the Almohads arrived, and those who had rejected al-Ghazālī's books read them again and realised that they were in accordance with religious law. The conclusion reached by Ibn Ṭumlūs was a commonsense one: it was clear that Andalusis started by rejecting the doctrines that they in the end accepted, albeit with reservations. Thus, he did not abandon logic, being sure that sooner or later it too would become acceptable to the *fuqahāʾ*.

1 See M. I. Fierro and S. Faghia, "Un nuevo texto de tradiciones escatólogicas sobre al-Andalus", *Sharq al-Andalus*, 7, 1990, Nos. 14 and 13.

2 Neither al-Ḥumaydī nor al-Fakhkhār make reference to the fact that ʿUmar b. Ḥafṣūn, at the time of his alliance with the Fāṭimids, is alleged to have practised the Shiʿite rites of the call to prayer, which included the disqualification of the first caliphs: see M. I. Fierro, *La Heterodoxia en al-Andalus durante el periodo omeya*, Madrid, 1987, pp. 122-23.

3 See the Arabic text of the *Risāla* in al-Maqqarī, *Nafḥ al-ṭīb min ghuṣn al-Andalus al-raṭīb*, ed. I. ʿAbbās, Beirut, 1398/1968, III, 176; French translation by C. Pellat, "Ibn Ḥazm, bibliographe et apologiste de l'Espagne musulmane", *Al-Andalus*, 19, 1954, p. 90.

4 On heterodoxy in al-Andalus during the times of the party-kings, see my study in Vol. VIII of the *Historia de España fundada por R. Menéndez Pidal y dirigida por J. Ma Jover Zamora* (in preparation).

5 *Aḥsan al-taqāsīm fī maʿrifat al-aqālīm*, ed. M. J. De Goeje, 2nd ed., Leiden, 1906, p. 236. As I have shown in *Heterodoxia*, p. 176, al-Muqaddasī's view is influenced by the situation existing in al-Andalus during the times of al-Manṣūr b. Abī ʿĀmir (366/977-392/1002) .

6 See the studies by I. Goldziher, J. López Ortiz, E. Lévi-Provençal, H. R. Idris, H. Monès, M. A. Makki, J. Aguadé and M. I. Fierro noted in the bibliography following.

7 See M. Muranyi, *Materialen zur mālikitischen Rechtsliteratur*, Wiesbaden, 1984. The transmission of the *Mudawwana* in al-Andalus has been studied by J. M. Fórneas, "Datos para un estudio de la *Mudawwana* de Saḥnūn en al-Andalus", *Actas del IV Coloquio Hispano-Tunecino (Palma de Mallorca 1979)*, Madrid, 1983, pp. 93-118, and M. Muranyi, "Notas sobre la transmisión escrita de la *Mudawwana* en Ifrīqiya según algunos manuscritos recientemente descubiertos (Qairawāner Miszellaneen III)", *Al-Qanṭara*, 10, 1989, pp. 215-31.

[8] See A. M. Turki, "La vénération pour Mālik et la physionomie du malikisme andalou", *Studia Islamica*, 33, 1971, pp. 41-65.

[9] See two examples in M. I. Fierro, "La polémique a propos de *raf' al-yadayn fī 'l-ṣalāt*", *Studia Islamica*, 65, 1987, pp. 69-90, and "Los mālikíes de al-Andalus y los dos árbitros (*al-ḥakamān*)", *Al-Qanṭara*, 6, 1985, pp. 79-102.

[10] On the general question of the *ra'y* of the Mālikis, see R. Brunschvig, "Polémiques médiévales autour du rite de Mālik", *Al-Andalus*, 15, 1950, pp. 321-68. For the use of the term *ra'y* in Andalusī sources, see D. Urvoy, *Le monde des ulémas andalous du Ve/XIe au VIIe/XIIIe siècle. Etude sociologique*, Geneva, 1978, appendix.

[11] See J. Aguadé, "Some remarks about sectarian movements in al-Andalus", *Studia Islamica*, 64, 1986, pp. 54-62, and Fierro, *Heterodoxia*, pp. 33-37.

[12] See the percentages in L. Molina, "Lugares de destino de los viajeros andalusíes en el *Ta'rīj* de Ibn al-Faraḍī", *Estudios onomástico-biográficos de al-Andalus*, ed. M. Marín, Madrid, 1988, I, 585-610.

[13] See I. M. Lapidus, "The separation of state and religion in the development of early Islamic society", *IJMES*, 6, 1975, pp. 363-85, and M. Cook, "Activism and quietism in Islam: The Case of the Early Murji'a", *Islam and Power*, ed. A. S. Cudsi and A. E. H. Dessouki, London, 1981, pp. 15-23.

[14] See M. I. Fierro, "Mu'āwiya b. Ṣāliḥ al-Ḥaḍramī al-Ḥimṣī: historia y leyenda", *Estudios onomástico-biográficos*, pp. 281-411, and "The introduction of *ḥadīth* in al-Andalus (2nd/8th-3rd/9th centuries)", *Der Islam*, 66, 1989, pp. 68-93.

[15] On these, see M. Marín, "Baqī b. Majlad y la introducción del estudio del *Ḥadīṯ* en al-Andalus", *Al-Qanṭara*, 1, 1981, pp. 165-208, and my study accompanying my edition and translation of Ibn Waḍḍāḥ's *Kitāb al-bida'*, new ed., Madrid, 1988.

[16] See Fierro, *Heterodoxia*, sections 8.4. and 9.1.

[17] See Fierro, "La polémique" and "Los mālikíes de al-Andalus".

[18] See A. M. Turki, *Polémiques entre Ibn Ḥazm et Bāǧī sur les principes de la loi musulmane. Essai sur le littéralisme zahirite et la finalité malikite*, Algiers, 1973.

[19] For a detailed study of the whole affair see Ibn 'Aqīl al-Ẓāhirī's study accompanying his edition of al-Bājī's *Taḥqīq al-madhhab* (Riyadh, 1403/1983), written by al-Bājī to defend his position and counter the refutations written against him.

[20] See the study accompanying my edition and translation of Ibn Waḍḍāḥ's *Kitāb al-bida'*, especially pp. 92-117. See also M. I. Fierro, "Una refutación contra Ibn Masarra", *Al-Qanṭara*, 10, 1989, pp. 273-75.

[21] See the study accompanying my edition and translation of Ibn Waḍḍāh's *Kitāb al-bida'*, pp. 117-19.

[22] See *ibid.*, pp. 92-97. See also M. K. Masud, *Islamic Legal Philosophy. A Study of Abū Isḥaq al-Shāṭibī's Life and Thought*, Islamabad, 1977, on this late Andalusī author who also wrote a treatise against *bida'*.

[23] A section of the collection of *fatāwā* by al-Wansharīsī is devoted to the *bida'* and many Andalusī *fatāwā* are collected within it. It has been published as an independent work by H. Pérès under the title of *Al-Mustaḥsan min al-bida'* (Algiers, 1946). See also the collection of *fatāwā* given by Abū Isḥāq al-Shāṭibī (ed. M. Abū 'l-Ajfān, Tunis, 1405/1984) and my review in *Sharq al-Andalus*, 4, 1987, pp. 351-54.

[24] See Ibn Sahl, *Tres documentos sobre procesos de herejes en la España musulmana/ Thalāth wathā'iq fī muḥārabat al-ahwā' wa 'l-bida' fī 'l-Andalus*, ed. 'A. W. Khallāf, Cairo, 1981, pp. 25-38.

[25] See M. I. Fierro, "Accusations of *zandaqa* in al-Andalus", *Quaderni di Studi Arabi*, 5-6, 1987-88, pp. 251-58, and *Heterodoxia*, pp. 179-86.

[26] See his *Al-'Awāṣim min al-qawāṣim*, ed. 'Ammār Ṭālibī, in *Arā' Abī Bakr b. al-'Arabī al-kalāmiyya*, Argel, n. d., II, 493, and Fierro, *Heterodoxia*, p. 129. On Maslama b. Qāsim's doctrines see now M. I. Fierro, "The polemic about the *karāmāt al-awliyā'* and the development of Sufism in al-Andalus (4th/10th-5th/11th century)", forthcoming.

[27] See Fierro, "Accusations of *zandaqa*". There were two other Andalusis charged with *zandaqa*: the 'Āmirid 'Abd al-Raḥmān Sanchuelo, because of his attempt to be named heir to the caliphate, by the Umayyad Hishām II, and the Shu'ūbī Ibn García On these see Ibn Sa'īd, *Al-Mughrib fī ḥulā 'l-Maghrib*, ed. S. Ḍayf, Cairo, 1964, I, 208, and J. T. Monroe, *The Shu'ūbiyya*

in al-Andalus, Berkeley, 1970, pp. 17, 93-94, 98, also pp. 59 and 69. In their case, however, the accusation of *zandaqa* is not recorded in the early sources and seems to be a later charge.

[28] The available sources give no information as to the identity of the person or persons who made the accusation against Ibn Masarra, or the date on which it was made. The evidence, in any case, shows that the accusation of *zandaqa* took place in Ibn Masarra's youth on the grounds of his Muʿtazilism, and before he developed his Sufi doctrine after his travel to the East. There is no hint that he suffered any persecution between his return to al-Andalus and his death in 319/931. See Fierro, *Heterodoxia*, section 7.5.

[29] See Fierro, *Heterodoxia*, section 8.4.

[30] See Marin, "Baqī b. Majlad", and Fierro, *Heterodoxia*, section 6.2.

[31] See Fierro, *Heterodoxia*, section 10.2.

[32] On these see Fierro, *Heterodoxia*, sections 7.2. and 9.1.

[33] On Ibn Ḥātim see my forthcoming study in *Anaquel de Estudios Arabes*, "El proceso contra Ibn Ḥātim al-Ṭulayṭulī (años 457/1064-464/1072)".

[34] On this attitude, see H. E. Kassis, "Muslim Revival in Spain in the Fifth/Eleventh Century. Causes and Ramifications", *Der Islam*, 67, 1990, pp. 78-110. For a parallel attitude in the trials for blasphemy that took place in al-Andalus when some Mozarabs were seeking martyrdom by insulting the Prophet, see M. I. Fierro, "Andalusī *fatāwā* on Blasphemy", *Annales Islamologiques*, forthcoming.

[35] See my study mentioned in the *Historia de España* (see note 4 above), section 2.3.1.

[36] *Ibid.*, section 2.3.8.

[37] On "false prophecy", see Y. Friedmann, *Prophecy continuous. Aspects of Aḥmadī Religious Thought and its Medieval Background*, Berkeley-Los Angeles-London, 1989, pp. 65-68.

[38] See Fierro, *Heterodoxia*, section 5.1.

[39] See *ibid.*, section 5.6.

[40] See *ibid.*, section 7.3.

[41] See *ibid.*, section 8.2.

[42] See *ibid.*, section 10.3.

[43] See *ibid.*,, section 1.2.

[44] See *ibid.*, section 2.2.

[45] *Al-ʿAwāṣim*, II, 490-91.

[46] M. Benaboud, "El papel político y social de los *ʿulamāʾ* en al-Andalus durante el periodo de los Taifas", *Cuadernos de Historia del Islam*, 11, 1984, pp. 7-52, points in the same direction.

[47] *Kitāb al-madkhal li-ṣināʿat al-manṭiq*, ed. and trans. M. Asín Palacios, *Introducción al arte de la lógica por Abentomlús de Alcira*, Madrid, 1916, pp. 8-9 and 8-10.

BIBLIOGRAPHY

Abū Bakr b. al-ʿArabī (d. 543/1148), *Al-ʿAwāṣim min al-qawāṣim*, ed. ʿAmmar Ṭālibī, in *Arāʾ Abī Bakr b. al-ʿArabī al-kalāmiyya*, Argel, n. d., 2 vols.

Aguadé, J., "Some remarks about sectarian movements in al-Andalus", *Studia Islamica*, 64, 1986, pp. 53-77.

Al-Bājī, d. 474/1081, *Taḥqīq al-madhhab yatlūhā ajwibat al-ʿulamāʾ bayna muʾayyid wa-muʿāriḍ ḥawla daʿwā kitābat al-rasūl, (ṣlʿm) li-smihi yawm ṣulḥ al-Ḥudaybiyya*, ed. Abū ʿAbd al-Raḥmān b. ʿAqīl al-Ẓāhirī, Riyadh, 1403/1983.

Benaboud, M., "El papel polítíco y social de los *ʿulamāʾ* en al-Andalus durante el periodo de los Taifas", *Cuadernos de Historia del Islam*, 11, 1984, pp. 7-52.

Brunschvig, R., "Polémiques médiévales autour du rite de Mālik", *Al-Andalus*, 15, 1950, pp. 321-68.

Cook, M., "Activism and Quietism in Islam: The Case of the Early Mujiʾa", in *Islam and Power*, ed. A. S. Cudsi and A. E. H. Dessouki, London, 1981, pp. 15-23.

Fierro, M. I., "Accusations of *zandaqa* in al-Andalus", *Quaderni di Studi Arabi*, 5-6, 1987-8, pp. 251-58.

——, "El derecho mālikí en al-Andalus, ss. II/VIII-V/XI)", *Al-Qanṭara*, 12, 1991, forthcoming.

——, *La heterodoxia en al-Andalus durante el periodo omeya*, Madrid, 1987.

——, "The introduction of *ḥadīth* in al-Andalus (2nd/8th-3rd/9th centuries)", *Der Islam*, 66, 1989, pp. 68-93.
——, "Los mālikíes de al-Andalus y los dos árbitros (*al-ḥakamān*)", *Al-Qanṭara*, 6, 1985, pp. 79-102.
——, "Mu'āwiya b. Ṣāliḥ al-Ḥaḍramī al-Ḥimṣī: historia y leyenda", *Estudios onomástico-biográficos de al-Andalus*, I, ed. M. Marín, Madrid 1988, pp. 281-411.
——, "La polémique a propos de *raf' al-yadayn fī 'l-ṣalāt* dans al-Andalus", *Studia Islamica*, 65, 1987, pp. 69-90.
——, "Religion", section VI of volume VIII of the *Historia de España fundada por R. Menéndez Pidal y dirigida por J. Ma Jover Zamora*, devoted to *Los Reinos de Taifas, desde comienzos del s. XI hasta la conquista almorávide* (in preparation).
Fierro, M. I., and S. Faghia, "Un nuevo texto de tradiciones escatológicas sobre al-Andalus", *Sharq al-Andalus*, 7, 1990, pp. 99-111.
Fórneas, J. M., "Datos para un estudio de la *Mudawwana* de Saḥnūn en al-Andalus", *Actas del IV Coloquio Hispano-Tunecino (Palma de Mallorca 1979)*, Madrid 1983, pp. 93-118.
Friedman, Y., *Prophecy continuous. Aspects of Aḥmadī Religious Thought and Its Medieval Background*, Berkeley, Los Angeles-London. 1989.
Goldziher, I., "Mohammed ibn Toumert et la théologie de l'Islam dans le Maghrib au XIe siècle", introduction to the edition by D. Luciani of *Le livre de Mohammed Ibn Toumert, Mahdi del Almohades*, Algiers, 1903.
Ibn Ḥazm (d. 456/1064), *Kitāb al-fiṣal fī 'l-milal wa 'l-ahwā' wa 'l-niḥal*, in the margins *al-Milal wa 'l-niḥal* of al-Shahrastānī, Cairo 1347-8, 5 volumes in one; partial trans. by M. Asín Palacios, *Abenházam de Córdoba y su Historia crítica de las ideas religiosas*, Madrid, 1929, 5 vols.
——, *Risāla fī faḍā'il ahl al-Andalus*, Arabic text in al-Maqqarī, *Nafḥ al-ṭīb*, ed. I. 'Abbās, Beirut, 1398/1968, III, 156-79, and in his *Rasā'il*, ed. I. 'Abbās, Beirut, 1980-3, II, 171-88; French translation by C. Pellat, "Ibn Ḥazm, bibliographe et apologiste de l'Espagne musulmane", *Al-Andalus*, 19, 1954, pp. 53-102.
Ibn Sahl (d. 486/1093), *Tres documentos sobre procesos de herejes en la España musulmana/ Thalāth wathā'iq fī muḥārabat al-ahwā' wa 'l-bida' fī 'l-Andalus*, ed. 'A. W. Khallaf, Cairo, 1981.
Ibn Sa'īd (d. 685/1286), *Al-Mughrib fī ḥulā 'l-Maghrib*, ed. S. Ḍayf, Cairo, 1964, 2 vols.
Ibn Ṭumlūs (d. 620/1223), *Kitāb al-madkhal li-ṣinā'at al-manṭiq*, ed. and transl. M. Asín Palacios, *Introducción al arte de la lógica por Abentomlús de Alcira*, Madrid, 1916.
Ibn Waḍḍāḥ (d. 287/900), *Kitāb al-bida'*, new edition, translation and study by M. I. Fierro, Madrid, 1988.
Idris, H. R., "Réflexions sur le Malikisme sous les Omayyades d'Espagne", *Atti del 3o Congresso di Studi Arabi e Islamici (Ravello 1966)*, Naples 1967, pp. 397-414.
Kassis, H. E., "Muslim Revival in Spain in the Fifth/Eleventh Century. Causes and Ramifications", *Der Islam*, 67, 1990, pp. 78-110.
Lapidus, I. M., "The Separation of State and Religion in the Development of Early Islamic Society", *IJMES*, 6, 1975, pp. 363-85.
Lévi-Provençal, E., "Le malikisme andalou et les apports doctrinaux de l'Orient", *RIEEIM*, 1, 1953, pp. 156-71.
——, *Histoire de l'Espagne musulmane*, Paris-Leiden, 1950-53, 3 vols.
López Ortiz, J., *La recepción de la escuela malequí en España*, Madrid, 1931.
Makki, M. A., *Ensayo sobre las aportaciones orientales en la España musulmana y su influencia en la formación de la cultura hispano-árabe*, Madrid, 1968, pp. 90-140.
Marín, M., "Baqī b. Majlad y la introducción del estudio del *Ḥadīṯ* en al-Andalus", *Al-Qanṭara*, 1, 1981, pp. 165-208.
Masud, M. K., *Islamic Legal Philosophy. A Study of Abū Isḥāq al-Shāṭibī's Life and Thought*, Islamabad, 1977.
Molina, L., "Lugares de destino de los viajeros andalusíes en el *Ta'rīj* de Ibn al-Faraḍī", *Estudios onomástico-biográficos de al-Andalus*, ed. M. Marín, Madrid, 1988, pp. 585-610.
Monès, H., "Le rôle des hommes de religion dans l'histoire de l'Espagne musulmane jusqu'à la fin du califat", *Studia Islamica*, 20, 1964, pp. 47-88.
Monroe, J. T., *The Shu'ūbiyya in al-Andalus*, Berkeley. 1970.

Al-Muqaddasī (d. after 375/985), *Aḥsan al-taqāsīm fī ma'rifat al-aqālīm*, ed. M.J. De Goeje, 2nd ed., Leiden 1906, *BGA*, Vol. III.
Muryani, M., *Materialien zur mālikitischen Rechtsliteratur*, Wiesbaden, 1984.
——, "Notas sobre la transmisión escrita de la *Mudawwana* en Ifrīqiya según algunos manuscritos recientemente descubiertos (Qairawāner Miszellaneen III)", *Al-Qanṭara*, 10, 1989, pp. 215-31.
Turki, A. M., *Polémiques entre Ibn Ḥazm et Bāǧī sur les principes de la loi musulmane. Essai sur le littéralisme zahirite et la finalité malikite*, Algiers, 1973.
——, "La vénération pour Mālik et la physionomie du malikisme andalou", *Studia Islamica*, 33, 1971, pp. 41-65.
Urvoy, D., *Le monde des ulémas andalous du Ve/XIe au VIIe/XIIIe siècle. Etude sociologique*, Geneva, 1978.
Al-Wanṣharīsī (d. 914/1508), *Al-Mi'yār al-mu'rib wa 'l-jāmi' al-mughrib 'an fatāwī ahl Ifrīqiya wa 'l-Andalus wa 'l-Maghrib*, Rabat, 1401/1981, 13 vols.

ANDALUSĪ MYSTICISM AND THE RISE OF IBN ʿARABĪ

CLAUDE ADDAS

Disappointment, and even indignation, was the reaction of the famous Andalusī mystic Muḥyī 'l-Dīn b. ʿArabī (Ibn ʿArabī) when, on his arrival in Egypt in 598/1200, he viewed the behaviour of Eastern Sufis. "The moment I arrived in this part of the world," he told his master and friend Shaykh ʿAbd al-ʿAzīz al-Mahdawī two years later, "I enquired after those men following the Ideal Way, in the hope of finding among them the breath of the Supreme Companion. I was taken to an assembled *khanqāh*, in a quite enormous building, where I noted that their greatest care and their chief preoccupation was cleaning their clothes and combing their beards ... In this country I met [Sufis] who, with no feelings of shame before the All Merciful, decked themselves out in the gowns worn by *fityān*s, while neglecting all question of obligatory and supererogatory acts. They would not be fit even to clean latrines."[1]

There is something a little disconcerting about the scathing severity of Ibn ʿArabī's judgement on first sight of his Eastern colleagues. Are we to see, in this virulent outburst, no more than an exaggerated expression of Andalusī patriotism, or does his harshness rather reflect a genuine malaise in relations between the Western and Eastern Sufi communities?

It should be made clear, first of all, that Ibn ʿArabī was neither the first nor the last Andalusī to express disapproval of the sometimes rather ostentatious religious bearing of Easterners. We might, for instance, recall the biting irony with which his contemporary Ibn Jubayr, in his *riḥla*, denounces the Eastern *ʿulamā*'s taste for solemn procedure, and the pretension displayed in their clothes and in the pompous appellations they assume.[2]

To be absolutely fair, Ibn ʿArabī's opinion of Eastern Sufism was a good deal less cut and dried than these two references, taken out of context, would suggest. He himself, in the same pages, owns that authentic gnostics are also encountered in the East, and he did not, finally, hesitate, once settled in the region, to adopt the practices appropriate to Eastern *taṣawwuf* whenever he judged this to be necessary or advisable. We are in fact dealing, at bottom, with a misunderstanding which was to evaporate as his acquaintance with Eastern Sufism deepened.

Initially, nevertheless, he very naturally judged the Cairo Sufis on the basis of Sufism as he himself had experienced it in the Muslim West; and while the two Sufi traditions might have aims and doctrinal bases in common, they exhibited wide differences with regard to form and methods.

In the Muslim West *ṣuḥba*, or spiritual companionship, was still an informal practice; it had not assumed the institutionalised and more or less regulated character that it was beginning to take on at thc cnd of the 6th/12th century (and still more markedly in the 7th/13th century) in the East, with the establishment of the organised and therefore more rigid system subsequently understood by the term *ṭarīqa*.

There was in fact, at this period, an evident divergence between the two traditions, with Eastern Sufism, for various reasons, manifesting a progressive structurisation—this being particularly reflected in the increasingly communal nature of spiritual life, evidenced by the widespread establishment of *khanqāhs*—while the search for God in Andalusī Sufism still remained a largely individual matter, free and flexible in its practice. Such differences of emphasis could lead to mutual incomprehension, and this was sometimes aggravated by a rather contemptuous attitude taken by Easterners towards Maghribis—an attitude experienced by Ibn ʿArabī himself when, barely arrived in Cairo, he was told by a Sufi from Irbil that there were no true gnostics in the West.[3] At this point incomprehension gave way to indignation, for this son of al-Andalus could not endure such scoffing at the expense of the shining companions and enlightened guides of his quest.

Initially, it must be said, Ibn ʿArabī was to some extent an *Uwaysī*, one of those whose spiritual development occurs spontaneously, without the intervention of any living earthly guide. There was no master by his side when, at about 15 years old, he was suddenly and even brutally summoned by God: it was by searching into the depths of his own self, and into the *baraka* with which certain prophets—particularly Jesus—surrounded him, that Ibn ʿArabī travelled down the dazzling and hazardous path of divine illumination. However, about five years after this spectacular conversion he discovered in al-Andalus, almost, so to speak, on his very doorstep, some *ʿārifūn bi Llāh,* men and women whose outstanding spiritual development often went unsuspected by their contemporaries.

Totally won over by the greatness of soul that lay hidden behind the commonplace appearance of these persons, Ibn ʿArabī placed himself under their tutelage. This was the beginning, for him, of a long period of *ṣuḥba*, in the course of which he kept company with many Andalusī masters; it was in fact only ten years later, during his first visit to the Maghrib in 590/1194, that he became the companion of a certain number of Maghribi Sufis, most of them disciples of Abū Madyan, who was himself of Andalusī origin.

Some of these Maghribi masters—notably ʿAbd al-ʿAzīz al-Mahdawī, with whom Ibn ʿArabī was to consort in Tunis—did indeed play a certain part in his spiritual development. Yet their moulding influence was, finally, a sporadic one, for when Ibn ʿArabī first met them his training and personality were already fully complete, bearing the definitive imprint of the teaching of Andalusī Sufis and the spiritual models they embodied. Thus, if he had, initially, been a "self-taught" saint, he was now heir to an Andalusī mystical tradition which profoundly influenced both his spiritual and his literary development.

We should not allow ourselves to be deceived by the profound originality characterising various aspects of the Shaykh al-Akbar's writings; this originality did, it is true, spring essentially from solitary meditation, yet his work was also steeped in the teachings of generations of earlier exemplars of Muslim spirituality, both from the East and from the West. Particularly instructive in this respect are the *Futūḥāt makkiyya*: the allusions to past masters with which the work is strewn are conclusive testimony, if any such be needed, that he did not disdain to listen to them, and they reveal, also, two basic features of his relation to those who had gone before him in the Way.

On the one hand we may see that he had—hardly surprisingly—been more marked by the teaching of Western, and especially Andalusī Sufis than by their Eastern brothers: there are, it is true, quite frequent references to writers like al-Ghazālī, al-Niffarī and Ḥakīm al-Tirmidhī, but they are far fewer in number than the countless passages on the experience of Andalusī masters which are scattered through the 560 subdivisions of the *Illuminations of Mecca*. On the other hand, a close reading of these latter passages reveals that he was fascinated less by the doctrinal ideas of his masters than by the spiritual virtues they embodied.

If one is to believe the view prevalent among specialists in the field, the local tradition with which the Shaykh al-Akbar thus became involved was a relatively recent one—Andalusī Sufism having, according to them, emerged only at the end of the 3rd century of the Hegira with Ibn Masarra (d. 319/931) and his disciples. The sources presently at our disposal do not, it is quite true, indicate any kind of homogeneous mystical trend in al-Andalus before the appearance of the Masarrī movement. Yet let us, nevertheless, guard against hasty conclusions. The absence of surviving written evidence by no means implies that the land of Spain had produced no *awliyāʾ* up to this point. Would we after all, without Ibn ʿArabī's testimony, ever have heard of Shams al-Fuqarāʾ, or Ṣāliḥ al-Barbarī, or so many other admirable Andalusī saints of whom no chronicle or epitaph preserves the memory or the name?

It would, moreover, be extremely imprudent to conclude from its geographical position on the Western edge of the Muslim community that al-Andalus was a closed world. We know that the pilgrimage made each year to Mecca by Andalusis and Maghribis was an opportunity for these outlying Muslims to follow the teaching of Eastern *ʿulamāʾ* as they visited Mecca, Alexandria, Baghdad, Cairo, Basra—the whole classic itinerary of Western pilgrims in search of knowledge; and it is highly likely, in the circumstances, that a number of these pious emigrants (who generally spent several years in the East) would have met and consorted with mystics such as Sarī al-Saqaṭī

(d. 253/867), Maʿrūf al-Karkhī (d. 200/815), Sahl al-Tustarī (d. 283/896) and Junayd (d. 298/910), or with some of their disciples. This particular aspect of the history of Muslim Spain remains, it must be admitted, a very obscure one, so that we are, finally, reduced to conjecture. Curiously, this whole question of relations between East and West during the centuries immediately following the conquest, and, more especially, of the penetration of Eastern mystical teaching into al-Andalus by the medium of the *ḥajj,* has never, to the best of my knowledge, been the subject of any really detailed study.

This is a serious handicap when it comes to research on the school of Ibn Masarra and its origins; nor is it by any means the only barrier to a proper study of this movement, whose major importance for the history of ideas in al-Andalus is universally recognised. This is made emphatically clear in a remarkable—and, unfortunately, unpublished—piece of work produced in 1973 by James W. Morris,[4] who collated and analysed most of the Arab and orientalist sources concerning Ibn Masarra al-Jabalī and his disciples. The results of this inventory are somewhat surprising, showing that the picture painted of Ibn Masarra and his school by Asín Palacios and his predecessors is in fact considerably at variance with the information actually contained in the sources on which they basically relied. This discrepancy essentially springs, Morris believes, from the fact that orientalists have derived their initial viewpoint on Ibn Masarra from a passage of the *Taʾrīkh al-ḥukamāʾ* of al-Qifṭī (d. 646/1248), who lived three centuries after the Shaykh al-Jabalī himself; in this account Ibn Masarra is linked with the *bāṭiniyya*, and with the neo-Platonic writings attributed by the Arabs to Empedocles and Pythagoras. On the basis of this observation—which is taken from a *single line* of Ṣāʿid (d. 462/1070)—Dozy, in his history of Muslim Spain, manages to convince himself of Ibn Masarra's "Bāṭinism" and of the latter's role as "a secret emissary of Fāṭimid propaganda in Spain".[5] Goldziher regards him as a "free thinker"—in other words a Muʿtazila—stating that "11th-century Spanish Islam was soon penetrated by a latent movement of free thought which came to be called Masariyya".[6] Neither Dozy nor Goldziher, however, made the connection between the Masarrī school and later Andalusī Sufism.

It was Asín Palacios who attempted to establish this relationship, in a work which first appeared in Madrid in 1914 under the title "Abenmasarra y su escuela". It would be impossible to overestimate the importance of this work, which has exerted a decisive and lasting influence on the whole approach taken towards Andalusī Sufism by orientalists. Even today many works on medieval Sufism are based on the two main theses developed by Asín in this work, the first of which was that Ibn Masarra, "under the Muslim guise of Muʿtazilism and Bāṭinism, was the defender and propagator, within Islamic Spain, of the Plotinian system of pseudo-Empedocles and of the notion most associated with him, namely that of the hierarchy of the five substances, preceded by a spiritual *Materia Prima*".[7] The second thesis was that Andalusī Sufism subsequent to Ibn Masarra, from Ismāʿīl al-Ruʿaynī to Ibn ʿArabī by way of Ibn al-ʿArīf and Ibn Qasī, sprang from the Masarrī school and itself represented the continuation of this school.

The first of these two hypotheses has been severely questioned, notably by S. M. Stern,[8] the arguments set out in "Abenmasarra y su escuela" being all the easier to refute in that they were, by the author's own admission, based on *mezquinas fuentes*.[9] What do these poor sources tell us about Ibn Masarra? The main biographical points to emerge from the *Taʾrīkh* of Ibn al-Faraḍī (d. 403/1012)[10] and the *Muqtabas* of Ibn Ḥayyān (d. 469/1076)[11] are as follows:

Ibn Masarra was born at Córdoba in 269/883, in the reign of the Umayyad prince ʿAbd al-Raḥmān. His father, ʿAbd Allāh b. Masarra was a learned man; he transmitted *ḥadīth*—four of his students are mentioned in a note in Ibn al-Faraḍī's *Taʾrīkh*[12]—and the same writer records that he enjoyed great fame at Mecca. ʿAbd Allāh b. Masarra twice made extended visits to the East, notably to Basra, where he came into contact with Muʿtazila circles. His contemporaries clearly had little relish for the interest he took in studies then regarded as unorthodox. However, as Morris very correctly notes, "Muʿtazila" was at this time used as a convenient blanket term for a huge area of theological or philosophical ideas regarded as suspect because they failed to fit into the rigid framework of Mālikī orthodoxy, and the suspicion of Muʿtazilism attached to Ibn Masarra and those around him (beginning with his father) should not be taken literally.

At the time of ʿAbd Allāh b. Masarra's death, which took place in 286/899, during his second visit to the holy places, his son, Muḥammad b. ʿAbd Allāh b. Masarra was about fifteen years old, and had, Ibn al-Faraḍī tells us, studied under the direction of his father, of Muḥammad b. Waḍḍāḥ and of one "al-Khushanī". The first of the two last-named *fuqahāʾ* poses no problem of identification: Muḥammad b. Waḍḍāḥ (d. 287/900) was in fact one of the first and most illustrious representatives of Andalusī Mālikism and played a considerable part in developing the science of *ḥadīth* in al-Andalus. During his second visit to the East he received, according to Ibn al-Faraḍī, transmitted material from 175 masters in Baghdad, Cairo, Damascus, etc.,[13] and it was, so Ibn Farḥūn tells us, thanks to him and to Baqī b. Makhlad[14] that al-Andalus became the *dār al-ḥadīth*.[15] Still more interestingly, he was also a great ascetic *(zāhid)*, and Ibn al-Faraḍī stresses that his first visit to the East in 218/833 was not made in the traditional quest of *ḥadīth*, but rather of *zuhd*, and with the wish to meet *ʿubbād*, or devotees. As such it is possible, and even likely, that he would, in the course of his journeying, have met such Eastern Sufis as Dhū 'l-Nūn (d. 245/859), Sarī al-Saqaṭī and Bishr al-Ḥāfī (d. 227/841) or some of their disciples. It is clear, in any case, that his teaching was not limited to *ḥadīth*; he also, so the author of the *Dībāj* reports, liked to "relate the history of saints ... and the masters are unanimous in stating that it was he who brought knowledge and ascesis [*al-*

ʿilm wa ʾl-zuhd] to the Andalusis". This sheds new light on the possible influence exerted by Eastern mystics on Ibn Masarra—a more decisive influence, in my view, than any pseudo-Empedocles might havc had—and on the precise channels through which this Eastern tradition was transmitted to al-Andalus. There is reason to suppose, indeed, that Ibn Waḍḍāḥ himself was one of these channels.

As for "al-Khushanī", this is probably Muḥammad b. ʿAbd al-Salām al-Khushanī (d. 286/899), another major transmitter of *ḥadīth* and author of several commentaries on the subject.[16] According to al-Nubāhī, who devotes a long passage to him in his *Kitāb al-marqaba ʾl-ʿulyā*,[17] he risked his life by his stubborn refusal to take on the post of *qāḍī* of Jaén which the Umayyad *amīr* attempted to impose on him. Possibly this refusal of a prestigious post coveted by so many bears the stamp of *zuhd*. We may note, in any case, that he too spent a long period in the East.

These two *ʿulamāʾ*, together with his father, instructed Ibn Masarra in the traditional religious sciences, and particularly in *ḥadīth*—it should be noted in this respect that Shams al-Dīn al-Qurṭubī (d. 671/1173), in his famous *Tadhkīra*, cites a *Kitāb al-tabyīn* of Ibn Masarra which, he says, contains a *ḥadīth* on the Day of Judgement that Ibn Masarra himself derives from his father and Ibn Waḍḍāḥ[18] (this detail is all the more interesting in that the work in question is not, to the best of my knowledge, mentioned elsewhere). However, his father—who, as noted above, was suspected of Muʿtazila opinions—certainly also introduced him to less orthodox fields of investigation. Did the library he bequeathed his son contain "suspect" works? Ibn al-Faraḍī's reference to this library does at least suggest that it was noteworthy either for the nature of the works involved or by reason of their number.[19]

It is also probable that—through Muḥammad b. Waḍḍāḥ and perhaps also through al-Khushanī, who spent no fewer than 25 years in the East—Ibn Masarra learned something of the ascetic, and even specifically mystical tradition of the East. This is clearly a matter of importance, given the place assumed by *zuhd* in his teaching and in the way of life embraced by himself and the first generation of his disciples. Moreover, Ibn Ḥayyān states—though on what basis is very far from clear—that Ibn Masarra had knowledge of medicine, philosophy, astrology, and so on.

All the principal persons among whom Ibn Masarra grew up had, then, visited the East and studied there, thereby coming into contact, directly or indirectly, with the various mystical, theological and philosophical doctrines circulating in that part of the Muslim world, and likely to appear suspicious in the eyes of the Andalusī *fuqahāʾ*. There is no reason, nevertheless, to suppose (as Ibn al-Faraḍī's informant does) that Ibn Masarra was actually accused of *zandaqa*, or heresy, in his own lifetime, and forced to "flee" al-Andalus[20] —though he did indeed follow his elders' example by himself visiting the East, and so had ample opportunity to consort with Sufis and gain a wider knowledge of their doctrine. Did he perhaps come into contact with disciples of Sahl al-Tustarī? A close study of his *Kitāb al-ḥurūf* reveals, as we shall see, numerous borrowings from al-Tustarī's treatise on the science of the letters.

Ibn al-Faraḍī and Ibn Ḥayyān insist that Ibn Masarra maintained relations with theologians and Muʿtazila in the East, and say that, on his return to al-Andalus, he passed himself off as a pious and devout man, so that his bearing deceived those who began to consort with him and listen to him. Nevertheless, they continue, when Ibn Masarra revealed his hateful doctrine and made open profession of his ideas, all men of intelligence and learning drew away from him, leaving him only with those too ignorant to know better.

Eleven of these companions who continued to follow the teaching of the Shaykh al-Jabalī are mentioned in a note in the *Takmila* of Ibn al-Abbār (d. 638/1260),[21] which was, it is true, written three centuries afterwards, but whose information is based on a work entitled *Kitāb akhbār Ibn Masarra wa aṣḥābihī*,[22] which, to the best of my knowledge, is mentioned by no other source.

A study of the relevant biographical details reveals that, while a number of these disciples were, unsurprisingly, from Córdoba, four of them in fact came from Toledo. Four of the disciples, moreover, accompanied Ibn Masarra on pilgrimage, and one of these relates how Ibn Masarra, when in Medina, made his way to the house of Māriya, the Prophet's Coptic concubine, and took scrupulous note of the dimensions and configuration of one of the two upper rooms,[23] then, on his return to al-Andalus, built an exact replica in the mountain retreat where he had his hermitage.[24] There is no indication in the sources why the house of Māriya should have held such a particular attraction for Ibn Masarra, as against any other place frequented by the Prophet, but M. I. Fierro pertinently notes that authors link this rather disconcerting action with the practice of *ittibāʿ āthār al-nabī*, of which his master Ibn Waḍḍāḥ disapproved.[25] Finally, most of Ibn Masarra's disciples are portrayed by Ibn al-Abbār as ascetics, being constantly referred to by such terms as *nāsik*, *wariʿ* and *zāhid*—which is particularly interesting when we consider the absence of this connotation in the biographical notes concerning the second generation of disciples in Ibn al-Faraḍī's *Ta'rīkh*.[26]

What exactly was the "odious doctrine" that sent such shudders through Ibn al-Faraḍī's interlocutor? One point is quite clear from the outset, namely that the accounts of it put forward by Arab authors are widely different, if not contradictory. Ṣāʿid,[27] followed by al-Qifṭī[28] and Ibn Abī Uṣaybiʿa (d. 668/1270),[29] portrays Ibn Masarra as a "*Bāṭinī* philosopher" seized by the philosophy of pseudo-Empedocles, while al-Ḥumaydī (d. 488/1095) attributes to him *ishārāt ṣūfiyya*.[30] Ibn al-Faraḍī and (still more) Ibn Ḥayyān stress his Muʿtazilī views; they claim that he favoured notions of free will, believing in the actual carrying out of punishment and reward and denying intercession.[31] This was also the view of Ibn Ḥazm (d. 456/1064), who claimed that Ibn

Masarra shared Muʿtazilī viewpoints on *qadar* and that he subscribed to the notion of divine knowledge as something adventitious and created.[32] The author of the *Fiṣal* also provides precious details on the *Masarriyya* [*sic*] of his time and on the dissension excited within their group by the theses of Ismāʿīl al-Ruʿaynī, who regarded himself as the Shaykh al-Jabalī's successor (he is said to have taken the title of *imām* and to have demanded that his adepts pay the *zakāt*) and the authorised interpreter of his works. He stated, in particular, that it was the Throne which ruled the world, God being too sublime to perform actions; "he ascribed this theory to Ibn Masarra on the basis of certain passages in his works", and retorted to anyone who contested this interpretation: "you have not understood the *shaykh*'s meaning".[33] Al-Ruʿaynī further admitted the possibility of *iktisāb al-nubuwwa*, the acquisition of prophecy, basing himself on propositions which, according to Ibn Ḥazm, are indeed to be found in Ibn Masarra's writings.[34]

These works of Ibn Masarra would appear to be four in number: the *Kitāb al-tabyīn* noted above, the *Kitāb al-tabṣira* mentioned by Ibn al-Abbār, the *Kitāb al-ḥurūf*, which is several times referred to by Ibn ʿArabī, and the *Kitāb tawḥīd al-mūqinīn* cited by Ibn al-Mar'a,[35] an Andalusī Sufi contemporary with Ibn ʿArabī. The two first were identified by Dr. Kamāl Ibrāhīm Jaʿfar, who published an edition of them in 1978, thereby resolving many puzzles and putting an end to numerous controversies.[36]

The first thing to be revealed is that the true title of the *Kitāb al-tabṣira* is in fact the *Kitāb al-iʿtibār*, *iʿtibār* being the word used by, among others, al-Fārābī, the *Ikhwān al-Ṣafā'* and Ibn Sīnā to denote the inductive method. In the treatise bearing this name, Ibn Masarra undertakes to demonstrate that *iʿtibār* and *waḥy* (revelation through the prophets) lead, by different paths, to the same certain truths. *Iʿtibār*, for Ibn Masarra, consists of using *ʿaql*, the intellect, to consider the Signs of God and so rise step by step to the knowledge of *tawḥīd*: "The world, its creatures and its signs constitute a ladder climbed by those who apply themselves to *iʿtibār* in order to attain the topmost heights of the great signs of God."[37] The choice of the term *iʿtibār* in the title and text can, it seems to me, be very simply explained by its appearance in several divine injunctions laid on man in the Quran (3:13; 12:111; 16:66; 23:21, etc.); Ibn Masarra is quite clearly setting out to clarify a divine command. The Quran, he emphasises, expressly and repeatedly invites us to use this faculty and reflect on the Signs of His creation, especially when "God said *with reference to his awliyā'*: 'and they meditate on the creation of the heavens and the earth [and declare] "Lord, You did not create all this in vain!"' (Quran 2/191)".[38] The specific reference to the *awliyā'*, i.e., the saints, excludes all possibility of ambiguity: the kind of intellectual activity set forth by Ibn Masarra is of a different order from the speculation of the *falāsifa*. It is a kind of meditation which leads, he says, to *baṣīra*—another Quranic term (12: 108) widely employed in the Sufi vocabulary—that is, to enlightenment (*laqad aṭlaʿat-hum al-fikra ʿalā ʾl-baṣīra*),[39] and, from there, to apprehension of the One God: "Through reflection they attain enlightenment, and, when they have become enlightened, they gain awareness of the Divine Oneness of which the prophets have told."[40] In this way *iʿtibār* allows us to decipher the universe, which is "in its entirety a book whose letters are His word",[41] and it confirms what the prophets tell us; so that, while *iʿtibār* proceeds from the manifest world to arrive at a higher world, and prophecy, by an exactly reverse process, moves from the higher to the lower, the two are in fact identical in their ultimate validity.[42]

Given the climate of the time, such statements might well seem inadmissible to the *fuqahāʾ*. Ibn Masarra does, however, firmly dissociate himself from the *falāsifa*, whose *iʿtibār* does not spring from an honest intention: "they have deceived themselves and become lost in mazes without light."[43] For all that, however, he does maintain in the *Kitāb al-ḥurūf* that the philosophers and the Ancients of the misguided nations had attained knowledge of *tawḥīd* without the mediation of prophecy.[44] Ibn Masarra is apparently making a distinction between the purely speculative reflection of the *falāsifa*, which leads to perdition, and the *iʿtibār* of the *ḥukamāʾ*, or sages, such as Plato, which may lead to a knowledge of the divine—a position, it should be said, held by many Sufis, notably by Ibn ʿArabī.[45] We may note, nevertheless, that this insistence on *iʿtibār* already prefigures one of the most singular manifestations in Islam of what might be called "a mystic way of wisdom", which Ibn Ṭufayl was to develop in his *Ḥayy b. Yaqẓān*. Ibn ʿArabī (though he never, as far as I know, mentioned Ibn Ṭufayl either favourably or unfavourably) recognised the legitimacy of this way of the *ḥukamāʾ*, a way involving rigorous initial ascesis with a view to drawing aside the "veils" inherent in human nature, but deemed it imperfect because it had not been made complete by faith and revelation.[46]

The second treatise of Ibn Masarra has the very precise title *Risālat khawāṣṣ al-ḥurūf wa ḥaqāʾiquhā wa uṣūluhā* and is concerned with the meaning and interpretation of the *nūrāniyyāt*, the fourteen separate letters which introduce certain Suras of the Quran. As such it is a basically esoteric work in the purest tradition of Islamic gnosis. In Islam *ʿilm al-ḥurūf*, the science of the letters,[47] which represents the quintessence of those spiritual sciences accessible solely to the élite of the *awliyāʾ*, inspired two major hermeneutic trends: one, of Hellenistic origin, whose most celebrated representative was undoubtedly Jābir b. Ḥayyān,[48] tended to search out knowledge of a cosmological, alchemical and even divinatory kind; the other, which had its basis in *taṣawwuf*, viewed *ʿilm al-ḥurūf* as the royal path to attaining a knowledge of metaphysical truths. Ibn Masarra's interpretation, which takes its inspiration on a number of points from Sahl al-Tustarī's treatise on the letters[49] (referred to by him on a number of occasions),[50] follows the second of these lines.

This text not only demonstrates Ibn Masarra's attachment to the tradition of *taṣawwuf* (so that it is within this framework that his doctrine and movement should be viewed), but also the fact that he was one of the major figures within this tradition and the precursor of an Andalusī mysticism which was to reach its high point with Ibn ʿArabī two-and-a-half centuries later. The influence of pseudo-Empedocles (and that of the neo-Platonists generally), is, to say the least, not obvious in these two texts, while that of Sahl al-Tustarī is, by contrast, clearly present.

How, in these circumstances, are we to explain the divergent opinions expressed on the Shaykh al-Jabalī, and judge the doctrine which some regard as belonging to philosophy and others as belonging to mysticism?[51] The varying interpretations no doubt spring from the difference of emphasis reflected in the two treatises in question. A superficial reading of the *Kitāb al-iʿtibār,* where ideas specifically concerning *taṣawwuf* are only lightly sketched in, might give the impression that the author is a philosopher rather than a mystic, while the treatise on the secrets of the separate letters reveals a master of *taṣawwuf* and a subtle interpreter. Certain remarks of Ibn Ḥazm, moreover, give the impression that Ibn Masarra had been studied in different intellectual circles, with the particular focus of interest changing over the centuries.

One thing at least is certain: for all the various efforts made by the *fuqahāʾ* to halt the impetus of Masarrī thought (such as the auto-da-fé of his works in 350/961, and the forced recantation of some of his disciples),[52] Ibn Masarra's writings continued to circulate and be studied—openly by some, discreetly by others—in the centuries following his death. This is clear from the notes Ibn al-Faraḍī devotes to his second generation disciples,[53], and from the reference of Ibn Ḥazm to the "*Masarriyya*" of his time, i.e. roughly around the beginning of the 5th century of the Hegira. How exactly this Masarrī tradition was handed down after the time of Ismāʿīl al-Ruʿaynī we do not know, but its visible presence in the 6th/12th century, in the context of the two Sufi authors Ibn al-Mar'a and, especially, Ibn ʿArabī, shows that it had not been extinguished. Ibn ʿArabī mentions Ibn Masarra, with evident admiration, on at least four occasions in his writings. In section 13 of the *Futūḥāt*, writing on the "Bearers of the Throne", he states: "I am told that Ibn Masarra al-Jabalī, *who was among the truly great men of the Way in knowledge, state and revelation*, once said ...".[54] In this passage Ibn ʿArabī is basing himself on oral tradition, but elsewhere he makes explicit reference to the *Kitāb al-ḥurūf*, notably in his *Kitāb al-mīm wa 'l-nūn*, when he informs the reader of his intention to treat the science of letters without exploring the operative aspect of their properties, "in the manner of Ibn Masarra in his *Kitāb al-ḥurūf*".[55] These passages, together with the two others mentioning Ibn Masarra in section 272 of the *Futūḥāt*[56] and in the *Fuṣūṣ*,[57] shows that Ibn ʿArabī was familiar with at least some aspects of Ibn

Masarra's doctrine and had very probably read his *Kitāb al-ḥurūf*. How far in fact had he been influenced by his ideas?

Referring to certain passages in the *Kitāb al-ḥurūf*, we cannot fail to be struck by the similarities. When, for instance, Ibn Masarra brings up the notion of *kawn*, the existential *fiat*, or *habāb*, the primordial dust which he and others regard as constituting the *materia prima*, or the connection between the manifestation of creatures arising out of this *materia prima* and the setting out of the letters, or when he underlines the connection between the 28 letters of the Arabic alphabet and the lunar cycles, every reader familiar with the Shaykh al-Akbar's works will recognise subjects running through his writings.

It should, however, once more be stressed that these ideas were not exclusive to Ibn Masarra: they were already present in Sahl al-Tustarī's treatise on the science of the letters, which served as an inspiration both to Ibn Masarra and to Ibn ʿArabī, and, in some cases, in the *Rasāʾil*s of the *Ikhwān al-Ṣafāʾ*. For this reason, and for others to be considered shortly, it would be wise not to exaggerate (but also not to minimise) the influence of Ibn Masarra on the thought of Ibn ʿArabī.

In the light of the relevant texts, then, Asín's thesis concerning Ibn Masarra and his doctrine is seen to be without foundation. But what of this Spanish orientalist's work on the Almería School (where he has, once more, undertaken pioneer work,[58] and as such merits our profound respect)? Here, too, it has to be said that his investigative methods appear highly debatable and his conclusions often incautious.

For Asín the Almería School basically represents a resurgence of the Masarrī movement, and, while admitting that there is no available documentation to support such a thesis,[59] he nonetheless undertakes his study from this viewpoint. It is, of course, true that Ibn Masarra, by virtue of works and teaching which had continued to circulate for centuries in Sufi circles in particular, was the source of a specifically Andalusī *taṣawwuf*. Nevertheless, it would seriously undervalue the inestimable wealth of post-Masarrī Sufism to consider it as a mere prolongation of the Masarrī school; if Ibn ʿArabī, Ibn al-ʿArīf, Ibn Barrajān, and many other Andalusī spiritual figures not mentioned in this study, were in varying degrees influenced by Ibn Masarra, this does not alter the fact that they also derived their inspiration from other sources, notably from Eastern writers and, still more, from their own spiritual experience.

Another of Asín's preconceptions, which was long to dog the approach of orientalists to this movement, was his belief that, of the school's three principal representatives, Abū 'l-ʿAbbās b. al-ʿArīf (d. 536/1141), Abū 'l-Ḥakam b. Barrajān (d. 536/1141) and Abū Bakr al-Mayūrqī (d. 537/1142), it was the first who was the leader of the group. Initially, indeed, he thought, and wrote, that the other two were Ibn al-ʿArīf's disciples;[60] and if he became a little less categorical on the point subsequently, he still persisted in regarding Ibn al-ʿArīf as the central figure. He also took it for granted that the revolt of the *murīdūn* under the leadership of Ibn Qasī (d. 546/1151) (again assumed to be a disciple of Ibn al-ʿArīf) represented the political outcome of the doctrine preached first by Ibn Masarra, then by Ibn al-ʿArīf.

How far does this viewpoint, which is still shared by a number of scholars today, correspond to what the texts have to tell us about the principal characters involved? It should be noted at the outset that the very expression "Almería School", convenient though it is, is a mere extrapolation. Some writers do indeed bring up the incident in Almería at the beginning of the century, when the Almoravid sultan ʿAlī b. Yūsuf b. Tāshfīn ordered an auto-da-fé of al-Ghazālī's *Iḥyāʾ*. This decision—which, according to the *Ḥulal*,[61] was taken on the insistence of certain *fuqahāʾ*, particularly the *qāḍī* Ibn Ḥamdīn, who even pronounced an anathema against anyone reading the work—was certainly not approved of by all the *ʿulamāʾ*. One of them, ʿAlī al-Barjī, reciter of the Quran in Almería, was courageous enough to express open written disagreement in the form of a *fatwā*, and according to Ibn al-Abbār several of his colleagues added their signature to his.[62] Such a joint condemnation was undeniably noteworthy and significant, but does it really justify notions of a "centre of Sufi resistance" to the Almoravid ruling power? It should be pointed out that the author of the *Muʿjam* refers to the protesters as *fuqahāʾ*: they were, in other words, Mālikī *fuqahāʾ* opposing other *fuqahāʾ*. Protests were in fact also raised in various Sufi circles in the Maghrib and al-Andalus, though these were, as Asín quite rightly notes, on an individual level and more discreetly expressed—which is not to say they were necessarily less effective.[63] In any case, the name of Ibn al-ʿArīf, who was at least 22 years old at the time,[64] is never associated with this particular event, and nor are those of Ibn Barrajān and Abū Bakr al-Mayūrqī.

What above all led Asín to suppose the existence of a core of Sufi rebels gathered around Ibn al-ʿArīf in Almería was the fact that the three were summoned to Marrakesh by the Almoravid sultan ʿAlī b. Yūsuf b. Tāshfīn—an event, which, it must be admitted, remains a puzzle for scholars.

Let it be stressed, first of all, that nothing we know of the antecedents of these three Sufis from their biographers would lead us to expect so dramatic a turn of events.

All the biographers of Ibn al-ʿArīf stress his competence in the *traditional* religious disciplines.[65] He was the son of a poor weaver, and had, so we are told, to defy the authority of his father in order to pursue his Quranic studies. Quickly excelling in the latter, he taught *qirāʾa* at Saragossa and Almería, and Ibn al-Abbār notes that he also practised *ḥisba* in Valencia.

Al-Mayūrqī is portrayed as a Ẓāhirī *faqīh*, expert in genealogy and *ḥadīth*.[66] He travelled to the East, where he met, in particular, Abū Bakr al-

Ṭurṭūshī, an Andalusī who apparently played an important and still relatively little-known role as a link between Eastern Sufism and that of the Muslim West.[67]

Ibn Barrajān, according to the *Takmila*, was not only skilled in Quranic studies and *ḥadīth*, but had knowledge of *taṣawwuf* and *kalām*, and Ibn al-Abbār also notes his two works, a commentary on the Quran and a commentary on the divine names.[68]

Just why, then, were these three *ʿulamāʾ* so brusquely summoned before the authorities? All three, it is true, were notorious ascetics, but that was nothing so very extraordinary in al-Andalus at this time. The relevant authors are somewhat imprecise as to the reasons.

Ibn Bashkuwāl, who had corresponded with Ibn al-ʿArīf, merely says of the latter's arrest that "he was denigrated to the Sultan, who accordingly ordered him to appear in Marrakesh".[69] Ibn al-Abbār, in his *Muʿjam*, initially connects Ibn al-ʿArīf's summons to Marrakesh with the fact that he was so popular and had gathered so many disciples round him: "those loyal to him in his Sufi path had become so numerous that the matter was reported to the Sultan." Yet immediately afterwards he introduces an "it is said" (*yuqāl*) to the effect that "the Almería *fuqahāʾ* unanimously condemned his doctrines and denounced him to the Sultan, warning the latter against him. The Sultan then ordered that he should be brought from Almería, together with Abū Bakr al-Mayūrqī of Granada and Abū 'l-Ḥakam b. Barrajān of Seville, who professed the same ideas". He then adds an interesting remark: "Abū 'l-Ḥakam was the major figure of the three, and had in fact been called 'the Ghazālī of al-Andalus'."[70] In 1956 Nwyia published three letters from Ibn al-ʿArīf to Ibn Barrajān[71] which leave one in no doubt whatsoever as to the relationship between the two Sufis, Ibn al-ʿArīf presenting himself as the humble disciple of his master Ibn Barrajān.

The latter, according to al-Shaʿrānī, had himself recognised as *imām* in 130 villages.[72] Al-Shaʿrānī is indeed a late source, but a similar reference has been located by D. Gril in the *Waḥīd* of Shaykh ʿAbd al-Ghaffār al-Qūsī, a 7th/13th century Egyptian Sufi.[73] The impression given is that the Almoravid powers had become anxious about his success and feared a coalition with Ibn al-ʿArīf, who also enjoyed great popularity. Why, though, should al-Mayūrqī too have been considered dangerous? The only indication we have on the subject is Ibn al-Abbār's statement that he shared the others' ideas.

Whatever the reasons, the three Sufis were brought to Marrakesh, where they did not, however, receive the same treatment. Al-Mayūrqī, according to Ibn ʿAbd al-Malik al-Marrākushī (d. 703/1303),[74] was arrested, whipped and then released; after which misadventure he spent some time in the Mashriq, then returned to the Maghrib, teaching *ḥadīth* at Bougie.

As for Ibn Barrajān, the *Takmila* merely notes that he met his death in Marrakesh,[75] without giving precise details as to his fate. However, al-Tādilī

(d. 624/1230) provides the following account in the *Tashawwuf*: "When Abū 'l-Ḥakam b. Barrajān was brought from Córdoba to Marrakesh, he was questioned as to certain matters of which he had been accused, and he defended himself against them in accordance with *ta'wīl*. He dissociated himself from the one who had stirred up criticism, declaring: 'I shall not live [long], but the one who caused me to come will not live on after my death.' He died, and the Sultan commanded that his body be thrown on the city's refuse dump." However, al-Tādilī continues, Ibn Ḥirzihim, who was one of the masters of Shaykh Abū Madyan, being informed of the Sultan's decision, called out the population of Marrakesh to attend Ibn Barrajān's funeral.[76]

Ibn Bashkuwāl is extremely evasive on the causes of of Ibn al-ʿArīf's death, but very precise as to the date of the event: "He died on the night of the Friday, and was buried during the day on Friday the 23rd in the month of *Ṣafar* in the year 536."[77]

Ibn al-Abbār gives two versions of the facts. According to the first, the Sultan, convinced of Ibn al-ʿArīf's excellence and piety, ordered him to be released and conveyed to Ceuta, where he died as the result of illness. The second version, to which the author attaches little credit, has Ibn al-ʿArīf poisoned on his return, during the sea crossing.[78]

The first version derives from Abū ʿAbd Allāh al-Ghazāl, who is identified by Ibn al-Abbār as a close disciple of the Shaykh of Almería.[79] However, al-Ghazāl is also the source cited by al-Tādilī for the second version of the facts in the *Tashawwuf*, where it is stated that Ibn al-Aswad, the *qāḍī* of Almería, had Ibn al-ʿArīf poisoned.[80] However, hagiographers, among whom al-Tādilī is to be numbered, do have a tiresome tendency to portray the most famous Sufis as the victims of sovereigns and of the latters' precious allies, the doctors of the Law.

A third event—supplementing the condemnation of the auto-da-fé of the *Iḥyā'* carried out by the Almerian *fuqahā'* and the summoning of three famous Sufis to Marrakesh—has been used to reinforce the thesis of dissidence on the part of a group of Andalusī Sufis, namely the revolt of the *murīdūn* unleashed a year after Ibn al-ʿArīf's death by his "disciple" Ibn Qasī.[81]

The conclusion to Nwyia's 1956 article on the three letters from Ibn al-ʿArīf to Ibn Barrajān very much reflects the general interpretation of this event on the part of orientalists: "The prevailing spirit in the Sufi School of Almería", he writes, "and the feelings of its members towards the Almoravids become very clear when we consider the behaviour of one of the most illustrious disciples of Ibn al-ʿArīf, the celebrated Abū 'l-Qāsim Ibn Qasī. The latter, we may well believe, was doing no more than put the ideas of his master into practice ..."[82]

In 1978, however, Nwyia discovered and published other letters of Ibn al-ʿArīf which led him to revise his judgement.[83] This correspondence, extracted from the *Kitāb miftāḥ al-saʿāda,*[84] notably includes two letters addressed to

Ibn Qasī. The first, dated by Nwyia between 525 and 529 A. H. (ca. 1131-34 A. D.), represents the first contact between the two Sufis, and Ibn al-ʿArīf expresses his surprise at learning, through a third party, that his name is familiar to Ibn Qasī. The latter clearly already enjoys a degree of fame and several disciples have gathered round him, including Abū 'l-Walīd b. Mundhir, later to be one of his principal lieutenants during the rebellion.

In the second letter Ibn al-ʿArīf expresses the pleasure with which he has read certain passages from the writings of Ibn Qasī, praising his intelligence, erudition and mastery of the spiritual sciences.[85] As Nwyia very justly remarks, the language used bears not the slightest resemblance to that of a *shaykh* towards his *murīd*.[86] These letters further show that, at the time they came to know one another, Ibn Qasī was an accomplished master whose spiritual and intellectual authority was already recognised by a certain number of disciples. It seems difficult, in view of all this, to ascribe to Ibn al-ʿArīf a decisive influence on Ibn Qasī's doctrinal training or mystical thought.

These two letters do not invalidate Ibn al-Abbār's claim that Ibn Qasī visited Ibn al-ʿArīf in Almería before his departure for Marrakesh.[87] But nor does the fact of this meeting, which probably did take place, by any means allow us to presume that Ibn al-ʿArīf was in some way implicated in the revolt of the *murīdūn*.

In fact another letter, addressed this time to Ibn Mundhir, actually precludes any such hypothesis.[88] In this text—in my view the most important and the most noteworthy among the correspondence in question—Ibn al-ʿArīf expresses his views on the question of submission to power legitimately held by an unjust sovereign, and he certainly does not mince his words on the subject: "No judicious man," he begins, "and no Muslim who is not weak [-minded] is in favour of striking at the government and waiting for a *mahdī* to come and reform it." He continues by saying, in substance, that Muslims have in all periods denigrated their rulers. During the reign of the Umayyads people complained and wished for the advent of a *mahdī*—and when this happened, in the form of the Abbasid dynasty, Muslims looked longingly back to the Umayyads, and "realised that the flow of blood and the violation had had the opposite result to the one they anticipated". The same state of affairs, he remarks, came about in Ifrīqiya, where the longed-for *mahdī* was "a Rāfiḍī Shiʿite, a *kāfir*"—an allusion, of course, to the reign of the Fāṭimids. In the light of this text, it is impossible to suppose that Ibn al-ʿArīf would ever—even verbally or from a distance—have encouraged the political ambitions of Ibn Qasī and the *murīdūn* rebellion. His remarks constitute an unqualified condemnation of any millenarian attempt to unseat any sovereign, however unjust; such a position being, in fact, characteristic of the line taken by all Sunni Sufis on this question.

Let us, then, sum up the conclusions emerging from all this. First of all, there is a vast discrepancy between the state of affairs reconstructed by Asín and that actually authorised by the relevant texts. Ibn Barrajān was the master of Ibn al-ʿArīf, not the reverse; and if it really is necessary to specify a leader of the group, then it was he, and not his disciple, who played this role. Moreover, Ibn Qasī, contrary to the currently accepted viewpoint, was not the disciple of the Shaykh of Almería, who only in fact came to know Ibn Qasī at a late date, when the latter had already established the *murīdūn* group; and, what is more, the *rasāʾil*s in the *Kitāb miftāḥ al-saʿāda* clearly indicate that Ibn al-ʿArīf was in no way implicated in the insurrection which broke out shortly after his death.

Having said that, it is of course obvious that the emergence of the *murīdūn* and their participation in the armed struggle against the Almoravid ruling power was in some way connected with immediately prior events. The opposition, whether discreet or openly proclaimed, to the auto-da-fé of the *Iḥyāʾ*, the success gained by Ibn Barrajān and ʿAlī b. Tāshfīn's decision to summon him to Marrakesh along with Ibn al-ʿArīf and al-Mayūrqī, are so many signs of the climate of tension prevailing in al-Andalus when Ibn Qasī's revolt broke out.

Finally, it seems to me that the whole notion of an "Almerian School" is in need of reconsideration. While the 5th century of the Hegira did, indisputably, witness a recrudescence of Andalusī Sufism, with Almería as one of its principal centres, nothing indicates that the city played a clearly pivotal role.

It is perfectly probable that some elements among the Sufis disapproved of certain decisions taken by the Almoravid ruling power, and criticised them either privately or publicly; it is also, frankly, something quite commonplace. Sunni Sufis adopted, according to circumstances and personal temperament, three types of attitude towards those holding the temporal power. Some turned entirely to the Divine Wisdom, avoiding any participation in the affairs of the State and any contact with its auxiliaries. Others, calculating that their participation would be beneficial, chose to cultivate relations with the agents of the ruling power in order better to control and guide them—this, for instance, was clearly the case with Abū 'l-ʿAbbās al-Qanjāʾirī al-Marī, an Andalusī Sufi contemporary with Ibn ʿArabī, whose influence over the Almohad sovereigns, and intimate relations with them, are stressed by all the biographers.[89]

The majority, however, maintained strict observance of the divine command: "Religion is the proper counsel in the service of God, of His Messenger, of the leaders of the Muslims and of the community in general."[90] They acted as the censors of princes, exhorting them to good and not hesitating to reprimand them, publicly if necessary, when they strayed from the right path and contravened the Law. Chronicles and works of hagiography teem with delightful portrayals of a ragged mystic insolently denouncing the exactions of some prince, or even, sometimes, of the Caliph in person.[91]

We must, at any rate, admit that the information presently available to us does not conclusively indicate the existence of a "school" in Almería. In the case of Ibn Masarra several documents attest to the existence of a homogeneous group associated with his name and doctrine, both during his life and after his death; nothing of the kind, however, exists for any "Almerian School". Finally, our only indication in this connection is the text in which Ibn al-Abbār states that Ibn al-ʿArīf, Ibn Barrajān and al-Mayūrqī professed the same doctrine; and this, it seems to me, is insufficient evidence.

We may note in any case that Arab writers do not treat Ibn al-ʿArīf, Ibn Barrajān and Ibn Qasī in any kind of uniform way. There is openly expressed sympathy for the Shaykh of Almería, who is portrayed as an authentic Sufi and ascetic; there is only slightly tempered esteem for Ibn Barrajān; but there is frank aversion to Ibn Qasī, who is seen by one and all as a charlatan and a cunning, ambitious opportunist.[92] These differences of attitude are also to be found in Ibn ʿArabī's judgement on the three Andalusī Sufis, made on the basis of their writings.

It is difficult, given the present state of our materials, to determine just how many works Ibn Barrajān actually produced. We know for certain that he wrote at least two books: a commentary on the Divine Names and a commentary on the Quran, specifically mentioned in the *Takmila*. However the title of these works varies from manuscript to manuscript, and we cannot be sure that all the titles in question refer to them. The commentary on the Divine Names appears in Brockelmann under the title *Sharḥ maʿānī asmāʾ Allāh al-ḥusnā*,[93] while Gril refers to a manuscript entitled *Tarjumān lisān al-ḥaqq al-mabthūth fī 'l-amr wa 'l-khalq*.[94] As for the *tafsīr*, it seems to have circulated under various titles. Brockelmann cites a manuscript entitled *Kitāb tanbīh al-afhām ilā tadabbur al-kitāb*,[95] while Gril notes the existence of various manuscripts of this *tafsīr* in Istanbul which may refer to two different works, and mentions, too, a *Kitāb al-irshād*, also classed with the *tafsīr*.[96] Finally, Ibn ʿArabī twice refers to a work by Ibn Barrajān entitled *Kitāb īdāḥ al-ḥikma*, which he studied in Tunis in 590/1194 under the direction of ʿAbd al-Azīz al-Mahdawī—and this too seems to denote his commentary on the Quran.[97]. It is in this book, he notes in his *mawāqiʿ* that there occurs the celebrated foretelling of the reconquest of Jerusalem in 583/1187[98] —a prediction which struck people very forcibly, as the following eye-witness account by Ibn Khallikān testifies: in 579/1183 A. H. the *qāḍī* of Damascus, Muḥyī 'l-Dīn b. Zakī addressed to Saladin (who had just taken Aleppo) a poem foretelling the latter's coming victory in Jerusalem, explaining, subsequently, that he was following the interpretation of the first four verses of the *Sūrat al-Rūm* given by Ibn Barrajān in his *tafsīr*.[99]

In the *Futūḥāt* Ibn ʿArabī stresses that knowledge of this event could be obtained through recourse to the science of the letters, and notes that Ibn

Barrajān, by not basing himself on this science, committed an error (*ghalaṭ*) which escaped his readers.[100]

For all that, the Shaykh al-Akbar always mentions Ibn Barrajān with respect and esteem, classing him among the "men of God".[101] Nevertheless, the tone is less warm than that which he employs when speaking of Ibn al-ʿArīf, whom he places in the ranks of "men of spiritual fulfilment" (*muḥaqqiqūn*), and so venerates as to regard him as one of his masters.[102] I wonder, incidentally, how far this preference on the part of the author of the *Futūḥāt* for the Shaykh of Almería helped persuade Asín of the latter's central role.

Apart from a certain number of letters appearing in the *Kitāb miftāḥ al-saʿāda*, the only work of Ibn al-ʿArīf known today is the *Maḥāsin al-majālis*, a quite short treatise in which he enumerates and analyses the principal "dwellings" the traveller encounters along the way. His objective, however, is not a humdrum listing of the stages of the Way, of the kind many others had undertaken before him; it is rather designed for the spiritual élite, and its primary purpose is to demonstrate how—with the exception of the dwelling of knowledge and, up to a certain point, that of love—all the dwellings represent veils interposed between the traveller and God, in that they proceed from illusion. Patience, resolution, sobriety, etc. are indeed praiseworthy virtues in themselves, but finally they reflect a persistent illusion in the individual, inducing him to recognise a reality in *mā siwā Llāh*, in that which is "other than God". Interesting though this vision of spiritual journey is, it is in fact less original than might at first be thought: B. Halff, indeed, has shown that, with the sole exception of the passage on knowledge, the whole work is inspired by two treatises of Shaykh ʿAbd Allāh al-Harawī 'l-Anṣārī, namely the *Manāzil* and, especially, the *ʿIlal*, which he often reproduces almost word for word and whose content is closely copied even in the final sentence: "Until that which has never been is annihilated and that which has never ceased to be subsists."[103] However the question of the *Maḥāsin*'s originality is less important, finally, than the lively interest aroused by the work in Sufi circles; the quite numerous references to the *Maḥāsin* in Ibn ʿArabī's *Futūḥāt*,[104] the commentary written on it by another great Andalusī Sufi, Ibn al-Mar'a[105] and, above all, the chain of transmission given for it by al-Wādī Ashī in his *Barnāmaj*[106] are indications of the degree of success the work enjoyed.[107]

I have written elsewhere of Ibn ʿArabī's scathing criticism of Ibn Qasī and his *Khalʿ al-naʿlayn*.[108] The commentary he wrote on this work shows how his point of view, contrary to what might be suggested by certain passages in the *Futūḥāt*,[109] does in the event coincide with that of Arab historians, although for radically different reasons: when, like them, he describes Ibn Qasī as an impostor,[110] it is not a matter of reliance on malicious gossip, but rather of judgement based on a considered assessment of the *Khalʿ*, which leads him to some categorical pronouncements on Ibn Qasī's spiritual knowledge and the authenticity of his vaunted divine inspiration.

From the very beginning, in fact, the author of the *Khalʿ* claims that his book is inspired: "I have not," he declares, "sought to produce a work in the [ordinary] manner of writers, but have simply conveyed what illumination [*fatḥ*] brought me."[111] The work is divided into four *ṣuḥuf*s, or "small books", in which cosmological, eschatological and angelological subjects are mixed together in a rather confused manner. The work as a whole is marked by a profusion of metaphorical expressions and a vocabulary referring ceaselessly to cosmology. To read the *Khalʿ* is to gain the impression, at times, that Ibn Qasī is a conjurer dazzling his reader with an ephemeral firework.

Whether venerating or reprimanding these representatives of the main tendencies of Andalusī Sufism—whose works he has studied, and whose first and second generation disciples he has in some cases consorted with—Ibn ʿArabī never remained indifferent to their doctrinal propositions. This should not though, in my opinion, be taken to imply that they decisively affected his own doctrine.

It is true, as I stressed at the beginning of this article, that Ibn ʿArabī's thought is profoundly marked by the Muslim mystical heritage, both Western and Eastern, on which it constantly reflects and which it embraces in an extraordinary synthesis. It is, too, indisputable that ideas can be found here and there in his writings which spring directly from these masters of Andalusī *taṣawwuf*. Nevertheless, when we set alongside these the richness and diversity of the doctrinal areas developed by Ibn ʿArabī, we see that such borrowings constitute, finally, only a tiny part of his works.

Anecdotes and accounts found, in his writings, on the subject of his Andalusī past make it clear that the Shaykh al-Akbar's debt to the saints of his native land lies in other areas. It is, quite clearly, not so much through their doctrinal teaching but through their actual personalities, and the example of their exceptional qualities, that these persons have mostly left their mark on his works. The first *murshid* under whose direction he placed himself, Abū 'l-ʿAbbās al-ʿUryānī was, we should remember, *ummī*, that is, illiterate. By contrast, Mūsā al-Mīrtulī, with whom he began to consort shortly afterwards, was a highly educated man and even an occasional poet, who figures in a number of compilations. However, what Ibn ʿArabī speaks of with such admiration is not so much his learning and his poetic gifts as the compassion which characterised both his spiritual state (he was, said Ibn ʿArabī, one of those "men who are assisted by God, and, who, in their turn, assist the creatures ... with goodness, gentleness and pity")[112] and the way he bore himself to those around him: "If a man was in need, he would sell a book from his considerable library and feed the wretch with the proceeds of the sale ... When he had sold them all, he died."[113] But the virtues of self-denial, compassion and love implicit in *futuwwa* were not exclusive to al-Mīrtulī: they appear, like a leitmotiv, on every page, on every line even, of the *Rūḥ al-quds*. Thus, Muḥammad al-Khayyāṭ, for example, "endured all evils, while forbidding himself to inflict any. ... He habitually attended to the poor in person, distributing food and clothing to them. He was, in truth, a man of profound goodness, full of compassion, benevolence and care for others ..."[114] Of Shaykh Ḥasan al-Shakkāz, Ibn ʿArabī recalls how "he never said 'I' "; "never," he insists, "have I heard him use that word."[115] And of Shaykh al-Qabāʾilī, to give one last example, he relates how "his prayers extended to all the inhabitants of heaven and earth, even to the fish in the sea."[116]

These human qualities which moved Ibn ʿArabī so deeply were accompanied by spiritual features of which they were the natural fruit, and three such features, apparently, specially marked the spiritual profile of the Sufis of al-Andalus: ascesis, poverty and devotion to the Quran; at least, these are the things which constantly spring to Ibn ʿArabī's mind when he remembers his country.

Ijtihād, *jidd* and *zuhd* are terms flowing ceaselessly from the Shaykh al-Akbar's pen to describe the zeal and ardour of the men who made up the spiritual élite of al-Andalus. Muḥammad al-Sharafī, for example, for example, "remained so long in prayer that his feet became swollen. ... He lived in the same house for forty years and never lit either fire or light."[117] As for ʿAbd Allāh al-Baghī, he had sticks in readiness "to thrash his legs when they were tired from so much praying".[118]

The deprivation, austerity and, often, misery they imposed on themselves leave us speechless. Fāṭima bint al-Muthannā lived in a hut of reeds made for her by Ibn ʿArabī and another disciple and fed herself on the refuse the Sevillians left at their doors.[119] Some of them filled honoured (if not well remunerated) positions, such as teacher or *imām*, but most of them, it should be stressed, gained their livelihood from humbler occupations: as sellers of pottery, camomile, opium or acorns, as cobblers, etc. Some finally chose to give up all idea of providing for their needs and placed their trust in Providence.

Whether learned or illiterate, whether they worked or held back from work, Andalusī Sufis set recitation of the Holy Book before all other study and all other reading. Thus, to quote just one example, Yūsuf al-Shuburbalī —who was so absorbed in contemplation of the Divine Presence that he never noticed an olive tree which had been in his garden since his earliest childhood—never, according to Ibn ʿArabī, read any other book but the Quran till the day he died.[120]

Ibn ʿArabī had certainly not been insensible to the doctrinal teaching lavished on him by his masters. Nevertheless, the things he retained from them above all, it seems to me, were the *makārim al-akhlāq*, the noble virtues they embodied; it was in these, clearly, that he perceived the superior quality of the Andalusī Sufism for which he was to strive, particularly in his *Rūḥ al-quds*, to command respect. All this largely explains the exasperation he felt, and expressed so bluntly, on his arrival in Egypt: his indignation was all the greater for the enormous feelings of admiration he cherished towards his Andalusī brothers. No doubt, too, the signs of change affecting Sufism in the East—necessary changes, perhaps, but harbingers, too, of the disappearance of a particular kind of world—filled him with painful presentiments that the extraordinary spiritual universe he had just left for good was about to suffer deep and irreversible upheaval.

A testimony to the gratitude he felt towards those men and women who had shared his spiritual odyssey, the *Rūḥ al-quds* stands like a memorial set in the midst of chaos, to recall, for the generations to come, the *fityān*, the heroic saints, who were the Sufis of al-Andalus.

1 *Rūḥ al-quds*, Damascus, 1970, p. 21.

2 *Journeys*, trans. M. Gaudefroy-Demombynes, Paris, 1949, p. 344.

3 *Rūḥ*, p. 27.

4 J. W. Morris, *A Reconsideration of the Primary Sources*, 1973. I am grateful to him for communicating this work to me.

5 *Histoire des musulmans d'Espagne*, 2nd ed., Leiden, 1932, II, 127-28.

6 *Le livre d'Ibn Toumert*, Algiers, 1903, pp. 66-69.

7 "Abenmasarra y su escuela", in *Obras escogidas*, Madrid, 1946, I, 113.

8 S. M. Stern, "Ibn Masarra, Follower of Pseudo-Empedocles—an Illusion", *Actas do IV Congresso de Estudos Arabes e Islámicos*, Coimbra-Lisbon, 1968, Leiden, 1971, pp. 325-39.

9 Asín Palacios, *op. cit.*, p. 113.

10 *Ta'rīkh 'ulamā' al-Andalus*, ed. F. Codera, Madrid, 1891-92. Cf. the note on Ibn Masarra (No. 1202) and that concerning his father (No. 650).

11 Ibn Ḥayyān, *Al-Muqtabas*, Vol. V, ed. P. Chalmeta, Madrid, 1979, pp. 20-36. See also, in connection with the notes of Ibn al-Faraḍī and Ibn Ḥayyān, M. Cruz Hernández, "La persecución anti-masarrī durante el reinado de 'Abd al-Raḥmān al-Nāṣir li Dīn Allāh según Ibn Ḥayyān", *Al-Qanṭara*, 2, 1981, pp. 52-67.

12 *Ta'rīkh 'ulamā'*, Nos. 306, 1068, 895, 1216.

13 *Ibid.*, No. 1136. See also N. Mu'ammar, *Muḥammad b. Waḍḍāḥ al-Qurṭubī mua'ssis madrasat al-ḥadīth bi 'l-Andalus ma'a Baqī b. Makhlad*, Rabat, 1983.

14 On this figure, see M. Marín, "Baqī b. Majlad y la introducción del estudio del ḥadīṯ en al-Andalus", *Al-Qanṭara*, 1, 1980, pp. 165-208, and M. I. Fierro, "The introduction of ḥadīth in al-Andalus", *Der Islam*, 66, 1989, pp. 68-93.

15 *Dībāj*, Beirut, n.d., pp. 204-41.

16 Ibn al-Faraḍī, *Ta'rīkh 'ulamā'*, No. 1135. See also Fierro, *op. cit.*, pp. 82-83. This study refers the reader to her work *La Heterodoxia en al-Andalus durante el periodo omeya*, Madrid, 1987, which I have not, unfortunately, been able to consult.

17 *Kitāb al-marqaba 'l-'ulyā*, Beirut, 1983, pp. 13-14.

18 Shams al-Dīn Qurṭubī, *Al-Tadhkīra fī aḥwāl al-mawtā*, Beirut, n. d., p. 341.

19 *Ta'rīkh 'ulamā'*, No. 650.

20 On the question of the anti-Masarrī persecutions, see Cruz Hernández, *op. cit.*; M. I. Fierro, "Accusations of *zandaqa* in al-Andalus", *Quaderni di Studi Arabi*, 5-6, 1987-88, pp. 255-56; al-Nubāhī, *Kitāb al-marqaba 'l-'ulyā*, pp. 78, 201.

21 *Al-Takmila li-kitāb al-ṣila*, ed. Husani, Cairo, 1955, No. 8, 17, 529, 530, 562; and ed. Codera, Madrid, 1886, 113, 186, 326, 347, 339; see also notes 281 and 389.

22 *Takmila*, No. 8.

23 For details of this house, known as *mashrab umm Ibrāhīm*, see *Encyclopédie de l'Islam*, 2nd ed., *s.v. Māriya*.

24 *Takmila*, No. 339. See also al-Maqqarī, *Nafḥ al-ṭīb min ghuṣn al-Andalus al-raṭīb*, ed. I. 'Abbās, Beirut, 1968, II, 354.

25 M. I. Fierro, "Una refutación contra Ibn Masarra", *Al-Qanṭara*, 10, 1989, pp. 273-75.

26 *Ta'rīkh 'ulamā'*, Nos. 897, 127, 1329, 179, 434, 54, 1359, 1364, 834.

27 *Ṭabaqāt al-umam*, ed. L. Cheiko, Beirut, 1912, pp. 20-21; trans. Blachère, Paris, 1935, pp. 58-60.

28 *Ta'rīkh al-ḥukamā*, Leipzig, 1903, pp. 16-17.

29 *'Uyūn al-anbā'*, Göttingen, 1884, pp. 32-33.

30 *Jadhwat al-Muqtabis*, Cairo, 1952, pp. 58-59, No. 83.

31 On this subject see E. Tornero, "Nota sobre el pensiamento de Abenmasarra", *Al-Qanṭara*, 6, 1985, pp. 503-06.

32 *Al-Fiṣal fī 'l-milal*, Cairo, 1903, IV, 198-200. See also IV, 80 and II, 128-29.

33 *Ibid.*, IV, 199.

34 *Ibid.*

35 L. Massignon, *Recueil de textes inédits*, Paris, 1929, p. 70.

36 *Min qaḍāyā 'l-fikr al-Islāmī*, Cairo, 1978, *Kitāb al-ḥurūf*, pp. 311-44 and *Kitāb al-i'tibār*, pp. 346-60.

37 *I'tibār*, p. 350.

38 *Ibid.*, p. 344.

39 *Ibid.*; the recurrence of this notion of *baṣīra* may perhaps explain why this treatise circulated under the title *Kitāb al-tabṣira*. In this connection, see *Takmila*, ed. Codera, No. 113.

40 *Ibid.*, p. 350.

41 *Ibid.*, p. 346.

42 *Ibid.*, pp. 350-51.

43 *Ibid.*, p. 357.

44 *Kitāb al-ḥurūf*, p. 315.

45 *Futūḥāt*, II, 523.

46 *Futūḥāt*, section 73, questions 12 and 13.

47 On the science of the letters in Islam, and in Ibn 'Arabī's work in particular, see the excellent analysis by D. Gril in *Les Illuminations de la Mecque*, Paris, 1988, pp. 385-487.

48 On Jābir b. Ḥayyān see Paul Kraus, *Ibn Jābir, contribution à l'histoire des idées scientifiques dans l'Islam*, Cairo, 1943; P. Lory, *Jābir ibn Ḥayyān. Dix traités d'alchimie*, Paris, 1983, and *Alchimie et mystique en terre d'Islam*, Paris, 1989.

49 *Risālat al-ḥurūf*, ed. Kamāl Ja'far, in his study *Sahl b. 'Abd Allāh al-Tustarī*, Cairo, 1974

50 *Kitāb al-ḥurūf*, pp. 317, 335, 339.

51 For a comparison of the opinions ascribed to Ibn Masarra and those to be found in the two treatises, see Kamāl Ja'far's "Min mu'allaffāt Ibn Masarra 'l-mafqūda" in *Majallat kulliyat al-tarbiya*, Vol. III, 1972, pp. 27-63.

52 See note 20 above.

53 *Ta'rīkh 'ulamā'*, Nos. 897, 127, 1329, 179, 437, 54, 1359, 1364, 834.

54 *Futūḥāt*, I, 149.

55 *Kitāb al-mīm*, Hyderabad, 1948, p. 7.

56 *Futūḥāt*, II, 581.

57 *Fuṣūṣ al-ḥikam*, ed. 'Afīfī, Beirut, 1946, I, 84.

58 *Obras escogidas*, I, 219-42.

59 "Abenmasarra y su escuela", pp. 142-43.

60 *Ibid.*, p. 143.

61 *Ḥulal*, Rabat, 1979, p. 104.

62 *Mu'jam*, Cairo, 1967, p. 283, No. 253.

63 On this subject, see: al-Tādilī, *Tashawwuf*, Rabat, 1984, pp. 96, 145, 169; and Ibn 'Arabī, *Rūḥ*, No. 40, in *Sufis of Andalusia*, trans. R. W. J. Austin, 2nd ed., Sherbone, 1988, pp. 136-37.

64 According to Ḥafnāwī, *Ta'rīkh al-khalaf*, Algiers, 1907, I. 94, the auto-da-fé was ordered in 503 A. H., and Ibn al-'Arīf born in 481 A. H.

65 For the biography of Ibn al-'Arīf, see: Ibn al-Abbār, *Mu'jam*, No. 14, pp. 15-20; Ibn Bashkuwāl, *Kitāb al-ṣila fī ta'rīkh a'immat al-Andalus*, ed. F. Codera, Madrid, 1883, No. 175; *Tashawwuf*, No. 18; 'Abbās b. Ibrahīm, *Al-I'lām bi man ḥalla Marākush wa Aghmāt min al-a'lām*, Rabat, 1974, I, 5-24; and 'Abd al-Wahhāb b. Manṣūr, *A'lām al-Maghrib*, Rabat, 1983, III, 231 *et seq.*

[66] On al-Mayūrqī, see Ibn al-Abbār, *Muʿjam*, No. 123, and *Takmila*, ed. Codera, No. 608; and Ibn ʿAbd al-Malik al-Marrākushī, *Al-Dhayl wa 'l-takmila*, Beirut, 1973, VI, No. 452, pp. 169-71.

[67] On al-Ṭurṭūshī see *Encyclopédie de l'Islam*, 2nd ed., *s. v. Ibn Abī Randaqa*; and V. Lagardère, "L'unification du mâlikisme oriental et occidental à l'Alexandrie: Abū Bakr al-Ṭurṭūshī", *Revue de l'Occident Musulman et de la Méditerranée* (Aix-en-Provence), 31, 1980-81, pp. 47-61.

[68] *Takmila*, No. 1797.

[69] *Ṣila*, No. 175.

[70] *Muʿjam*, No. 14, p. 19.

[71] P.Nwyia, "Notes sur quelques fragments inédits de la correspondance d'Ibn al-ʿArīf avec Ibn Barrajān", *Hespéris*, 43, 1956, pp. 217-21.

[72] Al-Shaʿrānī, *Ṭabaqāt*, I, 15.

[73] D. Gril, "Une source inédite pour l'histoire du *taṣawwuf*", *Livre du centenaire de l'IFAO*, Cairo, 1980, p. 463.

[74] *Dhayl*, VI, 171.

[75] Contrary to what I wrote in my biography of Ibn ʿArabī, *Ibn ʿArabī ou la quête du Soufre Rouge*, Paris, 1989, p. 74, it cannot be assumed that Ibn Barrajān was executed.

[76] *Tashawwuf*, p. 170.

[77] *Ṣila*, No. 175.

[78] *Muʿjam*, No. 14, pp. 19-20.

[79] Ibn ʿArabī also mentions Abū ʿAbd Allāh al-Ghazāl on several occasions, specifying, invariably, that he was a companion of Ibn al-ʿArīf. See, for example, *Futūḥāt*, 1228, II, 201, IV, 550, and *Sufis of Andalusia*, pp. 66, 1021, 104.

[80] *Tashawwuf*, No. 18, p. 120.

[81] On Ibn Qasī see: Ibn al-Abbār, *Kitāb al-ḥulla*, Cairo, 1963, No. 142, p. 197; *Aʿlām al-Maghrib*, III, 257; V. Lagardère, "La tarīqa et la révolte des murīdūn", *Revue de l'Occident Musulman et de la Méditerranée* (Aix-en-Provence), 35, 1983, pp. 157-70; P. Joseph Dreher, "L'Imâmat d'Ibn Qasī à Mertola", *MIDEO*, 18, 1988, pp. 195-210.

[82] "Notes", p. 219.

[83] "Rasā'il Ibn al-ʿArīf ilā aṣḥāb thawrat al-murīdīn fī 'l-Andalus", *Al-Abḥāth* (Beirut), 27, 1979, pp. 43-56.

[84] This work, Nwyia notes, gathers together various letters, including those of Ibn al-ʿArīf, but the latter is not the author of the work.

[85] Ibn al-ʿArīf's enthusiasm at reading these few passages from the writings of Ibn Qasī recalls that expressed by the Shaykh al-Akbar in the *Futūḥāt*, before a deeper study of the *Khalʿ al-naʿlayn* led him radically to revise his opinion (see below).

[86] In "La tariqa et la révolte des murīdūn" (p. 163), Lagardère, who repeats—often closely—Nwyia's brief analysis (in Arabic) of these letters in *Al-Abḥāth*, has clearly misunderstood the sentence where Nwyia states that it is "difficult to regard the language of these letters as being that used by a master to his disciple", rendering it in a diametrically opposed way: "In spite of the difficulty in interpreting this epistolary language of the guide towards his disciple".

[87] *Kitāb al-ḥulla*, Cairo, 1963, No. 142, p. 197.

[88] "Rasā'il Ibn al-ʿArīf", p. 53.

[89] For the details of his life, see the long note devoted to him by the *Dhayl*, I, No. 34, pp. 46-58.

[90] Al-Bukhārī, *Ṣaḥīḥ* "Īmān", 42.

[91] An example of this is ʿAbd Allāh al-Qaṭṭān, one of the Andalusī masters of Ibn ʿArabī, and called by the latter "the scourge of tyrants". Cf. *Sufis of Andalusia*, No. 16, pp. 112-13.

[92] See, for example, Ibn al-Abbār, *Kitāb al-ḥulla*, Cairo, 1963, p. 197, and al-Marrākushī, *Muʿjib*, Amsterdam, 1968, p. 150.

[93] C. Brockelmann, *GAL*, I, 434. See also Toufic Fahd, *La divination arabe*, 2nd ed., Paris, 1987, p. 236.

[94] Gril, "La science des lettres", in *Les illuminations de la Mecque*, p. 623, n. 239.

[95] Brockelmann, *op. cit.*

[96] Gril., *op. cit.*

[97] "*Risāla*", ed. H. Taher, in *Alif*, No. 5, p. 31.

[98] *Mawāqiʿ al-nujūm*, Cairo, 1965, p. 142.

[99] *Wafayāt al-aʿyān*, ed. I. ʿAbbās, Beirut, n.d., Vol. lv, No. 594, pp. 229-30.

100 *Futūḥāt*, IV, 220. In another passage (*Futūḥāt*, I, 60), Ibn ʿArabī specifies that Ibn Barrajān based his prediction on astrology.

101 *Futūḥāt*, II, 649. For other references to Ibn Barrajān, see also *Futūḥāt*, II, 104, 577 and III, 77.

102 See, for example, *Futūḥāt*, II, 97, 318.

103 B. Halff, "Le *Maḥāsin al-majālis* d'Ibn al-ʿArīf et l'oeuvre du soufi hanabalite al-Anṣārī", *Revue des Etudes Islamiques*, 39, fasc. 2, 1972, pp. 321-35.

104 See, for example: *Futūḥāt*, I, 93, 279; II, 97, 290, 318, 325; III, 396; IV, 92-93.

105 On this Sufi (who was the master of Ibn Sabʿīn) and his links with the *Shūdhiyya*, see Massignon, *La passion de Hallāj*, 2nd ed., Paris, 1975, II, 326 *et seq.*; *Aʿlām al-maghrib*, No. 81, 1, p. 77, where there is a bibliography.

106 *Barnāmaj*, Beirut, 1981, p. 302.

107 It is of some interest to note that the work was known by the illiterate *shaykh* Abū 'l-ʿAbbās al-ʿUryābī. Cf. *Rūḥ*, No. 1, in *Sufis of Andalusia*, p. 66.

108 *Ibn ʿArabī, ou la quête du Soufre Rouge*, p. 78

109 See, for example, *Futūḥāt*, I, 136, 312, 749; II, 52, 257, 686, 693, etc.

110 *Sharḥ kitāb khalʿ al-naʿlayn*, Istanbul, MS Shehit ʿAlī, 1174, fo. 111b-112a. See also fo. 99b.

111 *Ibid.*, fo. 6a.

112 *Futūḥāt*, II, 13.

113 *Al-Durra 'l-fākhira*, in *Sufis of Andalusia*, No. 8, p. 91; French trans., p. 96.

114 *Rūḥ*, in *Sufis of Andalusia*, No. 9, p. 93; French trans., p. 99.

115 *Durra*, in *Sufis of Andalusia*, No. 12, p. 98; French trans., p. 106.

116 *Rūḥ*, in *Sufis of Andalusia*, No. 20, p. 123; French trans., p. 137.

117 *Ibid.*, No. 4, p. 77; French trans., p. 78.

118 *Ibid.*, No. 15, p. 111; French trans., p. 122.

119 *Ibid.*, No. 55, p. 143; French trans., p. 160.

120 *Ibid.*, No. 6, pp. 79-83; French trans., pp. 82-86.

BIBLIOGRAPHY

Addas, C., *Ibn Arabī ou la Quête du soufre rouge*, Paris, 1989; English translation by Peter Kingsley, Oxford, in press.

Asín Palacios, Miguel, "Abenmasarra y su escuela: origines de la filosofía hispano-musulmana", in *Obras Escogidas*, Madrid, 1946, I, 1-216.

——,"El místico ibn al-ʿArīf y su *maḥāsin al-majālis*", in *ibid.*, I, 219-42.

Cruz Hernández, M., "La persecución anti-masarrī durante el reinado de ʿAbd al-Raḥmān al-Nāṣir li Dīn Allāh según Ibn Ḥayyān", *Al-Qanṭara*, II, 1981, pp. 52-67.

Dreher, P. Joseph, "L'Imâmat d'Ibn Qasī à Mertola", *Mélanges de l'Institut Dominicain des Etudes Orientales*, 18, 1988, pp. 195-210.

Fierro, M. I., *La heterodoxia en al-Andalus durante el periodo omeya*, Madrid, 1987.

——, "The introduction of *ḥadīth* in al-Andalus", *Der Islam*, 66, 1989, pp. 68-93.

——, "Una refutación contra Ibn Masarra", *Al-Qanṭara*, X, 1989, pp. 273-75.

——, "Accusations of *zandaqa* in al-Andalus", *Quaderni di Studi Arabi*, 5-6, 1987-88, p. 250 *et seq.*

Gril, D., "La science des lettres", in *Les Illuminations de la Mecque*, Paris, 1988, pp. 385-487.

Halff, B., "Le *Maḥāsin al-majālis* d'Ibn al-ʿArīf et l'oeuvre du soufi hanbalite al-Anṣārī", *Revue des Etudes Islamiques*, XXXIX, 1972, fasc. 2, pp. 321-35.

Ibn al-Abbār, *Al-Takmila li-kitāb al-ṣila*, ed. F. Codera, Madrid, 1886, and ed. Hourani, Cairo, 1955.

——, *Muʿjam*, Cairo, 1967.

——, *Kitāb al-ḥulla*, Cairo, 1963.

Ibn ʿArabī, *Al-Futūḥāt al-makkiyya*, Bulāq, Cairo, 1329 A. H.

——, *Fuṣūṣ al-ḥikam*, ed. ʿAfīfī, Beirut, 1946.

——, *Rūḥ al-quds*, Damascus, 1970, in *Sufis of Andalusia*, trans. R. W. J. Austin, Sherbone, 1988.

——, *Sharḥ kitāb khalʿ al-naʿlayn*, Istamnbul, MS Shehit Alī 1174, f. 1. 88b.

Ibn al-ʿArīf, *Maḥāsin al-majālis*, ed. and trans. M. Asín Palacios, Paris, 1933.
Ibn Bashkuwāl, *Kitāb al-ṣila fī taʾrīkh aʾimmat al-Andalus*, ed. F. Codera, Madrid, 1883.
Ibn al-Faraḍī, *Taʾrīkh ʿulamāʾ al-Andalus*, ed. F. Codera, Madrid, 1891-92.
Ibn Ḥayyān, *Al-Muqtabas*, Vol. V, ed. P. Chalmeta, Madrid, 1980.
Ibn Ḥazm, *Al-Fiṣal fī 'l milal*, Cairo, 1903
Ibn Masarra, *Kitāb al-ḥurūf*, ed K. I. Jaʿfar, in *Min qaḍāyā 'l-fikr al-islāmī,* Cairo, 1978, pp. 311-44.
——, *Kitāb al-iʿtibār*, in *ibid.*, pp. 346-60.
Ibn Qasī, *Kitāb khalʿ al-naʿlayn*, Istanbul, MS Shehit Alī 1174, f. 89-175.
Lagardère, V., "La tarīqa et la révolte des murīdūn", *Revue de l'Occident Musulman et de la Méditerranée*, 35, 1983, pp. 157-70.
Marín, M., "La transmisión del saber en al-Andalus hasta 300/912", *Al-Qanṭara*, VIII, 1987, pp. 87-97.
Morris, James W., *A Reconsideration of the Primary Sources*, 1973, unpublished.
Al-Nubāhī, *Kitāb al-marqaba 'l-ʿulyā*, Beirut, 1983.
Nwyia, P., "Notes sur quelques fragments inédits de la correspondance d'Ibn al-ʿArīf avec Ibn Barrajān", *Hespéris*, 43, 1956, pp. 217-21.
——, "Rasā'il Ibn al-ʿArīf ilā aṣḥāb thawrat al-murīdīn fī 'l Andalus", *Al-Abhāth*, Beirut, 27, 1979, pp. 43-56.
Al-Qifṭī, *Taʾrīkh al-ḥukamāʾ*, Leipzig, 1903.
Ṣā id, *Ṭabaqāt al-umam*, ed. L. Cheiko, Beirut, 1912, pp. 20-21; trans. Blachère, Paris, 1935.
Stern, S. M., "Ibn Masarra, Follower of Pseudo-Empedocles—An Illusion", *Actas do IV Congresso de Estudos Arabes e Islámicos*, Leiden, 1971, pp. 325-39.
Al-Tādilī b. al-Zayyāt, *Al-Tashawwuf ilā rijāl al-taṣawwuf*, ed. A. Tawfīq, Rabat, 1984.
Tornero, E., "Nota sobre el pensamiento de Abenmasarra", *Al-Qanṭara*, VI, 1985, pp. 503-06.

SCIENCE, TECHNOLOGY AND AGRICULTURE

NATURAL AND TECHNICAL SCIENCES IN AL-ANDALUS

J. VERNET

I. *The heritage of the late Roman period*

The Arab armies which conquered the Iberian Peninsula did not suddenly alter the existing culture which they encountered. They could not have done so: composed as they were of soldiers who were good warriors and officials who knew how to command an army and administer the conquered provinces, they did not aim to do more than live off the land and obey, in a rough and ready manner, the orders which they received from the Caliph in Damascus. Consequently they had, for their everyday needs, to rely on the practical knowledge of their new subjects: if they fell ill, they were attended by a Christian doctor; if they had problems in the cultivation of their newly acquired lands, it was their labourers or co-proprietors who had to resolve them. The sciences of Muslim Spain were those which had been studied in the Late Roman Empire, perceived through the prism formed by the encyclopaedic work of St. Isidore of Seville.

Immediately after the triumph of the Abbasid rulers, a member of the Umayyad family, ʿAbd al-Raḥmān I, managed to reach Córdoba and thus save his life. He swiftly gained power and declared himself to be independent of Baghdad. He introduced certain Eastern customs and tastes such as one might expect from a prince who had been educated at the court of the last Umayyad caliphs of Damascus, but he continued to depend upon Christian professional advisers, except in matters connected with warfare and the Muslim religion: military and civil engineers might be charged with the task of excavating a mine, building a bridge or a water channel, or determining, approximately, the direction of Mecca, so that the faithful might be able to turn their faces towards it at the time of prayer. Also during the reign of ʿAbd al-Raḥmān I it would seem that, among Spanish Muslims, there was a growing interest in the prophecies and predictions of soothsayers—an interest innate among all peoples—since we know the name of an astrologer who flourished in the last years of his rule: al-Ḍabbī.

During this period the non-mathematical sciences remained firmly within the Isidoran tradition: consider, for example, the T-map conserved in a manuscript in the Biblioteca Nacional, Madrid, the Arabic text of which shows that the author was very familiar with the work of St. Isidore, or the translation into Arabic of the *Historia* of Orosius, completed in Córdoba at a later date. Judging by the testimony of Ibn Juljul, who was writing in the second half of the 4th/10th century, doctors at this time studied the aphorisms of Christian doctors which had been translated into Arabic, and these should not be confused with the *Aphorisms* of Hippocrates. For the most part, they are short, penetrating observations, enabling a doctor to make a quick differential diagnosis within the limits of what was then possible. Ibn Juljul mentions six doctors who were practising medicine during the reigns of the *amīr*s Muḥammad I, al-Mundhir and ʿAbd Allāh. Five are Christians and two of them have names that betray their origins: Ḥamdīn b. ʿUbba (Opas) and Khālid b. Yazīd b. Rumān (Roman). One of them, Jawād, invented a medical remedy which must have been famous, for it was known as "the monk's medicine". In the middle of the 4th/10th century the situation began to change in favour of the Muslim doctors, but even so, when ʿAbd al-Raḥmān III fell ill with an inflammation of the ear, he was treated by Yaḥyā b. Isḥāq, the son of a Christian doctor. The prestige of this traditional medicine endured among the Arabs, so much so that Saʿīd b. ʿAbd Rabbihī (d. 366/977) states in his *Urjūza fī 'l-ṭibb* ("Didactic Poem on Medicine") that a proper knowledge of this science can only be attained by a person familiar with the ancient (i.e. Latin) texts which had been translated into Arabic.

It would seem—but this is still open to dispute—that just as astrologers continued to use the techniques of late Roman antiquity to make horoscopes, so farmers—by which I mean the owners of large country estates—cultivated their lands in accordance with the norms of classical agriculture. Until recently it was generally accepted that Iunius Moderatus Columela (1st century A.D.), a native of Cádiz, exercised a direct influence on the agricultural methods that were employed four or five centuries after the Muslim conquest, and it was also believed that his *De Re Rustica* had been translated into Arabic. These ideas were based on the words of a certain Yūnyūs cited by Ibn Ḥajjāj (fl. 5th/11th century), which happen to coincide with those of the above-mentioned Latin author. But, as in so many cases, the topic in question has by its very nature to be defined in *almost* the same words and in the same sequence, regardless of the author and the period to which he belongs. And since the opinions attributed to Yūnyūs now seem to be closer to those of Vindanius Anatolius of Berito, conserved in an Arabic text which derives from an earlier Syriac translation, Yūnyūs would be the distorted form of Vindanius.

Be that as it may, the only thing about which we can here be sure is that certain Roman agricultural practices survived in Muslim Spain, and this inevitably raises the question whether the introduction of certain specific techniques (the excavation of subterranean conduits or water-channels) should be credited to the Arabs, or whether the Arabs found such excavations already in existence and recognised them to be of the same type as the hydraulic devices which their compatriots had employed in the Yemen for centuries (*qanāt* in the West; *fajj* in Arabia).

II. *The first Eastern influences*

In the middle of the 3rd/9th century the first scientific and technical influences of Eastern origin were introduced into Muslim Spain. A few examples may be given by way of illustration. First we should note the arrival in Córdoba of the doctor al-Ḥarrānī, who soon became chief physician to the *amīr* ʿAbd al-Raḥmān II. Ibn Juljul gives us this information and mentions al-Ḥarrānī's two nephews (?), Aḥmad and ʿUmar b. Yūnus al-Ḥarrānī, who studied in Baghdad between 330/941 and 351/962 with T͟hābit b. Sinān b. T͟hābit b. Qurra. It was at this same time, that is to say in the 4th/10th century, that magic talismanic doctrines of Egyptian origin seem to have reached Muslim Spain. We now enter a period—that of the Cordoban Caliphate—during which an attempt was made to gather the maximum amount of information, regardless of its provenance, for the purposes of enlightenment. This was the policy which enabled science in al-Andalus to make great strides from the 5th/11th century onwards.

A precursor of all those whom we have hitherto mentioned was ʿAbbās b. Firnās (d. 274/887). Not only was he a poet and an astrologer, but he attempted to fly by leaping from the Ruṣāfa palace in Córdoba—a feat reminiscent of the later attempts made in this direction by the English monk Aylmer of Malmesbury. Unfortunately, Ibn Firnās could not understand the role played by the tail when birds alight on the ground, and he injured himself. But he was an enterprising man: he modified and, in so doing, perfected the technique of cutting rock crystal (quartz), which was already known to the Sassanians and the Romans; in one room of his house he built a kind of planetarium; and he invented a clepsydra (or water clock) capable of indicating the times of prayer, albeit without a high degree of accuracy. This machine (*minqāna* in the Arabic text) may perhaps be regarded as the prototype of those machines that were invented in the 5th/11th century.

In Spain the ancient and unsatisfactory theories of popular pharmacology, of late Roman origin, were displaced by Eastern theories; these were likewise inspired by classical Graeco-Roman and Indian texts, but they had passed through the filter of the East. The most interesting work which reached Córdoba was the *Materia Medica* of Dioscorides, translated into Arabic by Iṣṭifān b. Basīl. In about the year 337/948 the Byzantine Emperor presented the caliph ʿAbd al-Raḥmān III with a magnificent copy of Dioscorides in Greek. The readers—some of whom must have known colloquial Greek—could not understand the text. Since the Caliph did not have any hellenists at hand, he urged the Emperor to send him a specialist who could teach scientific Greek to his physicians. His petition was heeded, and it was thus that the monk Nicholas arrived in Córdoba.

With the latter's help it was possible to carry out a systematic revision of the Eastern Arabic version of the *Materia Medica* and to identify most of the plants, or "simples", mentioned therein. This is of some importance, since henceforward scientific Greek became part of the legacy of a group of scholars, such as Ḥasday b. S̲h̲aprūt, Ibn Juljul and Maslama of Madrid, each of whom had his own disciples—a group which was active in the first half of the 5th/11th century. Simultaneously, the first signs of a native Andalusī art of medicine began to appear: in about 353/964 ʿArīb b. Saʿīd wrote a treatise on obstetrics and pediatrics, the *Kitāb k̲h̲alq al-janīn*, which contains some information of an astrological kind, but which nonetheless offers evidence that a portion of Aristotle's writings was already known in Córdoba. A more important author is Abū 'l-Qāsim al-Zahrāwī (d. ca. 404/1013). He wrote a medical encyclopaedia in which there are prominent sections devoted to surgery (soon to be translated into Latin) and pharmacology. In the latter he displays a knowledge of the Egyptian and Iraqi techniques used by Eastern perfume dealers, the distant origins of which are to be found in the Mesopotamian tradition. We are equally indebted to these scholars for some of the first good clinical descriptions of leprosy and haemophilia; the introduction of cauterisation and numerous surgical instruments such as one frequently finds represented in the engravings of Renaissance doctors; and the stitching of wounds by means of ants.

At the end of the 4th/10th century botanical observations of the Eastern type were already known in Muslim Spain: in the work of Ibn Samajūn (fl. ca. 390/1000) one finds echoes of the *Nabataean Agriculture* and the *Kitāb al-nabāt* ("Book of Plants") of Abū Ḥanīfa al-Dīnawarī (d. 150/767). There is also a commentary on the latter by Ibn Uk̲h̲t G̲h̲ānim of Almería.

III. *The golden age of science in al-Andalus*

The beginning of the political decline of a country often occurs before it has attained its cultural pinnacle. This is what happened in Muslim Spain: the political and military hegemony of the caliphs was succeeded by the impotence of the "petty kings" (*mulūk al-ṭawāʾif*). The Muslims of the Iberian Peninsula were now grouped within ten or twelve independent states. Unable to fend off the attacks of the Christians of the North, they purchased peace in exchange for the payment of an annual tribute, and their sovereigns devoted themselves to the pursuit of a luxurious life, opposing one another and indulging their whims, so that they were sometimes encouraged to offer their patronage to specialists in different branches of learning. Thus, the kings of Saragossa, the Banū Hūd, favoured philosophers and men of letters; those of Toledo, the Banū D̲h̲ī 'l-Nūn, favoured scientists; those of Seville, the Banū ʿAbbād, favoured poets, etc. But their generosity was not exclusively limited to those who cultivated such disciplines; it was bestowed upon all deserving men, whether they were residents or travellers in their dominions.

For example, al-Bājī and Ibn al-Sīd found temporary asylum in Saragossa. Al-Kirmānī, a disciple of Maslama of Madrid, made known the *Rasāʾil Ik̲h̲wān al-Ṣafāʾ* ("Epistles of the Brethren of Purity"), the contents of which—by means as yet unknown—filtered into Europe. The astronomer Azarquiel of Toledo, who was probably apprehensive about the Christian assault on his country, sought and obtained refuge in Córdoba, which, at that time, belonged to the Sevillian al-Muʿtamid. The Sicilian poets Abū 'l-ʿArab and Ibn Ḥamdīs, who witnessed their own country fall into the hands of the Normans, found a new home in Seville. On the other hand—and this phenomenon was to become very apparent in the 6th/12th century—a considerable number of scholars and scientists emigrated from Muslim Spain to North Africa and the Middle East because they were frightened by the continuous defeats suffered by their sovereigns. It was probably as a result of this emigration that the work of Maslama of Madrid (d. ca. 397/1007) came to be known centuries later to the Easterner Ibn al-Shāṭir, and the *Kitāb al-qaṣd wa 'l-bayān* by the agriculturalist Ibn Baṣṣāl came to be used by the *rasūlī* sovereign of Yemen, al-Malik al-Afḍal, etc.

We are quite well informed about the development of science during this period thanks to the writings of the *qāḍī* of Toledo, Ṣāʿid, sometimes called Ibn Ṣāʿid (d. 462/1070), published under the title *Kitāb ṭabaqāt al-umam* (usually translated as the "Book of the Categories of Nations", but which is really a Universal History of the Sciences). There are obviously some inaccuracies, but, even in the state and condition in which it has survived, it constitutes a veritable archive of information, giving us the names of those young men who, at the time of the work's compilation, seemed to have the most promising future.

One of Ṣāʿid's contemporaries was the alchemist Abū Maslama of Madrid (not to be confused with the astronomer who is his near-namesake). He wrote a book entitled *Rutbat al-ḥakīm*, which, incidentally, contains a description of some experiments made by the author, from one of which one can infer that he was aware of the principle of the preservation of matter. Among this group of authors—it is difficult to know whether to call them technicians or scientists—one must include Aḥmad or Muḥammad b. Khalaf al-Murādī, a person unknown twenty years ago, who was "discovered" through the study of his *Kitāb al-asrār fī natāʾij al-afkār*, conserved in a single manuscript copied by the hand of Isḥāq b. al-Sīd, the chief astronomer of Alfonso X (the Wise).

The work of al-Murādī is of great interest. In spite of the fact that the single manuscript in which it is conserved has been approximately 40% destroyed, it can be almost completely reconstructed. It describes various clepsydras capable of being set in motion at specified intervals of time—so that they could have been used as clocks—and capable of performing predetermined motions. This means that we have found the only book hitherto known in al-Andalus which is comparable to the works of Heron, the Banū Mūsā brothers and al-Jazarī. There is another interesting detail about this work: the manner in which al-Murādī treats his subject-matter seems to be without precedent; in a couple of key words, the terminology is quite different from that which one finds in the above-mentioned works, and everything seems to suggest that we are here in the presence of a true inventor, or else someone who represents a native Andalusī tradition of artesan-mechanics. Similarly, in his clepsydras he seems to be working independently from Ibn Firnās and Azarquiel. Moreover, and this is important to emphasise, in order to produce hysteresis in his mechanical "toys", al-Murādī uses mercury (al-Jazarī uses metal balls) which is displaced inside the arms of the main balance, or master-balance of the system. Machine number one, which has recently been reconstructed, demonstrates the efficacy of a mechanism which had never before been used in this way.

It is now worth mentioning, to avoid having to insist upon it later, that the manuscript to which I have been referring contains treatises by different authors, one of the most remarkable of which is an account of six machines capable of producing perpetual motion. At least one of these was reproduced by the French artesan-architect Villard de Honnecourt (fl. ca. 1220).

On the subject of agriculture, we may proceed with more confidence, since the history of agriculture in Muslim Spain has recently been rewritten by Lucie Bolens.[1] First in Toledo, under the patronage of al-Maʾmūn b. Dhī 'l-Nūn, and later in Seville, there were, we know, several agriculturalists. Their dates are uncertain, but their activities seem to exist within the framework of the *ṭāʾifa* period, or, at the latest, up to the beginning of that of the Almoravids. The texts which have survived are, for the most part, incomplete, since they are included in much later anthologies compiled by North African writers. We should note the works of the doctor Ibn Wāfid (398/1007-467/1074) and Ibn Baṣṣāl of Toledo; of Abū 'l-Khayr and Ibn Ḥajjāj of Seville; and of al-Tighnarī, who, after studying in Seville, moved to Granada and, moreover, must have been a distinguished man of letters because his biography is to be found in *Al-Dhakhīra* by Ibn Bassām (d. 542/1147). The last of them, Ibn al-ʿAwwām (he lived some time between 512/1118 and 663/1265), composed his writings by a grafting process: it is a mosaic of what his predecessors had written on agriculture.

An analysis of these treatises shows that we are here faced with a mixture of agricultural traditions, the origins of which date back to Babylonian and Egyptian antiquity, and which reach the medieval period through the *Filāḥa nabaṭiyya* of Ibn Waḥshiyya. The Carthaginian, Roman and Hellenistic influences merge with the earlier sources as a consequence of the Arabic version of the Byzantine *Geoponika*. The majority of quotations by authors whose names are mentioned in these Hispano-Arab works are indirect. In other words, as in the case of the astrologer Ibn Abī Rijāl, these writers have not seen the original texts from which they cite. Furthermore, they mention sources like the *Filāḥa rūmiyya* and the *Filāḥa hindiyya*. The first may be attributed to a certain Qusṭūs, who is probably an imaginary person invented in the middle of the 4th/10th century by ʿAlī b. Muḥammad b. Saʿd. In any case, we know that in the 5th/11th century, in places such as Toledo and Seville, Andalusī agriculturalists planted botanical gardens and sought to investigate how well exotic plants might adapt to the climate of the districts in which they were working. Also, by keeping these plants under constant observation and by analysing the properties of the soil in which they grew, they considered how to improve their cultivation.

In order to do this, these scholars had to rely on the more advanced sciences: botany, pharmacology and medicine. The first of the above disciplines had attained its peak in Muslim Spain with the anonymous work entitled *ʿUmdat al-ṭabīb fī maʿrifat al-nabāt li-kull labīb*, written at the end of the 5th/11th century. In it one finds an excellent attempt to classify plants into categories (*jins*), species (*nawʿ*) and varieties (*ṣinf*), which is far more developed than any other system previously conceived of, even including those of Aristotle and Theophrastus. The work of this unknown author does not appear to have had a direct influence on the agriculturalists, even though the latter were particularly interested in the science of grafting. Ibn Baṣṣāl, for example, had noted that grafting is only successful between plants of the same kind: and he had likewise outlined a system of classification, as had Ibn al-ʿAwwām some years later, which is of much less value than that of *ʿUmdat al-ṭabīb*.

Medicine, like botany, is linked to astronomy owing to the interest of pharmacologists in obtaining "simples", that is to say, plants which might be employed as remedies, without adulteration. Al-Tighnarī and Ibn Wāfid were both doctors concerned with this question. The latter is said to be the author of a treatise on agriculture—nowadays one is inclined to attribute it to Abū 'l-Qāsim al-Zahrāwī—which has been largely preserved in a Spanish translation and was used by the Renaissance agriculturalist Gabriel Alonso de Herrera (d. ca. 1539). The agriculturalists of Muslim Spain studied the composition of the soil and endeavoured to make untilled land cultivable: they tried to define the characteristics of the manure best suited to each situation, and they analysed the water and examined how land could be irrigated by means of water-channels, wells, water-wheels (*nāʿūras*) and other devices. Their machinery and primitive wheels, articulated by a winding gear which was very imperfect, since it was only required to draw water in an irregular fashion, probably provided mechanics such as al-Murādī with the inspiration to develop their mechanical "toys"—toys which would eventually become clocks.

The agriculturalists were aware of the importance of rotating crops and leaving land to lie fallow; they knew that, in some cases, the mixing of manure was of paramount importance; and thus they managed to raise the standard of agriculture in Muslim Spain to a level which was only surpassed in the 19th century with the development of chemistry. During the Enlightenment (18th century) the Spanish authorities became so convinced of this decline in agriculture that they commissioned a Spanish translation of the works of Ibn al-ʿAwwām—a work which, a good many years later, was translated into French to make it accessible to French Algerian farmers.

If, from the medical point of view, agriculture reached its maturity at the end of the 4th/10th century with the work of al-Zahrāwī, and remained at a reasonably high level in the Iberian Peninsula throughout the 5th/11th century, the initial influence which it exercised on Christian Europe was slight. Here the chief influence was that of the Latin translations of the Salerno school made by Constantinus Africanus in the 5th/11th century.

However, at the end of the *ṭāʾifa* period, the situation changed: ʿAbd al-Malik b. Zuhr (d. 470/1078) took advantage of his pilgrimage to Mecca to study medicine at Qayrawān and Cairo, and in the first of these cities he may have met Constantinus Africanus. At all events, on his return to Spain, he became the physician of Mujāhid of Denia. His son, Abū 'l-ʿAlāʾ (the Aboali or Abulelizor of the Latin texts) received a solid schooling in medicine and literature, and, owing to these circumstances, was summoned to Seville, where he became physician to the ruler, al-Muʿtamid, and when the latter was deposed by the Almoravids, he changed sides to lend his services to the victor Yūsuf b. Tāshfīn. He died in Córdoba in 525/1131. At about this time the text of the *Qānūn* of Ibn Sīnā (Avicenna) reached Muslim Spain, parts of it commented upon by Abū 'l-ʿAlāʾ. His son Abū Marwān (487/1094-557/1161) was known to the Christians as Abhomeron Avenzoar. Abū Marwān was a contemporary of Ibn Rushd (Averroes). The latter regarded him as his equal in medicine and perhaps as a better pharmacologist, since at the end of his *Kitāb al-kulliyāt* (the *Colliget* of the Latin translators), with regard to pharmacological questions, Ibn Rushd refers his readers to *Al-Taysīr* by his colleague and friend Abū Marwān. This last work was translated into Latin by Paravicini in about 679/1280. It describes for the first time an abscess of the pericardium; it recommends, in some cases, feeding a patient through the oesophagus or the anus; and it gives one of the first descriptions of the mite which causes scabies (*sarcoptes scabiei*).

Meanwhile great progress was achieved in pharmacology as a consequence of the Arabic version of the *Materia Medica* of Dioscorides, established by doctors in Córdoba in the 4th/10th century. This, in turn, was twice summarised in Latin in 7th/13th century Toledo, while Ibn Wāfid's books on balneology (the scientific study of bathing and medicinal springs) and simple plant remedies were translated into Christian tongues: the first into Latin (*De Balneis*) and the second into Catalan (*Libre de les medicines particulars*). In the second of these works, the fruit of twenty years of research, he follows Dioscorides and Galen, but at the same time he makes his own personal observations, alleging that he prefers simples to compounds and that, as far as possible, he would do without either, limiting himself to the prescription of well-proven dietetic treatments.

However, the greatest pharmacologist in Muslim Spain seems to have been al-Ghāfiqī (fl. ca. 545/1150), who made detailed observations on the flora of al-Andalus. Al-Nabātī', Ibn Ṣāliḥ and Abū 'l-Ḥajjāj did the same, while their disciple, Ibn al-Bayṭar, continued this work in the north of Morocco and in all those regions through which he travelled. The text of Dioscorides known in Córdoba during the 4th/10th century was gradually augmented as a result of the contributions made by others over the centuries up to the time of Ibn al-Bayṭar (d. 646/1248). The latter, in his *Jāmiʿ al-mufradāt*, lists more than three thousand simples in an alphabetical order, using the information collected by his predecessors, but adding his own comments. This work alone describes more than twice the number of species of plants mentioned in the original Arabic version of Dioscorides.

IV. *The century of the philosophers*

Traditionally it used to be thought (possibly through the influence of Dozy) that the landing of African Berber tribes on the Iberian Peninsula—the Almoravids and the Almohads—was the direct cause of the cultural decline of Muslim Spain from the apex attained during the *ṭāʾifa* period. This may be true with regard to literature, but it is obviously not true as regards the development of science. Whereas in the 5th/11th century, the century of the *ṭāʾifa* kings, there were some outstanding astronomers, in the 6th/12th and 7th/13th centuries, when philosophers such as Ibn Bājja (Avempace) and Ibn Rushd were prominent, scientists also played an important role, since the former did not merely cultivate philosophy in the sense in which that word is understood nowadays: at that time the term comprised everything which until the 18th century was known as natural philosophy, including those sciences—such as mathematics and astronomy—which had still not become separated from the Aristotelian concept of science.

Without entering into a detailed analysis of the contributions to science at this period, it should be noted that it was during this century of philosophy (6th/12th century) that Muslim Spain *exported* most of its ideas to the East (Egypt, Syria, Persia and China) and to Europe (France, Italy, Germany and England). These invisible exports, which had started unobtrusively at the end of the 4th/10th century, now grew as a result of the scientific progress achieved in the Iberian Peninsula during the 5th/11th century: the flow of imported books—or at least of Eastern ideas—virtually came to a halt, while the scholars who emigrated eastwards personally conveyed their knowledge to those parts (as in the case of Abū Ṣalt of Denia), or else their works reached Cairo and Damascus in the hands of merchants, many of whom were Jewish. A contributory factor in this whole process was the expansion of maritime trade, which, by the 7th/13th century, had reached all the coasts of the Mediterranean, leading to growing competition between the Italian city-states—Venice, Genoa, Pisa—and the chief "autonomous" ports—Barcelona and Marseilles.

Let us look at an example of how science was exported to Egypt from Muslim Spain. There was a Jew of Saragossa named Abū 'l-Faḍl b. Ḥasday. He wrote well in Arabic and already in about 457/1065, when he was still a young man, he was familiar with two works by Aristotle: the *Physics* and *On the Heavens*. He converted to Islam and, some years later, emigrated to Egypt. A person of almost the same name is cited in that country as a correspondent of Ibn Bājja (Avempace) at the beginning of the 6th/12th century. But Ibn Bājja was also from Saragossa and we know that he died, perhaps as a result of poisoning, around 533/1138. I believe one may plausibly maintain that Abū 'l-Faḍl b. Ḥasday, who travelled east *before* 478/1085, was a friend and disciple of Ibn Bājja. But he also studied under the mathematician Ibn al-Sayyid of Denia, a person who is likewise cited in eastern lists of names.

Abū 'l-Faḍl (= Abū 'l-Faraj) b. Ḥasday deserves much more attention than he has hitherto received. Ibn Ṣā'id of Toledo had seen in him a young man with a promising future and he was in fact to become a great writer employed in the chancery of al-Muqtadir and al-Mu'taman of Saragossa. As a cultivated man, he probably aimed to display more erudition than that which one finds in the satirical letter (*hazaliyya*) addressed by Ibn Zaydūn, the great poet of Córdoba (394/1003-463/1070), to his rival in love, Ibn 'Abdūs. Just as Ibn Zaydūn began to discuss in his work everything which a cultured person in Córdoba in the first half of the 5th/11th century ought to know, so Abū 'l-Faḍl did the same for the second half of the century with reference to Saragossa, a city in which Ismā'īlī doctrines, introduced there by al-Kirmānī, were well known, as we shall immediately demonstrate. This fact is important.

Shi'ite commentaries on the following Quranic verse (24:35) were known in Saragossa:

> God is the Light of the heavens and the earth. The parable of His light is, as it were, that of a niche containing a lamp; the lamp is in a *container* of glass which is like a radiant star: it is lit by the *grace* of a blessed tree, an olive-tree that is neither of the east nor of the west, the oil whereof almost gives light although the fire does not touch it. Light upon light. God guides whomsoever He wills to His light, and God forms parables for men. God has full knowledge of all things.

Shi'ite commentaries on this verse reached Europe by way of Saragossa and they contributed to the formation of an ideological substratum which would later infiltrate Catharism and some European literary works (Chrétien de Troyes, *Parsifal*, etc.).

Abū 'l-Faḍl b. Ḥasday must have been born in about 436/1045. After falling in love with a Muslim girl, he became a Muslim and married her. In the course of his administrative work he must have known the chief figures of his age, including the Cid, Hugo, Abbot of Cluny, al-Bājī, the young Ibn

Bājja (Avempace, who, the writer Leo Africanus informs us, was of Jewish origin), Moses ha-Sefardī, who became Pedro Alfonso, Bahya b. Paqūda, the astrologer Ibn al-Khayyāṭ and many others. The bad relations which existed between al-Muqtadir of Saragossa and his brother Yūsuf Ḥussām al-Dawla of Lérida perhaps gave Abū 'l-Faḍl the idea of creating a fictitious exchange of letters between a doctor of Lérida named Burduqūn (Perdigón, from the Romance Perdix, the modern Perdiz; the surname Perdices ["Partridges"] is still widespread in that region) and an astrologer of Lérida nicknamed al-'Āfiya ("the healthy one") because he has lost an eye. The latter writes a letter to the doctor Perdigón, who has lost one of his testicles, saying that his way of walking reminds him of mechanical toys (*ḥiyal*) and mentions Philo and a certain Tālās as inventors of these devices; the doctor's remaining testicle was as large as a spherical astrolabe; his penis was similar to the alidad or index of a flat astrolabe; the astrologer knows that in their construction work masons use a level and architects use a plummet; he has seen an armillary sphere and geometrical instruments like cylinders and cones; he refers to the *Book of Animals* (probably that of Aristotle, *not* that of al-Jāḥiẓ); he mentions Galen and Aesculapius and enters fully into the subject of optics —although obliquely, as in the case of everything treated in these epistles: in a couple of words he speaks about the emission of rays of light and proceeds to assert that "if the light of all the stars were gathered together, they would shine brighter than the full moon".[2] The interpretation of the text will here depend on whether one regards this as a simple literary metaphor or a precedent of Olbers' paradox. He lists several constellations, notes that persons with good eyesight can count as many as seven stars in the Pleiades, alludes to moon-spots, demonstrates awareness that the lunar month does *not* begin at the time of the real conjunction of the moon and the sun, etc.

There is another aspect of these epistles which is especially interesting and which perhaps may explain why, at the time of al-Mu'taman, Abū 'l-Faḍl emigrated to Egypt, where he died before 515/1121, that is to say when he was about seventy-five years of age. It is the letter in which Perdigón mocks al-'Āfiya, saying: "There is some truth in that, since you are [the constellation of] the Whale (Cetus), the beast (*dābba*) of the sea that swims in the waves and in the celestial sphere. It is like that because Galen created it by gathering together a group of stars known as 'the sea-beast', whose belly sinks into the River (Eridanus); its tail goes behind Aquarius and it is in the place where Aquarius lets the water flow into the mouth of the Southern Fish. At the highest point of its mane are to be found the stars of the Fish, the sign of the zodiac... You [Perdigón] are certainly the one-eyed Antichrist (*Dajjāl*), the long-awaited *Qā'im*! We beg God to give us strength to face your banners, that He may assist us under your rule! We appeal to God that we may be able to breathe beneath your reins and that your aggressiveness and crimes may be kept far away from us, whether you are unjust or tyrannical, whether you are capricious or go astray! God is certainly forgiving and merciful to His slaves."[3]

The Beast (*al-Dābba*), the Antichrist (*al-Dajjāl*) and *al-Qā'im*, all explicitly mentioned by Abū 'l-Faḍl, place us directly in touch with the Ismā'īlī atmosphere which must have existed in Saragossa in the second half of the 5th/11th century. And in the background there is the exegesis which must have been applied to a key passage in the Quran.

Another example—and one which is more significant—is that of Ibn Rushd and Maimonides. Both were born in Córdoba: the first in 520/1126, the second in 535/1140. Ibn Rushd wrote his first commentary on Aristotle in 554/1159. At that time Maimonides was in Fez on his way to Cairo, which he reached in 560/1165. One may deduce from this that Maimonides had not read the works of his fellow-citizen Ibn Rushd while he was in the West. These reached him in the hands of learned merchants, such as the Jew Josef ben Yehuda ben Isḥāq ben 'Aqrūn, named in Arabic Abū 'l-Ḥajjāj Yūsuf b. Yaḥyā b. Isḥāq al-Sabtī 'l-Maghribī, who arrived in Cairo in about 580/1185. Since we know that Ibn 'Aqnīn and Maimonides studied the book of al-Mu'taman together, it must have already been in Cairo when they arrived (perhaps it was Ibn Ḥasday who brought it?); and since, during this period, they also read the works of Ibn Rushd and Jābir b. Aflaḥ, one must assume that books were then travelling swiftly from West to East. On the other hand, the *Astronomy*, which al-Biṭrūjī must have been composing at that time, arrived later, since, according to J. Samsó, it was completed between 580/1185 and 588/1192.

But the route from East to West was also quickly traversed. Whereas previously the route had reached north of the Pyrenees across Muslim Spain, now it crossed Christian Spain: this explains why the religious and philosophical works of Maimonides were known very early in Catalonia and Provence, giving rise to a heated controversy in the Jewish communities of those regions—a controversy comparable to that which the works of Ibn Rushd produced in Christian Europe, where they came to be known very soon, chiefly through the translations of Michael Scot.

It would be very interesting to know whether, as is generally said, Ibn Rushd had *no* disciples in the Muslim world. Since his name is missing in almost all subsequent biographical dictionaries, this is something which is hard to prove, but one must add that the names of many important mathematicians, doctors and astronomers are also missing. Officially Ibn Rushd only had two Arab disciples: his son Abū Muḥammad b. 'Abd Allāh (who was physician to the Almohad sultan al-Nāṣir) and Ibn Ṭumlūs of Azila. But if one accepts the definition of "disciple" given by the alchemist Abū 'l-Qāsim Maslama of Madrid in his *Rutbat al-ḥakīm* with reference to Jābir b. Ḥayyān, we might find another. Abū Maslama says that "one hundred and fifty years separate me from Jābir b. Ḥayyān, but, despite that, I regard myself as a true disciple of his because of the great esteem in which I hold his works".[4] By this criterion, Ibn Rushd had a magnificent disciple in the figure of Ibn Khaldūn. Al-Maqqarī, who in this instance is faithfully copying Ibn al-Khaṭīb's *Iḥāṭa*, informs us that Ibn Khaldūn "explained and summarised a large number of books by Ibn Rushd".[5] Since Ibn Khaldūn finished his *Muqaddima* three years after the assassination of Ibn al-Khaṭīb, it would seem that he went on gathering together materials from Ibn Rushd, whom he cites ten times and with whom, at one point, he takes issue. Similarly, Ibn Rushd himself did not always agree with Aristotle. To conclude, Ibn Khaldūn regarded himself as a disciple of Ibn Rushd a full two hundred years after the latter's death.

Furthermore, if we consider that Europe ends at the Urals and that Constantinople (Istanbul) belongs to the Western World, since it is situated to the west of the chain of mountains, one should count the number of Ibn Rushd's manuscript works which are located today in western libraries. If one does some statistics, on the basis of the information supplied by Miguel Cruz Hernández,[6] it will be found that the libraries of the Maghrib—from Istanbul to the West—contain more works than those situated to the east of the above-mentioned meridian.

One may therefore conclude that mutual intellectual contacts between East and West were at their height in the 6th/12th and 7th/13th centuries. We may proceed to inquire whether certain institutions, the origins of which lie in Iraq, took as long to reach Muslim Spain as is commonly supposed. Take, for example, the mental asylums and the colleges called *madrasa*s. Mental asylums and, in a broader sense, hospitals, existed in Muslim Spain at least a hundred years before the date generally given (Granada, 769/1367). A year after the conquest of Valencia (636/1238) by Jaime I ("the Conqueror") one already finds Latin documents donating grants to maintain beds (for patients) in the Hospital of Saint Vincent in the said city. It would be very strange indeed if it had occurred to the Aragonese and Catalans accompanying the King to *create* a new institution, unknown in their realms, unless they found it already functioning in the newly conquered city. We learn from the documents that in this hospital there was one room for men and another for women, and that the doctors only came to visit the sick in the morning or in the evening, in exactly the same way as they do nowadays. Moreover, in the *Vocabulista in arabico* by Ramón Martí (627/1230-682/1284), a writer from Barcelona, the word *malestan/maristán* (in Arabic *māristān* or *bīmāristān*) already appears. This would not have happened if the word were not in constant use in the regions known to the author.

The *madrasa* or school of higher education appears in an embryonic form in the Near East at the beginning of the 5th/11th century. Soon afterwards we already find it as an institution in its own right under the jurisdiction of the Seljuq minister Niẓām al-Mulk. This was a real university college, comprising a place of prayer, some pupils with scholarships, a rector, and some teachers who relied on income deriving from a foundation trust which was technically inalienable and protected by the law governing religious endowments (Arabic *waqf* or *ḥabs*, Spanish *habiz*). It took time for this institution to reach the West because Mālikī law had a different theory of how the goods of the deceased should be administered. However, endowments of this kind definitely existed in the 7th/13th century in Naṣrid Granada, and the building of what is supposedly the earliest *madrasa* in Muslim Spain (750/1349) is still standing. There are nevertheless grounds for suspecting that the administrative "model" for this college was utilised a century earlier and that the school founded by Alfonso the Wise in Murcia, which was governed by al-Riqūṭī, was already a *madrasa*, since the Christian king was not at all concerned about the juridical theories of the different Sunni schools of law and saw only the didactic results which might be achieved by the new institution, with its remote resemblance to a cathedral school.

This sovereign, Alfonso the Wise, never reckoned what his contemporaries and posterity might think of him as a scientist (posterity unjustly attributed to him the saying that "If God had consulted me at the time of the Creation about how to make the heavens, I would have advised Him to do so in a simpler way"). This is proved by the fact that throughout his whole reign (1252-1284) he kept in touch with the scholars of the Near East, regardless of the sect or religion to which they belonged. His embassies to the Mamlūks and the Mongols—and those which he received from them—not only had a political objective but also sought to procure materials to further his scientific projects. He was a learned king, but he was not very prudent—*savant* rather than *sage*. Thus he witnessed not only his son Sancho's rebellion against him but, what is more interesting from our point of view, the consolidation of Granada's independence under the rule of the Naṣrids.

V. *The end: the Naṣrid kingdom*

This last bastion of Islam in Spain attained its final moment of splendour in the 8th/14th century during the reign of Muḥammad V. From 748/1348 to 751/1351 it had to endure the scourge of plague, so well described by two polymath writers, Ibn Khātima and Ibn al-Khaṭīb, who give information on how the epidemic spread from the East to the West. It is to this period that one must assign the start of the transition from clepsydras to mechanical clocks, which, according to textual accounts, were operating up to a point in Granada, Fez, Tlemcen, etc., and the appearance of the first Arab nautical map which is extant (of the Western Mediterranean and the Atlantic Coast from Cape Bojador to England), usually called the Maghrib Map. This map may be dated about 730/1330, that is to say approximately fifty years later than the oldest known nautical map, which is that of Pisa. It is also certain that during this period scientific contacts with the Near East remained strong and there was still a keen interest in agriculture and medicine. Ibn Luyūn (681/1282-750/1349), for example, wrote a didactic poem on agriculture. With regard to medicine, we know that one doctor from al-Andalus emigrated to serve in Christian lands and that others, such as Muḥammad b. al-Shafra (d. 761/1360), had non-Muslim pupils in their classes.

[1] Lucie Bolens, *Agronomes andalous du Moyen Âge*, Geneva-Paris, 1981. See also J. Vernet, J. Samsó, *Les développements de la science arabe en Andalousie* (in press).

[2] Taken from Ibn Bassām, *Al-Dhakhīra fī maḥāsin ahl al-jazīra*, ed. Iḥsān 'Abbās, Beirut, 1974, I, 3, 456-94.

[3] *Ibid.*

[4] See J. Vernet, *Historia de la ciencia árabe: la alquimía*, Madrid, 1981, pp. 181-83.

[5] *Nafḥ al-ṭīb*, ed. Iḥsān 'Abbās, Beirut, 1968, VII, 180-81.

[6] M. C. Hernández, *Abū-l-Walīd ibn Rushd (Averroes). Vida, obra, pensamiento, influencia*, Córdoba, 1986, pp. 316-24.

BIBLIOGRAPHY

Comes, M., R. Puig and J. Samsó (eds.), *De Astronomia Alphonsi Regis*, Barcelona, 1987.

Comes, M., H. Mielgo and J. Samsó (eds.), *"Ochava Espera" y "Astrofísica". Textos y estudios sobre las fuentes árabes de la Astronomía de Alfonso X*, Barcelona, 1990.

García Sánchez, E. (ed.), *Ciencias de la naturaleza en al-Andalus. Textos y estudios*, I, Granada, 1990.

Glick, Thomas F., *Irrigation and Society in Medieval Valencia*, Cambridge (Mass.), 1970.

Kennedy, E. S., Colleagues and Former Students, *Studies in the Islamic Exact Sciences*, Beirut, 1983.

Kennedy, E. S., *A Survey of Islamic Astronomical Tables*, Philadelphia, 1956.

King, D. A., *Islamic Astronomical Instruments*, London (Variorum Reprints), 1987.

Millás-Vallicrosa, J. M., *Estudios sobre historia de la ciencia española*, Barcelona, 1949.

——, *Nuevos estudios sobre historia de la ciencia española*, Barcelona, 1960.

——, *Estudios sobre Azarquiel*, Madrid-Granada, 1943-50.

Samsó, J., *Las ciencias de los Antiguos en al-Andalus* (in press, to appear Madrid, 1992).

Vernet, J., *Estudios sobre historia de la ciencia medieval*, Barcelona-Bellaterra, 1979.

——, *De 'Abd al-Raḥmān I a Isabel II*, Barcelona, 1989.

——, *La cultura hispanoárabe en Oriente y Occidente*, Barcelona, 1978. There is a French translation (*Ce que la culture doit aux Arabes d'Espagne*, Paris, 1985) and a German translation (*Die spanische-arabische Kultur im Orient und Okzident*, Zurich and Munich, 1984).

——, *La ciencia en al-Andalus*, Seville, 1986.

—— (ed.), *Estudios sobre historia de la ciencia árabe*, Barcelona, 1980.

—— (ed.), *Textos y estudios sobre astronomía española en el siglo XIII*, Barcelona, 1981.

—— (ed.), *Nuevos estudios sobre astronomía española en el siglo de Alfonso X*, Barcelona, 1983.

THE EXACT SCIENCES IN AL-ANDALUS

JULIO SAMSÓ

I. General Remarks

Andalusī civilisation, which extended, approximately, from 93/711 to 897/1492, witnessed no scientific development in the field of the exact sciences until the reign of the *amīr* ʿAbd al-Raḥmān II (206/821-238/852), who, according to a late anonymous Maghribi source, was the first to introduce astronomical tables in al-Andalus.[1] Before that period we can only discern the survival of a Latin astrological tradition and suppose that it probably coexisted with an Arabic tradition of folk astronomy dealing mainly with weather predictions based on the *anwāʾ* system and with *mīqāt* problems, such as determining the *qibla* in order to establish the more or less correct orientation of the *miḥrāb* in the new mosques.[2] The middle of the 3rd/9th century saw the beginning of a period of easternisation in Andalusī culture, favoured both by the common practice of a *riḥla* to the East designed to complete the education of young men from any family which could afford it and, also, by the cultural policy of the Umayyad *amīr*s, who encouraged Eastern scholars to establish themselves in Córdoba and did their best to buy the new books published in the great capitals of the Mashriq. This period lasted at least until the fall of the Umayyad Caliphate (422/1031), which entailed the loss of political unity, but was followed by a subsequent period of fifty years (422/1031-479/1086) which may be regarded as the Golden Age of the exact sciences and of all the other manifestations of Andalusī cultural life. Sovereigns of the "petty kingdoms" (*mulūk al-ṭawāʾif*) encouraged the development of science, and one of them, Yūsuf al-Muʾtaman of Saragossa (474/1081-478/1085), was probably the most important mathematician in the history of al-Andalus. This period also witnessed the scientific activity, in Toledo and Córdoba, of Abū Isḥāq Ibrāhīm b. Yaḥyā ʾl-Naqqāsh, known as Ibn al-Zarqālluh or Ibn al-Zarqiyāl (d. 493/1100), who became, without any doubt, the most original and influential astronomer in al-Andalus. On the other hand, this golden half-century also entailed a progressive slowing down in contacts with the Mashriq, which meant that the development of the exact sciences in al-Andalus from the middle of the 5th/11th century on became somewhat original and independent of the East. This loss of contact with a cultural area which, especially from the 7th/13th century onwards, was producing new ideas in the field of astronomy was also one of the main reasons for the decay of Andalusī science, the first symptoms of which appeared during the 6th/12th century.

II. Mathematics

Mathematics did not, it should be stressed, have anything like the same importance in al-Andalus as astronomy. The oldest extant Andalusī mathematical text is the unpublished treatise on land surveying (*taksīr*) written by the physician Muḥammad b. ʿAbdūn al-Jabalī towards the middle of the 4th/10th century; the book is of a practical nature, and this seems, indeed, to be one of the main characteristics of the first manifestations of Andalusī mathematics. The second half of the 4th/10th century witnessed the important mathematical and astronomical school founded by Abū 'l-Qāsim Maslama b. Aḥmad al-Majrīṭī (d. 397/1007), three members of which—Maslama himself, Abū 'l Qāsim Aḥmad b. Muḥammad b. al-Samḥ (d. 426/1035) and Abū 'l Ḥasan ʿAlī b. Sulaymān al-Zahrāwī—wrote treatises on commercial arithmetic (*muʿāmalāt*). These texts do not seem to be extant, but we can gain an idea of their contents through the *Liber Mahameleth*, a Latin translation, ascribed to John of Seville, of an Andalusī treatise on the same subject.[3] The authorities quoted in it (Euclid, Archimedes, Nichomachos of Gerasa, Muḥammad b. Mūsā al-Khwārizmī and Abū Kāmil Shujāʿ b. Aslam al-Miṣrī) are precisely those one would expect to be known in al-Andalus in the second half of the 4th/10th century. The book deals with elementary arithmetic (addition, subtraction, multiplication, division and extraction of the square root, together with adequate methods for obtaining good approximations to imperfect square roots) and algebra (equations of the first and second degrees), and ends with a long collection of practical problems which might be of interest to a merchant.

Ibn al-Samḥ himself seems, apart from his *Kitāb al-muʿāmalāt,* to have written extensively on arithmetic and geometry, but his works on these subjects are apparently lost. Nothing, on the other hand, is known of the development of algebra in al-Andalus in this period, apart from what we can gather from the *Liber Mahameleth* and, possibly, from an analysis of the treatises on division of inheritance (*ʿilm al-farāʾiḍ*).[4] We have to wait till the last stage of Andalusī history, the Granada of the Banū Naṣr (631/1232-897/1492) to find an abridgement of algebra (*Ikhtiṣār al-jabr wa 'l-muqābala*), written by one Abū ʿAbd Allāh Muḥammad b. ʿUmar b. Muḥammad b. Badr,[5] of whom we know only that he wrote this book before 744/1343 and was (perhaps) an Andalusī author. The *Ikhtiṣār* is a treatise on elementary algebra dealing, among other things, with indeterminate equations in the Diophantine tradition, which are here documented for the first time in al-Andalus. Far more interesting is the work of the last important Andalusī mathematician, Abū 'l-Ḥasan ʿAlī b. Muḥammad al-Basṭī al-Qalaṣādī (b. ca. 815/1412, d. 891/1486 or 912/1506),[6] who wrote extensively on arithmetic, algebra and *farāʾiḍ*.[7] His mathematical works seem to have been strongly influenced by those of the Moroccan mathematician Abū 'l-ʿAbbās Aḥmad b. Muḥammad, known as Ibn al-Bannāʾ al-Marrākushī (654/1256-725/1321), but his originality has been exaggerated by modern scholarship. Thus, although he did indeed make interesting improvements to the method of successive approximations of imperfect square roots, the way he dealt with summations of series of squares and cubes merely followed the lead of Abū Manṣūr al-Baghdādī (d. 429/1037) and al-Umawī al-Andalusī (fl. 8th/14th century). Again, although he has been regarded as the man who introduced algebraic symbolism—and it is obvious that he did use it—he had numerous predecessors in this, both in the Mashriq and in the Maghrib.

If this brief survey of arithmetic and algebra in al-Andalus is somewhat unencouraging, a different picture emerges when we consider geometry and spherical trigonometry. Apart from the lost geometrical works of Ibn al-Samḥ, we should here consider three important figures of the 5th/11th century: King Abū ʿĀmir Yūsuf b. Aḥmad al-Muʾtaman of Saragossa, Abū Zayd ʿAbd al-Raḥmān b. Sayyid[8]—who flourished in Valencia between 456/1063 and 490/1096 and was the master of the famous philosopher and physicist Muḥammad b. Yaḥyā b. al-Ṣāʾigh, known as Ibn Bājja (463/1070?-533/1138)—and the *qāḍī* of Jaén Abū ʿAbd Allāh Muḥammad b. Muʿādh al-Jayyānī (d. 486/1093). About al-Muʾtaman we only knew, until very recently, that he had written an important treatise called *Al-Istikmāl*, but this situation has now changed as a result of important works by A. Djebbar and J. P. Hogendijk.[9] The latter has discovered four incomplete manuscripts of the *Istikmāl,* containing fragments of the work dealing with number theory, plane geometry, study of the concepts of ratio and proportion following books V and VI of Euclid's *Elements*, and the geometry of the sphere and of other solid bodies and conic sections. The extant parts of the *Istikmāl* prove that al-Muʾtaman had an important royal library containing the best books available in the 5th/11th century for the study of higher mathematics: Euclid's *Elements* and *Data*, Archimedes' *On the Sphere and Cylinder* (and, also, Eutocius' commentary on the second book of this work), the books on *Spherics* by Theodosius and Menelaos, Appolonius' *Conics*, Ptolemy's *Almagest*, Thābit b. Qurra's treatises on amicable numbers and on Menelaos' theorem, the treatise of the Banū Mūsā on the measurement of plane and spherical figures, Ibrāhīm b. Sinān's book on the quadrature of the parabola, Ibn al-Haytham's *Optics*, etc. Nevertheless, al-Muʾtaman's treatment of geometrical problems is not limited to mere reproduction of his sources, but, quite often, offers original solutions which prove that he was an excellent geometer.

Our knowledge of the works of Ibn Sayyid is more limited, as none of his books seem to be extant. He wrote on arithmetical series, following the tradition of the *Arithmetic* of Nichomachos of Gerasa, and his disciple Ibn Bājja gives us some information about his research in geometry, in which he studied conic sections—giving new definitions equivalent though not identical to those of Apollonius—plane curves higher than those of the second degree and which were not conic sections, and also such classical problems as the trisection of the angle and the determination of the two mean proportionals.

Two of the works of our third mathematician, Ibn Muʿādh, have been published and studied, namely his *Maqāla fī sharḥ al-nisba* ("Commentary on the concept of ratio")[10] and his *Kitāb majhūlāt qisī al-kura* ("Unknown arcs of the sphere").[11] The former deals with a question which, as we have seen, interested al-Mu'taman: Greek mathematicians considered that a ratio existed only when the result of the division between two magnitudes was a rational number, although Euclid seems to have accepted the possibility of a ratio existing in the case of a relation between two quantities the division of which gives an irrational number. This Euclidian line of research was followed by such Arab mathematicians as Ibn al-Haytham and ʿUmar al-Khayyāmī, and Ibn Muʿādh's book is a brilliant defence of Euclid's definition of ratio—the first known instance, it seems, of an adequate comprehension of it (we should bear in mind that this definition was rarely understood in Europe until the 17th century). The *Kitāb al-majhūlāt*, on the other hand, is the first treatise on spherical geometry compiled in Western Islam, and also the first known instance of this mathematical discipline existing independently of astronomy. While Greek mathematicians and astronomers used only one trigonometrical tool, the so-called Menelaos' theorem (*shakl al-qaṭṭāʿ* in Arabic) which established relations between six magnitudes (arcs and angles) belonging to two spherical triangles, Arab mathematicians in the Mashriq had, towards the end of the 4th/10th century and the beginning of the 5th/11th century, developed a series of new theorems which possessed the obvious advantage of establishing relations between four magnitudes belonging to the same spherical triangle. This entailed a kind of "trigonometrical revolution", and Ibn Muʿādh introduced six of these new theorems into the West. His *Kitāb al-majhūlāt* is a complete treatise on spherical trigonometry, in which he studies the solution of all possible cases of spherical triangles. He is clearly aware of the mathematical and astronomical work carried out in the East by al-Bīrūnī and his predecessors and contemporaries, and the sources he uses belong to a group which very rarely reached al-Andalus and Latin Europe. He was the first, in the West, to use a method of quadratic interpolation and to compute a tangent table in which the value of the gnomon used was 1. It is difficult to establish the extent of the *Kitāb al-majhūlāt*'s originality until his sources have been properly studied, but it does seem, for example, that his use of a polar triangle is independent of that of his Eastern predecessor Abū Naṣr Manṣūr b. ʿIrāq (d. ca. 428/1036).[12] Ibn Muʿādh's book was not translated into Latin, its influence on Medieval Europe being exerted indirectly through the *Iṣlāḥ al-majisṭī* written by Abū Muḥammad Jābir b. Aflaḥ (fl. ca. 545/1150) towards the middle of the 6th/12th century; this work was translated into both Latin and Hebrew, and four of Ibn Muʿādh's trigonometrical theorems appear in it.[13]

III. Astronomy

III.1 *Astrology, sundials and the survival of a Latin tradition*

If the Andalusī heritage in the field of mathematics is, with a few exceptions, not too rich, the situation changes entirely when we consider astronomy and astrology, two branches of knowledge which were closely related in the Middle Ages. ʿAbd al-Wāḥid b. Isḥāq al-Ḍabbī (fl. ca. 184/800) is probably the first Andalusī astrologer to have left a written work, and it gives an idea of the situation of the discipline towards the end of the 2nd/8th century. He composed an astrological *urjūza* of which only 39 verses are extant[14] and in which astrological predictions are based on the late Latin "system of the crosses" (*ṭarīqat aḥkām al-ṣulūb*). This Latin astrological tradition was much cruder than the standard Hellenistic one adopted by the Eastern Arabs and later introduced into al-Andalus: it identifies astrological houses with zodiacal signs, predictions are based on the positions of the planets (mainly Saturn, Jupiter, Mars and the Sun) in the four triplicities of air, water, fire and earth, only mean positions of the planets are taken into consideration and, obviously, it ignores the precession of equinoxes. Astrologers of this period, who did not have *zīj*es (astronomical tables), probably used approximate rules and diagrams allowing them to compute mean planetary longitudes:[15] such rules and diagrams are documented in Latin *computus* treatises, and they may be the origin of the zodiacal scale which appears in the back of Andalusī and Maghribi astrolabes, providing a simple means of calculating the solar longitude for a given date of the solar year. Such zodiacal scales appear in the oldest extant Andalusī astrolabes and are described in the first Andalusī treatises on this instrument. Eastern references to such diagrams are much later, and I suspect that this diagram was introduced into the Mashriq by the Andalusī polymath Abū 'l-Ṣalt Umayya b. Abī 'l-Ṣalt (ca. 460/1067-529/1134), who, in Alexandria (Egypt) in 503/1109-10, wrote a treatise on the use of the astrolabe in which he describes two different methods of determining the solar longitude (a solar ephemeris for a given year and the zodiacal scale).

A second example of the survival of a Latin astrological tradition in al-Andalus is to be found, probably, in sundials. The oldest extant Islamic sundials of the standard Hellenistic type (horizontal sundials in which the solar shadow for the solstices describes two arcs of a hyperbola, while in the equinoxes it describes a straight line) are Andalusī, but they are, in general, crude and poorly made,[16] and it is not until the end of the 7th/13th century that we find a *Risāla fī ʿilm al-ẓilāl* ("Epistle on the science of shadows"), in which an Andaluso-Tunisian astronomer, Abū ʿAbd Allāh Muḥammad b. Ibrāhīm al-Awsī, known as Ibn al-Raqqām (d. 715/1315), demonstrates considerable competence in gnomonics and describes the way to construct all kinds of sundial using the Hellenistic mathematical tool known as *analemma*.[17] There is, however, a second kind of Andalusī sundial known as *bilāṭa*, or *balāṭa* (the word does not seem to be of Arabic origin), whose description appears in several sources: Qāsim b. Muṭarrif's *Kitāb al-hay'a* (written towards the middle of the 4th/10th century), extant in manuscript Istanbul Carullah 1279;[18] a passage ascribed to Abū 'l-Qāsim Aḥmad b. ʿAbd Allāh, known as Ibn al-Ṣaffār (d. 426/1035) in the mechanical treatise *Kitāb al-asrār fī natā'ij al-afkār* (probably written in the 5th/11th century by a certain Aḥmad or Muḥammad b. Khalaf al-Murādī); a passage in Ibn Muʿādh's *Tabulae Jahen* quoted in the *zīj* of Ibn Isḥāq al-Tūnisī (fl. beginning of the 7th/13th century);[19] and, finally, a quotation of the famous Andalusī Jewish philosopher and scientist Mūsā b. Maymūn (Maimonides) (530/1135-601/1204).[20] All these texts describe what seems to be a very primitive kind of horizontal sundial in which the vertical gnomon is fixed in the centre of a semicircle—or two gnomons appear in the centres of two quadrants—and the limits of the hours are determined by radii that divide the circle equally (?) into 15 degree arcs. I believe this primitive kind of sundial corresponds to a Latin tradition related to the kind of dial often found in churches, and called a "mass clock" in England.

III.2 *Other astronomical instruments: equatoria, observational instruments and universal astrolabes*

Equatoria, the pseudo-*torquetum* designed for observation by Jābir b. Aflaḥ and universal astrolabes all seem to be instruments of Andalusī origin. Equatoria are apparently first found in al-Andalus at the beginning of the 5th/11th century, although a possible Eastern ancestor designed by Abū Jaʿfar al-Khāzin (d. between 350/961 and 361/971) has been suggested by D. A. King.[21] The first Andalusī treatises on this instrument were written by Ibn al-Samḥ, Ibn al-Zarqālluh and Abū 'l-Ṣalt.[22] Abū 'l-Ṣalt was, perhaps, responsible for the diffusion of this instrument in the Mashriq during his long stay in Egypt: the only published Eastern treatise on the equatorium was written by the 9th/15th century astronomer Jamshīd Ghiyāth al-Dīn al-Kāshī, and we find in it details reminiscent of the work of Ibn al-Zarqālluh and Abū 'l-Ṣalt.[23] The introduction of the new instrument into Latin Europe was earlier and more productive, for the first treatises belong to the 13th century and the tradition of building them, both in metal and in paper, lived on up to the 17th century.[24]

The birth of equatoria probably sprang from the development of astrology as a profession. The standard astrolabe solved, quite easily, the problem of the division of the houses necessary to cast a horoscope,[25] but the computation of planetary longitudes using a set of astronomical tables (*zīj*) entailed quite a lot of work. An equatorium solved this problem graphically, because it consisted of a set of Ptolemaic planetary models made to scale. The user of the instrument needed only to obtain the mean longitudes and mean anomalies of the planets from a *zīj*, and these data enabled him to establish the position of the centre of the planetary epicycle on its deferent, and also that of the planet on its epicycle. An alidade rotating around a point corresponding to the centre of the earth would, then, materialise the imaginary line connecting the earth and the planet, and would determine, on the ecliptic, the true longitude of the planet in question. The precision obtained with this kind of instrument was enough for the needs of a professional astrologer.

The three Andalusī equatoria are fairly straightforward and easy to understand for anyone basically acquainted with Ptolemaic astronomy. Ibn al-Samḥ's instrument seems to be narrowly related to the astrolabe, and it used a set of plates (one for each planet, plus another for the epicycles) which were kept within the "mother" (*umm*) of an astrolabe, using the scale engraved on the rim of the instrument as an ecliptic scale on which the true longitude of the planet was measured. However, in an effort to make his equatorium self-contained, he engraved mean motion tables in longitude and anomaly for each planet in the empty spaces of every plate. With Ibn al-Zarqālluh the equatorium becomes independent of the astrolabe, and we find, in his instrument, an attempt to represent all the planetary deferents and related circles on a single plate, engraved on both sides. A second plate, with all the epicycles, was superimposed on it. Furthermore, the complexity of the Ptolemaic Mercury model led him to take a revolutionary step and represent Mercury's deferent not as a circle but as an oval curve practically equivalent to an ellipse. Ibn al-Zarqālluh only represented graphically what was already implied in the Ptolemaic model,[26] but he seems to have been the first astronomer with the courage to cross the boundary of an astronomy based on circles and introduce a new astronomy of non-circular curves. Abū 'l-Ṣalt seems to have continued along similar lines, but his efforts to represent on one side of his basic plate all the planetary deferents and related circles (except for those of the Moon, which appear in the back of the same plate) in the Ptolemaic order suggest an attempt to make a real picture of the universe and to transcend the attitude of his predecessors, who were only interested in the practical applications of their mathematical models.

Andalusī astronomers were extremely interested in the development of astronomical instruments, most of which were, like the equatorium, analog computers. Only in two exceptional instances do we see them designing instruments meant for use in observations. One of these is Ibn al-Zarqālluh's armillary sphere, on whose construction he wrote a treatise which is extant in a 7th/13th century Spanish translation.[27] This instrument seems to be a development of the *astrolabon* described by Ptolemy in the *Almagest*, V, 1: Ibn al-Zarqālluh adds six rings to those of Ptolemy and states that the armillary sphere can be used to determine the longitudes and latitudes of the sun, moon , planets and stars. The second observational instrument described in Andalusī sources was designed by Jābir b. Aflaḥ,[28] and consists of a large graduated ring (Jābir mentions a diameter of about six spans) with an axis in its centre on which rotates a graduated quadrant with an alidade and two sights. The instrument can be mounted on the plane of the meridian, on that of the equator or on that of the ecliptic, and it has been regarded as a predecessor of the *torquetum*, first described towards the end of the 13th century by Bernard of Verdun and Franco of Poland, although the similarities between the two instruments are not very clear.

Our third group of Andalusī astronomical instruments comprises the so-called universal astrolabes designed in the 5th/11th century by Ibn al-Zarqālluh and his contemporary Abū 'l-Ḥasan ʿAlī b. Khalaf al-Shajjār, or al-Ṣaydalānī, and, in the 7th/13th century, by Ḥusayn b. Aḥmad b. Bāṣo. These universal astrolabes claim to correct the main defect of the standard astrolabe: being the result of a stereographic projection of the celestial sphere on the plane of the equator with the centre of projection in the South Pole, the horizon appears in it as an arc of a circle, and a special plate is therefore required for each latitude. The standard astrolabe is obviously the most useful analog computer applied to solving problems of spherical astronomy, or those related to the motion of the sun and the fixed stars, if an adequate plate is available; if this is not the case, however, it requires the use of approximate methods yielding insufficiently accurate results.[29] This problem was solved by Ibn al-Zarqālluh and ʿAlī b. Khalaf, both of whom designed instruments in which the projection used was also stereographic but the centre of projection was the equinoctial point (both Aries 0 degrees and Libra 0 degrees, which appear superimposed on the centre of the plate) and the plane of projection the solsticial colure. With this projection the horizon becomes a diameter of the plate, and a rotating ruler can easily become a movable horizon and be adapted to any required latitude.

Ibn al-Zarqālluh seems to have been the first to design a universal instrument of this kind:[30] 440/1048-9 saw his treatise, divided into 100 chapters, on the instrument called *al-ṣafīḥa al-ʿabbādiyya*, for it was dedicated to the future al-Muʿtamid b. ʿAbbād, king of Seville, who was then only eight or nine years old. This instrument had, on its face, a double grid of equatorial and ecliptical coordinates and a ruler-horizon, while, in its back, it had a zodiacal scale, an orthographic projection of the celestial sphere, a sine quadrant and a diagram which, combined with a most elaborate alidade, allowed the computation of the geocentric distance of the moon for a given time.[31] At a later date he seems to have dedicated a new version of his instrument to the same al-Muʿtamid. This second species of *ṣafīḥa* is usually called *al-shakkāziyya*, and appears described in treatises divided into 60 chapters. It is a simplified version of the *ʿabbādiyya* type, with only one complete grid of equatorial coordinates (the ecliptical grid is limited to the projection of the great circles of longitude which correspond to the beginnings of the zodiacal signs) in its face, while its back resembles that of a standard astrolabe because the orthographic projection, the sine quadrant, the lunar diagram and the sophisticated alidade have disappeared.[32]

There is some evidence that Ibn al-Zarqālluh conceived his two instruments—especially the *shakkāziyya*—as an auxiliary plate to be used when an astrolabe did not have a standard one for the adequate latitude, and as such it sometimes appears in the back of both Islamic[33] and European[34] astrolabes. Its use was more difficult and entailed a greater effort of the imagination than that of the standard astrolabe, mainly because it lacked a rete or spider (*ʿankabūt*) the rotation of which represented that of the celestial sphere around the earth. This is probably why ʿAlī b. Khalaf, in 464/1071-2, designed a new instrument which he called *al-asṭurlāb al-maʾmūnī* and dedicated to king al-Maʾmūn of Toledo (435/1043-467/1074). The front of this instrument consists of a single grid of coordinates on which he superimposed a rotating rete one half of which corresponded to a second grid of coordinates and the other half to the projection of a few stars as in the spider of an ordinary astrolabe. This instrument, like those of al-Zarqālluh, was well-known both in the Maghrib and in the Mashriq, and, at the beginning of the 8th/14th century, it influenced the work of the Syrian astronomer Shihāb al-Dīn Aḥmad b. Abī Bakr, known as Ibn al-Sarrāj.[35]

The last Andalusī attempt to design a universal astrolabe was made towards the end of the 7th/13th century by the Granada *muwaqqit* and instrument maker Ḥusayn b. Aḥmad b. Bāṣo, who invented a plate, to be used with a standard astrolabe, which he called *al-ṣafīḥa al-jāmiʿa li-jamīʿ al-ʿurūḍ* ("a general plate for all latitudes"). In this *ṣafīḥa* two well-known traditions converge: on the one side the efforts of Ibn al-Zarqālluh and ʿAlī b. Khalaf, who influenced Ibn Bāṣo in both the design and the use of his instrument; and, on the other, the Eastern tradition of the *ṣafīḥa āfāqiyya* ("plate of horizons"), whose invention is ascribed to Ḥabash al-Ḥāsib (d. ca. 250/864). This plate exerted its influence throughout the Islamic world, and similar solutions were applied by late European instrument makers—the last instance in which the rich Andalusī tradition of instrument design was influential.[36]

III.3 Zīj*es and astronomical theory*

The first set of astronomical tables (*zīj*) was introduced, as we saw in section I above, at the time of the *amīr* ʿAbd al-Raḥmān II; this *zīj* was probably the famous *Sindhind* in the recension made by Muḥammad b. Mūsā al-Khwārizmī (fl. ca. 215/830). Al-Khwārizmī's *Sindhind* was the object of new versions made by Maslama and his disciples Ibn al-Ṣaffār and Ibn al-Samḥ. Only a fragment of Ibn al-Ṣaffār's Arabic version is extant, in a manuscript written in Hebrew script in the Bibliothèque Nationale in Paris. As for Maslama's work, we know it through two Latin translations made by Adelard of Bath (fl. 1116-42) and Petrus Alfonsus (fl. 11th-12th century).[37] It is difficult to establish the precise innovations Maslama introduced in the *zīj*, since al-Khwārizmī's original work does not seem to be extant. Secondary sources, however, ascribe to Maslama an important change in the mean motion tables: al-Khwārizmī used as a *radix* date the era of the last Sassanian king Yazdijīrd III (midday of 16.6.632) and his years were Persian years of 365 days without fraction. Following Maslama's revision, however, the *radix* date is the beginning of the *Hijra* (midday of 14.7.622) and the tables are adapted to the Muslim calendar, using lunar years of 354 or 355 days. As al-Khwārizmī's calendar, in its present state, is composed from materials derived from Indian, Hellenistic and Andalusī sources, it has generally been accepted that Maslama introduced such Andalusī materials as the use of the Spanish era (which corresponds to -37), intercalation of a supplementary day in bissextile years at the end of December instead of February, a correction of the difference in geographical latitude between Arin and Córdoba which amounts to 63 degrees in our text and implies a displacement of the western meridian 17;40 degrees to the west of the Fortunate Islands,[38] adaptations of several tables to the geographical coordinates of Córdoba, etc. It seems, however, that Maslama also dealt with Indian materials and introduced unfortunate modifications in the tables of eclipses and in those which allow the computation of planetary latitudes.[39] He may also have been responsible for the introduction of such Ptolemaic materials as the right ascension table and the sine table. Finally, Maslama seems to have added a certain number of astrological tables such as those concerned with the projection of rays (*maṭraḥ al-shuʿāʿāt*), which constitute about a third of the whole *zīj*;[40] here he has been fully successful, and has improved on al-Khwārizmī's tables for the same purpose, for those of Maslama are easier to use and give exact results, whereas al-Khwārizmī only gave approximations. We should, however, be very cautious before ascribing to Maslama materials not found in al-Khwārizmī's original *zīj*, since Adelard of Bath's Latin translation also has later interpolations, such as, for example, the table for the visibility of the new moon which is computed for the latitude of Saragossa, a city in which the exact sciences were not seriously cultivated until the 5th/11th century.[41]

The time of Maslama not only saw a serious study of the Indian astronomical tradition represented by al-Khwārizmī's *Sindhind*, but also the introduction of the more elaborate Ptolemaic astronomy. We know that Maslama studied Ptolemy's *Almagest*, and his disciple Ibn al-Samḥ wrote a summary of this work. Maslama also wrote on al-Battānī's *zīj*, and parameters derived from this work were used by Ibn al-Samḥ in his treatise on the equatorium. Ptolemy's *Geography* was also known, being quoted by Ibn al-Ṣaffār in his epistle on the astrolabe, and Maslama wrote an important commentary on Ptolemy's *Planisphaerium*, in which he provided new and elegant solutions to problems of stereographic projection.[42] Finally, an older contemporary of Maslama, Qāsim b. Muṭarrif al-Qaṭṭān, seems to be aware of the size of the Universe according to Ptolemy's *Planetary Hypotheses*.

However, if Andalusī astronomers knew Ptolemy's works, they still never fully abandoned the Indian tradition. We have a good example of this in Ibn Muʿādh's *Tabulae Jahen* (the *zīj* of Jayyān, i.e. Jaén in the south of Spain), of which only the canons are extant, in a Latin translation by Gerard of Cremona. These tables were, fundamentally, an adaptation of al-Khwārizmī's *Sindhind* to the coordinates of Jaén,[43] but Ibn Muʿādh seems to be using a different version of the work from that of Maslama and introduces new materials which are either original or derive from Ptolemaic sources. Thus, his lunar and planetary models, and also the numerical parameters quoted in the canons, derive from al-Khwārizmī, but his table of the solar and lunar equations was not calculated, as al-Khwārizmī's was, according to the Indian "method of the declinations", but rather employed a Ptolemaic exact method. Al-Khwārizmī's *zīj* entirely ignores the precession of the equinoxes, while Ibn Muʿādh's canons have a description of a table of constant precession calculated for years and months. In other instances, Ibn Muʿādh—who is, let it be remembered, the author of the trigonometrical treatise *Kitāb majhūlāt qisī al-kura* (see II above)—demonstrates awareness of developments in the Mashriq associated with al-Bīrūnī and his immediate predecessors: his method for the division of the astrological houses of the horoscope is strongly reminiscent of a similar method specially favoured by al-Bīrūnī,[44] and he also gives an adequate description, with personal comments, of the so-called "Method of the *zīj*es" to determine the azimuth of the *qibla*, a method in which al-Bīrūnī and his "school" were strongly interested.[45]

The *Tabulae Jahen* were not as successful as the *Toledan Tables*, which, once again, we know only through a Latin translation, extant in an enormous number of manuscripts. These tables seem to have been the result of a hasty adaptation of all the available astronomical material (al-Khwārizmī, al-Battānī and the *Almagest*) to the coordinates of Toledo. This work must have been carried out in little more than one year, around 1069, by a group of Toledan astronomers led by the famous *qāḍī* Abū 'l-Qāsim Ṣāʿid b. Aḥmad b. ʿAbd al-Raḥmān b. Muḥammad b. Ṣāʿid (d. 462/1070), others of the group including Ibn al-Zarqālluh and ʿAlī b. Khalaf.[46] Even if the results were not brilliant—indeed, they can on the whole be considered a fiasco—we should consider that the mean motion tables are original and are the result of a programme of observations which must have begun earlier than 1069 and was continued by Ibn al-Zarqālluh until much later. This personage, whose work on universal astrolabes is considered in III.2 above, is the most original and influential Andalusī astronomer, but he started as an instrument maker; his interest in observations and astronomical theory was probably aroused by the collective work of *qāḍī* Ṣāʿid's team, and he must have continued as leader of the group after the latter's death. In any case, we know that he observed the sun over a period of twenty-five years,[47] and according to the *Al-Zīj al-kāmil fī 'l-ta'ālīm* of Abū Muḥammad 'Abd al-Ḥaqq al-Ghāfiqī al-Ishbīlī, known as Ibn al-Hā'im (fl. 601/1204-5) he also observed the moon for thirty-seven years.

The *Toledan Tables* bear witness to the first original development of Andalusī astronomy, which was extremely influential in Europe up to the Scientific Revolution, namely the theory of trepidation. This theory claims to design geometrical models capable of justifying two facts attested by more or less precise observation: (1) that the obliquity of the ecliptic is not constant, but is submitted to a slow diminution (Indian astronomers mentioned an obliquity of 24 degrees, Ptolemy of 23;51,20 degrees and the astronomers of Caliph al-Ma'mūn, ca. 215/830, of about 23;33 degrees); (2) that the velocity of precession is not constant (Hipparchus and Ptolemy established that it amounted to 1 degree in every 100 years, while al-Ma'mūn's astronomers considered that it was about 1 degree in every 66 years). Trepidation, as formulated by Muslim astronomers, had clear predecessors both in Classical Antiquity[48] and in the echoes of Greek astronomy in India;[49] these early formulations established that the equinoctial and solstitial points had a very slow movement forwards and backwards along a limited arc of the ecliptic (8 degrees according to Theon of Alexandria, ca. 370 A.D.), but no geometrical model justifying such a motion is known; one has to wait in fact until the first half of the 4th/10th century, when Ibrāhīm b. Sinān (296/908-335/946), the grandson of the famous Eastern mathematician and astronomer Thābit b. Qurra, designed the first known trepidation model.[50] Either this formulation of the theory or a different one was introduced in al-Andalus through the *Kitāb naẓm al-'iqd* written by Ḥusayn b. Muḥammad b. Ḥāmid, known as Ibn al-Adamī and published by one of his disciples in 338/949. This book was known to *qāḍī* Ṣā'id, and the latter probably dealt with the topic of trepidation, which was one of the main concerns of the group of Toledan astronomers; according to Ibn al-Hā'im, one of them, Abū Marwān al-Istijī, wrote a *Risālat al-iqbāl wa 'l-idbār* ("Epistle on accession and recession"), and he is one of the candidates—Ṣā'id being another—for the authorship of the famous *Liber de Motu Octave Spere* ("Book on the motion of the eighth sphere") traditionally ascribed to Thābit b. Qurra.[51] The authorship of *De Motu* is extremely difficult to establish, but it seems probable that the trepidation tables which appear in some manuscripts together with the Latin text, and which are also extant within the *Toledan Tables*, are independent of the *De Motu* and can be related to the work of the Toledan astronomers.[52] This work was continued by Ibn al-Zarqālluh, who, around 478/1085, wrote his treatise on the fixed stars (extant in a Hebrew translation),[53] in which he successively studied three different trepidation models, the third of these being an improvement, from a practical point of view, on that of the *Liber de Motu*, in that variable precession became independent of the oscillation of the obliquity of the ecliptic.

Ibn al-Zarqālluh dedicated twenty-five years of his life to solar observation, and, between 468/1075 and 473/1080, he wrote a book entitled either *Fī sanat al-shams* ("On the solar year") or *al-Risāla al-jāmiʿa fī 'l-shams* ("A comprehensive epistle on the Sun"). This book seems to have been lost, but we know of its contents through secondary sources,[54] both Arabic and Latin. Analysis of these sources proves a number of things: (1) Ibn al-Zarqālluh established, in observations of 467/1074-5, that the longitude of the solar apogee was 85;49 degrees, and this not only led him to confirm the common opinion of Muslim astronomers since around 830 that the solar apogee moved with the velocity of precession, together with the fixed stars, but also made him the first to state that the solar apogee had its own motion of about 1 degree in 279 Julian years; (2) he confirmed the length of the sidereal year (6,5;15,24 days) previously used in the Toledan Tables; (3) his observations led him to establish that the solar eccentricity for his time amounted to 1;58P. Given the fact that Hipparchus had, around 150 B.C., determined the solar eccentricity to be 2;30P, and that both Thābit b. Qurra and al-Battānī had established new values for that parameter (the former 2;2,6P, using observations of ca. 830, and al-Battānī 2;4,5P for the year 883), Ibn al-Zarqālluh concluded that the solar eccentricity was variable, and designed a geometrical model able to justify its variability and compute the value of the solar eccentricity for a given date. This model was well known in Europe up to the time of Copernicus.

Finally, we should remember that Ibn al-Hā'im furnishes new evidence concerning the thirty-seven years of lunar observation, involving a slight modification of Ptolemy's lunar model: according to this source, Ibn Zarqālluh stated that the centre of the Moon's mean motion in longitude was not the centre of the Earth, but was placed on a straight line linking the centre of the Earth with the solar apogee. This entailed the introduction, for the Moon, of an equant point which moved with the rotation of the solar apogee, and which forced him to introduce a correction in the mean longitude of the moon amounting to a maximum of 24 minutes. Ibn al-Zarqālluh's correction appears in Andalusī (Ibn al-Kammād) and Maghribi (Ibn Isḥāq, Ibn al-Bannā') *zīj*es, and also in the Spanish canons of the first version of the *Alfonsine Tables*.

Trepidation, a solar model with variable eccentricity, the correction in the lunar model and some Zarqāllian parameters appear in a family of characteristic Andalusī *zīj*es. The first of these is Ibn al-Zarqālluh's own *Almanac*,[55] which is, perhaps, less influenced by such peculiarities than other sets of tables in this group, although the solar tables seem to derive from Toledan parameters. The *Almanac* is based on a Greek work computed by a certain Awmātiyūs in the 3rd or 4th century A.D., and its purpose is to furnish astrologers with astronomical tables enabling them to obtain planetary longitudes without all the computation involved in the use of a *zīj*; to this end, Awmātiyūs and Ibn al-Zarqālluh used the Babylonian planetary cycles usually called "goal years". After the completion of one of these cycles, the longitudes of a given planet will be the same on the same dates of the year as at the beginning of the cycle. The elaboration of perpetual almanacs of this kind also appears to be characteristic of Andalusī astronomy; astronomers of the Mashriq, in contrast, computed ephemerides which were valid for only one year.

The other *zīj*es seriously influenced by Ibn al-Zarqālluh's astronomical theories are those composed by Abū Jaʿfar Aḥmad b. Yūsuf b. Yūsuf, known as [Ibn] al-Kammād (fl. beginning of the 6th/12th century), Ibn al-Hāʾim and Ibn al-Raqqām, but Ibn al-Zarqālluh's ideas also exerted a strong influence on such Maghribi astronomers as Ibn Isḥāq al-Tūnisī (fl. beginning of the 7th/13th century) and Ibn al-Bannāʾ al-Marrākushī. [Ibn] al-Kammād was probably a direct disciple of Ibn al-Zarqālluh, and composed three *zīj*es entitled *Al-Kawr ʿalā 'l-dawr*, *Al-Amad ʿalā 'l-abad* and *Al-Muqtabis*. Only the third of these (which is a summary of the other two) seems to be extant, in the Latin translation made by John of Dumpno in Palermo in 1262 (which also contains fragments of *Al-Kawr ʿalā 'l-dawr*); this *zīj* awaits detailed study, but [Ibn] al-Kammād seems to have followed his master's theories, although he introduced corrections in the parameters and computation procedures. The *Muqtabis* seems to be the main source of the astronomical tables prepared for King Peter IV of Aragon in the 14th century.[56]

[Ibn] al-Kammād was strongly criticised by Ibn al-Hāʾim, who, in 601/1204-05, dedicated his *Al-Zīj al-kāmil fī 'l-taʿālīm* to the Almohad caliph Abū ʿAbd Allāh Muḥammad al-Nāṣir (596/1199-610/1213). This work, extant in MS Marsh 618 of the Bodleian Library in Oxford, is not a standard *zīj*, for it contains an extremely elaborate set of canons (173 pages) but no numerical tables. These canons are mainly concerned with computational procedures to solve astronomical problems, and they include careful geometrical proofs which show their author to have been a good mathematician, perfectly aware of the new trigonometry introduced into al-Andalus by Ibn Muʿādh. This *zīj*, which is an extremely important unexplored astronomical source, contains a great deal of historical information on the work carried out by the Toledan school in the 5th/11th century, but Ibn al-Hāʾim, for all his obvious fidelity to Ibn al-Zarqālluh's theories, introduces what he considers to be improvements in the Zarqāllian parameters. Such changes, he states, are simply practical (*ʿamalī*) and have no theoretical (*ʿilmī*) implications.

The last of these "Toledan" *zīj*es are the two composed by the Andaluso-Tunisian astronomer Muḥammad b. al-Raqqām, whose treatises on sundials were noted in III.1 above. These are *Al-Zīj al-shāmil fī tahdhīb al-kāmil*, extant in a manuscript of the Kandilli Museum of Istanbul, and *Al-Zīj al-*

qawīm fī funūn al-taʿdīl wa 'l-taqwīm, of which just a few sheets survive in a manuscript in the Museo Naval in Madrid. The former was composed in 679/1280-1 in Tunis, with the aim of simplifying the canons of Ibn al-Hāʾim's *Al-Zīj al-kāmil*, adding the numerical tables lacking in this work and renewing the parameters so as to obtain a better agreement between computation and observation. The *Al-Zīj al-qawīm* was probably an adaptation of the previous *zīj* to the geographical coordinates of Granada, composed after Ibn al-Raqqām's arrival in the city in the time of Muḥammad II (672/1273-702/1302). Interestingly, Ibn al-Raqqām must have made a very careful determination of the latitude of Granada, for the table permitting determination of the visibility of the new moon explicitly mentions 37;10 degrees, which is precisely the modern value for the latitude of this city.

III.4 *The criticism of Ptolemy's astronomy and the birth of Andalusī cosmology*

We have seen that Andalusī astronomy, like Islamic astronomy in general, was not purely Ptolemaic, but introduced important modifications in the parameters and models of the *Almagest*. This obviously implied a degree of criticism, which reached its peak with the *Iṣlāḥ al-majisṭī* ("Revision of the *Almagest*") written towards the middle of the 6th/12th century by Jābir b. Aflaḥ, who has already been mentioned in II and III.2 above. Jābir's criticisms are purely theoretical in character, pointing mainly to such inconsistencies, in the *Almagest*, as the Ptolemaic order of the planets (Moon, Mercury, Venus, Sun, Mars, Jupiter and Saturn), which, as Jābir shows, necessarily implies transits of Mercury and Venus in front of the solar disk. As such transits have not been observed,[57] Jābir concludes that Mercury and Venus must rotate above the Sun and not below it. On another occasion Jābir is led to criticise Ptolemy by his own mathematical scruples: Ptolemy assumed the bissection of the eccentricity for the superior planets without giving any proof, and calculated the parameters for them by a long iterative process for which his starting point was three observations of oppositions between the planet and the mean Sun. As Jābir considers Ptolemy's method also has methodological defects, he proposes a new one in which he uses two pairs of oppositions, avoids Ptolemy's flaws and obtains sound results from a mathematical point of view. Unfortunately, however, the conditions he requires for his two pairs of oppositions are such that they cannot be observed in a period of time sufficiently short for the planetary apogee not to have altered its position substantially. It seems, then, that Jābir was a competent mathematician, but did not have much practical sense.[58]

On the other hand, the 6th/12th century saw the birth, in al-Andalus, of an important school of philosophers , including such figures as Ibn Bājja, Ibn Ṭufayl (before 504/1110-581/1185) and Ibn Ru<u>sh</u>d (520/1126-595/1198) and

Maimonides, which regarded the Ptolemaic system of the world as a mere mathematical tool, capable of accurately computing planetary positions, but unable to represent the physical structure of the Universe, mainly because it employed geometrical lines and points rather than solid spheres, and because it contradicted Aristotelian physics. Ptolemy himself tried to overcome the first of these "defects" in his *Planetary Hypotheses*, a work in which he conceived solid rings instead of mathematical circles and tried to estimate the size of the Universe.[59] These hypotheses were, as noted above (III.3), apparently known in al-Andalus towards the middle of the 4th/10th century, since Qāsim b. Muṭarrif, in his *Kitāb al-hay'a*, gives a list of the distances and sizes of the planets which is the same as that of Ptolemy's work.[60]

Ptolemy's *Planetary Hypotheses* was still, however, at variance with Aristotelian physics, and, indeed, with any kind of physics known in the 6th/12th century, and several attempts were therefore made by Ibn Bājja, Ibn Ṭufayl and Ibn Rushd to create a cosmological system with a physical capacity to exist. We do not have a sufficiently detailed knowledge of the results obtained by Ibn Bājja and Ibn Ṭufayl, while Ibn Rushd himself recognised the total failure of his efforts in this direction.[61] It is only with the *Kitāb fī 'l-hay'a* of Abū Isḥāq Nūr al-Dīn [b.] al-Biṭrūjī[62] (a disciple of Ibn Ṭufayl), probably composed between 581/1185 and 588/1192, that a complete cosmological system appears. With a limited knowledge of the astronomical literature available,[63] he conceives a homocentric universe in the tradition of Eudoxus,[64] and, using geometrical models which—as Goldstein has shown—derive ultimately from Ibn al-Zarqālluh, displaces Ptolemaic deferents and epicycles to the zone of the north pole of each planetary sphere. His planets are thus always kept at the same distance from the centre of the Earth, but, although al-Biṭrūjī shows a certain ingenuity in the conception of his models, his system is purely qualitative, has too many defects and inconsistencies and could never have formed the basis for the computation of a set of tables. However, as his main interest has been to create a cosmological system compatible with physical reality, it is important to say a few words about his physical, mainly dynamical, ideas. Both Ibn Rushd and al-Biṭrūjī were concerned with the problem of justifying how a single first motor can transmit motions in two contrary directions: daily motions from East to West (as a result of the rotation of the Earth) and motions in longitude from West to East. To explain this, al-Biṭrūjī uses notions taken from neo-Platonic, not Aristotelian dynamics: the daily rotation is transmitted from the first motor to the planetary spheres—even though the former is separated from them—and this transmission is explained through an allusion to the neo-Platonic *impetus* theory, which states, for example, that when an archer shoots an arrow he impregnates the projectile with a certain amount of force (*impetus*) which allows the arrow to move even if it is separated from its motor (archer and bow). The arrow progressively loses its *impetus*, and this entails a slowing down of its movement until it stops and falls to the earth. Such slowing down also affects the planetary spheres as a result of their distance from the motor; and this is why the starry sphere is the fastest of all, followed, in decreasing order of velocity, by the spheres of Saturn, Jupiter, Mars, through to the Moon. The motions in longitude, from West to East, of the stars (precession of the equinoxes) and planets are analysed as the delay (*taqṣīr*) which corresponds to this diminution of velocity. The *taqṣīr* (motion in longitude) is, then, maximum for the Moon and minimum for the sphere of the fixed stars. To this al-Biṭrūjī adds that each planetary sphere feels a desire (*shawq*) to imitate (*tashabbuh*) the motion of the sphere immediately above and tries to reach the perfection (*kamāl*) of the motion transmitted by the first motor. This *shawq*, again a neo-Platonic idea, compensates for the *taqṣīr*, and is identified by al-Biṭrūjī with the motion in anomaly of each planet on its epicycle. The result is, therefore, what one would expect: a complete failure to explain the physical world, due, mainly, to the inadequacy of the available physical notions. Despite his interest for the history of philosophy, al-Biṭrūjī's astronomy does not stand comparison with the great developments of Ibn al-Zarqālluh and his school, with whom Andalusī astronomy attained its highest level.

It is, perhaps, premature to attempt any kind of conclusion from this short survey of the development of the Exact Sciences in al-Andalus. I would, however, say that our knowledge of the subject has changed considerably over the past twenty years. Until fairly recently we should have said there was no such thing as Andalusī mathematics, but, following research undertaken on King al-Muʾtaman and Ibn Muʿādh al-Jayyānī, this is now no longer the case. Ibn Muʿādh appears to be original in his study of the Euclidean concept of ratio (*nisba*), and, if his treatise on trigonometry seems to derive mainly from sound assimilation of Eastern sources largely unknown in the western Islamic countries, his work in the field was, nevertheless, probably extremely significant for the development of the subject both in the Maghrib and in Latin Europe. As for al-Muʾtaman, it is still much too early to judge him, but Hogendijk's research clearly points in the direction of originality. These two figures are, however, exceptions; Andalusī mathematics does not seem to have had the importance and, especially, the continuity of its eastern counterpart. If we do in fact have to change our minds in the future, this will probably entail the discovery of new manuscripts like those of al-Muʾtaman's *Istikmāl*.

The situation is entirely different when we consider the history of Andalusī astronomy. Here we have a clear continuity of astronomical studies from the 4th/10th to the 8th/14th century at least, and also a central figure: the famous Toledan astronomer Ibn al-Zarqālluh, whose astronomical ideas and lines of research dominate the development of the subject for more than three centuries, both in al-Andalus and in the Maghrib. Until the 5th/11th century, al-Andalus remained an offshoot of Eastern Islam in astronomy, and the fact that the Indian tradition of al-Khwārizmī's *Sindhind* was strongly influential at a time when it had become obsolete in the Mashriq did little to raise the country's reputation in the field. The arrival of Ibn al-Zarqālluh, however, changed the situation entirely, in that he contributed to the development of a new kind of Andalusī astronomy characterised by a peculiar mixture of Indian elements (*Sindhind*), Greek elements (Ptolemy) and Islamic elements (al-Battānī), to which he added certain new ideas (trepidation, motion of the solar apogee, solar model with variable eccentricity, correction to the Ptolemaic lunar model) which were extremely influential both in the Maghrib and in Latin Europe, and even, sometimes, in the Mashriq. To this one should add the design of new calculating devices (equatoria, universal astrolabes), the recovery of perpetual almanacs and the appearance of a new cosmology attempting to create a new astronomical system compatible with a kind of physics which, again, was the result of a peculiar mixture of Aristotelian and neo-Platonic elements. The picture as a whole is highly original within the general frame of Islamic astronomy.

[1] L. Molina, *Una descripción anónima de al-Andalus*, Madrid, 1983, I, 138.

[2] J. Samsó, "Sobre los materiales astronómicos en el 'Calendario de Córdoba' y en su versión latina del siglo XIII", in *Nuevos estudios sobre astronomía española en el siglo de Alfonso X*, ed. J. Vernet, Barcelona, 1983, pp. 125-38; *idem*, "En torno al problema de la determinación del acimut de la alquibla en al-Andalus en los siglos VIII y IX. Estado de la cuestión e hipótesis de trabajo", in *Homenaje a Manuel Ocaña Jiménez*, Córdoba, 1990, pp. 207-12.

[3] J. Sesiano, "Le *Liber mahameleth*, un traité mathématique latin composé au XIIe siècle en Espagne", *Actes du Premier Colloque International d'Alger sur l'Histoire des Mathématiques Arabes*, Algiers, 1988, pp. 69-98; *idem*, "Survivance médiévale en Hispanie d'un problème né en Mésopotamie", *Centaurus*, 30, 1987, pp. 18-61.

[4] A. Djebbar, "Quelques aspects de l'Algèbre dans la tradition mathématique arabe de l'Occident Musulman", *Premier Colloque International d'Alger*, pp. 102-06.

[5] Edition and Spanish translation by J. A. Sánchez Pérez, *Compendio de Algebra de Abenbéder*, Madrid, 1916. See also Djebbar, *op. cit*, pp. 108-11

[6] M. Souissi, "'Ālim riyāḍī Andalusī. Al-Qalaṣādī", *Ḥawliyyāt al-jāmi'a 'l-Tūnisiyya*, 9, 1972, pp. 33-49; *idem*, "Un mathématicien tuniso-andalou: al-Qalaṣādī", *Actas del II Coloquio Hispano-Tunecino de Estudios Históricos*, Madrid, 1973, pp. 147-69; A. S. Saidan, "al-Qalaṣādī", in *Dictionary of Scientific Biography*, XI, New York, 1975, pp. 229-30; A. Djebbar, "Al-Qalaṣādī: 'ālim Andalusī-Maghribī min al-qarn al-khāmis 'ashar", *Al-'ilm wa-l-tiknūlūjiyā (Revue Arabe des Technologies)*, Paris, 1, No. 9, July 1990, pp. 12-23.

[7] His *Kashf al-asrār 'an 'ilm ḥurūf al-ghubār* has recently been edited and translated into French by M. Souissi, Tunis, 1988.

[8] See A. Djebbar, *Deux mathématiciens peu connus de l'Espagne du XIe siècle*, Paris, 1984, which provides a general survey of the secondary sources on al-Mu'taman and Ibn Sayyid.

[9] J. P. Hogendijk, "Discovery of an 11th-Century Geometrical Compilation: the *Istikmāl* of Yūsuf al-Mu'taman ibn Hūd, king of Saragossa", *Historia Mathematica*, 13, 1986, pp. 43-52; *idem*, "Le roi-geomètre al-Mu'taman ibn Hūd et son Livre de la Perfection (Kitāb al-Istikmāl), *Premier Colloque International*, pp. 53-66; *idem*, "The Geometrical Parts of the *Istikmāl* of Yūsuf al-Mu'taman ibn Hūd (11th century). An Analytical Table of Contents", to be published in *Archives Internationales d'Histoire des Sciences*.

10 E. B. Plooij, *Euclid's conception of ratio and his definition of proportional magnitudes as criticized by Arabian commentators. Including the text in facsimile with translation of the commentary on ratio of Abū ʿAbd Allāh Muḥammad ibn Muʿādh al-Djajjānī*, Rotterdam, 1950.

11 M. V. Villuendas, *La trigonometría europea en el siglo XI. Estudio de la obra de Ibn Muʿāḏ*, Barcelona, 1979. See also J. Samsó, "Notas sobre la trigonometría esférica de Ibn Muʿāḏ", *Awrāq*, 3, 1980, pp. 60-68; and M. G. Doncel, "Quadratic Interpolations in Ibn Muʿādh", *Archives Internationales d'Histoire des Sciences*, 32, 1982, pp. 68-77.

12 M. T. Debarnot, "Introduction du triangle polaire par Abū Naṣr b. ʿIrāq", *Journal for the History of Arabic Science*, 2, 1978, p. 132, n. 30.

13 R. Lorch, "The Astronomy of Jābir ibn Aflaḥ", *Centaurus*, 19, 1975, pp. 85-107. In spite of this, N. G. Hairetdinova ("On Spherical Trigonometry in the Medieval Near East and in Europe", *Historia Mathematica*, 13, 1986, pp. 136-46) has postulated a direct influence of Ibn Muʿādh's trigonometry on Regiomontanus.

14 Edition and Spanish translation by J. Samsó, "La primitiva versión árabe del Libro de las Cruces", in Vernet (ed.), *Nuevos estudios sobre astronomía española en el siglo de Alfonso X*, pp. 149-61. See also J. Samsó, "The Early Development of Astrology in al-Andalus", *Journal for the History of Arabic Science*, 3, 1979, pp. 228-43.

15 J. Samsó, "En torno a los métodos de cálculo utilizados por los astrólogos andalusíes a fines del s. VIII y principios del IX: algunas hipótesis de trabajo", *Actas de las II Jornadas de Cultura Arabe e Islámica*, Madrid, 1985, pp. 509-22.

16 D. A. King, "Three Sundials from Islamic Andalusia", *Journal for the History of Arabic Science*, 2, 1978, pp. 358-92; C. Barceló and A. Labarta, "Ocho relojes de sol hispano-musulmanes", *Al-Qanṭara*, 9, 1988, pp. 231-47; J. Carandell, "Dos cuadrantes solares andalusíes de Medina Azara", *Al-Qanṭara*, 10, 1989, pp. 329-42.

17 See the edition and Spanish translation by J. Carandell, *Risāla fī ʿilm al-ẓilāl de Muḥammad ibn al-Raqqām al-Andalusī*, Barcelona, 1988. See also J. Carandell, "An analemma for the Determination of the Azimuth of the Qibla in the *Risāla fī ʿilm al-ẓilāl* of Ibn al-Raqqām", *Zeitschrift für Geschichte der Arabisch-Islamischen Wissenschaften*, 1, 1984, pp. 61-72.

18 I am most grateful to Professor Fuat Sezgin of the University of Frankfurt for his generosity in providing me with a microfilm of this manuscript.

19 Ibn Isḥāq's *zīj* is extant in manuscript Hyderabad Andra Pradesh State Library 298. It was discovered by D. A. King, who sent me a photocopy.

20 The descriptions ascribed to Ibn al-Ṣaffar and Maimonides have been edited by King in "Three sundials".

21 D. A. King, "New Light on the 'Zīj al-Ṣafā'iḥ' of Abū Jaʿfar al-Khāzin", *Centaurus*, 23, 1980, pp. 115-17 (reprint in King, *Islamic Astronomical Instruments*, Variorum Reprints, London, 1987, No. XI).

22 See M. Comes, *Los ecuatorios andalusíes*, Barcelona, 1991.

23 E. S. Kennedy, *The Planetary Equatorium of Jamshīd Giyāth al-Dīn al-Kāshī (d. 1429)*, Princeton, 1960.

24 E. Poulle, *Les instruments de la théorie des planètes selon Ptolémée: Equatoires et horlogerie planétaire du XIIIe au XVIe siècles*, Geneva-Paris, 1980, 2 vols. On Hebrew equatoria cf. B. R. Goldstein, "Descriptions of Astronomical Instruments in Hebrew", in *From Deferent to Equant. A Volume of Studies in the History of Science in the Ancient and Medieval Near East in Honor of E. S. Kennedy*, ed. G. Saliba and D. A. King, New York, 1987, pp. 105-41.

25 See J. North, *Horoscopes and History*, London, 1986.

26 W. Hartner, "The Mercury Horoscope of Marcantonio Michiel of Venice. A Study in the History of Renaissance Astrology and Astronomy", *Oriens-Occidens* (Hildesheim, 1968), pp. 440-95.

27 M. Rico y Sinobas, *Libros del Saber de Astronomía del Rey D. Alfonso X de Castilla*, Vol. II, Madrid, 1863, pp. 1-24. Cf. J. Samsó, "Tres notas sobre astronomía hispánica en el siglo XIII", in *Estudios sobre historia de la ciencia árabe*, ed. J. Vernet, Barcelona, 1980, pp. 175-77.

28 R. P. Lorch, "The Astronomical Instruments of Jābir ibn Aflaḥ and the Torquetum", *Centaurus*, 20, 1976, pp. 11-34.

29 On the history of the standard astrolabe in al-Andalus, see M. Viladrich, R. Martí, "En torno a los tratados hispánicos sobre construcción de astrolabio hasta el siglo XIII", in *Textos y estudios sobre astronomía española en el siglo XIII*, ed. J. Vernet, Barcelona, 1981, pp. 79-99;

idem, "En torno a los tratados de uso del astrolabio hasta el siglo XIII en al-Andalus, la Marca Hispánica y Castilla", in Vernet (ed.), *Nuevos estudios sobre astronomía española en el siglo de Alfonso X*, pp. 9-74; M. Viladrich, *El "Kitāb al-ʿamal bi 'l-asṭurlāb" (Llibre de l'ús de l'astrolabi) d'Ibn al-Samḥ. Estudi i traducció*, Barcelona, 1986.

30 For the chronology of the three instruments designed by Ibn al-Zarqālluh and ʿAlī ibn Khalaf I follow the evidence furnished by D. A. King, "On the Early History of the Universal Astrolabe in Islamic Astronomy and the Origin of the Term 'Shakkazīya' in Medieval Scientific Arabic", *Journal for the History of Arabic Science*, 3, 1979, pp. 244-57. Reprint in D. A. King, *Islamic Astronomical Instruments*.

31 On this instrument, cf. R. Puig, *Los Tratados de Construcción y Uso de la Azafea de Azarquiel*, Madrid, 1987; *idem*, "La proyección ortográfica en el *Libro de la Açafeha* alfonsí", *De Astronomia Alphonsi Regis*, Barcelona, 1987, pp. 125-38; *idem*, "Al-Zarqālluh's Graphical Method for Finding Lunar Distances", *Centaurus*, 32, 1989, pp. 294-309.

32 R. Puig, "Concerning the ṣafīḥa šakkāziyya", *Zeitschrift für Geschichte der Arabisch-Islamischen Wissenschaften*, 2, 1985, pp. 123-39; *idem*, *Al-Šakkāziyya. Ibn al-Naqqāš al-Zarqālluh. Edición, traducción y estudio*, Barcelona, 1986.

33 On the echoes of Ibn al-Zarqālluh's instruments in the Mashriq, cf. D. A. King, *Islamic Astronomical Instruments*, London, 1987, Nos. VII-X; *idem*, "Universal Solutions in Islamic Astronomy", in *From Ancient Omens to Statistical Mechanics*, Copenhagen, 1987, pp. 121-32; *idem*, "Universal Solutions to Problems of Spherical Astronomy from Mamluk Egypt and Syria", in *A Way Prepared. Essays on Islamic Culture in Honor of R. B. Winder*, New York-London, 1988, pp. 153-84; J. Samsó and M. A. Catalá, "Un instrumento astronómico de raigambre zarqālī: el cuadrante šakkāzī de Ibn Ṭībugā", *Memorias de la Real Academia de Buenas Letras de Barcelona*, 13, 1971-75, pp. 5-31; J. Samsó, "A propos de quelques manuscrits astronomiques des bibliothèques de Tunis: contribution à une histoire de l'astrolabe dans l'Espagne Musulmane, *Actas del II Coloquio Hispano-Tunecino de Estudios Históricos*, Madrid, 1973, pp. 171-90; *idem*, "Una hipótesis sobre cálculo por aproximación con el cuadrante šakkāzī", *Al-Andalus*, 36, 1971, 383-90.

34 On the European diffusion of Ibn al-Zarqālluh's instruments, see E. Poulle, "Un instrument astronomique dans l'Occident Latin. La 'Saphea'", in *A Giuseppe Ermini*, Spoleto, 1970, pp. 491-510.

35 E. Calvo, "La lámina universal de ʿAlī b. Jalaf (s. XI) en la versión alfonsí y su evolución en instrumentos posteriores", in *"Ochava Espera" y "Astrofísica". Textos y estudios sobre las fuentes árabes de la Astronomía de Alfonso X*, Barcelona, 1990, pp. 221-38.

36 See Calvo's paper, "La lámina universal de ʿAlī b. Jalaf", mentioned above.

37 See H. Suter, *Die Astronomischen Tafeln des Muḥammed ibn Mūsā al-Khwārizmī in der Bearbeitung des maslama ibn Aḥmed al-Madjrīṭī und der latein Uebersetzung des Athelhard von Bath*, Copenhagen, 1914; O. Neugebauer, *The Astronomical Tables of al-Khwārizmī. Translation with Commentaries of the Latin version edited by H. Suter supplemented by Corpus Christi College MS 283*, Copenhagen, 1962; R. Mercier, "Astronomical Tables in the Twelfth Century", in *Adelard of Bath. An English Scientist and Arabist of the Early Twelfth Century*, ed. C. Burnett, London, 1987, pp. 87-118.

38 M. Comes, "The "Meridian of Water" in the Tables of Geographical Coordinates of al-Andalus and Northern Africa", *XVIII International Congress of History of Science. Abstracts*, Hamburg-Munich, 1989, P2, No. 1.

39 E. S. Kennedy and W. Ukashah, "Al-Khwārizmī's Planetary Latitude Tables", in E. S. Kennedy *et al.*, *Studies in the Islamic Exact Sciences*, Beirut, 1983, pp. 125-35.

40 E.S. Kennedy and H. Krikorian-Preisler, "The Astrological Doctrine of Projecting the Rays", in Kennedy *et al.*, *op. cit.*, pp. 151-56; J. P. Hogendijk, "The Mathematical Structure of Two Islamic Astrological Tables for "Casting the Rays", *Centaurus*, 32, 1989, pp. 171-202.

41 E. S. Kennedy, M. Janjanian, "The Crescent Visibility Table in al-Khwārizmī's Zīj", in Kennedy *et. al.*, *op. cit.*, pp. 151-56; D. A. King, "Some Early Islamic Tables for Determining Lunar Crescent Visibility", in Saliba and King (eds.), *From Deferent to Equant*, pp. 189-92; J. P. Hogendijk, "Three Islamic Lunar Crescent Visibility Tables", *Journal for the History of Astronomy*, 19, 1988, pp. 32-35.

42 J. Vernet and M. A. Catalá, "Las obras matemáticas de Maslama de Madrid", in *Estudios sobre historia de la ciencia medieval*, ed. J. Vernet, Barcelona-Bellaterra, 1979, pp. 241-71.

[43] H. Hermelink, "Tabulae Jahen", *Archive for the History of the Exact Sciences*, 2, 1964, pp. 108-12.

[44] North, *op. cit.*, p. 32 *et seq.*

[45] J. Samsó and H. Mielgo, *Ibn Isḥāq al-Tūnisī and Ibn Muʿādh al-Jayyānī on the Qibla* (forthcoming)

[46] On the *Toledan Tables* see G. J. Toomer, "A Survey of the Toledan Tables", *Osiris*, 15, 1968, pp. 5-174; F. S. Pedersen, "Canones Azarchelis. Some Versions and a Text", *Cahiers de l'Institut du Moyen Age Grec et Latin* (Copenhagen), 54, 1987, pp. 129-218; L. Richter-Bernburg, "Ṣāʿid, the *Toledan Tables*, and Andalusī Science", in Saliba and King (eds.), *From Deferent to Equant*, pp. 373-401; Mercier, *Astronomical Tables in the Twelfth Century*, pp. 104-12.

[47] The basic book on Ibn al-Zarqālluh is still J. M. Millás-Vallicrosa, *Estudios sobre Azarquiel*, Madrid-Granada, 1943-50.

[48] O. Neugebauer, *A History of Ancient Mathematical Astronomy*, Berlin-Heidelberg-New York, 1975, II, 631-34.

[49] D. Pingree, "Precession and Trepidation in Indian Astronomy before A.D. 1200", *Journal for the History of Astronomy*, 3, 1972, pp. 27-35.

[50] In his *Kitāb fī ḥarakāt al-shams*, ed. A. S. Saʿīdān, *Rasāʾil ibn Sinān*, Kuwait, 1983, pp. 274-304.

[51] This text has been published several times by J. M. Millás-Vallicrosa. See, for example, his *Estudios sobre Azarquiel*, pp. 496-509; English translation and commentary by O. Neugebauer, "Thābit ibn Qurra 'On the Solar Year' and 'On the Motion of the Eighth Sphere'", *Proceedings of the American Philosophical Society*, 106, 1962, pp. 290-99.

[52] On the geometrical model of the *Liber de Motu*, cf. B. R. Goldstein, "On the Theory of Trepidation according to Thābit b. Qurra and its Implications for Homocentric Planetary Theory", *Centaurus*, 10, 1964, pp. 232-47; J. Dobrzycki, "Teoria precesji w astronomii sredniowiecznej", *Studia i Materialy Dziejow Nauki Polskiej*, Seria Z.Z. II, 1965, pp. 3-47 (in Polish, with a long summary in English); J. North, "Thebit's Theory of Trepidation and the Adjustment of John Maudith's Star Catalogue", in *Richard of Wallingford. An Edition of his Writings with Introductions, English Translation and Commentary*, III, Oxford, 1976, pp. 155-58; R. Mercier, "Studies in the Medieval Conception of Precession", *Archives Internationales d'Histoire des Sciences*, 26, 1976, pp. 197-220, and 27, 1977, pp. 33-71.

[53] Millás-Vallicrosa, *Estudios sobre Azarquiel*, pp. 250-343. On this book, cf. Goldstein, *Trepidation* and J. Samsó, "Sobre el modelo de Azarquiel para determinar la oblicuidad de la eclíptica", in *Homenaje al Prof. Darío Cabanelas O.F.M.*, II, Granada, 1987, pp. 367-77. see also J. Samsó, *Trepidation in al-Andalus in the 11th century* (forthcoming).

[54] See G. J. Toomer, "The Solar Theory of al-Zarqāl: A History of Errors", *Centaurus*, 14, 1969, pp. 306-36, and "The Solar theory of al-Zarqāl: an Epilogue", in Saliba and King (eds.) *From Deferent to Equant*, pp. 513-19; J. Samsó, "Al-Zarqāl, Alfonso X and Peter of Aragon on the Solar Equation", in Saliba and King (eds.), *From Deferent to Equant*, pp. 467-76, and "Azarquiel e Ibn al-Bannāʾ", in *Relaciones de la Península Ibérica con el Magreb (siglos XIII-XVI*, Madrid, 1988, pp. 361-72. See also J. Samsó and E. Millás, *Ibn Isḥāq, Ibn al-Bannāʾ and al-Zarqālluh's Solar Theory* (forthcoming).

[55] Millás-Vallicrosa, *Estudios sobre Azarquiel*, pp. 175-234. See also M. Boutelle, "The Almanac of Azarquiel", *Centaurus*, 12, 1967, pp. 12-19.

[56] J. M. Millás-Vallicrosa, *Las Tablas Astronómicas del Rey Don Pedro el Ceremonioso*, Madrid-Barcelona, 1962.

[57] On presumed observations of transits see B. R. Goldstein, "Some Medieval Reports of Venus and Mercury Transits", in *Theory and Observation in Ancient and Medieval Astronomy*, Variorum Reprints, London, 1985, No. XV.

[58] R. Lorch, "The Astronomy of Jābir ibn Aflaḥ", *Centaurus*, 19, 1975, pp. 85-107; N. M. Swerdlow, "Jābir ibn Aflaḥ's Interesting Method for finding the Eccentricities and Direction of the Apsidal Line of a Superior Planet", in Saliba and King (eds.), *From Deferent to Equant*, New York, 1987, pp. 501-12; H. Hugonnard-Roche, "La théorie astronomique selon Jabir ibn Aflah", *History of Oriental Astronomy*, (IAU Colloquium 91), Cambridge, 1987, pp. 207-08.

[59] B. R. Goldstein, "The Arabic Version of Ptolemy's Planetary Hypotheses", *Transactions of the American Philosophical Society*, N. S. 57, No. 4, 1967.

60 F. Sezgin, *Geschichte des Arabischen Schrifttums. Band VI. Astronomie*, Leiden, 1978, p. 197.

61 F. J. Carmody, "The Planetary Theory of Ibn Rushd", *Osiris*, 10, 1952, 556-86; A. I. Sabra, "The Andalusian Revolt against Ptolemaic Astronomy", in E. Mendelsohn (ed.), *Transformation and Tradition in the Sciences*, Cambridge (Mass.), 1984, pp. 133-53.

62 B. R. Goldstein, *Al-Biṭrūjī: On the Principles of Astronomy*, New Haven-London, 1971, 2 vols.; F. J. Carmody, *Al-Biṭrūjī. De motibus celorum. Critical edition of the Latin translation of Michael Scott*, Berkeley, Los Angeles, 1952. On the European diffusion of al-Biṭrūjī's ideas see R. S. Avi-Yonah, "Ptolemy vs. al-Bitruji. A Study of Scientific Decision-Making in the Middle Ages", *Archives Internationales d'Histoire des Sciences*, 35, 1985, pp. 124-47.

63 The sources he quotes are the *Almagest*, Ibn al-Zarqālluh's lost book on trepidation and Jābir's *Iṣlāḥ*. He may also have read Theon's *Commentary of the Almagest*.

64 See E. S. Kennedy in *Speculum*, 29, 1954, pp. 246-51, and his note *Alpetragius' Astronomy* in *Journal for the History of Astronomy*, 4, 1973, pp. 134-36.

BIBLIOGRAPHY

Full bibliographical references are given in the footnotes. I have, however, compiled a list of a few general books which might prove of interest to the reader.

Comes, M., R. Puig and J. Samsó (eds.), *De Astronomia Alphonsi Regis*, Barcelona, 1987.

Comes, M., H. Mielgo and J. Samsó (eds.), *"Ochava Espera" y "Astrofísica". Textos y estudios sobre las fuentes árabes de la Astronomía de Alfonso X*, Barcelona, 1990.

Kennedy, E. S., Colleagues and Former Students, *Studies in the Islamic Exact Sciences*, Beirut, 1983.

Kennedy, E. S., *A Survey of Islamic Astronomical Tables*, Philadelphia, 1956.

King, D. A., *Islamic Astronomical Instruments*, London (Variorum Reprints), 1987.

Millás-Vallicrosa, J. M., *Estudios sobre historia de la ciencia española*, Barcelona, 1949.

——, *Nuevos estudios sobre historia de la ciencia española*, Barcelona, 1960.

——, *Estudios sobre Azarquiel*, Madrid-Granada, 1943-50.

Samsó, J., *Las ciencias de los Antiguos en al-Andalus* (in press, to appear Madrid, 1992).

Vernet, J., *Estudios sobre historia de la ciencia medieval*, Barcelona-Bellaterra, 1979.

——, *De ʿAbd al-Raḥmān I a Isabel II*, Barcelona, 1989.

——, *La cultura hispanoárabe en Oriente y Occidente*, Barcelona, 1978. There is a French translation (*Ce que la culture doit aux Arabes d'Espagne*, Paris, 1985) and a German translation (*Die spanische-arabische Kultur im Orient und Okzident*, Zurich and Munich, 1984.

——, *La ciencia en al-Andalus*, Seville, 1986.

—— (ed.), *Estudios sobre historia de la ciencia árabe*, Barcelona, 1980.

—— (ed.), *Textos y estudios sobre astronomía española en el siglo XIII*, Barcelona, 1981.

—— (ed.), *Nuevos estudios sobre astronomía española en el Siglo de Alfonso X*, Barcelona, 1983.

HYDRAULIC TECHNOLOGY IN AL-ANDALUS

THOMAS F. GLICK

Introduction

Although the remarks that follow are primarily concerned with hydraulic techniques, mainly those related to irrigation systems and to irrigation agriculture and a "technology" that includes both mechanical and institutional elements, they are also directed to broader questions of the place of technology within Islamic culture and in the historiography of that culture.

I. *Irrigation agriculture and the Arab "green revolution"*

Although the Romans irrigated in Spain, dry-farming was the basis of Roman agriculture and the artificial supply of water was supplementary. The considerable hydraulic works of the Romans (which the Arabs later admired as being monuments to the engineering prowess of the ancients—*al-uwal*), such as the Aqueduct of Segovia, were designed for urban water supply only, not for agriculture, although certain storage dams in Extremadura may indeed have stored water for agricultural use. In any event, the Muslims must have found that much of the pre-existing irrigation infrastructure was buried in subsoil. Such was no doubt true of the Valencian *huerta*, which had suffered a catastrophic population loss after the political turmoil of the 3rd century A. D.

The Muslim settlers, therefore, whether Arab or Berber, either took over or extended pre-existing channels or else installed them anew, basing themselves on practices learned in the Near East or North Africa. The context in which irrigation agriculture was established, however, was peculiar to the circumstances of the Arab conquest and the world it created. The conquests of the 2nd/8th century promoted a vast East-to-West movement of crops mainly grown in India under Monsoon conditions and which could not be grown in the Mediterranean world, with its characteristic summer droughts, without irrigation. The most notable of these crops, in order of their economic importance, were rice, sugar cane and such fruits as oranges and related citrus, the banana and the watermelon.[1] We therefore confront a richly complex diffusion which included: irrigated cultivars, mainly of Indian origin; a doctrine of agricultural knowledge—Indian agriculture (*filāḥa hindiyya*)—on how to cultivate them; and the theoretical and practical knowledge of irrigation required to grow them in the Mediterranean. The irrigation component of the new agriculture was itself a complex amalgam of technology (in the form of hydraulic appurtenances required to divert, conduct and raise water for irrigation) and institutions (the arrangements necessary for distributing the water among communities of farmers, including notions of water rights, principles of allocation and measurement, and mechanisms for administration, adjudication of disputes and social control of water distribution). The customary and legal principles according to which hydraulic agriculture was organised do, I wish to emphasise, constitute a technology, because without them the mechanical and physical structures of irrigation could not be put into use.

II. *Sources for the study of irrigation in al-Andalus*

In view of the paucity of documentation dealing directly with hydraulics, the study of Andalusī irrigation requires a mixture of techniques and approaches. Certain hydraulic appurtenances such as *qanāt*s and *norias* are dealt with in technical treatises, so we have some information on how they were in fact constructed. Such descriptions can then be checked against both archaeological evidence and recent ethnographic information, which must be considered a valid source of information in view of the conservativeness of agricultural practices and their resistance to change in traditional societies. Place names also provide complementary evidence on the distribution of hydraulic structures, such as dams and *qanāt*s, as well as providing some evidence as to their dating, as do the frequent arabisms by which irrigation techniques and practices continued to be called in Spain. So far as institutions of water distribution are concerned, the few Arabic documents antedating the Christian conquest that have been discovered[2] nevertheless reveal enough information to validate the vast documentary evidence of Islamic irrigation systems that survived into the Christian period. In general, wherever the Christians encountered functioning irrigation systems these were ordered to continue functioning "just as they were in the times of the Saracens" (to cite a typical formula). Two documental genres have proven particularly rich in yielding information concerning pre-existent Islamic systems: the first are the books of *repartimiento*, or land division, which record the human landscape of al-Andalus (though not without distortion) as the Christians encountered it;[3] and second are the registers of the properties of religious endowments ("habices") and related documents—translations into Spanish of Arabic land registers in Granada—on the basis of which the irrigation institutions of Naṣrid Granada can be at least in part reconstructed.[4] Finally, comparative study of past and present Islamic irrigation systems, both in Syria and Yemen (the two areas of the eastern Islamic world whose imprint was salient in Andalusī irrigation) and North Africa, can be expected to yield important clues as to the cultural filiation of irrigation in al-Andalus.

In the past ten years a number of coincident circumstances have joined to stimulate an avalanche of new historical studies of irrigation agriculture in

Spain, many of which reflect upon the Islamic period and the Muslim contribution.[5] Among these stimuli I might note: (1) the *régimen de autonomías*, which has both stimulated and financed numerous high-quality studies of local history; (2) the dissolution of an older consensus of Spanish medievalism, which concentrated on cereal farming as the basis of agriculture; and (3) the flowering of medieval archaeology, which has generated numerous new hypotheses concerning the social organisation of al-Andalus, including some interesting notions about hydraulic agriculture.[6] Here, I will limit my discussion to one archaeological study because it shows both the strengths and the limitations of the genre. Recently, Karl Butzer, Joan Mateu and a group of archaeologists and medievalists began to study a number of irrigated sites in the province of Castellón in order to study the origin and historical and cultural patterns of successive irrigation in Roman, Islamic and Christian agrarian régimes. Their conclusions were that the Islamic conquest "did not fundamentally alter the available range of cultivars and technology" and that, because of the depopulation and pattern of farm abandonment of late imperial times, "the Islamic cycle of renewed intensification and improved productivity gains undue prominence because of this ultimately catastrophic decline".[7]

Such a conclusion (of "undue" prominence) introduces a value judgement which distorts the meaning of cultural change and requires a short historiographical digression. Spanish Arabists and medievalists of the generation of Miguel Asín Palacios and Claudio Sánchez Albornoz held that the Islamic conquest only added superficial cultural gloss to a native population which continued to display "Hispanic" cultural and character traits, a "pan-Hispanic" view which was raised to the level of national ideology under the Franco régime, which embraced the historiography of Sánchez Albornoz, a republican exile, even as it excoriated his political stance. This view, which I call "pan-Hispanism", is currently known in historian's argot as "continuism". Following the lead of Américo Castro, who held that there was a sharp socio-cultural break caused by the Arab invasion, many historians of my generation and virtually all of the younger Spanish medievalists have argued that the acculturation of Muwallads was complete and that their culture should be called "Andalusī" in preference to misleading hyphenates like "Hispano-Arab". Following Don Américo we hold that what is "Hispanic" cannot be "Arab" and vice-versa.[8] The successful attack on pan-Hispanism, however, has now produced a new kind of rigidity which dissuades from any re-evaluation of institutional continuity between Roman and Islamic Spain, because any hint of "Roman survivals" smacks of continuism. This leaves a new generation of medieval archaeologists hanging on a limb, because there is no theoretical structure in place for putting such evidence (on irrigation régimes, or on pottery, to cite the two most salient examples) in a viable explanatory context.

Butzer's findings must, therefore, be reckoned with. Yet I challenge the notion that "undue prominence" has been given to the Arab (and possibly Berber) role in the renewal of the Peninsula's agricultural base. Such a view runs the risk of reviving the old canard that Arab civilisation, because of its genius for the synthesis of disparate cultural elements, was somehow lacking in originality, as if synthesis were not a culturally creative act. Our view is quite different: the melding of Indian agriculture, Roman and Persian hydraulic techniques, and a legal régime of water distribution combining elements of Arab and Berber tribal norms, Islamic law and Roman provincial customary law (a complex mixture that needs to be unravelled) constituted something quite different from its antecedent Roman irrigation agroecosystem, in terms of both water use and norms of distribution, let alone the kind of economy into which it was integrated.

Such strictures aside, we can say that the merit of Butzer's approach is to have provided a model for the study of such systems, by factoring them into a scale of analysis. The macrosystems of the great alluvial *huertas* were rebuilt by the Muslims on top of a Roman skeleton. Mesosystems (a village irrigating from one or more springs) and microsystems (tank, cistern or *noria* irrigation of family parcel) have different origins:

> The meso- and micro-scale networks in the adjacent mountains, were not superimposed on pre-Islamic irrigation layouts. They represent a significant expansion of irrigation into new eco-habitats, presumably during the second half of the economic revival (11th and 12th centuries) and were probably the work of settlers whose forebears had already been acculturated as Arabic-speaking Muslims.[9]

The over-definition of "origins", with its consequent cultural loadings, vitiates the otherwise perceptive findings of this study (although it describes the agriculture of Eastern Spain only).[10]

III. *Macrosystems*

The southern alluvial plain of the Mijares river provides the best archaeological evidence. The westernmost sector, now dry-farmed, has the remains of several Roman canals. The middle sector is irrigated by canals built by Christian settlers in the 1270s. The eastern third is rich in Arabic place names, was the focus of Muslim settlement and was described by Idrīsī as a prosperous irrigated district.[11] Although Butzer believes that Arabic toponyms have been overworked as cultural markers,[12] such studies yield results not much different from the archaeological survey of Burriana, the chief irrigated settlement of Muslim La Plana. Place-name evidence yields similar results. Further south, in Lorca, Robert Pocklington finds that 68% of the canals have pre-Islamic names, those with Arab names being found on the periphery and representing Muslim-built extensions of a pre-existing system. In Murcia, on the other hand, only 22% of the canals have pre-Islamic names. Those with Arab names form a coherent network, while those with pre-Arab names display a scattering pattern.[13] The inference is that the intensification of the irrigation system built by the Muslims blotted out the much more modest canal network they encountered there. In these cases, archaeological and toponymic evidence yield comparable results: the Muslims took over an area which had been modestly irrigated (the *huerta* of Lorca is much smaller than that of Murcia), rebuilt and extended the systems and, to the extent that the Arab and/or Berber settlers were tribal groups, they reorganised the allocation and administration procedures in accordance with tribal norms (a fundamental point not alluded to by the aforementioned authors).

The *huerta* of Valencia presents a similar picture. There is no clear picture of the extent to which the Romans irrigated there.[14] Although ceramic canal checks clearly identifiable as Roman have been excavated, continuous use of the *huerta* since at least the 4th/10th century has obliterated earlier remains, or made them inaccessible. Of the major canals and branches about half have Arabic names, including Mislata (*Manzil* ʿAṭāʾ), Favara (Hawwāra—a Berber tribe), Rascanya (in Arabic *rās al-qanāh* "head of the canal"), Faitanar (*k͟hayṭ al-nahr*, literally "thread of the river", in Arabic), Benatger (after a tribal segment), Algiròs (from *al-zurūb*, "the canals") and so forth.[15] I have made the case for the Arab nature of the irrigation system of the Valencian *huerta* based on the similarity of distribution arrangements there with those of Barada river of the Ghūṭa of Damascus. In each case the water of the river is considered to carry 24 units of water (*qīrāṭ*s in Damascus; *fila*s in Valencia) at each stage of diversion.[16] Guichard has challenged my interpretation on the basis of his supposition that the *huerta* was settled mainly by Berbers, e.g. the Hawwāra, who at some time irrigated along the Favara Canal.[17] Others have criticised his hypothesis of Berber settlement (see discussion, below), but for me the controversy serves to illustrate an elementary point about irrigation systems and their diffusion. The Arabs and Berbers who settled in al-Andalus did not bring canals, *qanāt*s, dams or *norias* with them; they only brought ideas. In assessing the hydraulic technologies of al-Andalus, therefore, the physical origin of canals is irrelevant: whatever the Muslims found they integrated into a quite different social, cultural and economic system than that prevailing before, according to norms they brought with them. And, even if Berbers vastly outnumbered Arabs in the *huerta* of Valencia (which cannot be demonstrated), the presence of just *one* Arab who knew the Syrian system could have sufficed to introduce it. To suppose that ideas and techniques can only diffuse via a folk migration is simply ingenuous.

The meaning of the common term in which measurement units of water are expressed in Eastern Spain, *fila* (Valencia; *hila* or *hilo* in Castilian) merits a brief discussion apart. The word means "thread", and we know both from place names like Faitanar or Alfeitami[18] and from documentation[19] that *fila* is simply a Romance translation of Arabic *khayṭ*. The *fila* is virtually everywhere a twelve-base unit of account (that is, it is imaginary) which expresses the water right of an individual, collectivity or town as a proportion of the total amount of water in the stream, in some segment of the stream, or at some stage of it. Whenever it had to be measured, as in the case of a water shortage, it was converted, logically, into time units (hours or days of water). The universality of twelve-base measurement units for irrigation throughout the Islamic world makes the *fila* the lynchpin of the case for Arab imprint upon distribution arrangements, along with the terms for irrigation turn, *tanda* (of uncertain origin, but presumed an arabism) in Valencia, *dula* (from *dawla*, the nearly universal expression for "turn" in the Yemen and in the Saharan chain of oases), *ador* (from *dawr*), and so forth. In the canals water was divided into aliquot portions by means of physical structures called divisors (*partidor* in Catalan and Castilian, but a number of synonymous arabisms are also found in post-conquest Christian systems—*almatzem*, from *maqsam*, in Gandia, and *sistar*, from *shaṭara*, in the Vall de Segó, both from Arabic words meaning "to divide").[20]

The diversion dam, a structure built across a stream to divert its water into a canal, is a universal technique known throughout the ancient Mediterranean and Middle East, and no cultural paternity can be assigned to it, even though Christian witnesses in court cases in 14th century Valencia were able to recognise those dams built before the conquest by their masonry. But the hydraulics of diversion dams were understood by all, as is suggested by the semantic equivalence of Catalan *resclosa* and Arabic *sudd* (which yields the common arabism *assut* in Catalan, *azud* in Castilian), both indicating closure. The current wheel, a compartmented *noria* which lifts water from a stream and discharges it into an elevated canal, is associated both with macrosystems (e.g. in Murcia) and with mesosystems (e.g. in Teruel). In the former, it was used to integrate lands of high elevation into the wider *huerta* system.

IV. *Mesosystems*

Those that Butzer studied in the Sierra de Espadàn are quite small—villages irrigated by one or two springs and with a dense packing of hydraulic techniques closely associated with Arab settlement, including terraced fields, cisterns, *shādūfs*, *norias* and measurement by clepsydra.[21] Thus in Ahín water from a perennial spring is stored in three cisterns and then distributed to fields on each bank in a weekly rotation. At Chóvar, one irrigation system consisted of a spring, two cisterns and canals irrigating some nine hectares; a second, distinct system irrigates around five hectares with spring water stored by storage dam and distributed in time-units measured with a clepsydra. This second system required that water be lifted onto some fields, and ruins of both a *shādūf* and a *noria* remain. From this evidence, Butzer's group concludes that "the lift and storage technology of the sierra in particular and the Valencian irrigation sphere in general indicates a combination of classical and Islamic roots. Introduction of the animal-driven water-wheel implies greater efficiency and will have facilitated Islamic intensification of agriculture in previously unirrigated areas."[22]

A larger mesosystem, in this case of distinctly Arab introduction, is that of Banyalbufar, Mallorca. This area of 60 hectares is irrigated by water from a *qanāt* and then distributed into cisterns or holding tanks of two varieties, uncovered (*ṣahrīj* in Arabic, *safareiq* in Catalan) and covered (*jubb* in Arabic, *aljub* in Catalan), from which terraced fields are watered in weekly turns. The fields are embanked in terraces called *marjades*, a *marqa* being the sustaining wall. These terms are thought to be derived from Arabic *maʿjil* and to have been introduced, along with the associated repertory of hydraulic techniques, from South Arabia under the Banū Ghāniya in the late 6th/12th century.[23] The turn procedure in Banyalbufar is broadly consonant with those of South Arabia (seven day turns, with days counted from sunrise to sunset), although it is also somewhat anomalous. In Yemen water is usually distributed to irrigators by time-units measured with clepsydras or other devices and overseen by an official. In Banyalbufar there is no formal irrigation community and no official designated to oversee the turn, which is executed by agreement of the irrigators.[24] This is a rare procedure in Eastern Spain, but not unheard of.

The *qanāt*, or filtration gallery, is a Persian technique widely diffused in Islamic Spain in meso-level irrigation systems. *Qanāt*s are sometimes described as vertical wells, but a true filtration gallery is built to skim along a water table and is provided with vertical shafts to supply access and air to workers engaged in maintaining the tunnel. In fact, the Arabs used a variety of related techniques to transport water underground, particularly in difficult terrains, not all of which captured water by filtration, and also built filtration galleries in river beds, not a topography characteristic of *qanāt*s. Archaeologists have recently studied *qanāt*s in Mallorca and Crevillente (Valencia);[25] river-bed galleries or *cimbra*s in Andarax (Almería), shorter than *qanāt*s usually are, without breathing wells, and which are not tunnels but rather covered trenches.[26] In Cocentaina there are *alcavon*s, tunnels with breathing wells, but which carry water from the Alcoi river to irrigation canals without collecting water by filtration.

V. *Microsystems*

Those studied by Butzer were fields sited above the communal mesosystems and irrigated by tanks.[27] But by far the most common type of microsystem was the single family farm watered by an animal-powered *noria*. The larger current wheel, which lifts water by means of a compartmented rim rather than a chain of pots, lifts large amounts of water and is characteristic of macro- or mesosystems where they are found on perennial streams or rivers or, as in the *huerta* of Murcia, on main irrigation canals.[28] A current wheel can be converted into an undershot vertical mill simply by connecting it to a horizontal axis. Thus the two techniques are closely related, and an artisan who can make a current wheel can also make a vertical mill.

But the *noria* that concerns us here is the smaller kind, powered in the Islamic Middle Ages by burros or oxen. Among the Andalusī agronomical writers, both Ibn al-ʿAwwām and Abū ʾl-Khayr provide specifications on tapping wells and on building *norias*.[29] For all their ubiquity, *norias* have not been much studied[30] and now have practically disappeared from Spain. Only their sites, therefore, can be studied, both from an archaeological and an engineering perspective. A recent archaeological survey in Villacañas (La Mancha), an area of the Islamic kingdom of Toledo where *norias* were densely implanted, reveals many *noria* wells provided with staircases or tunnels leading to the surface of the water. This technique is related to that of tunnelling for a *qanāt*, and indeed, as its name suggests, there was also a *qanāt* in Villacañas.[31] In a recent article, Robert Pocklington has suggested that the *qanāt* was also called *naqb* in Andalusī Arabic, as in the phrase *naqb al-bīr*, "the tunnel of the well", and, on this basis, suggests that the etymology of the place name Moncófar is *manqūba*, that is, a well with a gallery—a *qanāt*.[32] This might be so, but it is also true that wells could be tunnelled not only horizontally, as in a *qanāt*, but also vertically, and indeed diagonally as in the access staircase of a *noria*.

The large-scale introduction of the animal-driven *noria* made it possible for a family farm to produce a surplus for the market. The "*noria* revolution" was, therefore, intimately involved with the expansion of regional economies that characterised the *ṭāʾifa* period.[33] A *noria* site continuously used from the first half of the 4th/10th century to the mid 800s/1400s has recently been excavated at Oliva (Valencia). The chief interest of the site is that it yielded more than 5000 fragments of *noria* pots (*arcaduz* in Spanish, from Arabic *qādūs*) which show, first, that the perforation in the base recommended by Ibn al-ʿAwwām as a way to prevent breakage resulting from the impact of the pot on the surface of the water was introduced towards the end of the 5th/11th century, and, second, that the form of the pots suggests Syrian prototypes.[34] I might also add that in those areas of Spain where *norias* were used, the *noria* pot, required in huge numbers for replacement, was the basis of the local pottery industry.[35]

VI. *Mills*

The origin of the water mill is uncertain. The common horizontal (vertical axis) gristmill which is generically called the "Norse mill" in the West was also known in the East at an early date.[36] Documentary evidence for mills in al-Andalus is not abundant. The *Repartimientos* (Castilian; *Repartiments* in Catalan), land registers which recorded elements of the Andalusī landscape in parcels granted out to Christian settlers, show that al-Andalus was amply endowed with mills. That of Valencia mentions more than one hundred mills, with thirty-five in the city and *huerta* of Valencia itself, and nineteen in Játiva.[37] These were horizontal mills, many with more than one millstone (an indication of the abundance of hydraulic energy available in rivers or irrigation canals) and many belonged to important officials (for example, to a *rā'is* and a *qā'id*; also, in Játiva, two mills are recorded as belonging to the state—*almaczem*).[38] These mills are presumed all to be horizontal gristmills, first because no industrial mills (which were generally vertical) are specified, and second because in Valencia there are no mill sites provided with the millponds that overshot, vertical mills require. That would not rule out undershot vertical mills which involve an easy adaptation of the current wheel, but none are clearly documented. It may be that horizontal mills could be adopted for simple industrial purposes, and al-Qazwīnī mentions a horizontal mill in Mallorca which, in times of water shortage, was connected to a *noria* wheel (*dūlāb*) and run as an overshot vertical mill fed by a chute.[39]

The *Repartiment* of Mallorca similarly documents 162 mills, and Miquel Barceló estimates that just before the Christian conquest of 626-7/1229 there were around 197 mills in all.[40] In consonance with the limited water resources of the island, these were small, very few having more than one millstone. Almost one-quarter of these horizontal mills were powered by *qanāts*. As in Játiva, the *makhzan* owned mills, as did the *ḥabūs* (three mills) and an unnamed shaykh. Barceló believes that the tribal pattern of collective control of water prevented the formation of groups that monopolised mills.

Complementary evidence on Andalusī mills comes from place names. The *Repartiment* of Valencia mentions places with the elements *Raal, Rahal, Arreha, Raha,* etc. from Arabic *raḥā*, pl. *arḥā'*.[41] In spite of the salience of mills with multiple stones on the *Repartiment* of Valencia, simpler, one-stone mills must have been the most common and were typically massed at points of concentrated hydraulic energy, whether on suitable watercourses or near the heads of irrigation canals. Such a place was the Faḥṣ al-raḥī, "field of the mills", near Córdoba.[42]

Conclusion

No doubt the diffusion of mills and irrigation systems was linked. According to Miquel Barceló, in al-Andalus the mill was an afterthought to irrigation and subordinate to it, in contrast to the situation in feudal Catalonia, where milling was an end in itself (as a feudal monopoly) and irrigation a mere by-product.[43] The contrast in the two systems is a marker, for Barceló, of two different kinds of rural social organisation, the feudal and hierarchical Christian system and the egalitarian, tribal Muslim one. The model is promising, at least as a working hypothesis, and serves to underscore a central issue in the history of technology, namely the linkage between social systems and techniques. Mills and irrigation canals, both nearly universal techniques, nevertheless acquired different economic, social and cultural meanings when adopted in sharply different societies and cultures. Techniques are artefacts which, in their mechanical sense, can be analysed and classified without respect to their ambient culture. But *technologies*, techniques as cognitive systems, are specific to particular societies and cultures. Al-Andalus stood astride Europe and Asia geographically, and between Roman Hispania and Spain historically. But the patterns of diffusion, invention and innovation which history and archaeology reveal have to be interpreted on the basis of what we know of the social organisation of Andalusī society. Inasmuch as rural Andalusī society can only be known archaeologically and through comparative analysis, advances in the history of its technology must await the generation of hypotheses concerning the social structure within which these techniques were deployed.

[1] See Andrew M. Watson, *Agricultural Innovation in the Early Islamic World*, Cambridge (England), 1983, and his earlier summary, "The Arab Agricultural Revolution and its Diffusion, 700-1100", *Journal of Economic History*, 34, 1974, pp. 8-35.

[2] See below, notes 4 and 19. Most of the pre-conquest documentation is from Naṣrid Granada and, hence, late.

[3] See, for example, the *repartimientos* of Valencia and Murcia: M. D. Cananes and R. Ferrer Navarro, *Repartiment de València*, Saragossa, 1979, 2 vols.; Juan Torres Fontes (ed.), *Repartimiento de Murcia*, Madrid, 1960. Texts of the *repartiment* of Mallorca survive in Latin, Catalan and Arabic versions; see Angel Poveda, "Toponimia árabe-musulmana de Mayurqa", *Awrāq*, 3, 1980, pp. 75-101. See also Poveda's studies of water-related place names in Mallorca, "Aigües i corrents d'aigua a la toponimia de Mayurqa segons el *Llibre del repartiment*", *Butlleti de la Societat d'Onomàstica*, 10, 1982.

[4] On the utility of the *Libros de Habices* for deciphering Andalusī irrigation systems, see Juan Martínez Ruiz, "Terminología árabe del riego en el antiguo reino de Granada (siglos XV-XVII), según los libros de habices", in *El agua en zonas áridas: Arqueología e historia* (Acts of the I Coloquio de Historia y Medio Físico), Almería, 1989, II, 143-65.

[5] See Thomas F. Glick, "Historia del regadío y las técnicas hidráulicas en la España medieval y moderna: Bibliografía comentada", *Chronica Nova*, Granada (in press).

[6] The most interesting theories have been generated by Miquel Barceló and his group. See Barceló, "El diseño de espacios irrigados en al-Andalus: Un enunciado de principios generales" in *El agua en zonas áridas*, I, xiii-l; and Ramon Martí, "Hacia una arqueología hidráulica; la génesis del molino feudal en Cataluña", in *Arqueología medieval. En las afueras del "medievalismo"*, ed. Miquel Barceló, Barcelona, 1988, pp. 165-94.

[7] Karl W. Butzer *et al.*, "Irrigation Agroecosystems in Eastern Spain: Roman or Islamic Origins?", *Annals of the Association of American Geographers*, 75, 1985, p. 482. An agroecosystem is defined as "successfully 'tested' packages of technology, domesticates, and organisational strategies" (p. 479). In the view expounded here, I regard irrigation technology as including both the specific crops grown and the strategies for managing the hydraulic system.

[8] I have discussed the anthropological ramifications of the debate between Castro and Sánchez Albornoz in "Acculturation as an Explanatory Concept in Spanish History", *Comparative Studies in Society and History*, 11, 1969, pp. 136-54 (with Oriol Pi-Sunyer); "The Ethnic Systems of Premodern Spain", *Comparative Studies in Sociology*, 1, 1978, pp. 157-71; and "Américo Castro: La historia como antropología cultural", *Anthropos*, Barcelona, 21-22, Jan.-Feb. 1983, pp. 84-91.

[9] Butzer *et al.*, *op. cit.*, p. 499.

[10] See, on this account, Miquel Barceló's comments in "La questió de l'hidraulisme andalusi", in *Les aigües cercades (Els qanat(s) de l'illa de Mallorca)*, Palma de Mallorca, 1986, pp. 9-36.

[11] Butzer *et al.*, *op. cit.*, p. 487; André Bazzana and Pierre Guichard, "Irrigation et société dans l'Espagne orientale au Moyen Age", in *L'homme et l'eau en Méditerranée et au Proche-Orient*, ed. J. Metral and P. Sanlaville, Lyon, 1981, p. 138.

[12] Butzer *et al.*, *op. cit.*, p. 480.

[13] Robert Pocklington, "Acequias árabes y pre-árabes en Murcia y Lorca: Aportación toponímica a la historia del regadío", *Xé Colloqui General de la Societat d'Onomàstica. 1er d'Onomàstica Valenciana*, Valencia, 1986, pp. 462-73. Although I believe that toponyms have an archeological value, I do not believe that such evidence justifies the kind of naive generalisations which mar Pocklington's otherwise interesting study. Water was sold in Lorca, he says, because of the "capitalist" nature of "Romano-Visigothic" society (p. 468). See also Barceló's comment on this article, in "La questió de l'hidraulisme andalusí" (note 10, above), p. 14.

[14] Anti-continuists deny the existence of macrosystems in Roman and Islamic Spain alike. Thus for Ramon Martí, Butzer's Roman macrosystems never existed ("Oriente y occidente en las tradiciones hidráulicas medievales", in *El agua en zonas áridas*, I, 434), while for Patrice Cressier, "Archéologie des structures hydrauliques en al-Andalus", *ibid.*, pp. li-xcii, on p. lxxiii, there are no documentable macrosystems in al-Andalus. Cressier's conclusion is tendentious, because he, like Guichard and Bazzana, has a stake in demonstrating the tribal nature of all irrigation systems in al-Andalus.

[15] On the etymology of Faitanar and Rascanya, see Glick, *Irrigation and Society in Medieval Valencia*, Cambridge (Mass.), 1970, pp. 227-28. *Zarb* (pl. *zurūb*) yields both the canal name Algiròs and the technical term for drainage ditch, *assarb* (in Valencian; *azarbe* in Castilian).

[16] The argument is laid out in *Irrigation and Society*, chapter 11, and defended in *Islamic and Christian Spain in the Early Middle Ages*, Princeton, 1979, pp. 68-73; and in "Las técnicas hidráulicas antes y después de la conquista", in *En torno al 750 aniversario: Antecedentes y consecuencias de la conquista de Valencia*, Valencia, I, 53-71.

[17] P. Guichard, *Al-Andalus: Estructura antropológica de una sociedad islámica en occidente*, Barcelona, 1976, p. 305; and Bazzana and Guichard, *op. cit.*, pp. 122-25.

[18] Alfeitami: either "a thread of water" (*khayṭ al-māʾ*) (Glick, *Irrigation and Society*, p. 367, n. 54) or "the two threads [of water]" (*al-khayṭān*) (Carmen Barceló, *Toponimia árabe del País Valencià. Alqueries i castells*, Valencia, 1983).

[19] E.g., an Arabic document from Torres (Valencia) dated 1223 and sewn into a 16th-century court case; see Glick, *Irrigation and Society in Medieval Valencia*, p. 227 and note 45.

[20] On the Arabic etymologies for terms denoting irrigation turns, see Glick, *Irrigation and Society*, pp. 221 (*tanda*, *ador*), 222 (*almatzem*, *dula*), 223 (*sistar*). On *dula*, see also Manuel Espinar Moreno, Thomas F. Glick and Juan Martínez Ruiz, "El término árabe *dawla* 'turno de riego', en una alquería de las tahas de Berja y Dalias: Ambroz (Almería)", in *El agua en zonas áridas*, I, 121-41, a study based on the Libros de Habices.

[21] Thomas F. Glick, "Medieval Irrigation Clocks", *Technology and Culture*, 10, 1969, pp. 424-28.

[22] Butzer *et al.*, *op. cit.*, pp. 491-96.

[23] Maria Antonia Carbonero Gamundi, "Terrasses per al cultiu irrigat i distribució social de l'aigua a Banyalbufar (Mallorca)", *Documents d'Anàlisi Geogràfica*, 4, 1983, pp. 32-68; Jacqueline Pirenne, *La maîtrise de l'eau en Arabie du Sud antique*, Paris, 1977, pp. 21-34.

[24] Carbonero, *op. cit.*, p. 60.

[25] See the multi-authored volume *Les aigües cercades* (note 10 above); and Miquel Barceló *et al.*, "Arqueología: La Font Antiga de Crevillent: Ensayo de descripción arqueológica", *Areas, Revista de Ciencias Sociales* (Murcia), 9, 1988, pp. 217-31.

[26] Maryelle Bertrand and Patrice Cressier, "Irrigation et aménagement du terroir dans la vallée de l'Andarax (Almería): Les réseaux anciens de Ragol", *Mélanges de la Casa de Valázquez*, 21, 1985, pp. 122-23. On *cimbras* supplying the fountains of Almería from the Andarax river, see Manuel Gómez Cruz, "Las ordenanzas de riego de Almería año 1755", in *El agua en zonas áridas*, II, 1101-26. The *cimbra* feeding the Fuente Redonda had a vaulted ceiling, recognised in the 18th century as of "Arabic construction" (*de fábrica árabe*); *ibid.*, p. 1106.

[27] Butzer *et al.*, *op. cit.*, pp. 496-99.

28 Glick, *Irrigation and Society*, p. 178.

29 Lucie Bolens, "L'eau et l'irrigation d'après les traités d'agronomie andalous au moyen-âge (XIème-XIIème siècles)", *Options Méditerranéennes*, 16, December 1972, pp. 71-72.

30 But see the classic studies of Julio Caro Baroja, "Sobre la historia de la noria de tiro", *Revista de Dialectología y Tradiciones Populares*, 1, 1955,, pp.15-79; and Jorge Dias and Fernando Galhano, *Aparelhos de elevar a água de rega*, 2nd ed., Lisbon, 1986.

31 See Francisco García Martín and Thomas F. Glick, "Norias of La Mancha: A Historical Reconnaissance in Villacañas, Spain" (in press).

32 Robert Pocklington, "Toponimia y sistemas de agua en Sharq al-Andalus", in *Agua y poblamiento musulmán*, ed. Mikel de Epalza, Benissa, 1988, p. 106.

33 Glick, *Islamic and Christian Spain in the Early Middle Ages*, pp. 74-76. On the agricultural expansion of the *ṭā'ifa* period, see *ibid.*, pp. 76-78. Note that in La Mancha, an area of very dense noria concentration in modern times, the Romans had irrigated by gravity flow from perennial and intermittent streams. The Arabs replaced the system entirely with another based on norias and wells; see Almudena Orejas Saco del Valle and F. Javier Sánchez Palencia, "Obras hidráulicas romanas y explotación del territorio en la provincia de Toledo", in *El agua en zonas áridas*, I, 59.

34 André Bazzana, Salvador Climent and Yves Montmessin, *El yacimiento medieval de "Les Jovades"-Oliva (Valencia)*, Gandia, 1987.

35 Thomas F. Glick, "Noria Pots in Spain", *Technology and Culture*, 18, 1977, pp. 644-50.

36 The horizontal mill may have diffused simultaneously to Western Europe and the Islamic world from the same unknown hearth, "presumably north and east of the Roman Empire", Lynn White, Jr., *Medieval Technology and Social Change*, Oxford, 1962, p. 81.

37 Interestingly, none of the Játiva mills were paper mills, always presumed to have been vertical, because the famous paper industry of Islamic Játiva was not mechanised; see Robert I. Burns, *Society and Documentation in Crusader Valencia*, Princeton, 1985, p. 163.

38 Carmen Barceló, "Toponymie tribale ou familiale et organisation de l'espace dans l'aire valencienne à l'époque musulmane", *Revue de l'Occident Méditerranéen et Musulman*, 40, 1985, pp. 32-36.

39 Al-Qazwīnī, *Kosmographie*, ed. Wustenfeld, II, 381.

40 Miquel Barceló, "Els molins de Mayurqa", *Les illes orientals d'al-Andalus*, Palma de Mallorca, 1987, pp. 253-62.

41 *Ibid.* , p. 33. Some of these Rafal names, distorted to Real in Castilian, have been presumed to be residences of aristocrats, from *raḥl*, rural house, "maison hors d'une ville" (R. Dozy, *Supplément aux dictionnaires arabes*, 2nd ed., Leiden, 1927, I, 516); Miguel Asín Palacios, *Contribución a la toponimia árabe de España*, Madrid, 1944, pp. 128-29.

42 Glick, *Islamic and Christian Spain*, pp. 232-33.

43 These roles are evident in the physical lay-outs of canal/mill systems. See Barceló, "La arqueología extensiva y el estudio de la creación del espacio rural", in *Arqueología medieval* (note 6, above), pp. 234-38.

BIBLIOGRAPHY

Aigües cercades, Les (Els qanat(s) de l'illa de Mallorca), Palma de Mallorca: Institut d'Estudis Baleárics, 1986.

Agua en zonas áridas, El (Acts of the First Colloquium on History and Physical Environment), Almería: Instituto de Estudios Almerienses, 1989, 2 vols.

Barceló, Miquel (ed.), *Arqueología medieval. En las afueras del "medievalismo"*, Barcelona: Crítica, 1988.

Bazzana, André, and Pierre Guichard, "Irrigation et société dans l'Espagne orientale au Moyen Age", in *L'homme et l'eau en Méditerranée et au Proche-Orient*, ed. J. Metral and P. Sanlaville, Lyon: Maison de l'Orient, 1981.

Butzer, Karl W. *et al.*, "Irrigation Ecosystems in Eastern Spain: Roman or Islamic Origins?", *Annals of the Association of American Geographers*, 75, 1985, pp. 479-509.

Carbonero Gamundi, María Antonia, "Terrasses per al cultiu irrigat i distribució social de l'aigua a Banyalbufar (Mallorca)", *Documents d'Anàlisi Geogràfica* (Barcelona), 4, 1983, pp. 32-68.

Glick, Thomas F., *Irrigation and Society in Medieval Valencia*, Cambridge: Harvard University Press, 1970.

——, *Islamic and Christian Spain in the Early Middle Ages*, Princeton: Princeton University Press, 1979.

Guichard, Pierre, *Al-Andalus: Estructura antropológica de una sociedad islámica en occidente*, Barcelona: Barral, 1976.

Pocklington, Robert, "Acequias árabes y pre-árabes en Murcia y Lorca: Aportación toponímica a la historia del regadío", *Xé Colloqui General de la Societat d'Onomàstica Valenciana*, Valencia, 1986, pp. 462-73.

Watson, Andrew M., *Agricultural Innovation in the Early Islamic World*, Cambridge: Cambridge University Press, 1983.

AGRICULTURE IN MUSLIM SPAIN

EXPIRACIÓN GARCÍA SÁNCHEZ

Introduction

The importance of agriculture in human life has been obvious since earliest times. One of the many to stress this importance is the agronomer al-Tighnarī from Granada (5th/11th-6th/12th century), who writes that "agriculture constitutes the basis of subsistence for men and animals", so permitting "the preservation of life and the sustaining of the spirit".

The arrival of the Arabs marked the beginning of a profound development in Peninsular agriculture, which, in the last years of Visigothic rule, had regressed and decayed from the high level achieved during the Roman period. The new arrivals encountered a land whose fertility was described and celebrated by the Arab chroniclers and geographers, and they not only quickly perfected techniques inherited from the Hispano-Romans and Visigoths, but added their own specialised expertise in the fields of applied botany, agronomy, pharmacology and medicine—an expertise which, once it had been integrated and applied in practice, produced the great agricultural richness with which al-Andalus was blessed.

This expertise was acquired from different sources and transmitted in various ways. The first and most important source was the Eastern Graeco-Byzantine tradition, the second source was the Latin tradition and the last was local knowledge, possibly a Latin-Mozarabic substratum, which was perfectly assimilated. To this collection of diverse knowledge must be added, at a later date, the learning collected and transmitted in the *Nabataean Agriculture*, the first great Arabic work of agriculture, which was considered at that time to represent the Mesopotamian tradition.

I. *The Andalusī school of agronomy*

It was in the 4th/10th century that Andalusī scientists, having assimilated the knowledge of the Abbasid East, began to make original contributions to science, and this incipient tendency on the part of pre-eminent figures to make themselves independent of Eastern culture and science, together with a confluence of other elements and circumstances, led to the beginnings of a so-called "Andalusī school of agronomy", which achieved its highest point in the following 5th/11th and 6th/12th centuries.

One event which particularly favoured the development of pharmacology and botany, and hence of agronomy, was the acquisition of a copy of the

Materia Medica of Dioscorides,[1] sent as a gift from the Byzantine emperor Constantine VII Porphyrogenitus to the ruler of al-Andalus, ʿAbd al-Raḥmān III. However, the really decisive step towards the birth of an Andalusī school of agronomy was the composition, by ʿArīb b. Saʿīd, of the *Calendar of Córdoba*,[2] a work dedicated to the ruler al-Ḥakam II and containing agricultural data—inserted, usually, at the end of the description of each of the months of the year—in the areas of arboriculture, horticulture and gardening. There are also indications that ʿArīb wrote a treatise on agriculture, now lost, which was the source of the agronomical references in the *Calendar*. If this theory were confirmed, it would make his book the first Andalusī treatise on agriculture.[3]

To another great contemporary figure, Abū 'l-Qāsim Khalaf b ʿAbbās al-Zahrāwī, is attributed the authorship of a new treatise on agriculture, *Mukhtaṣar kitāb al-filāḥa*. This man, the "Abulcasis" of the medieval Latin texts, was the well-known court physician who served both al-Ḥakam II and al-Manṣūr, the general who succeeded him as ruler of al-Andalus. Although no Arabic source mentions the work, it is not surprising, given the inter-relation of the different disciplines we know today as the natural sciences, that al-Zahrāwī should, like other Andalusī physical scientists, have been attracted by agronomical studies; and, in that he was unquestionably the teacher, if indirectly, of later authors, he is considered by some[4] as the initiator of the Andalusī school of agronomy.

Another 4th/10th century text on agronomy was recently published as an anonymous work,[5] although the evidence seems to point to the authorship of a certain Ibn al-Jawād, about whom nothing is known. This work is divided into ten chapters and limits itself to the three agronomical fields of arboriculture, horticulture and gardening, the most interesting part, undoubtedly, being the fifth chapter, which deals with instructions for the cultivation of the most important ornamental plants known in al-Andalus at the time, and so supplements the information given in the *Calendar of Córdoba*.

Another important element in the later and most spectacular development of Andalusī agronomy is the appearance of botanical or experimental gardens, in which attempts were made to grow (from seeds, roots or cuttings) new plants brought from the most remote parts of the Near East, or to improve varieties of plants already known in the Peninsula. It happened frequently that agronomers collected plants in their travels to use later in their experiments.

The first known botanical garden was al-Ruṣāfa,[6] a kind of country estate devoted to recreation, built near Córdoba on the orders of the first Umayyad ruler of al-Andalus, ʿAbd al-Raḥmān I. The Arabic sources give a splendid account of the construction and agricultural activity there, laying special emphasis on the introduction of new plants which were later to spread throughout al-Andalus.[7]

The same kind of agricultural activity must have taken place at Madīnat al-Zahrā', the palatine city of the caliph ʿAbd al-Raḥmān III, although information from Arabic sources is here very scarce—by and large, the study of agricultural and botanical information in contemporary works permits only a vague notion of the activity in question.[8]

Following the disintegration of the central Caliphal government and the formation of the *ṭā'ifa* kingdoms, the petty kings hastened to imitate the customs of the dethroned caliphs, and experimental gardens accordingly sprang up in each individual court. Examples of such gardens were al-Ṣumādiḥiyya in Almería, the garden of the mill, or of the king, in Toledo and the garden also called the garden of the king, or of Sultan al-Muʿtamid, in Seville, each of these three gardens being directed by a theoretical agronomer. The contemporary Almerian historian and geographer Aḥmad b. ʿUmar al-ʿUḏrī (d.477/1085) thus describes al-Ṣumādiḥiyya: "In the outskirts of Almería, al-Muʿtaṣim constructed a garden (*bustān*) of artistic appearance with beautiful palaces. In this garden, in addition to the usual plants, exotic fruits are grown, like the various kinds of banana, and sugarcane."[9]

This tradition was to continue throughout the history of al-Andalus, with, for example, the garden of al-Buḥayra in Seville during the Almohad period, or the garden of the Jannat al-ʿArīf (Generalife) in Granada during the Naṣrid period.[10]

II. *The high point (5th/11th-7th/13th centuries)*

The high point of this school of agronomy, giving rise to what has come to be called "the Andalusī agricultural revolution", occurred at a very specific historical moment: that of the decentralisation of the Peninsula following the fall of the Caliphate and the establishment of the *ṭā'ifa* kingdoms, together with the new politico-economic balance this entailed. Very disparate efforts, knowledge and interests were to unite to bring about this development in agriculture: in the first place there were the rulers, who, as said above, sought the importation of new plants to acclimatise in their botanical gardens; there were their advisers, who were well aware of the importance of agriculture for the prosperity of the country; there were the jurists who created the interpretative legal framework for the needs of an expanding sector; and, finally, there were the agronomers, generally people of encyclopaedic knowledge who, to a greater or lesser degree, poured both theory and actual practical experience into their writings.

This agricultural expansion was clearly influenced by socio-cultural factors, as contacts between two separate civilisations brought forth new fashions and tastes. Eastern society was luxurious and refined compared to Peninsular society, and this led to a desire, in the latter, to surpass or at least to equal the East. On the level of material culture, and more specifically on that of food, this necessitated a range of agricultural products not previously found in al-Andalus, and there was a consequent attempt to import and acclimatise them. These and other factors led to the creation of an Andalusī agriculture wisely and rationally exploited, and reflecting a clear Mediterranean influence.

The 5th/11th and 6th/12th centuries were, as noted above, the period of the most important agricultural treatises: those of Ibn Wāfid, Ibn Baṣṣāl, Abū 'l-Khayr, Ibn Ḥajjāj, al-Tighnarī and Ibn al-ʿAwwām. However, the Arabic sources, and specifically the biographies, give little information on these authors, and this, together with the dispersed and summary nature of Andalusī manuscripts on agriculture, has made a study of them somewhat difficult.[11]

Of these Andalusī agronomers, the first, chronologically, is Ibn Wāfid (398/1008-466/1074). The abundance of biographical notices dedicated to this "Abenguefith", as medieval pharmacologists called him, is in contrast to the sparseness of information for the rest, although there are, it must be said, very serious doubts about the authorship of the "Compendium on Agriculture" (*Majmūʿ fī 'l-filāḥa*) which has been attributed to him. Whoever the actual author, however, this work was widely known and regarded, as is evident from its translation into two of the Peninsular romance languages, Catalan[12] and Castilian, and from its later influence on the great Renaissance work of agronomy , the *Agricultura General* of Gabriel Alonso de Herrera.

Another agronomer born in Toledo was Ibn Baṣṣāl, who must have succeeded Ibn Wāfid as head of the botanical garden in the grounds of King al-Maʾmūn of Toledo. His treatise, which was also translated into medieval Spanish,[13] stands apart from the other Andalusī works, first because his knowledge appears to be based exclusively on his own personal experience, with no other source at any rate mentioned, and second because he does not, as the other agronomers do, include matters extraneous to the practice of agriculture . When the *ṭāʾifa* kingdom of Toledo fell into Christian hands in 477/1085, Ibn Baṣṣāl, along with the other intellectuals of the city, moved to Seville. Here he offered his services to the king al-Muʿtamid, who, influenced by his prestige, gave him the directorship of the so-called "Garden of the Sultan" (*Ḥāʾiṭ al-Sulṭān*), where he continued with his agronomical task of acclimatising new plants.

Here in Seville there formed, around the figure of Ibn Baṣṣāl, the descendant of the primitive agronomical school which had arisen in the Córdoba of the Caliphate around the physician al-Zahrāwī, and had later moved temporarily to Toledo. Ibn Baṣṣāl managed to bring together a series of individuals with connected if not identical scientific interests, who considered him an eminent man (*māhir*)—in other words, a master—for his knowledge of agronomy.

One of this circle was Abū 'l-Khayr al-Ishbīlī[14] (a native of Seville, as his *nisba* indicates), of whom little is known; we have only indirect notices from other authors who used his book, these particularly mentioning his master-disciple relationship with Ibn Baṣṣāl. As with the works of so many of his contemporaries, his *Kitāb al-filāḥa*, which reflects the practical-theoretical dualism of his method, has come down to us incomplete.

One of the Andalusī authors most representative of the theoretical focus is Ibn Ḥajjāj, who may have been a member of the noble Sevillian family of the Banū Ḥajjāj, although we have few biographical facts concerning him. In contrast to the work of his contemporary, Ibn Baṣṣāl—with whom he must have been in contact, although no specific reference to this exists in the sources—his treatise, composed in 466/1073-4 and entitled *Al-Muqniʿ fī 'l-filāḥa* ("The Handbook of Agriculture"),[15] constitutes a veritable mosaic of quotations from ancient authors, with comparisons made, in some cases, with his own experience. Some scholars have detected, in this work, the persistence of the Latin agronomical tradition, in the form of direct influence from the *De re rustica* of the Hispano-Roman author Columela of the first century A.D. This is an extremely attractive thesis, but also a distinctly controversial one.[16]

The last 5th/11th century author chronologically (he actually wrote his book in the 6th/12th) was al-Tighnarī, who was born to a noble family, the Banū Murra, in a small village near Granada. According to the historian, Lisān al-Dīn Ibn al-Khaṭīb, al-Tighnarī was a clever literary man and an excellent poet who lived during the reign of the Zīrid prince ʿAbd Allāh b. Bulughghīn, although, possibly because of a disagreement with this ruler, he left Granada for the *ṭāʾifa* kingdom of Almería, where, in the gardens of the royal residence, al-Ṣumādiḥiyya, he undertook various types of agricultural experiment. Later, after travelling to various parts of North Africa and the East, he returned to al-Andalus, alternating his residence between Granada and Seville and forming part of Ibn Baṣṣāl's circle of agronomers and botanists in the latter.

Al-Tighnarī dedicated his treatise *Kitāb zahrat al-bustān wa-nuzhat al-adhhān* ("Splendour of the garden and recreation of the minds") to the Almoravid governor of Granada, Abū 'l-Ṭāhir Tamīm b. Yūsuf b. Tāshfīn. Even though something less than half the original work has come down to us, it clearly emerges as one of the most ordered and systematic of the Andalusī agronomical treatises, in which theory joins with actual practical experimentation, and it also reveals the breadth and depth of its author's knowledge on various subjects, including medicine, botany and linguistics.[17]

The treatise of Ibn al-ʿAwwām was, for a long time, the only reference work on Hispano-Muslim agronomy, yet, paradoxically, the personality of the author is almost entirely unknown; he is mentioned by only two authors, the historian Ibn Khaldūn and the Eastern geographer al-Qalqashandī, and they seem to know very little about him.

It seems clear, from the internal evidence of his work, that the author lived in Seville and, more specifically, in the Aljarafe district, which is mentioned as the place where he carried out his agricultural work: "I planted rice in Aljarafe" or "I have never seen fig trees planted among vines in the mountains of Aljarafe" are just two among many references. The impression is also given that he was a local aristocratic landowner, living in the 6th/12th and 7th/13th centuries, although the exact dates are not known.[18]

The *Kitāb al-filāḥa* is a large collection of excerpts from Andalusī and Eastern texts, and this is in itself a source of the work's interest and value, since, quite apart from being a compendium of previous theories of agronomy, it can help us reconstruct the original texts of certain authors, especially Hispano-Muslim authors, whose work has come down to us only in condensed or fragmented form. In this work, one of the few which have been completely preserved, Ibn al-ʿAwwām gathers all the knowledge of his period in the fields of agriculture and animal husbandry ; he brings together all the previous traditions of geoponics, comparing them and recreating them in the course of his summary; and he establishes an accepted tradition, a process of thought, which, as he himself affirms, is accompanied by experimentation: "I establish no principle in my work that I have not first proved by experiment on repeated occasions."[19]

III. *The final period (8th/14th century)*

With this century we encounter the last known work of Andalusī agriculture: the *urjūza,* or didactic poem, composed by the Almerian Ibn Luyūn (died 749/1349). The composition totals 1365 lines, and, in the words of its editor and translator J. Eguaras Ibáñez,[20] "it is far from the poetic elegances of the work of Virgil, even if some have gone so far as to call it the Andalusī *Georgics*"; it simply contains agricultural material—taken basically from the works of Ibn Baṣṣāl and al-Tighnarī—and there is no personal poetic element. Only when he speaks of the layout of the gardens, and the dwellings and country houses linked to them, does the author exhibit a degree of inspiration; for the rest it is a work without lyricism or rhetorical adornment. Eguaras also acknowledges its importance as being one of the few agricultural works (along with that of Ibn al-ʿAwwām) to have been preserved in its complete form; this is, indeed, something almost unknown in Andalusī agronomical literature.

Other Andalusī works on agronomy, apart from those mentioned above, are known to exist, but only through indirect references collected from later treatises. Such is the case with Ibn ʿArrāḍ and with an anonymous Andalusī manuscript from the 6th/12th century.[21]

IV. *Themes and content of Andalusī agricultural treatises.*

The Andalusī treatises—especially those which have been more completely preserved—generally follow the structure adopted by classical and Eastern works. The first chapters are devoted to soils, water and fertilisers, and these are followed by material on the raising of plants and the rearing of animals, and on veterinary science. It is not unusual for them to include calendars of agricultural tasks, accompanied at times by others of an astronomical and meteorological character, mixed with references to magic, local traditions and accounts taken directly from the statements of rural dwellers. Finally, they tend to record practical principles of domestic economy, methods of controlling disease and sickness in plants, and also indications of the factors, both physical and moral, which should be taken into account when selecting workers and people in charge of agricultural exploitation.

The treatises reflect, generally speaking, both a theoretical and a practical outlook, with a clear balance achieved between a rigorously pursued bookish culture on the one hand and personal experimentation on the other; they exhibit a harmonious and integrated concept of agriculture, considered as a balanced development of nature. Analysis of the treatises provides us with a picture of the agricultural geography of al-Andalus, and of its plant landscapes—although not a highly detailed one, since there are few specific mentions of place names and even fewer instances of both place and crop being noted.

The treatise of Ibn al-ʿAwwām, for instance, brings us nearer to a geography of al-Andalus, at least with regard to its interior arable land and the valley of the Guadalquivir river, transformed by intensive agricultural activity, with its cereals and vegetables grown on unirrigated land by dry farming, and its olive groves, vineyards, fruit-trees and horticultural products, these two last mixed in gardens of varying structure within a landscape filled with trees. In the same way, the *Zahrat al-bustān* of al-Tig͟hnarī shows us the fertile plain or vega (*faḥṣ*) of Granada, bounded on its north-east and north-west edges by high plateaus, which are cold climate districts set to the cultivation of extremely varied species of wheat and other cereals; and, on the coastal strip from Almería to Málaga, new cultivations involving agricultural techniques which, in the case of sugar cane and some citrus crops, recall those of the present day.

Nevertheless, if the treatises provide indications helping us to evaluate the diversity of Andalusī agriculture, especially up to the 7th/13th century, it should be emphasised that the majority of the works are in a summarised and incomplete form.

Cultivated species appear grouped according to the following categories:

cereals and leguminous plants;
vegetables and greens;
woody-stemmed plants and fruit trees;
industrial plants;
aromatic plants;
ornamental and flowering plants.

These categories will be considered separately in the following sections.

IV.1 *Cereals and leguminous plants*

Of the most widely grown grains, wheat and barley, a number of varieties are mentioned, according to the colour of the kernel, the planting cycle and the quality of the bread made from them. As for the leguminous plants —broad beans, chick peas, french beans, peas, lentils and lupins—these occupy a paramount position in Andalusī agriculture, since, in addition to their use in fixing nitrogen in the soil and thus aiding the system of crop rotation, they also played an important role in the nutrition of the Andalusī people.

IV.2 *Vegetables and greens*

The products of kitchen gardens were extremely varied, contrasting strongly with the invariable poverty of kitchen gardens in the Christian zone. Andalusis could consume fresh vegetables and greens practically all the year round, since those of summer (squash, eggplants, kidney beans, water melons, cucumbers, melons and garlic) rotated with those of winter (turnips, cabbages, carrots, leeks, Swiss chard, spinach and artichokes)—a situation which naturally favoured a nutritionally rich diet.

IV.3 *Woody stemmed plants and fruit trees*

Olive groves and vineyards seem to have covered a large part of al-Andalus, very much as they do in today's agricultural landscape; and, given the high degree of attention devoted to them in agronomical treatises, the importance of these two crops for the economy of the period is very clear. Among the fruit-trees, pomegranate and fig, Mediterranean trees *par excellence*, are also objects of special attention, and one might reasonably say that they cultivated the same kinds, and even a few more kinds, than is the case today. As for citrus fruits, a number of trees introduced by the Arabs are mentioned: the grapefruit (the earliest arrival in the Mediterranean west), the lemon, the bitter orange and the lime. The date palm, previously cultivated only as an ornamental plant, also makes its appearance in the Peninsula with the new settlers. Some of these trees were utilised not so much for their fruit as for their shade, for the scent of their flowers, for their wood (used for carving), for their medical properties, as condiments added to food, for industrial use (as food for silkworms, for instance), or simply for decorative purposes.

IV.4 *Industrial plants*

This group included a series of plants used for textiles and for the production of oil, sugar and dyes. The most important textile plants appear to have been cotton, flax and hemp, while dyeing plants mentioned include safflower, saffron, wild madder and sumach. Some plants had a number of different industrial applications, a case in point being hemp, which was used not only for weaving cloth but to make writing paper and various kinds of rope.

Another plant the Arabs introduced into al-Andalus, whence it spread to the rest of Europe, was the sugar cane, whose cultivation is already mentioned, along with that of rice, in the *Calendar of Córdoba* in the 4th/10th century, although some recent studies refuse to accept that it was introduced so early. In fact, while its area of cultivation might well have been very limited in that early period, it is not unreasonable to suppose that it could have been acclimatised in one of the botanical gardens in al-Andalus.

IV.5 *Aromatic plants*

The account of spices used as condiments and flavourings for food is very extensive, some of these, like saffron, giving rise to an active commerce. The Andalusis used saffron both as a perfume and as an ingredient in cooking, and they also used pennyroyal, caraway, marjoram bee-balm, fennel, cumin, coriander, caper, dill, mint and sesame. Liquorice, aniseed and wormwood were used to make sweetmeats and aromatic drinks.

IV.6 *Ornamental and flowering plants*

Andalusī treatises on agronomy provide much valuable data in this area, permitting us to reconstruct the species cultivated, and also the distribution, function, symbolism and many other aspects of the Hispano-Muslim garden, which was to have such an enormous influence on Spain and the rest of Europe during the Renaissance.

Fruit trees were highly valued, as they gave not only fruit, but also flowers, scent, colour and shade, but Andalusī gardens also contained willows, elms, cypresses, pines, oaks, palms, planes, myrtles, jasmine, and so on. Trees producing citrus fruit, such as bitter orange, cedrat and lemon, were very common. Among flowering plants, we find references to roses, carnations, violets, wallflowers, chrysanthemums, iris and waterlilies.

The agronomical treatises also give us some idea of the general characteristics and layout of gardens—they recommend, for instance, that cedrat trees should be protected against cold weather, and they provide the gardener with details of spacing between trees and the selection of the appropriate species for each particular part of the garden.

In the light of these treatises, the Andalusī garden appears as a mixture of garden and orchard, containing both aromatic and flowering plants. Shade-giving trees were found near walls and thorny plants placed at boundaries.

We may conclude, from this short review of the agricultural botany of al-Andalus, that the application of new techniques enabled a great variety of previously unknown species to be acclimatised, while others, which had once been cultivated but had now, for various reasons, dropped out of use or been left in a vestigial state, were replanted. To the species already known to pre-Andalusī Iberian agriculture, there were progressively added other, Eastern species documented by the Andalusī agronomers.

V. *Agricultural techniques*[22]

V.1 *Irrigation*

The extensive development and use of irrigated land produced by Andalusī knowledge and practice is, of course, extremely well known; indeed, the terminology connected with it has left its imprint on the Castilian language, and on a great many place names scattered throughout the Iberian region. The Hispano-Arabic people were experts in channelling and distributing the waters of their rivers by means of dams with a sluice or floodgate (Spanish *azudes*, from Arabic *asdād*), irrigation ditches (Spanish *acequias*, from Arabic *sāqiya*), water wheels (Spanish *noria*, from Arabic *nāʿūra*), water-mills (Spanish *acenas*, from Arabic *sāniya*) and other irrigation procedures, and at adapting and perfecting both the systems of the Western past and, more especially, the concepts and devices of the Eastern world.

Examination of the Andalusī treatises immediately reveals the primary role given to water, which, as noted above, is treated along with two other aspects—soils and fertilisers—at the very beginning of the works. On this subject—and, more specifically, in connection with the establishment of wells and the discovery of underground water—one may say that al-Tighnarī is one of the most original authors. He follows very closely the techniques described in the *Nabataean Agriculture*, though not the theosophical part which is developed alongside them throughout the latter work. In al-Tighnarī's treatise, the magical elements appear reformed and united with the rational, and he also includes accounts of personal experiences, sometimes contrasted with techniques learned in his journeys through Syria and Tunisia.

V.2 *Agricultural instruments*

This is an area where the Roman tradition is more deeply felt, although that is not to say that Eastern elements are absent. Instruments are generally simple, and usually made of iron, but also very diverse. A recent study[23] making a systematic and painstaking account of all the instruments mentioned in all the Andalusī works (both those edited and those still in manuscript) reveals an enormous variety of instruments, eighty in all, of which sixty are properly speaking tools, while the rest are accessories. Some of them, recorded only in the Andalusī texts, have etymologies indicating a Mozarabic origin, certain of these being quite advanced. Most noteworthy are those used to level the ground, like the *murjīqal*[24], derived from Spanish *murciélago* meaning "bat", which is mentioned by al-Tighnarī and subsequently taken up by Ibn Luyūn; this may be the same instrument that Ibn al-ʿAwwām (following Abū 'l-Khayr) uses in levelling waters and calls *marḥīfal*. Another instrument, used to scratch the earth around the roots of trees, is the *shanjūl*, possibly derived from *sanchuelo*, a term of romance origin, documented by Abū 'l-Khayr to designate a utensil which is "a kind of human hand with three cutting clubs".[25] Along with these and others of undoubted Spanish origin (the most numerous) may be mentioned one of

Eastern origin, the astrolabe, which, curiously, is recommended by Ibn al-ʿAwwām for the purposes of levelling land.

V.3 *Grafting*

One of the most interesting aspects of agricultural technique is the desire to classify, rationalise and systematise—a desire obvious from the study of soils, water and fertilisers, but seen above all in connection with plants. Ibn Baṣṣāl, in Chapter VIII of his treatise, sets out an original and detailed system of botanical classification, in which he mentions the different trees growing in the seven climes (*aqālīm*) into which the earth is divided and classifies them as aqueous, oleaginous, milky or gummy. This system was subsequently perfected by one of his disciples, the anonymous botanist of Seville, whose work *ʿUmdat al-ṭabīb fī maʿrifat al-nabāt li kulli labīb* has been noted as clearly prefiguring the system of classification adopted centuries later by Cuvier. The taxonomic classification of plants into genus (*jins*), species (*nawʿ*) and variety (*ṣinf*) is already present in this work.

It is perhaps in the field of grafting that one can best appreciate the high level of botanical knowledge displayed by the Andalusī agronomers. They were familiar with many forms of grafting—shield budding, scion grafting, budding, wedge grafting and tubing covered splice grafting, and also with the most efficient combinations of stocks and scions, some of them involving such surprising pairings as squash seed on squill onion or date tree on parsnip.

Conclusion

Hispano-Arabic agronomy from the 5th/11th to the 7th/13th centuries was, beyond all doubt, the most important and significant in the Islamic world of the time, though that is not to say it was the only one in existence; and it must, furthermore, be given the credit for having left its imprint on the knowledge and practice of the Christian West.

One last feature to be noted in these Andalusī treatises is their "experimental" character, which is what most attracted the attention of later Christian authors like Gabriel Alonso de Herrera, and which contained the germ of the modern experimental spirit. It was this real and direct knowledge of the land which underlay all the steps taken for the purpose of obtaining good crops; and from it sprang all the technologies based on their knowledge of previous traditions of agriculture, which they received, always, in a critical spirit, and applied to the earth of al-Andalus on which they stood.

[1] On this, see J. Vernet, *La cultura hispanoárabe en Oriente y Occidente*, Barcelona, 1978, pp 69-72.

[2] *Le Calendrier de Cordoue de l'année 961*, published R. P.Dozy, ed. and trans. with notes by Charles Pellat, Leiden, 1961.

[3] On this question, see A. C. López, "Vida y obra del famoso poligrafo cordobes del siglo X, ʿArīb Ibn Saʿīd", *Ciencias de la naturaleza en al-Andalus*, I, 1990, especially pp. 338-340.

4 This is the idea expressed by J.Vernet and J.Samsó in their work, "Panorama de la ciencia andalusí en el siglo XI", *Actas de las Jornadas de Cultura Arabe e Islámica* (1978), Madrid, 1981, pp. 135-63.

5 A. C. López y López, *Kitāb fī tartīb awqāt al-girāsa wa-l-magrūsāt. Un tratado agrícola andalusí anónimo*, Granada, 1990.

6 On this garden, see J.Samsó, "Ibn Hišām al-Lajmī y el primer jardín botánico en al-Andalus", *RIEEI*, 21, 1981-2, pp. 135-41.

7 This description of the Ruṣāfa and the activities taking place there has been transmitted to us by the historian al-Maqqarī, basing himself on the testimony of Ibn Ḥayyān. See al-Maqqarī, *Nafḥ al-ṭīb min ghuṣn al-Andalus al-raṭīb*, ed I.'Abbās, Beirut, 1968, I, 466-67.

8 See J. E. Hernández Bermejo, "Aproximación al estudio de las especies botánicas originariamente existentes en los jardines de Madīnat al-Zahrā'", *Cuadernos de Madīnat al-Zahrā'*, I, 1987, pp. 61-81.

9 Al-'Udhrī, *Tarṣī' al-akhbār*, ed 'Abd al-'Azīz al-Ahwānī, Madrid, 1965, p. 85.

10 On the subject of Andalusī botanical gardens, E. García Sánchez and A. C. López presented a paper now in press at the *International Symposium: "The Authentic Garden"*, celebrated in Leiden, May 8-11, 1990, to commemorate the fourth centenary of the founding of the botanical garden of the city of Leiden. The title of their paper was "The Botanical Gardens in Muslim Spain".

11 There is at present a Project of Investigation underway at the *Escuela de Estudios Arabes*, which has as its object the global study of the agronomy of al-Andalus. This requires a preliminary historiographical and philological study of the Andalusī manuscript texts, which is now being undertaken.

12 The text of the Castilian version was edited by J. M. Millás Vallicrosa, a pioneer and promoter of the study of Andalusī agronomy, under the title "La traducción castellana del 'Tratado de Agricultura' de Ibn Wāfid", *Al-Andalus*, 8, 1943, pp. 281-332. The medieval Catalan version upon which we are presently working is contained in a codex of miscellaneous manuscripts of the Bibliothèque Nationale de Paris, given the number 93 by A. Morel Fatio, *Catalogue des manuscrits espagnols et des manuscrits portugais*, Paris, 1892, pp. 332-33. As for the Arabic original of Ibn Wāfid's treatise, it is collected, also in an incomplete form, in two editions of agricultural texts of a miscellaneous character: Abū 'l-Khayr al-Andalusī, *Kitāb fī 'l-filāḥa*, ed. Sīdī Tuhāmī, Fez, 1358 A. H.; Ibn Ḥajjāj al-Ishbīlī, *Al-Muqni' fī 'l-filāḥa*, ed. S. Jarrār and Y. Abū Ṣāfiya, Amman, 1982 (the treatise of Ibn Wāfid is on pages 6-84 and 2-86 respectively); the Spanish translation by J. M. Carabaza Bravo, *Aḥmad b. Muḥammad b. Ḥajjāj al-Ishbīlī: al-Muqni' fī 'l-filāḥa*, doctoral dissertation, University of Granada, 1988, I, 178-281.

13 Ibn Baṣṣāl, *Kitāb al-qaṣd wa 'l-bayān*, ed. and trans. with notes by J. M. Millás Vallicrosa and M. Aziman, *Libro de Agricultura*, Tétouan, 1955; its medieval Castilian translation has been published by J. M. Millás Vallicrosa, "La traducción castellana del 'Tratado de agricultura' de Ibn Baṣṣāl", *Al-Andalus*, 13, 1948, pp. 347-430.

14 On this author see J. M. Carabaza, "Un agrónomo del siglo XI: Abu l-Jayr", *Ciencias de la naturaleza en al-Andalus*, I, 1990, pp. 223-40.

15 The Arabic text of his treatise is in a Jordanian edition mentioned previously, pages 85-123, and translated into Spanish by J. M. Carabaza, *Aḥmad b. Muḥammad*, I, 283-329.

16 Professor Lucie Bolens provides a detailed argument for this thesis in her excellent work *Agronomes andalous du Moyen Age*, Geneva, 1981, especially p. 44 *et seq.*

17 On this author, whose treatise I have edited, see my articles as follows: "El tratado agricola del granadino al-Tignarī", *Quaderni di Studi Arabi*, 5-6, 1987-88, pp. 278-92; "Al-Tignarī y su lugar de origén", *Al-Qanṭara*, 9/1, 1988, pp. 1-11.

18 On Ibn al-'Awwām, see the preliminary study by E. García Sánchez and J. E. Hernández Bermejo included in the facsimile edition published Madrid, 1988, I, 11-46.

19 Ibn al-'Awwām, *Kitāb al-filāḥa*, ed., with a Spanish translation, J. A. Banqueri, Madrid, 1802, I, 10.

20 Ibn Luyūn, *Tratado de agricultura*, ed., with a Spanish translation, J. Eguaras Ibáñez, Granada, 1975, p. 21.

21 There are quotations from the treatise of Ibn 'Arrāḍ in Ibn Luyūn and his annotator. Of the second author, the anonymous Andalusī, there is material in codicile number XXX of the "Colección Gayangos" of the Real Academia de la Historia in Madrid, folios 141v-143v.

[22] It is impossible, given the purpose and size of this essay, to deal with all the different agricultural techniques developed by the Andalusī agronomers. For this reason I shall only note certain interesting aspects of some of them.
[23] See M. D. Guardiola, "Instrumental agricola en los tratados andalusíes", *Ciencias de la naturaleza en al-Andalus,* I, 1990, pp 107-49.
[24] According to Simonet, this word corresponds to *murciegal* or *murciélago* because of the similarity between the animal and the instrument, which, like the bat, has the form of an isoceles triangle. See F. J. Simonet, *Glosario de voces ibéricas y latinas usadas entre los mozárabes.* Madrid, 1888, pp. 390-391.
[25] This is the opinion of M. Asín, the editor and partial translator of the work. See M. Asín Palacios, *Glosario de voces romances registradas por un botánico anónimo hispano-musulmán (siglos XI-XII),* Madrid-Granada, 1943.

BIBLIOGRAPHY

Abū 'l-Khayr, *Kitāb fī 'l-filāḥa,* ed. Sīdī Tuhāmī, Fez, 1358 A. H.
Asín Palacios, M., *Glosario de voces romances registradas por un botánico anónimo hispano-musulmán (siglos XI-XII),* Madrid-Granada, 1943.
Bolens, Lucie, *Agronomes andalous du Moyen Age,* Geneva, 1981.
Calendrier de Cordoue de l'année 961, ed. R. P. Dozy, trans. C. Pellat, Leiden, 1961.
Carabaza, J. M., "Un agrónomo del siglo XI: Abū l-Jayr", *Ciencias de la naturaleza en al-Andalus,* I, 1990, pp. 223-40.
García Sánchez, E., "Al-Tignarī y su lugar de origen", *Al-Qanṭara,* 9/1, 1988, pp. 1-11.
——, "El tratado agricola del granadino al-Tignarī", *Quaderni di Studi Arabi,* 5-6, 1987-88, pp. 278-92.
García Sánchez, E., and A. C. López, "The Botanical Gardens in Muslim Spain", paper presented at the international symposium on *The Authentic Garden,* Leiden, 1990 (in press).
Guardiola, M. D., "Instrumental agrícola en los tratados andalusíes", *Ciencias de la naturaleza en al-Andalus,* I, 1990, pp. 107-49.
Hernández Bermejo, J. E., "Aproximación al estudio de las especies botánicas originariamente existentes en los jardines de Madīnat al-Zahrā'", *Cuadernos de Madīnat al-Zahrā',* 1, 1987, pp. 61-81.
Ibn al-ʿAwwām, *Kitāb al-filāḥa,* ed., with Spanish translation, J. A. Banqueri, Madrid, 1802, 2 vols.
Ibn Baṣṣāl, *Kitāb al-qaṣd wa 'l-bayān* (*Libro de Agricultura*), ed., with translation and notes, J. M. Millás Vallicrosa and M. Aziman, Tétouan, 1955; medieval Castilian translation edited by J. M. Millás Vallicrosa, "La traducción castellana del 'Tratado de agricultura' de Ibn Baṣṣāl", *Al-Andalus,* 13, 1948, pp. 347-430.
Ibn Ḥajjāj al-Ishbīlī, *Al-Muqniʿ fī 'l-filāḥa,* ed. S. Jarrār and Y. Abū Ṣāfiya, Amman, 1982; Spanish translation by J. M. Carabaza Bravo, *Aḥmad b. Muḥammad b. Ḥajjāj al-Ishbīlī: al-Muqniʿ fī 'l-filāḥa,* doctoral dissertation, University of Granada, 1988, 2 vols.
Ibn Luyūn, *Tratado de agricultura,* ed., with Spanish translation, J. Eguaras Ibáñez, Granada, 1975.
Ibn Wāfid: "La traducción castellana del 'Tratado de Agricultura' de Ibn Wāfid", ed. J. M. Millás Vallicrosa, *Al-Andalus,* 8, 1943, pp. 281-332.
López, A. C., *Kitāb fī tartīb awqāt al-girāsa wa-l-magrūsāt. Un tratado agrícola andalusí anónimo,* Granada, 1990.
——, "Vida y obra del famoso poligrafo cordobes del siglo X, ʿArīb Ibn Saʿīd", *Ciencias de la naturaleza en al-andalus,* I, 1990.
Al-Maqqarī, *Nafḥ al-ṭīb min ghuṣn al-Andalus al-raṭīb,* ed. I. ʿAbbās, Beirut, 1968.
Samsó, J., "Ibn Hišām al-Lajmī y el primer jardín botánico en al-Andalus", *RIEEI,* 21, 1981-82, pp. 135-41.
Simonet, F. J., *Glosario de voces ibéricas y latinas usadas entre los mozárabes,* Madrid, 1888.
Al-ʿUdhrī, *Tarṣīʿ al-akhbār,* ed. ʿAbd al-ʿAzīz al-Ahwānī, Madrid, 1965.
Vernet, J., *La cultura hispanoárabe en Oriente y Occidente,* Barcelona, 1978.
Vernet, J., and J. Samsó, "Panorama de la ciencia andalusí en el siglo XI", *Actas de las Jornadas de Cultura Arabe e Islámica* (1978), Madrid, 1981, pp. 135-63.

THE USE OF PLANTS FOR DYEING AND CLOTHING

COTTON AND WOAD IN AL-ANDALUS: A THRIVING AGRICULTURAL SECTOR (5TH/11TH-7TH/13TH CENTURIES)

LUCIE BOLENS

I. *The roots of Mediterranean sensibility*

I.1 *Nature, passion of nature and poetry*

Clothing and dyeing are, finally, a necessity for prince and private citizen alike; and the physical and cultural form these things take, in the context of the everyday welfare of a given society, will naturally reflect the place where they are undertaken. This element of place must be considered if we wish fully to understand the influence of al-Andalus and the binding force of its civilisation within the particular human framework of the distant past. The crucial role of clothing in relation to the tender passions of love is indeed in accordance with Islam, which, both as a religion and as a temporal power, forbade direct representation of the human body, so that personal adornment came to be all the more valued. Yet monotheistic religion could not eliminate the ancient mythological aspects; natural beauty was inseparable from a strange sense of nature, which made mythical heroes rise up from the very landscape, from the shimmering ocean air, or from the clear air over the blue hills, with their silvery olive trees, by the shores of the Meseta. Plant and light must be seen together, as harmonious aspects of the vanished culture that bequeathed such glories as the Alhambra or the Alcázar of Seville, and the courtyards crossed by ancient *saetas*,[1] or *ghaitas*, which are still preserved to this day in the Constantine region of Algeria.

"Colour," writes Michel Pastoureau, "is indissolubly linked to culture, and cannot be envisaged outside a particular time and place." This is because "it is neither a substance (as was sometimes thought in the Ancient World), nor a breaking up of light (as medieval scholars believed), but a sensation, the sensation of something coloured by a light illuminating it, which is received by the eye and communicated to the brain; and, like all sensations, it springs at once from biological mechanism and from cultural heritage."[2]

Important though they are, optics and mineralogy will remain in the background of my endeavour to celebrate al-Andalus in 1992. Rather, the link (more earthy and more poetic, in the rural, Virgilian sense of the term) with a still mythical cosmos, with the sun and the water, will lead us, as we study our sources, from furrow to colour, from soil to garment, from the "face of earth" (as the earth is called in Andalusī Arabic) to the cotton and sky-blue woad used for weaving and dyeing by the Andalusis. If Spain was famed for its mercury—for the ore which, Ibn Sīnā said, was like cinnabar and was obtained through fire—and if the alembic remained in daily evidence for perfumes and cosmetic materials, I shall rather pursue the subject between heaven and earth, in the realm of the unyielding sun and the merciful moon, and in the music of the running water used for irrigating and steeping, so inextricably bound up with the ancient linens and blue dyes.

I.2 *A koine: knowledge in the service of humanity*

While agronomic and botanical records in Hispano-Arabic, Romance, Hebrew and Latin demonstrate the emergence and establishment of cotton, they also speak of fibres already known in the Ancient World: flax, hemp, esparto and palm fibre, in addition to wools and leathers. As for colours, they standardly include costly mineral dyes, but pay special attention to the development of vegetable dyes; sky-blue (*samāwī*) is more in evidence than lapis lazuli and azurite (*lāzaward*), while the indigo brought from such distance, and capable of dyeing a full marine purple, was to become famed through the whole Mediterranean world. Jews—with their special predilection for the Biblical *tekhelet*, or night horizon-blue—and Muslims and Christians (whether from Septem-Ceuta or Cyrene, from Córdoba, Granada, Seville, Andarax, Sousse, Cirta-Constantine or Fez) were, for all the maltreatments and discriminations in status, united by a single passion, one determined neither by religion nor by politics, but rather the gift of nature: a passion for light. "Here is vital strength at its median point," writes Antoni Gaudì, "and indeed 'Mediterranean' means 'centre of the earth'. The median light is found, at 45 degrees, on its shores, offering the best definition of bodies and forms; and it is here that artistic cultures have flourished, by very reason of this balanced light." It is here that the blue of the Armenian stone joined with the *varmeau ou varmillon* of the old Provençals, and the pastel cosmetics of the Ancient World with the gilded vermilion which is the simple gift of the light.

1.3 *Technique and transmission: the assurance of continuity*

Before the advent of Andalusī Islam and its brilliant school of agronomists,[3] the 7th-century writer Isidore of Seville, at the crossroads of two eras, had handed down a vast repository of ancient knowledge on plants and on vegetable and mineral dyes.[4] In 1250, following the first Christian reconquest, the *Lapidary* found at the home of a Toledo Jew by the Infant Alfonso el Sabio[5] was translated from Arabic into Castilian by his Jewish physician Ihuda Mosca el Ménor (*este judio su físico*, says the Prologue). This work, in which colours are said to receive their particular qualities from the heavenly bodies, was to be supervised by one of the king's Christian clerks, Garcì Perez; with its unbroken Greco-Persian and Arabo-Jewish history, it is thoroughly representative of the way things were handed down through al-Andalus. Andalusī agronomists and physicians, whether Jews, Muslims or "others", aspired to kinship with Aristotle, Galen, Rāzī and Ibn Sīnā, and, indeed, with such very obscure alchemical dyers as the Alexandrian Bolos Democritos and with the early Syriac work of which Bachir Attié has revealed so much.[6] This history of different viewpoints and cultural interlinking is also a history of techniques, and the transformation we call agriculture may be perceived in terms of alchemical knowledge linked with the distant Chaldean past: the *Book of Agriculture* by the 5th/11th century Sevillian Abū 'l-Khayr (in folio 64 of the Paris manuscript, placed after Abū 'l-Qāsim al-Baghdādī b. Buṭlān) quotes an Eastern Babylonian-Baghdadi alchemy which places agriculture under the aegis of the transformation of sublunary bodies.

Techne and *sania* cannot be divided: a brilliant sherbet will be offered in a glass cup and the thick flesh of fruits is at once healing and pleasurable; nothing, finally, separates usefulness and beauty. Andalusī civilisation would not have enjoyed the artistic achievements it did without a sophisticated agriculture of which we are now more aware. Much was already known about soils in the light of combined Eastern and Western traditions, and this knowledge was further, and excitingly, advanced by the repeated experiments carried out on the Aljarafe around Seville,[7] today a wide plain, but then described as a hilly site from which came the oil called *jabalī*; here Ibn Wāfid of Toledo reproduced, on the model of Toledo, one of the first experimental gardens of the Western world.[8] The high level of botany reflected in the "Andalusī school" became still higher with the subsequent introduction of new plants brought from the East, or else acclimatised in vegas irrigated from the higher plateaus or sierras—techniques and production of water for agrarian purposes being the essential foundation of Andalusī agriculture's rise in the 5th/11th century.[9] A textile civilisation can be discerned through the gifts of garments made by the ruling hierarchy and through what archaeology is able to tell us about the various concerns of the home: bedding and cloths, hangings and linen robes soaked in woad, green or black *santabarras* worn by Spanish sailors,[10] indigo turbans, nets for women's hair (*raṭāfil*, or *alvanega de red*),[11] pearls and other gems studding the clothing.

It is from the 5th/11th century on that scholarly works begin to reflect a further development of plants used for textiles and colouring.

II. *Plant fibres: a thriving agriculture*

II.1 *Eastern cultural precedents*

In his *Letter on the Elixir* and the *Avicennae ad Hasen Regem Epistula de Re Recta*,[12] Ibn Sīnā sets out the principle, and the outcome, of transcending the normal limits of nature. Following Jābir b. Ḥayyān[13] and the *Nabataean Agriculture* practised in the same (number 4) climate as that of al-Andalus, Ibn Sīnā places within the category of art (*ṣināʿa*) everything which modifies the way matter is arranged in order to make what is hidden appear, without any supplementation by extranatural or supernatural means; directed by

Saturn-Hermes, which, according to alchemical theory, presides over those fermentations responsible for blackening physical substances, the peasant also follows the phases of the moon and the progress of the sun through the zodiac; for anyone grafting one plant on to another must know of the affinities between the terrestrial and the astral. There is, therefore, no modification to the ancient heritage of Aristotle and Ptolemy; we are dealing, basically, with the metaphysical principle of divine primacy as the source of all energy. All Andalusis quoted Ibn Sīnā as a major authority, and Ruska believes the *Letter on the Elixir* to have been itself Andalusī. The conclusion of this work describes the alembic[14] and sums up the efficacity of the elixir of colours: "It colours [*ṣabagha*] by means of its colouring, immerses by means of its fatty matter and fixes with its lime. The fat [*duhn*] is the binding force between colouring, which is very subtle, lime, which is very thick, and water. The colouring is borne by mercury. If the fat which sets in the lime colours in the colouring, the two become immersed in this mercury, and if the lime is set, the two set with the mercury by virtue of the mixture."

While holding back from invention, Ibn Sīnā innovates as the Andalusī agronomists—at once traditional and innovative[15]—were themselves to do. Agriculturalists took their inspiration from physicians, "geoponics" and physicists alike; apart from Ibn Sīnā, who figures equally with Aristotle, knowledge was handed on by al-Dīnawarī al-Nabaṭī, al-Ghāfiqī and the *Nabataean Agriculture*. In its chapter devoted to the *Ars Magna*, the latter work, which is designed to provide instruction on ancient precedents in Mesopotamia, takes up the *Book of the Secrets of the Moon* supposedly written by Adam, and, on the basis of this venerable authority, attributes to humans the power to imitate nature by producing new plant and animal species.[16] Water in agriculture was to play the role of mercury in alchemy, a fluid vehicle for other substances, the intermediary element in transmutations.[17]

II.2 *Agrarian expansion and practices*

Let us consider what specific underlying patterns can be discerned with respect to the rise of the rural economy following the Muslim conquest.

Scholarly treatments of textile plants include plants effectively used for the purposes of dyeing. Chapter 22 of Ibn al-ʿAwwām's *Book of Agriculture*, for instance, first considers, at some length, the various methods of cultivating cotton, moves on to flax and hemp, then deals with saffron, henna, madder, woad and the card thistle used for teaseling. Lucerne and poppy are included in the chapter on account of their new importance for the rearing of horses, and there are brief looks at rosemary for human consumption. Industrial cultivation of cotton, flax, saffron and woad moves parallel with the rise of the merchant bourgeoisie of the *ṭā'ifa* period (5th/11th century) and the Berber empires (5th/11th-7th/13th centuries) through these three centuries of Hispano-Arab power.

Al-Wansharīsī's *Kitāb al-mi'yār* (literally: "Book of Standards")[18], insofar as agricultural practices can be reconstructed from it, is not specific on industrial cultivation. *Munāṣafa* (share-cropping) and tenant cultivation gave rise to multiple contracts based on the traditional *sharīka* ("share contract"); this appears once, with particular reference to hemp (according to the jurist Ibn Lubāba), with no public or notarial authority involved. All this confirms the overall impression of a considerable increase in free private property.[19] If wool was the object of frequent legal wrangling on account of the many small flocks of sheep in the general economy, the irrigated squares planted with cotton, woad or madder, the fields of henna and the sloping beds of saffron were no doubt a source of continual quarrels, in peasant or semi-rural circles, over the problems of administering the water supply,[20] for legal cases mention such problems only in connection with fibres. Contracts involving *muzāra'a* (agricultural associations) and *musāqāt* (settlement with rent part-paid in produce) are characteristic of the overall agrarian system, and it is sometimes difficult to distinguish Andalusī from African practices.

The settler owning his own land paid the *zakāt*, the Islamic state tax paid by Muslims; because of the numerous and complex tiny associations involved in medium and small-scale cultivation for the investment and sharing of profits, this was due on the property of the official owner.[21] The People of the Book (*Ahl al-Kitāb*) also paid the *kharāj*, a source of frequent complaint due to the need to wait for agents to come and assess the crop. Jointly-owned property seems to have been no less common than in the foodcrop sector, and recent investigation from juridical sources suggests aspects more in keeping with the commercial agricultural sector: fields are placed not directly around houses, but are rather arranged in squares where conditions are best for irrigation, at the foots of hills or on alluvial coastal lands.

III. *Cotton* (quṭn)*: a highly profitable sector*

III.1 *The names and the thing*

While the fibres of flax and hemp come from the stem, and through steeping, cotton derives from a capsule enclosing a multitude of hairy seeds. The cotton plant is a hardy sub-tropical one linked with Indian and Arab civilisations, and when it spread to the Western Mediterranean, the name of the new fibre, for all the differences in the process of derivation, became linked with that of flax.

The word *quṭn* or *quṭun* (*al-quṭun*) (Spanish *algodón*) comes from Old Arabic *qaṭana*. Originally from Northern India (*Gossypium herbaceum L.*) and Southern India (*Gossypium arboreum L.*), it is semantically distinct from the Sanskrit *karpasa*, which has given Hebrew *carpas*, Greek *karpasos* ("fine gauze") and Latin *carbasus*. Strabon describes cotton as being wool from a tree.[22] Although the plant had spread to the Mediterranean, India was to remain the large-scale exporter of the commodity through the High Middle

Ages, and Marco Polo was to witness the preparation of great bales destined for the West. From the Maghrib it was to spread deep into Africa, as far as Ghana and the Sudan—although the latter did in fact already possess a wild cotton from which brightly-coloured loincloths were made for local use. A crossing of this wild variety with the North African one produced *Gossypium obtusifolium Roxb*, which was highly suitable for spinning and weaving.[23]

Cultivation in al-Andalus is first mentioned in the 4th/10th century, notably in the *Calendar of Córdoba*, although the *Kitāb fī tartīb awqāt al-ghirāsa wa 'l-maghrūsāt* says nothing of it.[24] Andalusī agronomists generally speak of it, and detailed treatments are provided by Abū 'l-Khayr of Seville (5th/11th century), Abū ʿAbd Allāh Muḥammad b. Ibrāhīm b. al-Baṣṣāl, who speaks of a "Sultan's garden" in his *Kitāb al-qaṣd wa 'l-bayān*, Abū 'l-Muṭarrif ʿAbd al-Raḥmān b. Muḥammad b. ʿAbd al-Kabīr b. Yaḥyā b. Muḥammad al-Lakhmī b. Wāfid (389/999-467/1074) (the last two coming to Seville in the 5th/11th century, following the capture of Toledo by Alfonso VI in 1085), Ibn al-ʿAwwām of Seville (6th/12th-7th/13th century), al-Ṭighnarī of Granada (author of a voluminous treatise written under the Almoravid king Yūsuf b. Tāshfīn, which provides valuable information on Ibn Baṣṣāl),[25] the Sevillian Ibn Ḥajjāj, author of *Al-Muqniʿ*, and Ibn Luyūn of Granada (681/1282-750/1349).[26]

Cotton is sown in February or March, at the same time as safflower, in irrigated or cool soils fertilised with sheep manure. The field must be ploughed up to ten times, according to the system of tillage and hoeing known as *qalīb*, for the point of breaking up the soil is not to open it (*filāḥa*), but to close the surface and so avoid capillarity and evaporation. The preparation of the cotton field (*ḥawḍ*), in flattened squares and in "dried out" ground, was undertaken by hand. It was important to level out any slope which might exist, so as to derive maximum benefit from the irrigation.

III.2 *The pattern of agricultural yields under intensive irrigated cultivation*

The crucial notion here—as with the rest of agriculture during this favourable economic period—is that of the *optimum mean yield*. Efforts are focused on those crops which are most profitable at the particular moment, foremost among which, in this case, are textile plants and plants used for dyeing. Underlying this situation is the rise of the merchant bourgeoisie, whose particular way of life, as I have described it in *La cuisine andalouse*, would have been unthinkable without the infrastructure such cultivation provided.

Whether crops were open field or horticultural, and whether properties were collective or private, exemption from paying the *kharāj* was always granted on the basis of historical background (for having supported the Almohads, for example)[27], or of tribal origins in connection with the period immediately following the conquest. The unit of cultivated land called the *faddān* referred to tribal or individual property, while the Sevillian *marjaʿ*,

again a unit of land under cultivation, designated private lands around the city. Ibn Ṣāḥib al-Ṣalāh gives the figure of 800 *marja*ʿs for Seville, i.e., 3,000 dinars, and Ibn al-ʿAwwām says that the *marja*ʿ represents the area of land worked by heavy tillage (*qalīb*) on easy land (following Banqueri's translation *llano* for *sahla*).[28] The *ḍay*ʿ*a* (Spanish *aldea*) consisted of about 10 *faddān*s, and also possessed a *noria*, a mosque and a *madrasa*. The profitability of Maghrebo-Andalusī agriculture between the 5th/11th and 7th/13th centuries depended on the existence of a large workforce of slaves controlled according to a strict Taylorism. Several *ḍay*ʿ*as* made up a *qarya* (Spanish *alquería*), a large rural settlement plus surrounding district, with a hydraulic system; this was, in principle, a royal property granted on a life interest basis to important figures—Almohads and Andalusī jurists responsible for maintaining the law.[29]

III.3 *Care in cultivation*

The flower bud appeared in August and the heads were picked in September, first thing in the morning and with great care, by peasant women who would also undertake the subsequent stages. In Iraq the heads would be picked in the month of *tammūz* (July), i.e., in hotter conditions earlier in the season. The next stage would be to separate the fine strands from the heads (in the shade), then lay them in the sun and finally press them into bales. We know, from the Andalusis themselves, that a similar process took place in Syria, with a difference of one month (indicating the nature of the respective climates) and that the field was prepared a year beforehand. On the ecological side, the *Nabataean Agriculture* informs us that the earth (*turāb*), or upper living layer, should be without residual saline traces. When the heads had been picked, the plant was pruned with a knife, in the same manner as a vine creeper, and would come up again the following year. The crop was, finally, a profitable one, and was dispatched into Spain and the Mediterranean Basin, yet the inverse movement of imported Indian cotton continued. Economic life was already complex.

III.4 *Knowledge and stimulation to production*

These two aspects of expansion had never become separated: slavery and profits combined to keep this society a distinctively ancient one, enjoying surplus and making good use of its best scholars.

On the Aljarafe, the Mount of Seville, Ibn al-ʿAwwām experimented with new or disputed kinds of cultivation,[30] having first established the scholarly antecedents for each species; in the case of cotton the transmitted tradition began not with the Ancients, but with medieval figures: Abū Ḥanīfa al-Dīnawarī, the *Nabataean Agriculture*, Abū 'l-Khayr, Ibn Baṣṣāl, Ibn Wāfid and authorities from Sicily, Egypt, the Persian Gulf and the Arab Peninsula; Dioscorides[31] is most unusually absent. In contrast, the Andalusī school of agronomy tailored matters to its own requirements, for the sector was a new one and innovation essential. This movement, focused on al-Andalus itself —where the countryside was, incidentally, highly variable, as can be seen if we compare the climates of Almería and Seville, or Campo de Níjar[32] and the Algarve—is particularly evident within the commercialised sectors encouraged by the urban power of the kings and the *fuqahāʾ*.

III.5 *Spinning and weaving: the control of the souks*

Cotton was a precious commodity; "cotton," says Ibn al-ʿAwwām, "has been provided among us for some years."[33] Ibn al-Bayṭār of Málaga speaks in similar vein: the newly-picked cotton is called *qūr*, the *khishfūj* seed, which, according to Rāzī, has aphrodisiac qualities. Cotton clothing is said to be softer and warmer than linen clothing. According to al-Idrīsī (493/1100-560/1166), "rich people [*khāṣṣa*] wear cotton clothes and short cloaks", while wool is worn by the poorest people.[34] Treatises on *ḥisba* and regulations for the souks closely control spinning and weaving, and talk is no longer of agricultural but of technical matters: we hear of spinning with a "wheel", or *miftal*, which is perhaps a spinning wheel, for the Indian spinning wheel appeared between the 5th and the 9th century A.D.; in the regulations for Seville, at the beginning of the 7th/13th century, standards correspond to those in force in Paris, namely two heddles, two threads, combs with 24 ligatures and 40 *bayt*s, or widths of thread, per piece.[35] Deficiencies in the dimensions of the web are punishable, according to the number of *bayt*s missing, where insufficient picking off of the carders has attracted rats.[36] Half a century later the Establishments of Saint-Louis were to make markets liable to regulation for the same reasons.

IV. *The ancient fibres: flax and hemp* (kattān *and* shahdānaj) (Linum Usitatisimum L. *and* Cannabis sativa L.)

IV.1 *Flax holds its own*

The fibre of flax and hemp is derived from steeping of the stems. Conditions for cultivation were the same, and linen held its ground in the markets. Growing well in a temperate climate, flax had already been introduced during Roman times, into Galicia, Lusitania and the marshy regions of the south, towards Ampurias, Tarragona and Játiva, and the tradition was continued under the Hispano-Arabs; its ancient status explains the presence of Bolos Democritos among the traditional authorities. According to the *Nabataean Agriculture* it was of Coptic origin. From the 5th/11th century onwards it no longer seems to be found in the best-placed sites at the foot of the sierras, contemporary documents rather referring to the Southern coastal regions, around Málaga, in the Plain of Granada and in the wonderful Andarax valley, catering for Almería[37], where coloured linen sails were manufactured.

Ibn al-ʿAwwām conducted successful experiments with thick sowing in non-watered ground, and with refertilisation using pigeon dung. In the favourable economic conditions prevailing, the introduction of cotton did not drive out Spanish flax, which remained highly esteemed, and even came to be more densely planted around Seville, on the Aljarafe. Linen was woven and dyed both for the home market and for export. The flax had to be sown when the moon was waxing, and the stems were immersed for steeping, weighed down with heavy stones to keep them below the water, then beaten on the water. The quality of the water was regarded as crucial for the relative whiteness of the finished product; if the water was flowing and warm, the fibre would be white; in polluted water it would be almost black; slight impregnation with sheep manure would make it reddish-brown. When steeping had been completed, the tow would come away of itself, and it was then laid out to dry, as with cotton. Steeping took 50 days in cold countries, 30 in warm parts of al-Andalus.[38]

IV.2 *Hemp for use in the fields*
Brought originally from Persia, hemp, or *shahdānaj*, kept its ancient name of "royal seed". As with flax, the tow is derived from the stem, and it was grown in the same soils, being sown thinly to obtain the seed and thickly to obtain the fibre. The *Nabataean Agriculture* calls the Suse seed the "China seed".[39] The tow was coarser, but cultivation was also less delicate, with less watering needed; it was used for many things: sackcloth, thick-textured clothing, paper, ropes for rural use and for every kind of marine work. The labour of growing hemp, and also cotton, was performed by women. Almería, Saragossa, Bocairente and Jódar were well-known for their textiles, but are not mentioned for linen.

Whether applied to the woollen garments of the common people or the silks of the rich, plants for dyeing were easily available and could be used on an industrial scale. Their importance was to grow spectacularly within the general context of economic and cultural expansion.

V. *The reign of colour*

V.1 *Strange delights*
Byssus, a silky-haired marine substance, appears in the Bible under the name of *butz*; it is called *byssos* in Greek, *byssus* in Latin and *bisso guacara* in Italian, and also *lanna Pinna*. It is derived from a mollusc[40] which may itself be reddish-brown, black or green, but whose filaments are characteristically iridescent and golden. Apparently found at Sfax, Djerba and in Southern Iberia, it was worth its weight in gold (as was the cloth itself, which could replace the metal for the purposes of paying taxes). The finished material was called *abū qalamūn*[41], meaning Brocade of Rūm, and only the Sultan had the right to a garment made from it (it took several years to obtain the necessary amount, and it might cost several thousand dinars). Also called "marine wool", byssus seems to have been abundant off the shores of Sfax,

and it was said that "the colour of this mollusc is that of the mollusc which gives pearls".

They were gathered off Santarem, on the Atlantic, and they were golden-coloured and silky-soft to the touch, being in fact treated like silk. Material made from it had the property of changing its colour according to the time of day (in Perrault's story, we may remember, the girl "Peau d'Ane" asked her father for a dress which was "the colour of the weather", elusive and constantly shifting). It was pricelessly valuable, and its export forbidden. In 387/997, following his escapade at Saint James of Compostella, al-Manṣūr presented his Christian allies with Ṭirāz silks subject to royal monopoly, and the chronicle cites a vizier as making a gift of the same kind to the king of Seville, al-Muʿtamid for the festival of Nawrūz. In 392/1002, following a raid on Santarem, al-Manṣūr bestowed twenty-one tunics (*kisā'*s) *of sea wool*, two amber cloaks, one of scarlet (*siqlāṭūn*), fifteen plumes, seven brocade carpets, two garments of Byzantine brocade and two skins (*farwa*s) of fennec.

In May 961 (A.H. 350), according to the *Calendar of Córdoba*,[42] the fiscal agents in the provinces requisitioned alkermes (*qirmiz*, Latin *grana*) for the royal monopoly, in August sky-blue (*ṣibāgh al-samāwī*, Latin *tinctura celesti*) and in September madder (*fuwwa*, Latin *rubia*), and there are market regulations to the same effect in Seville (in the 6th/12th century) and Málaga (in the 7th/13th century)—i.e., two or three centuries later. Agriculture continued to provide the basis for dyes on an industrial scale.

V.2 *Blue: woad or indigo?*

Still, today, sugar is whitened with "aniline". In fact, aniline is indigo, and this word is found throughout 5th/11th-7th/13th century sources. It is essential to go to the texts themselves (avoiding translations, like those by Banqueri or Clément-Mullet of Ibn al-ʿAwwām, by Leclerq of Ibn al-Bayṭār and by Meyerhof of Maimonides), and the following treatment is based on detailed lexicological verification. I will give here a very short summary of the relevant findings, focusing on the colour blue with particular reference to the roles of woad and indigo, and with brief information on other plants used in dyeing.

Lapis lazuli, or "azure of Acre" (*azurium ultra-marinum*), remains the term for bright blue; it is the *cyanos autophyes*, or natural blue, brought from Scythia (*lāzaward* in Arabic). The copper-based blues (*azurro della magna, azurro citramarinum*) were too well-known (according to Layard, the azure used by the Assyrians will have been of this kind) for references to the colour not to continue to be used—thus, for example, flax flowers are called, in poetry, "lapis lazuli"! As such, we must proceed with care. The pure blue of The Ancient Phoenicians and Hebrews was obtained from a mollusc called *ḥilzon* or *hilazon* (Arabic: *ḥalazūn*) (murex or cuttle-fish) found on the shores of Tyre and Haifa.

Meanwhile the "indigo" brought from India and East Africa became all the rage: we hear of *anīl*, *nīl*, and, soon, qualifying terms in connection with *nīl* for various types of blue; however, the local plant used to produce the colour was woad, called, in the North-West, *guesde*. As such, the colour blue, and the particular plant, woad or indigo, need be considered in the light both of botanical considerations and of linguistic cross-referencing, the relevant terms, *nīl*, *anīl*, *lāzaward*, *wasma*, *khiṭr*, or *khaṭr*,[43] and *ʿiẓlim*, being sometimes used synonymously and sometimes distinctively.

Lāzaward is the stone, azurite or lapis lazuli, and is used in this sense in lapidaries. Ibn al-Bayṭār notes that *ʿiẓlim* is *Indigofera*, the plant which produces *nīl* or *nīlaj*, in other words indigo;[44] while some, like Maimonides, take indigo to be the male woad flower. In 6th/12th century Seville, to sell woad as indigo was punishable as fraud; it was a well-known and therefore, presumably, a common practice.

The terms *wasma* and *samāwī* allowed agronomists to bypass lexicological vagueness, the lapidary Castilian *azul* or *cardeño* being, initially, inadequate. Ibn al-ʿAwwām calls woad *al-bustānī*[45] or *al-samāwī*, which may have been used only with reference to *bustānī* (translated by Banqueri as "hortense").

As for *khiṭr*, Ibn al-Bayṭār regards it as a synonym of *wasma*, while Maimonides takes it to refer to the leaves of the indigo plant, or *nīlaj*: "*It is al-khaṭr, that is, the leaves of the indigo plant [nīlaj], and it is al-ʿiẓlim; it is what the people call al-nīl, which is used as a black dye*" (this is in accordance with Michel Pastoureau's idea of blue as the dark colour).

The leaves of woad (*Isatis tinctoria*, cruciferous) and of the indigo plant (*Indigofera tinctoria*, leguminous) dye blue by virtue of their indigotin, and it is the actual content of the latter in the leaves which determines the darker or lighter shade—which explains the lexical and scientific discrepancies, and why indigo could be taken to be the male woad plant. The 6th/12th century manuscript of Ibn Buklārish calls woad *wasma*, with the Castilian gloss translating *folium* because it is blue by virtue of its leaves.[46] *Ḥinnā 'l-majnūn*, or "fool's henna", a mixture of woad and henna, dyed black. *Isatis tinctoria L.* is given considerable prominence in the *Ethnographic Museum of Istanbul*. The mordant was alum (*shabb*), and we learn that, with iron as mordant, the Medes achieved a consistent black; the Levant provided Anatolian alum. The weeping gum benzoin (*anjudān*), was also used in colouring. This was thought to have been lost in Cyrenaica in Roman times, but had simply come to be known under another name (*silphium*).[47]

Conclusion

The term blue, which is at present a subject of discussion among other historians of colour, embodies a degree of systematic meaning, but there are also traps involved. To consider words and things, and to separate the reality from the image pursued by the Ancients, remains an absorbing venture for the scholar, especially if the picture is a coloured one. Soon the cochineal of Cádiz would be neither alkermes nor the cochineal already known, but American cochineal, adding another page, another debate and another horizon, to the image of our present time.

It is clear that economic progress was maintained in the period of the *ṭā'ifa* kingdoms (so called after the regions of Ancient Persia) which followed the decentralisation of the Caliphate. In these kingdoms, ruled by Yemenis, Syrians, Persians, "Slavs" who were often in fact African or Nordic, and Berbers,[48] there was indeed a spectacular advance from the 4th/10th century on. Trading with the Abbasid Empire continued to take place, and it is also known that merchandise and fashions passed freely between the south and the north of the Peninsula.

As for the crucial question of the relationship between various sources of knowledge and practical application, I have already indicated the complex nature of Andalusī agronomic science. Despite a strong admixture of elements from the Graeco-Latin, Persian, Indian, Iberian (i.e., Carthaginian and Roman Baetican) heritages, it finally evolved a rich and complex tradition of its own which amounted to true creativity on the technical and scientific level. Generally speaking it was a case of "practical application being Roman and knowledge Eastern".[49] The politicisation of the subject has led certain of my young Catalan colleagues to regard as insulting any notion of a Roman contribution; yet—quite apart from the need to accept historical fact—it is clear from many examples that the Rome of the recent past, mighty, imperial and effective, held a considerable appeal for the Hispano-Arab imagination.[50]

On the technical and scientific level, the most original feature was soil science,[51] which was of a modernity so marked and so surprising that it is still little acknowledged or understood by specialist geo-historians, whatever their particular viewpoint; and, moreover, this pedology, combined with botanical knowledge derived from the East, was applied in countless areas in al-Andalus, both in subsistence agriculture and in commercial agriculture, the latter being exemplified by oil and by clothing as considered in this essay.

Eastern fashions arrived with Ziryāb in the 3rd/9th centuries, and were to revolutionise customs of dress and table manners alike—six centuries in advance of the North (including Russia) in the case of table manners, and long before the Crusades, from the late 11th century on, introduced the West to Eastern magnificence.

These cultural contacts had, finally, an overriding effect with respect to humanistic culture in Mediterranean societies, with the lapse of time noted above allowing people to grow accustomed to difference. In the Mediterranean region, particularly in Sicily and Andalus, the habit of communal feeling and living together disappeared less quickly than in the North, where the need for a single, distinctive consciousness closed Christian society against Jews and Muslims alike, leading, subsequently, to the persecution of Christian "heresies".

In the South, there continued up to the so-called Renaissance a tolerant and unfanatical way of life finding its essential expression in the street and the public places—a kind of "patio civilisation"[52]—and in a taste for leisure and conviviality. Ibn Khaldūn was right to fear for the liberty of peoples when such an unfanatical way of life prevailed. It seems, though—for neither progress nor regression is linear—that this humanist ideal is attempting to be reborn today, here and there, among the embers of the colonial empires.

[1] *Ghaïta* is *saeta* in Castilian, and denotes the distinctive ancient manner of singing, with the voice raised, in which notes were released like arrows shot from a bow. It was an eagerly awaited feature of evenings during the Andalusī period. The term *ghaïta* is still used, in this vocal sense, in 20th-century Algeria, and is no doubt an Andalusī archaism.

[2] Michel Pastoureau, "Vers une histoire de la couleur bleue", in *Sublime Indigo*, Fribourg, 1987, p. 20. See also the same author's *Figures et couleurs. Etude sur la symbolique et la sensibilité médiévale*, Paris, 1986.

[3] L. Bolens, *Agronomes andalous du Moyen Age*, Geneva, 1981, Vol I. For agriculture, see J. Vallvé, "La agricultura in al-Andalus", *Al-Qanṭara*, 3, 1982, pp. 261-97; E. García Sánchez, J. M. Carabaza Bravo and Manuela Marín, in García Sánchez (ed.), *Ciencias de la naturaleza en al-Andalus*, Granada, 1990. For details of ordinary daily life, see L. Bolens, *La cuisine andalouse, un art de vivre, XIe-XIIIe siècles*, Paris, 1990, I, 17-50.

[4] Isidore of Seville, in J. Oroz Reta, *Etimologias*, Madrid, 1982, Vol. II, books XVI, XVII and XIX.

[5] Alfonso X el Sabio, *Lapidario*, ed. S. Rodríguez and M. Montalvo, Madrid, 1981.

[6] B. Attié, "L'ordre chronologique probable des sources directes d'Ibn al-ʿAwwām", *Al-Qanṭara*, 3, 1982, pp. 299-332.

[7] Bolens, *Agronomes andalous*, p. 33.

[8] L. Bolens, "Les jardins d'al-Andalus", in Flaran 9, *Jardins et vergers en Europe occidentale VIIIe-XVIIIe siècles*, Auch, 1987; and *L'Andalousie du quotidien au sacré, 11e-13e siècles*, Aldershot-Vermont, 1991, chapter 16.

[9] See: T. F. Glick, *Islamic and Christian Spain in the Early Middle Ages*, Princeton, 1979; A. Watson, *Agricultural Innovation in the Early Islamic World*, Cambridge (England), 1983; L. Bolens, "La révolution agricole du XIe siècle", *Studia Islamica*, 42, 1978, pp. 121-41.

[10] R. P. A. Dozy, *Noms des vêtements chez les arabes*, Amsterdam, 1845, p. 211.

[11] Dozy, *op. cit.*, p. 189, under *rutfil*; called *capillejo de muger* by Pedro de Alcala (Elena Pezzi, *El vocabulario de Pedro de Alcala*, Almería, 1989, under *alvanega*).

[12] Ibn Sīnā, *Risālat al-iksīr*, in G. Anawati, *Oriente e Occidente, scienze e filosofia*, Rome, 1973, pp. 285-346, and medieval Latin translation.

[13] P. Kraus, *Jābir ibn Ḥayyān, contribution à l'histoire des idées scientifiques dans l'Islam*, Paris, 1986, p. 121 *et seq.* On Nabataean agriculture, see T. Fahd, "Histoire de l'agriculture en Iraq", in *Handbuch der Orientalistik, Geschichte der Islamischen Länder*, I, Leiden-Cologne, 1977, pp. 276-377.

[14] L. Bolens, "Les parfums et la beauté en Andalousie médiévale, 11e-13e siècles", *Les Soins de Beauté*, 3e colloque international de Grasse, Nice, 1987, pp. 145-69.

[15] Bolens, *Agronomes*, II, 88 *et seq.*, "Les jardins andalous", pp. 71-96, and *L'Andalousie du quotidien au sacré*, chapter 16.

[16] *Nabataean Agriculture*, Fo. 236r, in Fahd, *op. cit.*, p. 266, 12 and p. 353, 4.

[17] Bolens, *La cuisine andalouse*, under *couscous* (pp. 155-71) and *sorbets jāwārish* (pp. 239-64).

[18] L. Bolens, "Al-Andalus: les structures foncières d'après les sources juridiques", in *Mélanges Duby*, 1991. For the original source, see al-Wansharīsī, *Kitāb al-miʿyar* (9th/15th century), Fez lithographed edition, Al-Zaouia el Hamel MS, T, VI, 132.

19 See Ibn ʿAbdūn, *Traité de ḥisba*, in E. Lévi-Provençal, *Séville musulmane au début du XIIe siècle*, Paris, 1947, III, 9-10; Spanish translation by E. García Gómez and E. Lévi-Provençal, *Sevilla a comienzos del siglo XII*, Seville, 1981, No. 3, pp. 42-43.

20 See T. Glick, *The Old World background of the Irrigation System of San Antonio*, Texas, 1972; and Bolens, "L'irrigation en Andalus: une société en mutation; analyse des sources juridiques", *I Colloquio de Historia y Medio Físico*, Almería, 1989, pp. 69-95.

21 Al-Wanṣharīsī, *Kitāb al-miʿyar*, following ʿUmar al-Iṣhbīlī, VIII, 92.

22 Strabon, *Geography*, XV, 1, 10-21.

23 See A. G. Haudricourt and L. Hédin, *L'homme et les plantes cultivées*, Paris, 1943, p. 137; M. Lombard, *Les textiles dans le monde musulman, VII-XIII siècles*, Paris-Leiden, 1978, p. 76, note 3; A. Watson, *Agricultural Innovation in the Early Islamic World*, Cambridge (England), 1983, pp. 31-41. There are between 40 and 50 varieties of cotton.

24 *Calendrier de Cordoue*, ed. C. Pellat, Leiden, Brill, 1961, p. 61; A. C. López y López, *Kitāb fī tartīb awqāt al-girāsa wa 'l-magrūsāt. Un tratado agrícola andalusí anónimo*, Granada, 1990.

25 On the 5th/11th century agronomists, see H. Pérès, *Kitāb al-filāḥa*, Algiers, 1946, p. 10. On Ibn Baṣṣāl, see J. M. Millás-Vallicrosa and Muḥammad Azimān, *Ibn Baṣṣāl, Libro de agricultura* (text, translation and notes), Tétouan, 1955, Arabic text, p. 114.

26 See García Sánchez, *Ciencias de la naturalezza*; Bolens, *Agronomes*, p. 44; Ibn Luyūn, *Kitāb ibdāʾ al-malāḥa wa inhāʾ al-rajāḥa fī usūl ṣināʿat al-filāḥa*, MS 1352, Rabat; J. Eguaras Ibañez, *Tratado de agricultura*, Granada, 1975 (new ed. 1988).

27 See Ibn Abī Zarʿ, *Rawḍ al-qirṭās fī akhbār mulūk*, Rabat, 1936, p. 111. For advantages conferred in the Almohad period (in the Almohad capitals of Marrakesh, Seville and Bougie), see Rhozali Ben Younes, *Recherche sur le mode de production au temps Almohades*, Thèse de 3e cycle, Paris, 1986, p. 112.

28 Bolens, *Agronomie*, p. 82 *et seq.* and chapter on soils; Ibn Ṣāḥib al-Ṣalāt, *Al-Mann bi 'l-imāma*, ed. A. Tazī, Beirut, 1957, p. 466; Ibn al-ʿAwwām, *Kitāb al-filāḥa, Libro de agricultura*, ed. J. Banqueri, Madrid, 1802, I, 531; Bolens, *Cuisine andalouse*, pp. 17-50.

29 See Ibn Baṣṣāl, *Libro de agricultura*, pp. 114-15 (text) and 151-52 (trans.); Marrākushī, *Akhbār al-Maghrib*, Cairo, 1948, pp. 237, 376; Ibn Abī Zarʿ, *Rawḍ al-qirṭās*, p. 146.

30 Ibn al-ʿAwwām, *Kitāb al-filāḥa*, II, 103 *et seq.*

31 R. T. Günther, *The Greek Herbal of Dioscorides*, New York, 1959; Juan Vernet, "La ciencia en el Islam y Occidente", in *L'Occidente e l'Islam nell'Alto Medioevo, Settimane di Spoleto*, April, 1964, II, 537-72.

32 See D. Provansal and P. Molina, *Campo de Níjar: conijeros y areneros*, Almería, 1989. For the Maghrib, see Ben Younes, *op. cit.*, p. 125 *et seq.*

33 *Kitāb al-filāḥa*, p. 105.

34 See al-Idrīsī, *Description of Africa, Spain and the Maghreb*, ed. R. Dozy and J. de Goeje, Leiden, 1968, pp. 3, 16; Ibn al-Bayṭār al-Mālaqī, *Kitāb al-jāmiʿ li mufradāt al-adwiya wa 'l aghdhiya*, Būlāq ed., 1291 A. H., IV, 24.

35 See al-Saqaṭī, *Manuel hispanique de ḥisba*, ed. G. S. Colin and E. Lévi-Provençal, Paris, 1931, *bayt*, 3-23; *baʿa* 7, 18; on unbleached fabric, *Khām*, 29; Spanish translation by P. Chalmeta, *Al-Andalus*, 32, 1967, pp. 1-38, 39-77; 33, 1968, pp. 78-120, 131-98.

36 Al-Saqaṭī, in Chalmeta, *op. cit.*, n. 134, 138, 139, 145.

37 Al-Ḥimyarī, *Al-Rawḍ al-miʿṭār*, ed. E. Lévi-Provençal, Leiden, 1938, p. 40, No. 29; Ibn al-Bayṭār, *Kitāb al-jāmiʿ*, n. 39.

38 See Ibn al-ʿAwwām, *Kitāb al-filāḥa*, Arabic text, p. 113; Ibn al-Bayṭār, *Kitāb al-jāmiʿ*, note 41, IV, 51; M. Asín Palacios, *Glosario de voces romances*, Madrid-Granada, 1942, No. 1, p. 116: *el-abertal*; and 305, p. 56 *lino*, Latin *linu* and *Kattan.*

39 See Ibn al-ʿAwwām, *Kitāb al-filāḥa*, Arabic text, p. 118.

40 See Lombard, *op. cit.*, p. 113 ; Ibn al-Bayṭār, *Kitāb al-jāmiʿ*, n. 39, II, 386-87, No. 1423; J. Vallvé, "La industria en al-Andalus", *Al-Qanṭara*, 1, 1980, p. 229.

41 See H. Pérès, *La poésie andalouse en arabe classique*, p. 217, n. 4 and p. 317; J. Vallvé, "La industria en al-Andalus", pp. 228-29.

42 *Calendrier de Cordoue*, pp. 90-91, 132-33, 144-45; al-Saqaṭī, trans. Chalmeta, n. 138; Ibn ʿAbdūn, *Traité de ḥisba*, n. 174.

43 See Ibn al-Bayṭār, *Kitāb al-jāmiʿ*, *s. v. Wasma*, IV, 194; also Maimonides, *Sharḥ asmāʾ al-ʿuqqār*, MS 33711, Istanbul, Aghya Sofia, fo. 83v-84ro, *s. v. Wasma.*

44 See Ibn al-Bayṭār, *Kitāb al-jāmiʿ*, 1562; *nīl, nīlaj*, 2244, IV, 186-87; Ibn al-ʿAwwām, *Kitāb al-filāḥa*, II, 28; V, 307.

45 See Ibn al-ʿAwwām, *Kitāb al-filāḥa*, II, 129; Clément-Mullet reads *samāwī* and translates as "pastel" (i.e., pastel blue associated with woad), while Ibn al-ʿAwwam follows Abū 'l-Khayr in making pastel blue synonymous with sky-blue; Ibn al-Bayṭār, *Kitāb al-jāmiʿ*, II, 64 (*nīl* = indigo), IV, 186-87; Maimonides, *Sharḥ asmāʾ al-ʿuqqār*, Fo. 74b-102a, and see also Meyerhof, *Un glossaire de matière médicale de Maïmonide*, Cairo, 1940, n. 126; ʿAbd al-Razzāq al-Jazāʾirī, *Kashf al-rumūz fī bayān al-aʿshāb (Révélations des Enigmes)*, trans. L. Leclerc, Paris, 1874, n., 25, see also *terre verte* and *zirqūn*, blue bordering vermilion red.

46 See Ibn Buklārish (late 6th/12th century), *Al-Mustaʿīnī*, MS Leiden Univ. Library, Or 15, fo. 34r.

47 Reply to J-P. Bouquet, "Le silphium, nourriture des Dieux, plante miraculeuse aujourd'hui disparue", *Dossiers d'Histoire et d'Archéologie*, 123, Jan. 1988, pp. 88-91.

48 P. Guichard, *Les Musulmans de Valence et la Reconquête (XIe-XIIIe siècles)*, Damascus, 1990; D. Wasserstein, *The Rise and Fall of the Party Kings, Politics and Society in Islamic Spain, 1002-1086*, Princeton, 1985; A. Huici Miranda, *Historia política del imperio almohade*, 1956, and *Historia musulmana de Valencia*, 1970.

49 L. Bolens, "La conservation des grains en Andalousie médiévale d'après les traités d'agronomie hispano-arabes", in *La conservation des grains*, ed. F. Sigaut, Paris, 1986, Vol. II; and Bolens, *Agronomes andalous*, p. 281.

50 L. Bolens, "L'agronomie et al-Andalus: Orient, occident, ou l'Andalousie?", *Al-Qanṭara*, 11/2, 1990, pp. 367-78.

51 Bolens, *Agronomes andalous*, pp. 58-123.

52 Bolens, *Cuisine andalouse*.

BIBLIOGRAPHY

Primary sources

Alfonso el Sabio, *Lapidario (según el Ms Escurialiense H. I, 15)*, ed., with introduction and notes, S. Rodríguez and M. Montalvo, Madrid, 1981.

Calendrier de Cordoue, ed. C. Pellat, Leiden, 1961.

Al-Ḥimyarī, *Al-Rawḍ al-miʿṭar*, ed. E. Lévi-Provençal, Leiden, 1938.

Ibn ʿAbdūn, *Traité de ḥisba*, in *Séville au XIIe siècle*, ed. E. Lévi-Provençal, Paris, 1947.

Ibn al-ʿAwwām, *Kitāb al-filāḥa, Libro de agricultura*, ed. J. Banqueri, Madrid, 1802, 2 vols.; reprinted Ministerio de Agricultura, Pesca y Alimentación, Madrid, 1988.

Ibn Abī Zarʿ, *Rawḍ al-qirtās fī akhbār mulūk al-Maghrib wa taʾrīkh madīnat Fās*, Rabat, 1936.

Ibn al-Bayṭār al-Mālaqī, *Kitāb al-jāmiʿ li mufradāt al-adwiya wa 'l aghdhiya*, Būlāq edition, IV, 1291 A. H., 2 vols.

Ibn Baṣṣāl, *Libro de agricultura*, ed. and Spanish translation J.-M. Villás Vallicrosa and M. Aziman, Tétouan, 1955.

Ibn Buklarīsh, *Al-Mustaʿīnī*, MS Leiden University Library, Or 15, fo. 34r.

Ibn Luyūn, *Kitāb ibdāʾ al-malāḥa wa-inhāʾ al-rajāḥa fī usūl ṣināʿat al-filāḥa*, MS 1352, Rabat; J. Eguaras Ibañez, *Tratado de agricultura*, Granada, 1975.

Ibn Ṣāḥib al-Ṣalāt, *Al-Mann bi 'l-imāma*, Beirut, 1957.

Ibn Sīnā, "Risālat al-iksīr" ("Letter on the Elixir"), in P. Anawati, *Oriente e Oriente scienze e filosofia*, Rome, 1973, pp. 285-346.

Ibn Wāfid, *Libro de agricultura*, ed. J.-M. Villás Vallicrosa, *Al-Andalus*, 8, 1943.

Al-Idrīsī, *Description de l'Afrique et de l'Espagne*, ed. and trans. R. Dozy-de Goeje, Leiden, 1968.

Isidore of Seville, *Etimologiarum Libri Viginti*, *Patrologia Latina*, Vol. 82, or J. Oroz Reta, Madrid, Lib 16, 17, 19, 1982.

ʿAbd al-Razzāq al-Jezāʾrī, *Kashf al-rumūz fī bayān al-aʿshāb (Révélations des énigmes)*, trans. L. Leclerc, Paris, 1874.

Maimonides, *Sharḥ asmāʾ al-ʿuqqār*, MS 33711 Istanbul, Aghya Sofia, Fo. 74 b-102a.

Al-Marrākushī, *Akhbār al-Maghrib*, Cairo, 1948.

Nabataean Agriculture, from T. Fahd, "Histoire de l'agriculture en Iraq", in *Handbuch der Orientalistik, Geschichte der Islamischen Länder*, Leiden, 1977, pp. 276-377.
Pedro de Alcala, in E. Pezzi, *El Vocabulario de Pedro de Alcala*, Almería, 1989.
Risāla fī awqāt al-sana, Un calendario anónimo andalusí, ed., with translation and notes, M. A. Navarro, Granada, 1990.
Al-Saqaṭī, *Manuel hispanique de ḥisba*, ed. G. Colin and E. Lévi-Provençal, Paris, 1931.
——, *Al-Kitāb fī adab al-ḥisba (Libro del buen gobierno del zoco)*, ed. P. Chalmeta, *Al-Andalus*, 32/1, 1967, pp. 1-38; 33/1, 1968, pp. 78-120; 33/4, 1968, pp. 131-98.
Al-Wansharīsī, *Kitāb al-miʿyar*, lithograph edition of Ms al-Zaouia el Hamel, Fez, 11 vols.

Secondary works
Arié, R., *España musulmana (siglos VIII-XV)*, Vol. III of *Historia de España*, ed. M. Tuñon de Lara, Barcelona, 1982.
Asín Palacios, Miguel, *Glosario de voces romances registradas por un botánico anónimo hispano-musulmán (siglos XI-XII)*, Madrid-Granada, 1943.
Attié, B., "L'ordre chronologique probable des sources directes d'Ibn al-ʿAwwām", *Al-Qanṭara*, 3, 1982, pp. 299-332.
Ben Younes, R., *Recherche sur le mode de production au temps des Almohades*, Thèse 3e cycle, Paris, 1986.
Bolens, L., *Agronomes andalous du moyen âge*, Geneva, 1981.
——, *La cuisine andalouse, un art de vivre, XIe-XIIIe siècles*, Paris, 1990.
——, *L'Andalousie, du quotidien au sacré, XIe-XIIIe siècles*, Aldershot-Vermont, 1991.
——, "L'irrigation en al-Andalus", *I Coloquio de Historia y Medio Físico*, Almería, 1989, pp. 69-95; also in *L'Andalousie du quotidien au sacré*, chapter 3.
——, "Les jardins andalous", in *Flaran 9, Jardins et vergers en Europe occidentale, VIII-XVIII siècles*, Auch, 1987; also in *L'Andalousie du quotidien au sacré*, chapter 17.
——, "Le soleil pulvérisé sur les tables andalouses", in *Manger des yeux*, ed. R. Stern, Pully, 1989; also in *L'Andalousie du quotidien au sacré*, chapter 12.
——, "Les parfums et la beauté en al-Andalus", in *Les Soins de Beauté, 3e Congrès International de Grasse*, Nice, 1987, pp. 145-69; also in *L'Andalousie du quotidien au sacré*, chapter 15.
Chalmeta, P., *El señor del zoco*, Madrid, 1973.
Dozy, R., *Noms des vêtements chez les Arabes*, Amsterdam, 1845.
García Sánchez, E. (ed.), *Ciencias de la naturaleza*, Granada, 1990.
Glick, T. F., *Islamic and Christian Spain in the Early Middle Ages*, Princeton, 1979.
Haudricourt, A. G., and I. Hédin, *L'homme et les plantes cultivées*, Paris, 1843.
Kraus, P., *Jābir ibn Ḥayyān, Contribution à l'histoire des idées scientifiques dans l'Islam*, Paris, 1986.
Lombard, M., *Les textiles dans le monde musulman, VII-XIIe siècles*, Paris-Leiden, 1978.
Miquel, A., *Géographie humaine du monde musulman jusqu'au 11e siècle*, Paris-Leiden, 1967-88, 4 vols.
Pastoureau, M., "Vers une histoire de la couleur bleue", in *Sublime Indigo*, Fribourg, 1987, pp. 19-27.
——, *Figures et couleurs*, Paris, 1986.
Pérès, H., *La poésie andalouse en arabe classique au 11e siècle*, Paris, 1953.
Provansal, D. Molina P., *Campo de Nijar: cortijeros y areneros*, Almería, 1989.
Vallvé, J., "La industria en al-Andalus", *Al-Qanṭara*, 1, 1980, pp. 109-238.
——, "La agricultura en al-Andalus", *Al-Qanṭara*, 3, 1982, pp. 261-97.
Vocabulista in arabico, ed. da Schiapparelli, Florence, 1871.
Watson, A., *Agricultural Innovation in the Early Islamic World*, Cambridge (England), 1983.

THE HISPANO-ARAB GARDEN: NOTES TOWARDS A TYPOLOGY

JAMES DICKIE (YAQUB ZAKI)

The Hispano-Arabic garden, unlike its Perso- and Indo-Islamic counterparts, suffers from a lack of pictorial documentation; reconstruction has to base itself on surviving or excavated examples as supplemented by contemporary description. The holocaust of Arabic manuscripts following the conquest of Granada ensured that surviving literary sources would be scanty, and the garden carpets of 18th-century Persia have no Spanish equivalent. Writers on the subject rely overmuch on the present appearance of gardens on Muslim sites, choosing to ignore that the garden is of its nature the most evanescent of art forms, one season alone sufficing to effect a change. In Spain the issue is further complicated by the coincidental discovery of America in the same year as the fall of Granada, an event which was decisively to alter the flora of Europe. No less serious was the italianisation of Spanish palaces and gardens under Renaissance influences in a process which erased the indigenous tradition in less than a century.

The Islamic garden is a variant of the Paradise garden, a concept variously conceived according to the cultural context, and the Hispano-Arab garden is a regional variation of the Islamic. The Hispano-Arab garden affords the only physical evidence as to the nature of the pre-Timurid Islamic garden. Basic components are a raised grid, irrigation under gravitational pressure, central collecting pool or system head (*taqsīm*), and formal walkways incorporating channels by which irrigation is accomplished. The walks define the zone formally, leaving room for a less formal approach within the areas so defined. A quadripartite arrangement seems to have been standard, but not *de rigueur*. Verdure and water are disposed axially and geometrically, but this symmetry derives from the formal arrangement of palace architecture, where a defined relationship of correspondences (*jawābāt*) exists between the different parts; a less formal relationship doubtless obtained elsewhere.

The Samarrā᾽ Bowl reproduced by Herzfeld,[1] although dating from around 2000 B. C., depicts the prototypal garden to which all subsequent planning conformed, that is to say, the quadripartite (*chahār-bāgh*) division of space. The persistence of the *mandala* plan is explicable in Jungian terms (*Man and His Symbols*), but in practical terms is only an elegant solution to the problem of how to irrigate a square or rectangular area, a device for the economic use of water. Symbolically read, the crossed axes could correspond to the four rivers of Paradise (Jayḥān, Sayḥān, Nīl, Furāt) specified in

Prophetical Tradition.[2] Alternatively they could be the four rivers of wine, sweet water, clarified honey and milk unvarying in taste referred to in the Quran (47:15), although the point of confluence makes this hypothesis seem less likely.

If we are to credit Marco Polo, such streams literally existed in the garden the Old Man of the Mountain laid out in Alamūt, following the eschatological descriptions in the Quran:

> The Old Man (*shaykh*) was called in their language Aloadin ('Alā' al-Dīn). He had caused a certain valley, between two mountains, to be enclosed, and had turned it into a garden, the largest and most beautiful that ever was seen, filled with every variety of fruit. In it were erected pavilions and palaces, the most elegant that can be imagined, all covered with gilding and exquisite painting. And there were runnels too, flowing freely with wine and milk and honey and water; and numbers of ladies of the most beautiful damsels in the world, who could play on all manner of instruments and sing most sweetly, and danced in a manner that it was charming to behold. For the Old Man desired to make his people believe that this was actually Paradise. So he had fashioned it after the description that Mahommet gave of his Paradise, to wit, that it should be a beautiful garden running with conduits of wine and milk and honey and water, and full of lovely women for the delectation of all its inmates.[3]

One commentator believes that this garden may now have to be discarded from our stock of Oriental images because in the late 1950s a British expedition to the spot could find no trace of the enchanted setting where the Assassins were seduced into absolute obedience.[4] But it is obvious from the account of the expedition that the excavators did not look in the right place, in "a valley between two mountains", where *qanāt*s would have tapped the water that collects at the foot of any rock and led it to a walled enclosure.[5]

This attempt to literalise the ingredients of the Quranic Paradise is important because the Quranic texts, whether literally or metaphorically read, depict a *sensual* Paradise, a garden (*janna*) of moisture and shade. Although a servile imitation of the Quranic account, the Alamūt formula was being followed, albeit less slavishly, more or less everywhere.[6] Thus the basic Islamic garden plan arises from a convergence of two notions of how Paradise should look, the Persian and the Arabian: fusion followed by diffusion (through conquest). In Spain, such gardens would become places where people could enjoy the sensations a prodigious nature afforded them: "contemplation, the sounds of water and the nightingale's song, the scents of flowers, the cool feel of flowers against the skin, all in an atmosphere of Quranic paradise."[7] The invention of the fourfold plot was decisive, for it meant that water became the organisational principle of the Islamic garden.

The courtyard house, which compresses and formalises the garden concept, was not introduced into Spain by the Arabs but was standard Iberian procedure which the Arabs found congenial. Formal gardens functioned within palaces not only as courtyard space but intervening between palatial elements conceived of as units within an overall scheme less tectonic than horticultural. Such palaces existed *intra* as well as *extra muros* but were confined to the suburbs. The presence of gardens inside the Alhambra, which was densely urbanised, is not in doubt, for we have the contemporary evidence of the Venetian ambassador, Andrea Navagiero, who, after visiting the Alhambra, writes in a letter dated the end of May, 1526, that in addition "to these sumptuous palaces [i.e., Comares and the Court of the Lions] those infidel kings had many other places of recreation, in towers, palaces, orchards and private gardens, alike inside as outside the walls of the Alhambra."[8] If small, such places approximated to villas, and, if large, formed palatine cities, after the manner of Hadrian's Villa at Tivoli. Examples are Madīnat al-Zahrā' and the Alhambra, whilst the Alamiría (Umayyad) and the Generalife (Naṣrid) represent the smaller, villa-type, recreative (i.e., protocol-free) palace. Generally, rulers dwelt in a fortified Alcázar (*al-qaṣr*) with a system of interlocking courtyards, a life-style less congested than that of the city outside but not substantially different. Private cemeteries and dynastic mausolea were attached to palaces. The royal pantheon, always figuratively referred to as *al-Rawḍa*, was so in actuality as well as in metaphor, because ancillary garden space accommodated the less important burials. Navagiero's reference to gardens inside the Alhambra does not, however, help us to locate them, and any attempt to identify them with existing sites is fraught with problems.

Although Hispano-Arabic texts bristle with references to gardens, descriptions are rare. There is, however, an invaluable account dating from the 5th/11th century that describes a garden of the period in Córdoba, in which the key word *ḥayr* appears. A *ḥayr* is a hunting park, but it is also a pleasure garden. Careful collation of passages in which this word occurs leaves little doubt that *ḥayr*, a walled enclosure, is the Arabic equivalent of the Greek *paradeisos*, because *paradeisos* is from the Old Persian *pairidaeza*, a compound noun formed from *pairi* ("around") and *daeza* ("wall"). The term is familiar from the names of those palace *cum* caravanserai establishments in the Syrian desert like Qaṣr al-Ḥayr al-G͟harbī and Qaṣr al-Ḥayr al-S͟harqī. *Ḥayr* is a corruption of *ḥā'ir* (pl. *ḥawā'ir*), meaning "tank", which by metonymy comes to signify the plantation watered from it. The word is used by Ibn al-K͟haṭīb (713/1313-776/1375) in his description of the Alhambra:

> The city, which is the seat of the ruler, towers over Granada's inhabited area on the south. It overlooks the city [of Granada] with its gleaming [lit. "white"] battlements, lofty towers, redoubtable bastions and exquisite palaces which blind [both] sight and mind. Watercourses [*jadāwil*] pouring down the hillside from its abundant waters and overflowing cisterns [*ḥawā'ir*] produce a noise that can be heard afar off.[9]

A *ḥayr* is a *paradeisos*, that is, an enclosed garden, or *hortus conclusus*. Thus *ḥayr al-ḥayawānāt* is a zoological garden, walled to keep in the animals. Arab kings delighted in assembling rare species, both animal and vegetable, in their palaces, so *ḥayr* can also mean botanical garden. A *ḥayr* was an essential adjunct to an Umayyad palace, at least in the desert, where produce could not be had from a market. Bastioned walls enclosed agricultural and horticultural land supportive to the palace and fed by either *qanāt*s or aqueducts. The park at Malmaison in Josephine's time, with its menagerie, hothouses and exotic plantations, would count as a *ḥayr*, as might also the Petit Trianon for a time, under Louis XV. Although stocked with rare plants and animals for the express delectation of the ruler, essentially a *ḥayr* is functional: its purpose is to provide food for the royal table.

Referring to a literary interment that took place in 426/1035, al-Fatḥ b. Khāqān describes a garden belonging to Córdoba's Golden Age, the 4th/10th-early 5th/11th century. The poet who was fortunate enough posthumously to enjoy its amenities, Ibn Shuhayd (382/992-426/1035), was no stranger to them in life, for he and the owner had oft disported themselves there, if we are to believe Ibn Khāqān. The scene of these dissipations was a park known as Ḥayr al-Zajjālī after its proprietor, the vizier Abū Marwān al-Zajjālī. Ibn Khāqān refers in his description to "files of trees symmetrically arranged", an arrangement clearly arboricultural, and singles out a courtyard (*ṣaḥn*), a watercourse (*jadwal*) serpentine in outline, and a central collecting basin (*jābiya*), all in addition to a pavilion exquisitely executed in gold and azure. *Ṣaḥn* indicates an open space or paved area, and the basin would have been fed by a serpentine stream traversing this courtyard.

A similar arrangement seems to have been obtained in al-Muʿtaṣim's palace (the Ṣumādiḥiyya) in Almería in the 5th/11th century, where serpentine channels linked various basins one to another. This prince (443/1051-484/1091), who was a poet, in one of his compositions compares the water in his garden to a snake twisting as it slithers away.[10] In the Alcazaba at Málaga there is a piece of Visigothic masonry reworked in Arab times as a waterspout with a serpentine channel; the Arabs were evidently fascinated by water which described a serpentine motion. It is this same term, *jadwal* (pl. *jadāwil*), that Ibn Sirāj,[11] writing to Fatḥ b. Khāqān about the channels, or runnels, of al-Zahrā', uses to distinguish an artificial watercourse from a natural stream (*nahr*), and Ibn al-Khaṭīb uses the term for the artificial channels that carry off the surplus water from the Alhambra in the passage already quoted. The pavilion in Ḥayr al-Zajjālī probably resembled one of around the same date in the Alcazaba of Málaga, where a wooden roof is supported on cantilevered arches similar to those in the vicinity of the *miḥrāb* (prayer-niche) in the Mosque of Córdoba.

The essential parts of Ibn Khāqān's description read as follows:

> This *ḥayr* is one of the most wonderful, beauteous and complete of places. Its courtyard of pure white marble is traversed by a stream wriggling like a snake. In it is a tank (or reservoir) into which all waters tumble. The roof [of its pavilion] is

> adorned in gold and blue, likewise the sides and walls. The garden had files of trees symmetrically aligned, and its flowers smiled from their [open] buds, and [so dense was the foliage] the sun couldn't glimpse the ground, and the breeze, blowing over it night and day, was impregnated with perfume. I myself have passed nights and days there, and it was as if they were composed of lovers' glances or cut from the pages of youth.

The passage concludes on a personal note:

> Abū ʿĀmir b. Shuhayd enjoyed there spells of well-being and rest, morning and evening. Fate gave him whatever he desired, and he combined [the pleasures of] sobriety and intoxication. He and the owner of the garden buried alongside him were companions in infantile pursuits and allies in inebriation. They persisted in this course, behaving thus in their pride and vanity until death overtook them and Fate decreed their limits. Thus they became neighbours in death as they had been in life, and the shade of these shady spots drew away from them ...[12]

Apart from indicating that the garden was viewed as a place suitable for voluptuousness, a character it has always retained, the passage conveys almost a French sense of *volupté*, a combination of love and death. The two friends emparadised here obviously sought to recapture in a favourable milieu something of the joys of youth, although Ibn Khāqān leaves us to imagine the bowers where they gratified their senses before their passions subsided into dust. These corporeal delights (*jismiyyāt*) anticipate the spiritual ones (*ruḥāniyyāt*) of Paradise. But, at the same time, Ibn Khāqān's censorious language evokes another garden, that of rebellion and lost innocence.

From the description it is clear that al-Zajjālī's pleasure grove was a paradise garden, or duplicate heaven, a divine framework of reference which does not necessarily preclude profane use. Files of trees symmetrically arranged in regular plots go back to ancient Persia. Although the paradise garden is a Near Eastern notion, the key word in the evolution of the idea as it travelled west is the Greek *paradeisos*, the word the Septuagint uses for the Garden of Eden and which recurs in the Quran (18:107 and 23:11).[13] The Hebrew uses *gann* (Ar. *janna*), which is simply "garden", but as the garden whence our First Parents were excluded had a wall and a guarded gate to prevent their return, the Greek translation was felicitous.

In a *paradeisos* the wall had a twofold purpose: to keep the game in and the common herd out. This indicates that the main objects of a paradise were (a) sport, (b) privacy. (More coy but less elusive game could also be pursued in such a setting, where intimate bowers disposed the mind to dalliance, for by this time the concept had been modified to include a profane as well as sacred desire.) There is, however, a contradiction here, for the game would soon ruin any ornamental scheme, so that "paradise" was not slow to acquire other connotations. This could account for the semantic shift whereby game preserve became pleasure garden. After the revelation of Islam, theological factors may have contributed to the shift, pleasure (*niʿma*) being the central experience of Paradise. *Naʿīm* (delight, bliss), from the same root, used definitely, is a synonym for Paradise. This way the garden became a mirror image of Paradise, and its role is allegorical but without the aid of statuary to point the allegory, as in European gardens.

Xenophon (d. after 353 B.C.E.) is credited with introducing the paradise garden to the West, but a Damascene toponym, Ḥayr Sarjūn, records the site of a palace belonging to the Assyrian king Sargon II, whose father overran the whole of West Asia in the 8th century B.C.E. This would seem to show that such gardens not only antedate Cyrus the Younger (d. 401 B.C.E) but had reached the Levant more than three centuries before Xenophon met the Persian king. As Ḥayr Sarjūn lay within the city walls, it cannot have been a hunting park but only a pleasure grove.[14] Certainly the garden idea came from the East; it was in the hot climate of Asia that the idea of grouping productive trees with flowers for fragrance or appearance irrigated from wells or canals first occurred. It was only after his defeat of Mithridates in 63 B.C.E. that Lucullus, no less famous as an epicure than as a general, laid out the first park in Rome, the Horti Luculliani, where Messalina later disported herself, round about his palace. The connection between gardens and sybaritism was by now well established; but the important point is that in either case, Greece or Rome, the first gardeners were generals who had seen service in the East. Lucullus also takes the credit for the introduction of the cherry (from Northern Anatolia).

Referring to the Umayyad caliph Hishām I (72/691-125/743), the Greek historian Theophanes (ca. 752-817) says: "And he began to found palaces in open country and town, and to create sown fields and *paradeisoi*, and to make water channels."[15] This shows *ḥayr* to be the same thing as *paradeisos*. As it moved out of the Levant, the concept merged with the Latin *hortus* and acquired functional apanages. A similar semantic shift was undergone by *ḥayr*, which, by the time it reaches Spain with the Arabs, denotes a walled enclosure for horticulture rather than a game preserve. From Xenophon, through the Alexandrian translators of the Septuagint and crossing the linguistic boundaries into Arabic as *firdaws*, the word retains its primary meaning of enclosure. Arabic, however, uses *firdaws* mainly for eschatological description whilst retaining *ḥayr* for its mundane equivalent. All this would seem to make the Greeks or Romans the vehicle of the idea's transmission, with the Arab diaspora the decisive factor in its ultimate diffusion.

Abū Marwān al-Zajjālī had bequeathed his garden to the city for use as a public amenity. Pérès[16] hazards the guess that this is probably the first instance of such a bequest in history and concludes that public parks were an invention of the Arabs, but he had evidently forgotten Julius Caesar:

> Moreover he hath left you all his walks,
> His private arbours, and new-planted orchards.
> On this side Tiber, he hath left them you,
> And to your heirs for ever: common pleasures
> To walk abroad and recreate yourselves.

In these five lines Shakespeare somehow manages to communicate the essence of a *waqf* (religious endowment) and does so much better than his source (North's Plutarch). Al-Zajjālī's bequest could only have taken the form admissible under Islamic Law, a *waqf*, the nature of which precludes restriction on its use, so Pérès was mistaken in supposing that only the elegant society of the capital would have had the *entrée*; the garden ceased to be privileged space the moment its owner's testament came into effect.[17]

In spite of Ibn Shuhayd's burial there beside his statesman friend, recalling Horace's next to Maecenas on the Esquiline, the Ḥayr al-Zajjālī was not a funerary enclosure (*rawḍa*); it is an *hortus*, or combination of flower garden and orchard after the Roman fashion, no different in fact from the Horti Maecenatiani or the Horti Sallustiani in Rome. The ornamental garden is a legacy of the Renaissance; prior to that date gardens were functional and recreational at the same time. Whether in Rome or Spain these *horti* formed, along with countless courtyards, the lungs through which a city breathed: in Ancient Rome *horti* represented one eighth of the total urban area; in modern London the parks represent one twenty-ninth! Although only Julius Caesar's testamentary bequest was public property, the Roman public had the right of entry into all the royal gardens. These included the Horti Luculliani referred to, which had been made over to Claudius as a gift by their proprietor (the Valerii) to avert the emperor's wrath over their abuse by Messalina and her paramours.

Another and greater poet, Ibn Zaydūn (394/1003-463/1070), describes the pools of al-Zahrā' as so deep as to appear blue and surrounded with umbrageous margins:

> There may [be found] blue waters whose margins are kept moist by shade, [by the side of which] I entered into a compact with Time respecting a compliant youth.[18]

Whilst from another poem we know that the pools were lilyponds:

> By night, waterlilies exhaled a perfume which diffused itself, drowning until morning opened their eyes.[19]

An earlier verse from the same poem alludes to the droplets shed by fountains:

> And the gardens smiled with silver water as if you had torn necklaces from your throat.[20]

A pool conforming to Ibn Zaydūn's description was discovered by Félix Hernández Giménez in 1944; it separates a large *salle d'apparat* (*majlis*) from a pavilion sited opposite and reflects the architecture of both. The city, 120 hectares in extent, is disposed on graduated terraces descending the hillside, with the palatine quarters (*al-qaṣr*) on the uppermost. A similar arrangement is also found in Mughal India (e.g., the Shālāmār Bāgh, Lahore) and may reflect the hierarchically organised heavens of Muslim eschatology (Quran, 3:163). Seven terraces are found in Persia as well as in India. Eight corresponds to the eight heavens; seven symbolises the planets and twelve the signs of the zodiac (as in the Nis͟hāṭ Bāg͟h in Kashmir). All spatial arrangements assume charged significance, for they seek to follow the divine scheme of the Creator. The pavilion in Madīnat al-Zahrā' marks the spot where the two axes intersect in a huge quadripartite garden, the outline of whose beds is clearly visible. Of the four arms one is taken up by the hall and reflection pool.[21] The north side of the pavilion is reflected in the pool whilst three smaller pools to the east, west and south, effect the same for the remaining sides. These pools supply runnels (Ibn K͟hāqān's *jadāwil*) in the kerbing of the beds on all four sides. Apertures, closed off by means of bungs, allowed the beds to be periodically flooded. All four tanks are sufficiently deep to justify Ibn Zaydūn's reference to azure depths.

Córdoba's loss of political hegemony following the *fitna* (422/1031 saw the final collapse of the Cordoban Caliphate) led to a diffusion of talent and the simultaneous emergence all over the Peninsula of multiple cultural foci as the new city states vied one with another for the attention of the learned or fashionable. The cases of Almería and Málaga have already been cited, but in the Aljafería of Saragossa (seat of the Banū Hūd, 431/1039-540/1146), now rescued from the ignominy of having served as the city gaol since 1772, a courtyard garden has come to light. Pools at opposite ends of a court obviously intended to reflect the delicate tracery of the porticoed sides are linked by a straight watercourse without any transverse.

Heir to Córdoba as cultural capital of Spain was Seville, and parts of the famed al-Mubārak Palace of the poet king al-Muʿtamid (431/1040-487/ 1095) have recently come to light in the Alcázares Reales. An impressive Almoravid (6th/12th century) garden has been superimposed on an earlier one of 5th/11th century date, all but obliterating it. The primitive arrangement included three sunken flower beds on one side and three more corresponding on the opposite side. If, as seems probable, the central one on either side were not a bed but a tank, the original arrangement would differ little from that at Saragossa. The beds are however much deeper than at al-Zahrā', where the subsoil rock is high; the sides are stuccoed and painted in imitation of arches. In the garden which was superimposed on this one the arches are real, blind and made of brickwork. Crossed axes incorporate channels lined with tiles radiating from a central pool. The flowerbeds are deep; formerly dwarf orange trees grew in each corner, four to a bed.

Deeper still were the beds in another Almoravid garden growing only orange trees, one side of which was excavated in the Alcázares and then reburied. This garden had the luck to be recorded by the local historian Rodrigo Caro in the 17th century before it was thrown down by the local tremors of the Lisbon earthquake (felt even in Scotland!) in 1755. Caro describes the crossed axes as so tall as to form a viaduct, or rather an aqueduct, supported on arches, so that to get from one part of the garden to another all one had to do was walk underneath them.[22] Water descended to the level of the beds through clay pipes embedded in the brickwork. The unusually deep beds were intended for the planting of orange trees.

Another Almoravid garden, discovered in 1924 in a palace (the Castillejo) in the Vega of Murcia, furnishes a link between these earlier gardens and those of the Granadine epoch. This palace, precariously perched atop a pinnacle of rock rising dramatically out of the level land of the Vega, must have presented its builders with formidable hydraulic problems. Torres Balbás attributes it to a local chieftain, Ibn Saʿd b. Mardanīsh (d. 572/1172), who resisted the Almohads.[23] The plan as excavated is identical to that of the Court of the Lions two centuries later: a rectangular court bisected both longitudinally and transversally, with the main axis emphasised by terminal pavilions. Pavilions would seem to have replaced the tanks of the Saragossan example. In Granada, and probably at Murcia too, the tank contracted into a fountain sheltered by a pavilion.

This relieves us of the need to describe the over-familiar Court of the Lions, whose sole innovation consists of a fountain at the convergence of the axes where in Seville there had been a depressed basin. Orange trees formerly in the corners recall the case of Seville and point to a tradition in this regard. The trees were seen in 1502 by a Flemish traveller, Antoine de Lalaing, and in view of the date must be presumed to have belonged to the original planting.[24] Lalaing refers to six, but these are likely to have been survivors out of an original total of eight. This last was the number settled on by Torres Balbás when he replanted the trees in the course of his restoration around 1928. They were removed when the governing body, the Patronato, decided to replant the garden with flowers. This proved unsatisfactory, and four (!) orange trees have been put back.

The so-called court is really a palace, and but one of a number of discrete residential entities within the walls of a palatine city representing successive building phases that waxed and waned as the state alternately prospered or languished. The Palace of the Lions is a *villa urbana* as distinct from a *villa rustica*, which type is represented by the Generalife on the opposite side of the gorge.[25] In Spain one can never get very far away from Ancient Rome. Muslim Spain made use of both the *domus urbana* and the *villa rustica*, but long before Palladio the Arabs had hit upon an idea which otherwise had to await the Renaissance for its introduction in Europe: the *villa urbana*. Arab historians never refer to the Alhambra as a *qaṣr* (palace) or *qalʿa* (citadel) but only as *madīnat al-Ḥamrāʾ* (as opposed to *madīnat Gharnāṭa*, the bourgeois city).[26] This means that everything inside the Alhambra is urban by definition: the Court of Comares is a *domus urbana*, and the Court of the Lions a *villa urbana*, built alongside the main palace for feasting, soirées and parties, with gardens for recreation attached. The Generalife is a *villa rustica* but with the plan of a *domus urbana* and with immense estates—ten to twelve times the size of the Alhambra. Though fortified, the Generalife is extramural; intramural villas existed, but only in the *arbāḍ* (suburbs), never within the *madīna*. Where urbanisation was thin, as in the Potters' Quarter (Rabaḍ al-Fakhkhārīn), such estates could be extensive. This was the case with the Manjāra al-Kubrā and the Manjāra al-Ṣughrā (respectively the Greater and Lesser Orchards), the dwelling house of the former of which survives in part (Cuarto Real de Santo Domingo). These were suburban villas. Following villa precedent, the Court of the Lions has the kind of garden one might expect to find in a regular villa. The sense of enclosure in the Generalife was originally every bit as tight as in the Court of the Lions, with *miradors* to release the eye, two in the Generalife, one in the Court of the Lions. In the Generalife, one *mirador* frames the urban landscape to the west whilst another traps a view of the Alhambra to the south. This last was a combined garden/landscape. The garden it overlooked was the one where the Venetian ambassador saw rabbits frolicking amongst the myrtle bushes.[27] The Court of the Lions shares the same arrangement but reverses the direction; it looks over a lower terrace toward the Albaicín. The reciprocal entrapment of the Generalife was the work of another *mirador*, in the palace known as the ex-Convento de San Francisco. Today, overgrowth prevents this *mirado*r from fulfilling its function; but, originally, it returned the compliment from the opposite side of the gorge. Both of these were terraced gardens. In reality, the Generalife had three *miradors*; the third was an internal one, for regarding the garden in the Patio de la Acequía. The Lions quadrangle had the same number, two to regard the courtyard and one to regard the garden. This was a water garden and would have reflected the *mirador* of Lindaraja as well perhaps as the Tower of Abū Ḥajjāj. Since Charles V, none of this has been visible, and it is impossible for today's visitor to grasp the visual ensemble intended by the Arabs.

The Generalife was one of three fortified *munya*s (villas) that had the job of protecting the approaches to the Alhambra from the rear, the others being the Alixares (demolished to make room for a cemetery in the 19th century) and the House of the Bride (Dār al-ʿArūsa) on the Cerro de Santa Elena. Under its present camouflage of Romantic garden it is not a little difficult today to visualise the Generalife as the fortress it once was, fortified from before and behind, yet the fortifications are still there and visible provided one take the trouble to look for them, even if no longer so conspicuous as Ibn al-Khaṭīb found them in the 8th/14th century. "There surround", says the great historian, "the walls of the [Alhambra] city extensive orchards [*basātīn*], which are the private property of the sultan, and trees with intertwining branches such that from behind the hedges white battlements gleam like stars amidst the verdure."[28] Nor, for that matter, so conspicuous as Bermúdez de

Pedraza was still to find them 270 years later: "The gardens [of the Generalife] are planted on the slopes of the hill of the Sun, which they call *Santa Elena*, and are so fortified with great walls of mortar that this alone would attest to the greatness of the founders."[29] "Mortar" here refers to the construction of boundary walls in concrete, which renders them invulnerable to siege engine or cannon. Naṣrid cities were seldom taken by assault; practically all had to be starved into submission.

All three palaces mentioned are examples of the *villa rustica*, that is an *hortus*, and stood embowered amidst orchards, as did the Generalife till the last century. These are real villas, extra-mural arcadias fusing rural idyll and economic income in a tradition going back to Pliny and Hadrian *via* Iberia. Ibn al-Khaṭīb describes these rural paradises in rapturous terms:

> Farms [*qurā*] and gardens [*jannāt*] were in such number that Granada resembled a mother surrounded by children, with luxuriant herbiage adorning her sides as if she had donned a necklace covering the upper part of her breasts, whilst winds embalmed her with zephyrs. Villas [*munan*] and royal properties [*mustakhliṣāt*] encompassed the city like bracelets. Nuptial thrones [i. e., buds] were set up for the brides of the gardens [i.e., the flowers]. The sultan of the spring [i.e., the rose] took his seat to review the rebels [the other flowers]. The nightingale of the trees preached a sermon, whereupon [all] listeners fell attentive. [Acres of] vines waved like billows, and the [whole] neighbourhood overflowed with their juice. Like the sky of the world beautified with innumerable stars so lay [the plain] with towers of intricate construction and equipped with staircases. The winds exhaled perfumes, bringing Paradise to mind for whoso hopes for what God has in store for him by way of requital. ... The reminders of Granada's muezzins vied with one another at daybreak [to wake people] with melodies like [those of] turtle doves. With its glorious kings, Granada exercised a jurisdiction proceeding from authority and government in a place filled with charms free of [any] blemish, [indeed] surpassing all metonymy and metaphor, where there were ancient and venerable mosques, canals ensuring continuous irrigation and numerous bridges, together with taxes levied on the valuable goods [for sale] in the markets, and the faces of flowers and graceful people [dressed in] garments as to surpass those worn by the horizons, filling the hearts of believers with compassion.[30]

Ibn al-Khaṭīb paints a picture of snug farms, prosperous villages and a contented, devout folk, but he also stresses the importance of the villa economy in a way that cannot but remind us of economic conditions in the late Roman Empire:

> There is no space not taken up with gardens [*jannāt*], vineyards [*kurūm*] and orchards [*basātīn*]. But as for the land where the plain extends on the north there are to be found villas of such magnitude and prohibitive cost that none but a member of the royal family could afford to own them, for some yield crops worth half a thousand dinars notwithstanding the low prices vegetables fetch in this city. Of these, nearly thirty are the private property of the sultan. Round about them and right up to their boundaries there is valuable real estate which is never idle and each unit of which never fails to produce around 25 dinars for the exchequer. There too the sultan has properties in good order from which the state's coffers regularly benefit, all dotted about with gleaming houses, tall towers, broad thresh-

ing-floors and comparable enclosures for pigeons and domestic animals. Within the city boundaries and the circuit of its walls the number of the private properties of the sultan does not exceed twenty. Therein are employed vast numbers of labourers and nimble stallions reserved for his personal use or for ploughing. Many of these [properties] are provided with strongholds, mills and mosques. And this happy state of affairs, which is due to the excellence of the husbandry and the prime nature of the terrain, pervades the remaining villages and towns belonging to subjects [of the crown], amongst which figure large towns and populous villages adjoining the boundaries of the royal domains, not a few of which are extensive in size and endowed with all the benefits of civilisation. In this [economy] some thousands are involved and these exhibit great variety of type, whilst others there are which have one or two proprietors and upward. The number of such places exceeds 300, some fifty whereof have Friday pulpits, [mosques] wherein pale hands are extended and eloquent voices raised. The walls of this city and its environs enclose more than 130 mills driven by water.[31]

We have rendered *qarya* (Sp. *alquería*) as farm or village according to context. Both are admissible, a *qarya* being by definition any place neither a *madīna* (settlement) or *ḥiṣn* (stronghold); Ibn al-Khaṭīb himself stresses how the population can vary from several people to several thousand, that is to say, all the way from smallholding to small town. Münzer, referring to one particular plain, says: "This plain also is filled with hamlets—which we call villas—and Saracens occupied in tilling the soil."[32] *Munya* is villa, but *burj* we have translated as tower, although in Valencian Arabic it means villa. *Burj* indicates a fortified villa. Münzer, writing in 1494, confirms this interpretation: "... orchards, I repeat, full of houses and towers, occupied during the summer. ..."[33] *Munya*, translated by Dozy (*Supplément aux dictionnaires arabes*) as *(h)ortus*, is, literally, an object of desire: hence a place whither one goes to recreate, i.e., a pleasance or rural retreat. An *hortus* would happily accommodate both functions. Horticulture being a branch of agriculture, the art of landscape architecture is but a refinement of the science of agriculture. "Villa" suffered semantic distortion at the hands of the Renaissance: *villa* is primarily an economic term indicating a self-sufficient rural enterprise, an integrated economic unit; in Latin the word means a farm.[34] Italy and Spain were dotted about with innumerable such economic units. Villas such as Ibn al-Khaṭīb keeps referring to comprised herbiage and pasturage, viniculture or horticulture, with a decorative zone separating the house from its ancillary economy, as may still be seen in Vélez Benaudalla (Valley of the Banū ʿAbd Allāh), midway between Granada and Motril, where a garden of this period survives.[35] Villas could be rural, urban or suburban, depending on location; architecturally, the first and last probably differed little if at all, unlike their Roman counterparts, for the Roman suburban villa put its country cousin to shame.

Ibn al-Khaṭīb's raptures are echoed by early Christian writers. Describing the site of the House of the Bride in the 17th century, Bermúdez de Pedraza comments:

> This hill of Santa Elena was so famous in the time of the Moors that when they took this city, says Ibn Ṭāriq, it seemed a paradise, and, even though it is now stripped of its lustre, it retains traces of its beauty and in Moorish times so dense was it with houses and fruit trees that it resembled a Flemish canvas.[36]

The location of the House of the Bride testifies to the formidable hydraulic skills of the Arab agronomers, as to raise water to such a height it was necessary to tap the Darro and then hollow out the centre of the hill so that water could be raised by a system of interlocking paternosters. Endless chains working buckets, or perhaps water skins, brought the water up halfway, where it decanted into a cistern whence it was carried to the surface by a second chain.[37] Where once a hill stood smothered in smiling orchards, today an exhausted soil can barely produce the nourishment to sustain a clump of stunted olive trees. The Alcázar Genil on the outskirts of Granada was another such *hortus*, with a huge pool measuring 121 x 28 metres for the irrigation of a very large area, now all built over in the last ten years, including even the pool in which the architecture of the little palace was reflected. The pool was used for aquatic spectacles, a form of entertainment popular with Moorish kings.

Rules for the management of such estates are given by Ibn Luyūn (681/1282-750/1349), the Andalusī Varro, in his poem on agriculture.[38] This is a metric treatise dealing with such practical matters as what the Romans called *cognitio fundi*, the natural situation of the villa, its soil and climate; *instrumenta*, the tools, fertilisers, etc.; *res quibus arva coluntur*, the different operations that require doing and the crops that form the object of such operations; and, lastly, *tempora*, the seasons at which these operations are to be performed. Of the 157 sections into which the poem is divided no fewer than 70 deal with horticulture. From Ibn Luyūn various quondam features of the Generalife, like the cistern, and others still extant, like the Water Stairway (Escalera de Agua), can be identified, making up a productive villa, as far removed in function as in appearance from the Romantic garden that occupies the site today. As a villa, its courtyard is organised along quadripartite lines but with the emphasis on perspective. (Cf. Ibn Luyūn, sect. 157, "And let its length exceed its breadth so that the gaze may roam freely", something that could not happen with a normal courtyard where space was constricted by the urban location.) Of its planting, Navagiero refers only to myrtle and (dwarf) orange trees, the same as in the Court of Comares.[39]

In Almería, which formed part of the sultanate of Granada, the term for a villa was *burj*; in Córdoba it was *munya*; but in Granada *manjāra* ("orchard") was common. The word survives in local toponyms, e.g., Almanjayara on the outskirts of the city, an area where till recently there were huge orchards. Ibn al-Khaṭīb, in the second of our extensive quotations from his *oeuvre*, distinguishes between garden, vineyard and orchard; visibly, they could be distinguished, but a *munya* embraced all three. Royal properties boasted poetic or hyperbolic appellations, like the name of some constellation. In North Africa a *villa urbana* is *riyāḍ* (gardens), pointing thereby to its distinguishing characteristic. In Granada the term *carmen* (*karma*: vine; *karm* vineyard) is still used for a modest *villa urbana*, the grapevine being the only productive plant whose culture was economically feasible under such restricted conditions.

The numerous royal demesnes in and around the capital to which Ibn al-Khaṭīb refers were all *horti*, as were the country houses noblemen had on their estates outside the city, to which they retreated during the summer. Typical was the royal estate of the Generalife; its extensive lands afforded pasturage for the royal herds, both ovine and bovine. Properly understood, the relationship between the Alhambra and the Generalife is that between a manor house and the home farm. The Alhambra was, as already observed, a city, and the urban setting accounts for the Court of Comares in the shape of a *domus urbana*. The so-called Court is really an independent palace and as the seat of government rejoices in a *majlis* (reception hall) located in the tower that gives the palace its name. This is a courtyard house with central pool. In urban architecture, pools are axial, placid and ample, not just to reflect the two porticoed sides but to cool the surrounding apartments during the summer. A town house differs from a villa in having no garden, only a paved surface relieved by shrubbery and with a pool occupying the centre of the court. Domestic courtyards are described by Navagiero as adorned with "fountains, myrtles and trees, and in some there are large and beautiful fountains."[40]

Most pools were rectangular, although a lobulated one in the Court of Machuca in the Alhambra recalls comparable features in Persia; but Spanish pools never attained to the Baroque exuberance of curvilinear pools in Persia or India. The pebble mosaic surrounding many pools today is unlikely to be original; excavated examples are framed in terracotta tiles with ceramic inserts to form a pattern. The garden survived vestigially in courtyards as marginal strips of greenery with climbing plants, particularly jasmine, although myrtle hedges may have flanked the pool where space allowed. Both in the Courtyard of Comares and the Generalife Navagiero[41] remarked the presence of orange trees as well as myrtle bushes, and Münzer, who visited the Alhambra on October 23, 1494, saw "indescribable palaces, floored with the whitest marble, most beautiful gardens adorned with lemons and myrtles, [equipped] with pools and marble benches off to the sides,"[42] which latter feature ties in with Roman precedent. The decorative marble borders of these beds can still be seen in the Alhambra Museum (now redesignated Museo Nacional de Arte Hispanomusulmán and awaiting transfer to purpose-built accommodation in the Generalife). Fountains, often with conch-shaped bowls set in flat basins at one or both ends of the pool, lent animation to the courtyard. Sometimes, as in the Palace of Yūsuf III (built 810/1407-820/1417), called after the Count of Tendilla, governor of the Alhambra after the conquest, the overflow is ingeniously led around the margin of the tank by runnels, Madīnat al-Zahrā'-fashion, to fccd thc pool from thc oppositc cnd, so that both placidity and movement were present. In the Alhambra, water knows three states: horizontal (static), vertical (kinetic) and transitional, where the fountain overflow produces hemicyclical ripples as it discharges into the pool. Jets were flag-shaped, unlike today, and bowls were perforated so they could not overflow, the Arabs relishing the dry sound of water against stone. This policy is not followed in restoration: water against water and overflowing the sides like a curtain appeals to our sensibility more, just as the jets in the Patio de la Acequía (Court of the Watercourse) in the Generalife, although an innovation of the last century, are admitted by all to be an improvement. Navagiero refers with awe to an immense fountain in one of the lower courtyards of the Generalife, with a jet ten cubits high and shedding its droplets far and wide so that any who paused to contemplate it were refreshed.[43] Zoomorphic fountains offer another parallel with Persia: apart from the lions in the court of that name two others, now in the Partal, stood in the Māristān (hospital) formerly in the Albaicín. Horses' heads, probably of bronze, discharge into a pool in a miniature of a Hispano-Arab garden.[44] The miniatures in this manuscript are tentatively dated to the 8th/14th century, the period of the two examples quoted. Normally, fountains were of marble and resisted erosion, but an anomalous one of serpentine in the Alhambra museum is of importance as showing that the Alhambra was never for a moment static but in a constant state of flux and hence impossible to fix, let alone restore, at any one moment in history, unless we unwisely settled on 897/1492.

897/1492 is not just the year of final catastrophe but the date of a botanical revolution without parallel in European history before the 19th century. Columbus's chance discovery of America led to the introduction of exotica on an unprecedented scale, but botanical lists record the pre-Columban flora of the Iberian Peninsula. John Harvey[45] supplies classified lists derived from the works of Ibn Baṣṣāl (c. 473/1080) and Ibn al-ʿAwwām (*c.* 586/1190), whereas Sta. Eguarras organises the material alphabetically under the Arabic name. These two studies, both published in 1975, were preceded by García Gómez's magisterial "Sobre agricultura arábigo-andaluza."[46] Ibn Luyūn's work is based on an earlier manual of husbandry, *Kitāb al-qaṣd wa 'l-bayān* ("The Book of Thrift and Clarity") by Ibn Baṣṣāl, itself an abridgement of an earlier work by the same author. Ibn Baṣṣāl, though from Toledo, was a contemporary of al-Muʿtamid of Seville, for whom he designed a garden; it is not known whether this be the garden of which remains were discovered in the Alcázares Reales. Botany was a field in which Spanish Muslims excelled; the greatest of all Oriental botanists was Ibn al-Bayṭār (593/1197-646/1248) of Málaga, who botanised in the area of Seville. He was preceded by a Sevillian, Abū 'l-ʿAbbās b. al-Rūmiyya (558/1163-636/1239), whose mother was evidently Christian. There was also the latter's colleague, ʿAbd Allāh b. Ṣāliḥ. Ibn ʿAwwām, already mentioned, was a farmer from the same region. Such lists were drawn up with horticultural or pharmaceutical intent; an exception was al-Ḥimyarī's list of floral metaphors in Arabic poetry, *Al-Badīʿ fī waṣf al-rabīʿ* ("Novelties in Description of the Spring"), which is a compilation of the floral metaphors most frequently encountered in Hispano-Arabic poetry.[47]

The reason for the demise of the Hispano-Arab garden is a hypothesis poised midway between demography and aesthetics. If the thesis advanced here be correct, that the art of garden design is but an extension of the science of agriculture, on which it remains dependent, then the expulsion of the Moriscos would have killed off the tradition of Islamic gardening in Spain even had the conquest of Granada not coincided with changes in fashion prompted by the Renaissance. The Renaissance viewed gardens as supplementary to architecture, whereas Muslims have tended to view the palace as subordinate to the garden. No synthesis was possible between opposites so diametrical, besides which patronising Islamic art in any form would have rendered a person suspect in the eyes of the Inquisition. The manuals of husbandry were all in Arabic at a time when the mere possession of a page of Arabic script was enough to incur a charge of apostasy. Estates were expropriated, and the villa system that had rendered Spain prosperous gave way to vast latifundias and overall mismanagement: within two centuries, deforestation and soil erosion produced an arid landscape where once a squirrel could have travelled from Gibraltar to the Pyrenees without ever having to dismount. Yet the Arabs left an indelible impression on the horticulture of Europe: besides the ubiquitous jasmine, which riots all over Spain in the spring, they introduced the pomegranate, the artichoke and the cultivation of the date palm and sugar cane, besides the precious thuja (Ar. *thuyya*) wood, all in addition to oranges, apricots and asparagus as well as the staple rice. Such a list shows how much our present diet owes to the Muslim conquerors of Spain.

Like Islamic architecture, Hispano-Arab garden design defies categorisation in Western terms: not only does it stand outside European chronology, when for eight centuries Spain belonged to an alien civilisation; conceptually, it does not belong either, for it is neither classical nor romantic. The Anglo-Chinois garden, eschewing the French linear style, eschewed likewise rational symmetry of thought. Islamic art was never under the spell of the fertile antitheses that inform European aesthetics, which may explain why gardens "resurrected" on Islamic sites so rarely satisfy: neither the classical parterres in the Alcázares Reales at Seville nor the Romantic garden hung on the terraces of the Generalife in the 19th century nor the trimmed box-edging Torres Balbás introduced in the Alhambra and the Generalife in any way represent, or even approximate to, what was there before.

[1] *Die Ausgrabungen der Samarra*, Hamburg, 1948, Vol. V, plate 16.

[2] Muslim, *Ṣaḥiḥ, Kitāb al-janna*, 6,807.

[3] *The Book of Ser Marco Polo*, trans. Henry Yule, London, 1903, I, 139-40.

[4] A. C. Kimmens, *Tales of Hashish*, New York, 1977, pp. 25-26.

[5] P. R. E. Willey, *The Castles of the Assassins*, London, 1963, pp. 204-26.

[6] In the *Zafarnāmeh*, Sharaf al-Dīn ʿAlī Yazdī cites a case almost as slavish: "Along the way [to Kish, i. e., Shahr-i Sabz] is a mountain approximately seven parasangs from Samarqand, and at the pass flows a river. When the mighty emperor [Timur] reached that mountain, since his realm-adorning mind never missed an opportunity to build something in any place that was worthy of a structure, he ordered a garden laid out there in such a way that the sweet waters of the river would flow through the garden in remembrance of the divine words 'beneath which rivers flow'." (*apud* Wheelan Thackston, *A Century of Princes: Sources on Timurid History and Art*, Cambridge (Mass.), 1989, p. 88). This garden, known as the Takht-i Qarāchār, may have been a paradisal mount, following Quranic antecedent. A pyramidal shape can be inferred both from the hierarchical arrangement of the eight concentric heavens of Muslim eschatology and from the reiterated phrase always used in the Quran in conjunction with the word *jannāt, tajrī min taḥtihā 'l-anhār* ("with rivers flowing underneath them"), which would seem to indicate gardens cooled by subterranean streams. Without consulting Yazdī's text, we have taken the liberty of emending Professor Thackston's transliteration. "Qaracha" is obviously Qarāchār, a cousin of Chenghiz Khan and grandfather of Timur, in whose honour it is clear from the text that the garden was created.

[7] Francisco Prieto-Moreno, in Luis Seco de Lucena and Francisco Prieto-Moreno, *La Alhambra. El Generalife*, Madrid, 1980, p. 72.

[8] Navagiero, 5th letter, *apud* Francisco Javier Simonet, *Descripción del reino de Granada*, Madrid, 1872, p. 255. Navagiero's letters were published along with his collected works in Padua in 1718 with the title *Andreae Naugerii patricii Veneti, oratoris et poetae clarissimi opera omnia*.

[9] *Al-Lamḥa 'l-badriyya fī 'l-dawla 'l-Naṣriyya*, Cairo, 1347/1927, p. 14.

[10] *Apud* Ibn Khāqān, *Qalāʾid al-ʿiqyān fī maḥāsin al-aʿyān*, ed. Muḥammad al-ʿInnābī, Tunis, 1966, p. 55.

[11] Ibn Khāqān, *op.cit.*, p. 11.

[12] *Ibid.*, p. 174.

[13] The Quranic *firdaws* is a loan-word. Those who derive it from Greek, *via* the Arabic plural, *farādis*, are almost certainly mistaken, as the word could easily have entered Arabic directly from Old Persian. See Arthur Jeffery, *The Foreign Vocabulary of the Quran*, Baroda, 1938, pp. 223-24. In the Quran the word appears first genitively (*Jannāt al-Firdaws*), then absolutely (*al-Firdaws*). It is sometimes unclear whether Quranic terms referring to Paradise be synonymous or indicate different levels of glory. On this, commentators and traditionists are at variance, some making *al-Firdaws* out to be the topmost level whilst others reserve this honour for the Garden of Eden (*Jannāt ʿAdn*, the phrase (*Gann Eden*) used in Genesis (2:15)), consigning al-Firdaws to the second level. See Ṭabarī's *tafsīr* on 17:107.

[14] See Ghassān Sbāno, *Taʾrīkh Dimashq al-qadīm*, Damascus, 1984, p. 232.

[15] *Apud* K. A. C. Creswell, *Early Muslim Architecture*, New York, 1979, Vol. I, pt. II, p. 537. Creswell also quotes two instances of the use of the word *ḥayr*, in Samarrāʾ and Baghdad, with the clear meaning of game preserve; although the Baghdad example may have been a zoological, not a hunting, park.

[16] *La poésie andalouse en arabe classique au XI siècle*, Paris, 1953, pp. 128-29.

[17] *Ibid.*, p. 129.

[18] *Dīwān*, Cairo, 1375/1956, *qaṣīda* in *ḥāʾ*, v. 15, p. 206.

[19] *Ibid.*, *qaṣīda* in *qāf*, v. 7, p. 172.

[20] *Ibid.*, v. 3, p. 171.

[21] This garden and another similar alongside were excavated by the late Félix Hernández Giménez. Although D. Félix did not live to publish his plan and report of the excavations, a plan by Basilio Pavón Maldonado appeared in *Al-Andalus*, 43, 1968, p. 21 ("Influjos occidentales en el arte del califato de Córdoba", pp. 205-20).

[22] Caro's description is quoted in an earlier study by the present writer, "The Islamic Garden in Spain", in *The Islamic Garden*, ed. R. Ettinghausen and E. MacDougal, Washington (DC),

1976, pp. 87-105, in which the writer expanded on an earlier paper on the subject, "The Hispano-Arab Garden: its Philosophy and Function", *Bulletin of the School of Oriental and African Studies*, 31, 1968, pp. 237-48, which was a translation from the Spanish, "Notas sobre la jardinería árabe en la España musulmana", *Miscelánea de Estudios Arabes y Hebraicos*, 14-15, 1965-66, pp. 75-87.

23 "Patios de Crucero", *Al-Andalus*, 23, 1958, pp. 171-92. See particularly p. 177.

24 See *Collections des voyages des souverains des Pays-Bas*, ed. M. Gachard, Brussels, 1876, I, 206.

25 The derivation usually given for "Generalife", from *jannat al-ʿarīf*, is clearly impossible, because though *t* relaxes to *d* it cannot produce *r*, whereas *nūn* in final position yields *a*, *n* or *r*. The name comes from the plural, *jinān al-ʿarīf*, "the gardens of the overseer (or architect)". This is the form given by Alonso de Castillo, and is almost certainly a colloquial usage, since Ibn al-Khaṭīb uses the singular. It would make sense for the Spanish to come from a colloquial rather than classical usage.

26 See, for example, *Al-Lamḥa*, p. 14, and *Kitāb nubdhat al-ʿaṣr fī akhbār mulūk Banī Naṣr aw taslīm Gharnāṭa wa nuzūḥ al-Andalusiyyīn ilā 'l-Maghrib*, an anonymous chronicle of the fall of Granada edited by Alfredo Bustani and translated by Carlos Quirós under the title *Fragmento de la época sobre noticias de los Reyes Nazaritas o capitulación de Granada y emigración de los andaluces a Marruecos*, Larache (Morocco), 1940, Ar. text, pp. 3, 41, 42.

27 "In it [the Patio de la Acequía] there is a gallery, outside which there grow myrtles so tall as to reach, or almost reach, level with the balconies, so uniformly trimmed and so dense as to appear not treetops but a level, green meadow. These myrtles are planted the whole length of the gallery, some six to eight paces off, and in the vacant space so left innumerable rabbits are visible through the undergrowth, gleaming and presenting a beautiful picture." *Apud* Simonet, *op.cit.*, pp. 239-40. Navagiero is referring to a screen of arches introduced by the Christians; before the arches were inserted the scene he describes would have been visible only from the *mirador*.

28 *Al-Lamḥa, loc. cit.*

29 From the *Historia eclesiástica, principios y progresos de la ciudad y religión católica de Granada* of Francisco Bermúdez de Pedraza, published Granada, 1638. *Apud* Simonet, *op. cit.* p. 269.

30 *Miʿyār al-ikhtibār fī dhikr al-maʿāhid wa 'l-diyār* apud *Mushāhadāt Lisān al-Dīn b. al-Khaṭīb fī bilād al-Maghrib wa 'l-Andalus*, a collection of Ibn al-Khaṭīb's epistles ed. Aḥmad Mukhtār al-ʿAbbādī, Alexandria, 1958, pp. 90-91. Dr. ʿAbbādī's text is defective: for *quṣāt* read *ʿuṣāt* (rebels). "And like the sky of the world": the simile is from the Quran (67:5); white towers peeping out of the verdure bring to mind the famous Quranic metaphor. "... as to surpass": this refers to the colour of the sky at dawn and sunset; Granada is famed for the beauty of its sunsets. Ibn al-Khaṭīb is not exaggerating; the Spanish Muslims wore very colourful garments.

31 *Al-Lamḥa*, pp. 14-15. "Unit": the *marjiʿ ʿamalī* is a unit of agrarian measurement equivalent to eight cubits square, applied to cultivable land for fiscal purposes. By "city boundaries" Ibn al-Khaṭīb means the walls of the urban perimeter, not those of the *madīna*. The reference to pulpits is indicative of size; a mosque where a preacher (*khaṭīb*) is installed only exists where there is a sizeable population. The other liturgical reference is to *duʿāʾ* (petitionary prayer), which follows the *ṣalāt* (ritual prayer), when the worshipper raises his hands in token of supplication and repeats the response (Amen) after each petition made by the prayer-leader or preacher.

32 Münzer, *Viaje por España y Portugal. Reino de Granada*, Granada, 1987, p. 47. This is the second of two reprints of the Madrid edition of 1951 which both appeared in the same year, with different pagination.The hamlets to which he refers would be *qarya*s or *munya*s.

33 *Ibid*, p. 46.

34 Farm or estate; the meaning overlaps with *fundus*. To complicate matters further, all the farms in Latium were called *horti*, not *fundi*, yet they cannot all have been fruit gardens. Since the farms in the vicinity of Rome were known as *horti*, this implies that the *horti* within the city may have been no less utilitarian, at least in part.

35 A ruined *qarya* garden in the Alpujarras has been studied by Patrice Cressier. See "Un jardin d'agrément 'chrétien' dans une campagne de tradition morisque: le *cortijo* de Guarros (Almería, Espagne)", *Flaran* 9, Jardins et vergers en Europe occidentale (VIIIe- XVIIIe siècles), 1987, pp. 231-37.

[36] *Apud* Simonet, *op. cit.*, p. 269.

[37] Torres Balbás ("Dār al-ʿArūsa y las ruinas de palacios y albercas granadinos situados por encima del Generalife", *Al-Andalus*, 13, 1949, pp. 185-203) does not address the question of hydraulics, although his plan shows the trough in which a waterwheel worked and which evidently formed part of the system. Situated on the north side of the palace, this wheel must have been intended to irrigate the palace gardens.

[38] *Ibn Luyūn: tratado de agricultura*, ed. and trans. Joaquina Eguarras Ibáñez, Granada, 1965, pp. 171-72. Spanish trans. p. 254.

[39] Andrea Navagiero, 5th letter, *apud* Simonet, *op. cit.*, p. 239.

[40] *Ibid.*, p. 245.

[41] *Ibid.*, p. 329.

[42] *Viaje*, p. 39.

[43] *Op. cit.*, p. 240.

[44] A.R. Nykl, *Historia de los amores de Bayād y Riyāḍ*, New York, 1941, p. 21.

[45] "Gardening and Plant Lists of Moorish Spain", *Garden History*, 3, 1975, pp. 10-22.

[46] *Al-Andalus*, 10, 1945, pp. 127-46.

[47] Ed. Henri Pérès, Rabat, 1940. John Harvey succeeded in convincing the present writer that al-Ḥimyarī's work has less value as a source than he formerly attributed to it. (See n. 21, *supra.*) I take the liberty of quoting Mr. Harvey's very interesting comments. "I rather wonder about accepting a list of floral metaphors in poetry as being a guide to the botany of gardens. Even in the straightforward realm of English prose, it is the 'literary' sources that are misleading and suspect, so far as the correct identification of species grown is concerned. Arabic, without vowels and with easily misunderstood diacritical points, gives rise to more ambiguities than the Roman alphabet, as well. I am far from under-rating the importance of poetry, but have found that poets do tend to run along certain tracks of well-trodden similes in regard to nature generally, birds, flowers, etc. I regard Ibn Baṣṣāl as an almost archival source, based on direct observation; Ibn al-ʿAwwām was more literary, so less likely to be precise." (personal communication dated March 24, 1987).

BIBLIOGRAPHY

Book of Ser Marco Polo, The, trans. Henry Yule, London, 1903.

Cressier, Patrice, "Un jardin d'agrément 'chrétien' dans une campagne de tradition morisque: le *cortijo* de Guarros (Almería, Espagne)", *Flaran* 9, Jardins et vergers en Europe occidentale (VIIIe- XVIIIe siècles), 1987, pp. 231-37.

Creswell, K. A. C., *Early Muslim Architecture*, New York, 1979.

Dickie, James, "Notas sobre la jardinería árabe en la España musulmana", *Miscelánea de Estudios Arabes y Hebraicos*, 14-15, 1965-66, pp. 75-87; translated into English as "The Hispano-Arab Garden: its Philosophy and Function", *Bulletin of the School of Oriental and African Studies*, 31, 1968, pp. 237-48.

——, "The Islamic Garden in Spain", in *The Islamic Garden*, ed. R. Ettinghausen and E. MacDougal, Washington (DC), 1976, pp. 87-105.

García Gómez, E., "Sobre agricultura arábigo-andaluza", *Al-Andalus*, 10, 1945, pp. 127-46.

Harvey, John, "Gardening and Plant Lists of Moorish Spain", *Garden History*, 3, 1975, pp. 10-22.

Herzfeld, E., *Die Ausgrabungen der Samarra*, Hamburg, 1948.

Al-Ḥimyarī, *Al-Badīʿ fī waṣf al-rabīʿ*, ed. Henri Pérès, Rabat, 1940.

Ibn K͟hāqān, *Qalāʾid al-ʿiqyān fī maḥāsin al-aʿyān*, ed. Muḥammad al-ʿInnābī, Tunis, 1966.

Ibn al-K͟haṭīb, *Al-Lamḥa 'l-badriyya fī 'l-dawla 'l-Naṣriyya*, Cairo, 1347/1927.

——, *Miʿyār al-ik͟htibār fī d͟hikr al-maʿāhid wa 'l-diyār* apud *Mus͟hāhadāt Lisān al-Dīn b. al-K͟haṭīb fī bilād al-Mag͟hrib wa 'l-Andalus*, ed. Aḥmad Muk͟htār al-ʿAbbādī, Alexandria, 1958.

Ibn Luyūn, *Tratado de agricultura*, ed. and trans. Joaquina Eguarras Ibáñez, Granada, 1965.

Ibn Zaydūn, *Dīwān*, Cairo, 1375/1956.

Jeffery, Arthur, *The Foreign Vocabulary of the Quran*, Baroda, 1938.

Kimmens, A. C., *Tales of Hashish*, New York, 1977.

Kitāb nubdhat al-ʿaṣr fī akhbār mulūk Banī Naṣr aw taslīm Gharnāṭa wa nuzūḥ al-Andalusiyyīn ilā 'l-Maghrib, ed. Alfredo Bustani, trans. Carlos Quirós under the title *Fragmento de la época sobre noticias de los Reyes Nazaritas o capitulación de Granada y emigración de los andaluces a Marruecos*, Larache (Morocco), 1940.

Lalaing, Antoine de, "Voyage de Philippe le Beau en Espagne, en 1501", in *Collection des voyages des souverains des Pays-Bas*, ed. M. Gachard, Brussels, 1876.

Münzer, Hieronymus, *Viaje por España y Portugal. Reino de Granada*, Granada, 1987.

Nykl, A. R., *Historia de los amores de Bayād y Riyāḍ*, New York, 1941.

Pavón Maldonado, Basilio, "Influjos occidentales en el arte del califato de Córdoba", *Al-Andalus*, 43, 1968, pp. 205-20.

Pérès, Henri, *La poésie andalouse en arabe classique au XI siècle*, Paris, 1953.

Sbāno, Ghassān, *Ta'rīkh Dimashq al-qadīm*, Damascus, 1984.

Seco de Lucena, Luis, and Francisco Prieto-Moreno, *La Alhambra. El Generalife*, Madrid, 1980.

Simonet, Francisco Javier, *Descripción del reino de Granada*, Madrid, 1872.

Thackston, Wheelan, *A Century of Princes: Sources on Timurid History and Art*, Cambridge (Mass.), 1989.

Torres Balbás, L., "Dār al-ʿArūsa y las ruinas de palacios y albercas granadinos situados por encima del Generalife", *Al-Andalus*, 13, 1949, pp. 185-97.

——, "Patios de Crucero", *Al-Andalus*, 23, 1958, pp. 171-92.

Willey, P. R. E., *The Castles of the Assassins*, London, 1963.

THE TRANSLATING ACTIVITY IN MEDIEVAL SPAIN

CHARLES BURNETT

I

In considering the translating activity in respect of Islamic Spain I shall mainly be looking at Islamic Spain from beyond its borders. Adventurers and scholars were attracted to al-Andalus because of the splendour of Islamic culture and the superiority of Arabic learning. The spoil of the Christian reconquest was not only silks and damask, but also valuable manuscripts. Refugees from Muslim-dominated areas and the intelligentsia who remained in cities reconquered by the Christians were able to impart to those who had been educated in Latin schools the scientific knowledge of a superior culture and to act as interpreters of Arabic texts. Important, too, were the Jewish communities in al-Andalus which absorbed much of Arabic scientific culture and remained largely undisturbed after the Christian reconquest.[1]

Translation, of course, had been taking place at all levels of society within Islamic Spain. The community was multilingual. The official language of the government and of higher education was the literary Arabic of the Quran. Occasionally the colloquial Arabic would be written down—for example, in the poetic form known as the *zajal*. However, the majority of the populace spoke a Romance language. This is apparent in another poetic form which originated in Spain—the *muwa<u>sh</u><u>sh</u>aḥ*—in which the refrain (*<u>kh</u>arja*) is sometimes in a Romance dialect.[2] This refrain is usually sung by a girl: it is significant that the vernacular should be regarded as appropriate to wives and daughters. Another vernacular was the dialect (or rather, dialects) of the Berbers who had come across the Straits of Gibraltar in large numbers with their Arabic leaders. Berber words occur in surprising places, such as in the names of one set of the sixteen figures used in the form of divination called "geomancy", and in the earliest European names for the "Arabic" numerals.[3] Beside Arabic, Latin continued in use as the language of the Church.[4] Many educated Christians, however, adopted the literary language of the Muslims, and incurred disfavour for doing so from the more fanatical of their brethren. Finally the Jewish population still used Hebrew alongside Arabic. Having no special regard for the Arabic of the Quran, they wrote Arabic as they spoke it (while using the Hebrew script), so giving further evidence of the dialect of Arabic used in al-Andalus. The Christian, Jewish and Islamic societies were largely self-governing and had their own laws and judges. However, on many occasions there must have been a need for interpreters. At least one judge for the Christian community in Córdoba also served as their interpreter.[5]

This multilingual society was inherited by the Christian rulers of Spain. One can see this by the number of legal documents in which both Arabic and Latin occur, the Arabic often being a translation or summary of the Latin text for the benefit of an Arabic-speaking plaintiff or defendant.[6] Interpreters would have been present at the proceedings. Sometimes they translated the Latin into the Romance vernacular which would have been understood by both parties. For example, at the end of a Latin act issued by the archbishop of Toledo in 1178, there is a note in Arabic indicating that "Jalid ben Solaiman ben Gasan ben Servando" and "Domingo Salwat" had heard the archdeacon repeat in "Roman" the text of the act.[7] The Muslim community (Mudejars) would continue to use Arabic script even when the Romance language became their mother tongue, so producing the literature known as *aljamía*.

Under Islamic domination several Latin texts were translated into Arabic, including a book on agriculture by Columella, a history by Orosius, a "Roman book" on astrology, and (apparently) Isidore's *Etymologies*.[8] Christians were responsible for making some of these translations, and a large number of works were translated into Arabic specifically for the 'Arabicised' element of the Christian community (though not exclusively, for Muslim scholars also refer to these texts). At least three versions of the Psalms were made, including a verse translation completed by Ḥafṣ al-Qūṭī in 276/889, which was specifically meant to replace the inelegant prose version in circulation at the time. A church calendar was translated and combined with a distinctly Arabic division of the year based on the rising of twenty-eight constellations known as the "lunar mansions", resulting in the *Calendar of Córdoba* (357/967).[9] Arabicised Christians (called Mozarabs by other Christians) continued to use Arabic under Christian domination and even into the 14th century. This is evident from the number of Latin manuscripts, mainly of Christian content, with Arabic translations or glosses in them. The well-known Arabic-Latin/Latin-Arabic Leiden glossary was most likely written to enable a community whose first literary language was Arabic to understand the Latin rite of the Roman church.[10]

Occasionally Arabic glosses appear in scientific and philosophical works; for example, in a copy of the medical encyclopaedia of Oribasius which was in the cathedral library of Chartres in the Middle Ages,[11] and an 11th-century manuscript of Boethius's *On Arithmetic* in the monastery of Ripoll in Catalonia.[12] This is significant, for Boethius's work was the most advanced text on arithmetic before the advent of Arabic learning, and Ripoll was the earliest centre outside al-Andalus to show the influence of this learning.[13] The Mozarab (as he must have been) who wrote Arabic equivalents to Boethius's definitions of the five species of inequality in that Ripoll manuscript was familiar with the technical terms of Arabic mathematics. It was men such as these who would have been conduits through which Arabic culture reached the rest of Europe. The transmission of this culture and the information that it imparted concerning Islamic Spain will be the focus of our attention in this article.

II

Before the days of mass education and universal literacy the ability to read and the possession of magical powers often merged in the popular imagination. If the books were not directly concerned with the truths of religion, then the gift of understanding them was thought to be due to the inspiration of demons. Scholars who dealt with Islamic science were regarded with particular suspicion. Gerbert d'Aurillac, one of the first Latin scholars to enquire about Arabic science, according to a story current in the early 13th century, "was the best necromancer in France, whom the demons of the air readily obeyed in all that he required of them by day and night, because of the great sacrifices he offered them."[14] These demons taught him how to use an astrolabe.

But to a certain extent the scholars themselves fitted this popular image. In our first encounters with the transmission of Arabic science we find the exact sciences inextricably mixed up with astrology and magic and their transmission hedged with language redolent of a mystery religion. The same scholar would see nothing incongruous in solving a quadratic equation one moment and predicting from the stars whether a man might be killed by falling masonry the next: he might even make a talisman to prevent such a contingency. Thus Adelard of Bath, the early 12th-century English Arabist, translated the raw materials of mathematics—Euclid's *Elements* and al-Khwārizmī's astronomical tables—and also provided versions of an introduction to astrology, a set of astrological aphorisms and a work on making talismans which includes prayers to mice, bidding them to leave a property, and a method for driving scorpions out of his city of Bath.[15]

When we turn to the situation in al-Andalus we find scholars associated with both the exact sciences and magic. One of these was Adelard's main authority for the astrolabe, Maslama al-Majrīṭī (ca. 400/1000). It was his revision of the tables of al-Khwārizmī for the meridian of Córdoba that Adelard had translated, and his text on the astrolabe on whose Latin translation Adelard based his own work *On how to use the Astrolabe*. Yet, from an early date, a comprehensive text on magic (*Ghāyat al-ḥakīm*) and another on alchemy (*Ruṭbat al-ḥakīm*) were ascribed to Maslama. Moreover Maslama introduced to al-Andalus the *Letters of the Brethren of Purity* which are heavily imbued with neo-Platonic and Hermetic religio-philosophical ideas, and imply a kind of intellectual brotherhood.[16]

The earliest translations from Arabic are in the fields of divination and astrology and those parts of mathematics which prepare the student for these subjects, such as geometry and astronomy. Western visitors to Muslim towns may have come across crude versions of these techniques. Michael Scot refers to skilled women in the streets and alleys of Tunis who invite newly arrived merchants to ask about their situation, their families and the outcome of their business dealings.[17] Adelard of Bath and his "nephew" had spent a few days with an old sorceress (*anus praestigiosa*) learning how to perform incantations.[18] Others may have been shown or offered an astrolabe. If the "Carolingian" astrolabe described by Destombes is genuine, the artefact may have paved the way for the Latin texts describing its construction and use.[19]

Divinatory techniques could have been picked up from Arabs by example rather than through texts. For instance, one could learn how to cast lines of dots randomly on the ground and join them together in pairs in order to form the figures used in "the science of the sand", which became known by the literary Latin term "geomancy".[20] Or one could learn how to turn the letters of the names of each of two protagonists in a battle or a contest into numbers, to determine which of them would win.[21] Or one could learn how to find out hidden things or predict the future by observing various marks on the shoulder-blade of a sheep which had been slaughtered and boiled until the flesh had fallen from the bone.[22] Most of these techniques could be learnt with the aid of a good memory or, at most, a sheet of parchment giving the names and meanings of the sixteen geomantic figures, a list of the number-letter equivalents, or a plan of the shoulder-blade with the significations of each of its areas written in.

At some stage, however, more detailed explanations were written down. Our earliest Latin text containing information from Arabic sources happens to be of this kind. It was written in the late 10th century, and is known variously as *Liber Alchandrei, Mathematica Alhandrei summi astrologi*, and *Mathematica Alexandri summi astrologi*—all these names implying some connection with Alexander the Great of Macedon.[23] A large part of this text consists of "interrogations" posed by the client and "judgements" given by the astrologer on matters of every-day concern, such as marriage, business dealings, the sex of one's unborn child and the outcome of an illness. The judgement is found by applying to the celestial "places" a number derived from the names of the client and of his mother. This form of judgement is distinctly Arabic, and survives to this day in North Africa.[24] The Arabic origin of the text is made explicit by references to "Saraceni" and "the Arabic language". The text includes the earliest Latin form of twenty-eight lunar mansions whose appearance in the *Calendar of Córdoba* has already been mentioned. In fact, the two texts may be contemporary. The *Liber Alchandrei* recalls the polyglot atmosphere of the capital of al-Andalus, for it includes, alongside Arabic names for the zodiac signs and the planets, Hebrew names for the same terms and for the letters in which the names of the client and his mother must be written, and a letter of Petosiris to Nechepso which was probably translated from Greek in the late Classical period and part of the surviving Latin culture in Spain.

The earliest manuscript of the *Liber Alchandrei* closes with several circular diagrams which show the names of the twenty-eight lunar mansions, their constellations and the number-letter equivalents used in making astrological judgements.[25] The numbers here are written in Roman numerals, but in an Italian manuscript of medical works similar circular diagrams are filled with the forms of Arabic numerals which are found on the counters of the abacus associated with Gerbert d'Aurillac.[26] Richard Lemay has pointed out that Arabic numerals (which technically should be called "Indian" numerals, and were so called by the Arabs) were used in very restricted contexts in the Islamic world in the Middle Ages. One of these contexts was precisely the form of divination in which numbers were substituted for letters.[27] The Western equivalents of the "Indian" numerals are the *g̲h̲ubār* ("dust") numerals which appear to have originated in Spain since the forms of 5, 6, and 8 are derivable from Visigothic script. Ibn K̲h̲aldūn in the 8th/14th century states that the "*g̲h̲ubār* letters" are used for the *zā'iraja*, or magical circle made up of all kinds of letters and numbers.[28] There is, on the other hand, no evidence that Arabic merchants or administrators in Spain made use of *g̲h̲ubār* numerals.[29] It is possible that Gerbert, or one of his followers, got the idea of marking the abacus counters with Arabic numerals from a magical or divinatory context in which numbers were used as ciphers, as they are in the Latin medical manuscript.

The earliest Latin texts on the abacus do not depend on Arabic texts, but the names of the nine different counters which represented the nine digits appear to be Arabic and Berber words for the numerals in distorted forms which suggest an oral transmission.[30] This Gerbertian abacus was popular throughout Western Europe during the 11th and early 12th century. It was a teaching tool, enabling students to see how numbers functioned. It was impractical as a calculating instrument for real-life transactions, and was probably never used as such. It was the means, however, by which many European scholars first became aware of Arabic *g̲h̲ubār* numerals and some of their Arabic names, and, at least for the Abbot of Malmesbury, the instrument itself had been "snatched from the Saracens".[31]

Towards the middle of the 6th/12th century the abacus began to be replaced by a method of calculation with Arabic numerals not marked on counters but written directly on a board thinly covered with sand, or on parchment. This was the algorism, in which the same Arabic *g̲h̲ubār* numerals were used, and which had been taken, along with the method of calculation, from a single text by al-K̲h̲wārizmī—his *On Indian Calculation*.[32] Arabic numerals did not cease to have a magical aura; in fact they continued for some centuries to be regarded as a secret code and edicts proscribing their use were promulgated in several cities.[33]

The introduction of the algorism is symptomatic of the change in the process of transmission of Arabic science in the 6th/12th century. The transmission acquires a firm literary basis. This is hinted at in the injunction of Ibn ʿAbdūn, the jurist writing in Seville in the early years of the century, who forbids the selling of books to Jews and Christians, because they translate them and pass them off as their own compositions.[34]

III

One of the earliest of these translators was Hugo of Santalla working in the 12th century in Aragon. He dedicated all the works that have dedications to Michael, bishop of Tarazona from the time of its reconquest (513/1119) until 1151. A near Arabic neighbour of bishop Michael was the last of the Banū Hūd dynasty of Saragossa, Sayf al-Dawla. After the fall of Saragossa to the Christians in 512/1118 the Banū Hūd took up residence in Rueda de Jalón, some 55 kilometres from Tarazona. Sayf al-Dawla himself established quite friendly relations with the king of Aragon, Alfonso VII, whose coronation as Emperor he attended. In 534/1140 or 535/1141 he was obliged to relinquish Rueda de Jalón in exchange for some lands near Toledo.[35] What is interesting is that he had a library from which bishop Michael was able to choose some works for Hugo to translate.[36]

The Banū Hūd had a reputation for their patronage of learning. Both the botanist Ibn Biklari<u>sh</u> and the philosopher Ibn Bājja (Avempace) were in Saragossa. Two members of the dynasty themselves achieved reputations for their remarkable mathematical talents: Aḥmad al-Muqtadir bi-llāh (who ruled from 438/1046 to 474/1081) and his son Yūsuf al-Muʾtaman b. Hūd (474/1081-478/1085).[37] The latter composed a truly comprehensive book on geometry known as "The Perfection" (*Al-Istikmāl*), which drew on a large number of sources, including Euclid's *Elements* and *Data,* the *Spherics* of Theodosius and Menelaus, the *Conics* of Apollonius, Archimedes' *On the Sphere and Cylinder*, Eutocius's commentary on this work, <u>Th</u>ābit b. Qurra's treatise on amicable numbers and Ibn al-Hay<u>th</u>am's *Optics*. Probably during the reign of Aḥmad al-Muqtadir bi-llāh, whose renown extended to astronomy and philosophy, a pupil of Maslama al-Majrīṭī called al-Kirmānī (died 457/1065) introduced the *Letters of the Brethren of Purity* into Saragossa.[38] Perhaps he too brought Maslama's revision of the tables of al-<u>Kh</u>wārizmī from Córdoba to Saragossa, for the lunar visibility tables that survive in Latin only have been recomputed for a latitude which is that of Saragossa.[39]

Some idea of which texts remained in the library of the Banū Hūd when they moved to Rueda de Jalón can be gauged from the evidence of Hugo's translations. In only one preface does he mention this library (*armarium Rotense*), but that is precisely his preface to a commentary on the tables of al-Khwārizmī which must have been known in Saragossa (it was also translated by Abraham b. Ezra, a Jewish scholar from neighbouring Tudela).[40] Hugo goes on to write that the manuscript was found "among the more secret depths of the library" (*inter secretiora bibliotece penetralia*). This suggests a part of the library specially designated for the non-Muslim sciences and magic. One hundred years later the French bibliophile, Richard of Fournival, "kept his 'secret texts' (*tractatus secreti*) on astrology, alchemy, and magic in a separate room to which, he claims, only he had access".[41] Hugo certainly wishes to foster the impression that he is passing on secret knowledge which must not be divulged to other than worthy individuals.

Like his predecessor in Southern Italy, the translator Constantine of Africa, Hugo subsumes his Arabic author's preface into his own preface, so that it is sometimes difficult to distinguish the words of his source from his own words, where the Arabic origin is unavailable for comparison.[42] But it is apparent that he is in agreement with the tone of his Arabic authors. In the preface to a large book on horoscopic astrology Hugo, following his source, lists some 125 astrological books, whose gist is preserved in two comprehensive volumes. These, we read, "were placed in the hands of a certain wise and most dependable man (for no access to them was allowed to any unworthy or foolish person); thus neither the translation of these books nor their teaching is further granted either to us or to anyone of this generation except to one who is endowed with complete honesty and philosophical understanding".[43] These are the books whose secret the Arabic author unlocks and Hugo, in turn, reveals to the Latin world.

In his preface to Pseudo-Ptolemy's *Centiloquium* (astrological aphorisms), Hugo exhorts Michael "not to commit the secrets of such wisdom (*tante sapiencie archana*) into the hands of any unworthy individual, or to allow anyone to share in the secrets who rejoices in the number of his books rather than delights in their teaching".[44] Again, in another preface, he says he has tried to find amongst the Arabs the four species of divination mentioned (and, incidentally, condemned) by Isidore of Seville: divination respectively by earth, water, air and fire. In encountering the Arabic "science of the sand" he thought he had discovered Isidore's geomancy ("earth-divination"), and he promises to find and to translate texts on the the other "mancies".[45] But secrets could also be found in the shoulder-blades of sheep for (as we read in Hugo's preface to one of his two translations of an Arabic text on scapulimancy—a preface which incorporates Arabic material) "the rain brings down the secret (*archanum*) of God's teaching and an interior power into the very plants and herbs of the earth, like the manna of God's own grace and wisdom, and this secret is transferred to the shoulder-blades of the sheep eating this grass".[46]

Hugo's interest in secrets and "mancies" suggests more than idle curiosity; he seems to believe (or at least acquiesce to beliefs stated in his sources) in the secret society of an intellectual élite . This belief is most fully stated in the preface to the text on geomancy where we read:

> God the Creator of things, who founded everything as a new creation without an exemplar, deciding in his mind about the future state of things before their actual coming-into-being, distributes to each man as He wishes what he thinks it right to bestow upon the rational creature from the treasury of His whole being. Hence all created beings, whether rational or irrational or inanimate, show the same obedience to Him, and, although in their lives they have descended to the rank of mortal beings, they venerate Him as a result of unity alone. Holding all things in the form of images before they come into being, He pours a kind of intuitive and intellectual notion of them into the secret place [*arcanum*] of men's hearts. Eventually such a state of creation comes into being that God is able to associate by a kind of bond the foremost and most venerable teachers ... so that all discord having been put aside, the rational or "positive justice" can join them together through an equable bond.[47]

The high-flown language is difficult to follow, but we have here a picture of a special bond between men who have been privileged to receive God's gift of intuitive knowledge. This bond which produces a state of peace in human society is parallel to the bonds which govern and preserve the universe. It is to this latter topic that Hugo's most interesting translation is devoted. This is the *Secret of Creation* of Pseudo-Apollonius, which purports to be Hermes Trismegistus's account of God's creation of the world, and of the origins of minerals, plants, animals and men. Throughout the work there is an emphasis on the idea of an underlying unity in nature and of bonds connecting every level of creation. For all things derive from one substance and one seed. This philosophy is epitomised in the document known as the Emerald Tablet which became the credo of the alchemists and of which the earliest known Latin version is within Hugo's translation of The *Secret of Creation*.[48]

Hugo's text is closest to an Arabic manuscript copied in 485/1092, another Arabic copy of which is still in Spain.[49] We have no independent Arabic testimony that the *Secret of Creation* was in the library of the Banū Hūd, but it is worth noting that the text comes from the same milieu and shares some of the same Hermetic and neo-Platonic sources as the *Letters of the Brethren of Purity* which *were* in Saragossa.[50] In turn, we have no translation of the *Letters* attributed to Hugo. However, there are anonymous Latin translations of at least two of these letters,[51] and further evidence may eventually be found of their influence on Latin scholars in the North of Spain.

IV

Not far from Tarazona was Tudela on the river Ebro. This town had important Jewish and Muslim communities and was the home of the Jewish scholars Abraham b. Ezra (1086-1164) and Judah Halevi (d. 1141).[52] The translators Hermann of Carinthia and Robert of Ketton are said to have been working in the region of the Ebro in 1141,[53] and could well have been in Tudela; Robert was later canon of the church there. Hermann knew several of the same sources as Hugo, and perhaps also had access to the library of the Banū Hūd. For he knows the works of Theodosius and Archimedes, and made versions of Euclid's *Elements* and al-Khwārizmī's astronomical tables, all of which were apparently in the Banū Hūd's possession. In his major original work, the cosmogony called *On the Essences* (*De essentiis*), Hermann cites the Emerald Tablet from the *Secret of Creation* (he is the only Latin scholar besides Hugo who appears to know the latter work), and refers to several other Hermetic works.[54] However, in the preface to *On the Essences*, which is addressed to Robert, he makes a significant contrast between the "secrets" (*secreta*) and the "public schools". Robert and he have been labouring together night and day on the "intimate treasures of the Arabs" (*intimi Arabum thesauri*) in the "inner sanctuaries of Minerva" (*adyta Minerve*), and Hermann is now considering whether it is appropriate to make the fruits of their research public. He is afraid of committing the crime of Numenius, who divulged the Eleusinian mysteries and consequently saw the Eleusinian goddesses in a dream dressed as prostitutes available for use to all and sundry. In Hermann's case the Goddess Minerva reassures him—also in a dream—that *her* attributes are not diminished by being made freely available and should be given out liberally.[55]

Whether Hermann's decision to make public the secrets of Arabic science represents a change of policy from that of Hugo depends on how much trust we place in the literary style adopted in these translators' prefaces. It is a fact that Hugo's translations had a very limited diffusion. Hermann and Robert, on the other hand, advertised their work to the highest European authorities of the time. Robert promises to Peter the Venerable, abbot of Cluny, who was responsible for promoting the Cluniac reform of the Christian church in Spain, "a celestial gift which embraces within itself the whole of science" —i.e., a work on astronomy, whereas Hermann sent one of his translations (that of Ptolemy's *Planisphere*) to Thierry of Chartres, the foremost educator in France of the second quarter of the 12th century. In the preface to this translation Hermann sketches a history of astronomy, refers to the basic textbooks on the subject, and advertises three of his own works, and one of Robert's.[56] Thierry was engaged in compiling an annotated "library" of texts on the seven liberal arts, and included two translations from Arabic, which may be in Robert and Hermann's versions.[57]

A decade or two after Robert and Hermann's project to translate and send to France texts on geometry and astronomy, an even more comprehensive programme of translations was planned and undertaken, this time in Toledo. The motive force for this programme seems to have been an archdeacon resident in Toledo called Dominicus Gundissalinus. Perhaps in reaction to the idea of a secret intellectual élite, Dominicus considers that it is no longer possible to be a sage (*sapiens*); one can only aspire to be proficient in certain sciences, or at least to know something about a few of them.[58] To facilitate this he describes each of the sciences in turn in his *On the Sciences*, drawing largely on the translation of al-Fārābī's *Classification of the Sciences* made by Gerard of Cremona.

It is reasonably certain now that Gerard of Cremona worked closely with Dominicus. He is probably to be identified with a "Girardus" described as a deacon in a document of the Cathedral of Toledo of 11 March 1162, and as "Girardus called master" (*Girardus dictus magister*) in two later documents of the Cathedral (March 1174 and March 1176). All three documents are also signed by Dominicus.[59] Al- Fārābī's *Classification of the Sciences* provided a template for Gerard on which to pattern the programme of his own translations, several of which were used in turn by Dominicus when he adapted al-Fārābī's text into a comprehensive account of philosophy and its parts—*On the Division of Philosophy*—patterned on schemata developed by Thierry of Chartres and his pupils.[60] With Dominicus and Gerard of Cremona we see not only a high public profile given to translations from Arabic, but also an expansion of the range of texts into medicine and philosophy. Gerard translated several of Aristotle's works and some commentaries on Aristotle by Arabic authors or Greek commentators whose work had been translated into Arabic.[61] On the other hand, Dominicus and his associates Avendauth and Johannes Hispanus translated the works of Arab and Jewish scholars who had summarised and reinterpreted Aristotle's philosophy in the light of neo-Platonic trends—i.e., Ibn Sīnā, Ibn Gabirol and al-Ghazālī.[62]

The advertisements of Robert of Ketton and Hermann of Carinthia were clearly effective. John of Salisbury regarded the Arabs as being more advanced than the Latins in geometry and astronomy.[63] Toledo was the natural place where this Arabic learning could be found. Gerard of Cremona had been attracted to Toledo because of his desire for Ptolemy's *Almagest*, the 2nd-century A.D. textbook on astronomy. Another scholar, Daniel of Morley, tells a more detailed story about how he came to Toledo. He had at first left England to seek learning in Paris, but, disappointed by what he found there and hearing that "the learning of the Arabs" (*doctrina Arabum*), which consisted almost entirely of the scientific works he was interested in, was in vogue in Toledo, he hurried there, and was not disappointed. He recounts a lecture given by Gerard, on astrology.[64]

V

Gerard of Cremona died in 1187. At his death his pupils (*socii*) drew up a list of his many translations from Arabic, since he had been too humble to put his name to many of them.[65] These *socii* could have included Dominicus and Johannes Hispanus, for the former was still alive in 1181 (and there is no evidence that he died soon after this), and the latter lived until 1215.

The 7th/13th century witnessed a continuation of the translating activity. Two conspicuous elements about this activity should be noted: first, the transmission of the results of the last flowering of philosophy in Islamic Spain; and second, the rise of "official translation", i.e., translation as part of public policy, either to aggrandise the newly emerging Spanish nation, or to convert the Muslim.

To turn to the first of these: Under the Almohads there occurred an Indian summer for philosophy in Islamic Spain. This took the form of a burst of "fundamentalist" Aristotelianism unparalleled elsewhere in the Arabic word.[66] The central figure is Ibn Ṭufayl (d. 581/1185), the court physician of the Almohad leader in Córdoba and the composer of the philosophical novel *Ḥayy b. Yaqẓān*—the story of an orphan on a desert island who discovers the truths of philosophy and religion entirely by a process of deduction. Ibn Ṭufayl had introduced to the Almohad ruler the philosopher Ibn Rus͟hd (Averroes, d. 594/1198), and inspired al-Biṭrūjī (Alpetragius) to write his book on astronomy. This book, *On the Movements of the Heavens* (written ca. 600/1200), was a revolutionary attempt to replace Ptolemy's astronomical system with a model which was compatible with Aristotelian physics. Averroes in his turn undertook the most ambitious project ever conceived for interpreting Aristotle: three levels of commentaries for the whole of Aristotle's works, to which a commentary on Plato's *Republic* was added. These consisted of: a) summaries of the texts; b) paraphrases; and c) line by line exegeses.[67]

Andalusī Aristotelianism appears to have had little influence on subsequent Arabic scholarship. Its influence on Latin and Hebrew philosophy and science was, on the other hand, immense. It was in this intellectual climate at Córdoba that the philosophy of Maimonides (d. 600/1204) was formed. And within a few years of their composition the works of both al-Biṭrūjī and Ibn Rus͟hd were being translated into Latin and Hebrew. The first translations were made in Spain. Michael Scot translated *On the Movements of the Heavens* in Toledo in 1217, five years after the defeat of the Almohads in the battle of Las Navas de Tolosa. To Michael Scot are also attributed the earliest translations of Averroes, which he probably began in Spain, and continued when he moved to Italy in the 1220s.[68]

The radical nature of this new Aristotelianism and its origin in Spain is indicated by the extreme reaction that it provoked in Paris—in particular, the prohibition promulgated in the University of Paris in 1215 against Aristotle's works on metaphysics and natural science, the *summae* of these works (i.e., presumably, the works of Avicenna and Averroes) and the writings of "Mauritius Hispanus", amongst others.[69] The most plausible explanation of the identity of the latter is that he is Mauritius, archdeacon of Toledo, who sponsored translations of other texts of the Almohads, as we shall see.[70]

The continuation of interest in Aristotelianism in Christian Spain in the 13th century has not yet been explored by scholars, but is evident from the following facts: Alvaro of Toledo (floruit 1267 until after 1286) copied out Michael Scot's translation of al-Biṭrūjī's *On the Movements of the Heavens* and wrote a commentary on Averroes' *On the Substance of the Globe*. He dedicated the latter to the Archbishop of Toledo, Gonzalo García Gudiel, who himself had collected several manuscripts of the works of Aristotle, Avicenna and Averroes by 1273.[71] The archbishop commissioned a translation of those books on natural science in Avicenna's *Shifā'* which had not been translated by Dominicus Gundissalinus.[72]

With García Gudiel we come to the very end of the 13th century. If we retrace our steps we can follow the course of "official translations" through the century. The battle of Las Navas de Tolosa (609/1212) and the subsequent capture of Seville and Córdoba, leaving as the only Islamic kingdom in Spain the vassal state of Granada, gave the Christian bishops and kings a great feeling of confidence. We see at least one archbishop and two kings who produce texts in their own names to further the Hispanicisation and Christianisation of the Iberian Peninsula.[73]

Rodrigo Jiménez de Rada, Archbishop of Toledo from 1210 to 1247, wrote the *Historia Gothica* and the *Historia Arabum*, both of which rely heavily on Arabic sources.[74] A canon in his cathedral called Mark was asked by his archdeacon, Mauritius (mentioned above), to translate the Quran and the Profession of Faith of the founder of the Almohad movement.[75] James the Conqueror, king of Catalonia (d. 1276) was more a warrior than a cultural hero, and added Valencia, Murcia and the Balearic Islands to the kingdom of Catalonia. But he also wrote a unique biography, in Catalan—the *Llibre dels feyts*—and set up a school for training missionaries.[76]

The most remarkable instance, however, is of course that of Alfonso X, "el Sabio", king of León and Castile from 1252 until 1284.[77] His nationalism is evidence in his great law-codes and histories (of Spain and of the world), which build on the earlier histories of Rodrigo Jiménez and even on the Islamic literature translated by Hermann of Carinthia and Robert of Ketton. Above all, it is evidenced by the fact that he chose to use Castilian as the literary language of his court. He was not so interested in Aristotle, but sponsored the translation of texts on magic, the science of the stars, entertaining stories, and games (including chess, draughts and backgammon). Not only was the language of these translations Spanish, but also he made it seem that the authors themselves were Spanish, calling for example the author of the *Ghāyat al-ḥakīm*, "Picatrix Hispanus".[78] Of course, in a way, they were. The author of *Ghāyat al-ḥakīm*, though not Maslama al-Majrīṭī himself, lived in al-Andalus in the 5th/11th century. One or two of the texts on the science of the stars appear to have been written by the translators themselves. The absence of any Muslim involvement in the translations is notable. Most of Alfonso's translators were Jews, and those who were not Jews were Christians who sometimes translated the Castilian text into Latin.

VI

What could Europeans learn of Islamic Spain from these translations? It must be said, first of all, that works on philosophy and the exact sciences are not likely to give much information about the society in which they were written. However, an informative introduction to the Islamic religion itself could be gained from reading the texts that Peter the Venerable commissioned in the 1140s from Hermann of Carinthia, Robert of Ketton and Peter of Toledo. These were all translations of Arabic texts on Islam, and included the Quran, a life of Muḥammad, a history of the world from the Islamic point of view from the Creation to the time of the Prophet, an account of the early caliphs, and a debate between a Muslim and a Christian.[79]

For all the extremely negative attitude towards Islam shown by Robert of Ketton in his prefaces, the translations themselves are quite faithful to their originals. Peter the Venerable had attached to his team of translators a Muslim called Muḥammad, presumably to help in matters of doctrine. The translator of the debate between the Muslim and the Christian (the *Apology* of al-Kindī), even left in a sentence in which the caliph al-Maʾmūn, the judge of the debate, comes down in favour of the Muslim.[80] He considered Christianity to be a religion for enjoying life in the world to come, whereas Islam enabled one to enjoy both this world *and* the next. Unfortunately an early editor of the Latin text erased this approbation of Islam which, consequently, is not found in later manuscripts. Nevertheless the "Toledan collection", as the works commissioned by Peter the Venerable are called, remained a valuable dossier for Westerners wishing to understand Islam. In the 17th century Robert of Ketton's translation of the Quran was still being used by Christian missionaries, and the *Apology* of al-Kindī has become popular in modern times at the interface of Islam and Christianity in North Africa.[81]

Other sources for gaining knowledge of Spanish Islamic society are the works of astrology and divination. Richard Lemay has pointed out that in some manuscripts of John of Seville's translation (529/1135) of Abū Maʿshar's *Greater Introduction to Astrology* (235/849) there are annotations explaining some of the terms used, including: "Note that Abū Maʿshar calls 'aldea' the habitations (*villulae*) in which the more noble of the Arabs dwell, i.e., the places of tents, since noble Arabs always dwell in tents and not in cities"; the same annotator interprets "cities and halls" (*civitates et aulas*) as *alcasares* (the Spanish word from *al-qaṣr*, "castle").[82]

Associated with astronomical tables in two manuscripts of the 6th/12th century is a bilingual Arabic-Latin fortune-telling table which indicates the activity someone should be engaging in depending on the sign of the zodiac in which each of the planets is situated.[83] The activities are all pleasant and presumably recall the recreations of a leisured inhabitant of al-Andalus: e.g., hearing or playing musical instruments (including the *rabāb*, the shawm, the horn, various kinds of drum, and singing), riding through beautiful places, resting in the shade, buying or building a house or guest-quarters, decorating a reception room, buying slippers, smelling roses or irises, entering a bath, wearing multi-coloured clothing or silks or brocade or a long-sleeved gown, hunting ducks or hares and hunting with a falcon, playing with a girl, drinking by a river (either grape-wine—*khamr*, or date-wine—*nabīdh*), and finally eating all kinds of delicious food. These include lamb, chicken, a young dove, partridges, thrushes, dates, a pie made of borage, a cake (*ḥalwā*), aubergines, artichokes, dill, *tafāyā* (interpreted in Latin as "meat with coriander") and mushrooms.[84]

Other astrological works refer to the best time to learn to play the "lyre" (presumably the *ʿūd*), the drum (*ṭanbūr*) and trumpets,[85] and give advice on digging irrigation ditches, which includes descriptions of the *shadūf* (translated as "stork" in Latin), the *sāniya* or "water scoop", and the *nāʿūra* or water-wheel:

> In digging beds for irrigation channels, let the Moon be in a good position ... [If all this is done] hindrance from digging the channel is avoided and the abundance and the salubrity of the water is assured ... In making certain machines which are accustomed to be used by certain peoples for drawing up water, and which, because of their appearance, they call in the vernacular [*vulgari nomine*] "storks", let the Ascendent and the Cardines be firm ... For the manufacture of wheels which the Arabs call *azeniae* or *annorae* the aforesaid method for wells should be followed. Both machines are useful for drawing forth water for irrigating fields.[86]

More immediately relevant to Islamic Spain are the texts on divination by sheeps' shoulder-blades.[87] These seem to have been elaborated on Spanish soil. For in both Arabic and Latin texts there are references to Córdoba, Saragossa and other capitals of the *ṭāʾifa* kingdoms of al-Andalus. In one Arabic text the two main divisions of the Arabs in Spain—the family of Fihr and the family of Marwān—are mentioned. In both an Arabic and a Latin text the tribal divisions of the Berbers—the Butr and Barānis—are also named. The texts give intimate details of family life, indicating whether the husband will dominate his wife or *vice versa*, how many servants there are in the house and whether they are black, Arabs or Christians, and have straight or curly hair.

Latin-reading Europeans, however, did not read these texts in order to find out more about Islamic Spain. They were interested in the texts for practical purposes or for making progress in mathematics or philosophy. The Arabs were not mere conduits of Ancient Greek learning. Admittedly, translators were searching out Ancient Greek works and occasionally complained when they could only find an Arabic translation of a Greek work.[88] Gerard of Cremona, Robert of Ketton and Hermann of Carinthia were all aiming for the *Almagest* of Ptolemy, Constantinc of Africa wanted to introduce to the Latins Galen and Hippocrates. But it was acknowledged that scholars writing in Arabic had developed, added to, or made more accessible, the texts of Antiquity. Understanding the *Almagest* may have been the aim of every aspiring astronomer, but most scholars in the Middle Ages, including Dante, found it easier to use the shorter *Elements of Astronomy* of al-Farghānī.[89] Ptolemy's *Tetrabiblos* was regarded as the fountainhead of teaching on astrology; yet the works of Abū Maʿshar and al-Qabīṣī were much more frequently copied and cited.[90] Avicenna's *Sufficiency* (*Shifāʾ*), as its title implied, provided a full curriculum in philosophy and, partly because it gave clear-cut answers rather than left questions hanging in the air, it was easier to manage than the several books of Aristotle's philosophy and was consequently popular. Averroes, on the other hand, with his three tiers of commentary to each of Aristotle's works, provided a thorough-going method for a detailed study of Aristotle and a model for Latin commentaries from the mid-7th/13th century onwards.[91] A mark of his success is the fact that a far greater number of his commentaries survive in Latin than in the original Arabic.[92]

The Arabs of the Middle Ages seem to have had a special flair for mathematics, and the Latin translations in this field provide only a dim reflection of the true splendour of the achievements of men like al- Muʾtaman b. Hūd or Omar Khayyam.[93] The translations did, however, introduce into the West calculation with Arabic numerals, algebra, trigonometry and advanced geometry. In medicine, above all, Arabic works held sway in the Middle Ages. One need only mention the names which became familiar in the Latin forms of Avicenna (this time as author of the *Canon of Medicine*), Rhazes, Mesue, Isaac, and Abulcasim.[94]

Most of these texts had originally been translated in Spain.[95] Many of them had been written by Muslims (or, to a lesser extent, Christians or Jews) resident in Spain. We have already mentioned Maslama al-Majrīṭī, al-Biṭrūjī, Averroes, and Ibn Bājja, the last of whose views were known through the commentaries of Averroes. But there were others, such as ʿArīb b. Saʿd, who contributed to the composition of the *Calendar of Córdoba*, Abraham bar Ḥiyya (d. c. 531/1136), the author of a book on trigonometry translated by Plato of Tivoli under the title *Liber embadorum* ("Book of areas"),[96] the 5th/11th-century mathematician and astronomer Ibn Muʿadh of Jaén whose works on atmospheric refraction (*De crepusculis*) and *Tables of Jaén* were translated by Gerard of Cremona,[97] and Ibn al-Zarqālluh whose astronomical tables composed for Toledo in ca. 462/1070 became the standard tables in use in Latin translation in the West between the late 12th and early 14th centuries.[98] But Arabic texts also arrived in al-Andalus from the furthest parts of the Islamic world, and this, in itself, testifies to the brilliance of the academic society in Islamic Spain. Adelard of Bath had regarded Arabic learning as synonymous with rational thought.[99] What Hugo of Santalla said of his own subject would have been echoed by many of his fellow Latins concerning other subjects:

> It befits us to imitate the Arabs especially, for they are as it were our teachers and precursors in this art.[100]

[1] For general accounts of the translation process see M.-T. d'Alverny, "Translations and Translators", in *Renaissance and Renewal in the Twelfth Century*, ed. R. L Benson and G. Constable, Oxford, 1982, pp. 421-62; C. Burnett, "Some Comments on the Translating of Works from Arabic into Latin in the Mid-Twelfth Century", in *Orientalische Kultur und europäisches Mittelalter*, ed. A. Zimmermann, Berlin, 1985, pp. 161-71, and "Literal Translation and Intelligent Adaptation amongst the Arabic-Latin Translators of the First Half of the Twelfth Century", in *La diffusione delle scienze islamiche nel Medio Evo Europeo*, ed. B.-M. Scarcia Amoretti, Rome, 1987, pp. 9-28; N. Daniel, *The Arabs and Medieval Europe*, London, 1975; D. C. Lindberg, "The Transmission of Greek and Arabic Learning to the West", in *idem* (ed.), *Science in the Middle Ages*, Chicago, 1978; M. R. Menocal, *The Arabic Role in Medieval Literary History*, Philadelphia, 1987; and J. Vernet, *La cultura hispanoárabe en Oriente y Occidente*, Barcelona, 1978. Catalogues or lists of translations are included in F. J. Carmody, *Arabic Astronomical and Astrological Sciences in Latin Translation*, Berkeley, 1955 and L. Thorndike and P. Kibre, *A Catalogue of Incipits of Mediaeval Scientific Writings in Latin*, revised and augmented ed., London, 1963.

[2] S. M. Stern, *Hispano-Arabic Strophic Poetry*, Oxford, 1974.

[3] For Berber involvement in geomancy see F. Klein-Franke, "The Geomancy of Aḥmad b. ʿAlī Zunbul: A study of the Arabic Corpus Hermeticum", *Ambix*, 20, 1973, pp. 26-36; "Arabic" numerals are discussed below.

[4] Roger Wright, *Late Latin and Early Romance*, Liverpool, 1982, pp. 151-63.

[5] P. S. Van Koningsveld, *The Latin-Arabic Glossary of the Leiden University Library*, Leiden, 1977, p. 57. The judge is Aṣbagh b. Nabīl (362/971). Another judge—Ḥafṣ b. Albar al-Qūṭī—was a translator from Latin into Arabic (see below).

[6] Examples of documents in which Arabic and Latin occur can be found in F. J. Hernández, *Los cartularios de Toledo*, Madrid, 1985, plates 6, 7, 9, 11 and 13.

[7] M.-T. d'Alverny, "Les traductions à deux interprètes: d'arabe en langue vernaculaire et de langue vernaculaire en latin", in *Traductions et traducteurs au moyen âge*, ed. G. Contamine, *Colloque internationale du CNRS*, Paris, 1989, p. 197.

[8] Van Koningsveld, *Latin-Arabic Glossary*; J. Samsó, "The Early development of Astrology in al-Andalus", *Journal for the History of Arabic Science*, 3, 1979, pp. 228-43.

[9] C. Pellat (ed.), *Le Calendrier de Cordoue*, Leiden, 1961.

[10] Van Koningsveld, *The Latin-Arabic Glossary of the Leiden University Library*, Leiden, 1977.

[11] Paris, Bibliothèque nationale, lat. 10233 (s. viii).

[12] Ripoll MS 168, fol. 42r; the notes are to the the text of Boethius, *De arithmetica*, I. 32.

[13] J. M. Millás Vallicrosa, *Assaig d'història de les idees físiques i matemàtiques a la Catalunya medieval*, Barcelona, 1931, discussing the texts on the astrolabe in Ripoll MS 225.

[14] Michael Scot, *Liber introductorius*, quoted in L. Thorndike, *Michael Scot*, 1965, pp. 93-94.

[15] For the life and works of Adelard of Bath, see C. Burnett (ed.), *Adelard of Bath: An English Scientist and Arabist of the Early Twelfth Century*, *Warburg Institute Surveys and Texts XIV*, 1987. Adelard spent some time in Southern Italy, Sicily and, possibly, the Middle East, but probably passed most of his life in the region of the Severn valley in England.

[16] Vernet, *op. cit.*, pp. 32 and 154, and J. Thomann, "The Name Picatrix: Transcription or Translation?", *Journal of the Warburg and Cortauld Institutes*, 53, 1990, pp. 289-96.

[17] C. H. Haskins, *Studies in the History of Mediaeval Science*, 2nd ed., Cambridge (Mass.), 1927, p. 290, n. 114, and Daniel, *The Arabs and Mediaeval Europe*, p. 285.

[18] M. Müller (ed.), Adelard of Bath, *Quaestiones naturales*, Beiträge zur Geschichte der Philosophie des Mittelalters, 31.2, Münster, 1934, p. 53, lines 27-30.

[19] Marcel Destombes, "Un astrolabe carolingien et l'origine de nos chiffres arabes", *Archives Internationales d'Histoire des Sciences*, 58-59, 1962, pp. 3-45. The genuineness of this astrolabe has been discussed at a recent conference in Paris.

[20] T. Charmasson, *Rechereches sur une technique divinatoire: la géomancie dans l'occident médiéval*, Geneva-Paris, 1980.

[21] C. Burnett, "The Eadwine Psalter and the Western Tradition of the Onomancy in Pseudo-Aristotle's *Secret of Secrets*", *Archives d'Histoire Doctrinale et Littéraire du Moyen Âge*, 55, year 1988, pp. 143-67.

[22] C. Burnett, "Arabic Divination and Celtic Lore: Some Aspects of the Theory and Practice of Scapulimancy in Western Europe", *Cambridge Mediueval Celtic Studies*, 6, 1983, pp. 31-42.

[23] Millás Vallicrosa, *Assaig*, pp. 67-40; A. Van de Vyver, "Les plus anciennes traductions latines médiévales (Xe-XIe siècles) de traités d'astronomie et d'astrologie", *Osiris*, 1, 1936, pp. 666-84. This work should be viewed as part of the large body of apocryphal literature couched in the form of correspondence between Aristotle and his royal pupil Alexander the Great; see C. Burnett, "Arabic , Greek and Latin Works on Astrological Magic Attributed to Aristotle", in *Pseudo-Aristotle in the Middle Ages*, ed. Jill Kraye, W. F. Ryan and C. B. Schmitt, London, 1986, pp. 84-96.

[24] L. Veccia Vaglieri and G. Celentano, "Trois Epîtres d'al-Kindī", *Instituto Orientale de Napoli. Annali*, 34, 1974, p. 525.

[25] Paris, Bibliothèque nationale, lat. 17868, fol. 16v. The diagrams are reproduced in E. Wickersheimer, "Figures médico-astrologiques des IXe, Xe et XIe siècles", *Janus*, 19, 1914 , p. 175.

[26] Rome, Biblioteca Alessandrina, MS 1.f.18, N.171, fol. 3r, reproduced in M. Pasca (ed.), *La scuola medica Salernitana*, 1988, p. 53.

[27] R. Lemay, "Arabic Numerals", in *Dictionary of the Middle Ages*, ed. J. R. Strayer, I, New York, 1982, p. 384: "the number of Arabic ... manuscripts that use the Hindu numerals for divination and for magic far exceeds those that deal seriously with mathematics proper".

[28] *Ibid.*, p. 385.

[29] A. Labarta and C. Barceló, *Números y cifras en los documentos arábigohispanos*, Córdoba, 1988.

[30] W. Bergmann, *Innovationen im Quadrivium des 10. und 11. Jahrhunderts*, Stuttgart, 1985.

[31] William, Abbot of Malmesbury, described Gerbert as "the first to snatch the abacus from the Saracens and give it rules for use"; N. Bubnov, *Gerberti Opera Mathematica*, Berlin, 1899, p. 387.

[32] A. Allard (ed.), Moḥammed ibn Mūsā al-Khwārizmī, *Le Calcul indien*, Paris-Namur, 1991.

[33] A. Murray, *Science and Society in the Middle Ages*, Oxford, 1978.

[34] E. Lévi-Provençal and E. García Gómez, *Sevilla a comienzos del siglo XII*, Madrid, 1948, p. 173.

[35] E. Lévi-Provençal, revision of R. Dozy, *Histoire des musulmans*, Leiden, 1932, III, 154, n. 1.

[36] Haskins, *op. cit.*, pp. 67-81.

[37] J. P. Hogendijk, "Discovery of an 11th-Century Geometrical Compilation: the *Istikmāl* of Yūsuf al-Mu'taman ibn Hūd, King of Saragossa", *Historia Mathematica*, 13, 1986, pp. 43-53.

[38] Vernet, *op. cit.*, p. 32.

[39] I owe this information to Dr Jan Hogendijk.

[40] Haskins, *op. cit*, p. 73; B. R. Goldstein, *Ibn al-Muthannâ's Commentary on the Astronomical Tables of al-Khwârizmî*, New Haven-London, 1967.

[41] D. Pingree, "The Diffusion of Arabic Magical Texts in Western Europe", in *La diffusione delle scienze islamiche nel Medio Evo Europeo*, ed. B.-M. Scarcia Amoretti, Rome, 1987, p. 80.

[42] On Constantine's practice see D. Jacquart, "Le sens donné par Constantin l'Africain au *Pantegni*: les prologues latin et arabe", in *Constantine the African and ʿAlī ibn al-ʿAbbās al-Majūsī*, ed. C. Burnett and D. Jacquart (in press).

[43] C. Burnett and D. Pingree (eds.), Hugo of Santalla, *Liber Aristotilis* (in preparation), Prologue, sentences 42-43.

[44] Haskins, *op. cit.*, p. 70.

[45] Preface to his *Art of Geomancy*, edited in Haskins, *ibid.*, pp. 78-79.

[46] Burnett, "Arabic Divination and Celtic Lore", p. 35.

[47] Haskins, *op. cit.*, p. 78.

48 C. Burnett, "Hermann of Carinthia", in *A History of Twelfth-Century Philosophy*, ed. P. Dronke, Cambridge (England), 1988, pp. 398-400.

49 U. Weisser (ed.), Pseudo-Apollonios von Tyana, *Buch über das Geheimnis der Schöpfung und die Darstellung der Natur*, Aleppo, 1979, pp. 10-12 and 30.

50 For example, both cite the Hermetic book *Kitāb al-iṣṭamāṭīs* and both have a detailed account of the development of the embryo according to the influence of the planets.

51 I.e., the letter on logic (*Posterior Analytics*), Beirut edition, I, 429-52, Latin version in A. Nagy, *Die philosophischen Abhandlungen des Ja'qūb ben Isḥāq al-Kindī*, Beiträge zur Geschichte der Philosophie des Mittelalters, 2.5, Münster, 1897, pp. 41-64; and the letter on geography, Beirut edition, I, 158-82, Latin version ed. P. Gautier Dalché, "*Epistola fratrum sinceorum in cosmographia*: une traduction latine inédite de la quatrième risāla des Iḫwān al-Ṣafā'", *Revue d'histoire des textes*, 18, 1988, pp. 137-67. The letter on talismans (Beirut edition, IV, 283-462) includes material which is also found in Latin texts; see Burnett, "Arabic, Greek and Latin works on Astrological Magic Attributed to Aristotle", p. 89, n. 6.

52 See "Ibn Ezra" in *Encyclopaedia Judaica*, 8, 1971, pp. 1163-70.

53 Haskins, *op. cit.*, p. 55.

54 C. Burnett, "Hermann of Carinthia and the *Kitāb al-isṭamāṭīs*: further evidence for the transmission of Hermetic magic", *Journal of the Warburg and Cortauld Institutes*, 44, 1981, p. 167.

55 C. Burnett, *Hermann of Carinthia, De Essentiis: a Critical Edition with Translation and Commentary*, Leiden, 1982, pp. 70-73.

56 *Ibid.*, pp. 6, 8-9.

57 Thierry's collection of texts on the seven liberal arts, entitled *Heptateuchon*, is discussed in E. Jeauneau, "Note sur l'Ecole de Chartres", *Studii Medievali*, 3rd series, 5, 1964, pp. 821-65. The recent editors of the version of Euclid's *Elements* in the *Heptateuchon* have proposed that it is by Robert (see H. L. L. Busard and M. Folkerts (eds.), *The Latin Translation of Euclid's Elements known as Version II* (in press)), whereas the tables of al-Khwārizmī could be Hermann's revision of Adelard's version; see H. Suter, with A. Bjørnbo and R. Besthorn, *Die astronomischen Tafeln des Muḥammad ibn Mūsā al-Khwārizmī in der Bearbeitung des Maslama ibn Aḥmed al-Majrīṭī und der lateinischen Uebersetzung des Athelard von Bath*, Copenhagen, 1914, p. xiii.

58 L. Baur (ed.), Dominicus Gundissalinus, *De Divisione Philosophiae*, Beiträge zur Geschichte der Philosophie des Mittelalters, 4.2-3, Münster, 1903, p. 3 and J. Jolivet, "The Arabic Inheritance", in Dronke, *A History of Twelfth-Century Western Philosophy*, pp. 135-36.

59 Hernández, *op. cit.*, Nos. 134, 165 and 174.

60 The translations of Gerard used by Dominicus include al-Kindī's *On the Five Essences*, Isḥāq Isrā'īlī's *Book of Definitions*, Euclid's *Elements*, Anaritius's commentary on the latter, and Avicenna's *Canon*. Dominicus is also aware of the mathematical text "mahamelech" (*k. al-mu'āmalāt*) and Menelaus' *On Spherical Figures*, both translated by Gerard. P. M. J. E. Tummers' suggestion ("Some Notes on the geometry Chapter of Dominicus Gundissalinus", *Archives Internationales d'Histoire des Sciences*, 34, 1984, pp. 19-24) that Dominicus used the Arabic original of Anaritius's commentary is less plausible. The relationship of *On the Division of Philosophy* to the Chartrian schemata is shown by K. M. Fredborg, *The Latin Rhetorical Commentaries by Thierry of Chartres*, Toronto, 1988, pp. 14-20.

61 See C. C. Gillispie, *Dictionary of Scientific Biography*, New York, 1970-80, Supplement I, pp. 173-92 (article by R. Lemay on "Gerard of Cremona").

62 Jolivet, *op. cit*

63 *Metalogicon*, IV.6, ed. C. C. J. Webb, Oxford, 1929, p. 171.

64 G. Maurach (ed.), Daniel von Morley, *Philosophia*, in *Mittellateinisches Jahrbuch*, 14, 1979, pp. 212 and 244-45.

65 The list has been printed several times and is most conveniently reproduced in E. Grant (ed.), *A Source Book in Medieval Science*, Cambridge (Mass.), 1974, pp. 35-38.

66 A. I. Sabra, "The Andalusian Revolt against Ptolemaic Astronomy: Averroes and al-Biṭrūjī", in *Transformation and Tradition in the Sciences*, ed. E. Mendelsohn, Cambridge (England), 1984, pp. 133-53.

67 P. W. Rosemann, "Averroes: A Catalogue of Editions and Scholarly Writings from 1821 Onwards", *Bulletin de Philosophie Médiévale*, 30, 1988, pp. 153-221.

68 Thorndike, *Michael Scot*, pp. 22-31, and R. Gauthier, "Notes sur les débuts (1215-1240) du premier Averroïsme", *Revue des Sciences Philosophiques et Théologiques*, 66, 1982, pp. 321-74.

69 H. Denifle (ed.), *Chartularium Universitatis Parisiensis*, I, Paris, 1899, pp. 78-79.

70 M.-T. d'Alverny, "Deux traductions latines du Coran au moyen âge", *Archives d'Histoire Doctrinale et Littéraire du Moyen Âge*, 16, 1947, pp. 129-30.

71 M. Alonso Alonso, "Bibliotecas medievales de los Arzobispos de Toledo", *Razón y Fé*, year 41, 1941, pp. 295-309.

72 S. Van Riet (ed.), *Avicenna Latinus: Liber Tertius Naturalium, de Generatione et Corruptione*, Louvain-Leiden, 1987.

73 It is debatable to what extent these men can be called the "authors" of the works published under their names. However, what is important is that they wanted it to be known that these texts were their own.

74 J. F. Valverde (ed.), Rodrigo Jiménez de Rada, *Historia de Rebus Hispaniae* [=*Historia Gothica*], Corpus Christianorum continuation mediaevalis, 72, Turnhout, 1987, p. xi.

75 M.-T. d'Alverny and G. Vajda, "Marc de Tolède, traducteur d'Ibn Tūmart", *Al-Andalus*, 16, 1951, pp. 99-140, 259-307; 17, 1952, pp. 1-56.

76 M. de Riquer, *Història de la literatura Catalana*, I, Barcelona, 1964, pp. 394-429, and R. I. Burns, *Emperor of Culture: Alfonso X the Learned of Castile and His Thirteenth-Century Renaissance*, Philadelphia, 1990.

77 R. I. Burns, *The Worlds of Alfonso the Learned and James the Conqueror*, Princeton, 1985, and *Emperor of Culture*; and M. Comes, R. Puig and J. Samsó (eds.), *De astronomia Alphonsi regis*, Barcelona, 1987.

78 Thomann, "The name Picatrix".

79 D'Alverny, "Deux traductions latines du Coran au moyen âge".

80 *Ibid.*, p. 95.

81 For further information on the *Apology* see P. S. Van Koningsveld, "La Apología de al-Kindī en la España del siglo xii. Huellas toledanas de un 'animal disputax'", in *Estudios sobre Alfonso VI y la Reconquista de Toledo. Actas del II Congreso Internacional de Estudios Mozárabes*, 3, 1990, pp. 107-29.

82 R. Lemay, *Abū Maʿshar and Latin Aristotelianism in the Twelfth Century*, Beirut, 1962, p. 14.

83 P. Kunitzsch, "Eine bilingue arabisch-lateinische Lostafel", *Revue d'Histoire des Textes*, 6, 1976, and C. Burnett, "A Note on Two Astrological Fortune-Telling Tables", *Revue d'Histoire des Textes*, 18, 1988, pp. 257-62.

84 The activities are described in single words or short phrases consisting of a *maṣdar* construction in Arabic and an infinitive construction in Latin: "to eat a cake", "to hear a drum", "marriage", etc. Similar culinary ingredients can be found in the 7th/13th-century Andalusī cookery-book published by A. Huici Miranda, *La cocina hispano-magrebí en la época almohade según un manuscrito anónimo*, Madrid, 1965.

85 C. Burnett, "Teoria e pratica musicali arabe in Sicilia e nell'Italia meridionale in età normanna e sveva", *Nuove Effemeridi* (Palermo), 11, 1990, p. 86.

86 Oxford, Bodleian Library, MS Bodley 430, fol. 75vb.

87 Burnett, "Arabic Divination and Celtic Lore".

88 This was the case with Eugene of Palermo (6th/12th century) who was obliged to use the Arabic version of Ptolemy's *Optics*; see d'Alverny, "Translations and Translators". The Greek version has yet to be found.

89 The version of al-Farghānī used by Dante is edited by R. Campani, Città di Castello, 1910.

90 This is the case, for example, in the large-scale introduction to philosophy, the *Liber Introductorius* of Michael Scot.

91 D. A. Callus, "Introduction of Aristotelian Learning to Oxford", *Proceedings of the British Academy*, 29, 1943, shows how Latin commentators were influenced by the methodology of Avicenna and Averroes; see also J. Marenbon, *Later Medieval Philosophy (1150-1350)*, London, 1987, pp. 50-62.

92 Rosemann, *op. cit.* Averroes' popularity continued into the Renaissance when several more of his works were translated into Latin: C. B. Schmitt, "Renaissance Averroism Studied through the Venetian Editions of Aristotle-Averroes", *Convegno internazionale, L'Averroismo in Italia*, Rome, 1979, pp. 121-42.

[93] H. Suter, *Die Mathematiker und Astronomen der Araber und ihre Werke*, Leipzig, 1900.

[94] These being Ibn Sīnā, al-Rāzī, Ibn al-Māsawaih, Isḥāq al-Isrā'īlī and Abū l'Qāsim; see D. Jacquart and F. Micheau, *La médecine arabe et l'occident médiéval*, Paris, 1990.

[95] J. A. Sánchez Pérez, *Biografías de Matemáticos Arabes que florecieron en España*, Madrid, 1921.

[96] J. M. Millás Vallicrosa, *Estudios sobre historia de la ciencia española*, Barcelona, 1949, pp. 219-26.

[97] A. I. Sabra, "The Authorship of the *Liber de crepusculis*, and eleventh-century Work on Atmospheric Refraction", *Isis*, 58, 1967, pp. 77-85 and 560.

[98] J. M. Millás Vallicrosa, *Estudios sobre Azarquiel*, Madrid-Granada, 1943-50.

[99] Müller (ed.), *Quaestiones Naturales*, p. 11, lines 23-24.

[100] C. Burnett, "A Group of Arabic-Latin Translators working in Northern Spain in the mid-twelfth Century", *Journal of the Royal Asiatic Society*, year 1977, p. 90.

BIBLIOGRAPHY

Allard, A. (ed.), Moḥammed ibn Mūsā al-Khwārizmī, *Le Calcul indien*, Paris-Namur, 1991.

Alonso Alonso, M., "Bibliotecas medievales de los Arzobispos de Toledo", *Razón y Fé*, year 41, 1941, pp. 295-309.

Alverny, M.-T. d', "Deux traductions latines du Coran au moyen âge", *Archives d'Histoire Doctrinale et Littéraire du Moyen Âge*, 16, 1947, pp. 69-131.

——, "Avendauth?" in *Homenaje Millás Vallicrosa*, Barcelona, 1954, I, 19-43.

——, "Translations and Translators", in *Renaissance and Renewal in the Twelfth Century*, ed. R. L. Benson and G. Constable, Oxford, 1982, pp. 421-62.

——, "Les traductions à deux interprètes: d'arabe en langue vernaculaire et de langue vernaculaire en latin", in *Traductions et traducteurs au moyen âge*, ed. G. Contamine, *Colloque internationale du CNRS*, Paris, 1989, pp. 193-206.

D'Alverny, M.-T. and G. Vajda, "Marc de Tolède, traducteur d'Ibn Tūmart", *Al-Andalus*, 16, 1951, pp. 99-140, 259-307; 17, 1952, pp. 1-56.

Baur, L. (ed.), Dominicus Gundissalinus, *De Divisione Philosophiae*, Beiträge zur Geschichte der Philosophie des Mittelalters, 4.2-3, Münster, 1903.

Bergmann, W., *Innovationen im Quadrivium des 10. und 11. Jahrhunderts*, Sudhoffs Archiv, Beiheft 26, Stuttgart, 1985.

Bossong, G., *Probleme der Übersetzung wissenschaftlicher Werke aus dem Arabischen in das Altspanische zur Zeit Alfons des Wiesen*, Tübingen, 1979.

Bubnov, N., *Gerberti Opera Mathematica*, Berlin, 1899; reprinted Hildesheim, 1963.

Burnett, C., "A Group of Arabic-Latin Translators working in Northern Spain in the mid-twelfth Century", *Journal of the Royal Asiatic Society*, year 1977, pp. 62-108.

——, "Arabic into Latin in Twelfth-century Spain: the Works of Hermann of Carinthia", *Mittellateinisches Jahrbuch*, 13, 1978, pp. 100-34.

——, "Hermann of Carinthia and the *Kitāb al-Isṭamāṭīs:* further evidence for the transmission of Hermetic magic", *Journal of the Warburg and Courtauld Institutes*, 44, 1981, pp. 167-69

——, *Hermann of Carinthia, De Essentiis: a Critical Edition with Translation and Commentary*, Leiden, 1982.

——, "Arabic Divination and Celtic Lore: Some Aspects of the Theory and Practice of Scapulimancy in Western Europe", *Cambridge Medieval Celtic Studies* 6, 1983, pp. 31-42.

——, "Some Comments on the Translating of Works from Arabic into Latin in the Mid-twelfth Century", in *Orientalische Kultur und europäisches Mittelalter*, ed. A. Zimmermann, Miscellanea Mediaevalia 17, Berlin, 1985, pp.161-71.

——, "Arabic, Greek and Latin Works on Astrological Magic Attributed to Aristotle", in *Pseudo-Aristotle in the Middle Ages*, ed. Jill Kraye, W. F. Ryan and C. B. Schmitt, London, 1986, pp. 84-96.

——, *Adelard of Bath: An English Scientist and Arabist of the Early Twelfth Century*, ed. C. Burnett, Warburg Institute Surveys and Texts XIV, 1987.

——, "Literal Translation and Intelligent Adaptation amongst the Arabic-Latin Translators of the First Half of the Twelfth Century", in *La diffusione delle scienze islamiche nel Medio Evo Europeo*, ed. B.-M. Scarcia Amoretti, Rome, 1987, pp. 9-28.

——, "Hermann of Carinthia", in *A History of Twelfth-Century Western Philosophy*, ed. P. Dronke, Cambridge (England), 1988, pp. 386-406.

——, "The Eadwine Psalter and the Western Tradition of the Onomancy in Pseudo-Aristotle's *Secret of Secrets*", *Archives d'Histoire Doctrinale et Littéraire du Moyen Age*, 55, year 1988, pp. 143-67.

——, "A Note on Two Astrological Fortune-Telling Tables", *Revue d'Histoire des Textes*, 18, 1988, pp. 257-62.

——, "Teoria e pratica musicali arabe in Sicilia e nell'Italia meridionale in età normanna e sveva", *Nuove Effemeridi*, 11, Palermo, 1990, pp. 79-89.

Burnett, C and D. Pingree (eds.), Hugo of Santalla, *Liber Aristotilis* (in preparation).

Burns, R. I., *The Worlds of Alfonso the Learned and James the Conqueror*, Princeton, 1985.

——, *Emperor of Culture: Alfonso X the Learned of Castile and His Thirteenth-Century Renaissance*, Philadelphia, 1990.

Busard, H. L. L., and M. Folkerts (eds.), *The Latin Translation of Euclid's Elements known as Version II* (in press).

Callus, D. A., "Introduction of Aristotelian Learning to Oxford", *Proceedings of the British Academy*, 29, 1943, pp. 229-81.

Campani, R. (ed.), *Al-Farghānī, Il "Libro dell'aggregazione delle stelle"*, Città di Castello, 1910.

Carmody, F. J., *Arabic Astronomical and Astrological Sciences in Latin Translation*, Berkeley, 1955.

Charmasson, T., *Recherches sur une technique divinatoire: la géomancie dans l'occident médiéval*, Geneva and Paris, 1980.

Comes. M., R. Puig and J. Samsó (eds.), *De astronomia Alphonsi regis*, Barcelona, 1987.

Daniel, N., *The Arabs and Mediaeval Europe*, London, 1975.

Denifle, H. (ed.), *Chartularium Universitatis Parisiensis*, I, Paris, 1899.

Destombes, Marcel, "Un astrolabe carolingien et l'origine de nos chiffres arabes", *Archives Internationales d'Histoire des Sciences*, 58-59, 1962, pp. 3-45.

Encyclopedia Judaica, Jerusalem, 1971-2.

Fredborg, K. M., *The Latin Rhetorical Commentaries by Thierry of Chartres*, Toronto, 1988.

Gauthier, R., "Notes sur les débuts (1215-1240) du premier Averroïsme", *Revue des sciences Philosophiques et Théologiques*, 66, 1982, pp. 321-74.

Gautier Dalché, P., "*Epistola fratrum sincerorum in cosmographia*: une traduction latine inédite de la quatrième risāla des Ikhwān al-Ṣafā'", *Revue d'Histoire des Textes*, 18, 1988, pp. 137-67.

Gillispie, C. C. (ed.), *Dictionary of Scientific Biography*, New York, 1970-80.

Goldstein, B. R., *Ibn al-Muthannā's Commentary on the Astronomical Tables of al-Khwārizmī*, New Haven and London, 1967.

Grant, E. (ed.), *A Source Book in Medieval Science*, Cambridge (Mass.), 1974.

Haskins, C. H., *Studies in the History of Mediaeval Science*, Cambridge (Mass.), 1924, second ed., 1927.

Hernández, F. J., *Los cartularios de Toledo*, Madrid, 1985.

Hogendijk, J. P., "Discovery of an 11th-Century Geometrical Compilation: the *Istikmāl* of Yūsuf al-Mu'taman ibn Hūd, King of Saragossa", *Historia Mathematica*, 13, 1986, pp. 43-53.

Huici Miranda, A., *La cocina hispano-magrebí en la época almohade según un manuscrito anónimo*, Madrid, 1965.

Ikhwān al-Ṣafā', *Rasā'il*, Beirut, 1957, 4 vols.

Jacquart, D., "Le sens donné par Constantin l'Africain au *Pantegni*: les prologues latin et arabe", in *Constantine the African and ʿAlī ibn al-ʿAbbās al-Majūsī*, ed. C. Burnett and D. Jacquart (in press).

Jacquart, D., and F. Micheau, *La médecine arabe et l'occident médiéval*, Paris, 1990.

Jeauneau, E., "Note sur l'école de Chartres", *Studi Medievali*, 3rd series, 5, 1964, pp. 821-65.

Jolivet, J., "The Arabic Inheritance," in *A History of Twelfth-Century Western Philosophy*, ed. P. Dronke, Cambridge (England), 1988.

Klein-Franke, F., "The Geomancy of Aḥmad b. ʿAlī Zunbul: A Study of the Arabic Corpus Hermeticum", *Ambix*, 20, 1973, pp. 26-36.
Kunitzsch, P., "Eine bilingue arabisch-lateinische Lostafel", *Revue d'Histoire des Textes*, 6, 1976.
Labarta A., and C. Barceló, *Números y cifras en los documentos arábigohispanos*, Córdoba, 1988.
Lemay, R., *Abū Maʿshar and Latin Aristotelianism in the Twelfth Century*, Beirut, 1962.
——, "Arabic Numerals", in *Dictionary of the Middle Ages*, ed. J. R. Strayer, I, New York, 1982, pp. 382-98.
Lévi-Provençal, E., revision of R. Dozy, *Histoire des musulmans*, Leiden, 1932.
Lévi-Provençal, E., and E. García Gómez, *Sevilla a comienzos del siglo XII*, Madrid, 1948.
Lindberg, D. C., "The Transmission of Greek and Arabic Learning to the West", in *idem* (ed.), *Science in the Middle Ages*, Chicago, 1978.
Marenbon, J., *Later Medieval Philosophy (1150-1350)*, London, 1987.
Maurach, G.(ed.), Daniel von Morley, *Philosophia*, in *Mittellateinisches Jahrbuch*, 14, 1979, pp. 204-55.
Menocal, M. R., *The Arabic Role in Medieval Literary History*, Philadelphia, 1987.
Millás Vallicrosa, J. M., *Assaig d'història de les idees físiques i matemátiques a la Catalunya medieval*, Barcelona, 1931.
——, *Estudios sobre Azarquiel*, Madrid and Granada, 1943-50.
——, *Estudios sobre historia de la ciencia española*, Barcelona, 1949.
Müller, M. (ed.), Adelard of Bath, *Quaestiones naturales*, Beiträge zur Geschichte der Philosophie des Mittelalters, 31.2, Münster, 1934.
Murray, A., *Science and Society in the Middle Ages*, Oxford, 1978.
Nagy, A., *Die philosophischen Abhandlungen des Jaʿqūb ben Isḥāq al-Kindī*, Beiträge zur Geschichte der Philosophie des Mittelalters, 2.5, Münster, 1897.
Pasca, M. (ed.), *La scuola medica Salernitana*, Naples, 1988.
Pellat, C., *Le Calendrier de Cordoue*, ed. R. Dozy, new ed. C. Pellat, Leiden, 1961.
Pingree, D., "The Diffusion of Arabic Magical Texts in Western Europe", in *La diffusione delle scienze islamiche nel Medio Evo Europeo*, ed. B.-M. Scarcia Amoretti, Rome, 1987, pp. 57-102.
Riquer, M. de, *Història de la literatura Catalana*, I, Barcelona, 1964.
Rosemann, P. W., "Averroes: A Catalogue of Editions and Scholarly Writings from 1821 Onwards", *Bulletin de Philosophie Médiévale*, 30, 1988, pp. 153-221.
Sabra, A. I., "The Authorship of the *Liber de crepusculis*, and eleventh-century Work on Atmospheric Refraction", *Isis*, 58, 1967, pp. 77-85 and 560.
——, "The Andalusian Revolt against Ptolemaic Astronomy: Averroes and al-Biṭrūjī", in *Transformation and Tradition in the Sciences*, ed. E. Mendelsohn, Cambridge (England), 1984, pp. 133-53.
Samsó, J., "The Early Development of Astrology in al-Andalus", *Journal for the History of Arabic Science*, 3, 1979, pp. 228-43.
Sánchez Pérez, J. A., *Biografías de Matemáticos Árabes que florecieron en España*, Madrid, 1921.
Stern, S. M., *Hispano-Arabic Strophic Poetry*, Oxford, 1974.
Suter, H., *Die Mathematiker und Astronomen der Araber und ihre Werke*, Abhandlungen zur Geschichte der mathematischen Wissenschaft, 10, Leipzig, 1900.
Suter, H., with A. Bjørnbo and R. Besthorn, *Die astronomischen Tafeln des Muḥammad ibn Mūsā al-Khwārizmī in der Bearbeitung des Maslama ibn Aḥmed al-Majrīṭī und der lateinischen Uebersetzung des Athelard von Bath*, Copenhagen, 1914.
Thomann, J., "The Name Picatrix: Transcription or Translation?" *Journal of the Warburg and Courtauld Institutes*, 53, 1990, pp. 289-96.
Thorndike, L., *History of Magic and Experimental Science*, Vols. 1-2, New York, 1923.
——, *Michael Scot*, London and Edinburgh, 1965.
Thorndike, L., and P. Kibre, *A Catalogue of Incipits of Mediaeval Scientific Writings in Latin*, revised and augmented ed., London, 1963.
Tummers, P. M. J. E., "Some Notes on the Geometry Chapter of Dominicus Gundissalinus", *Archives Internationales d'Histoire des Sciences*, 34, 1984, pp. 19-24.

Valverde, J. F. (ed.), Rodrigo Jiménez de Rada, *Historia de Rebus Hispanie* [=*Historia Gothica*], Corpus Christianorum continuatio mediaevalis, 72, Turnhout, 1987.
Van de Vyver, A., "Les plus anciennes traductions latines médiévales (Xe-XIe siècles) de traités d'astronomie et d'astrologie", *Osiris*, 1, 1936, pp. 658-91.
Van Koningsveld, P. S., *The Latin-Arabic Glossary of the Leiden University Library*, Leiden, 1977.
——, "La Apología de al-Kindī en la España del siglo xii. Huellas toledanas de un 'animal disputax'", in *Estudios sobre Alfonso VI y la Reconquista de Toledo, Actas del II Congreso International de Estudios Mozárabes*, 3, 1990, pp. 107-29.
Van Riet, S. (ed.), *Avicenna Latinus: Liber Tertius Naturalium, de Generatione et Corruptione*, Louvain-Leiden, 1987.
Veccia Vaglieri, L., and G. Celentano, "Trois Epîtres d'al-Kindī", *Istituto Orientale de Napoli. Annali*, 34, Naples, 1974, pp. 523-62.
Vernet, J., *La cultura hispanoárabe en Oriente y Occidente*, Barcelona, 1978.
Webb, C. C. J. (ed.), John of Salisbury, *Metalogicon*, Oxford, 1929.
Weisser, U. (ed.), Pseudo-Apollonios von Tyana, *Buch über das Geheimnis der Schöpfung und die Darstellung der Natur*, Aleppo, 1979.
Wickersheimer, E., "Figures médico-astrologiques des neuvième, dixième et onzième siècles", *Janus*, 19, 1914, pp. 157-77.
Wright, Roger, *Late Latin and Early Romance*, Liverpool, 1982.

ISLAMIC CIVILISATION IN AL-ANDALUS: A FINAL ASSESSMENT

Initially Islam was regarded by the Christian world as the expression of one more heretical sect of Christianity. When, however, the speed and magnitude of its spread and the political and religious threat it might pose to Western interests became apparent, relations between the two worlds became increasingly distant, till, finally, they stood in clear confrontation.

From the 8th and 9th centuries on, Western Christians viewed Islam and the Islamic world as an enemy that must be opposed so as to preserve the solidarity of Western cohesion, which had been broken following the fall of the Western Roman Empire, and the image of this enemy was one heavily laden with ideology.

Behind all this, however, was another reality which must be taken into account: commercial and diplomatic relations with the Islamic world (both in the East and in the West, i. e., in al-Andalus), continued despite the hostilities, so that the antagonists were in fact brought together through consistently important trade relations.

In al-Andalus, to which the Arabs and the Berbers had come in 92/711, an authentic political and cultural empire was formed under the rule of the Umayyad dynasty whose founder in al-Andalus, ʿAbd al-Raḥmān I, known as al-Dākhil or the eagle of Quraysh, had fled from Damascus.

Islam, which had created a syncretism and a cultural fusion based not only on its idea of universality and the tolerant nature of its religious conceptions but also on its prodigious capacity for assimilation and creativity and its characteristically experimental tendency, bore splendid fruit in al-Andalus, and it was there that the most important ethnic and cultural fusion of East and West took place. In the 4th/10th century, under the caliphs ʿAbd al-Raḥmān III and al-Ḥakam II, Córdoba was the most brilliant Islamic capital of the period, and also, as the celebrated historian Ramón Menéndez Pidal has pointed out, the most civilised city in Europe.

From al-Andalus there emerged a cultural transmission between civilisations in conflict; the very soil of the Iberian Peninsula provided an example of this, but transmission also extended to the main continent of Europe beyond. The modes of communication were simple:

— The transmission of oral versions of Arab stories and poetry, which were spread by itinerant minstrels, in ignorance of their origin, among Western peoples.
— Europeans travelling to al-Andalus in search of Arab-Islamic cultural lore.
— Frequent trade relations and political contacts through diplomatic embassies.

— Political refugees such as the Mozarabs, who, although tolerated by the Muslims for a time, emigrated in times of intransigence and fanaticism to be with their co-religionists in the north of the Peninsula.
— The *scriptoria* of the monasteries in the Peninsula, especially that of Santa María de Ripoll, which, in the 12th and 13th centuries, acquired a large number of Arabic scientific works which were then translated by monks, many of Mozarab origin.
— The schools for translators that were established in Toledo, following the Christian conquest of that city in 478/1085, by Christian kings and prelates like Archbishop Rodrigo Ximénez de Rada and the King of Castile and León, Alfonso X, "The Wise", with the purpose of digesting the Arab knowledge accumulated in the great libraries of the former Muslim sovereigns.

The resulting translations represented an indirect but very concrete means of transmitting Islamic culture from al-Andalus to Europe, and the schools attracted a stream of intellectuals to the Peninsula from various parts of Europe, and from the three monotheistic religions (Muslims, Christians and Jews), who had of necessity to coexist in the course of their work, and who distributed the results of these translations of Arabic manuscripts in their countries of origin. Such names as Gerard of Cremona, Robert of Chester, Adelard of Bath and Michael Scot remain historically linked to the indirect diffusion of the knowledge contained in the various Arab-Islamic sciences.

The flood of translations centred around the preferred fields of mathematics and science. It is to Islamic culture that we owe our knowledge of numbers, including the zero, of Indian origin but transmitted by a Muslim from Persia named al-Khwārizmī, and Muslims also developed geometry, demonstrated the position and movements of the planets and made many other scientific and medical discoveries, such as the discovery of the minor circulation of the blood, in the 7th/13th century, by the Arab doctor Ibn al-Nafīs.

This brilliant cultivation, by Muslims, of various branches of science (the "rational sciences" as they called them) corresponded to the Islamic conception of man, as a being endowed with intelligence who does not belong to one single nation but to all civilisations, and who needs to cultivate science and the habit of precise thinking so as to help develop the mind, lending order and coordination to its thoughts.

Muslim philosophical and mystical thought was also transmitted to European Western culture through translations of the works of the mystic al-Ghazālī, the Cordoban philosopher Ibn Rushd (Averroes) and other Muslim philosophers. Ibn Rushd inaugurated the line of equilibrium in the Faith-Reason dialectic, so founding a kind of medieval intellectualism.

The Andalusī Muslims were famous for their skill in hydraulic technology, which they broadened and perfected on the base left by the Romans. They built *norias*, water-driven mills, irrigation canals and current wheels, and established a network of irrigation systems throughout the Peninsula, so substantially modifying the agricultural profile of Roman Spain, which had till then been limited to production of the Mediterranean agricultural triad of olives, wheat and grapes. With the opening of new agricultural areas capable of producing other crops, the Arabs introduced and acclimatised such Eastern innovations as date palms and lemon trees, and these in turn changed the Peninsular landscape.

They also promoted the production of silk and paper, which they had learned from the Chinese. Both these products were truly revolutionary factors in the rising manufacture of books and textiles, such high levels of perfection being attained that some of the brocaded textiles and calligraphic and illustrated manuscripts are today preserved as genuine treasures in our museums.

This development of diverse technologies within the Muslim world reflects the well-known Islamic theory that man must know how to avail himself of the useful properties of what the Creation offers, but in a way always geared towards social utility.

Their universal vision was reflected in an art which was similarly the product of the Muslim capacity for wholeness and synthesis; they knew how to assimilate the technical advances of the now politically dominated civilisations, such as the Roman-Byzantine and the Persian, and at the same time how to imprint the stamp of their own genius, which in many cases surpassed that of their teachers. All this benefited Europe.

One example of this inspired capacity for synthesis is the famous Great Mosque of Córdoba, in which Roman columns and arch systems are used together with Visigothic and Corinthian capitols and Byzantine mosaics. But Muslim artists also knew how to impart perfect organisation to all these elements, supplying a magnificent solution to the fragmentation of space based on a system of double arches over a forest of columns, together with the lovely cupolas, with their cosmic significance—all contrived in such a way that few works of art can be likened to this building.

In the industrial arts their skill and creative genius is obvious. In Toledo they introduced the technique of damascene work, the inlaying, that is, of filaments of silver and gold on to metal, a craft which is still practised in the city. Workshops in Córdoba produced beautiful chests of marble and both opaque and transparent glassware. The city of Granada was famous for its marquetry, in which ivory or bone was inlaid on wood, and even today Granada's artesans continue to create beautiful boxes in this style. The Muslims also left a heritage of ceramics in Granada and Málaga, the latter being famous for its production of lustreware in Islamic times.

There was also of course cultural exchange, in the field of art, through imitation: the embroideries on the ceremonial robes of some Christian kings contained copies of Kufic inscriptions (Quranic eulogies or verses) which were generally believed to be simply decorative motifs.

Such influences went beyond academic and erudite transmission; they were also very important factors at the level of social influence, resulting, generally, from intercultural contacts within the context of a régime of co-existence among peoples and cultures, as was undoubtedly the case in al-Andalus.

It should be said, in conclusion, that these factors of cultural interpenetration cannot always be measured, as has been the tendency in recent times, by the yardstick of cold statistics. Nor can they be evaluated at the moment they are produced, since cultural influence is not for the most part quantitative, but rather depends on the receptivity of the assimilating culture and the extent of contact on the two sides—the side that influences and the side that is influenced—so that the process can only be evaluated from a distance, after a certain amount of time has passed.

MARGARITA LÓPEZ GÓMEZ

BIOGRAPHIES OF CONTRIBUTORS

Claude Addas gained her doctorate from the University of Paris I in 1987, with a dissertation entitled *Ibn ʿArabī ou la quête du Soufre rouge*. This work, which was published in 1989, is a substantial biography of Ibn ʿArabī, and has been highly praised for its treatment both of Ibn ʿArabī's own thought and teaching and for the place this thought and teaching assumes within the wider religious and intellectual framework of its time.

Jamal al-Din al-ʿAlawi is Professor of the History of Islamic Philosophy and Chairman of the Department of Philosophy, Sociology and Psychology at the University of Muhammad Ben ʿAbdalla at Fez. He has published *Essays in Logic and Natural Science of Ibn Rushd* (1983); *The Works of Ibn Bājja* (1983); *Philosophical Treatises by Ibn Bājja* (1983); *Epitome of De Caelo by Ibn Rushd* (1984); *Extracts from the Physics of Aristotle by Ibn Rushd* (1983-84); *Theory of Demonstration and its Significance for the Philosophic Discourse of Ibn Rushd* (1986); "Al-Ghazālī and the 'Formation of Philosophic Discourse' by Ibn Rushd", *Review of the College of Art*, Fez, 8, 1986; "Problematic of the Relation between Physics and Metaphysics", *Review of the College of Art*, Fez, 3, 1988.

Aziz al-Azmeh is Professor of Islamic Studies at the University of Exeter. A specialist in Arabic and Islamic cultural and intellectual history in medieval and modern times, he has published two works on Ibn Khaldūn, *Ibn Khaldūn in Modern Scholarship* (1981) and *Ibn Khaldūn: An Essay in Reinterpretation* (1982), both in English, and a number of works of more general scope, *Historical Writing and Historical Knowledge* (1983) and *The Politics and the History of "Heritage" (1987)*, both in Arabic, and *Arabic Thought and Islamic Societies* (1986), in English.

Roger Boase was formerly Senior Lecturer at the University of Fez, Morocco, and is now Honorary Research Associate at Westfield College, University of London, where he has given seminars on the Arabic lyric of the Andalusian Courts. A hispanist and cultural historian with a special interest in the influence of the Arab world on Europe, his publications include *The Origin and Meaning of Courtly Love* (1977), *The Troubadour Revival: A Study of Social Change and Traditionalism in Late Medieval Spain* (1979, this work being subsequently translated into Spanish) and various articles on Spanish, Islamic and other subjects. At present he is engaged in research on the Spanish convert to Islam Anselm Turmeda.

Lucie Bolens is Professor of Medieval History at the University of Geneva. She has published widely on aspects of medieval agriculture and related subjects, with a special emphasis on Andalusī agriculture and dietary history. She is the author of *Les méthodes culturales au Moyen-Age d'après les traités d'agronomie andalous: traditions et techniques* (1974, a second enlarged edition appearing under the title *Agronomes andalous du Moyen Age* in 1981), *Elixirs et merveilles, un manuscrit inédit de cuisine suisse romande* (1984), *La cuisine andalouse, un art de vivre, 11e-13e siècle* (1990), *L'Andalousie du quotidien au sacré: 11e-13e siècle* (1991), *La Bible et l'histoire: au féminin* (1991) and numerous articles and contributions to scholarly volumes.

Charles Burnett is Lecturer in the history of Islamic influence in Europe in the Middle Ages and early modern period at the Warburg Institute of the University of London. His publications include *Hermann of Carinthia, De Essentiis: A Critical Edition with Translation and Commentary* (1982), *Pseudo-Bede: De Mundi Celestis Terrestrisque Constitutione: A Treatise on the Universe and the Soul* (edited and translated with the collaboration of members of a seminar group at the Warburg Institute, London) (1985), *Adelard of Bath: An English Scientist and Arabist of the Early Twelfth Century* (1987) and numerous articles concerning Islamic culture in Europe.

Johann Christoph Bürgel was assistant to Professor A. Dietrich at the *Seminar für Arabistik* at Göttingen from 1960 to 1970, and in 1970 he was appointed to the chair of Islamic Studies at the University of Bern, where he is now Head of Department. His main areas of research are Arabic and Persian literature and the history of Islamic culture, and he has published a dozen books and over 70 articles, his most recent major publication being *The Feather of Simurgh. The "Licit Magic" of the Arts in Medieval Islam* (1988). Professor Bürgel has organised three international symposia (1980, 1983, 1986) on contemporary literature in the Islamic world, and has lectured on various occasions in the USA and in a number of European and Oriental countries. In 1983 he received the Friedrich Rückert Award of the town of Schweinfurt for his translation of Arabic, Persian and Urdu poetry.

Pierre J. E. Cachia taught at the American University in Cairo and at the University of Edinburgh, and has, since 1975, been Professor of Arabic Language and Literature at Columbia University. His main books are: *Ṭāha Ḥusayn: His Place in the Egyptian Literary Renaissance* (1956); a critical edition of the *Kitāb al-burhān* of Eutychius of Alexandria (1960, 1961); *History of Islamic Spain* (with W. Montgomery Watt) (1965); *Islam: Past Influence and Present Challenge* (ed., with Alford T. Welch) (1979); *Popular Narrative Ballads of Modern Egypt* (1989); and *An Overview of Modern Arabic Literature* (1990). He has also contributed to the *Dictionary of Orien-*

tal Literatures, the *Encyclopaedia Britannica*, the *Encyclopaedia of Islam* and the *Encyclopaedia Americana,* and published articles in various scholarly journals. Professor Cachia is the co-founder and joint editor of the *Journal of Arabic Literature* and of its Translations and Literary Studies series of books.

Pedro Chalmeta has been a member of the Spanish National Centre for Scientific Research, Director of the Seminario Historia, Dercho y Economía of the Instituto Hispano-Arabe, a professor at the Universidad Complutense de Madrid, Visiting Professor at the University of California at Los Angeles, the Maison des Sciences de l'Homme (Paris) and the Collège de France (Paris), and is at present Professor at the University of Saragossa. He is a member of the Academy of History of Iraq. Professor Chalmeta is the author of *El Libro del buen gobierno del zoco de al-Saqaṭī* (1969), *El "señor del zoco" en España: edades media y moderna. Contribución al estudio de la historia del mercado* (1973), *Concesiones territoriales en al-Andalus (hasta la llegada de los almorávides)* (1976) and *La formación de al-Andalus: los primeros 80 años* (1991), and, in collaboration with F. Corriente, of *Al-Muqtabas (V) de Ibn Ḥayyān* (1979) and *Kitāb al-wat̲h̲āʾiq wa ʾl-sijillāt li Ibn al-ʿAṭṭār* (1983). He has also written numerous articles in Spanish and French on varied aspects of Islamic Spain.

Olivia Remie Constable was educated at the Universities of Yale and Princeton, obtaining a Ph.D. from the latter in 1989, has held various fellowships in the United States and is now Assistant Professor in the Department of History at Columbia University. She has a special interest in the subject of trade in Muslim Spain, and has produced a number of articles and papers in this area.

Federico Corriente is full Professor of Arabic and Islamic Studies at the University of Madrid. He has previously taught at establishments of Higher Education in Cairo, Tétouan, Rabat, Philadelphia and Saragossa, and has undertaken research in several areas of Arabic and Semitic studies, including pre-Islamic and Modern Arabic Literature, Andalusī Arabic Literature, Semitic Linguistics, Ethiopian Studies and, above all, Andalusī and Western Arabic dialectology, which has been his main concern in recent years. He has written more than twenty books and forty articles, including translations from Arabic and Ethiopic into Spanish (including the *Muʿallaqāt*, Ibn Quzmān's *Dīwān*, al-Ḥakim's *Ahl al-kahf*, The Book of Henoc and The Book of Jubilees), editions of Arabic texts (such as Ibn Ḥayyān's *Muqtabas V*, Ibn al-ʿAṭṭār's Legal Formularies and the *Dīwāns* of Ibn Quzmān and As̲h̲s̲h̲us̲h̲tarī), Arabic grammars and dictionaries for the use of students and grammatical and lexical treatises on Andalusī Arabic.

Miguel Cruz Hernández is Professor of Islamic Thought at the Universidad Autónoma de Madrid. He has published very widely in the field of Spanish Muslim philosophy and other areas, his publications including such major general works as *Filosofía hispano-musulmana* (1957, 2 vols.), *La filosofía árabe* (1963), *Historia del pensamiento en el mundo islámico* (ed.) (1981, 2 vols.) and *Historia del pensamiento en al-Andalus* (ed.) (1986, 2 vols.), and editions or critical works in connection with such specific figures as: Ibn Sīnā: *La Metafísica de Avicena* (1949) and *Avicena: Sobre Metafísica* (Introduction, Translation and Notes) (1950); Ibn ʿArabī: *Ibn Arabi de Murcia* (1968); Ramon Llull: *El pensamiento de Ramon Llull* (1977); and Ibn Rushd: *Abu-l-Walid Ibn Rušd, Averroes: vida, obra, pensamiento, influencia* (1986) and *Averroes: Exposición de la "Republica" de Platon* (Introduction, Translation and Notes) (1987).

James Dickie (Yaqub Zaki) has held academic appointments at the Universities of Manchester, Lancaster and Harvard-MIT. He was Chief Adviser to the World of Islam Festival, 1974-76. His main research interests are in the field of Muslim Spain and Islamic theology and liturgiology. In 1975 he published an edition (with translation) of the *dīwān* of Ibn Shuhayd al-Andalusī, a version without translation also being published in Cairo in 1969, and he has also published articles in various academic journals and has contributed to the Encyclopaedia Britannica. He is currently engaged on a monograph on the Alhambra, entitled *The Alhambra. A Functional Analysis.*

Jerrilynn Dodds was Assistant Professor in the Department of Art History and Archeology at Columbia University from 1980 to 1989 and is now Associate Professor at the School of Architecture at the City College of the City University of New York. She has also held visiting lectureships and professorships at the University of Minnesota (1978), the University of North Carolina (1978-79 and 1979-80) and Duke University (1980). A specialist in Medieval Art and Architecture, with particular concentration on the Spanish and Islamic fields, her publications include *Architecture and Ideology in Early Medieval Spain* (1990) (which won her the ASHAHS Publication award), *Essays in Honor of Whitney Stoddart* (ed.) (1986), *Al-Andalus: The Islamic Arts of Spain* (ed., with Daniel Walker) (forthcoming, 1992), and numerous articles on Andalusī art and architecture.

Mikel de Epalza has taught at the universities of Barcelona, Lyon, Tunis, Algiers, Oran and Madrid, and is at present Professor of Arabic and Islamic Studies at the University of Alicante, Spain. He has published widely in the fields of Islamic-Christian relations, the history of al-Andalus, relations between Spain and the Arab world, and Islamic urbanism, his publications including *La Tuhfa. Autobiografía y polémica islámica contra el Cristianismo, de Abdalla at-Taryumān (Fray Anselmo Turmeda)* (1971), *Jésus otage.*

Juifs, chrétiens et musulmans en Espagne (VIIe-XVIIe siècles) (1987) and *La rábita islámica. Historia institucional* (in press).

Antonio Fernández-Puertas has held Spain's only chair in Islamic Art, at Granada University, since 1980. Previously he was, until 1975, an official researcher of the Consejo Superior de Investigaciones Científicas, and in 1974 he became curator and deputy director of the Museo Nacional de Arte Hispanomusulmán in the Alhambra, being director of the Museum from 1978 to 1987. He has been appointed a member of Spain's Archaeological Mission in the Islamic Near East, a member of the Governing Board of the Alhambra, a member of the Board of State Museums and a member of the Committee of Artistic Acquisitions and Export Control, and is a fellow of the Royal Asiatic Society. Dr Fernández-Puertas has published over 60 works in specialised journals on Islamic art, architecture, epigraphy, calligraphy, numismatics, decoration, geometric design and proportion, and he has written the only major work on the kufic calligraphy of the palaces of Comares and the Riyāḍ (Lions) in the Alhambra and a further monograph on the façade of the palace of Comares.

María Isabel Fierro was Reader in the Department of Arabic at the Universidad Complutense in Madrid from 1983 to 1987, and has, since 1987, been a researcher in the Arabic Department at the Institute of Philology at the Consejo Superior de Investigaciones Científicas in Madrid, her main areas of research interest being Mālikī law, treatises against religious innovation, early *ḥadīth*, heresy in Islam and the history of al-Andalus. She is the author of *La heterodoxia en al-Andalus durante el periodo omeya* (1987), has provided an edition, translation and study of Muḥammad b. Waḍḍāḥ al-Qurṭubī's *Kitāb al-bidaʿ* (1988), and has published numerous articles in the field of Andalusī religious studies.

Madeleine Fletcher has taught at the Universities of Harvard (1966-69), Princeton (1972-73) and Columbia (1975-80), and now teaches Spanish Literature and Civilisation, and also courses on Islamic Law, at Tufts University, Medford, Massachusetts. She is presently working on a study of the history of the Almohad dynasty in Spain and North Africa, to be published by the University of South Carolina Press under the title *Western Islam: The Twelfth-Century Renaissance.*

Expiración García Sánchez taught in the Department of Islamic History at the University of Granada from 1979 to 1985, and has, since 1985, been a researcher in the Arabic Department at the Consejo Superior de Investigaciones Científicas in Madrid, becoming its vice-director in 1989. She is a specialist in the history of Andalusī science, with particular reference to alimentation and agriculture, together with the related fields of botany, pharmacology and dietetics. Dr García Sánchez has been principle researcher in connection with a number of projects, such as that investigating agronomic knowledge and techniques in Islamic Spain, and has headed a group conducting research into the Natural Sciences in Muslim al-Andalus.

Lois A. Giffen has taught at New York University and Portland State University, and is at present Associate Professor of Arabic Literature and Islamic Studies at the University of Utah. She is the author of *Theory of Profane Love among the Arabs: The Development of the Genre* (1971, 1972) and of "Love Poetry and Love Theory in Medieval Arabic Literature" in *Arabic Poetry: Theory and Development*, ed. G. E. von Grünebaum (1973), these studies being based on research in Arabic manuscript collections in nine countries under an ACLS/SSRC Foreign Area Fellowship. In addition to other papers on courtly love or love theory, Dr Giffen has published on aspects of the Arabic zoological tradition, Islamic ethical attitudes towards the animal kingdom, ethical influences in Islamic ritual law, motifs in the heroic tales of the Oghuz Turks and brief accounts of medieval Arab or Arabo-Persian scholars, and has, in papers and seminars, explored humour and satire in the Arabic tradition up to modern times.

Thomas F. Glick is Professor of History and Geography at the University of Boston. He is a historian of science and technology and has written on the diffusion of Islamic technology in Christian Spain. He is the author of *Irrigation and Society in Medieval Valencia* (1970) and *Islamic and Christian Spain in the Early Middle Ages* (1979).

Oleg Grabar was formerly Professor of Fine Arts at Harvard University and Aga Khan Professor of Islamic Art and Architecture, and is now Professor in the School of Historical Studies, Institute for Advanced Study, Princeton. He is the author of numerous works on historical subjects. His book, *The Formation of Islamic Art* (1973) has been translated into German (1979) and French (enlarged edition, 1987), a revised and enlarged edition in English appearing in 1987. His other writings include: *The Coinage of the Tulunids* (1957); *Persian Art Before and After the Mongol Conquest* (1959); *Sassanian Silver, Late Antique and Early Medieval Arts of Luxury from Iran* (1967); *Studies in Islamic Art and Archaeology* (1976); *The Alhambra* (1978); *City in the Desert* (with Renata Holod, James Knustad, William Trousdale) (1978); *Epic Images and Contemporary History* (1980); and *The Great Mosque of Isfahan* (1990).

Pierre Guichard has taught at the Universities of Toulouse, Geneva and Lyon, and is at present Professor of Medieval History at the Université Lumière-Lyon II. He is a former member of the Casa de Velázquez of Madrid. Professor Guichard is the author of *Structures sociales "orientales" et "occidentales" dans l'Espagne musulmane* (1977), *L'Espagne et la Sicile musulmanes aux XIe et XIIe siècles* (1990) and *Les musulmans de Valence et la*

Reconquête (XIe-XIIe siècles) (1990), the last-named being the published version of the thesis submitted for his *doctorat d'Etat*, and has produced articles and contributions for various learned journals and larger scholarly works.

Abbas H. Hamdani was formerly Professor of Islamic History at the University of Karachi and Professor of Arabic Studies at the American University in Cairo, and is currently Professor of Middle Eastern History at the University of Wisconsin-Milwaukee, where he has for many years been Chairman of the University's Committee for Middle Eastern and North African Studies and of the Comparative Study of Religion Program. He has also held research fellowships at the Institute of Ismaili Studies, London, and the American Research Center in Egypt. A specialist in Fāṭimid Studies and the social and cultural history of medieval Islam, he is the author of *The Fāṭimids* (1962, the work appearing in a Persian translation in 1985) and the chapter on Fāṭimid History and Historians in the *Cambridge History of Arabic Literature (Vol. 2B)* (forthcoming), and has published numerous articles and scholarly contributions in North America and in various European, Asian and North African countries.

Leonard Patrick Harvey held lectureships in Spanish at Oxford (1956-58), Southampton (1958-60) and Queen Mary College, London (1960-63), was Head of the Spanish Department at Queen Mary College from 1963 to 1973 (being appointed Professor in 1967) and Cervantes Professor of Spanish at King's College, London, from 1973 to 1983. He became Emeritus Professor of Spanish in the University of London in 1983. He is the author of *Islamic Spain 1250 -1500* (1990), and edited and introduced S. M. Stern's posthumous book *Hispano-Arabic Strophic Poetry* (1974). A specialist on the Moriscos, he has published many seminal works on their history and culture, and has undertaken important pioneer work on the study of *aljamiado* texts.

Robert Hillenbrand has taught in the Department of Fine Art at the University of Edinburgh since 1971, and has been Professor there since 1989. He has also held Visiting Professorships at Princeton (1979), UCLA (1981) and Bamberg (1990). He is the author of *Imperial Images in Persian Painting* and *Islamic Architecture in North Africa*, has edited such works as *The Islamic Book* and *Proceedings of the Congress of European Arabists and Islamicists*, and has, among many other articles, contributed material on the major Islamic building types for the *Encyclopaedia of Islam*. He has been a board member of the journals *Art History* (1978-88), *Persica* and the *Bulletin of the Iranian Institute*, and has been on the editorial boards of *Studies in Islamic Art* (Los Angeles) and *Oxford Studies in Islamic Art*, and been Islamic art adviser to the Macmillan *Dictionary of Art*. He organised an exceptionally extensive exhibition of Persian miniature paintings at Edinburgh in 1977, and also organised major international conferences on Islamic art, in Edinburgh, in 1977, 1982, 1987 and 1990. He is secretary of the British Institute of Persian Studies.

Salma Khadra Jayyusi taught at a number of Arab and American universities, before, in 1980, leaving teaching to found the Project of Translation from Arabic (PROTA), designed to combat ignorance and misrepresentation of Arabic literature and culture in the wider world. Her poetry and critical writings have been widely published, her first collection of poems, *Return from the Dreamy Fountain*, appearing in 1960, and her two-volume critical history *Trends and Movements in Modern Arabic Poetry* in 1977. As Director of PROTA Dr Jayyusi has so far edited around thirty volumes, ranging from single author works to large anthologies of modern Arabic literature, the latter comprising *Modern Arabic Poetry* (1987), *The Literature of Modern Arabia* (1988), *An Anthology of Modern Palestinian Literature* (1992), *Modern Arabic Fiction* (in press) and (with Roger Allen as co-editor) *Contemporary Arabic Drama* (in press). Since 1989 she has been working on a new anthology, *Poets of the End of the Century (New Voices in Arabic Poetry)*, and is also preparing two collections of her critical articles in Arabic and English.

Luce López-Baralt teaches Spanish and Comparative Literatures at the University of Puerto Rico. She has held a number of fellowships and has been Visiting Professor and Scholar at Harvard, Yale, Brown and Rabat Universities. Her book *San Juan de la Cruz y el Islam* appeared in 1985, and her edition of the *Obras completas de San Juan de la Cruz* (in collaboration with Eulogio Pacho) is now under publication. She is also the author of *Huellas del Islam en la literatura española. De Juan Ruiz a Juan Goytisolo* (1985; Arabic translation 1990; English translation under publication) and *Un "Kama Sutra español". El primer tratado erótico de nuestra lengua (MS. S-2 BRAH Madrid)* (under publication) and has edited Miguel Asín Palacios's *Sadilies y alumbrados* (1990). Dr. López-Baralt is a member of the Academia de la Lengua Española de Puerto Rico and of the Academia de la Lengua Española de Madrid, and a member of the Board of Directors of the Asociación Internacional de Hispanistas, the Comité International d'Etudes Morisques, the *Nueva Revista de Filología Hispánica* (Mexico) and the *Journal of Hispanic Philology* (Florida).

Margarita López Gómez has been Director of the Department of History and Art of the Instituto Occidental de Cultura Islámica in Madrid since 1985, and, since 1991, has held the same post at the Fundación Occidental de Cultura Islámica. She has recently supervised two important expositions of Islamic art, in Toledo (1987) and Teruel (1988).

Mahmoud A. Makki is Professor of Andalusian Literature at Cairo University, having been commissioned, in 1982, to found the new Department of

Spanish Language and Literature at the University which he has headed up till now. Dr. Makki has many books and other works dealing with Andalusī history and literature, and also with with various other fields of Arabic literature. Among his works are *Shiʿism in al-Andalus* (1954); *Egypt and the Early Historical Sources on al-Andalus* (1957); *New Historical Documents from the Age of the Almoravids* (1959-1960); *The Dīwān of Ibn Darrāj of Castile* (1961); *A Study of Cultural Currents from the Arab East and their Influence on Andalusī Culture until the Fourth Century A.H.* (1967); and with Suhair al-Qalamawi, *Influence of Arabs and Islam in European Civilisation* (1971).

Manuela Marín has taught at the Universidad Complutense, Madrid, the Spanish Institute, Baghdad, and the Instituto Hispano-Arabe, Madrid, and has, since 1988, been a researcher in the Department of Arabic Studies at the Consejo Superior de Investigaciones Científicas in Madrid. She is the editor of the journal *Al-Qanṭara.* Her current research interests are the social and cultural history of al-Andalus and food in Islamic societies, her recent publications including *Individuo y sociedad en al-Andalus* (in press), *Kanz al-fawāʾid fī tawzīʿ al-mawāʾid* (ed., with D. Waines) (in press) and an edition, with introduction, of Ibn Bas̲h̲kuwāl's *Kitāb al-mustag̲h̲īt̲h̲īn* (1991). She has published articles, in various languages, in *Al-Qanṭara, Cahiers d'Onomastique Arabe, Studia Islamica, Quaderni di Studi Arabi, Manuscripts of the Middle East* and the *British Society for Middle Eastern Studies Bulletin.*

María Rosa Menocal was Associate Professor of Romance Languages at the University of Pennsylvania from 1980 to 1986, and has, since 1986, been Associate Professor in the Department of Spanish and Portuguese at the University of Yale, where she has been Director of Graduate Studies since 1987 and held a Senior Faculty Fellowship from 1989 to 1990. She is the author of *Primavera: An Introduction to Italian* (1983), *The Arabic Role in Medieval Literary History: A Forgotten Heritage* (1987) and *Writing in Dante's Cult of Truth from Borges to Boccaccio* (1991), and has published numerous articles on predominantly Romance subjects.

Dieter Messner is Professor of Romance Philology at the University of Salzburg and head of the Department of Ibero-Romance there. He is the author of *Dictionnaire chronologique de la langue portugaise* (1976), *Einführung in die Geschichte des französischen Wortschatzes* (1977), *Répertoire chronologique des mots français* (1977), *Geschichte des spanischen Wortschatzes* (1979), *Iberoromanisch, eine Einführung* (1983), *História do léxico português* (1990) and numerous other books and articles on the history of Romance languages. Professor Messner is also the editor of *Studien zur rumänischen Sprache und Literatur*, *Romanische Volksbücher* and *Salzburger Romanistische Schriften.*

James T. Monroe has taught at the University of Harvard and the University of California, San Diego, and is at present Professor of Arabic and Comparative Literature in the Departments of Near Eastern Studies and Comparative Literature at the University of California, Berkeley. Professor Monroe is the author of *The Shuʿūbiyya in al-Andalus: The Risāla of Ibn García and Five Refutations. Introduction, Translation and Notes* (1970), *Islam and the Arabs in Spanish Scholarship (Sixteenth Century to the Present)* (1970), *Risālat at-Tawābiʿ wa-z-zawābiʿ (The Treatise of Familiar Spirits and Demons) by Ibn Shuhaid al-Andalusī. Introduction, Translation and Notes* (1971), *Hispano-Arabic Poetry: A Student Anthology. Arabic Texts, Translations, and Notes* (1974) and *The Art of Badīʿ az-Zamān al-Hamadhānī as Picaresque Narrative* (1983), and, in collaboration with Benjamin M. Liu, of *Ten Hispano-Arabic Strophic Songs in the Modern Oral Tradition: Music and Texts* (1989). He has, in addition, published widely in scholarly journals and contributed to a number of larger academic works in the field of Hispanic-Arabic studies.

Julio Samsó is a full professor in the Department of Arabic at the Universidad Autónoma de Barcelona and the University of Barcelona. He is an effective member of the Real Academia de Buenas Letras de Barcelona and the Académie Internationale d'Histoire des Sciences (Paris) and a corresponding member of the Real Academia de la Historia (Madrid). He was Treasurer of the International Union of History of Science—Division of History of Science from 1982 to 1989 and a consulting member of Commission 41 (History of Astronomy) of the International Astronomical Union from 1982 to 1985. He has, together with Professor Juan Vernet, organised two exhibitions: "Astronomical Instruments in Medieval Spain and their Influence in Europe" (Sta. Cruz de la Palma, 1985) and "The Scientific Legacy of al-Andalus" (Madrid, March-May, 1992). Professor Samsó has published widely on Andalusī science and in other areas of Arabic scholarship, his publications including *Estudios sobre Abū Naṣr b. ʿAlī b. ʿIrāq* (1969), *Tratado de Astrología atribuido a Enrique de Villena* (with Pedro M. Catedra, 1980, 2nd edition 1983), *Antología de las Mil y Una Noches* (1976, further editions 1982 and 1986) and *Las ciencias de los antiguos en al-Andalus* (1992).

Raymond P. Scheindlin is Professor of Medieval Hebrew Literature at the Jewish Theological Seminary of America, and a former provost of the Seminary. His main field of research is medieval Hebrew poetry and its connections with Arabic literature. His publications include *Form and Structure in the Poetry of al-Muʿtamid Ibn ʿAbbād* (1975), *201 Arabic Words* (1978); *Wine, Women and Death: Medieval Hebrew Poems on the Good Life* (1986), *The Gazelle: Medieval Hebrew Poems on God, Israel and the Soul* (1991). He has also produced numerous articles and translations from Yiddish and Hebrew. Dr Scheindlin was a Guggenheim fellow in 1988.

Dominique Urvoy is Professor of Arabic Thought and Civilisation at the University of Toulouse-le-Mirail. He earlier pursued research work at the Casa de Velazquez in Madrid, at the Institut Français d'Etudes Arabes in Damascus and at the Centre National de la Recherche Scientifique in Paris, and has taught at the Universities of Damascus and Dakar. He is the author of *Le monde des ulémas andalous du V/XIe au VII/XIIIe siècle-Etude sociologique* (1978), *Penser l'Islam. Les présupposés islamiques de l' "Art" de Lull* (1980), *Pensers d'al-Andalus. La vie intellectuelle à Cordoue et Séville au temps des empires berbères (fin XIe siècle-début XIIIe siècle)* (1990) and *Ibn Rushd (Averroes)* (1991).

Rafael Valencia teaches Arabic Language, the History of Islam and the History of al-Andalus at the University of Seville. He is the author of *Sevilla entre dos mundos (711-1492): de Africa a América* (1983), *Ibn Jaldún. Introducción a la historia. Antología* (1985), *Latinoamérica y el mundo arabo-islámico en el horizonte del año 2000* (1986), *Sevilla musulmana hasta la caída del califato: contribución a su estudio* (1988) and *El espacio urbano de la Sevilla árabe* (1988).

Juan Vernet has, since 1954, held the Chair of Arabic Language and Literature at the University of Barcelona. He is a member of the Real Academia de la Historia (Madrid), the Academia de Buenas Letras (Barcelona) and the Académie Internationale d'Histoire des Sciences (Paris), and is also an Honorary Member of the Royal Asiatic Society (London). A distinguished Arabist and historian of science, his publications include *Astrología y astronomía en el Renacimiento. La revolución copernicana* (1974), *La cultura hispano-árabe en Oriente y Occidente* (1978, French version published 1985, under the title *Ce que la culture doit aux Arabes d'Espagne*), *La ciencia en al-Andalus* (1986) and *Simbad el Marino* (1987). He has produced Spanish translations of the Quran (1952, 1963) and the *Arabian Nights* (1967). In the realm of scientific history he has demonstrated, among other things, that the nautical map originated in China, that the compass was known in Spain in the 3rd/9th century and that, according to some Arab astronomers, the universe measured several light years.

María J. Viguera has held teaching posts at the Universidad Autónoma, Madrid, the Universidad Complutense, Madrid, and the University of Saragossa, and is now Head of the Department of Arabic at the Universidad Complutense, Madrid. She was also, for ten years, Chief of the Bibliographical Section at the Instituto Miguel Asín of the Consejo Superior de Investigaciones Científicas. Dr Viguera's publications include her doctoral dissertation on *Al-Musnad* of Ibn Marzūq al-Tilimsanī (published in Spanish in 1977 and Arabic in 1981), her translation *Gala de caballeros* from the Arabic original of Ibn Hudhayl (1977) and works on Andalusī history, such as *Aragón musulmán* (1981, 2nd edition 1988), and she is the editor of *Ana-*

quel de Estudios Arabes, initiated in 1990. Dr Viguera is also the editor of such Acts of Proceedings as *La mujer en al-Andalus. Reflejos históricos de su actividad y categorías sociales* (1985), and has published numerous articles and other scholarly contributions in the field of Arabic studies.

David Waines has held teaching posts at the American University in Cairo and Ain Shams University, Cairo (1972-74), at Simon Fraser University, British Columbia (1975), and, since 1976, at the University of Lancaster, first in the Department of Arabic and Islamic Studies and, since 1983, in the Department of Religious Studies. His current research interests are in the field of medico-culinary tradition and dietary theory in medieval Islamic culture, his book *In a Caliph's Kitchen: The Golden Age of the Arab Table* appearing in 1989, and he has also written *The Unholy War: Israel and Palestine 1897-1971* (1971, a second edition entitled *A Sentence of Exile* appearing in 1977) . His most recent book, *The Revolt of the Zanj*, Volume 36 of Tabari's *History of Kings and Prophets*, is in press.

Owen Wright is Reader in Arabic at the School of Oriental and African Studies of the University of London. His publications include *The Modal System of Arab and Persian Music, A. D. 1250-1300* (1978), a transcription with annotations of Demetrius Cantemir, *The Collection of Notations: i: text* (1992), *Words Without Songs: A Musicological Study of an Ottoman Anthology and its Precursors* (1992), a chapter on "Music and Verse" in the *Cambridge History of Arabic Literature (Vol. I)* (1983) and various other publications in the musicological field in scholarly volumes and journals.

INDEX

Except in the case of a few extremely well-known figures (e.g., the Emperor Hadrian, the Emperor Charles V), the following conventions are normally followed with regard to rulers:

- Effective rulers of al-Andalus are given their title alone, with no further designation (e.g., ʿAbd al-Raḥmān II, *al-Amīr*; Abū Yaʿqūb Yūsuf, Caliph);
- Caliphs outside al-Andalus are designated as appropriate (e.g., Abū Bakr, First Caliph of Islam; Hishām b. ʿAbd al-Malik, Umayyad Caliph in Damascus);
- Other rulers, within or outside al-Andalus, are designated with reference to the appropriate territory or tribal group (e.g., Al-Muʿtamid b. ʿAbbād, ruler of Seville; ʿAlī b. ʿUthmān, Abū ʾl-Ḥasan, of the Marīnids).

Main references are in bold.

ʿAbbās b. ʿAbd al-Muṭṭalib 18
ʿAbbās b. Firnās 31, 116, 939, 942
ʿAbbās b. al-Mundhir, Archbishop of Seville 138
ʿAbbās b. Nāṣiḥ 24, 26
Abbasids 18, 19, 20, 24, 25, 26, 35, 113, 117, 120, 122, 125, 130, 131, 133, 137, 265, 337, 370, 371, 399, 424, 508, 510, 559, 573, 603, 604, 610, 616, 617, 690, 712, 726, 777, 867, 880, 923, 937, 987, 1011
ʿAbd al-Aʿlā b. Wahb 900
ʿAbd Allāh b. ʿAbd al-Raḥmān ("al-Balansī") 21, 22
ʿAbd Allāh b. ʿAbd al-Raḥmān al-Nāṣir 854, 897
ʿAbd Allāh b. Badr 643
ʿAbd Allāh b. Bulluqqīn b. Bādīs, ruler of Granada 60, 61, 62, 63, 688, 694, 700, 717
ʿAbd Allāh b. Ḥusayn b. ʿĀṣim 888
ʿAbd Allāh b. Khālid 19
ʿAbd Allāh b. al-Mughallis 888
ʿAbd Allāh b. al-Muhājir 50
ʿAbd Allāh b. Muḥammad, *al-Amīr* 30, **32-34**, 49, 133, 137, 405, 463, 683, 744, 753, 777, 779, 880, 901, 938
ʿAbd Allāh b. Muḥammad b. Maslama 56
ʿAbd Allāh b. Muḥammad b. Qāsim 854
ʿAbd Allāh b. Mūsā, Abū Muḥammad 660
ʿAbd Allāh b. Naṣr 890
ʿAbd Allāh b. Ṭāhir 24
ʿAbd Allāh b. Zubayr 4, 18
ʿAbd Allāh, Fāṭimid propagandist 240
ʿAbd al-ʿAzīz al-Manṣūr 50
ʿAbd al-ʿAzīz b. Marwān 4
ʿAbd al-ʿAzīz b. Mūsā b. Nuṣayr, Governor 9, 10, 11, 744
ʿAbd al-Barr b. Hārūn 641
ʿAbd al-Ḥamīd b. Yaḥyā b. Saʿd 342
ʿAbd al-Karīm b. Mughīth 26
ʿAbd al-Malik b. ʿAbd Allāh b. Umayya 32
ʿAbd al-Malik b. ʿAbd al-Jawād 32
ʿAbd al-Malik b. Jahwar 52
ʿAbd al-Malik b. al-Manṣūr al-ʿĀmirī 606
ʿAbd al-Malik b. Marwān, Umayyad Caliph in Damascus 4, 18, 378, 639
ʿAbd al-Malik b. Umayya 34
ʿAbd al-Malik b. Zuhr, Abū ʾl-ʿAlāʾ 145, 944
ʿAbd al-Malik b. Zuhr, Abū Marwān 145, 944
ʿAbd al-Muʾmin, Caliph 68, **69-72**, 73, 238, 240, 241, 247, 611, 612
ʿAbd al-Muṭṭalib 902
ʿAbd al-Raḥmān I, called "al-Dākhil", *al-Amīr* 11, 13, 16, **19-21**, 22, 50, **113-14**, 116, 118, 129, 130, 137, 322, 510, 599, 600,

601, 602, 603, 640, 641, 682, 683, 684, 777, 903, 937, 988, 1059
ʿAbd al-Raḥmān II, *al-Amīr* **24-27**, 28, 29, 31, 115, 116, 130, 141, 144, 463, 557, 559, 601, 604, 641, 642, 710, 777, 896, 939, 954, 960
ʿAbd al-Raḥmān III, called "al-Nāṣir", *al-Amīr*/Caliph **33-38**, 41, 44, 45, 47, 50, 117, 124, 126, 130, 138, 143, 188, 189, 190, 264, 329, 330, 463, 510, 511, 587, 601, 603, 604, 605, 642, 643, 644, 684, 688, 690, 749, 750, 752, 754, 764, 779, 853, 854, 881, 886, 897, 900, 938, 939, 988, 989, 1059
ʿAbd al-Raḥmān b. Ibrāhīm b. Ḥajjāj 684
ʿAbd al-Raḥmān b. Jahwar 52
ʿAbd al-Raḥmān b. al-Manṣūr al-ʿĀmirī ("Sanchuelo") 42, 47, 50, 421
ʿAbd al-Raḥmān b. Marwān ("al-Jillīqī") 29, 30, 32
ʿAbd al-Raḥmān b. Rustum 27
ʿAbd al-Raḥmān b. Sayyid 954
ʿAbd al-Raḥmān b. Zayyān 608
ʿAbda, Princess *see* Teresa
Aben Abóo 224
Aben Humeya (Fernando de Válor) 224
Abraham b. Dāʾūd 197
Abraham b. Ezra 195, 517, 1042, 1043
Abraham b. al-Fakhkhār 198
Abraham bar Ḥiyya 197, 1050
Abraham b. Muhājir 190
Abū ʾl-ʿAbbās of Murcia 766
Abū ʾl-ʿAbbās b. al-Rūmiyya 1031
Abū ʿAbd Allāh Muḥammad ("Boabdil"), ruler of Granada 83, 84, 265, 664
Abū ʾl-Ajannas 888
Abū ʿAlī Yūnus 247
Abū ʿĀmir 784
Abū ʿAmr al-Dānī 860-61, 862, 863
Abū ʾl-ʿArab 941
Abū ʾl-Atāhiya 26, 326, 328, 337, 389
Abū Bakr, First Caliph of Islam 241, 242, 243, 639
Abū Bakr b. ʿAmmār 53
Abū Bakr b. ʿUmar 61
Abū Dabbūs, Caliph 77
Abū Dāwūd 241
Abū Faḍl b. Ḥasday 190, 191, 784, 946, 947
Abū ʾl-Fidāʾ 278
Abū ʾl-Ghamr b. ʿAzzūn 70
Abū ʾl-Ḥajjāj 945
Abū Ḥanīfa al-Dīnawarī, *al-Imām* 278, 331, 940, 1003, 1006
Abū ʾl-Ḥasan ʿAlī, Prince, of Granada 83
Abū ʾl-Ḥasan b. Buṭlān 785
Abū ʾl-Ḥazm b. Jahwar 49, 52, 344, 347, 348, 349
Abū ʾl-Khayr (of Seville) 145, 942, 990, 996, 1002, 1005, 1006
Abū ʾl-Khayr (heretic) 901
Abū Madyan 922
Abū Maʿshar 173, 527, 1048, 1050
Abū Maslama of Madrid 941
Abū ʾl-Mughīra b. Ḥazm 710
Abū Muḥammad ʿAbd al-Ḥaqq 655, 658
Abū ʾl-Naʿīm Riḍwān 81
Abū ʾl-Najm 324
Abū Nuwās 26, 326, 328, 332, 370
Abū ʾl-Qāsim b. ʿAbbād 53
Abū ʾl-Qāsim b. Buṭlān al-Baghdādī 1002
Abū ʾl-Qāsim b. Ṣāʿid (Ṣāʿid of Toledo) 252, 512, 778, 780, **784**, 785, 855, 912, 941, 946, 962, 963
Abū Saʿīd b. ʿAbd al-Muʾmin 788
Abū ʾl-Ṣalt Umayya 785, 945, 956, 957, 958
Abū Tammām 321, 326, 328, 332, 346, 372
Abū ʿUmar Aḥmad 648
Abū ʾl-Walīd b. Mundhir 923
Abū Yaʿqūb Yūsuf, Caliph 79, 140, 142, 144, 612, 789, 831, 838
Abū Yaʿza 236
Abū Yūsuf Yaʿqūb, Caliph 78, 79, 140, 792
Abulafia, Meir 198
Abulafia, Samuel Halevi 595, 596
Abulafia, Todros 198
Abulcasis *see* Al-Zahrāwī, Abū ʾl-Qāsim
Adelard of Bath 278, 961, 1038, 1039, 1051, 1060
Adobales 30
Aesculapius 947
Agadir 3
Aghlabids 30
Aghmāt 54, 60, 61, 63, 140, 357, 359
Agila, ruler of the Visigoths 113
Aguilar de la Frontera 32
Aḥmad b. Abī ʿAbda, Abū ʾl-ʿAbbās 33, 34
Aḥmad b. Baqī 883
Aḥmad b. Ḥakam b. Ḥafṣūn 784
Aḥmad b. Marwān 766
Aḥmad b. Naṣr 645
Aimeric de Peguilhan 475
ʿĀʾisha, Umayyad Princess 121

Ajarquía, Battle of 83
Al-Akhṭāl 324
Alani 5
Alanje 29, 75
Alarcos, Battle of 74, 75
Alava 22, 26, 32
'Alawis 48, 51, 59
Alba, Duke of 220
Albaicín Quarter (Granada) 84, 91, 99, 100, 101, 102, 1025, 1030
Albertus Magnus 278, 517
Albuquerque 30
Albuquerque, Affonso de 288
Alcaçer do Sal 43, 74
Alcalá de Guadaira 9
Alcalá de Henares 8
Alcalá la Real 80
Alcaraz, Battle of 55
Alcaudete 79
Alcira 76
Aledo 62, 64
Alemán, Mateo 520
Alexander II, Pope 465
Alexander VI, Pope 282
Alexander of Aphrodisia 781, 813, 814, 815, 816, 817, 818, 819, 823, 824, 825
Alexander the Great 1039
Alexandria 23, 69, 205, 207, 512, 702, 760, 763, 765, 766, 867
Alfaques, Puerto de los 231
Alfonso I, "the Warrior", of Aragon 55, 65, 67, 151, 156, 162, 462, 688
Alfonso I, of Asturias 17, 22
Alfonso II, of Aragon 196
Alfonso II, of Asturias 22
Alfonso III, of Aragon 76
Alfonso III, of Asturias and León 30, 33
Alfonso IV, of Asturias and León 36
Alfonso IV, of Portugal 80
Alfonso V, of Asturias and León 43
Alfonso VI, of Castile and León 51, 54, 56, 57, 58, 61, 62, 63, 64, 65, 123, 150, 172, 173, 174, 181, 196, 278, 462, 464, 465, 466, 609, 651, 705, 1005
Alfonso VII, of Aragon 1041
Alfonso VII, of Castile and León 66, 71
Alfonso VIII, of Castile 73, 74, 75, 588, 593
Alfonso IX, of León 75
Alfonso X, "the Wise", of Castile and León 78, 79, 128, 138, 143, 144, 146, 196, 198, 465, 509, 519, 566, 589, 596, 767, 874, 941, 950, 1001, 1047, 1048, 1060
Alfonso XI, of Castile and León 79, 80, 128, 184
Alfonso Henriquez II, of Portugal 72
Alfonso de Madrigal 476
Algarve 12, 68, 683, 698, 1007
Algeciras 8, 26, 27, 44, 52, 53, 60, 61, 62, 70, 78, 79, 80, 139, 184, 618, 748
Algiers 208, 224, 227
Alhama (near Granada) 83
Alhama (de Aragón) 181
Alhambra 71, 81, 84, 88, 89, 90, 95, 96, 99, 100, 102, 103, 109, 119, 262, 265, 280, 311, 513, 543, 587, 588, 589, 595, 596, **615-18**, **621-25**, 635, 649, 662, 663, 665, 1000, 1018, 1019, 1024, 1025, 1029, 1030, 1031
'Alī, Fourth Caliph of Islam 242, 899, 902
'Alī b. Abī Rijāl 527
'Alī b. Ḥammūd, Caliph 48
'Alī Iqbāl al-Dawla 51, 54, 58, 262
'Alī b. 'Īsa b. Maymūn 70
'Alī b. Muḥammad b. Sa'd 943
'Alī b. 'Uthmān, Abū 'l-Ḥasan, of the Marīnids 80
'Alī b. Yūsuf b. Tāshfīn, *al-Amīr al-muslimīn* 58, **64-66**, 67, 68, 69, 70, 275, 609, 610, 653, 655, 920, 924
Alicante 76, 452
Aljarafe 140, 145, 991, 992, 1002, 1006, 1008
Almeida, Francisco de 288
Almería 48, 50, 57, 59, 62, 63, 71, 79, 83, 84, 97, 251, 262, 420, 607, 647, 661, 692, 694, 698, 701, 702, 710, 741, 760, 765, 767, 768, 855, 860, 861, 895, 902, 921, 923, 924, 980, 989, 991, 993, 1007, 1008, 1019, 1023, 1028
Almohads 66, **68-77**, 99, 100, 102, 127, 128, 137, 138, 140, 141, 143, 144, 162, 176, 185, 188, 195, 196, 197, 199, **235-58**, 265, 312, 372, 511, 568, 596, 611, **612-14**, 615, 619, 645, 655, **658-63**, 666, 679, 686, 689, **696-705**, 716, 741, 765, 767, 789, 796, 798, 830, 865, 866, **868-72**, 904, 945, 965, 989, 1005, 1006, 1024, 1046, 1047
Almoravids 50, 51, 54, 57, 58, 59, **60-68**, 69, 70, 71, 127, 137, 139, 140, 143, 162, 176, 195, 238, 239, 264, 275, 357, 372, 379, 462, 511, 568, **609-11**, 612, 613, 615,

619, **651-58**, 659, 679, 686, 688, 689, **696-705**, 706, 716, 717, 741, 757, 765, 767, 792, 796, 859, **865-68**, 869, 920, 924, 942, 944, 945, 1023, 1024
Almuñécar 19
Alpuente 49, 686
Alpujarras 205, 207, 230
ʿAlqma b. ʿAbda 324
Alvaro, Bishop of Córdoba 28, 115
Alvaro of Toledo 1047
Amatus de Monte Cassino 465
Amaya 9
Al-Amīn, Abbasid Caliph 557
ʿĀmir b. Muʿāwiya 880
ʿĀmirids 36, **40-47**, 50, 57, 127, 191, 338, 420, 693, 694, 753
Amoy 284, 285
Ampurias 1007
ʿAmr b. al-ʿĀṣ 3
ʿAmr b. Qumaiʾa 324
ʿAmrūs, Governor of Toledo 23
Anatolia 1021
Andalucía 150, 156, 159, 161, 584, 682, 683, 689, 698, 704
Andarax 208, 980, 1001, 1007
Andreas Capellanus 400, 472, 474, 475
Andújar 75
Al-Anṣārī, ʿAbd Allāh al-Harawī 926
Al-Anṣārī, al-Ḥusayn b. Yaḥyā 20
Anselmo de Turmeda 314, 533
Antequera 82
Antilla 274, 275
Appolonius 954, 1041
Aqsa Mosque 131
Aquinas, St. Thomas 489, 509, 517, 797
Al-Aʿrābī, Sulaymān b. Yaqẓān 20
Aragon 9, 50, 64, 67, 76, 77, 81, 83, 128, 172, 176, 177, 181, 182, 184, 185, 196, 198, 203, 206, 209, 211, 220, 221, 222, 223, 227, 230, 231, 269, 273, 462, 465, 466, 471, 596, 691, 706, 766, 875, 1041
Archidona 12
Archimedes 953, 954, 1041, 1044
Archpriest of Hita *see* Ruiz, Juan
Arcos 51, 53, 60, 78
Arévalo 222
Arias Montano, Benito 538
Arīb b. Saʿīd 940, 988, 1050
Arin 961
Aristotle 127, 145, 249, 279, 408, 483, 499, 509, 516, 781, 785, 793, 795, 796, 807, 811, 815, 818, 819, 821, 826, 837, 839, 871, 943, 946, 947, 948, 949, 1001, 1003, 1045, 1046, 1050
Arjona 77
Aṣbag͟h b. Wānsūs 23
Al-Aṣg͟har, Aḥmad b. Burd 309
Al-Aʿs͟hā 324
As͟hʿaris 69, 238, 239, 252, 832, 833, 861, 868, 869, 895, 898, 900
Al-As͟htarkuwī, Abū ʾl-Ṭāhir 310
Al-Aṣīlī 899
Aslam b. ʿAbd al-ʿAzīz 884
Astorga 9
Asturias 9, 16, 17, 21, 22, 27, 30, 37, 39, 680
Ateca 181
Atienza 39
ʿĀtika, wife of Abū Bakr b. Ḥazm 431
Augustine, St. 188
Augustus, Emperor 112
Avempace *see* Ibn Bājja
Avenzoar family 140, 145, 944
Averroes *see* Ibn Rus͟hd
Avicenna *see* Ibn Sīnā
Avignon 16
Avila 180, 535
Awmātiyūs 964, 965
Al-Awzāʿī, *al-Imām* 21, 777, 850, 896
Aylmer of Malmesbury 939
Ayyūbids 196, 292
Azarquiel *see* Ibn al-Zarqālluh
Azeca 66
Al-ʿAzīz, Fāṭimid Caliph 44, 120
ʿAzīz b. K͟haṭṭāb 76
Aznalcázar 71
Azores 276, 277

Bacon, Roger 278, 512
Badajoz 162, 609, 686, 701, 861
Bādīs b. Ḥabbūs, ruler of Granada 57, 60, 88, 108, 190, 192, 651
Badr, Umayyad Princess 658, 665
Badr b. Aḥmad 33
Baetica *see* Bética
Baeza 71, 81, 665
Baghdad 25, 26, 35, 51, 53, 56, 61, 62, 63, 67, 71, 72, 75, 193, 262, 284, 289, 399, 410, 460, 463, 508, 509, 510, 512, 536, 558, 617, 618, 709, 725, 763, 778, 937
Al-Bag͟hdādī, Abū Manṣūr 954
Al-Bag͟hdādī, ʿAlī 524
Al-Bag͟hī, ʿAbd Allāh 928

Al-Baḥrī, Khashkhāsh 275
Al-Bājī, Abū 'l-Walīd 859, 861, 862, 863, 864, 866, 898, 900, 940
Bakiya, the Eunuch 120
Bakr b. Yaḥyā 33
Al-Bakrī, ʿUbayd Allāh 116, 118, 267, 293, 745, 746, 755, 764, 902
Balāṭ al-Shuhadā', Battle of 12
Balearic Isles 58, 59, 73, 74, 154, 184, 452, 703, 869, 1047
Balj b. Bishr al-Qushayrī 12, 13, 14, 19, 50, 137
Al-Ballūṭī, ʿAbd al-Malik 779
Al-Ballūṭī, Abū Ḥafṣ ʿUmar 24
Al-Ballūṭī, Ayyūb 881
Al-Ballūṭī, al-Ḥakam 779
Al-Ballūṭī, Mundhir b. Saʿīd 126, 691, 854
Al-Ballūṭī, Saʿīd 779
Banū ʿAbbād 50, 53, 190, 344, 647, 648, 684, 901, 940
Banū ʿAbd al-Wād 82
Banū Abī ʿAbda 20, 25
Banū Abī Qurra 51, 53
Banū 'l-Afṭas 51, 53, 56, 686
Banū 'l-Aghlab 35
Banū ʿAmrūs 689
Banū Ballūṭī 779
Banū Basīl 25, 690
Banū Birzāl 48, 51, 53
Banū Bukht 20, 25
Banū Dammar 48
Banū Dhī 'l-Nūn 33, 51, 53, 55, 647, 649, 686, 940
Banū Fuṭays 25
Banū Ghāniya 73, 74, 980
Banū Ghazlūn 686
Banū Gómez 43
Banū 'l-Ḥadīdī 901
Banū Ḥafṣūn 34
Banū Ḥajjāj 32, 683, 684, 991
Banū Ḥammūd 51, 53, 59, 421
Banū Hārūn 53
Banū Hūd 50, 51, 54, 63, 64, 75, 190, 647, 649, 940, 1023, 1041, 1043, 1044
Banū Jahwar 50, 53, 690
Banū Judhām 50
Banū Khaldūn 32, 683, 799
Banū Khalīʿ 684
Banū Khālid 20
Banū Khazrūn 51, 53
Banū Marīn *see* Marīnids
Banū Marwān 125
Banū Midrār 31, 44
Banū Mughīth al-Rūmī 20
Banū Murra 991
Banū Mūsā 954
Banū Muzayyin 53
Banū Nūḥ 51, 53
Banū Qasī 30, 157, 463, 684, 689
Banū Qāsim 686
Banū Quraysh 323, 426, 690, 884, 1059
Banū Razīn 51, 59, 64, 686, 691
Banū Rushd 792
Banū Salama 888, 889
Banū Shabrīt 689
Banū Shuhayd 20, 25, 690
Banū Sirāj 82
Banū Ṣumādiḥ 50, 647, 650
Banū Ṭāhir 50
Banū Tujīb 33, 50, 51, 684, 690
Banū ʿUbayd 35, 36
Banū ʿUdhra 423, 424, 460, 633
Banū ʿUthmān 20
Banū Uzdāja 48
Banū Wansūs 886
Banū Yafran 48
Banū Yannaq 30
Banū Zīrī *see* Zīrids
Banyalbufar 980
Baqī b. Makhlad 31, 854, 855, 879, 883, 888, 897, 900, 904, 913
Barānī Berbers 13, 14, 1049
Baray de Remincho 217, 221, 222, 223, 875
Al-Barbarī, Ṣāliḥ 911
Barbastro 46, 54, 55, 64, 265, 462, 465, 901
Barbieri, Giammaria 398, 435
Barcelona 9, 10, 15, 22, 23, 24, 27, 42, 47, 65, 156, 498, 741
Al-Barghawāṭī, Yūnus 902
Barghwāṭa Berbers 61
Al-Barjī, Abū 'l-Ḥasan 780, 867, 920
Barqa 3, 4
Barrios de Luna 46
Al-Bashīr, ʿAbd Allāh b. Muḥsin 69
Al-Bashīr, Muḥammad b. Muḥsin 245, 246, 247
Basques 160, 259
Basra 289, 323, 426, 763, 913
Bāṭinis 777, 855, 900, 912, 915
Al-Battānī 278, 964, 969
Bayazid II, of the Ottomans 207
Al-Baydhaq 245

Baza 84, 280, 283
Beatus, the Monk 172
Beja 9, 12, 32, 71, 73
Bellvís clan 177
Benegas, Yuce 218, 535
Benjamin of Tudela 766
Benveniste, Sheshet 196
Berbers 3, 4, 7, 12, 13, 14, 16, 17, 19, 20, 22, 23, 28, 32, 33, 36, 41, 45, **46-49**, 50, 51, 52, 115, 116, 125, 127, 137, 235, 236, 237, 238, 239, 240, 242, 245, 247, 249, 250, 251, 252, 259, 276, 277, 344, 615, 651, 658, 679, 682, 684, 685, 686, 691, 693, 694, 699, 705, 715, 732, 777, 800, 802, 849, 853, 886, 887, 902, 903, 974, 978, 1003, 1011, 1036, 1040, 1049
Bermúdez de Pedraza, Francisco 95, 96, 101, 1025-26, 1027
Bermudo II, of León 42, 43, 463
Bernard de Sédirac 705
Bernard of Verdun 959
Bernart de Ventadorn 467, 469, 470
Bertaut, François 98
Bética (Baetica) 5, 8, 680
Bint al-Marwaziyya 717
Al-Birūnī 265, 527, 529, 955, 962
Bis͟hr al-Ḥāfī 913
Biskra 4
Al-Bitrūjī, Abū Isḥāq Nūr al-Dīn 948, 967, 968, 1046, 1047, 1050
Al-Bitrūjī, Yūsuf 70
Bobadilla 282
Bobastro 32, 34, 154
Bocairente 1008
Boccanegra family 180, 181
Boethius 565, 1037
Bolos Democritos 1002, 1007
Boltaña 46
Bordeaux 15
Borja 65
Borrel, ruler of Barcelona 39, 42
Bougie 800, 921
Al-Buḥayra, Battle of 70, 247
Al-Buḥturī 321, 326, 330, 332, 347, 370, 372
Bukhara 507
Buluqqīn b. Zīrī 44
Burgos 39, 43, 180, 220, 588, 596, 655, 662
Burgos, Council of 174
Burgundy 15, 16
Burriana 977
Butr Berbers 13, 14, 1049
Byzantines 3, 4, 5, 24, 27, 38, 124, 263, 267, 321, 327, 436, 508, 585, 602, 886, 939, 942, 987, 1009, 1061

Cabra 80, 405, 748
Cáceres 72, 73, 766
Cádiz 27, 70, 76, 273, 490, 491, 763, 938, 1011
Cadrete 217, 221
Cagigas, Isidro de las 176
Cairo 88, 120, 122, 205, 220, 288, 289, 584, 585, 588, 702, 909, 910, 944, 945
Calahorra 36, 39
Calatalifa 30
Calatayud 11, 65
Calicut 287
Caliphate (in al-Andalus) **35-49**, 50, 52, **117-27**, 189, 462, 463, 510, 511, **601-06**, 607, 608, 619, **642-47**, 684, 685, 686, 687, 688, **690-693**, 695, 741, 751, 752, 753, 754, 854, 857, 939, 989, 1023
Calixtus III, Pope 286
Campo de Nijar 1007
Canales 30, 65
Canaries 276, 277
Cangas de Onís 17
Cantabria 17, 160
Cantemir, Demetrius 569, 571
Cantino, Alberto 275
Cape Verde 277
Carcassonne 15
Carmona 9, 51, 53, 60, 139, 748
Carpini, Giovanni di Plano 283
Carrión de los Condes 43
Carteya 7
Carthage 126
Casas, Bartolomé de las 280, 281, 492, 500, 519
Casas, Ignacio de las 209, 229, 538
Castellón 976
Castile 22, 26, 37, 42, 43, 46, 47, 67, 72, 76, 77, 78, 79, 80, 81, 82, 83, 84, 106, 137, 143, 171, 176, 177, 180, 181, 184, 185, 196, 198, 203, 204, 209, 220, 221, 222, 223, 225, 259, 262, 263, 269, 273, 281, 462, 463, 464, 466, 516, 528, 593, 594, 615, 661, 662, 663, 766, 767, 768, 769, 875
Castilla la Vieja 9
Castillo, Alonso del 228, 538

Catalonia 37, 46, 65, 171, 198, 220, 222, 462, 699, 706, 1037
Cervantes, Miguel de 146, 218, 231, 520, 521, 522, 527, 538, 543
Ceuta 6, 7, 12, 37, 44, 48, 71, 73, 79, 286, 1001
Charlemagne 20, 22, 509
Charles III, of Navarre 184
Charles V, Emperor 98, 109, 134, 220, 543, 589, 1025
Charles the Bald 31
Charles Martel 15, 16
Chaucer, Geoffrey 468, 509
Cheng Ho, Admiral 292
Chengiz Khan 283
China 7, 279, 280, 281, 282, 283, 284, 285, 507, 508
Chóvar 979
Chrétien de Troyes 946
El Cid (Rodrigo Díaz de Vivar) 58, 62, 64, 72, 139, 156, 181, 182, 263, 309, 464, 512, 688
Cintra 57, 63
Cirta 1001
Claudius, Emperor 1022
Clavijo, Ruíz González de 104
Clunia 43, 46
Cluny 1044
Cocentaina 980
Coimbra 10, 42, 56, 171, 901
Colomera 84
Columbus, Christopher 273, 274, 275, 278, 279, 280, 281, 282, 283, 286, 287, 291, 293, 491, 492, 496, 497, 499, 510, 1030
Columbus, Ferdinand 273, 274, 279
Columela, Iunius Moderatus 938, 991, 1037
Constance, Queen of France 705
Constantine VII, called "Porphyrogenitus", of the Byzantines 37, 124, 190, 988
Constantine of Africa 944, 1042, 1050
Constantinople 27, 82, 116, 286, 287, 327, 509, 510, 605
Copernicus 509, 964
Córdoba 6, 8, 12, 14, 16, 19, 23, 24, 25, 27, 29, 31, 32, 33, 34, 36, 37, 38, 39, 40, 41, 42, 43, 44, 47, 48, 49, 50, 52, 53, 60, 66, 68, 71, 72, 74, 76, 79, 81, 88, 98, **112-35**, 137, 139, 140, 153, 155, 156, 159, 161, 162, 172, 173, 251, 260, 261, 264, 275, 325, 336, 338, 342, 344, 348, 357, 400, 401, 402, 405, 420, 431, 460, 466, 498, 510, 511, 512, 518, 556, 558, 559, 568, 584, 585, 588, 589, 602, 603, 605, 606, 607, 608, 609, 611, 612, 635, 648, 655, 665, 680, 683, 685, 689, 692, 694, 695, 696, 698, 701, 716, 718, 731, 732, 741, 744, 746, 748, 750, 751, 752, 753, 755, 760, 763, 769, 777, 779, 792, 852, 855, 857, 858, 859, 865, 867, 868, 870, 878, 880, 881, 885, 889, 896, 915, 922, 937, 939, 941, 944, 952, 961, 982, 1001, 1005, 1018, 1019, 1023, 1028, 1036, 1037, 1038, 1041, 1046, 1047, 1049, 1059, 1061
Córdoba, Gaspar de 230
Córdoba, Great Mosque of 12, 21, 26, 38, 43, 45, 119, 128, **129-35**, 172, 584, 585, 586, 593, 596, **599-602**, 613, 618, 641, 643, 645, 658, 659, 881, 885
"Córdoba Martyrs" **28-29**, 115, 152, 157, 687, 853
Coria 22, 56, 61
Corunna 43
Cota, Rodrigo 474, 476
Covadonga, Battle of 17
Crespin, Robert 465
Crete 22
Cuba 281, 492, 510
Cuenca 33, 51, 55, 73, 74, 608, 649, 685, 686
Cullera 76
Cyprus 283, 293
Cyrenaica 1010

Al-Ḍabbī, ʿAbd al-Wāḥid b. Isḥāq 938
Al-Ḍabbī, Aḥmad 389, 763
Damascus 9, 10, 12, 25, 88, 114, 130, 131, 152, 153, 155, 260, 323, 507, 508, 510, 512, 600, 601, 602, 635, 640, 690, 937, 945, 978
Daniel of Morley 1045
Dante Alighieri 314, 494, 498, 529, 797, 842, 1050
Dapiera, Meshullam 198
Daroca 65
Davídiz, Sinando 156, 173, 705
Dāwūd b. ʿAlī 854
Delicado, Francisco 522, 523
Denia 54, 58, 76, 156, 161, 162, 262, 694, 765, 785, 859
Al-Dhahabī, Aḥmad al-Manṣūr, 227
Dhū 'l-Nūn al-Ikhmīmī 778, 913
Dhū 'l-Rumma 324, 388

Diaz, Bartholomeu 287
Al-Dimashqī, Abū 'l-Faḍl Ja'far 761
Diniz, King of Portugal 286
Dioscorides 38, 124, 145, 782, 939, 944, 945, 1006
Ditch, Battle of the 36, 37
Djerba 1008
Dom João II, of Portugal 287
Dunash b. Labrat 124, 193

Ecija 34, 78, 748
Egica, ruler of the Visigoths 188
Egypt 3, 4, 5, 11, 19, 23, 44, 81, 82, 120, 188, 195, 196, 206, 240, 280, 289, 759, 764, 896, 929, 1006
Elche 76
Elches 151, 162, 204
El-Congost de Martorell, Battle of 65
Eleanor of Aquitaine 466
Elipandus, Bishop 173, 174
Elizabeth I, of England 227
El Vacar, Battle of 67
Elvás 75
Elvira 10, 12, 19, 32, 34, 48, 88, 89, 155, 604, 682, 684, 693, 748
Emirate (in al-Andalus) **17-35**, **113-17**, 593, **599-601**, **641-42**, 645, 689, 692
Empedocles 855, 912
England 506
Enneco, ruler of Navarre 463
Enrique II de Trastamara, of Castile 81
Enrique IV, of Castile 82, 83
Escalada 172
Escalona 67
Los Escayuela 78, 79
Ethiopia 286
Euclid 781, 786, 953, 954, 955, 968, 1038, 1044
Eugenius IV, Pope 285
Eulogius 115, 116
Eutocius 1041
Evora 10, 34, 56, 72, 755, 766
Extremadura 29, 56, 974

Al-Fakhkhār 895, 900, 903
Fañez, Alvar 63, 64
Al-Fārābī 555, 561, 564, 565, 784, 785, 786, 788, 802, 821, 830, 834, 836, 838, 840, 843, 916, 1045
Faraj b. Sallām, Abū Bakr 777
Al-Farazdaq 323
Al-Farghanī 279, 1050
Faro 33, 53
Al-Fāsī, Abū 'Umrān 60
Fāṭima, wife of 'Abd al-Muṭṭalib 902
Fāṭima bint al-Muthannā 928
Fāṭimids 35, 38, 40, 44, 69, 120, 131, 195, 239, 240, 247, 289, 292, 332, 612, 642, 647, 901, 912
Favila 17
Al-Fazārī 895
Ferdinand I, of Castile and León 56, 57
Ferdinand II, "the Catholic", of Aragon 83, 84, 93, 97, 99, 106, 108, 195, 201, 205, 219, 220, 265, 273, 282, 535
Ferdinand II, of León 72, 73
Ferdinand III, of Castile and León 75, 76, 77, 78, 128, 146, 612, 767
Ferdinand IV, of Castile and León 79, 83
Ferdinand, Regent of Castile 82
Fernán González, ruler of Castile 56, 57
Ferrizuel, Joseph 196
Fez 23, 44, 61, 68, 81, 102, 140, 251, 265, 568, 609, 647, 651, 660, 789, 800, 1001
Al-Fihrī, 'Abd al-Malik b. al-Qaṭan, Governor 12, 13, 14
Al-Fihrī, Yūsuf b. 'Abd al-Raḥmān, Governor 13, 19, 20, 113, 684, 744
Fitna 265, 325, 326, 330, 334, 335, 336, 344, 421, 683, 685, 690, 777, 781, 858, 1023
Florence 483
Florencio, the Monk 172
Force, Duc de la 227
Fortun Garcés, ruler of Pamplona 463
Fortún b. Mūsā 29
Fraga, Battle of 67
France 462, 494, 506, 1044
Franco of Poland 959
Franks 5, 15, 16, 21, 23, 31, 58, 65, 174, 259, 265, 268, 686, 692
Frederick II, Emperor 669, 798
Frontiers *see* Lower Frontier; Middle Frontier; Upper Frontier
Fusṭāṭ 25

Galen 426, 509, 782, 786, 944, 947, 1001, 1050
Galera 224
Galicia 5, 16, 17, 22, 26, 27, 39, 42, 43, 171, 267, 268, 1007
Gama, Vasco da 278, 282, 287, 289
Gandía 221, 704

García I, of Navarre 36, 39
García Fernández, ruler of Castile 39, 42
García Gudiel, Gonzalo 1047
García Jiménez 62
García Ordoñez 64, 65
García Sánchez II, of Pamplona 43
Garcilaso 541
Gaul 12, 15, 16, 680, 683, 692
Generalife 88, 615, 621, 624, 635, 663, 989, 1018, 1024, 1025, 1026, 1028, 1029, 1030, 1031
Genoa 145, 768
Geraldo the Bold 72
Gerard of Cremona 278, 279, 962, 1045, 1050, 1060
Gerbert d'Aurillac 1038, 1040
Gerona 10
Al-Ghāfiqī, ʿAbd al-Raḥmān b. ʿAbd Allāh 12, 15, 16
Al-Ghāfiqī (pharmacologist) 945, 1003
Al-Ghafla, Khalīl 854
Ghālib al-Nāṣirī 39, 41, 42
Al-Gharnāṭī, Abū Bakr b. ʿĀsim 873, 874
Al-Gharnāṭī, Abū Isḥāq 873, 874
Al-Ghassānī, Ḥassān b. Nuʿmān 4
Al-Ghassānī, Jabala b. al-Ayham 8
Al-Ghazāl, Abū ʿAbd Allāh 922
Al-Ghazāl, Yaḥyā b. al-Ḥakam 24, 26, 27, 266, 267, **327-28**, 329, 330, 331, 332, 334, 358, 464
Al-Ghazālī, Abū Ḥāmid 63, 67, 69, 71, 238, 250, 251, 542, 633, 697, 698, 715, 780, 794, 835, 839, 866, 867, 869, 871, 872, 875, 904, 911, 920, 1045, 1060
Al-Ghāzī b. Qays 21
Gibraltar 7, 71, 79, 81, 82, 539, 612, 767, 1031
Gijón 9
Goa 288
Góngora, Luis de 541
Gormaz 39
Gorrico, Father 282
Goths *see* Visigoths
Governors, Period of the **10-17**
Gracián, Baltasar 520, 792
Granada 12, 48, 51, 53, 57, 63, 66, 77, **78-84**, **88-111**, 128, 140, 143, 146, 155, 156, 159, 162, 178, 180, 181, 192, 199, 201, 202, 203, 204, 205, 207, 218, 219, 220, 224, 225, 228, 229, 260, 262, 263, 266, 273, 311, 488, 491, 513, 535, 537, 568, 571, 595, 609, 614, 615, 635, 651, 653, 658, 684, 687, 688, 693, 700, 704, 711, 718, 741, 768, 800, 872, 874, 942, 953, 960, 966, 975, 987, 989, 991, 993, 1001, 1005, 1007, 1016, 1018, 1024, 1026, 1027, 1028, 1029, 1031, 1047, 1061
Grand Khān 277, **280-86**, 293, 510, 949, 950
Great Mosque of Córdoba *see* Córdoba, Great Mosque of
Guadalajara 8, 29, 30, 74
Guadalmellato 47
Guadix 79, 83, 154, 159, 162
Guazalete, Battle of 14, 29
Guilhem VIII, of Aquitaine 465, 466
Guilhem IX, of Aquitaine 464, 466, 467, 474
Guillaume de Montreuil 465
Gundissalinus, Dominicus 173, 564, 1044, 1045, 1047
Gundisalvi/Gundisalvo *see* Gundissalinus

Ḥabash al-Ḥāsib 960
Ḥabbūs b. Māksan b. Zīrī, ruler of Granada 60, 98, 101
Hadrian, Emperor 113, 1018, 1026
Ḥafṣa bint Ḥamdūn of Guadalajara 710, 718
Ḥafṣa al-Rakūniyya 514, 711
Ḥafṣids 81, 82, 204, 799
Haifa 1009
Al-Ḥāʾik 561, 568, 571
Al-Ḥajarī, Aḥmad b. Qāsim 227-28
Al-Ḥakam I, *al-Amīr* **22-24**, 114, 401, 463, 467, 642, 689, 746, 750, 852, 888, 896
Al-Ḥakam II, called "al-Mustanṣir", Caliph 36, **38-40**, 41, 44, 45, 50, 56, 118, 120, 122, 124, 126, 130, 132, 133, 138, 324, 330, 463, 467, 512, 601, 602, 604, 605, 606, 643, 644, 645, 647, 659, 691, 754, 852, 857, 884, 897, 901, 988, 1059
Ḥakīm al-Tirmidhī 911
Halevi, Judah 194, 195, 490, 516, 1043
Al-Ḥallāj 798
Al-Hamadhānī, Badiʿ al-Zamān 308, 309, 310, 311, 830
Al-Ḥamdānī, Abū Firās 330
Ḥamdīn b. ʿUbba 938
Ḥanafis 850, 851, 895, 896
Al-Ḥanash fortress 34
Hanokh, Rabbi 124
Hargha Berbers 68, 69
Al-Ḥarīrī, Abū Muḥammad al-Qāsim 197, 198, 307, 310, 313, 510, 830

Al-Ḥarīzī, Judah 193, 197, 198, 313, 516
Al-Ḥarra, Battle of 12
Al-Ḥarrānī, Aḥmad b. Yūnus 939
Al-Ḥarrānī, 'Umar b. Yūnus 939
Al-Ḥarrānī, Yūnus 939
Hārūn al-Rashīd, Abbasid Caliph 25, 263, 463, 508, 509, 556, 557, 725
Hārūn b. Sālim 885
Ḥasan b. 'Alī 633
Al-Ḥasan b. Jannūn 44
Al-Ḥasan b. Mufarrij 642
Ḥasday b. Shaprūt 124, 190, 192, 691, 751, 764, 940
Hāshim b. 'Abd al-'Azīz 28, 29, 30, 31, 32
Al-Hāshimī 533
Ḥassān b. Mālik, Abū 'Abda 50
Hawwāra Berbers 33, 51, 685
Helena, Empress of Byzantium 190
Henry II, of England 466
Henry IV, of France 227
Henry the Navigator 286, 287
Hermann of Carinthia 1043, 1044, 1045, 1046, 1047
Hermes Trismegistus 1043
Herrera, Gabriel Alonso de 943, 990, 997
Al-Ḥimyarī 118, 123, 146, 1031
Hintāta Berbers 238
Hipparchus 782, 964
Hippocrates 782, 938, 1050
Hishām I, *al-Amīr* **21-22**, 247, 601, 852, 1021
Hishām II, Caliph 40, 41, 47, 48, 118, 138, 139, 326, 330, 463, 606, 647, 900
Hishām III, Caliph 127
Hishām b. 'Abd al-Malik, Umayyad Caliph in Damascus 12, 19, 378, 599, 639
Hispaniola 280, 281
Holbein, Hans, the Younger 669
Homs 12, 137
Horace 1022
Hosius, Bishop 113
Hosteogis, Bishop 155
Hroswitha 118
Huelva 53, 781
Huesca 46, 54, 55, 64, 156, 161, 176, 466
Huéscar 80
Huete 33, 51, 73, 74, 686
Hugo of Santalla 1041, 1042, 1043, 1044, 1051
Al-Ḥumaydī 895, 915
Ḥusām al-Dawla 608
Al-Ḥuṭai'a 324
Ibiza 58, 65, 76, 540
Ibn 'Abbād of Ronda 512, 530
Ibn al-Abbār 354, 717, 763, 764, 765, 766, 852, 915, 916, 920, 921, 922, 925
Ibn 'Abd al-Barr, Abū 'Umar 714, 861, 862, 863, 899
Ibn 'Abd Rabbihī 38, 121, 122, 310, **328-30**, 334, 358, 410, 557, 714, 725
Ibn 'Abd al-Ra'ūf 409
Ibn 'Abdūn 125, 701
Ibn 'Abdūs, Abū 'Āmir 348, 349, 946
Ibn Abī Randaqa 310
Ibn Abī Rijāl 942
Ibn Abī Uṣaybi'a 915
Ibn Abī Zamanīn 860, 867
Ibn Abī Zar' 245
Ibn Abī Zayd al-Qayrawānī 899
Ibn al-Adamī 963
Ibn Aflaḥ, Jābir 948, 955, 957, 959, 966
Ibn Aḥlā 895
Ibn al-Aḥmar *see* Muḥammad I, of Granada
Ibn al-Aḥnaf, al-'Abbās 352, 424, 467
Ibn Amīr Ḥājib, Abū 'l-Ḥasan 'Alī 276
Ibn 'Ammār 139, 331, 346, **355-56**, 357, 358, 360, 372, 464, 717
Ibn 'Aqnīn 948
Ibn al-'Arabī, Abū Bakr Muḥammad 71, 140, 143, 145, 866, 868, 869-70, 900, 903
Ibn 'Arabī, Muḥyī 'l-Dīn 126, 236, 251, 470, 512, 529, 628, 778, 780, 798, 799, 839, 840, 843, 855, 872, **909-33**
Ibn al-'Arīf, Abū 'l-'Abbās 67, 251, 780, 867, 872, 913, **919-926**
Ibn 'Arrāḍ 992
Ibn al-Aswad 922
Ibn al-Athīr 245, 246
Ibn 'Attāb 870
Ibn al-'Awwām 145, 942, 943, 944, 990, 991, 992, 993, 996, 997, 1003, 1005, 1006, 1007, 1009, 1010, 1030, 1031
Ibn al-Azraq 205, 263
Ibn Badr, Abū 'Abd Allāh 953
Ibn Badrūn 125
Ibn Baghūnīsh 784
Ibn Bājja (Avempace) 412, 513, 555, 564, 573, 706, **785-88**, 796, 807, 809, 810, 811, 813, 814, 815, 816, 817, 821, 824, 825, 830, 838, 840, 843, 851, 945, 946, 954, 966, 967, 1041, 1050
Ibn Baqī 353
Ibn al-Bannā' al-Marrākushī 953, 964, 965

Ibn Barrajān, Abū 'l-Ḥakam 67, 780, 867, **919-26**
Ibn Bashīr, Muḥammad 114
Ibn Bashkuwāl 763, 764, 765, 852, 921, 922
Ibn Bāṣo, Aḥmad 612, 613, 959, 960
Ibn Baṣṣāl 942, 943, 990, 991, 992, 997, 1005, 1006, 1030
Ibn Bassām 310, 352, 409, 410, 411, 942
Ibn Baṭṭūṭa 872
Ibn al-Bayṭār 945, 1007, 1009, 1010, 1030
Ibn Bāz, Ibrāhīm b. Muḥammad 887, 888
Ibn Biklārīsh 1010, 1041
Ibn al-Dabbāgh 870
Ibn al-Darrāj al-Qasṭalī 45, **335**, 336, 349, 358
Ibn Diḥya 267
Ibn Faḍl Allāh al-'Umarī 95, 98, 276
Ibn Faḍlān 266
Ibn al-Faraḍī 763, 852, 868, 913, 915, 918
Ibn Faraj al-Jayyānī 354, 402, 472
Ibn Farḥūn 899, 913
Ibn al-Fāriḍ 529
Ibn Fawwāl 784
Ibn Furkūn 663
Ibn Fuṭays 120
Ibn Gabirol 409, 516, 784, 1045
Ibn García, Abū 'Āmir 262, 264
Ibn Ghālib 527, 746, 749, 755
Ibn Ḥabīb, 'Abd al-Malik 853, 882, 896, 897, 899
Ibn al-Ḥaddād, Muḥammad 354, 470
Ibn Ḥafṣūn, 'Umar 31, 34, 125, 154, 155-56, 158
Ibn al-Hā'im 963, 964, 965, 966
Ibn al-Ḥājj 403
Ibn Ḥajjāj 145, 938, 942, 990, 991, 1005
Ibn Ḥalīf 765
Ibn Ḥamdīn, Muḥammad b. 'Alī 67, 70, 780, 867, 920
Ibn Ḥamdīs 357, 941
Ibn Hamshuk 71
Ibn Ḥanbal, Aḥmad 854
Ibn Hāni' 117, 324, 328, 330, **332-34**, 335, 343, 349, 355, 358
Ibn Ḥātim al-Ṭulayṭulī 901
Ibn Ḥawqal 119, 293, 688, 744, 745, 751, 752, 753, 756, 763
Ibn al-Haytham 954, 955, 1041
Ibn Ḥayyān 125, 126, 127, 265, 465, 556, 557, 559, 642, 717, 764, 855, 856, 884, 913, 914, 915
Ibn Ḥazm, Abū Bakr 431
Ibn Ḥazm, 'Alī b. Aḥmad b. Sa'īd 119, 120, 121, 122, 123, 125, 139, 245, 250, 264, 311, 312, **342-43**, 401, **420-442**, 460, 461, 462, 463, 465, 467, 469, 470, 471, 472, 473, 487, 488, 527, 533, 633, 693, 695, 696, 697, 712, 716, 778, 779, **780-84**, 785, 789, 854, 855, 861, 862, 863, 864, 865, 866, 870, 896, 898, 901, 903, 915, 916, 918
Ibn Ḥirzihim 922
Ibn Hūd, ruler of Saragossa 265
Ibn Hūd al-Judhāmī 75, 716
Ibn 'Idhārī 127, 602, 744, 745, 750, 751, 752, 753
Ibn al-Iflīlī 900, 901
Ibn Isḥāq al-Tūnisī 957, 964, 965
Ibn Jābir al-Fārasī, 'Alī 538
Ibn Jaḥḥāf, Ja'far 58
Ibn al-Jawād 988
Ibn al-Jawzī 423, 426
Ibn al-Jayyāb 663, 665
Ibn Jubayr 909
Ibn Juljul 851, 937, 938, 939, 940
Ibn al-Kammād 964, 965
Ibn Khafāja 352, 355, 360, 369, **379-92**, 631, 632
Ibn Khalaf al-Shajjār 959, 960, 962
Ibn Khalāṣ 798
Ibn Khaldūn 32, 89, 119, 125, 141, 146, 177, 240, 246, 263, 266, 268, 269, 683, 691, 718, 726, 798, **799-802**, 866, 867, 873, 949, 991, 1012, 1040
Ibn Khallikān 925
Ibn Khāqān, al-Fatḥ 310, 1019, 1020, 1023
Ibn Kharūf 401
Ibn al-Khaṭīb, Lisān al-Dīn 81, 90, 96, 103, 260, 261, 263, 264, 310, 311, 515, 571, 663, 664, 666, 714, 716, 718, 745, 755, **798-99**, 873, 949, 950, 991, 1018, 1019, 1025, 1026, 1027, 1028, 1029
Ibn Khātima 950
Ibn Killis, Ya'qūb 190
Ibn al-Labbāna 325, 358, 360
Ibn Labīd 901
Ibn Lubāba 1004
Ibn Luyūn 951, 992, 996, 1005, 1028
Ibn Mājid, Aḥmad 287, 289, 291
Ibn al-Makwī 899
Ibn al-Mar'a 918
Ibn Mardanīsh, ruler of Valencia 68, 71, 72, 73, 76, 262, 610, 661, 689, 697, 699, 1024

Ibn Marzūq 872
Ibn Masarra, ʿAbd Allāh 777, 913
Ibn Masarra, Muḥammad b. ʿAbd Allāh **777-79**, 780, **855-56**, 890, 900, 911, **912-19**
Ibn Miskawayh 783
Ibn Muʿādh 954, 955, 957, 962, 965, 968, 1050
Ibn al-Mujāhid 871
Ibn al-Muqaffaʿ, ʿAbd Allāh 314, 342, 830
Ibn al-Murābiʿ al-Azdī 311
Ibn Muṭarrif, Qāsim 957, 967
Ibn al-Muʿtazz 326, 330, 370
Ibn al-Nabbāsh 784
Ibn al-Nafīs 1060
Ibn Naghrīla, Ismāʿīl 88, 190, 192, 193, 194, 615
Ibn Qasī, Abū ʾl-Qāsim 67, 70, 71, 698, 902, 913, 920, 922, 923, 924, 925, 926, 927
Ibn al-Qāsim 896
Ibn al-Qaṭṭān 241, 243, 245, 246
Ibn Qayyim al-Jawziyya 152, 423, 426, 427
Ibn al-Qiṭṭ al-Mahdī 33, 247, 685, 902, 903
Ibn Qutayba 52
Ibn al-Qūṭiyya, Abū Bakr Muḥammad 125, 376, 557
Ibn Quzmān 405, 406, 409, 411, 497, 710, 797
Ibn al-Raqqām 956, 965, 966
Ibn Rashīq 62, 265
Ibn Razīn, ʿAbd al-Malik 59
Ibn Razīn, Hudhayl b. Khalaf 59
Ibn Razīn al-Tujībī 731, 732, 733
Ibn al-Rūmī 326, 330, 370, 372
Ibn Rushd, Abū ʾl-Qāsim Aḥmad b. Muḥammad 792
Ibn Rushd, Abū Muḥammad b. ʿAbd Allāh 948
Ibn Rushd, Abū ʾl-Walīd Muḥammad b. Aḥmad b. Muḥammad, called "al-Jadd" 66, 704, 785, 792
Ibn Rushd (Averroes) 122, 127, 140, 244, 250, 252, 279, 408, 489, 509, 512, 704, 712, 785, 788, 789, 791, **792-97**, 800, 801, 802, **804-29**, 830, 838, 839, 843, 851, 868, 870, 871, 874, 944, 945, 948, 949, 966, 967, 1046, 1047, 1050, 1060
Ibn Sabʿīn **798**, 872
Ibn al-Ṣaffār, Abū ʾl-Qāsim Aḥmad b. ʿAbd Allāḥ 957, 960, 961
Ibn al-Ṣaffār, Yūnus b. ʿAbd Allāh 860
Ibn Ṣāḥib al-Ṣalāh, Abū Marwān 142, 641, 651, 699, 1006
Ibn Sahl al-Isrāʾīlī, Ibrāhīm 195, 360, 571
Ibn Sahl (jurist) 764, 899
Ibn Saʿīd al-Maghribī (al-Andalusī) 118, 120, 121, 122, 269, 514, 701, 711
Ibn Ṣāliḥ, ʿAbd Allāh 945, 1031
Ibn Samajūn 940
Ibn al-Samḥ, Abū ʾl-Qāsim 953, 954, 958, 960, 961
Ibn al-Saqqāʾ 52
Ibn Sāra 472
Ibn al-Sarrāj 960
Ibn Ṣayqal 889
Ibn al-Ṣayrafī 689
Ibn Sayyid, ʿAbd al-Raḥmān 946, 954
Ibn Sharaf al-Qayrawānī 310, 472
Ibn al-Shāṭir 941
Ibn Shuhayd 310, 311, 314, 325, 331, **335-42**, 376, 402, 420, 422, 428, 1019, 1020, 1022
Ibn al-Sīd 780, **784-85**, 940
Ibn Sīnā (Avicenna) 313, 472, 509, 555, 565, 789, 793, 796, 798, 799, 830, 836, 840, 843, 916, 944, 1001, 1002, 1003, 1045, 1046, 1047, 1050
Ibn Tāshfīn, Abū ʾl-Ṭāhir b. Yūsuf 991
Ibn Taymiyya 245
Ibn Tifilwīt, governor of Saragossa 706
Ibn Ṭufayl 252, 312, 313, 628, **788-92**, 796, **830-47**, 851, 917, 966, 967, 1046
Ibn Tūmart, Muḥammad 66, **68-70**, 77, **236-58**, 868, 869, 871
Ibn Ṭumlūs 798, 903, 904, 948
Ibn ʿUkāsha 53
Ibn Waḍḍāḥ, Muḥammad 854, 855, 878, 888, 897, 898, 913, 914, 915
Ibn Wāfid 942, 943, 944, 990, 1002, 1005, 1006
Ibn Waḥshiyya 942
Ibn Yazīd 714
Ibn Zamrak 513, 617, 663, 664, 665, 666, 798
Ibn al-Zarqālluh 941, 942, 952, 957, 958, 959, 960, 962, 963, 964, 965, 967, 968, 1050
Ibn Zaydūn 117, 125, 139, 331, **343-51**, 355, 357, 358, 359, 400, 401, 428, 469, 514, 709, 946, 1022, 1023
Ibn al-Zubayr 852
Ibn Zurayq al-Baghdādī, Abū ʾl-Ḥasan ʿAlī 350

Ibrāhīm b. Dhī 'l-Nūn 686
Ibrāhīm b. al-Ḥajjāj 32
Ibrāhīm b. 'Īsā b. Ḥayyawayh 889
Ibrāhīm b. Sinān 963
Ibrāhīm b. Ya'qūb 124, 266, 267, 268
Ibrāhīm b. Yūsuf b. Tāshfīn 65
Ice de Gebir 212, 213, 216, 223, 874
Idrīs II, of the Idrīsids 23
Idrīs, ruler of Málaga 48
Al-Idrīsī, Abū 'Abd Allāh 120, 268, 275, 276, 292, 293, 701, 765, 977, 1007
Al-Idrīsī, 'Alī b. Ḥammūd 48
Idrīsids 23, 44, 51, 59
Ifrīqiya *see* Tunisia
Ijillīz 69
Al-Ilbīrī, Abū Isḥāq 192
Al-Ilbīrī, Muḥammad 867
India 10, 278, 280, 510, 872, 1004, 1010, 1022, 1029
Innocent IV, Pope 283
Iran 18, 872
Iraq 18, 112, 117, 188, 584, 604, 766, 849, 896
Iria Flavia 43
'Īsā b. al-Ḥasan b. Abī 'Abda 28
'Īsā b. Manṣūr, Bishop of Córdoba 124
'Īsā b. Shuhayd 28
Isaac Moheb b. Ephraim 128
Isaac ben Zadok 196
Isabella I, "the Catholic", of Castile **83-84**, 93, 97, 99, 103, 106, 108, 195, 201, 220, 266, 273, 278, 282, 535
Isabella, Princess (daughter of above) 184
Al-Iṣbahānī, Abū 'l-Faraj 555
Isḥāq b. Ḥasday 190
Isḥāq b. al-Sīd 941
Isidore of Seville, St. 138, 539, 937, 1001, 1037, 1042
Al-Iskandarānī, 'Abd al-Wāhid b. Yazīd 27
Ismā'īl I, of Granada 79, 80, 663, 666
Ismā'īl b. Badr 784
Ismā'īl b. Mūsā 29
Ismā'īlis 69, 764
Al-Iṣṭakhrī 685
Iṣṭifān b. Basīl 939
Al-Istijī, Abū Marwān 963
Italy 277, 452, 692, 768
Izrāq b. Muntīl 29

Al-Jabalī, Muḥammad b. 'Abdūn 953
Jābir b. Ḥayyān 917, 948, 1002
Jacob ben Elazar 198
Jaén 12, 19, 32, 34, 48, 75, 76, 77, 79, 81, 264, 402, 647, 665, 701, 748, 914, 962
Jaén, Treaty of 77
Ja'far b. 'Abd al-Raḥmān 644, 645
Al-Jāḥiẓ 309, 310, 854, 947
Jaime I, "the Conqueror", of Aragon 76, 77, 176, 703, 767, 949, 1047
Jaime II, of Aragon 79
Jamaica 283
James, St. 228, 518, 537
James I, of England 226, 227
Jamīl b. Ma'mar al-'Udhrī (Jamīl Buthayna) 324, 460, 472
Japan 280
Jassās 889
Játiva 76, 154, 183, 264, 420, 607, 696, 701, 765, 769, 982, 1007
Al-Jazarī 942
Al-Jazūlī, 'Abd Allāh b. Yasīn 61, 68
Jeddah 288
Jehoseph b. Ismā'īl b. Naghrīla 192
Jerez 78, 79, 661, 732
Jerome, St. 283
Jerome of Moravia 564
Jerusalem 279, 282, 283, 519, 584, 600
Jesus 173, 188, 229, 242, 537, 910
Jews 5, 106, **124-25**, 127, 128, 138, 150, 153, 155, 156, 160, 178, **188-200**, 292, 313, 483, 490, 491, 492, 493, 500, 506, **515-17**, 519, 520, 595, 614, 686, 687, 691, 692, 702, 715, 759, 761, 766, 767, 777, 784, 849, 866, 879, 880, 901, 945, 1001, 1043, 1048
Jidāla Berbers 61
Al-Jidālī, Yaḥyā b. Ibrāhīm 60
Jimena, wife of El Cid 58
Jiménez de Cisneros, Francisco 84, 100, 101, 109, 204
Jiménez de Rada, Rodrigo 265, 1047, 1060
Joachim, Abbot 283
Jódar 32, 1008
Johannes Hispanus 1045
Johannes Tzimisces, Emperor of the Byzantines 39
John of Capua 314
John of the Cross, St. 520, 528, 529, 530, 537
John of Salisbury 1045
John of Seville 173, 279, 953, 1048
Joseph b. Shatnash 124

Joseph b. Zabara 197
Juan, Don, Bishop 138
Julian, Governor of Ceuta 6, 7
Julius Caesar 1021, 1022
Junayd 912
Jurumenha 72

Al-Kafīf, al-Ḥannāṭ 901
Kāfūr, ruler of Egypt 372
Al-Kalbī, Abū 'l-Khaṭṭār b. Ḥusām 12, 13
Al-Kalbī, ʿAnbasa b. Suḥaym 12, 15, 17
Al-Kalbiyya, Maysūn 368, 369
Al-Kāshī, Jamshīd Ghiyāth al-Dīn 957
Kashmir 1023
Al-Kātib, al-Ḥasan b. ʿAlī 559, 560
Khālid b. Hāshim 645
Khālid b. Yazīd b. Rumān 938
Khalīl b. Aḥmad 404
Khalil Pasha 227
Al-Khallāl, Abū Salama 18
Khanifra 236
Al-Kharā'iṭī 422
Khārijis 14, 18, 426, 435, 860, 868, 895, 902
Al-Khawlanī, al-Samḥ b. Mālik, Governor 12, 15, 112, 744, 747
Khayr b. Shākir 32
Khayrān al-ʿĀmirī 50, 57, 59
Khayrān al-Ṣaqlabī 48
Al-Khayyāmī, ʿUmar 955
Al-Khayyāṭ, Muḥammad 927
Khazars 124
Al-Khāzin, Abū Jaʿfar 957
Khurāsān 18, 764
Al-Khurāsānī, Abū Muslim 18
Al-Khushanī, Muḥammad b. ʿAbd al-Salām 879, 913, 914
Al-Khushanī, Muḥammad b. Ḥārith 114
Al-Khwārizmī, Muḥammad b. Mūsā 172, 278, 953, 960, 961, 962, 969, 1038, 1040, 1041, 1042, 1044, 1060
Al-Kilābī, al-Ṣumayl b. Ḥātim 13
Al-Kindī 555, 558, 561, 564, 784, 1048
Al-Kirmānī 784, 940, 946, 1041
Kufa 323, 763
Kulthūm b. ʿIyāḍ al-Qushayrī 12
Al-Kurdī, Mīr Ḥusayn 288
Kusayla 4
Kutāma Berbers 33, 240
Al-Kutandī 710
Kuthayyir ʿAzza 324

Labīb, ruler of Tortosa 51, 59
La Cartagena 5
La Higueruela, Battle of 82
Al-Lakhmī, ʿAbd al-Raḥmān b. ʿAlqama 16
Al-Lakhmī, ʿAlī b. Rabāḥ 8
Al-Lakhmī, Ayyūb b. Ḥabīb 11, 12
Al-Lakhmī, ʿIṭāf b. Nuʿaym 50
Lalaing, Antoine de 96, 1024
Lalla Taquandout 246
Lamtūna Berbers 61
Languedoc 435, 466, 498
La Plana 977
Laqant 684
Lara, Nuño de 78
Las Navas de Tolosa, Battle of 75, 77, 265, 1046, 1047
Al-Laythī, Yaḥyā b. Yaḥyā 21, 23, 116, 852, 853, 879, 880, 896
Leo X, Pope 288
León 9, 22, 27, 30, 34, 35, 36, 37, 39, 42, 43, 46, 72, 154, 156, 171, 452, 463, 596
Leovogildo, ruler of the Visigoths 5, 113
Lepanto, Battle of 208, 293
Lérida 9, 46, 49, 54, 156
Lerma, Duke of 230
Levant (Spanish) 703, 859, 861, 862, 865
Libya 765
Lisān al-Dīn *see* Ibn al-Khaṭīb
Lisbon 27, 57, 62, 63, 74, 274, 275, 276, 705, 902
Llull, Ramon 519, 525, 529, 537, 780, 799, 861
Loja 83, 84
Lope b. Mūsā 29
Lorca 32, 62, 403, 895, 977, 978
Louis I, of the Franks 22, 23
Louis VIII, of France 466
Louis IX (St. Louis), of France 283
Lower Frontier 23, 30, 31, 685
Lucena 83, 178, 792
Lucian 311
Lucullus 1021
Luis de León, Fray 517, 520
Luis de Torres 281, 492, 510
Luna, Alvaro de 82
Luna, Miguel de 538
Lyon 16

Al-Maʿāfirī 98, 337
Al-Maʿarrī, Abū 'l-ʿAlā' 311, 314, 326, 389
Madeira 276, 277

Al-Madīna 'l-ʿĀmiriyya 44
Al-Madīna 'l-Zāhira 44, 119, 127, 338
Madīnat al-Zahrā' 38, 44, 45, 47, 118, 119, 126, 143, 324, 338, 511, 586, 601, **603-04**, 605, 607, 616, 642, 643, 644, 658, 690, 693, 718, 989, 1018, 1019, 1022, 1023, 1030
Madrid 30, 74, 889
Maecenas 1022
Magacela 75
Al-Maghāmī, Fāṭima bint 718
Maghrāwa Berbers 48, 61
Al-Maghrāwī, Abū Zayd ʿAbd al-Raḥmān 179
Al-Maghrāwī, Khazrūn b. Fulfūl 44
Al-Maghrāwī, Ubaydallāh Aḥmad b. Bū Jumʿa 209, 210
Al-Maghrāwī, Zīrī b. ʿAṭiyya 44
Al-Mahdawī, ʿAbd al-ʿAzīz 909, 910, 925
Magio, the Monk 172
Mahdī b. Muslim 849
Al-Mahdiyya 71, 240, 764
Al-Mahrī, Sulaymān b. Aḥmad 289
Maimonides, Abraham 761
Maimonides, Moses 128, 195, 196, 313, 412, 517, 761, 788, 948, 957, 967, 1010, 1046
Majnūn, Qays b. al-Mulawwaḥ 841
Majorca (Mallorca) 26, 58, 59, 65, 76, 184, 704, 861, 980, 982
Majūs 153, 155, 160
Al-Makhzūmī 710
Makkī b. Abī Ṭālib 861
Málaga 10, 12, 31, 34, 52, 60, 68, 79, 83, 84, 97, 154, 155, 156, 159, 161, 178, 202, 262, 311, 336, 452, 539, 607, 614, 688, 701, 741, 744, 748, 767, 865, 895, 993, 1007, 1009, 1019, 1023, 1030, 1061
Al-Mālaqī, Yūsuf b. al-Shaykh 714
Al-Malaṭī 98
Al-Malik al-Afḍal, ruler of Yemen 941
Mālik b. Anas, *al-Imām* 21, 23, 116, 180, 850, 852, 853, 857, 873, 879, 895, 896, 899
Mālikis 21, 116, 212, 253, 428, 612, 643, 697, 777, 792, 850, 852, 853, 854, 855, 856, 857, 860, 861, 862, 863, 864, 866, 873, 879, 896, 897, 898, 899, 900, 903, 913, 950
Malindi 287
Mallorca *see* Majorca
Malta 224
Mamlūks 81, 82, 115, 205, 206, 208, 280, 287, 288, 289, 292, 401, 588, 950
Al-Ma'mūn, Abbasid Caliph 23, 25, 463, 509, 557
Al-Ma'mūn, Yaḥyā b. Dhī 'l-Nūn, ruler of Toledo 55, 56, 57, 901, 942, 960, 963, 990, 1048
Maʿn b. Ṣumādiḥ 57
El Mancebo de Arévalo 217, 218, 223, 535, 536, 875
Manresa 46
Manrique, Cardinal 223
Mansa Mūsā, ruler of Mali 276
Al-Manṣūr, Abū Jaʿfar, Abbasid Caliph 20, 21
Manṣūr b. ʿIrāq, Abū Naṣr 955
Al-Manṣūr, Muḥammad b. Abī ʿĀmir 40, **41-45**, 46, 47, 50, 51, 56, 122, 127, 133, 139, 326, 330, 344, 420, 463, 602, 606, 647, 651, 691, 693, 744, 755, 781, 854, 858, 861, 900, 988, 1009
Al-Manṣūr, Yaʿqūb, Abbasid Caliph 73, 74, 660
Al-Maqqarī, Abū ʿAbd Allāh 115, 118, 119, 134, 205, 207, 259, 260, 261, 421, 556, 557, 558, 568, 604, 745, 746, 756, 862, 949
Al-Maqrīzī 120
Maqueda 74
Marbella 80
Marcellus 112
Marco Polo 279, 284, 285, 292, 492, 1005, 1017
Marcos de Guadalajara 210, 211
Al-Marī, Abū 'l-ʿAbbās al-Qanjā'irī 924
Marīnids 75, 77, 78, 79, 81, 82, 245, 799
Mark, Canon of Toledo 1047
Marrakesh 61, 64, 69, 70, 102, 140, 251, 609, 610, 611, 613, 651, 658, 659, 660, 733, 792, 920, 921, 922, 923
Al-Marrākushī, ʿAbd al-Wāḥid 246, 612, 839, 852
Marseilles 231
Martel, Esteban, Fray 221, 223
Martí, Ramón 949
Martins, Fernão, Canon 274
Martos 80
Maʿrūf al-Karkhī 912
Marwān b. ʿAbd al-Raḥmān 400
Marwān b. Muḥammad 18

Marwān b. Mūsā 4
Al-Marwānī, Abū Muḥammad b. Muʿāwiya 763
Maslama, Abū 'l-Qāsim (Maslama of Madrid) 940, 941, 948, 960, 961, 962, 1038, 1041, 1047, 1050
Maslama b. Qāsim 900
Maṣmūda Berbers 61, 66, 68, 69, 140, 238, 651, 658
Al-Massūfī, Barrāz 70
Al-Massūfī, Muḥammad b. Ghāniya 73
Al-Masʿūdī 268, 275
Maurice of Nassau, *Stadtholder* 228
Mauritius, Archdeacon of Toledo 1046, 1047
Al-Mawṣilī, Ibrāhīm 557
Al-Mawṣilī, Isḥāq 25, 556, 557, 559, 560, 561
Maysara, called "al-Ḥaqīr" 14
Al-Mayūrqī, Abū Bakr 67, 780, **919-925**
Al-Māzarī 765
Mazdalī, ruler of Córdoba 65
Mazdalī b. Sulunkān 58
Mecca 286, 288, 289, 292, 640, 886, 887, 888, 911, 913, 937
Medellín 75
Medici, Lorenzo dei 483
Medina 12, 21, 134, 463, 556, 558, 584, 850, 870, 896, 915
Medinaceli 39, 42, 43, 44
Medinasidonia 9, 12, 14, 48, 78, 682
Mena, Juan de 520
Menahem b. Saruq 124, 193
Menelaos of Alexandria 954, 955, 1041
Mequinenza 67
Mérida 9, 22, 23, 29, 30, 31, 33, 75, 161, 601, 684, 689
Mértola 32, 53, 71
Messalina 1021
Meya 46
Michael, Bishop of Tarazona 1041, 1042
Middle Frontier 30, 39, 41, 44
Miknāsa Berbers 51, 56, 685
Minorca 26, 76, 699
Miranda, Count of 230
Al-Mīrtulī, Mūsā 927
Al-Miṣrī, Shujāʾ b. Aslam 953
Moclín 84
Monleón 32
Monmagstre 46
Montánchez 72, 75
Montefrío 84
Montemayor, Jorge de 520
Monzón 55, 64
La Mora de Ubeda 218, 535, 875
Moriscos 93, 95, 101, 109, 151, 173, 177, 181, 185, **201-34**, 453, 511, 1031
Morocco 4, 38, 44, 51, 59, 61, 235, 238, 239, 240, 251, 412, 462, 512, 541, 689, 691, 697, 698, 731, 732, 869, 879
Morón 48, 51, 60, 139, 748
Mosca, Ihuda 1001
Moses (the Jewish prophet) 236, 247, 832
Moses b. Ezra 191, 193, 194, 516, 527
Moses of Narbonne 791
Moses, Rabbi 124
Mozarabs 15, 23, 28, 29, 30, 66, 116, 124, 125, 138, **149-70**, **171-75**, 259, 262, 263, 410, 448, 452, 518, 687, 688, 689, 690, 691, 705, 715, 777, 879, 987, 1037, 1060
Muʿāwiya b. Abī Sufyān, Umayyad Caliph in Damascus 3, 368, 369, 426
Muʿāwiya b. Hishām 642
Muʿāwiya b. Lope 124
Al-Muʿayṭī, ʿAbd Allāh 48, 58
Mubārak, ruler of Valencia 50, 57
Mubashshir b. Sulaymān, Nāṣir al-Dawla 58, 59
Mudejars 128, 146, 151, 173, **176-87**, 202, 206, 220, 221, 222, 225, 448, 518, 526, 527, **592-98**, 661, **705-07**, 872, 874, 880, 1037
Al-Mughīra, brother of Caliph al-Ḥakam II 40, 41, 606, 608
Mughulṭāi 425
Muḥammad, the Prophet 134, 189, 210, 241, 242, 243, 247, 248, 250, 262, 333, 398, 421, 425, 426, 434, 507, 533, 537, 538, 639, 849, 850, 872, 879, 895, 898, 901, 1017, 1048
Muḥammad I, *al-Amīr* **27-31**, 32, 51, 601, 641, 642, 746, 852, 853, 854, 896, 897, 938
Muḥammad I, of Granada 76, 78, 88, 511
Muḥammad II, of Granada 78, 79, 660, 663, 666
Muḥammad III, of Granada 79, 660, 663, 666
Muḥammad IV, of Granada 80, 663
Muḥammad V, called "al-Ghanī bi-Llāh", of Granada 80, 81, 102, 104, 664, 665, 666, 667, 798, 950
Muḥammad VII, of Granada 82

Muḥammad IX, of Granada 83
Muḥammad b. ʿAbbād 139
Muḥammad b. ʿAttāb 899
Muḥammad b. Dāwūd al-Ẓāhirī 422, 424, 425, 426, 460, 467, 472
Muḥammad b. Fuṭays b. Wāṣil 882
Muḥammad b. al-Ḥājj 65
Muḥammad b. Hishām b. ʿAbd al-Jabbār 47, 718
Muḥammad b. Jahwar, Abū 'l-Walīd 52, 349
Muḥammad b. Maḥmūd al-Qabrī 405, 410, 411
Muḥammad b. Mūsā 763
Muḥammad al-Nāṣir, Caliph 74-75, 660, 965
Muḥammad b. al-Qāsim b. Ḥammūd 60
Muḥammad b. al-Shafra 951
Muḥammad b. Sulaymān 763
Muḥammad b. Tamlīkh 645
Muḥammad b. ʿUmar b. Lubāba 885
Muḥammad b. Yūsuf b. Naṣr *see* Muḥammad I, of Granada
Muḥyī 'l-Dīn b. Zakī 925
Al-Muʿizz, Fāṭimid Caliph 190, 332, 333
Mujāhid al-ʿĀmirī, ruler of Denia and the Balearics 48, 51, 57, 58, 262, 861, 944
Mu'min b. Saʿīd b. Qays 328
Al-Mundhir b. Muḥammad, *al-Amīr* **31-32**, 938
Münzer, Hieronymus 91, 93, 94, 98, 99, 101, 102, 103, 104, 105, 106, 1027, 1029
Al-Muqaddasī 118, 895, 903
Muqātil, ruler of Tortosa 51, 59
Al-Muqtadir, Aḥmad b. Hūd, ruler of Saragossa 54, 58, 649, 946, 947, 1041
Al-Murādī, Aḥmad (or Muḥammad) b. Khalaf 941, 942, 943, 957
Murcia 10, 12, 26, 32, 50, 53, 59, 62, 66, 67, 68, 72, 73, 76, 81, 231, 262, 264, 400, 401, 464, 498, 610, 661, 689, 697, 698, 701, 704, 865, 874, 950, 977, 978, 979, 1024
Al-Mursī, Abū 'l-Ḥusayn b. al-Ḥāsib 564
Al-Murtaḍā, ʿAbd al-Raḥmān b. Muḥammad 48
Al-Murtaḍā, Aghlab 58, 63
Mūsā b. Mūsā b. Qasī 29, 33, 689
Mūsā b. Nuṣayr al-Lakhmī 4, 7, 8, 9, 10, 13, 50
Al-Muṣāra, Battle of 19
Al-Muṣḥafī, Jaʿfar b. ʿUthmān 40, 41
Al-Mustaʿīn, Aḥmad b. Hūd, ruler of Saragossa 54, 55, 65
Al-Mustaʿīn, Sulaymān b. al-Ḥakam, Caliph 47, 48, 341, 468
Al-Mustaʿīn, Sulaymān b. Muḥammad, ruler of Saragossa 49, 54, 59
Al-Mustakfī, Muḥammad b. ʿAbd al-Raḥmān b. ʿAbd Allāh, Caliph 48-49, 401, 709, 717
Al-Mustaʿlī, Muḥammad II b. Idrīs 60
Al-Mustanṣir *see* Al-Ḥakam II
Al-Mustanṣir, Caliph (Almohad) 75
Al-Mustaẓhir, ʿAbd al-Raḥmān b. Hishām, Caliph 48, 468
Al-Muta'ayyid, Idrīs b. ʿAlī 60
Al-Muʿtadd bi-Llāh, Hishām b. Muḥammad, Caliph 49
Al-Muʿtaḍid b. ʿAbbād, ruler of Seville 51, 52, 53, 55, 60, 139, 265, 348, 349, 355, 357
Al-Mu'taman, Yūsuf b. Hūd, ruler of Saragossa 946, 947, 948, 952, 954, 955, 986, 1041, 1050
Al-Muʿtamid b. ʿAbbād, ruler of Seville 50, 52, 53, 54, 56, 59, 61, 62, 63, 139, 140, 141, 143, 145, 173, 198, 264, 265, 325, 331, 344, 346, 348, 349, 355, **356-60**, 462, 464, 465, 512, 514 , 526, 609, 648, 717, 941, 944, 959, 989, 990, 1009, 1023, 1030
Al-Mu'tamin, ʿAbd al-ʿAzīz 57, 59
Al-Mutanabbī 307, 321, 326, 332, 349, 372
Al-Muṭarrif, son of *al-Amīr* ʿAbd Allāh b. Muḥammad 33, 34, 901
Al-Muṭarrif b. ʿAbd al-Raḥmān, son of *al-Amīr* ʿAbd al-Raḥmān II 27
Muṭarrif b. ʿAbd al-Raḥmān, calligrapher 644, 645
Al-Muʿtaṣim, Muḥammad b. Ṣumādiḥ, ruler of Almería 57, 62, 63, 710, 989, 1019
Al-Mutawakkil, Abbasid Caliph 370
Muʿtazilis 69, 122, 777, 856, 868, 895, 900, 901, 912, 913, 914, 915, 916
Al-Muʿtazz bi-Llāh, Abbasid Caliph 370
Muwallads 15, 23, 28, 29, 31, 32, 33, 34, 49, 114, 116, 125, 137, 151, 262, 602, 687, 689, 690, 699, 747, 749, 779, 792
Muẓaffar, ruler of Valencia 50, 57
Al-Muẓaffar, ʿAbd al-Malik b. al-Manṣūr 44, **46**, 47, 59, 326, 330, 344, 420, 764, 858
Al-Muẓaffar, Muḥammad b. ʿAbd Allāh 56

Al-Nabātī 945
Al-Nābigha 'l-Dhubyānī 324
Al-Nābigha 'l-Ja'dī 324
Al-Nābulusī 529
Al-Naḍar b. Salama 880
Nāfi' 895
Nafza Berbers 19, 33, 247, 685
Al-Nahrajūrī 778
Nakūr 19
Narbonne 10, 16, 153
Al-Nāṣir, Caliph *see* 'Abd al-Raḥmān III
Nāṣir al-Mustanṣir, Caliph 75
Naṣr, ruler of Granada 79, 663
Naṣr, Abū 'l-Fatḥ 27, 116
Naṣr al-Dawla al-Ḥamdānī 117
Naṣrids **78-84**, **88-111**, 178, 199, 202, 207, 224, 262, 263, 265, 511, 513, **614-18**, 619, **621-25**, 642, 645, 655, 660, 661, 662, **663-69**, 714, 716, 717, 768, **872-74**, 950, 953, 975, 989, 1026
Navagiero, Andrea 93, 95, 104, 105, 107, 1018, 1029, 1030
Navarre 30, 34, 35, 36, 37, 39, 42, 176, 183, 184, 185, 202, 203, 220, 222, 452, 462, 463, 466
Nazhūn 710
Nebrija 78
Nefzāwī, Shaykh 524, 526, 542
New World 273, 278, 483, 499
Nicholas, the Monk 124, 939
Nichomachos of Gerasa 953, 954
Niebla 9, 12, 53, 70, 748
Al-Niffarī 911
Nîmes 15
Niẓām al-Mulk 949
Nobles, Battle of the 14
Normans 27, 39, 54, 55, 71, 265, 460, 462, 465, 587
Al-Nubāhī 914
Nuñez Muley, Francisco 224
Al-Nūrī, Abū 'l-Ḥasan 531, 532

Ocsonoba 9, 12, 53
Odo of Cluny 565
Olmos 30
Onneca, Princess, of Navarre 463
Oporto 30
Oran 209, 232
Ordoño I, of Asturias 29
Ordoño II, of Asturias and León 34, 36
Ordoño III, of León 38
Ordoño IV, of León 38, 39, 124, 463
Ordoño IV, of Navarre 126, 127
Oreja 74
Orihuela 68, 701
Orosius 937, 1037
Osma, Battle of 36, 37, 42
Otto I, of Germany 37, 124
Otto II, of Germany 39
Ottomans 82, 204, 208, 224, 226, 232, 269, 289, 293, 571
Oviedo 9, 22, 30, 172
Oxford 511

Padrón 43
Palermo 587
Palestine 74, 194, 462
Palestinians (in al-Andalus) 12, 19
Palos 273, 282, 491
Pamplona 15, 30, 35, 36, 37, 42, 43, 463
Paris 1007, 1045, 1046
Paterna, Battle of 57
Paul the Deacon 683
Peçanha, Manuel 286
Pechina 779
Pedro I, of Aragon 466
Pedro I, "the Cruel", of Castile 81, 143, 146, 177, 263, 588, 595, 596, 799
Pedro II, of Aragon 75, 76, 196
Pedro IV, of Aragon 81, 965
Peking 292
Pelayo 16, 17, 21
Peña de Cervera 43
Pepin II 16
Pereira, Gonçalho 286
Pérez del Pulgar, Hernán 98, 108
Perfecto 29
Persia 18, 263, 510, 561, 1008, 1016, 1020, 1023, 1029, 1060
Peter Martyr 205, 206, 207, 220
Peter of Toledo 1048
Peter the Venerable, Abbot of Cluny 1044, 1048
Petrarch, Francesco 497
Petrus Alfonsus 197, 961
Philip II, of Spain 223, 224, 230
Philip III, of Spain 511, 522
Philip of Evreux 184
Pierre d'Ailly, Cardinal 278, 279
Piri Reis 275, 289, 293
Pisans 58, 65
Pit, Battle of the 23

Pius II, Pope 285
Plato 311, 425, 426, 461, 509, 516, 781, 793, 837, 838, 839, 917, 1046
Plato of Tivoli 278, 1050
Pliny 1026
Plotinus 516, 840
Poitiers 12, 16
Poley 32
Polop 221
Porphyry 516
Portio, Camilio 288
Portugal 5, 9, 10, 12, 29, 33, 34, 43, 56, 72, 172, 184, 185, 204, 269, 273, 274, 275, 277, 286, 288, 289, 705
"Prester John" *see* Grand Khān
Priego 32, 80
Priscilian 856
Proclus 516
Provence 16, 195, 198, 462, 494, 497, 498
Pseudo-Appolonius 1043
Pseudo-Ptolemy 1042
Ptolemy 426, 527, 627, 782, 961, 962, 963, 964, 966, 967, 969, 1003, 1046, 1050
Pulgar, Hernando del 520
Pythagoras 912

Al-Qabā'ilī, Shaykh 928
Al-Qāḍī 'Iyāḍ 868, 884
Al-Qādir, Yaḥyā b. Dhī 'l-Nūn 55, 56, 57, 173
Qā'it Bey 205
Qal'a of Banī Ḥammād 251, 765
Qalam 558
Al-Qalaṣādī 953
Al-Qālī, Abū 'Alī 38, 45, 309, 324
Al-Qalqashandī 120, 991
Al-Qanāzi'ī, Abū 'l-Muṭarrif 860
Al-Qashshāsh, Abū 'l-Ghayth 541-42
Al-Qāsim b. Ḥammūd 48, 60
Qāsim b. Muḥammad b. Siyār 854
Qasmūna 711
Al-Qaṭṭān, Qāsim b. Muṭarrif 962
Qayrawān 3, 4, 23, 35, 37, 60, 119, 153, 584, 763, 764, 849, 852, 944
Al-Qaysī, Yaḥyā b. Muḍar 23
Qaysis 8, 13, 14, 16, 19, 26, 50
Al-Qazwīnī 268, 982
Al-Qifṭī 912, 915
Al-Qilfāṭ, Yaḥyā 328
Qudāma b. Ja'far 410
Quesada 79
Quevedo, Francisco Gómez de 519, 522
Quinsay 284, 285
Al-Qurashī, al-'Abbās b. 'Abd Allāh 26
Al-Qurṭubī, Shams al-Dīn 914
Al-Qūsī, 'Abd al-Ghaffār 921
Qutayba b. Muslim al-Bāhilī 7, 10
Al-Qūṭī, Ḥafṣ 1037

Rabadan, Muḥammad 875
Rabat 119, 140, 659, 660
Rabī', Count 115
Rabī' b. Zayd *see* Recemund
Al-Rāḍī, son of al-Mu'tamid of Seville 359
Raimundo, Archbishop 173
Al-Ramādī, Yūsuf b. Hārūn **330-32**, 358, 410, 411
Ramiro I, of Asturias 27, 29
Ramiro II, of Aragon 67, 138, 466
Ramiro II, of Asturias and León 36, 37
Ramiro III, of León 39, 42
Ramon Berenguer II, of Barcelona 464
Ramon Berenguer IV, of Barcelona 462
Ramon Borrel III, of Barcelona 46
Raqsh al-A'azz 275
Al-Rashīd, Abū Muḥammad 'Abd al-Wāḥid, Caliph 798
Al-Rashīd, son of al-Mu'tamid of Seville 464
Rayyo 682
Al-Rāzī, 'Īsā b. Aḥmad 114, 763
Recaredo, ruler of the Visigoths 6, 515
Reccafred, Archbishop of Seville 138
Recemund (Rabī' b. Zayd) 119, 688, 691
Ribagorza 4
Richard I, "the Lionheart", of England 466
Richard of Fournival 1042
Richard of St. Victor 473
Richelieu, Cardinal 511
Ricla 65
Riḍwān, vizier to Yūsuf I of Granada 99, 100
Río Salado, Battle of 80
Rioja, La 43
Ripoll, Santa María de 171, 172, 1037, 1060
Riquier, Giraut 471
Al-Riqūṭī, Muḥammad 874, 950
Robert of Ketton 1043, 1044, 1045, 1047, 1048, 1050
Roderic (Rodrigo), ruler of the Visigoths 6, 7, 8, 17, 153, 163, 265
Roger II, of Sicily 275, 292

Rojas, Fernando de 520
Roland 20
Romans 5, 6, 601, 614, 680, 755, 937, 938, 942, 974, 976, 977, 983, 987, 1011, 1021, 1022
Rome 280, 519
Roncesvalles 20
Ronda 51, 60, 78, 79, 80, 84, 684, 748
Roussillon 171
Al-Ruʿaynī, Abū Hārūn 779
Al-Ruʿaynī, Ismāʿīl b. ʿAbd Allāh 779, 902, 913, 916, 918
Al-Ruʿaynī, Saʿdūn 22
Al-Ruʿaynī, Yaḥyā 779
Rudel, Jaufre 465
Rueda 42, 65, 1041
Ruiz, Hernán 142
Ruiz, Juan (Archpriest of Hita) 202, 467, 475, 510, **526-28**, 543
Rumayk b. Ḥajjāj 717
Al-Rumaykiyya, Iʿtimād 357, 717
Rūmī, Jalāluddin 628
Al-Rūmī, Mughīth 8, 9, 113
Al-Rundī, Abu Bakr 714
Al-Rundī, Abū 'l-Baqā' 264, 325
Ruṣāfa 19
Al-Ruṣāfa (palace) 21, 599, 603, 939, 988
Rustumids 31

Saadiah b. Danan 199
Saadiah ben Joseph 193
Al-Sabīka, Battle of 71
Sābūr, Governor of the Lower Frontier 56
Sacromonte of Granada 228, 537, 539
Saʿd b. Muḥammad, ruler of Granada 82
Al-Ṣadfūrī, Abū Naṣr 881
Saʿdids 204, 227
Al-Safāqusī, Abū ʿAmr 861
Al-Saffāḥ, Abū 'l-ʿAbbās, Abbasid Caliph 18
Ṣafwān b. Idrīs 402
Al-Saghīr, Durrī 647
Sagrajas, Battle of 62
Sahagún 593, 594
Sahl b. Hārūn 309, 342
Saḥnūn, *al-Imām* 850, 896
Al-Ṣaḥrāwī, Yaḥyā b. ʿAlī 67
Saʿīd b. ʿAbd Rabbihī 938
Saʿīd b. Ayyūb 643
Saʿīd al-Baghdādī 45
Saʿīd b. Fatḥūn al-Saraqusṭī 784, 900, 901
Saʿīd b. Ḥakam 76
Saʿīd b. Hudhayl 32
Saʿīd b. ʿImrān b. Mushrif 888
Saʿīd b. Jūdī 32
Saʿīd b. Mastanna 32
Saʿīd b. Sulaymān 882
Ṣāʿid of Toledo *see* Abū 'l-Qāsim b. Ṣāʿid
Sajūma 4
Saladin 289
Salama b. Mufarrij 653
Salama b. Umayya b. Wadīʿ 886
Salamanca 41, 597
Saldaña 43
Salé 232, 765
Sālim, ruler of the Ottomans 293
Saltés 53
Salvatierra 75
Samarcand 507, 508
Samarra 119, 584, 603, 616, 1016
San Esteban de Gormaz 43
San Eulogio 28
San Juan 46
San Pedro, Diego de 520
San Vicente, Battle of 42
Al-Ṣanʿā'nī, Ḥanash b. ʿAbd Allāh 8, 9
Sancho I, of Aragon 466
Sancho I Garcés, of Navarre 34, 35, 36, 463
Sancho I, "the Fat", of León 36, 37, 38, 39, 124, 463
Sancho II Abarca, of Navarre 39, 42, 47, 463
Sancho IV, of Castile and León 79
Sancho, ruler of Navarre 75
Sancho, ruler of Portugal 74
Sancho, Prince, of Castile 64, 65, 465
Sancho García Fernández, ruler of Castile 43, 46, 466
Sancho Ramirez, ruler of Aragon 55
Sanchuelo *see* ʿAbd al-Raḥmān b. al-Manṣūr al-ʿĀmirī
Sansón, Abbot 28, 155
Santa Cruz 75
Santa Cruz, Alonso de 208
Santa Fé 84, 273
Santa María de Cortes 766
Santarem 10, 57, 62, 63, 73, 472, 705, 1009
Santaver 51, 64
Santiago de Compostela 43, 123, 466, 518, 1009
Sanudo, Marino 279
Ṣaqāliba (Slavs) 22, 40, 45, 50, 127, 151, 156, 157, 259, 262, **691-92**, 694, 699, 1011
Al-Saqaṭī 756

Sara the Goth 136, 683
Saragossa 9, 20, 22, 23, 29, 30, 33, 39, 46, 48, 50, **54-55**, 58, 65, 123, 156, 161, 162, 190, 265, 462, 588, 606, 607, 610, 613, 647, 650, 684, 690, 694, 698, 706, 860, 861, 940, 946, 954, 961, 1008, 1023, 1041, 1042, 1049
Sargon II, of the Assyrians 1021
Sarī al-Saqaṭī 911, 913
Al-Sarrāj, Abū ʿAlī 33
Al-Sarrāj, Jaʿfar b. Aḥmad 425
Sawār b. Ḥamdūn 32
Ṣawwāb, wife of Ibrāhīm b. Ismāʿīl al-Qabrī 886
Sayf al-Dawla, ruler of Aleppo 372
Sayf al-Dawla, ruler of Saragossa 71, 1041
Sayyida, wife of Alfonso VI of Castile and León 465
Scot, Michael 948, 1039, 1046, 1060
Segovia 212, 974
Segovia, Juan de 875
Seneca 518
Septimanie 16
Serpa 72
Seville 9, 10, 12, 27, 32, 34, 50, 52, **53-54**, 62, 63, 66, 71, 72, 73, 74, 75, 76, 77, 79, 104, 127, 134, **136-48**, 154, 162, 173, 177, 190, 273, 344, 348, 355, 357, 400, 462, 465, 498, 518, 540, 562, 568, 588, 589, 595, 597, 609, 612, 614, 642, 647, 648, 650, 651, 660, 663, 682, 683, 684, 694, 698, 701, 717, 731, 732, 748, 759, 792, 859, 860, 865, 870, 871, 928, 940, 941, 942, 943, 959, 989, 990, 991, 997, 1000, 1001, 1002, 1005, 1006, 1007, 1008, 1009, 1010, 1023, 1024, 1030, 1031, 1047
Seydī ʿAlī Reis 289
Sfax 126, 1008
Shabṭūn (Ziyād b. ʿAbd al-Raḥmān) 21, 22, 881, 885
Al-Shāfiʿī, *al-Imām* 31, 853, 897
Shāfiʿis 428, 853, 861, 862, 863, 864, 870, 895, 896, 897
Al-Shakkāz, Ḥasan 928
Al-Shāmī, Ibrāhīm b. Sulaymān 24
Al-Shāmī, Muʿāwiya b. Ṣāliḥ 850, 897
Al-Shāmī, Ṣaʿṣaʿa b. Sallām 850, 897
Al-Shammākh 324
Shams al-Fuqarāʾ 911
Al-Shaqundī, Abū ʾl-Walīd Ismāʿīl b. Muḥammad 310, 766
Al-Sharafī, Muḥammad 928
Al-Shaʿrānī 921
Al-Sharīshī, Abū ʾl-ʿAbbās 310
Al-Shāṭibī, Ibrāhīm b. Mūsā 873
Shiʿites 18, 33, 35, 37, 38, 40, 69, 211, 325, 332, 684, 799, 853, 868, 895, 899, 901, 923
Al-Shuburbalī 928
Shuqr 379, 389
Shurayḥ 870
Al-Shushtarī 571
Sicily 275, 452, 460, 461, 462, 509, 540, 587, 1006
Sí𝚌ulo, Lucio Marineo 95, 97, 109
Sidrāy b. Wazīr 71
Sijilmāsa 4, 31, 44, 61
Al-Silafī 766
Silves 53, 71, 73, 74, 355, 701
Silvester II, Pope 512
Ṣinhāja Berbers 40, 41, 44, 48, 51, 52, 60, 651, 685, 732
Al-Ṣinhājī, Abū ʾl-Ḥasan ʿAlī b. Taʿishshā 658
Al-Ṣinhājī, Mallūl b. Ibrāhīm b. Yaḥyā 246
Al-Ṣiqillī, ʿAbbās 73
Sīrāf 763
Sisibut, ruler of the Visigoths 188
Slavs *see Ṣaqāliba*
Socrates 783
Somontín 32
Sousse 1001
Straton of Sardes 400
Ṣubḥ, wife of Caliph al-Ḥakam II 463
Suevi 5
Sufis 69, 122, 337, 352, 380, 434, 461, 530, 531, 626, 697, 780, 798, 858, 859, 871, 873, 874, 879, 890, 895, **909-33**
Al-Suhrawardī, Shihāb al-Dīn 798, 830, 843
Al-Sukūnī, Muʿāwiya b. Ḥudayj 3
Sulaymān b. ʿAbd al-Malik, Umayyad Caliph in Damascus 9, 10
Sulaymān b. ʿAbd al-Raḥmān, brother of *al-Amīr* Hishām I 21
Al-Ṣumayl b. Ḥātim 19, 20
Al-Ṣunawbarī 326, 371, 386, 388
Sunnis 35, 69, 211, 212, 344, 950
Sunyer, ruler of Barcelona 37
Al-Surunbāqī, Saʿdūn 29
Syria 19, 112, 113, 117, 129, 289, 462, 507, 604, 605, 614, 682, 750, 850, 975, 996, 1018

Syrians (in al-Andalus) 12, 13, 19, 50, 137, 777, 1011

Tabarca 763
Tablada, Battle of 27
Al-Tādilī 921, 922
Ṭā'ifas 33, 48, **49-60**, 139, 161, 162, 190, 191, 265, 326, 327, 335, 344, 348, 379, 512, **606-08**, 615, 619, **647-50**, 659, 661, 686, 687, 688, **693-96**, 698, 702, 705, 716, 718, 741, 764, 765, 767, 860, 861, 865, 942, 944, 945, 989, 990, 1049
Talamanca 30, 853
Al-Ṭalamankī, Abū ʿUmar b. Lubb 860, 902
Talavera 9, 65, 74, 145, 853
Ṭālūt b. ʿAbd al-Jabbār 23
Tamerlane 799
Al-Tamīmiyya, Ḥassāna 328
Tangiers 3, 4, 6, 7, 8, 251
Tarazona 65, 1041, 1043
Ṭarīf b. Mulūk 7
Tarifa 7, 70, 75, 78, 79, 80, 653
Al-Ta'rīkhī 122
Ṭāriq b. Ziyād 4, 6, 7, 8, 9, 10, 13
Tarragona 10, 741
Ṭarūb, wife of *al-Amīr* ʿAbd al-Raḥmān II 463
Tāshfīn b. ʿAlī b. Yūsuf 66, 67, 68, 70, 71
Teba 80
Tejada 71
Tello Fernández 67
Teodofredo 6
Teodomiro 10, 11
Teresa, Princess of León, called ʿAbda, wife of al-Manṣūr al-ʿĀmirī 43
Teresa of Avila, St. 520, 530, 531, 532
Teruel 51, 685, 686, 979
Tétouan 568
Thābit b. Qurra 939, 954, 963, 964, 1041
Al-Thaghrī, Aḥmad 84
Al-Thaqafī, al-Ḥurr b. ʿAbd al-Raḥmān, Governor 12, 13, 113
Al-Thaqafī, Muḥammad b. al-Qāsim 7, 10
Themistius 813, 824
Theodosius 954, 1041, 1044
Theon of Alexandria 963
Theophilus, Emperor of the Byzantines 27
Theophrastus 145, 943
Theuda, Queen of Navarre *see* Toda
Theuda, Queen of the Normans 464
Thierry of Chartres 1044, 1045
Tiaret 31
Al-Tīfāshī, Aḥmad b. Yūsuf 411, 412, 555, 556, 560, 561, 562, 563, 564, 568, 569, 573
Al-Tighnarī 942, 943, 987, 990, 991, 992, 993, 996, 1005
Timbuktu 232
Tinmal 246, 659
Tivoli 1018
Tlemcen 4, 61, 68, 69, 70, 81, 82, 238, 568, 609, 610, 651, 653, 659
Toda (Theuda), Queen of Navarre 36, 38, 124, 463
Toledo 6, 8, 9, 14, 23, 26, 29, 30, 33, 34, 51, 53, 54, **55-56**, 61, 64, 65, 66, 74, 118, 149, 150, 151, 156, 157, 159, 160, 161, 162, 163, 171, 172, 173, 174, 176, 180, 196, 265, 278, 462, 465, 509, 512, 588, 592, 593, 594, 595, 596, 647, 649, 650, 661, 663, 685, 686, 688, 689, 698, 705, 731, 732, 853, 859, 860, 901, 915, 940, 943, 944, 952, 960, 962, 963, 964, 965, 986, 989, 990, 1001, 1002, 1005, 1037, 1041, 1044, 1045, 1046, 1047, 1060, 1061
Torres-Novas 74
Tortosa 51, 54, 57, 59, 76, 156, 161, 162, 231, 706
Toscanelli, Paolo Pozzo dal 274
Toulouse 15, 498
Tours 15
Trajan, Emperor 113, 518
Tripoli 3, 71
Trujillo 72
Tudela 55, 176, 184, 220, 400, 689, 706, 889, 1042, 1043, 1044
Tudmir 10, 26
Tudmīr of Oriola 153
Al-Tujībī, Mundhir b. Yaḥyā 48, 54
Al-Tujībī, Yaḥyā b. Muḥammad 39
Al-Tujībī, Yaḥyā b. Mundhir 54
Tunis 204, 208, 568, 800, 910, 966, 1039
"Tunis Exile" 541
Tunisia (Ifrīqiya) 3, 4, 11, 14, 31, 36, 44, 71, 81, 82, 212, 232, 240, 411, 412, 541, 584, 896, 996
Tunstede, Simon 564
Turkestan 7, 10, 507
Al-Ṭurṭūshī, Abū Bakr 63, 69, 71, 310, 744, 753, 872, 882, 883, 920
Al-Tustarī, Sahl 912, 915, 917, 918, 919
Al-Tuṭīlī, Aʿmā 400, 634
Tyre 1009

ʿUbāda b. Māʾ al-Samāʾ 405, 410, 411
ʿUbayd Allāh b. ʿAbd Allāh al-Balansī 26
ʿUbayd Allāh b. Abī ʿAbda 32
ʿUbayd Allāh al-Mahdī 35, 37, 240, 247
ʿUbayd Allāh b. Muḥammad 33
ʿUbayd Allāh b. Qāsim, Archbishop of Seville 138, 145
ʿUbayd Allāh b. Umayya b. S̲h̲āliya 32
ʿUbayd Allāh b. ʿUt̲h̲mān 19
ʿUbayd Allāh b. Yaḥyā 884, 886
Ubeda 71, 75, 81, 665
Uclés 33, 51, 64, 65, 74, 686
Uclés, Battle of 64-65, 465
Al-ʿUd̲h̲rī, Aḥmad b. ʿUmar b. Anas 141, 275, 744, 745, 746, 748, 751, 989
ʿUmar b. ʿAbd al-ʿAzīz, Umayyad Caliph in Damascus 12
ʿUmar b. Abī Rabīʿa 469
ʿUmar b. ʿAdabbas 641
ʿUmar b. al-K̲h̲aṭṭāb, Second Caliph of Islam 242, 421, 639, 881
ʿUmar al-Mālaqī 311
ʿUmar al-Mutawakkil b. al-Afṭas 55-56, 61, 63
Al-Umawī al-Andalūsī 954
ʿUmayr b. Saʿīd 136
Umayyads 4, 10, 11, 12, 13, 15, 17, 18, 19, 20, 25, 33, 37, 41, 50, 60, 112, 113, 153, 155, 159, 161, 191, 250, 264, 323, 325, 370, 371, 372, 378, 398, 420, 421, 426, 507, 510, 514, 556, 558, 573, 585, 586, 587, 588, 599, 600, 602, 604, 605, 614, 635, 639, 640, 645, 650, 682, 683, 684, 689, 690, 691, 709, 716, 745, 759, 764, 767, 777, 784, 796, 850, 862, 868, 880, 896, 900, 901, 902, 914, 923, 952, 988, 1018, 1019, 1021, 1059
Umm al-Ḥasan bint Abī Liwāʾ Sulaymān b. Aṣbag̲h̲ 887
Umm al-Kirām, Princess, of Almería 710
Uns al-Qulūb 710
Upper Frontier 11, 20, 22, 26, 29, 30, 33, 34, 48, 49, 50, 54, 55, 61, 63, 64, 65, 67, 75, 124, 131, 132, 683, 686, 689, 690, 752, 888, 889
ʿUqba b. al-Ḥajjāj, Governor 16, 744
ʿUqba b. Nāfiʿ 3
Al-Urmawī, Ṣafiyy al-Dīn 555, 560, 561
Urubba Berbers 3
ʿUrwa b. al-Ward 324
Al-ʿUryānī, Abū ʾl-ʿAbbās 927
Usāma b. Munqid̲h̲ 268
Al-ʿUtbī 853, 896
ʿUt̲h̲mān, Third Caliph of Islam 585, 639
ʿUt̲h̲mān b. Abī ʾl-ʿAlāʾ 80
ʿUt̲h̲mān Dey 541
ʿUt̲h̲mān b. Saʿīd b. ʿUt̲h̲mān 886
Utrera 81

Vaca de Castro, Pedro 537
Valdejunquera, Battle of 34
Valdés brothers 520
Valence 16
Valencia 21, 27, 48, 51, 56, 57, 58, 64, 65, 66, 67, 68, 76, 156, 162, 163, 173, 176, 177, 185, 206, 209, 220, 221, 222, 223, 225, 227, 230, 232, 262, 263, 264, 379, 420, 452, 464, 614, 685, 688, 698, 700, 701, 703, 704, 706, 859, 949, 974, 978, 979, 980, 982
Valladolid 42, 180, 182, 183
Valtierra, Battle of 55, 65
Vamba, ruler of the Visigoths 6
Vandals 5
Vascones 5, 8, 20
Vega, Lope de 218, 505, 533, 538, 541, 543
Venice 232, 1018
Vienne 16
Vikings 124
Villard de Honnecourt 942
Violante, Princess, of Aragon 76
Virgin Mary 537
Visigoths **5-6**, 15, 16, 149, 150, 153, 156, 157, 158, 160, 161, 163, 173, 188, 189, 265, 409, 506, 518, 680, 682, 686, 750, 849, 987, 1019
Vives, Juan Luis 520

Al-Wādī Ās̲h̲ī 926
Waḍīh al-Ṣaqlabī 44
Wahb b. ʿAbd Allāh b. Ḥazm 27
Wajjāj b. Zalū 61
Walīd b. ʿAbd al-Malik, Umayyad Caliph in Damascus 7, 9, 10, 129, 378
Walīd b. Yazīd, Umayyad Caliph in Damascus 640
Wallāda bint al-Mustakfī 121, 343, 347, 348, 349, 351, 401, 469, 514, 696, 709, 710, 711, 712
Al-Wans̲h̲arīsī, Aḥmad b. Yaḥyā al-Tilimsānī 179, 681, 764, 1004
Al-Waqqas̲h̲ī, Abū ʾl-Walīd His̲h̲ām b. Aḥ-

mad 901
Al-Washshā' 422
William, Abbot of Malmesbury 1040
Witiza, ruler of the Visigoths 6, 7, 136, 163, 683, 747, 750

Xenophon 1021
Ximénez de Urrea, Pedro Manuel 471

Yaḥyā b. 'Abd Allāh, Abū 'Īsā 880
Yaḥyā b. 'Alī, ruler of Ceuta 48
Yaḥyā b. Ḥajjāj 878
Yaḥyā b. Isḥāq 938
Yaḥyā b. Ma'mar 881
Yaḥyā b. Mujāhid 857
Yaḥyā b. Qāsim b. Hilāl 887, 888
Yáñez de la Almedina 669
Al-Ya'qūbī 685
Yemen 289, 938, 975, 980
Yemenis (in al-Andalus) 8, 13, 14, 16, 19, 20, 21, 50, 137, 446, 682, 683, 684, 1011
Young Man of Arévalo *see* El Mancebo de Arévalo
Yumn b. Rizq 889
"Yūnyūs" (Vindanius) 939
Yūsuf I, of Granada 80, 99, 100, 103, 104, 262, 663, 665, 666, 667, 872
Yūsuf II, of Granada 82
Yūsuf III, of Granada 82, 360, 635, 664, 1029
Yūsuf b. 'Abd al-Mu'min, Caliph **72-73**, 243
Yūsuf b. Bakht 19
Yūsuf Ḥusām al-Dawla 947
Yūsuf b. Tāshfīn, *al-Amīr al-muslimīn* 54, 56, 60, **61-64**, 78, 357, 359, 379, 380, 462, 609, 651, 688, 705, 944, 1005
Yūsuf b. Ya'qūb, Caliph 252, 789

Al-Ẓāfir b. Dhī 'l-Nūn, ruler of Toledo 650
Zafra, Hernando de 93
Al-Zaghal, Muḥammad b. Sa'd, ruler of Granada 83, 84
Al-Zāhid, Abū Wahb 890
Ẓāhiris 425, 428, 698, 781, 853, 854, 861, 862, 864, 868, 869, 901, 920
Al-Zahrāwī, Abū 'l-Ḥasan 953
Al-Zahrāwī, Abū 'l-Qāsim (Abulcasis) 122, 940, 943, 944, 988, 990
Zaidān, Muley 227
Al-Zajjālī, Abū Marwān 1019, 1020, 1021, 1022
Al-Zajjālī, *al-faqīh* 779
Al-Zajjālī al-Qurṭubī 715
Al-Zallāqa, Battle of 54, 63, 64, 74
Zamora 33, 42, 46
Zanāta Berbers 44, 48, 51, 60, 61, 685
Al-Zanātī, Khālid b. Ḥumayd 14
Zarrūq, Aḥmad 542
Zāwī b. Zīrī, ruler of Granada 48, 60, 89, 98, 101
Zaynab of Almería 711
Zaytūn 284, 285
Zayyān b. Mudāfi' 76
Zayyānids 81
El Zegrí 204
Al-Zīrī, Tamīm 62
Zīrids 51, 53, 60, 190, 192, 621, 651, 687, 694
Ziryāb (Abū 'l-Ḥasan 'Alī b. Nāfi') 25, 26, 117, 556, 557, 558, 559, 560, 561, 563, 564, 565, 573, 604, 709, 1011
Ziyād b. Abī Sufyān 426
Ziyādat Allāh I, of the Aghlabids 557
Zubayda, wife of Abbasid Caliph Hārūn al-Rashīd 508
Al-Zubaydī, Abū Muḥammad 138, 139
Zuhayr al-'Āmirī, ruler of Almería 50, 57, 59, 192
Zuhayr b. Qays 4
Zuwāgha Berbers 685

THE MUSLIM CONQUEST

ṬĀRIQ ------------------

MŪSÀ B. NUṢAYR ....

'ABD AL-'AZĪZ ._._._._._.

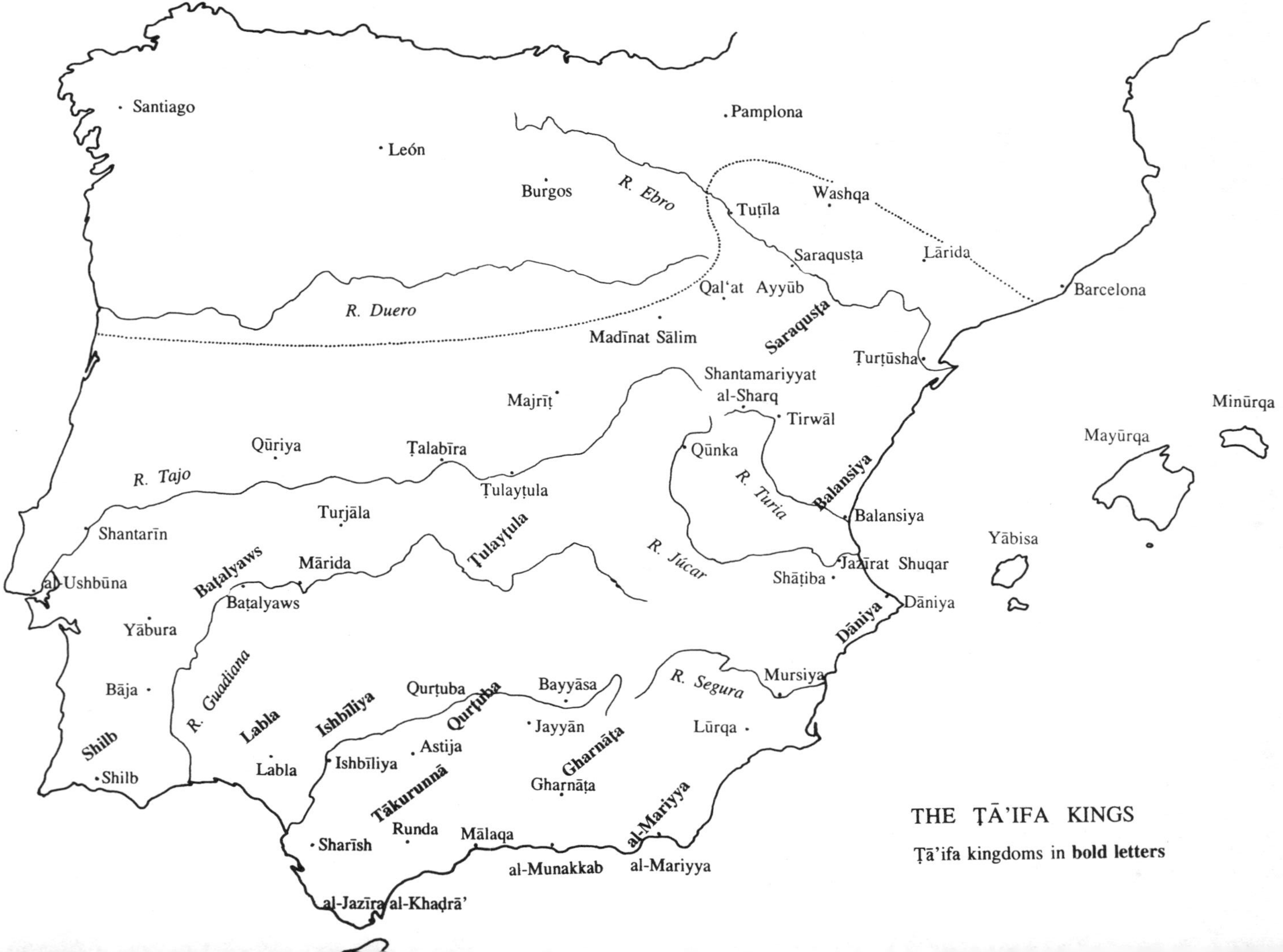

THE ṬĀ'IFA KINGS

Ṭā'ifa kingdoms in **bold letters**

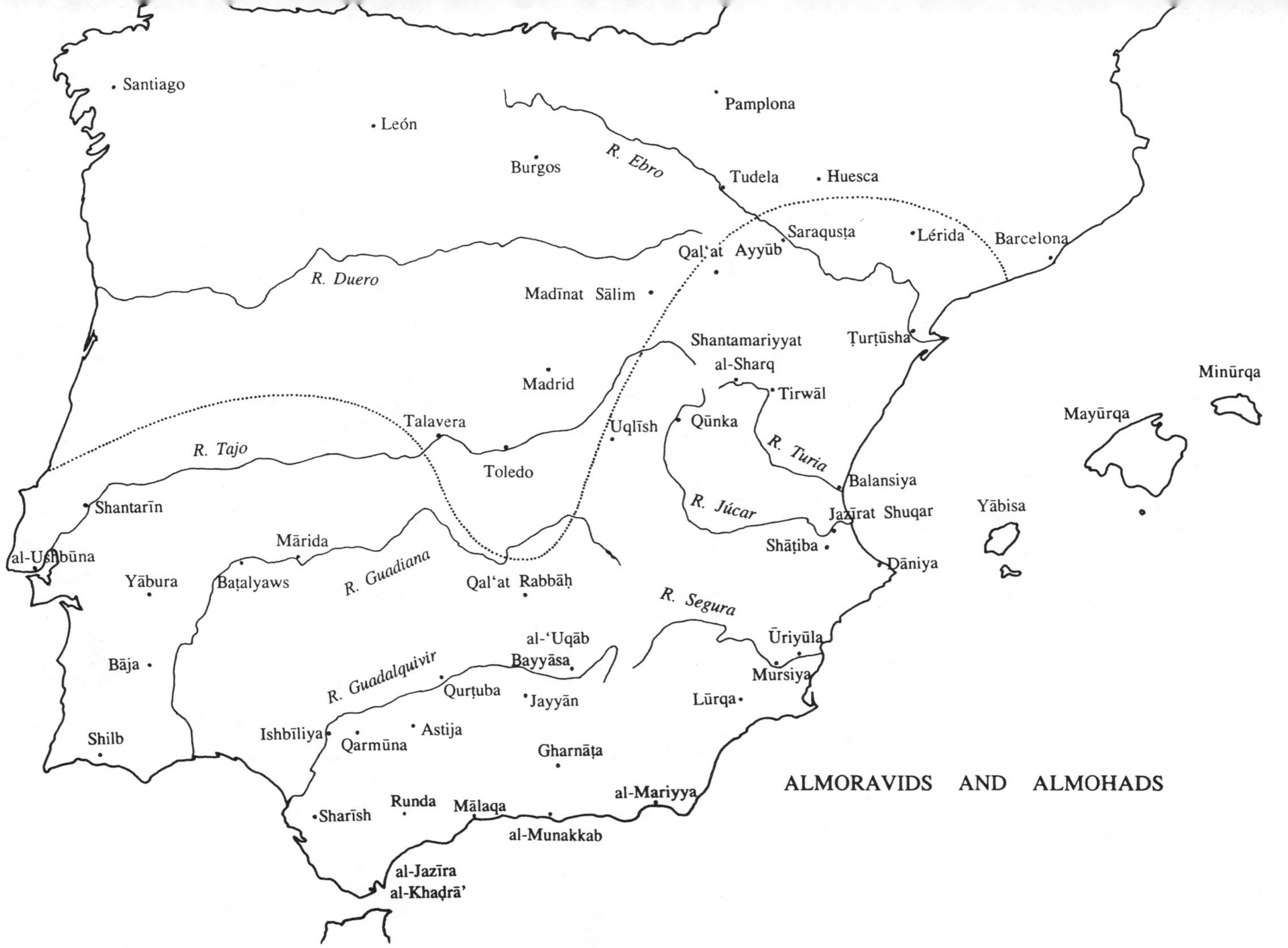

Santiago
León
Burgos
R. Ebro
Pamplona
Tudela
Huesca
Saraqusṭa
Lérida
Barcelona
Qal'at Ayyūb
R. Duero
Madīnat Sālim
Ṭurṭūsha
Shantamariyyat
al-Sharq
Tirwāl
Madrid
Minūrqa
Mayūrqa
Talavera
Uqlīsh
Qūnka
R. Tajo
R. Turia
Toledo
Balansiya
Shantarīn
R. Júcar
Jazīrat Shuqar
Yābisa
Mārida
Shāṭiba
al-Ushbūna
R. Guadiana
Dāniya
Yābura
Baṭalyaws
Qal'at Rabbāḥ
R. Segura
al-'Uqāb
Ūriyūla
Bayyāsa
Bāja
R. Guadalquivir
Mursiya
Qurṭuba
Jayyān
Lūrqa
Ishbīliya
Astija
Qarmūna
Shilb
Gharnāṭa
ALMORAVIDS AND ALMOHADS
al-Mariyya
Runda
Sharīsh
Mālaqa
al-Munakkab
al-Jazīra
al-Khaḍrā'

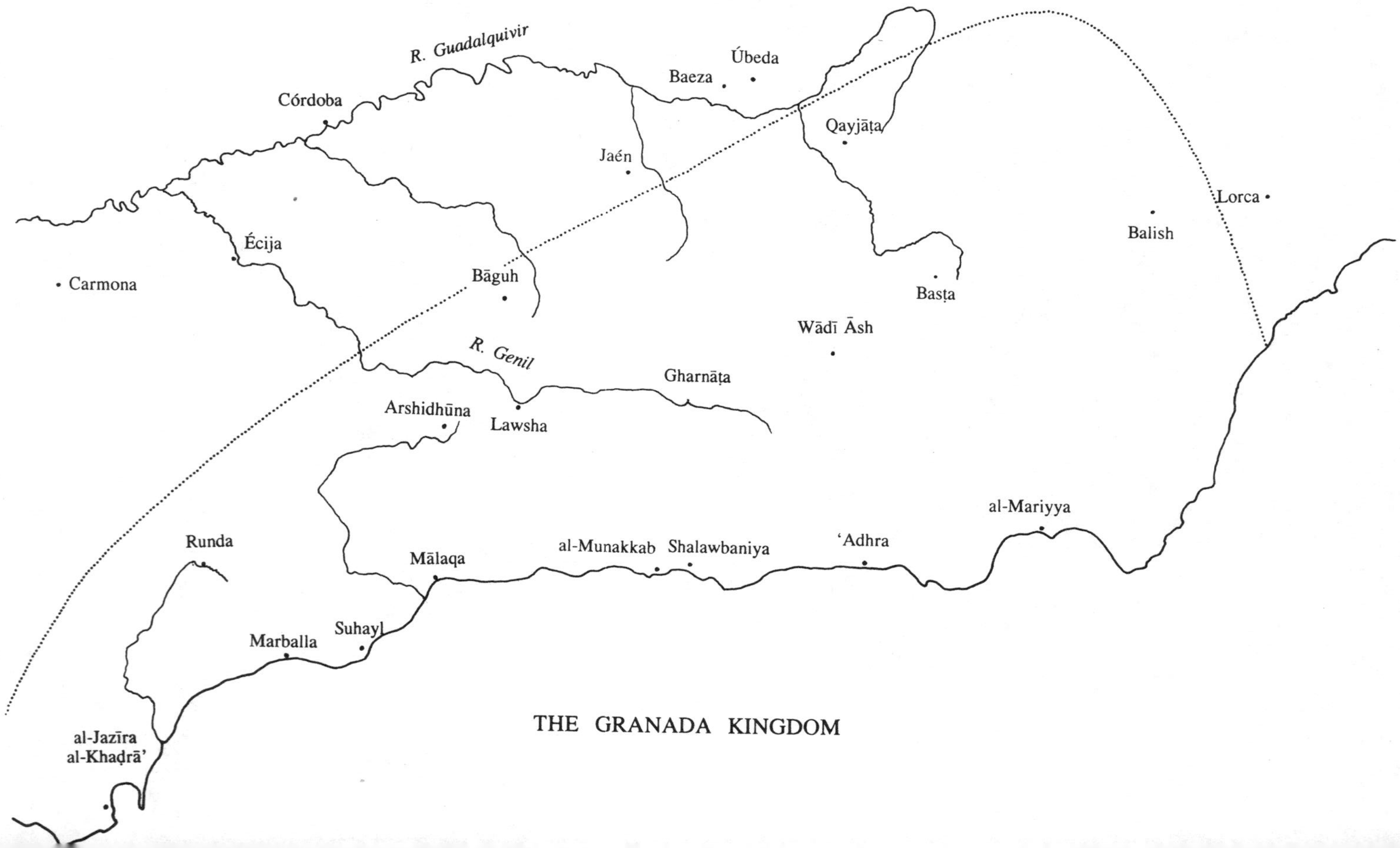

THE GRANADA KINGDOM

LOCATION OF CURRENT WHEELS IN THE IBERIAN PENINSULA (after Caro Baroja)

Site of current wheel x

Stabilized frontier of al-Andalus during the Umayyad Caliphate, 10th Century

Santiago
León
R. Duero
Majrīṭ
Qūriya
R. Tajo
Ṭulayṭula
Turjāla
Shantarīn
Mārida
al-Ushbūna
Baṭalyaws
R. Guadiana
Yābura
Bāja
al-Madīna al-Zahrā'
Qurṭuba
Jayyān
Ishbīliya
Astija
R. Guadalquivir
Qarmūna
Shilb
Bubashtir
Sharīsh
Mālaqa
al-Jazīra al-Khaḍrā'

THE UMAYYAD CALIPHATE

SCHOLARS' LIST

Through its Scholars' List Brill aims to make available to a wider public a selection of its most successful hardcover titles in a paperback edition.

Titles now available are:

AMITAI-PREISS, R. & D.O. MORGAN, *The Mongol Empire and its Legacy.* 2000. ISBN 90 04 11946 9, price USD 29.90

COHEN. B., *Not the Classical Ideal.* Athens and the Construction of the Other in Greek Art. 2000. ISBN 90 04 11712 1, price USD 39.90

GRIGGS, C.W., *Early Egyptian Christianity* from its Origins to 451 CE. 2000. ISBN 90 04 11926 4, price USD 29.90

HORSFALL, N., *A Companion to the Study of Virgil.* 2000. ISBN 90 04 11870 5, price USD 27.90

JAYYUSI, S.K., *The Legacy of Muslim Spain.* 2000. ISBN 90 04 11945 0, price USD 54.90

RUTGERS, L.V., *The Jews in Late Ancient Rome.* Evidence of Cultural Interaction in the Roman Diaspora. 2000. ISBN 90 04 11928 0, price USD 29.90

TER HAAR, B.J., *The Ritual and Mythology of the Chinese Triads.* Creating an Identity. 2000. ISBN 90 04 11944 2, price USD 39.90

THOMPSON, T.L., *Early History of the Israelite People* from the Written & Archaeological Sources. 2000. ISBN 90 04 11943 4, price USD 39.90

WOOD, S.E., *Imperial Women.* A Study in Public Images, 40 BC – AD 68 2000. ISBN 90 04 11950 7, price USD 34.90

YARBRO COLLINS, A., *Cosmology & Eschatology in Jewish & Christian Apocalypticism.* 2000. ISBN 90 04 11927 2, price USD 29.90